Kant's *Groundwork for the Metaphysics of Morals*

Kant's *Groundwork for the Metaphysics of Morals*

A Commentary

Henry E. Allison

OXFORD
UNIVERSITY PRESS

OXFORD

UNIVERSITY PRESS

Great Clarendon Street, Oxford OX2 6DP
United Kingdom

Oxford University Press is a department of the University of Oxford.
It furthers the University's objective of excellence in research, scholarship,
and education by publishing worldwide. Oxford is a registered trade mark of
Oxford University Press in the UK and in certain other countries

© Henry E. Allison 2011

British Library Cataloguing in Publication Data
Data available

Library of Congress Cataloging in Publication Data
Data available

ISBN 978-0-19-969154-8

Printed in the United Kingdom by
the MPG Books Group Ltd

To the memory of Lewis White Beck

Contents

Acknowledgments

I wish to express my thanks to Ann Margaret Baxley, Huaping Lu-Adler, Adrian Piper, Dieter Schönecker, Oliver Sensen, and Christian Wenzel for their helpful comments on various portions of this manuscript. Particular thanks are due to two anonymous readers from Oxford University Press whose insightful comments helped to make this a much better book than it would otherwise have been. I also want to thank Peter Momtchiloff for his encouragement of this project and Jens Timmermann for graciously making available to me a pre-publication version of his extremely useful bilingual edition of the *Groundwork* with his editorial notes and revision of the Gregor translation. Finally, I wish to thank Huaping Lu-Adler a second time for taking on the task of preparing the index.

Note on sources and key to abbreviations and translations

Apart from the *Critique of Pure Reason*, where references are to the standard A and B pagination, and *Eine Vorlesung über Ethik* (edited by Paul Menzer, Berlin: Rolf Heise, 1924) all references to Kant are first to the volume and page of *Kant's gesammelte Schriften* (KGS), herausgegeben von der Deutschen (formerly Könliglichen Preuissischen) Akademie der Wissenschaften, 29 volumes (Berlin: Walter de Gruyter [and predecessors], 1902ff.) and second (where applicable) to the volume and pagination in *The Cambridge Edition of the Works of Immanuel Kant* Cambridge: Cambridge University Press, 1998). Translations from the *Groundwork for the Metaphysics of Morals* are my own; although I have consulted most of the already existing English translations.

A	*Anthropologie in pragmatischer Hinsicht* [KGS 7] *Anthropology from a pragmatic point of view*, translated by Robert B. Louden, in *Anthropology, History and Education* (231–429), *The Cambridge Edition of the Works of Immanuel Kant*, edited by Günter Zöller and Robert B. Louden, Cambridge: Cambridge University Press (2007).
AM	*Anthropologie Mrongovius* [KGS 25].
BB	*Bemerkungen zu den Beobachtungen über das Gefühl des Schönen und Erhabenen* [KGS 20] *Remarks on the Observations on the Feeling of the Beautiful and the Sublime*, selections translated by Curtis Bowman, Paul Guyer, and Frederick Rauscher, in *Notes and Fragments* (1–24), *The Cambridge Edition of the Works of Immanuel Kant*, edited by Paul Guyer, Cambridge: Cambridge University Press (2005).
Br	*Kant's Briefwechsel* [KGS 10–12] *Correspondence*, translated and edited by Arnulf Zweig, *The Cambridge Edition of the Works of Immanuel Kant*, Cambridge: Cambridge University Press (1999).
EF	*Zum ewigen Frieden. Ein philosopischer Entwurf* [KGS 8] *Toward Perpetual Peace A Philosophical Project*, translated by Mary J. Gregor, in *Practical Philosophy*, *The Cambridge Edition of the Works of Immanuel Kant* (317–51), edited by Mary J. Gregor, Cambridge: Cambridge University Press (1996).
Ethik	*Eine Vorlesung Kants über Ethik*, edited by Paul Menzer, Berlin: Rolf Heise (1924). *Lectures on Ethics*, translated by Louis Infield, Indianapolis: Hackett (1981).
FI	*Erste Einleitung in die Kritik der Urteilskraft* [KGS 20] "First Introduction to the Critique of the Power of Judgment," translated by Paul Guyer and Eric Matthews, in *Critique of the Power of Judgment*, *The Cambridge Edition of the Works of Immanuel Kant* (3–51), edited by Paul Guyer, Cambridge: Cambridge University Press (2000).

Fort   *Welches sind die wirklichen Fortschritte, die die Metaphysik seit Leibnitzens und Wolfs Zeiten in Deutchland gemacht hat?* [KGS 20] *What Real Progress has Metaphysics Made in Germany since the Time of Leibniz and Wolff?* translated by Peter Heath, in *Theoretical Philosophy after 1781*, *The Cambridge Edition of the Works of Immanuel Kant* (353–424), edited by Henry Allison and Peter Heath, Cambridge: Cambridge University Press (2002).

GMS   *Grundlugung zur Metaphysik der Sitten* [KGS 4].

IAG   *"Idee zu einer allgemeinen Geschichte in weltbürgerlicher Absicht"* [KGS 8] "Idea of a universal history from a cosmopolitan point of view," translated by Allen Wood, in *Anthropology, History and Education* (231–429), *The Cambridge Edition of the Works of Immanuel Kant* (107–20), edited by Günter Zöller and Robert B. Louden, Cambridge: Cambridge University Press (2007).

JL   *Jäsche Logik* [KGS 9] *The Jäsche Logic*, translated by J. Michael Young, in *Lectures on Logic*, *The Cambridge Edition of the Works of Immanuel Kant* edited by J. Michael Young (527–640), Cambridge: Cambridge University Press (1992).

KpV   *Kritik der praktischen Vernunft* [KGS 5] Critique of Practical Reason, translated by Mary J. Gregor, in *Practical Philosophy*, *The Cambridge Edition of the Works of Immanuel* Kant (139–271), edited by Mary J. Gregor, Cambridge: Cambridge University Press (1996).

KrV   *Kritik der reinen Vernunft* [KGS 3–4] Critique of Pure Reason, translated and edited by Paul Guyer and Allen Wood, *The Cambridge Edition of the Works of Immanuel Kant*, Cambridge: Cambridge University Press (1998).

KU   *Kritik der Urtheilskraft* [KGS 5] *Critique of the Power of Judgment*, translated by Paul Guyer and Eric Matthews, *The Cambridge Edition of the Works of Immanuel Kant*, edited by Paul Guyer, Cambridge: Cambridge University Press (2000).

LB   *Logik Blomberg* [KGS 24] The Blomberg Logic, translated by J. Michael Young, in *Lectures on Logic*, *The Cambridge Edition of the Works of Immanuel Kant*, edited by J. Michael Young (5–246), Cambridge: Cambridge University Press (1992).

LD-W   *Logik Dohna-Wundlacken* [KGS 24]. *The Dohna-Wundlacken Logic* (381–423), translated by J. Michael Young, in *Lectures on Logic*, *The Cambridge Edition of the Works of Immanuel Kant*, edited by J. Michael Young (431–516), Cambridge: Cambridge University Press (1992).

LH   *Logik Hechsel* [KGS 24] The Hechsel Logic, translated (in part) by J. Michael Young, in *Lectures on Logic*, *The Cambridge Edition of the Works of Immanuel Kant* edited by J. Michael Young (431–516), Cambridge: Cambridge University Press (1992).

MAM   *"Muthsmasslicher Anfang der Menschengeschichte"* [KGS 8] "Conjectural beginning of human history," translated by Allen Wood, in *Anthropology, History and Education*, *The Cambridge Edition of the Works of Immanuel Kant*

	(163–75), translated and edited by Günter Zöller and Robert B. Louden, Cambridge: Cambridge University Press (2007).
MAN	*Metaphysische Anfangsgründe der Naturwissenschaft* [KGS 4] *Metaphysical foundations of natural science*, translated by Michael Freedman, in *Theoretical Philosophy after 1781*, *The Cambridge Edition of the Works of Immanuel Kant* (183–270), edited by Henry Allison and Peter Heath, Cambridge: Cambridge University Press, (2002).
Met Mongovius	*Metaphysik Mrongovius* [KGS 29], translated by Karl Ameriks and Steve Naragon, in *Lectures on Metaphysics*, *The Cambridge Edition of the Works of Immanuel Kant* (109–286), edited by Karl Ameriks and Steve Naragon, Cambridge: Cambridge University Press (1997).
ML_1	Metaphysik L_1 [KGS 28] translated by Karl Ameriks and Steve Naragon, in *Lectures on Metaphysics*, *The Cambridge Edition of the Works of Immanuel Kant* (19–106), edited by Karl Ameriks and Steve Naragon, Cambridge: Cambridge University Press (1997).
MM I	*Moral Mrongovius* (1) [KGS 27].
MM 2	*Moral Mrongovius* (2) [KGS 29] translated by Peter Heath, in *Lectures on Ethics*, *The Cambridge Edition of the Works of Immanuel Kant* (225–48), edited by Peter Heath and J.B. Schneewind, Cambridge: Cambridge University Press (1997).
MPC	*Moralphilosophie Collins* [KGS 27] translated by Peter Heath, in *Lectures on Ethics*, *The Cambridge Edition of the Works of Immanuel Kant* (41–222), edited by Peter Heath and J. B. Schneewind, Cambridge: Cambridge University Press (1997).
MS	*Metaphysik der Sitten* [KGS 8] *The Metaphysics of Morals*, translated by Mary J. Gregor, in *Practical Philosophy*, *The Cambridge Edition of the Works of Immanuel Kant* (365–603), edited by Mary J. Gregor, Cambridge: Cambridge University Press (1996).
MSV	*Metaphysik der Sitten Vigilantius* [KGS 27] *Kant on the Metaphysics of Morals*, translated by Peter Heath, in *Lectures on Ethics*, *The Cambridge Edition of the Works of Immanuel Kant* (251–452), edited by Peter Heath and J. B. Schneewind, Cambridge: Cambridge University Press (1997).
MV	*Metaphysik Vigilantius* [KGS 28], translated by Karl Ameriks and Steve Naragon, in *Lectures on Metaphysics*, *The Cambridge Edition of the Works of Immanuel Kant* (417–506), edited by Karl Ameriks and Steve Naragon, Cambridge: Cambridge University Press (1997).
Nachricht	*M. Immanuel Kants Nachricht von der Einrichtung seiner Vorlesungen in dem Winterhalbenjahre von 1765–66.* [GMS 2] *M. Immanuel Kant's announcement of the program of his lectures for the winter semester 1765–66*, translated by David Walford, in *Theoretical Philosophy, 1755–1770*, *The Cambridge Edition of the Works of Immanuel Kant* (287–300), edited by David Walford, Cambridge: Cambridge University Press (1992).
OP	*Opus postumum* [KGS 21–22].

P   *Pädagogik* [KGS 9] *Lectures on pedagogy*, translated by Robert Louden, in
                     Anthropology, History and Education (437–85), *The Cambridge Edition of the
                     Works of Immanuel Kant*, edited by Günter Zöller and Robert B. Louden,
                     Cambridge: Cambridge University Press (2007).

Pro   *Prolegomena zu einer jeden künftigen Metaphysik, die als Wissenschaft wird
                     aufterten können* [KGS 4] *Prolegomena to any future metaphysics that will be able to
                     come forward as science*, translated by Gary Hatfield, in *Theoretical Philosophy
                     after 1781*, *The Cambridge Edition of the Works of Immanuel Kant* (53–169),
                     edited by Henry Allison and Peter Heath, Cambridge: Cambridge
                     University Press (2002).

R   *Reflexionen* [KGS 17–19].

RGV   *Die Religion innerhalb der Grenzen der blossen Vernunft* [KGS 6] *Religion within
                     the boundaries of mere reason*, translated by George Di Giovani, in *Religion and
                     Rational Theology*, edited by Allen Wood and George Di Giovani, *The
                     Cambridge Edition of the Works of Immanuel Kant* (57–215), Cambridge:
                     Cambridge University Press (1996).

RSV   Recension of J. H. Schulz's *Versuch einer Anleitung zur Sittenlehre für alle
                     Menschen, ohne Unterschied der Religion, nebst einem Anhange von den
                     Todesstraffen* [KGS 8] "Review of Schulz's Attempt at an introduction to a
                     doctrine of morals for all human beings regardless of different religions,"
                     translated by Mary J. Gregor, in *Practical Philosophy*, *The Cambridge Edition of
                     the Works of Immanuel Kant* (7–10), edited by Mary J. Gregor, Cambridge:
                     Cambridge University Press (1996).

TP   *Über den Gemeinspruch Das mag in der Theorie richtig sein, taugt aber nicht für die
                     Praxis* [KGS 8] "On the common saying: That may be correct in theory, but
                     it is of no use in practice" (279–309), translated by Mary J Gregor, in *Practical
                     Philosophy*, *The Cambridge Edition of the Works of Immanuel Kant*, edited by
                     Mary J. Gregor, Cambridge: Cambridge University Press (1996).

U   *Untersuchung über die Deutlichkeit der Gründsatze der natüturlichen Theologie und
                     der Moral* [KGS 2] *Inquiry concerning the distinctness of the principles of natural
                     theology and morality*, translated by David Walford, in *Theoretical Philosophy,
                     1755–1770*, *The Cambridge Edition of the Works of Immanuel Kant* (248–75),
                     edited by David Walford, Cambridge: Cambridge University Press (1992).

UE   *Über eine Entdeckung, nach der alle neue Kritik der reinen Vernunft durch eine ältere
                     entbehrlich gemacht warden soll* [KGS 8] *On a discovery whereby any new critique of
                     pure reason is to be made superfluous by an older one*, translated by Henry Allison,
                     in *Theoretical Philosophy after 1781*, *The Cambridge Edition of the Works of
                     Immanuel Kant* (283–336), edited by Henry Allison and Peter Heath,
                     Cambridge: Cambridge University Press (2002).

VEF   *Vorarbeiten zum ewigen Frieden* [KGS 24] *Preliminaries to Perpetual Peace*.

VMS   *Vorarbeiten zu Die Metaphysik der Sitten* [KGS 23] *Preliminaries to the
                     Metaphysics of Morals*.

Introduction

Kant's *Groundwork for the Metaphysics of Morals*, which was first published in 1785 and will henceforth be referred to as GMS (*Grundlegung zur Metaphysik der Sitten*), is widely regarded as the most important work in modern moral philosophy. It is also generally recognized that the main reason for this lies in Kant's "discovery" or "invention" of the autonomy of the will, that is, the revolutionary and seemingly paradoxical idea that moral requirements are self imposed or, equivalently, that the ground of the authority of these requirements lies in the will of the agent.[1] In his own influential analysis of Kant's achievement, J. B. Schneewind depicts it as the radicalization of a conception of morality as self-governance, which attained prominence in the seventeenth and eighteenth centuries as an alternative to the traditional view of morality as obedience to law.[2] On Schneewind's view, Kant's conception of autonomy is a radicalization of this conception, because self-governance does not require that the source of the principles according to which agents supposedly govern themselves be regarded as stemming from the will.[3]

While I am in general agreement with Schneewind's account, I believe that it does not go far enough. Specifically, it ignores the fact that an essential part of the Kantian revolution in moral theory, which can be regarded as the practical counterpart of what is often referred to as Kant's "Copernican revolution in [theoretical] philosophy," is a radical reconfiguration of the universe of moral theories. Kant does not simply replace previous forms of morality as self-governance with a deeper and more powerful one

---

[1] In explaining the choice of the title for his book, Schneewind (1998, 3) remarks that he chose the term "invention" rather than "discovery" because autonomy for Kant requires a contracausal freedom, which he regards as a sheer invention on Kant's part in the manner of Leibniz's monads. But even if one shares Schneewind's skepticism regarding such freedom, this applies only to Kant's account of the conditions of the possibility of autonomy rather than to the conception of autonomy itself. Moreover, it seems clear that Kant himself viewed his principle of autonomy as a discovery rather than an invention, inasmuch as he supposedly arrived at it by means of a regressive analysis of what is implicit in a common, pre-philosophical conception of morality and of rational agency.

[2] Schneewind (1998, esp. 4–6).

[3] Although he does not use the term "self-governance," preferring instead expressions such as "self-determination," self-regulation," and especially "the internal ought," a rich and highly informative account of what can be described as theories of self-governance within British moral philosophy of the seventeenth and eighteenth centuries has been provided by Darwall (1995). Much like Schneewind, Darwall sees these theories as approaching Kant's conception of autonomy to various degrees without fully attaining the Kantian view. But since his focus is exclusively on the British tradition, he does not, except in passing, discuss Kant's own views.

(though he certainly does that). Although he does not put it in this way, Kant effectively argues that previous conceptions of self-governance occupy common ground with obedience-based conceptions of morality, as well as other conceptions, which do not fit neatly into either of these camps.[4] The term that Kant chose for this common ground is "heteronomy" and the result is that what was previously seen as a conflict between radically distinct conceptions of morality is reconceived as a family quarrel between various forms of heteronomy, all of which are united in locating the ground of morality in something external to the will of the agent. Moreover, this again may be regarded as the counterpart to a fundamental move that Kant made in theoretical philosophy, which in this case is the unification of all non-critical philosophies under the rubric "transcendental realism" to which he opposed his "transcendental idealism."[5]

Although Kant seems to have coined the term "heteronomy," or at least was the first to attribute to it a systematic significance, he did not invent the term "autonomy," which has a long history in juridical and political theory, reaching from the classical period to Kant's predecessor Christian Wolff.[6] In fact, the core of the Kantian notion was already expressed by Rousseau in a political context with his famous definition of freedom as "obedience to a law one prescribes to oneself."[7] Viewed in light of Rousseau's definition, Kant's achievement consists in having transformed this notion from one that was intended to account for the obligation to obey the juridical laws of a political state to one that grounds the obligation to obey an inner, moral legislation. And, as a direct result of this, the traditional question: "Why should I be moral?" was transformed from one concerning the benefits to be derived from obeying ethical requirements (whether in this world or the next) into one concerning the grounds of the legitimacy of these requirements.

This change also brought with it a reconceptualization of practical reason. Rather than being regarded as the vehicle for determining the nature of the good and of the best means for attaining it, as it was traditionally understood, Kant saw practical reason, in the form of "pure practical reason," as itself the source of universally valid normative principles, which hold independently of any ends chosen by a rational agent and therefore any object of the will. This idea is sometimes characterized in terms of the Rawlsean formula, "the priority of the right over the good."[8] This characterization is somewhat misleading, however, inasmuch as the priority for Rawls applies to his conception of justice as fairness; whereas for Kant it applies not only to duties of justice, but to all ethical duties. Thus, I believe that the Kantian view might be better

---

[4] We shall see in Chapter 9 that, though Kant's taxonomies of moral theories in GMS and the *Critique of Practical Reason* do not refer explicitly to either self-governance or obedience to law, they encompass such theories.

[5] For my analysis of this see Allison (2004, 20–49).

[6] See Pohlmann (1971, 701–19).

[7] Rousseau (1978, 56).

[8] For his discussion of the complex relations between the right and the good, see Rawls (1971, esp. 31f. and 446–52).

described as the priority of (the moral) law over the good. And it is the fact that GMS is the first work in which Kant expressed this priority, which is inseparably connected with his conceptions of autonomy and the categorical imperative, that makes it the single most important contribution to modern moral philosophy.[9]

Like any claim to philosophical importance, this one is highly controversial and it is clear that many moral philosophers of various stripes would contest it. What cannot be contested, however, is that GMS is the single most written about work in modern moral philosophy.[10] Indeed, given the vast amount of literature that has already been devoted to this relatively slim text, the first question that any putative commentator must address is what justifies adding to it.

My answer to this question is two-fold. The first stems from the nature of the text itself. Like any great philosophical work, GMS is inexhaustible. Thus, I am confident that, if two hundred years from now people are still studying and reflecting upon philosophical texts, GMS will continue to be prominent amongst them. Although this does not guarantee that one's own contribution will be of any import, it at least makes it possible to dismiss the worry that there is nothing further to be said on the matter.

My second, more personal, reason for believing that I have something to contribute is that I have studied, taught, and written about this seminal work for over forty years. The result of this ongoing engagement with GMS, however, turns out to have been something of a mixed blessing. On the one hand, each such engagement has resulted in a sense of having gained fresh insights and a deeper understanding of the work; while, on the other hand, as the unavoidable concomitant of this, I have been forced to abandon views to which I had previously adhered with some degree of confidence. Extrapolating from this result, it might reasonably be inferred that if I were to devote another forty years to the study of this text, I would gain an even deeper understanding and in the process discard many of the views that I presently hold. But inasmuch as it is highly unlikely that I shall have this opportunity, I think it best to express my views as of 2011.

Although it has no direct bearing on the import of what I have to say, I also think it should noted that the present may be regarded as something of a highpoint in the study of Kant's moral philosophy, at least in the Anglophone philosophical world. For example, the days are long past when one could regard GMS, perhaps together with the *Critique of Practical Reason* (1788), as containing all that one needed to be concerned with in order to comment in a serious way on Kant's moral theory.[11] Rather, it is now generally recognized that GMS is properly classified as a work in meta-ethics, having as its sole aim the two-part task of searching for and establishing the supreme principle of morality

---

[9] Actually Kant only makes this priority fully explicit in the second *Critique* (KpV 5: 62–65; 190–92); but it is implicit in GMS and underlies his account of the concept of a categorical imperative.

[10] One might argue that this honor, at least in the Anglophone literature, belongs to Hobbes' *Leviathan*; but I believe that the importance of this work lies largely (though not exclusively) in political theory, rather than moral philosophy or ethics in the narrower sense.

[11] Symptomatic of this tendency is the short work by Ross (1954), which purports to be a study of Kant's ethical theory, but is in fact a commentary on GMS.

(GMS 4: 392$_{3-4}$); whereas it is the long delayed *Metaphysics of Morals* (1796–97), for which GMS was originally intended to lay the foundation, that is Kant's major work in normative ethics. And it is currently likewise generally acknowledged that, in addition to these, any serious work on Kant's moral theory requires a knowledge of other texts, including (but not limited to) *Religion within the boundaries of mere reason* (1793), *Anthropology from a pragmatic point of view* (1798), and the various versions of his lectures on ethics.

The appreciation of the presence in the Kantian corpus of a division of labor between meta- and normative ethics, has also led to a better understanding of the nature and function of the categorical imperative. More specifically, it has resulted in increasing support for the view that Kant's famous and oft-criticized application of it in GMS 2 to tokens of the various types of duty are intended as illustrations of the fruitfulness of this imperative in ruling out certain maxims or proposed courses of action, rather than as failed attempts to derive particular duties from it.[12] And it is also now widely recognized that the categorical imperative should not be considered a kind of algorithm, from which duties are supposedly derivable in a quasi-mechanical manner, without any attention to circumstances or role for judgment.[13]

Nevertheless, once we move beyond these areas of broad agreement, which mainly concern how *not to read* Kant, we encounter fundamental disagreement on a number of major interpretive questions. One concerns the extent to which GMS and, more generally, Kant's practical philosophy, needs to be interpreted in light of his overall "critical" project. Since no serious commentator of whom I am aware goes so far as to assert that those working on Kant's practical philosophy need pay no attention to the latter, including the core teachings of the first *Critique*, it is usually a matter of degree and of philosophical interest. It does seem to be the case, however, that, as a matter of practice, some (but by no means all) of the most influential of today's Anglophone writers on Kant's ethics pay scant attention to the first *Critique*. By contrast, perhaps because my first serious encounter with Kant was with his theoretical philosophy, my own work emphasizes the close connection between his theoretical and practical philosophy.

In addition, there are a large number of hotly contested issues regarding the interpretation and evaluation of the argument of GMS. Prominent among these are: the nature and function of the categorical imperative; what Kant understands by a good will and the role that it plays in his argument; the identity of the unnamed first of the three propositions affirmed in GMS 1; Kant's conception of moral worth and the examples he uses to illustrate it; the alleged analyticity of hypothetical imperatives; Kant's controversial derivation of the formula for the categorical imperative from an analysis of its concept in GMS 2 and the relation between this and the other derivations

---

[12] It is sometimes thought that ruling out a course of action as impermissible is sufficient to establish a negative duty not to perform actions of this type, but I shall argue that this is not actually the case.

[13] For his own statement of this view, which I assume influenced the views of his former students, see Rawls (2000, 166).

of the imperative in the first and third sections of GMS; the universalizability test as applied to tokens of the four types of duty and the nature of the contradiction that maxims that fail this test supposedly involve; the number of formulas for the categorical imperative that Kant provides in GMS 2 and their relations to each other; the contrast between autonomy and heteronomy as foundational moral principles and the all-inclusiveness of this division; and, finally, the whole set of controversial issues regarding Kant's "deduction" of the categorical imperative and freedom in GMS 3. In the body of this commentary, I shall discuss each of these (and other questions), many of them in considerable detail.

One distinctive feature of this commentary is that it devotes more attention than is customary to the historical context in which Kant wrote. This encompasses both the internal development of Kant's thought leading to the composition of GMS and the major external influences on the work. With regard to the former, I do not attempt to trace the development of Kant's moral philosophy from his earliest recorded thoughts on the subject until GMS, since that is in itself a book-length task.[14] Rather, I focus mainly on the still not sufficiently appreciated fact that Kant's initial "critical" project, as articulated in the first edition of the *Critique of Pure Reason* (1781), included a projected work in moral theory, a metaphysics of morals to be precise, but did not envision the need for any preliminary work such as GMS. In other words, Kant initially regarded the first *Critique* as providing a sufficient foundation for both a metaphysics of morals and a metaphysics of nature. And it follows from this that, in order to understand the *raison d'être* of GMS, it is necessary to understand what led Kant to change his mind on that matter sometime between 1781 and 1784. To anticipate, I shall argue that Kant initially located the foundation for his projected metaphysics of morals in the postulates of God and immortality in the Canon of the first *Critique* and that it was his dissatisfaction with his account of these postulates, which may have been triggered by Garve's review, that led him to recognize the need for a distinct foundation for his moral theory.

My account of external influences likewise makes no pretence of completeness; rather, I devote the second chapter to a discussion of what I take to be the two most important of these for an understanding of GMS: (1) the Wolffian "universal practical philosophy," which was regarded by Wolff and his followers as a kind of propaedeutic to the various branches of practical philosophy distinguished by this school; and (2) the so-called "popular moral philosophy," which was closely associated with Christian Garve. In both cases, my interest lies not in their intrinsic philosophical merits, which at least in the latter case are slight, but in their importance for understanding Kant's project in GMS, which in both cases are substantial.

Since the work in universal practical philosophy of Alexander Baumgarten (*Initia philosophiae practicae primae acroamatice*), who was Wolff's most distinguished disciple,

---

[14] For such studies see Schlipp (1960), Schmucker (1961), and Ward (1972).

was one of the textbooks that Kant used for his lectures on ethics, these lectures contain abundant references to it and discussions of topics that pertain to universal practical philosophy, such as the nature of moral principles, obligation, imputation, and freedom, all of which bear directly on Kant's central concerns in GMS. Accordingly, it is evident that Kant's ongoing engagement with Baumgarten and, more generally, with universal practical philosophy, played an essential role in shaping his emerging moral theory.

Moreover, within the Preface to GMS itself, Kant devotes a lengthy paragraph to differentiating his project from that of universal practical philosophy, which I believe reflects his concern that his contemporary readers, most of whom were presumably familiar with the latter, might, in virtue of certain superficial similarities, fail to appreciate the radically different nature of his project. Thus, in order to understand how Kant conceived his own project in GMS it is essential to understand the respects in which he viewed it as differing from the Wolffian universal practical philosophy.

Although the relationship between Kant and Garve and the influence of the latter's translation of and commentary on Cicero's *De officiis* has been a subject of discussion in the secondary literature since an influential paper by Klaus Reich, it remains a highly controversial matter.[15] Reservations regarding the thesis of a significant influence of Garve's *Cicero* on Kant seem to be due partly to the fact that he nowhere refers to either Garve or Cicero by name within GMS, though he does refer to Wolff and universal practical philosophy, and partly to the fact that some of Reich's claims regarding Kant's adoption of Ciceronian or, more precisely Stoic ideas made use of by Cicero, are less than compelling.[16] Nevertheless, inasmuch as Kant entitled the second section of GMS "*Transition from popular moral philosophy to the metaphysics of morals*," and engaged in this section in an extended critique of the empirical and eudaemonistic views of this popular moral philosophy of which Garve was recognized as the chief spokesperson, there is a strong case for the thesis that he was among Kant's chief targets. And, as we shall see in the second chapter, this case becomes compelling when we factor in Hamann's reports of Kant's concern with Garve's *Cicero* at the time of the composition of GMS.

The main point for which I wish to argue, however, is that Kant saw in some of Garve's comments on Cicero a challenge to the very idea of a metaphysics of morals. Simply put, if, as Garve's empirical-anthropological approach and insistence on the need for philosophers (especially Kant) to express themselves in a popular (non-technical) manner imply, a metaphysics of morals is neither possible nor necessary, why should Kant waste his time trying to lay the foundation for one? Thus, if Kant's concern with the Wolffian universal practical philosophy was that it might itself be taken as already offering a metaphysics of morals, thereby making his own project redundant, his concern with the Garvean popular moral philosophy was that it might make such a metaphysics seem totally wrongheaded. And I submit that Kant saw these

---

[15] See Reich (1939b).
[16] See Schönecker (1999, 61–67).

two views as twin threats to the understanding and acceptance of his own radically novel project and, as such, concluded that they had to be dealt with in a direct and uncompromising fashion.

In order to evaluate this thesis, it is necessary to determine exactly what Kant's project was in GMS and what its novelty consists in. To begin with, there is no difficulty in defining the nature of Kant's project, since he unambiguously does it for us. As already noted, it consists of two parts: one devoted to searching for and the other to establishing the supreme principle of morality. Moreover, there does not appear to be anything particularly novel in either part of the project, so described. Accordingly, whatever novelty is involved must concern the method whereby Kant proposed to pursue these goals. Although we shall see that Kant's execution of the second part of his project, which is the subject matter of GMS 3, is highly problematic, it is relatively clear that he regarded it as grounding a synthetic *a priori* proposition, which takes the form of a practical analogue of a transcendental deduction.[17] Kant's method in the first part of his project is more difficult to specify, however, since it seems to involve two logically independent procedures, both of which are described as "analytic" or "regressive," and one of which is carried out in each of the first two parts of the work.[18]

In GMS 1, Kant starts from the premise that the true principle of morality must already be latent in the ordinary human understanding and that the task of the moral philosopher is to clarify this principle and give it a precise formulaic expression. Kant terms this procedure a "*Transition from common rational cognition to philosophical moral cognition*," and he appropriately compares it with that of Socrates. In GMS 2, by contrast, Kant proceeds to the formulation of the supreme principle of morality as the categorical imperative by means of an analysis of "the universal concept of a rational being as such" (GMS 4: 412_{3-4}). And if the procedure of GMS 1 occupies some common ground with popular moral philosophy, with its assumption that morality must fall within the purview of the ordinary human understanding, that of GMS 2 marks a decisive break with the former. Accordingly, the question becomes why this second and vastly more complex section is necessary and perhaps even whether it is compatible with the first, a claim which popular moral philosophy would likely deny.

Fortunately, the latter part of this question can be answered easily. There is no incompatibility between the thesis that the fundamental principle of morality is recognized and accepted as such by the ordinary human understanding and that it is

---

[17] We shall see, however, that there is some controversy regarding the synthetic *a priori* practical proposition that is "deduced." The candidates are the moral law, the categorical imperative, or both. I shall argue for the third alternative.

[18] Near the close of the Preface, Kant informs the reader that the method he will adopt proceeds "analytically from common cognition to the determination of its [common cognition's] supreme principle and, then, in turn synthetically from the testing of this principle and its sources back to common cognition in which its use is encountered" (GMS 4: 392_{18-21}). The proper interpretation of this methodological pronouncement remains highly controversial and I shall consider aspects of it at various points in this commentary. At present, I wish merely to point out that it glosses over the significant difference between the starting point of the analytic procedures that Kant adopts in GMS 1 and 2.

grounded in the extremely abstract concept of a rational being as such, because the recognition and acceptance of a moral principle does not rest upon a grasp of its ultimate grounding. If it did, only meta-ethicists could be moral! The first part of the question is more pressing, however, and though I address it at a number of points in the body of this work, I shall here attempt to provide the reader at least a taste of the line of argument I pursue.

At the most basic level, the problem can be described as the apparent redundancy of GMS 2. Given the fact that this is the longest, richest, and most complex of the three sections of GMS and that it contains Kant's best known and most discussed formulations of the categorical imperative, the suggestion that it is redundant might seem to border on the bizarre. Nevertheless, if we take seriously Kant's account of the two-part concern of the work, together with the fact that he had already arrived at a formulation of the categorical imperative (though it is not there referred to as such) by the end of GMS 1, it could be argued that he should have proceeded directly to the execution of the second part of his project in GMS 3.

In fact, a modified version of the redundancy thesis has been argued for by A. R. C. Duncan. Acknowledging the importance of Kant's derivation and illustration of the first formulation of the categorical imperative in the early portion of GMS 2, Duncan does not suggest that the section as a whole is redundant; rather, he maintains that the bulk of the remainder of the section, should be regarded as an "ethical interlude," which, as such, is peripheral to the meta-ethical concerns of GMS as a whole. And he explains its presence in the text largely along the lines suggested by Reich, that is, as an endeavor on Kant's part to show the affinity between his account of the categorical imperative and the basic principle found in Cicero's *De officiis*.[19] But while Duncan's reading has been widely rejected, it does not seem to me that a compelling alternative reading of the portion of the text that he dismisses as an interlude is to be found in the literature. Thus, providing one is among the central concerns of this commentary.

An important feature of my reading is a modalized interpretation of Kant's thesis that a supreme principle of morality, whatever it may turn out to be, must be regarded as absolutely or unconditionally binding. Unlike many present-day moral philosophers, Kant did not ask whether morality is unconditionally binding or, what amounts to the same thing, rests on a categorical imperative. Rather, he assumed that if there is such a thing as morality it must be binding in this way and sought to determine its possible ground, which he located in the concept of a rational being as such.

If one were to ask Kant why he thought that unconditional bindingness is contained in the very concept of morality, he would no doubt again appeal to the common understanding of morality.[20] But this common understanding obviously does not include the idea that the bindingness of morality is grounded in the concept of a

---

[19] See Duncan (1957, esp. 167–82).

[20] See, for example, GMS 4: 389_{11-23}. I shall discuss this passage in Chapter 1.

rational being or, more properly, a rational agent as such.[21] In the first chapter, I shall attempt to reconstruct and defend what I take to be Kant's argument that this grounding is a necessary condition of a moral principle possessing the requisite binding force. To anticipate, the claim will be that such force requires that the principle be binding on every *conceivable* rational agent and that this is possible only if it is grounded in what is common to every conceivable rational agent, which just is their rational agency. This, in turn, leads to the conditional: if there is such a thing as morality, its principle must be found in the concept of a rational agent as such.

The point that I wish to emphasize at present, however, is that this grounding project is the key to understanding the complex and seemingly bewildering structure of GMS 2, where, after presumably deriving the categorical imperative from an analysis of the concept of such an imperative (an unconditionally binding principle), Kant proceeds to distinguish at least three formulas for this allegedly single imperative. Once again to anticipate, I shall argue in Chapter 9 that the three formulas that Kant presents represent successive stages in the complete construction of the concept of the categorical imperative and that they are correlated with a progressive analysis of the concept of rational agency. In the first stage, rational agents are defined as beings who act according to their *representation* of laws or on principles; in the second, they are regarded as beings who determine themselves to act for the sake of an end; and in the third they are conceived as beings who act on the basis of self-given laws, that is, autonomously. The first of these is correlated with the formula of universal law (FUL) or, more precisely, its "typic," the formula of law of nature (FLN); the second with the formula of humanity as an end in itself or, more simply, the formula of humanity (FH); the third with the principle or formula of autonomy (FA).[22] This, then, likewise issues in a conditional, which is the implicit outcome of Kant's regress on the universal concept of a rational being as such, namely: if there is such a thing as morality, its addressees must be autonomous agents.

If this is correct, it seems reasonably clear that the task of GMS 3, entitled "*Transition from the metaphysics of morals to the critique of pure practical reason*," is to demonstrate that we must attribute to our wills the property of autonomy, from which it would follow that we are unconditionally bound by the categorical imperative. Although Kant himself does not frame the issue in quite this way, we shall see that this is what his "deduction" of the categorical imperative as a synthetic *a priori* practical proposition actually comes down to.

The commentary contains twelve chapters and is divided into four parts. The first part (Chapters 1 and 2) deals with the Preface and the discussion of universal practical and popular moral philosophy. The second part (Chapters 3 through 5) deals with the

---

[21] Although Kant usually refers simply to rational beings, since we shall see that it is important for him to maintain at least the notional possibility of rational beings *without wills*, that is, rational beings that are not rational agents, it is necessary to keep this distinction in mind.

[22] Like many commentators, I regard the so-called formula of a realm of ends (FRE) as a variant of the formula of autonomy rather than as a distinct formula.

argument of GMS 1, starting with the concept of a good will and proceeding to Kant's formulation of the fundamental principle of morality as it is latent in the common human understanding. The third part (Chapters 6 through 9) deals with GMS 2 and analyzes the various formulations of the categorical imperative and their relationship to each other. The fourth part (Chapters 10 through 12) deals with the second part of Kant's project: his attempt to establish the objective practical reality of the moral law and the bindingness of the categorical imperative.

PART I

Preliminaries

1

The Nature of and Need for a Metaphysic of Morals: An Analysis of the Preface of GMS

The Preface to GMS is divided into three parts: (1) a division of the various fields of philosophy, which is based partly on the classical Stoic division and is intended to find a place for a metaphysics of morals; (2) an argument for the necessity of such a metaphysics, which Kant here equates with a pure moral philosophy; (3) an account of the divisions and method of GMS, which is supposed to lay the foundation for such a metaphysics rather than to itself constitute it. But since an interpretation of the text requires some understanding of its place within the development of Kant's moral theory, particularly his long-standing project of writing a metaphysics of morals, I shall begin with a brief account of that topic. Accordingly, the chapter is divided into four parts: the first contains this historical sketch and the last three deal with the above-mentioned parts of the Preface.

I

Although the *Metaphysics of Morals* was Kant's latest systematic work, published in 1796–97, his concern with such a metaphysics can be traced back to early in his career and survived radical changes in his views on what it would contain. The first known reference to the matter is in a letter to his former student, Herder, dated May 9, 1767. In describing his own work at this time, Kant writes:

My principal aim is to know the actual nature and limits of human capacities and inclinations, and I think I have finally more or less succeeded as far as morals [*die Sitten*] is concerned. I am now working on a Metaphysics of Morals, in which I fancy I shall be able to present the evident and fruitful principles of conduct and the method that must be employed if the so prevalent but for the most part sterile efforts in this area of knowledge are ever to produce useful results. I hope to be finished with this work this year, unless my fragile health prevents it. (Br. 10, 74; 94–95)[1]

---

[1] In the interests of consistency, I have modified Zweig's translation, rendering "*Sitten*" as "morals" rather than "ethics." Occasionally Kant also uses the term "*Ethik*," which, at least at some points in Kant's work, has a narrower meaning.

In the letter, Kant is not particularly informative about either the contents or method of this supposedly nearly completed work; but his reference to "the actual nature and limits of human capacities and inclinations" suggests the naturalistic, empirical program in moral theory that he had outlined some two years earlier in his announcement of his courses of lectures for the winter semester of 1765–66. Indicating the influence of the British moralists and Rousseau (who is not mentioned), Kant there wrote:

I shall lecture on *universal practical philosophy* and the *doctrine of virtue*, basing both of them on *Baumgarten*. The attempts of *Shaftesbury*, *Hutcheson* and *Hume*, although incomplete and defective, have nonetheless penetrated furthest in the search for the fundamental principle of all morality. Their efforts will be given the precision and the completeness which they lack. In the doctrine of virtue I shall always begin by considering historically and philosophically what *happens* before specifying what *ought to happen*. In so doing, I shall make clear what method ought to be adopted in the study of *man*. And by *man* here I do not only mean *man* as he is distorted by the mutable form which is conferred upon him by the contingencies of his condition, and who, as such, has nearly always been misunderstood even by philosophers. I rather mean the unchanging *nature* of man, and his distinctive position within the creation. My purpose will be to establish which perfection is appropriate to him in the state of *primitive* [*rohen*] innocence and which perfection is appropriate to him in the state of *wise* [*weisen*] innocence. It is also my purpose to establish what, by contrast, the rule of man's behaviour is when, transcending the two types of limit, he strives to attain the highest level of physical and moral excellence, though falling short of that attainment to a greater or lesser degree. This method of moral enquiry is an admirable discovery of our times, which, when viewed in the full extent of its programme, was entirely unknown to the ancients. (*Nachricht* 2: 311–12; 298)[2]

In spite of the reference to the rationalist Baumgarten, whose works provided the texts for Kant's lectures on moral philosophy, it is clear from the above that his approach to the subject at the time was deeply anthropological in the sense that it was based on an empirical investigation of human nature.[3] Especially significant in this regard is Kant's methodological remark that he will consider "what *happens* before specifying what *ought to happen*." Kant's decisive turn from an empirical, anthropological to a rationalist, *a priori* approach to philosophy in general, which includes moral philosophy, is signaled in his Inaugural Dissertation: *On the form and principles of the sensible and intelligible world* (1770). In writing to Johann Heinrich Lambert on September 2 of that year, Kant again refers to a proposed "Metaphysics of Morals," this time characterizing it in quite different terms as an investigation in "pure moral philosophy, in which no empirical principles are to be found" (Br 10: 97; 108). This is virtually identical to the characterization that Kant later provided in the Preface to GMS.

---

[2] For accounts of the relation between Kant's *Nachricht* and his moral philosophy at the time, see Schlipp (1960, 75–78) and Schmucker (1961, 148–54).

[3] The works of Baumgarten, which provided the basis on which Kant structured his lectures are *Initia philosophiae practicae primae* (1760) and *Ethica philosophica* (1751 and 1763). The first of these is contained in KGS 19, 7–91 and the second in KGS 27, 737–1015. Kant was required by the Prussian government to use textbooks for all of his lectures.

Kant's final reference to a metaphysics of morals prior to the first *Critique* is in a letter to Marcus Herz in late 1773, which again indicates a significant development in his thought on the topic.[4] Kant promises with "almost certainty" that his work on transcendental philosophy, which he refers to for the first time as "a critique of pure reason," will be completed by a little after Easter (1774) and he informs Herz that he is looking forward to turning to metaphysics, which consists of two parts: the metaphysics of nature and the metaphysics of morals, the second of which he expects to complete first.

In this context, Kant also asks Herz about his own work in moral philosophy, expressing a hope that he will not include in it an application of the concept of reality [*realitaet*], since this concept is transcendental (a pure concept of the understanding), whereas moral philosophy is not part of transcendental philosophy, since its highest elements are pleasure and displeasure (Br 10: 144–45; 140). Although this might appear to suggest a eudaemonistic, or even hedonistic view, which would reflect at least a partial return to his earlier anthropological approach, Kant's subsequent remarks make it clear that this is not what he had in mind. His point is not that the highest ground of morality must be based on the feeling of pleasure and displeasure, but that it must stand in a relation thereto. This is because he held that a moral principle is distinguished from a merely speculative (theoretical) one by its possession of motivational force and that this requires that the principle stands in relation to feeling. As Kant puts it, "though the highest ground of morality is intellectual, it must itself be pleasing in the highest degree" (Br 10: 145; 140). Here Kant poses the problem that will become decisive for his subsequent treatment of moral philosophy and lead to the most distinctive aspect of his thinking on the subject: how can a purely intellectual principle, which the principle of morality is from that time on for Kant, have motivational force?

When viewed in light of Kant's remarks in the above-cited passage from his announcement of his lectures on ethics, it seems highly likely that Hume played a large role in posing this problem for Kant, just as he did in the case of the synthetic *a priori*. For while it may be assumed that, because of his lack of knowledge of English, Kant had little or no direct access to the not yet translated *Treatise*, where Hume launched his full-scale attack on the rational intuitionists such as Samuel Clarke, for whom the human mind has a direct insight into moral truths, the thesis that moral principles must have motivational force and a skepticism regarding the capacity of truths discovered by the intellect to have such force are clearly present in Hume's *An Enquiry concerning the Principles of Morals*, with which Kant is known to have been familiar.[5]

---

[4] In his earlier and more famous letter to Herz of February 1772, in which he is usually taken to have first expressed the essential critical problem of the justification of *a priori* cognitions, Kant does not refer explicitly to a projected work entitled "Metaphysic of Morals"; but he does note his efforts to separate the sensible from the intellectual in moral theory as well as theoretical philosophy (see Br 10: 29; 132).

[5] See Hume (1998, 74–76). Skepticism regarding the capacity of judgments of the intellect to motivate characterizes Hume's more moderate position in Hume (1999). In Hume (2000), by contrast, he straightaway denied any such capacity (op. cit. 265–71 and 293–302). In his discussion of rational intuitionism, Rawls

In Kant's mature formulation of the motivational problem, it takes the form of the question: how can pure reason be practical? (where reason's practicality consists in its capacity to determine the will). In his lectures on moral philosophy in the period leading up to and perhaps somewhat after the publication of the first *Critique*, however, Kant tended to frame the issue in terms of a distinction between two conditions that must be met by whatever is to count as the supreme principle of morality, or, alternatively, between two roles that such a principle must play. On the one hand, it must serve as the principle of moral appraisal [*principium dijudicationis*], which determines the permissibility or obligatory nature of an action or omission; on the other, it must function as the principle of execution [*principium executionis*], which provides an incentive [*Triebfeder*] to obey the former (MPC 27: 274; 65). It is clear that Kant's main problem lies with the latter. As he puts it at one point, "The understanding obviously can judge, but to give the judgment of the understanding compelling force, to make it an incentive that can move the will to action—this is the philosopher's stone" (*Ethik* 54; 45).

Although Kant eventually found his philosopher's stone in the principle of the autonomy of the will, according to which the binding force of the moral law is derived from its self-legislated nature and is manifested in a feeling of respect, at this time he envisaged a close connection between the moral incentive and a practical faith in God and a future life. Thus, in the Canon, which contains Kant's systematic discussion of morality in the first *Critique*, he writes: "[W]ithout a God and a world that is now not visible to us but is hoped for, the majestic ideas of morality are, to be sure, objects of approbation and admiration but not incentives for resolve and realization" (KrV A813/B841).

The idea here is not the crudely eudaemonistic one that we need an assurance of future rewards and punishments in order to have any incentive to follow the dictates of morality; it is rather the more sophisticated (though still ultimately eudaemonistic) view that the moral law specifies the condition under which alone one can be *worthy* of happiness [*Glückseligkeitwürdig*]. Accordingly, the worry, which is addressed by the postulates of God and a future life, is that one might be worthy of happiness and still not attain it, which Kant thought would tend to undermine moral endeavor. In other words, Kant's view at this time was that, while not itself a directly motivating factor, since this would destroy the purity of the moral disposition, the belief in a future life, in which happiness will be rewarded commensurately to its deservedness, provides an important source of moral encouragement, apart from which moral effort could not be sustained.[6]

---

notes that the thinkers to whom this label is applied saw moral thought as a form of theoretical rather than of practical reason. In the case of Clarke, who was the leading representative of this view, this involved a judgment of certain actions as fit to be done (or shunned) because they accorded (or conflicted) with the nature of things. The moral psychology connected with this position consists essentially in the assumption that the intellectual apprehension of the fitness of things or the principle of fitness is itself immediately motivating. As Rawls points out, this is denied (or at least called into question) by both Hume and Kant. See Rawls (2000, 69–78).

[6] For fuller discussion of this topic see Allison (1986a, esp. 103–9 and 1990, 54–70).

Although the issue remains controversial, Kant's view that morality is grounded in a practical faith in God and a future life helps to explain why in 1781 he thought that a critique of pure reason could provide an adequate foundation for a metaphysics of both morals and nature. With regard to the former, while denying the possibility of a dogmatic proof of either God or immortality, the *Critique* left ample room for a practical faith, which is all that morality supposedly requires. In any event, it is evident that Kant saw no need for either a critique of practical reason or, indeed, any separate grounding for a metaphysics of morals. As far as foundations were concerned, the way was clear for him to proceed directly to the latter task. It is also evident, however, that by 1784 Kant had second thoughts on the matter; for still with no thought of writing an additional critique of practical reason, he came to see the need for a separate work devoted to laying the foundations for the projected metaphysics of morals. The result was GMS.

II

The Preface of GMS is devoted to explaining the aim, importance, and structure of the work. And though the readers of the first *Critique*, at least those who had made it all the way to the chapter on the Architectonic, would have encountered the expression "metaphysics of morals" and a cryptic account of its subject matter, it was hardly a notion with which Kant could have assumed any general familiarity. In fact, at one point Kant virtually apologizes for using the "so much decried name" [*so verschrieenen Namen*] "metaphysics" with reference to moral philosophy (GMS 4: 410_{15}). Accordingly, Kant's initial task is to explain what he understood by such a metaphysics, which he attempts to do by relating it to the classical Stoic division of philosophy into physics, ethics, and logic. Kant accepts this division in principle; but under the guise of uncovering its principle, securing its completeness, and articulating its sub-divisions, interprets it in such a way as to make it roughly accord with the view of the Architectonic.[7]

Assuming that philosophy consists of rational cognition [*Vernunfterkenntnis*], Kant first divides such cognition into material and formal. Whereas the former is concerned with a determinate sphere of objects and their laws, the latter is concerned merely with "the form of understanding and of reason itself, and the universal rules of thinking in general, without distinction of objects" (GMS 4: 387_{9-11}). Kant identifies formal philosophy with logic. The two parts of material philosophy correspond to physics and ethics in the classical scheme; though Kant terms them respectively a "doctrine of nature" [*Naturlehre*] and a "doctrine of morals" [*Sittenlehre*].

After denying that logic, as purely formal, can have an empirical part, Kant sub-divides each of the two branches of material philosophy into a pure (*a priori*) and an

---

[7] I say that this division as Kant construes it is roughly in accord with the position of the Architectonic because there are some subtle differences, which we need not consider here. For a discussion of these differences, see Siep (1989, 34).

empirical part. In each case, the pure part is identified with metaphysics, yielding a metaphysics of nature and a metaphysics of morals. In the terms of the schema outlined in the Architectonic, the former is concerned with the laws of nature according to which everything happens; the latter with laws of freedom according to which everything ought to happen, even though it frequently does not (KrV A841–42/B869–70; GMS 4: $387_{25}388_3$).

In the case of physics or natural philosophy, there is no problem with the claim that it has an empirical part. The problem lies rather in Kant's claim that it has a pure or *a priori* part as well. Kant explicitly affirms this in the *Prolegomena* (1783), the second part of which is concerned with the question of how a pure natural science is possible, where he addresses this question by appealing to the transcendental principles of the Analytic of the *Critique* as *a priori* conditions of experience.

In the case of morals, it is the inclusion of an empirical part, which Kant characterizes as "practical anthropology," that is problematic.[8] Already in the *Critique*, Kant had affirmed that "pure morality [*die reine Moral*] is not grounded on any anthropology (no empirical condition)" (KrV A841–42/B869–70). In GMS he asserts that only the rational, that is, the pure or *a priori* part belongs to morals proper [*eigentlich Moral*] (GMS 4: 388_{12-14}). And, in the same context, he states emphatically, that "all moral philosophy rests entirely on its pure part, and applied to the human being [*den Menschen*] does not borrow the least bit from acquaintance with him (anthropology), but gives him as a rational being laws *a priori*" (GMS 4: 389_{26-29}).

Elsewhere, however, Kant offers a more nuanced view, suggesting that practical or moral anthropology constitutes a genuine component of moral theory, which complements the *a priori* metaphysics of morals by providing the basis for the application of moral principles to human beings. Thus, in a lecture roughly contemporaneous with the composition of GMS, he characterizes moral anthropology as "*philosophia moralis applicata*" or "moral philosophy applied to men" and terms it "the second part of morals." And he further states that, "The particular constitution of man and the laws based upon it, come to the fore in moral anthropology under the name of ethics [*Ethik*]" (MM II 29: 599; 226–27).[9] Moreover, later in GMS Kant states that while moral laws are derived from the universal concept of a rational being as such, "morality . . . needs anthropology for its *application* to human beings" (GMS 4: 412_{3-6}). But in a note attached to the previously cited passage in which he endeavors to explain why he chose the term

---

[8] This practical anthropology, which Kant never wrote as such and which presumably encompasses a detailed moral psychology, must be distinguished from the pragmatic anthropology, which was a subject on which Kant lectured repeatedly and a version of which (*Anthropology from a Pragmatic Point of View*) was published in 1798.

[9] Similarly, in a lecture, which dates from roughly the same time, Kant insists that "morality cannot exist without anthropology, for one must first know of the agent whether he is also in a position to accomplish what is required of him that he should do" (MPC 27: 244; 42). And later in the same set of lectures, in criticizing Baumgarten regarding the moral significance of gender differentiation, he writes: "In regard to sexual distinctions, one may look to anthropology, from which the duties can then be inferred" (MPC 27: 466; 217).

"metaphysics" to characterize pure moral philosophy, Kant adopts a more ambivalent tone regarding the relevance of the pure/applied distinction to moral theory:

One can, if one wishes, distinguish (just as pure mathematics is distinguished from the applied, and pure logic from the applied) pure philosophy of morals (metaphysics) from the applied (namely to human nature). By this terminology one is at once reminded that moral principles are not grounded on the peculiarities of human nature, but must be subsistent *a priori* for themselves; but that from such principles it must be possible to derive practical rules for every rational nature and therefore also for human nature. (GMS 4: 410$_{30-37}$)

Kant's main purpose in this note, indeed in his entire plea for a metaphysics of morals, is to guard against the intrusion of anthropological considerations into the derivation or grounding of moral principles. This includes both the supreme principle of morality and the particular obligations that would be derived from this principle in the metaphysics of morals for which GMS is to lay the foundation.

Kant's division of labor within the various sciences is rendered confusing, however, by his failure to distinguish clearly between two senses in which he uses the term "pure." In the main sense in which he uses it here, it is equivalent to *a priori* and, as such, it is contrasted with "empirical." Thus, Kant's claim that moral philosophy rests entirely on its pure part is intended to rule out seeking an empirical grounding for its principles. But, as is clear from the note cited above, Kant also uses it in the more familiar sense in which it is contrasted with "applied." And it is also clear that the two senses of "pure" are not co-extensive, since a pure physics or natural science is not equivalent to an *a priori* physics.

With regard to Kant's discussion of morality, it seems that what he wanted to say, but never quite succeeded in saying with sufficient clarity, is that morality does not have a non-pure (empirical) part, but it does have a non-pure (applied) part, namely, moral anthropology, which he insists must be subordinate to the pure part. Similarly, in the case of logic, while Kant denies that it can have an empirical part, he acknowledges in the *Critique* that it has an applied part, which is "directed to the rules of the use of the understanding under the subjective empirical conditions that psychology teaches us" (KrV A53/B77). As such, unlike applied mathematics, applied logic is really a branch of pedagogy or psychology rather than logic; and Kant notes that it is concerned with "attention, its hindrance and consequences, the cause of error, the condition of doubt, of reservation, of conviction, etc." (KrV A54–55/B79). In this respect, applied logic seems closer to applied moral philosophy, in the sense of moral anthropology, than it is to applied physics or mathematics.

Kant affirms a further parallelism between ethics and logic in the *Critique*, when he states that general and pure logic is related to applied

as pure morality [*die reine Moral*], which contains merely the necessary moral laws of a free will in general, is related to the doctrine of virtue proper, which assesses these laws under the hindrances of the feelings, inclinations, and passions to which human beings are more or less subject, and which can never yield a true and proven science, since it requires empirical and psychological principles just as much as applied logic does. (KrV A55/B79)

A somewhat different view regarding the systematic place of moral anthropology and its relationship to applied ethics is to be found in the *Metaphysics of Morals*. In the Introduction to this work, Kant first remarks that "a metaphysics of morals cannot dispense with principles of application, and we shall often have to take as our object the particular *nature* of human beings, which is cognized only by experience, in order to *show* in it what can be inferred from universal moral principles" (MS 6: 217; 372). Here, in contrast to GMS, an empirical element is itself part of the metaphysics of morals and, as such, of moral theory proper, insofar as the latter is concerned with duties incumbent upon human beings. But this empirical element is no longer identified with moral anthropology, since Kant proceeds to define the latter in terms that are reminiscent of his account of a doctrine of virtue in the first *Critique*. As he here puts it:

The counterpart of a metaphysics of morals, the other member of the division of practical philosophy as a whole, would be moral anthropology, which, however, would deal only with the subjective conditions in human nature that hinder people or help them in *fulfilling* the laws of a metaphysics of morals. It would deal with the development, spreading, and strengthening of moral principles (in education in schools and in popular instruction) and with other similar teachings and precepts based on experience. (MS 6: 217; 372)

This survey of Kant's shifting views regarding the relationship between moral anthropology and moral theory indicates the presence of an ongoing tension in his thought. On the one hand, there is the uncompromising aprioristic view, which predominates in the Preface to GMS and those places in GMS 2 where Kant emphasizes the distinctiveness of a metaphysics of morals, in which anthropological considerations play no role in either the grounding or the application to human beings of moral principles. On the other hand, there are places where empirical knowledge of human nature is deemed to play an essential, albeit subordinate, role in moral theory. In this strand of Kant's thought, though human nature is not viewed as the source of moral principles, empirical knowledge thereof is considered necessary for the application to human beings of principles, the scope of which is rational beings as such.

Although developing the point would take us well beyond the scope of the present work, it must at least be noted that the inclusion of an empirical component in the application of moral principles, which is an essential feature of Kant's later writings, was dependent on a development of a distinction in his theoretical work between the *a priori* and the pure *a priori*, which he first drew in the Introduction to the second edition of the *Critique* and is therefore not to be found in GMS.[10] After defining *a priori* cognitions as "those that occur absolutely independent of all experience," Kant notes

---

[10] The importance of this distinction for the understanding of Kant's project of a metaphysics of morals has been emphasized by Gregor (1963, 1–17).

that "Among *a priori* cognitions . . . those are called **pure** with which nothing empirical is intermixed." And, as an example of a cognition that is *a priori* without being pure, he cites the proposition "Every alteration has a cause" (KrV B3). This proposition is *a priori* because of its necessity and strict universality, but it is not *pure a priori* because it contains an empirical concept (alteration). Accordingly, this distinction leaves room for a class of "impure" *a priori* cognitions, which employ empirical as well as *a priori* concepts.

In Kant's theoretical philosophy, this distinction between the two classes of *a priori* cognition reflects the distinction between a general and special metaphysics of natural science, which Kant drew in the *Metaphysical Foundations of Natural Science*. The former constitutes the "pure" or transcendental part of such a metaphysics and is concerned with "the laws that make possible the concept of nature in general, even without relation to any determinate object of experience, and thus undetermined with respect to the nature of this or that thing in the sensible world" (MAN 4: 469; 185). The latter constitutes the "impure" or "applied" part and is concerned with "a particular nature of this or that kind of thing, of which an empirical concept is given." The basic idea is that the inclusion of an empirical concept, in this case the concept of matter, does not compromise the *a priori* nature of the enterprise, because "outside of what lies in this concept [which for Kant involves being movable in space], no other empirical principle is used for its cognition" (MAN 4: 469–70; 185). In other words, Kant claims that the minimal nature of the empirical component (a single concept) limits the scope of his metaphysical project without undermining its apriority.

Applying this schema to Kant's moral theory, GMS corresponds to its pure, general, or transcendental part, since it is concerned with the applicability of moral principles to *rational* beings as such and abstracts from whatever special considerations may be involved in their application to *human* beings.[11] The latter is the task of the *Metaphysics of Morals*, which considers duties incumbent upon and involving human beings considered as such rather than as male or female, young or old, aristocrat or commoner, rich or poor, educated or uneducated, etc.[12] Accordingly, the question becomes: what is it that pertains to the concept of a human being as such, which is analogous to mobility as a property of matter as such, in that it allows for the derivation of duties *a priori* through the application of the supreme principle of morality to this concept? Although Kant is largely silent on this topic, I believe that a reasonable conjecture is that it encompasses the three predispositions to good in human nature, which he

---

[11] I am not here claiming that the pure part of moral theory belongs to transcendental philosophy, since Kant explicitly denies this, albeit for somewhat different reasons in each edition of the *Critique* (see KrV A14–15 and B28–29). My point is merely that this part of moral theory is the practical analogue of the transcendental part of the metaphysics of nature. Kant notes the parallelism between the application of the pure *a priori* (transcendental) principles to experience in the metaphysics of nature and the application of pure practical principles to human nature in the metaphysics of morals at MS 6: 216–17; 372.

[12] In the *Metaphysics of Morals* , Kant deals briefly with the latter type of duty in a chapter entitled "On ethical duties of human beings toward one another with regard to their **condition**" (MS 6: 48–96; 584), which he treats as an appendix to his argument, because such duties cannot be specified systematically.

distinguished in *Religion*, namely, to animality, to humanity, and to personality (see RGV 6: 26–28; 74–76).[13]

Leaving that speculation aside, however, the main point is that at the time of the composition of GMS Kant lacked the tools for including an empirical element, however minimal, in a metaphysics of morals, as he then conceived it, since he had not yet arrived at the distinction between *a priori* and pure *a priori* cognitions. Moreover, given the focus of this work on the determination of the fundamental principle of morality rather than on the derivation of particular duties from this principle, there was no reason for Kant to include an empirical element in his account; for if anything in ethics is to be pure *a priori*, it is its supreme principle.

III

Having provided some sense of what he understands by a metaphysics of morals and assigned it a place in the taxonomy of philosophical disciplines in the first part of the Preface, Kant turns in the second part (GMS 4: 388_9–91_{15}) to the more difficult task of arguing for the indispensability of such a metaphysics. But since Kant's argument for this thesis extends beyond the Preface to portions of GMS 2, the analysis of this argument requires a consideration of these later texts as well. In fact, by considering not simply the argument as contained in the Preface but also its further development, I hope to be able to show that Kant not only provides an argument for the necessity of some (undetermined) metaphysics of morals but for a particular one or, more precisely, for a particular grounding for any such metaphysics. I shall further argue that this grounding provides the key to understanding Kant's unique meta-ethical standpoint. To anticipate, my contention is that what is unique about Kant's meta-ethics is the seemingly paradoxical combination of grounding the supreme principle of morality in the abstract concept of a rational being as such, while justifying this procedure by appealing to a supposedly shared pre-philosophical understanding of morality.[14] Although the latter part of this procedure is hardly unique, since it is adopted by the popular moral philosophy, as well as many other meta-ethical positions, the former part is distinctively Kantian, particularly given his understanding of the concept of a rational

---

[13] The predisposition to "animality" concerns humans taken as living beings and encompasses the pre-rational, instinctual basis of human nature. The predisposition to "humanity" concerns humans considered as rational animals and basically involves the capacity to use reason in the service of inclination. The predisposition to "personality" concerns humans as moral or accountable beings. Not only does Kant characterize these as "predispositions *toward good*," since they demand compliance with the moral law (RGV 6: 28; 76), but he maintains that they are sources of specific duties to ourselves (MS 6: 421–47; 546–67). We shall revisit these predispositions in Chapter 8 in connection with the analysis of Kant's conception of humanity [*Menschheit*]. For my previous discussion of them, see Allison (1990, 148–50).

[14] This initial characterization of Kant's meta-ethical position is somewhat of an over-simplification, since we shall see that it is crucial for Kant to distinguish between rational beings *simpliciter* and rational beings with wills, that is, rational agents, and that it is really in the latter concept that Kant attempts to ground morality. But since at this preliminary stage in his account he refers to rational beings, I shall here follow his usage.

being as such. Since Kant argues for the indispensability of a metaphysics of morals, so construed, on both theoretical and practical grounds, the discussion is divided into two parts: one examining Kant's argument for the theoretical and the other for the practical necessity of such a metaphysics.

Before proceeding, however, it is necessary to distinguish between three different senses in which Kant uses the expression "metaphysics of morals" in GMS.[15] First, we have already seen that in the Preface Kant equates it with pure or *a priori* moral philosophy. In this sense, GMS is itself part of a metaphysics of morals. Second, he uses it to refer to the projected work for which GMS is intended to lay the foundation. In this sense, GMS is obviously not a part of this metaphysics. Third, it refers to that to which a transition is made in GMS 2 and from which one is made in GMS 3. Equally obviously, construed in this sense, the metaphysics of morals is itself a part of GMS. Our present concern is with the first of these senses.

(A) The indispensability for moral theory of a metaphysics of morals

Kant initially formulates his methodological thesis by posing the following rhetorical question: "whether one does not think it a matter of the utmost necessity to work out once a pure moral philosophy, which is fully cleansed of everything that may be empirical and belong to anthropology"? Although this question constitutes a challenge to any empirically based moral theory, its specific target is the popular moral philosophy, which Kant accuses of not having any method at all, instead appealing indiscriminately to *a priori* or empirical (anthropological) considerations, as the situation seems to require.[16] In response to this question, which introduces a third sense of "pure," namely, uncontaminated or unmixed, that is clearly directed at the popular moral philosophy, Kant writes:

[T]hat there must be such [a philosophy] is already evident from the common idea of duty and of moral laws. Everyone must admit that a law, if it is valid morally, i.e., as ground of an obligation, must carry with it absolute necessity; that the command: thou shalt not lie, is valid not merely for human beings, as if other rational beings had no need to heed it; and likewise with all remaining genuinely moral laws; hence that the ground of obligation here is to be sought not in the nature of the human being [*des Menschen*] or the circumstances of the world in which he is placed, but *a priori* solely in concepts of pure reason, and that every other precept [*Vorschrift*] grounded on principles of mere experience, and even a precept that is universal in a certain respect, insofar as it rests in the smallest part on empirical grounds, perhaps only as to its motivating ground [*Bewegungsgrund*], can indeed be called a practical rule, but never a moral law. (GMS 4: 389$_{9-23}$).

This passage contains the gist of Kant's argument for the indispensability for moral theory of a pure moral philosophy, insofar as it is contained in the Preface. It consists of three claims, the first two of which supposedly entail the third. A striking feature of the

---

[15] See, for example, Bittner (1989, 14–15), and Schönecker and Wood (2004, 10–11).

[16] See, for example, GMS 4: 410$_{3-18}$.

passage is Kant's assertion that the first two of these claims are derived from the "common idea of duty and of moral laws," which implies that the conclusion must likewise be in accord with this common idea. This is the first indication that the ultimate basis both for Kant's claim of the necessity of a metaphysics of moral and the specific direction that it will take is provided by a supposedly shared pre-philosophical understanding of morality.

(1) Kant's initial claim is that a moral principle must involve "absolute necessity." I shall term this the "absolute necessity thesis." In spite of Kant's assertion that every one must admit it, the expression "absolute necessity" is ambiguous in its reference and obscure in its sense. With regard to the former, it can be taken to refer either to particular moral precepts such as "do not lie" or to the more general moral principles in which these precepts are supposedly grounded: for example the greatest happiness principle of classical utilitarianism or the categorical imperative. With regard to the latter, the expression can be understood in either a purely prescriptive or a modalized sense. In the case of moral principles, on the prescriptive (or normative) interpretation, the claim would be that in every possible world in which the principle holds, it holds with absolute necessity in the sense of allowing no exceptions. The modalized interpretation, by contrast, holds that a moral principle, if it is to be considered as such, must be thought as holding in all possible worlds, that is, every conceivable world containing rational beings capable of responding to moral requirements.[17] In what follows, I shall take "absolute necessity" to refer to moral principles and I shall understand it in the modalized sense.

(a) At first glance this reading may seem problematic, since in the passage under consideration Kant appears to be attributing absolute necessity to particular moral injunctions, such as the prohibition of lying, rather than to principles. Moreover, on this reading, the necessity to which Kant refers is most naturally taken in the prescriptive sense, which is built into every "ought" claim. This leaves unexplained, however, the meaning of the qualifier "absolute," which, on this reading would most likely be taken as an expression of Kant's notorious "rigorism," that is, the thesis that duties allow for no exceptions.[18] But if this is what Kant meant, he was wrong in claiming that everyone must agree, since the common view is that duties, even supposedly strict ones, such as the prohibition against lying, allow for exceptions under certain circumstances.

[17] According to Scarano, whose account has influenced this part of my analysis, the non-modalized formula for a moral principle is that any properly moral principle must have the following form: "For all objects x: if, and only if, x satisfies the criterion C, does x have the moral quality M." Correlatively, the modalized formula is that "Necessarily, for all objects x: if, and only if, x satisfies the criterion C, does x have the moral quality M." See Scarano (2006, 7–10). I believe that my formulation accords with this. The qualification limiting the scope of a moral principle to possible worlds containing beings capable of responding to moral requirements is necessary, since a moral principle obviously would not apply in a world in which there is no one to address.

[18] This is the view of Timmermann (2007a, 5).

The purely prescriptive, reading also fails to accord completely with the text; for it seems clear that, rather than equating "absolute" with not allowing exceptions in this familiar sense, Kant takes it to indicate the universal scope, that is, the application to all rational beings (without exception) of any particular duty claim. In other words, assuming that Kant is here referring to particular moral precepts, the denial of exceptions refers to the scope of their application rather than to the cases falling under them, e.g., particular instances of deliberate falsehood. I shall return to this issue below in connection with an analysis of what I term the "scope thesis," which is the second of the three theses that Kant enunciates in the passage before us.

(b) As already noted, however, I believe that "absolute necessity" refers not to specific duties (or at least not primarily to them), but to the underlying principle on which these duties are based. In the text currently before us, support for this reading is provided by Kant's reference to "the ground of an obligation," which is most naturally understood as referring to the general principle on which a particular duty is based. And we shall see that further support is provided by other passages as well. But the main basis for this reading is a consideration of Kant's overall project in GMS, namely, "the search for and establishment [*die Aufsuchung und Festsetzung*] of *the supreme principle of morality*" (GMS 4: 392$_{3-4}$). In fact, we shall see that the assumption that this principle, whatever it turns out to be, must have absolute necessity in the modalized sense is the first and essential step in this search.

(2) Kant's second claim is the previously referred to scope thesis, that is, the thesis that in order to be valid a moral principle must be applicable not only to human beings, but to all rational beings. Although the text before us does not address the issue, it must be noted that it is compatible with the modalized reading, which maintains that a moral principle must be applicable not only to every *actual* rational being, but to every *conceivable* one.

(3) Kant's third claim is that the ground of moral obligation is to be sought "not in the nature of human beings or the circumstances of the world in which they are placed, but *a priori* solely in concepts of pure reason." I shall term this the "apriority thesis." Assuming (a) that the two above-mentioned alternatives are empirical and are intended to represent all viable empirical grounding candidates, and (b) that the grounding of a principle must be either empirical or *a priori*, it follows (c) that the grounding of the principle that itself grounds all first-order moral principles must be *a priori*. And since an *a priori* grounding of a moral principle for Kant could only be in *a priori* concepts ("concepts of pure reason"), it follows (d) that this principle must be grounded in some such concept[s], which entails (e) that the quest for the supreme principle of morality must proceed by an *a priori* method.[19]

---

[19] I take it that this conclusion is independent of the question of whether the absolute necessity and scope theses are to be understood in the modalized sense. Moreover, on this point I differ from Scarano, who, after

Nevertheless, this argument for the apriority thesis is far from sufficient for Kant's larger purposes. The basic problem is that it shows only that a moral theory must be grounded in *some* concept(s) of pure reason and it is completely uninformative on the question of which one(s). In fact, many moral theories which Kant explicitly rejects meet this criterion. One example is Wolff's, whose views and Kant's critique thereof will be discussed in the next chapter. Another is Crusius', for whom moral obligations are grounded in the will of God, specifically in God's ends and perfections, of which we can supposedly acquire *a priori* knowledge because we are equipped with the appropriate innate ideas.[20]

A useful way of framing the problem, which has been suggested by Rüdiger Bittner, is in terms of a distinction that Kant later draws in passing between the seat [*Sitz*] and origin [*Ursprung*] of concepts. His claim is that in the case of moral concepts, which presumably include the not yet identified supreme principle of morality, both are to be found "completely *a priori* in reason" (GMS 4: 411$_{8-9}$). In discussing this contrast, Bittner points out that these are distinct: the *Sitz* of a concept is the place where it is located, which in the present case would be the faculty of reason; whereas its *Ursprung* refers to the ground of its validity. Thus, in the case of moral concepts, Kant's claim is not only that that they must be determined or found by purely rational means, but that they must also be grounded in pure reason. And, as Bittner notes, a concept could have its *Sitz* in pure reason but not its *Ursprung*.[21] A good example of this is the view of Crusius referred to above. While the *Sitz* of moral concepts on his view is in our innate ideas; their *Ursprung* is in God's ends and perfections, which are the grounds of obligation. Accordingly, Kant's task is to show that whatever is to count as the supreme principle of morality must have not only its *Sitz* but also its *Ursprung* in pure rational concepts.[22] And while the argument from the Preface considered above may be

---

arguing convincingly for interpreting Kant's absolute necessity thesis in a modal sense, proceeds to interpret Kant's apriority claim in light of Kripke's distinction between metaphysical and epistemological terms. Since this line of thought creates conceptual space for notions like the contingent *a priori* and the necessary *a posteriori*, which are oxymorons on the traditional view, Scarano finds in the text currently under consideration a substantive argument from necessity (in the modalized sense) to apriority. See Scarano (2006, esp. 12–15). Whatever intrinsic philosophical interest such an argument might possess, I find it hopelessly anachronistic as a reading of Kant, since he obviously would have had little sympathy for views such as Kripke's.

[20] See Crusius (1969, 166–67). For a brief account of Crusius' moral theory, see Schneewind (1998, 445–56).

[21] See Bittner (1989, 17–18).

[22] One of Bittner's main criticisms of Kant's procedure is his claim that the assignment of the *Ursprung* of moral concepts to pure reason is not only distinct from but incompatible with the assignment of their *Sitz* to the same reason. In support of this he maintains that it is only on the basis of experience that one can attribute reason to a being. As he puts it, "'*Vernunft*' ist kein reiner Vernunftbegriff." See Bittner (1989, 20). Although this may be true, it is irrelevant, since the issue concerns the kind of concepts or principles to which morality appeals, not the determination of whether a given being is rational, which is a matter of judgment, applying non-empirically determined criteria to a particular case.

sufficient to address the first task, it contributes relatively little to the second and more important one.[23]

Unfortunately, Kant does not address the second issue explicitly, a failure which is in a large part due to the fact that his discussion of the matters bearing on it is scattered between the Preface and portions of GMS 2 rather than spelled out in a single place. Indeed, it might even be questioned whether Kant actually argues for this second claim, as opposed to merely assuming (erroneously) that it follows from the first. Nevertheless, I believe it possible to construct such an argument on the materials that Kant provides, which turns on the modalization of the absolute necessity and scope theses. And since I also hope to show that Kant is best read as understanding these theses in their modalized sense in which they reciprocally imply one another, this will also amount to an argument for the hermeneutical thesis that this argument represents Kant's actual view. At the very least it should articulate the meta-ethical view to which Kant is rationally committed.

The essential point is that the non-modalized versions of absolute necessity and scope theses can account for the prescriptive necessity of courses of action *under a principle* (those prescribed by the principle in question), but not the necessity *of the principle itself*. Moreover, this is insufficient, since the latter is required if the principle is to have genuine normative force that can extend an unconditioned necessity to the particular requirements falling under that principle. But this is possible only if the necessity and universal scope of the principle are understood in the modalized sense.

Let us consider Kant's own example: the duty not to lie. Quite apart from the question of whether it allows for exceptions, in the cases in which it does apply, it does so unconditionally to all rational beings. For Kant, appealing again to the understanding of morality possessed by common human reason, this is simply what it means to be obligated. But this unconditionality means that it must be viewed as binding not merely on every actual rational being (human or otherwise), but on every *conceivable* rational being (existent or otherwise). In other words, such a principle's binding force must have a counterfactual reach; and it is just this reach that is accounted for by the modalized version of the scope thesis.[24] This also explains why the necessity to which Kant refers is qualified as *absolute*.[25] For Kant to say that something is absolutely

---

[23] I say that it contributes relatively little rather than nothing at all because it could be argued, *pace* Bittner, that having its *Sitz* in pure reason is a necessary, though not a sufficient condition of a concept or principle having its *Ursprung* there.

[24] Kant's view may be formally expressed as: (x) (Px → $\square$ (y) (Rx →Bxy)); that is, for any x, [if x is a moral principle, then necessarily: (for any y, if y is a rational being, then x unconditionally binds y)]. I am indebted to Huaping Lu Adler for this formalization.

[25] See KrV A324–25/B380–82. Kant here distinguishes between two senses of "*absolute*." One indicates that something is valid of a thing considered in itself or internally, which he claims is the least that one can say about a thing. The other affirms that it is valid of something in every relation, which is the most that can be said about it. It seems evident that, with reference to moral principles, Kant is taking the term in the second and stronger sense. Moreover, although in the first *Critique* passage Kant is referring to what is supposedly "absolutely possible," I think it also evident that this applies to what is supposedly absolutely necessary as well.

necessary is to say that it is necessary in every conceivable relation, which is the Kantian equivalent of every possible world. And lest one think that this modalization of Kant's claims involves reading something into the text that is not really there, we need only note the following passage:

[U]nless one wants to dispute whether the concept of morality has any truth and relation to any possible object, one cannot deny that its law [the supreme principle] is of such extensive significance that it would have to be valid not merely for human beings but for all *rational beings as such*, not merely under contingent conditions and with exceptions, but with *absolute necessity*. (GMS 4: 408$_{12-18}$)

Accordingly, the question becomes: what must be the *Ursprung* of any moral principle that could have the requisite scope and necessity? And when the issue is framed in this way the answer seems relatively clear. If it is to be valid for every conceivable rational being, it must have its origin in a concept for pure reason; for only such a concept could have this scope and necessity. More specifically, it must be the concept of something that is common to every conceivable rational being and to nothing else. But this is just the property of being a rational being. And from this it follows that, if a moral principle is to have the modal features that Kant's analysis requires, it could only have its *Ursprung* in "the universal concept of a rational being as such" (GMS 4: 412$_{3-4}$), which is precisely what Kant claims.

To summarize: if we consider Kant's initial argument in the Preface for the necessity for moral theory of a pure, that is, *a priori* moral philosophy, together with its extension in GMS 2, we find a two-part argument for the *Sitz* and *Ursprung* in pure reason of whatever could serve as the supreme principle of morality, which locates this *Ursprung* in the universal concept of a rational being as such. The first part of this argument, which is contained in the passage from the Preface cited above, yields the conclusion that the *Sitz* of any putative moral principle must be found in concepts of pure reason. Its premises are the absolute necessity and scope theses, understood in a manner which abstracts from the question of their modality. Its second part, which is contained mainly in GMS 2, presupposes the modalized versions of these theses and argues from this that the *Ursprung* of any putative supreme principle of morality must lie in the universal concept of a rational being as such.[26]

I shall conclude this analysis of Kant's argument for the necessity for moral theory of a metaphysics of morals with two observations, which I take to be crucial to the understanding of the overall argument of GMS. The first is that, contrary to what one might suppose, neither Kant's argument for the necessity of a metaphysics of morals nor the formulation of the concept on which such a metaphysics could alone be based rely on the tacit identification of the sought for supreme principle of morality with the

---

[26] Both Bittner and Siep, who together with Scarano are among the few commentators to have examined the argument of the Preface in any detail, conclude, albeit on different grounds, that the argument for the *Ursprung* thesis is fallacious. Neither, however, considers the issue of modality. See Bittner (1989, esp. 22–28) and Siep (1989, esp. 40).

categorical imperative. If it did, Kant's whole procedure in the portions of the text discussed above could be dismissed as question begging. Rather, Kant is here engaged in a meta-ethical reflection on the conditions that must be met by *anything* that could count as a supreme principle of morality. This leads down the road to the categorical imperative, but it does not presuppose it.

The second observation concerns the source of the premises on the basis of which Kant constructed his analysis, particularly the absolute necessity and scope theses in their modalized forms and the claim that moral concepts must have both their *Sitz* and *Ursprung* in concepts of pure reason. The text makes it quite clear that Kant regarded these as already found, albeit not in a clearly articulated form, in the common, pre-philosophical conception of morality; and it is to this conception that Kant consistently appeals in his search for the supreme principle of morality.[27] Kant's position is open to serious question on this point and we shall return to this issue in Chapters 3 through 5, which deal with the argument of GMS 1, where Kant explicitly claims to be doing nothing more than clarifying what he terms "common rational moral cognition." But whatever one's ultimate judgment on this matter, I think it evident that this is how Kant understood his own project. Otherwise expressed, while there are many *theories* of morality, for Kant there is only one true *concept* of morality and it is possessed by ordinary human reason. Accordingly, we shall see that, while Kant was willing to consider the possibility that the generally received concept of morality might be a mere phantom of the brain [*ein Hirngespinst*] (GMS 4: 445₉), he would not brook any challenge to the view that this phantom is what we both do and must understand by morality.

(B) The indispensability of a metaphysics of morals for moral practice

After presenting his case for the necessity for moral theory of a metaphysics of morals, Kant argues for its necessity for moral practice. He begins by noting that, even though human beings are equipped with the correct moral principles, because they are beset by so many inclinations they have difficulty applying them *in concreto*. And from this he concludes:

A metaphysics of morals is therefore indispensably necessary, not merely from a motive of speculation . . . but because morals themselves remain subject to all sorts of corruption as long as that guiding thread and supreme norm of correct moral judgment is lacking. For with regard to the morally good, it is not enough that it *conform* to the moral law, but it must also be done for the sake of this law [*um desselben willen geschehen*]; otherwise, that conformity is only very contingent and precarious, because the non-moral [*unsittliche*] ground will now and then produce lawful

---

[27] In my view, this applies to GMS 2 as well as GMS 1, even though Kant there makes a fresh start by attempting to derive the various formulas of the categorical imperative from an analysis of rational agency rather than directly from rational moral cognition. Since this second derivation rests on the assumption that the *Ursprung* of the supreme principle of morality is to be sought in the universal concept of a rational being as such, it is itself ultimately based upon an analysis of the common, pre-philosophical conception of morality or common rational moral cognition.

actions, but very often actions contrary to the law. But now the moral law in its purity and genuineness (which is precisely what matters most in the practical) is to be sought nowhere else than in a pure philosophy; therefore this (metaphysics) must come first, and without it there can be no moral philosophy at all; that which mixes these pure principles with empirical ones does not even deserve the name of a philosophy (for this distinguishes itself from common rational cognition precisely by the fact that it expounds in a separate science what the latter comprehends only confusedly [*nur vermengt*]), still less of that of a moral philosophy, because precisely through this mixture it undermines the purity of morals and proceeds contrary to its own end. (GMS 4: 389_{36}–90_{18})

This paragraph makes five basic points: (1) Morals, meaning the practice of morality, is susceptible to various corrupting influences, as long as it lacks the norm of correct moral judgment, that is, the right principles. (2) This openness to corruption stems from the fact that morality (presumably the common concept of morality referred to above) requires not merely a *de facto* agreement with its precepts, but one that is based on the recognition of their normative status. (3) The fundamental principle of morality (the moral law) is found in its unadulterated form only in a "pure philosophy" (a metaphysics of morals). (4) Therefore, any moral philosophy that is to be valid for moral practice, which is a necessary condition for counting as a moral philosophy, must be based on a pure philosophy, which expounds the moral law in its unadulterated form. (5) As a corollary of this, it follows that any purported moral philosophy that fails to adopt this procedure not only fails to count as a moral philosophy, but actually works contrary to the true end of such a philosophy, that is, it enhances rather than checks a tendency towards the corruption of morals. Since (1) appears to be non-controversial, (3) was presumably established in the previous part of Kant's analysis, and (5) evidently follows from (4), I shall limit my comments to (2) and (4).

The noteworthy feature of (2) is that it appears to rest on Kant's claim that the categorical imperative requires that our actions not only conform to duty but are performed from it, in the sense of being motivated by the recognition of their dutifulness. The problem is that this creates the worry that Kant is here engaged in circular reasoning, assuming that the categorical imperative is the supreme principle of morality in an argument that is supposedly intended to establish this result.

Any such worry is misguided, however, since the claim that to be morally good, an action must not only "*conform* to the moral law . . . it must also happen for the sake of this law" is not one that is unique to Kant's moral philosophy. On the contrary, many (if not most) moral theories would hold that, in order for an act to possess moral value, it not only must be the right thing to do in given circumstances, but it most be done for the right reasons. Otherwise, as Kant points out, the accord of the act with the principle would be purely contingent, a matter of chance for which the agent deserves no moral credit. For example, what serious consequentialist would argue that, in order to receive moral praise, it suffices that an act achieve a good result (however this goodness may be determined by the theory), even though the agent did not intend it or any other morally desirable result? Granted, Kant builds more into this claim than the relatively non-controversial thesis that morally worthy actions must be done for the right kind of reasons, since he has quite distinctive views about both the nature of the moral principle and what constitutes the (morally) right kind of reasons; but this does not affect the point at issue.

The problem with (4) is that it might be taken to yield an implausibly strong conclusion, namely, that in order to be morally good, a person must know and apply the correct moral theory. Such a view is implausibly strong because it seems to imply that only a moral philosopher, specifically one of a Kantian persuasion, is capable of acting morally. Moreover, this contradicts a central tenet of Kant's moral theory, since this theory holds not only that moral goodness (a good will) is within the capacity of any normal adult human being, but also that every such being already possesses the true concept of morality, albeit not in a clearly worked out form.[28] But if this is the case, one might well ask why philosophy should be required to provide us with something that we already possess apart from it.

The answer is two-fold, corresponding to the two parts of the objection. First, Kant never claimed that it is necessary to possess a fully worked out moral theory in order to be a morally good person. He did claim, however, that the latter required some grasp of the correct principles for the reason given above. Second, what makes this requirement reasonable is precisely the assumption that these principles are already contained in the concept of morality embedded in the understanding of every normal adult human being or, in Kant's terms, "common rational moral cognition." Finally, the fact that this implicit metaphysics is not fully worked out, but is combined with spurious and potentially harmful assumptions, creates the need for moral philosophy, which serves as a guardian against error rather than as an independent source of truth. We shall see in Chapter 5 that Kant returns to this issue at the end of GMS 1, where he examines the factors underlying what amounts to a propensity in human nature to corrupt moral principles.

IV

In the final portion of the Preface (GMS 4: $391_{16}-92_{28}$), Kant describes the aim and method of the work. He begins by informing the reader that it is intended to lay the groundwork [*Grundlegung*] for a projected metaphysics of morals, while noting that the only proper foundation [*Grundlage*] for the latter would be a critique of a *pure practical reason*. The situation, he suggests, is precisely parallel to theoretical metaphysics, the foundation for which has already been provided by a critique of pure speculative reason (GMS 4: 391_{16-20}).

---

[28] In the Introduction to the work to which he gave the title, Kant said of a metaphysics of morals that, "[I]t is itself a *duty* to *have* such a metaphysics, and every human being also has it within himself"; which he qualifies by adding "though as a rule only in an obscure way; for without a priori principles how could he believe that he has a giving of universal law within himself?" (MS6: 216; 371).

Some of the terminological features of this statement of intent call for comment, inasmuch as they reflect Kant's unsettled view of the overall structure of his emerging "critical" system. Specifically, the *Critique of Pure Reason* is now termed a critique of "pure speculative reason," while the not yet projected *Critique of Practical Reason* is described as a critique of "*pure* [my emphasis] practical reason."[29] The gist of the matter seems to be that Kant came to perceive the necessity for a separate foundation for moral philosophy and this required abandoning the original plan, which envisioned the *Critique of Pure Reason* as providing a foundation for both a metaphysics of nature and a metaphysics of morals. Accordingly, the task of the first *Critique* is reconceived as providing a foundation merely for the pure speculative use of reason and a parallel critique is claimed to be required for its pure practical use.

Having claimed that only a critique of pure practical reason would be fully adequate to the task at hand, Kant must explain why he is providing something less. He offers three reasons. First, in spite of what he has just said, he suggests that a critique in the practical domain is not as essential as it was shown to be in the speculative, "because with regard to the moral [*im Moral*] human reason, even the most common understanding, can readily be brought to a great correctness and completeness, whereas in its theoretical but pure use it is wholly and entirely dialectical" (GMS 4: 391$_{21-24}$). Here, as elsewhere, Kant is appealing to his Rousseauean view of the "common man" as fully capable of recognizing and applying the correct moral principles, at least under ideal conditions, when he is not corrupted by alien influences.

Kant's second reason for providing a groundwork rather than a full-scale critique is that the latter would require exhibiting the unity of pure practical with speculative reason by deriving them both from a common principle. This reflects Kant's view that there can be only a single reason, which is distinguished merely in its application (GMS 4: 391$_{25-28}$). Although Kant excuses himself from this task on the grounds of its complexity, he did eventually attempt to deal with it in the second *Critique*, where he argues that, through the moral law, conceived as a causal law governing a free will, practical reason gives content to the otherwise vacuous idea of an intelligible or noumenal causality, which reason requires in its theoretical function (KpV 547–50; 178–80).

Kant's third reason does not bear so much on GMS as on the projected metaphysics of morals. Since, in spite of its intimidating title, Kant suggests that the latter is "capable of a great degree of popularity and suitability for the common understanding," he

---

[29] Apparently, with the terminology of GMS in mind, Kant begins the Preface to the second *Critique* by explaining why it is entitled simply a *Critique of Practical Reason* rather than a *Critique of Pure Practical Reason*. The point is that the goal of this work is to show that "there is pure practical reason" or, as Kant generally puts it, that pure reason can be practical; and to this end it is necessary to criticize reason's entire practical faculty (KpV 5: 3; 139). In other words, what is criticized here is the pretension of *empirical* practical reason to be the only form of practical reason. By contrast, in GMS Kant does not launch a critique of empirical practical reason *per se*, since he does not examine it; though we shall see that he does criticize philosophical views that offer an empirical foundation for morality.

prefers to issue the preliminary foundational work separately, thereby making the work to be erected on this foundation easier to comprehend (GMS 4: 391_{34}–92_2). As we shall see in the next chapter, largely as the result of pressure from Christian Garve, Kant took seriously the issue of popularity, by which is understood intelligibility for the educated but not philosophically trained reader, rather than acceptance by a large segment of the general public, as the term is usually understood today.

According to Kant, what makes GMS incapable of such popularity is its aim, which, as already noted, is the search for and establishment of the supreme principle of morality. Clearly, this assumes that there is such a principle, which seems to be something that Kant never doubted, even though he had shifting views about its precise nature. Moreover, by presenting this as a distinct, self-contained project, Kant, in effect, introduces a further division of labor, this time within the already circum-scribed field of pure moral philosophy. The first part of this project (the search for this principle) is a matter of uncovering it and its presuppositions. This is basically what Kant endeavors to do in the first two sections of GMS. The second part (the establishment of this principle) is a matter of justification or grounding, that is to say, its deduction. This is the task of the third section.

The final paragraph, in which Kant spells out the method to be followed in GMS, together with the listing of the headings of its three sections, is among the more obscure of the Preface. Kant proposes a dual procedure, which he claims to be the most suitable, "if one wishes to proceed analytically from common [moral] cognition to the determination of its supreme principle and then, in turn, synthetically from the examination of this principle and its sources back to common cognition, in which its use is encountered" (GMS 4: 392_{18-22}). Kant does not explain why one would wish (or need) to proceed in this manner, but it seems reasonably clear that he thought it necessary to accomplish the above-mentioned two-fold goal of the work. Although the matter is somewhat controversial, it also seems reasonable to assume that the search for the principle of morality is the task of the analytic portion and its establishment that of the synthetic.[30]

Since Kant's fullest account of the distinction between the analytic and synthetic methods (which is not to be confused with that between analytic and synthetic judgments) is in the *Prolegomena*, it is customary to look there for the model to interpret his procedure in GMS.[31] Nevertheless, it takes only a brief glance

---

[30] This has been challenged, albeit in different ways, by Brandt (1988) and Miltz (1998).

[31] Kant also discusses the topic in the various versions of his lectures on logic. Thus, in the *Jäsche Logic* he states that the analytic method begins with the conditioned and grounded and proceeds to principles (the conditions), while the synthetic method proceeds from principles to consequences or the simple to the composite. Kant further notes that the former procedure can be called "regressive" and the latter "progres-sive" (JL 9: 149; 639). Kant's understanding of this methodological distinction seems to be fairly standard. The key features of all the formulations are the contrasts between conditioned and condition and regressive and progressive.

at this account to realize that the distinction, as he there characterizes it, cannot be straightforwardly applied to GMS.

In the *Prolegomena*, Kant emphasized that the synthetic method is that of the *Critique*, because it is the only one capable of establishing the possibility of metaphysics, which he there regarded as equivalent to establishing the possibility of synthetic cognition *a priori*. The *Critique* supposedly does this by an examination of pure reason, which uncovers the elements and laws of its pure use. As Kant puts it, the *Critique* "tries to develop cognition out of its original seeds without relying on any fact whatsoever" (Pro 4: 274; 70). Apparently, it is its not having to rely on any "fact" or unjustified presupposition that accounts for the power of the synthetic method of the *Critique*.

By contrast, the *Prolegomena*, which Kant characterizes as "preparatory exercises" (Pro 4: 274; 70), proceeds by the analytic method, which, as he here describes it, means that it assumes the actuality of a body of synthetic *a priori* cognition (mathematics and pure natural science) and investigates how (under what conditions) such cognition is possible. Kant further clarifies his view of the analytic method in an important footnote, where he writes:

> The analytic method, insofar as it is opposed to the synthetic, is something completely different from a set of analytic propositions; it signifies only that one proceeds from that which is sought as if it were given, and ascends to the conditions under which alone it is possible. In this method one often uses nothing but synthetic propositions, as mathematical analysis exemplifies, and it might better be called the *regressive* method to distinguish it from the synthetic or *progressive* method. (Pro 4: 276n; 73)

Unlike the *Prolegomena*, GMS does not begin with a body of synthetic *a priori* practical cognitions, as if it were given. If it did, it would have had to begin with the categorical imperative and regress to the conditions of its possibility.[32] Rather, GMS 1, which Kant characterizes as containing a "transition from common rational moral cognition to philosophical moral cognition," begins with the concept of a good will, which Kant takes to be the highest value recognized by the former mode of moral cognition and culminates in the uncovering of the supreme principle of morality, which in GMS 2 will be identified with the categorical imperative. This procedure is regressive in the sense that it moves from something conditioned (the concept of a good will) to the categorical imperative as its highest condition; but this regress is quite different than the one described in the *Prolegomena*. Whereas the latter is a regress from cognitions to their enabling conditions (space and time as forms of sensibility and the categories), the former is essentially an exercise in conceptual analysis, the aim of which is to make explicit what is already presupposed in ordinary moral cognition.

---

[32] The latter is essentially the procedure of the second *Critique*, which, qua critique, supposedly uses the synthetic method; but which affirms the moral law as a "fact of reason" and then argues for the reality of freedom as a necessary condition of this "fact."

The situation becomes more problematic when we consider the last two sections of GMS in light of Kant's own characterization of the relation between the analytic and synthetic portions of his procedure. As already noted, he suggests that the former proceeds from common moral cognition to its supreme principle and the latter from this principle back down to ordinary cognition. In other words, the circle is completed with the argument returning to the point from which it started. On the one hand, this appears to reduce GMS 2, which is usually viewed as the heart of the work, to a mere appendage, since it seems to suggest that it stands outside this circle; while, on the other hand, this characterization does not seem to fit the procedure of GMS 3, since it is not clear that this section closes this circle. I shall briefly discuss each problem in turn.

To begin with, although Kant characterizes the procedure in each of the first two sections of the work as analytic, they do not constitute consecutive steps in a single regressive argument. On the contrary, GMS 2 appears to change the subject and make a fresh start. Moreover, Kant's procedure in this section differs from that of the first in many ways, the most important of which being that the transition is there distinct from the regress. Whereas we have seen that the transition in GMS 1 is to an undefined philosophical moral cognition and is at the same time a regress from something conditioned (a good will) to its condition (the categorical imperative), the transition in GMS 2 is from popular moral philosophy to a metaphysics of morals, which are obviously not related as conditioned to condition. Since Kant understood by popular moral philosophy primarily the work of Garve, one possible reason for this procedure is that it provided him with an opportunity to incorporate remnants of his original "anti-Garve" project. A more systematically reputable explanation, however, is that Garve, like Kant, purported to base his moral theory on a pre-philosophical, commonsensical understanding of morality, which made it imperative for Kant to differentiate his project as sharply as possible from Garve's. But inasmuch as I shall discuss Garve's view in the next chapter, I shall say nothing further about the matter here.

Our immediate concern is rather with the regress in GMS 2. If it is not in the transition, where is it? The short answer is that it is in the metaphysics of morals, as it appears in this section. As we shall see, this regress starts not with our ordinary, pre-philosophical moral convictions, but with the abstract philosophical concept of a rational agent as such. We shall also see that the various steps in this regress, which Kant links with the various formulas of the categorical imperative, involve an increasingly deeper account of rational agency and its conditions, culminating in the uncovering of the principle of the autonomy of the will. Again, I shall postpone my analysis of these crucial moves for subsequent chapters; but it is worth noting that here the nature of the regress is much closer to that of the *Prolegomena* than that of GMS 1. This is because with the autonomy of the will we reach the supreme condition of the possibility of the categorical imperative and therefore of morality as Kant conceived it, just as with the *a priori* forms of sensibility and pure concepts of the understanding in the *Prolegomena* we supposedly arrive at the supreme conditions of the possibility of mathematics and natural science respectively.

To determine the nature of the supreme principle of morality as the categorical imperative is not, however, to establish the possibility or actuality of this imperative. Accordingly, for all that the analytic procedure purports to show, it remains possible that this imperative is a phantom of the brain, a merely chimerical idea without any truth. And since we are dealing with a synthetic *a priori* practical proposition, removing this possibility requires an additional transition, this time from the metaphysics of morals to a critique of pure practical reason. This is the subject matter of GMS 3, where we also find the shift from the analytic to the synthetic method. But since this argument will be the subject matter of the final three chapters of this commentary, I shall once again postpone my discussion of it.

Instead, I shall conclude this chapter with a brief comment on Kant's previously cited claim that the interplay of the analytic and synthetic methods in GMS describes a circular process that both begins and ends with common rational moral cognition. Since Kant's procedure as just described appears to culminate in a critique of pure practical reason rather than common rational moral cognition, it is sometimes wondered whether Kant's characterization of his procedure really meshes with what he actually does in GMS 3.[33] Nevertheless, a careful consideration of the text will show that Kant does deliver in GMS 3 what he promises in the Preface. To anticipate, the key text is a passage immediately following what Kant himself describes as the deduction of the categorical imperative, where he remarks that, "The practical use of the common human reason confirms the correctness of this deduction" (GMS 4: 454_{20-21}). Kant explains what he means by this in a lengthy passage, where he appeals to the distinction between the sensible and intelligible worlds on which the deduction turns and argues that the consciousness of standing under the categorical imperative leads even "the most malicious scoundrel" to think of himself in his better moments as a denizen of the latter (GMS 4: 454 21–27). I shall return to the issues raised by this claim in the final chapter; but for now the main point is simply that, assuming that this scoundrel possesses common rational moral cognition, the synthetic procedure in GMS 3 does in fact culminate in a descent to the common rational moral cognition in which the whole argument of GMS is rooted.[34]

---

[33] This questioned by Bittner (1989, 29).

[34] In highlighting the significance of this passage in the context of the present considerations, I am following Miltz (1998, 198–201).

2

Universal Practical Philosophy and Popular Moral Philosophy

Although the bulk of the present chapter constitutes a digression from direct commentary on the text of GMS, it is one which I believe to be necessary in order to understand this work in its historical context. As the title suggests, it is concerned with the two approaches to moral philosophy in relation to which Kant largely framed his project in GMS: the universal practical philosophy, which was initially formulated by Wolff and further developed by Baumgarten and the latter's student Georg Friedrich Meier, and the eclectic "popular moral philosophy," which was associated with Christian Garve, as well as figures in the Berlin enlightenment. In spite of their radically different methodologies (a systematic and dogmatic rationalism versus an eclectic empiricism), universal practical philosophy and popular moral philosophy share some common features to which Kant was deeply opposed, specifically, eudaemonism and an endeavor to ground morality in human nature. Accordingly, I believe that a sketch of the relevant features of these approaches and an analysis of Kant's reaction to them will put us in a better position to appreciate the reasoning behind some of the more distinctive and controversial features of GMS. The chapter is divided into two parts. The first examines the main tenets of universal practical philosophy and Kant's critique thereof. The second analyzes the views of Garve, as expressed in his notes to his translation of and commentary on Cicero's *De officiis*.

I

The discussion of universal practical philosophy is divided into three parts. The first attempts to provide an overview of its central tenets and methodology, which requires a consideration of its place within the Wolffian system of practical philosophy. The second considers Kant's fundamental criticisms of universal practical philosophy in the various lectures on ethics for which he used Baumgarten's treatment of it as his text. The third analyzes a single paragraph in the Preface to GMS, in which Kant endeavors to underscore the radical difference between universal practical philosophy and his own project of a metaphysics of morals. This paragraph, which was neglected in the preceding chapter, is important because it provides Kant's clearest statement of his understanding of the major differences between his project and its Wolffian counterpart, differences which Kant's Wolffian trained readers were likely to overlook because of certain superficial similarities.[1]

(A) The nature of universal practical philosophy

Both the name and the method of this discipline were inventions of Christian Wolff.[2] In his dissertation of 1703, entitled *Philosophia practica universalis*, Wolff attempted to provide practical philosophy with a new foundation, which was modeled on mathematics and the sciences that make use of the mathematical method. As such, it was intended as a challenge to the Aristotelian view that the level and kind of certainty attainable in a science is a function of the subject matter of that science and that full certainty is unobtainable in the study of human affairs. Abandoning a reliance on the mathematical method of demonstration, though not the goal of apodictic certainty, Wolff published in 1738 a work under the same title, which is concerned with the most general rules of human action and which purports to provide certain knowledge of the general principles governing our free actions, understood as the voluntary behavior of human beings. As concerned with such actions, it is a practical or, in Wolff's scholastic terminology, an "affective" science, which he defines it as "the affective practical science of directing free actions by the most general rules."[3]

Wolff's universal practical philosophy was put in textbook form by Alexander Baumgarten under the title *Initia philosophiae practicae primae acroamatice* in 1760, and it was this work that provided the text for Kant's own treatment of universal practical philosophy in the various versions of his lectures on ethics. But the subject matter was given its fullest treatment in a German work by Baumgarten's student, Georg Friedrich Meier, *Allgemeine practische Weltweisheit* (1764). Even though Kant does not refer to it explicitly in his lectures, referring instead to Baumgarten ("our author"), Kant was undoubtedly familiar with the latter work, and since it provides the most accessible and comprehensive treatment of the subject the following account will be largely based upon it.[4]

Within the Wolffian school, the importance of universal practical philosophy stems from its foundational role in the system of moral disciplines. Anticipating much of what Kant was to say about a metaphysics of morals, Meier claims that universal practical

---

[1] It should be noted that this is not limited to Kant's own contemporary readers, since Bittner emphasizes the similarities between the Wolffian universal practical philosophy and Kant's procedure in GMS, while questioning Kant's attempt to draw a sharp distinction between them. See Bittner (1989, 20–21).

[2] Much of this sketch of the history and nature of the project of a *philosophia practical universalis* up to the time of Kant is based on the account of Kobusch (1993, esp. 92–100).

[3] Wolff (1963, 37).

[4] Both the significance of Meier's work, which he characterizes as providing "*eine Metaphysik der Person*," and its influence on Kant are emphasized by Kobusch (1993).

philosophy is essential to both moral theory and practice. In both cases, this stems from the need for a demonstration of the basic duties that are incumbent on human beings as such.[5]

From a theoretical standpoint, this is necessary to secure a scientific status for practical philosophy comparable to that possessed by its theoretical counterparts. In this spirit, Meier characterizes universal practical philosophy as the metaphysics of all practical disciplines in the sense that it deals with "the universal predicates of all moral things."[6] The basic idea is that universal practical philosophy is concerned with the generic duties incumbent on human beings, of which those considered in the particular practical disciplines are specifications and on which their obligatory force ultimately depends.[7] As Meier puts it at one point, apart from a foundation in universal practical philosophy, which is alone capable of bringing the highest degree of completeness and certainty to the specific practical disciplines, the latter would be built on sand.[8] As such, universal practical philosophy is a kind of metaphysics of morals, inasmuch as it purports to provide the only viable foundation for a system of human duties.

Nevertheless, Meier insisted that the main import of universal practical philosophy falls on the practical rather than the theoretical side. In addition, he pointed out in a manner, which is at least not inconsistent with Kant, that a clear grasp of one's duties greatly facilitates their performance.[9] In sharp contrast to Kant, however, Meier held that the primary practical benefit of such knowledge, which is provided by universal practical philosophy, is that it provides an indispensable means to the attainment of happiness.[10]

Another feature of universal practical philosophy, which is partly reminiscent of Kant, is its focus on general rules governing free actions.[11] Because of their normative necessity these rules are laws, and since they reflect the nature of the agent rather than the dictates of an external authority, they are laws of (human) nature. Accordingly, the fundamental task of universal practical philosophy is to derive these laws, together with the closely related concepts of obligation and duty, from the nature of human beings considered as free agents.

---

[5] Meier (2006, 2–3).

[6] Ibid., 55.

[7] Although he does not discuss it in detail, Meier essentially adopts Wolff's taxonomy of the practical disciplines: ethics, politics, and economics. The first is concerned with human beings living in their natural (pre-political) condition, that is, in a state of nature in the traditional (non-Hobbesian) sense and with the duties encumbent upon them, so considered. Politics is that part of practical philosophy in which human beings are considered as living in a political condition or civil society and is concerned with the rules or duties governing their free actions in that condition. Economics [oeconomica] deals with individuals as living in smaller, non-political societies, such as the family and with the duties to which individuals, so considered, are subject. See Wolff (1963, 36).

[8] Meier (2006, 61).

[9] Ibid., 45–46.

[10] Ibid., 7–9. See also, 30, 34–35, 44–45.

[11] Ibid., 235–98.

This scope limitation to human beings constitutes a fundamental difference from the Kantian view as discussed in the previous chapter. This limitation is not the result of any skepticism on Meier's part regarding either the existence of other species of rational beings in the universe or their subjection to practical laws; it rather stems from his belief that, since we cannot know the ways in which other rational beings differ from humans, it would be futile to investigate their natural duties.[12] The latter point underscores the empirical, psychological orientation of universal practical philosophy, which not only puts it at the opposite end of the methodological spectrum from Kant's metaphysics of morals, but also stands in some tension with its rationalist underpinnings and claim to be a demonstrative science.

In spite of its empirical, naturalistic approach, universal practical philosophy's focus on the intimate connection between laws and freedom also calls to mind Kant's metaphysics of morals, with its appeal to moral laws as laws of freedom. Nevertheless, its underlying conception of freedom and the laws thereof are radically opposed to the Kantian view. Not surprisingly, its conception of freedom is essentially the Leibnizian one, as articulated by Wolff, according to which free actions are necessary in the sense that they are governed by the principle of sufficient reason.[13] For Wolff, Baumgarten, and Meier what renders an action "free" is not its lack of determining grounds (the so-called "liberty of indifference"), but the kind of determining grounds that it has. Specifically, free actions are those that are performed on the basis of what the intellect (correctly or incorrectly) perceives to be the best or most perfect course of action in a given situation. Since the will or appetitive faculty lacks any spontaneity of its own, it invariably chooses what the intellect perceives to be the best. In this respect, its choices are necessary; but inasmuch as these choices depend on the perception of the intellect, they are only morally rather than absolutely or unconditionally necessary, which supposedly suffices for freedom.

This compatibilist conception of freedom underlies Meier's claim that the fundamental concept of universal practical philosophy is that of a free action.[14] Thus, it is in light of this conception of freedom that universal practical philosophy analyzes the central concepts of the natural law tradition with which it is closely connected. A case in point is the concept of obligation [obligatio, Verbindung, Verpflichtung], which Kant, following Baumgarten, discusses at some length in his lectures. Eschewing complications such as the distinction between active and passive obligation, an act is obligatory within universal practical philosophy if it is morally necessary.[15] Baldly put,

---

[12] Meier (2006, 61), 3–5.

[13] The distinctive feature of the Wolffian view, which is shared by Baumgarten, is that it holds (contra Leibniz) that the principle of sufficient reason is itself viewed as a consequence of the principle of non-contradiction. Nevertheless, Wolff (and Baumgarten) did not believe that attributing logical necessity to the principle of sufficient reason rendered everything governed by the latter principle itself logically necessary.

[14] Meier (2006, 67–68).

[15] See Baumgarten (1934, 11) and Meier (2006, 137–42).

this seems non-controversial, since not only Kant but any philosopher who has any use for the concept of obligation would be inclined to accept it.

Complications begin, however, with universal practical philosophy's peculiar understanding of moral necessity and possibility, each of which is given both a broad and a narrow sense. Broadly construed, everything is morally possible that is compatible with freedom of the will and the physical capacities of the agent. As such, the category encompasses every act that can be performed voluntarily, including manifestly evil and immoral ones, which from a Kantian point of view would be deemed morally *impossible* in the sense of being impermissible or in violation of duty.[16] Correlatively, everything is morally necessary in the broad sense whose opposite is morally impossible.[17] But since the latter includes only what is either unconditionally or absolutely necessary or physically impossible, the morally necessary likewise includes all free actions.[18] In other words, taken in their broad senses, the morally possible and the morally necessary are extensionally equivalent; though they still differ intensionally, since the force of claiming that an action is morally necessary is to underscore the core Leibnizian thesis that it is *only* morally, as opposed to absolutely or unconditionally necessary.

This gives a strange turn to the identification of obligatoriness with moral necessity. Since all free or voluntary (morally possible in the broad sense) actions are morally necessary (again in the broad sense), it seems to follow that all such actions (including those that are manifestly evil or immoral) are not only permissible but obligatory. Thus, obligatoriness loses any special connection with what is morally required and instead characterizes the conditionally necessary character of free actions (including morally evil ones). Moreover, rather than endeavoring to deny or mitigate this result, Meier emphasizes it. In fact, he explicitly denies the usefulness of distinguishing between moral and non-moral obligation on the grounds that the essence of the latter consists in the will being necessitated, and that this applies whether or not its motivating grounds are specifically moral.[19]

Meier, again following Wolff and Baumgarten, attempts to deal with the seemingly paradoxical implication of the view that we may be obligated to perform not merely morally indifferent but immoral actions by introducing the concept of a motive [*Bewegungsgrund*] and appealing to the narrow senses of the notions of moral necessity and possibility. Motives, by which Meier understands desires and abhorrences [*Verabscheuunngen*], are the means through which a free will is determined.[20] Since, given the Wolffian primacy of the intellect, whatever is desired is thought to be good and abhorred to be bad or evil, this means that, in a situation of choice, whatever alternative has the preponderance of *Bewegungsgründe* in its favor is by that very fact deemed to be good or at least the best available choice. Accordingly, properly spelled out the thesis of universal practical philosophy is that an agent is obligated to choose what seems to that

---

[16] Meier (2006, 137–39).   [17] Ibid.   [18] Ibid., 139–40.
[19] Ibid., 176–77.   [20] Ibid., 143–45.

agent to be the best available option at a given time, all things considered. But it must also be noted that the obligatory force of choosing the best possible option and avoiding the less good alternatives, which is concisely expressed in the Baumgartian principle *"fac bonum, omitte malum"*[21] [Do good, omit evil], is inseparable from the connection of these choices with rewards and punishments, which reflects the eudae-monistic orientation of universal practical philosophy.[22]

The fact that what a particular agent takes to be the best may not objectively be the best creates conceptual space for a distinction between genuine or true and false obligations; the latter being those that arise through indistinct or inadequate ideas.[23] And in his endeavor to deal with a presumed obligation to evil or sinful actions, Meier notes that anything that contradicts a true obligation is morally impossible in the narrow sense, which entails that it cannot be morally necessary in that sense and therefore cannot constitute an obligation.[24]

As far as true obligations are concerned, the fundamental concept for the Wolffians is perfection [*perfectio, Vollkommenheit*]. Wolff construed the term in both an ontological and a practical sense, with the former being the key to the latter. Taken in its ontological sense, the perfection of a thing consists in the harmony of its manifold parts, their functioning together so as to constitute a unified whole.[25] Wolff's view of practical perfection stems from the application of this concept to the human will. Accordingly, he defines the perfection of the latter as "the harmony of all and every volition with one another, none running contrary to the others."[26] He also regarded perfection, so construed, as the ultimate end of human action.[27] Thus, in what is usually referred to as Wolff's "German Ethics," he states as a moral principle: "Do what makes you and your condition more perfect and omit what makes your and your condition less perfect."[28] In Baumgarten, this leads to the principle: "*Quaere perfectio-nem, quantum potes*" [Seek perfection as much as you can].[29] And for Meier the first principle from which every genuine obligation flows is to "Make yourself in all your free actions as perfect as possible," which is logically equivalent to Baumgarten's formula.[30]

In order to appreciate the import of this principle for Wolffian practical philosophy, it is essential to keep in mind that Wolffian perfectionism is rooted in its intellectualist view of the mind, according to which all its contents (including emotions and sensa-tions) are cognitions. Accordingly, to increase the mind's perfection is to increase its cognitive power, which involves the transformation of thoughts that are confused and indistinct into those that are clear and distinct. Inasmuch as this increases the power of the mind to recognize the true good, it also increases its power to accomplish it, since the main hindrance to this accomplishment lies in the indistinctness of its ideas of the

---

[21] Baumgarten (1934, 25).   [22] See Meier (2006, 145–46.)   [23] Ibid., 151–52.
[24] Ibid., 161–62.   [25] Wolff (2005, 78–79).   [26] Ibid., 562.
[27] Wolff (1979, 18–19).   [28] Wolff (1976, 16).
[29] Baumgarten (1934, 23).   [30] Meier (2006, 232–33).

good. Moreover, this increase in the power of the mind leads not only directly to the increase of its own perfection, but also to the recognition of the need to increase the perfection of the body (which is intimately related to that of the mind) and of the perfection of others as well. Finally, since the feeling of pleasure is itself a confused awareness of perfection, this automatically brings with it an increase in happiness, which underlies the eudaemonistic dimension of this approach.[31]

I shall discuss the Kantian critique of Wolffian perfectionism as a moral theory below; but before turning to that it is necessary to say a word about another moral principle to which the practitioners of universal practical philosophy were committed and which is intimately related to its perfectionism, namely, the Stoic principle: "*Naturae convenienter vivens,*" which in Baumgarten takes the form "*naturae convenienter vivens, quantum potest, quaerit perfectionem suam*" [Live according to nature, to the extent that you can in order to attain your perfection].[32] Although we shall see that Kant regarded this principle as a hypothetical imperative, for Baumgarten it had obligatory force as a principle of intrinsic or natural obligation, because it provides the means for attaining to the extent possible the perfections that constitute one's natural end. The basic idea is that to live according to nature is to live according to the laws of one's nature, which, since it has the sanction of reason, obligates independently of any external authority, including God. Moreover, since knowledge of one's nature and perfections rests upon experience, this links the program of universal practical philosophy closely with empirical psychology, a point which was not lost upon Kant.[33]

(B) Kant's critique of universal practical philosophy in his lectures on ethics during the 1780s[34]

Kant's main criticism of universal practical philosophy in these lectures is just that it purports to be a universal practical philosophy, that is, one which provides an analysis of the will or volition in general rather than of the "pure will," by which Kant understood a will considered independently of any motivation by sensuous impulses or desires and which he deemed essential to the possibility of morality. More specifically, Kant's complaint is that universal practical philosophy fails to deal adequately with moral concepts such as goodness, evil, obligation, duty, imputation, and the like because it ignores the morally specific features of these notions. In addition, Kant points out the tautological nature of many of the moral principles referred to above and

---

[31] Many of the points in this paragraph were suggested by the discussion of Schneewind (1997, xix–xx).

[32] Baumgarten (1934, 26).

[33] The Wolffians distinguished between rational and empirical psychology as two distinct branches of metaphysics. As the names suggest, the former is an *a priori* discipline, in which the human soul is investigated through rational concepts, whereas in empirical psychology it is cognized on the basis of experience. For the distinction, see Baumgarten (1926, 130). Kant followed Baumgarten in discussing both types of psychology in his lectures on metaphysics; though in the Dialectic of the first *Critique* he considers only rational psychology, arguing that in its treatment of the soul it is guilty of a series of paralogisms.

[34] I shall here limit my analysis to Kant's lectures from the 1780s because these are the ones that are most directly germane to the genesis and argument of GMS.

raises deep objections against the Wolffian view of free agency, which underlies its accounts of obligation and imputation.

(1) *The concept of obligation*: The difference between universal practical philosophy and the Kantian view is best approached through a comparison of their respective views on obligation. As we have seen, Meier, who closely followed his mentor Baumgarten, distinguished between genuine and spurious obligations, but explicitly refused to limit obligation to the sphere of morality. Moreover, in proceeding in this way, Meier was being true to the method of universal practical philosophy, which, qua universal, sought a generic and univocal conception of obligation of which moral obligation is merely a species. It is just this, however, that Kant emphatically denied.

Referring to Baumgarten ("our author"), Kant claimed that all obligation for him is "the coupling of the most superior grounds to my action [*die Verknüpfung der vorzüglichsten Gründe zu meiner Handlung*], for he says that the good contains impelling grounds [*bewegende Gründe*] to act, and the superior [*vorzügliche*] good has superior impelling grounds [*vorzüglicheBewegungs Gründe*] to act" (MPC 27: 264; 57). From Kant's point of view, the major difficulty with this characterization is that the nature of the good, which contains the impelling or motivating grounds for our actions, remains indeterminate, which means that we can be obligated to pursue non-moral as well as moral goods. At issue is not whether there are non-moral goods, but whether we may be properly said to have an obligation to pursue them. Expressing the matter in terms of imperatives, Kant remarks that not all imperatives yield obligations, as Baumgarten apparently thought. In support of this, Kant refers to *imperativi problematici*, which he had previously argued do not amount to obligations (MPC 27: 264; 57).

Elsewhere, Kant argues that obligation is not merely a necessity [*Notwendigkeit*] but also a *necessitation* [*Nöthigung*] (MM1 27: 1408). This is a direct challenge to the Wolffian view as formulated by Meier, for whom we have seen that obligation is defined in terms of the moral necessity (in the broad sense) of an action. Against this, Kant points out that, while God's actions are morally necessary, they are not necessitated. The latter requires constraint, which is not applicable to the divine or holy will, since it is not subject to any countervailing desires or interests. In other words, for Kant necessitation arises only in the case of human (or other finite rational) wills, for which what is objectively necessary is subjectively contingent. Furthermore, being necessitated is not equivalent to being obligated for Kant; since it is necessary to distinguish between a *pathological* necessitation, which is the product of impulses stemming from an agent's sensuous nature, and a *practical* necessitation, which is the product of an understanding of the good. And, finally, within the latter category, it is also necessary to distinguish between a pragmatic and a moral necessitation, only the second of which counts as an obligation because it is categorical or unconditioned (MM1 27; 1408–9 and MPC 27: 255–56; 50–51).

(2) *The moral principles of universal practical philosophy*: Closely related to Kant's critique of universal practical philosophy's account of obligation are his comments regarding

the three basic moral principles already referred to: *fac bonum, omitte malum*; *quaere perfectionem, quantum potes*; and *naturae convenienter vivens*. To begin with, Kant denies that the first even counts as a moral principle, since it leaves undefined the nature of the good that one should do and the bad (or evil) that one should omit. Since these goods might be regarded as good for any arbitrary purpose, say the acquisition of wealth or, more generally, for the attainment of happiness, as well as the morally good, it is just as easily regarded as a principle of skill or prudence as a moral principle. If, however, the principle is understood to refer specifically to the morally good, then it is tautologous, since it says no more than it is good that you do the good (MPC 27: 264–65; 57–58 and MM1 27: 1414).

Kant's response to the second principle is more nuanced, reflecting his view that of all the erroneous principles of morality, that of perfection is the best, since, unlike moral sense theories, it is based on reason rather than sentiment, while, unlike eudaemonistic ones, it at least does not infringe upon morality (MM2, 29: 626; 244 and GMS 4: 443_{20-27}). Thus, at one point Kant suggests that perfection is less indefinitely expressed than the other principles affirmed by universal practical philosophy and, as such, is not a "total tautology" but has a "degree of usefulness"(MPC 27: 265; 58). Apparently, this is because perfection, understood as "the completeness of man in regard to his powers and capacity, and readiness to carry out all the ends that he may have," has something to do with morality. Nevertheless, it is not equivalent to moral goodness, which is a quality (perfection) of the will, consisting in "the property of making good and proper use of all these perfections." The basic point is that since perfection, so understood, can be used for all sorts of ends, including evil ones, it cannot itself be identified with the morally good; but inasmuch as the good will needs the perfection of its powers to carry out what is willed, it is indirectly necessary to morality (MPC 27: 265–66; 58–59). Later, in GMS and the *Metaphysics of Morals*, Kant will argue for basically this reason that we have a duty to perfect ourselves; but for Kant this is seen as grounded in the categorical imperative rather than as itself the ground of moral obligation. Indeed, Kant insists that, taken in the latter sense, it is tautologous (MM2 29: 616; 236).

Unfortunately, Kant's account of the third principle of Wolffian moral theory (*Vive convenienter naturae*), or at least Collins' report of it, appears to be a bit garbled. Kant is recorded as claiming that if this proposition is read as stating: "Live according to the laws which nature gives you through reason," then it is still tautological, because "to live according to nature would mean to direct one's action according to the physical order of natural things" (MPC 27: 266; 59). The problem is that this advice does not seem tautologous, unless it is taken to mean something like "obey the law of gravity," in which case it would be better described as otiose.[35] Moreover, Kant also states that

---

[35] That Kant does not have the logical sense of tautology here in mind is clear from other passages. For example, he remarks that it would count as a "tautologous rule of decision" if a doctor advised someone suffering from constipation to make sure that his bowels are loose (MC 27: 265; 58).

this same principle is prudential rather than moral; and he adds that it is not even a good prudential principle, since one does not know if it is a good thing (presumably for oneself) that one's actions conform to nature (MPC 27: 266; 59).[36]

(3) *The concept of freedom in universal practical philosophy*: In the lectures with which we are currently concerned, Kant discusses freedom largely in connection with the topics (taken over from Baumgarten) of moral or practical compulsion [*Zwang*] and necessitation [*Nöthigung*]. Accordingly, Kant sets aside the whole transcendental dimension of his account, which is central to the first and second *Critiques*, as well as GMS 3. Moreover, even though the critique of the Wolffian view discussed above is obviously implicit in Kant's entire account, he does not explicitly thematize it, as he does, for instance, the notion of obligation and the various versions of the principle of morality. The fundamental contrast with which Kant operates in these lectures is between an *arbitrium brutum* and an *arbitrium liberum*, which resembles Baumgarten's distinction between an *arbitrium sensitivum* and an *arbitrium liberum*.[37] Since for both Kant and the Wolffians, a free will must in some way be determined or necessitated, a purely arbitrary choice (the liberty of indifference) being considered an absurdity, the difference between the two species of *arbitria* turns on the different types of necessitation to which they are subject. For Kant, the former is pathologically and the latter practically necessitated. And since the former is directly determined by the strongest stimulus, there is no place for freedom. As Kant puts it at one point, "Animals are necessitated *per stimulos*, so that a dog must eat if he is hungry and has something in front of him; but man, in the same situation can constrain himself"(MPC 27: 268, 60). By contrast, a being with an *arbitrium liberum* has this power of self-constraint, since it acts on the basis of motives [*per motiva* or *Bewegursachen*], which provide reasons for acting that may be independent of and in conflict with any impulses or inclinations that the being has. Moreover, these motives (whether moral or pragmatic) do not render the course of action they prescribe causally necessary, since the *arbitrium liberum* remains free to ignore them and to act instead on the basis of immediate inclination. Thus, Kant points out, in opposition to the Wolffian view, that "to act contrary to obligation is still

---

[36] In the Vigilantius lecture on the metaphysics of morals of 1793 Kant provides a clearer statement of his point. Referring to the same principle, he points to its ambiguity and suggests two possible interpretations: (1) it could mean live like an animal, in which case it would be a highly problematic prudential principle; or (2) it could mean "Live according to the precepts of reason," in which case it is tautologous, telling us nothing more than to do our duty because it is our duty (MSV 27: 518; 281). Since Kant was obviously aware that the principle was understood in the latter way, his critique closely parallels those of the other Wolffian principles. In each case, if made contentful, they do not qualify as principles of morality; while if they are taken as such principles they are tautologous in the sense of being uninformative.

[37] Baumgarten (1926, 135). It should also be noted, however, that, while for Baumgarten, with his Wolffian view of freedom, an *arbitrium sensitivum* and an *arbitrium liberum* are contrasted on the basis of whether the motivating cause is sensible or intellectual, for Kant the human will is both *sensitivum* and *liberum*, rather than *brutum*, because it is sensibly *affected* but not *determined* (KrV A534/562). Indeed, one way of contrasting the Wolffian and the Kantian views is that the latter has room for the contrast between being affected and being determined, while the former does not. Or, perhaps better, since the Wolffian view is deterministic, the difference could be understood only as a contrast between a partial and a complete cause.

an exercise of freedom" (MPC 27: 288; 82). Presumably, this thought underlies Kant's remark that, "freedom is a terrifying thing, since its actions are not determined at all" (MPC 27: 258; 52).

Later, in discussing duties to oneself, which pertains to ethics proper rather than to universal practical philosophy, Kant expands upon this. On the one hand, he emphasizes the supreme value of freedom by characterizing it as "the inner worth of the world," on the grounds that it is the source of all value; on the other hand, he notes that, "insofar as it is not restrained under certain rules of conditional employment, it is the most terrible thing there could be" (MPC 27: 344; 125).[38] In other words, freedom needs to be constrained by being brought under rules; but the difficulty is that the only power capable of constraining it is freedom itself (MPC 27: 346; 126). Kant further suggests that the rule according to which freedom must restrict itself is its "conformity with the essential ends of mankind" (MPC 27: 345, 126), and that "The *principium* of all duties is thus the conformity of the use of freedom with the essential ends of mankind" (MPC 27: 346; 127).

As far as compulsion is concerned, in the case of the of an *arbitrium liberum* it is likewise practical rather than pathological and it only enters the picture when there is a conflict between what reason dictates to be the best course of action (either morally or pragmatically) and the agent's inclination. Accordingly, as already noted, for a divine or holy will there is no necessitation or compulsion (though there is necessity), since there are no inclinations that conflict with the dictates of reason. And, for the same reason, there are no obligations or duties for such a will. Indeed, Kant claims that, "The more a man can be morally compelled, the freer he is; the more he is pathologically compelled, though this occurs only in a comparative sense, the less free he is" (MPC 27: 268; 60).

The qualification that the human will can be compelled only in a comparative sense is important for understanding Kant's view, since his position is that it cannot actually be compelled, which is itself an implication of the thesis that the only restriction on freedom (understood as freedom of choice not action) must be one imposed by freedom upon itself. As Kant puts it in a passage that sounds almost Sartrean:

[I]f a man . . . is forced to an action by numerous and cruel tortures, he still cannot be compelled to do these things if he does not will it; he can after all withstand the torture. Comparatively speaking, he can be compelled, indeed, but not strictly; it is still possible for him to refrain from action, regardless of all the sensory incentives—that is the nature of *arbitrium liberum*. (MPC 267; 60)

Here again there is a decisive difference with the Wolffian view, for which everything turns on the weight of the stimuli and there is no conceptual space for a will possessing a spontaneity that enables it to stand apart from its motivating grounds. To be sure, a Wolffian agent might be able to resist considerable physical pain, say the fires of the Inquisition; but this would be understood in terms of the model of an agent who is so

---

[38] See also R7202 19: 469 and R7217 19: 288.

engrossed in the thought of the heavenly bliss that is soon to be enjoyed that the present sufferings count as nothing.

For Kant, by contrast, if it is an imputable action it always involves an exercise of spontaneity on the part of an agent, through which the latter freely decides on the basis of some principle, rather than, like the Wolffian martyr, being irresistibly determined by the strongest belief or desire. Returning to Kant's own torture example, let us assume that the agent relents and gives the information being sought by the torturers. On the Kantian picture, we are to think of the unfortunate agent as acting on a principle (even if only implicitly) to the effect that it is not worth undergoing great suffering to save those whose identities and whereabouts are being sought by the torturers. It is thus a matter of the agent placing greater value on the cessation of personal suffering than on the fate of those being sought and perhaps the cause for which they are fighting. Even though the agent may not formulate such a thought to himself, it (or something like it) is the principle on which he acts, which is why Kant claims that the agent may be said to be compelled only in a relative and not in a strict sense.[39]

(C) Kant's remarks regarding universal practical philosophy in GMS

These remarks are contained in a single paragraph in the Preface, which follows immediately upon Kant's argument for the necessity of a metaphysics of morals and are intended to underscore the difference between his project and the Wolffian. I shall cite the paragraph in its entirety and then comment upon it:

It should not be thought, however, that what has here been called for is already found in the propaedeutic to his moral philosophy of the famous *Wolff*, namely, in what he called *universal practical philosophy*, and therefore do not need to break into an entirely new field. Precisely because it is supposed to be a universal practical philosophy, it has not taken into consideration a will of any particular kind, such as one determined fully from *a priori* principles, without any empirical motivating grounds [*Bewegungsgründe*] and which could be termed a pure will, but only volition as such, with all the actions and conditions that pertain to it in this general sense; and it is thereby distinguished from a metaphysics of morals in just the way that general logic is distinguished from transcendental philosophy, of which the former expounds the actions and rules of thinking *as such*, the latter merely the particular actions and rules of **pure** thinking, i.e., those through which objects can be cognized fully *a priori*. For the metaphysics of morals should investigate the idea and the principles of a possible *pure* will and not the actions and conditions of human volition in general, which for the most part are taken from psychology. That moral laws and duty are also spoken of in this universal practical philosophy (though without any warrant) is no objection to my assertion. For the authors of this science remain true to their idea of it in this too; they do not distinguish the grounds of motivation, which are represented as such fully *a priori*

---

[39] Kant's term for the principle that guides an agent's choice is "maxim." In order to avoid unnecessary duplication, I have delayed my initial discussion of this central Kantian conception for the next chapter. It should also be noted that in later chapters I shall spell out the conception of freedom at work here in terms what I call Kant's "incorporation thesis."

through reason and are genuinely moral, from the empirical ones, which the understanding raises to universal concepts through the comparison of experiences; rather they consider them only in terms of the greater or smaller sum of them, without attending to the difference in their sources (since they are all regarded as homogeneous); and through this they make for themselves their concept of *obligation*, which is to be sure anything but moral, although the way in which it is constituted is all that can be demanded in a philosophy that does not judge about the *origin* of all possible practical concepts, whether they also occur *a priori* or merely *a posteriori*. (GMS 4: 390$_{23}$–91$_5$)

The passage contains three main points, which largely recapitulate topics discussed at greater length in the lectures:

(1) First and foremost, Kant attacks universal practical philosophy's approach to moral philosophy, that is, its systematic attempt to ground key moral concepts such as obligation and imputation in an account of volition as such. His basic charge is that this procedure leads unavoidably to ignoring or abstracting from those aspects of agency or volition that are unique and essential to morality. As the above-cited text makes clear, these are its "purity" that is, the independence from anything stemming from our sensuous nature of its motivating grounds, and the *a priori* nature of its governing principles, both of which are ignored by universal practical philosophy because they are not components of volition as such. In short, by focusing exclusively on the genus (volition in general or as such) universal practical philosophy ignores the differentia, which, according to Kant, are essential to an understanding of morality.

In an effort to reinforce this point, Kant draws an analogy between universal practical philosophy and logic, suggesting that the former stands to a metaphysics of morals as the latter stands to transcendental philosophy, understood in the critical sense as an analysis of the pure (*a priori*) rules of the understanding. Although in the versions of Kant's lectures on ethics, which we have been considering, he does not refer to a metaphysics of morals, Kant draws essentially the same analogy, substituting metaphysics for transcendental philosophy, and suggesting that just as logic abstracts from the content of cognitions, so universal practical philosophy abstracts from the grounds of motivation (MM 2: 29: 598; 226).

A Wolffian would no doubt reject Kant's analogy between universal practical philosophy and logic. Within the Wolffian system, the true counterpart of universal practical philosophy is ontology rather than logic.[40] Following the Aristotelian-Scholastic tradition, Wolff defines ontology as "the science of being in general, or insofar as it is being."[41] Beneath ontology lie the three sciences that constitute the special branches of metaphysics: psychology (rational and empirical), rational (or transcendental) cosmology, and rational (or natural) theology, with their

---

[40] Wolff (1963, 35) defines logic as "the science of directing the cognitive faculty in the knowledge of truth." As such, it is much broader than syllogistics and might be equated with scientific method.

[41] Ibid., 39. Ontology, so understood, is equivalent to transcendental philosophy in the traditional (pre-Kantian) sense.

respective objects: the soul, the world, and God.[42] Accordingly, while logic stands apart from the Wolffian system of metaphysics, just as it does for Kant, the parallel between universal practical philosophy and ontology is both precise and intended, since the former stands in the same relation to the more specific practical sciences as the latter does to the branches of metaphysics.

Since Kant was intimately familiar with the Wolffian system, it may be assumed that he was well aware of this and that his intent in drawing a parallel between universal practical philosophy and logic was not to provide an account of the structure of this system, but to underscore what for him is the fatal flaw in its attempt to ground ethics in a universal practical philosophy, so conceived. Simply put, Kant's point is that just as logic abstracts from the question of the conditions or principles of *a priori* cognition, which is crucial for metaphysics for Kant, so universal practical philosophy abstracts from the conditions or principles of a metaphysics of morals, which is equally crucial for moral philosophy as he conceived it.

Moreover, Kant would not have been impressed by the Wolffian retort, since he regarded Wolffian ontology as itself essentially reducible to logic, in virtue of its endeavor to derive the supposedly metaphysical principle of sufficient reason from the logical principle of contradiction.[43] In fact, Kant's critique of this ontology closely parallels his critique of universal practical philosophy. In addition to its misguided attempt to derive a purportedly metaphysical from a logical principle, Kant's chief complaint against this ontology is that, because of its focus on the concepts of objects or things in general, which are the pure or unschematized categories in his account, it unavoidably abstracts from the spatiotemporal form of human experience. Since for Kant space and time have their ground in human sensibility, spatiotemporal properties and relations cannot be predicated of things in general. And since, as sensible conditions of human cognition, these forms cannot be abstracted from without depriving this cognition of its content (concepts without intuition are empty), Kant famously declared that "the proud name of ontology . . . must give way to the modest one of a mere analytic of the human understanding" (KrV A247/B303). Although in the practical domain it is not a matter of giving up a proud name for a more modest one, since Kant's title for his practical project is decidedly immodest, it is likewise a case of carving out a separate domain in which a distinct *a priori* principle (the moral law) is operative and in which we shall see there is reference to a distinct mode of sensibility, namely, moral feeling or respect.

(2) Kant expands on the difference between universal practical philosophy and a projected metaphysics of morals by noting that the principles of the former are taken largely from psychology, since it is concerned with the actions and conditions of

---

[42] Ibid., 41–42. Wolff does not here use this terminology, however, referring instead to natural theology and psychology as two species of "pneumatics" and cosmology or the science of the world as a whole as "general cosmology."

[43] Kant criticizes this move in UE 8: 193–98; 288–93. I discuss this in Allison (1973, esp.19–21, 51–52).

human volition as such, whereas the latter is concerned exclusively with "the idea and the principles of a possible *pure* will." Quite apart from the question of the viability of his own project, Kant is here correct on two counts. First, it is evident that any putatively generic account of human volition must look to psychology for its explanatory principles. Second, Wolff explicitly affirms that universal practical philosophy borrows principles from psychology, more specifically from empirical psychology.[44] Moreover, we have seen that this point was explicitly acknowledged by Meier.

(3) Although Kant could not accuse universal practical philosophy of ignoring concepts such as moral laws, duty, and obligation, which are integral to his own projected metaphysics of morals, he does object strenuously to the manner in which it treats them. Indeed, he goes so far as to suggest that its concept of obligation is "anything but moral." Some of the reasons for this, particularly the account of obligation, have already emerged from a consideration of Meier's account of universal practical philosophy and of Kant's discussions in his lectures. A point that calls for further notice, however, is that Kant attributes the failure of universal practical philosophy primarily to its inattention to the question of the origin of practical concepts, that is, whether they are *a priori* or merely *a posteriori*. Although this calls to mind the distinction discussed in the previous chapter between the *Sitz* and *Ursprung* of moral principles and Kant could certainly claim that universal practical philosophy does not locate the *Ursprung* of such concepts in the universal concept of a rational agent as such, his equation of the question of origin with that of apriority indicates that his concern here lies elsewhere, namely, in the fact that, as we have already seen, the Wolffians themselves acknowledge the psychological basis of their fundamental practical concepts.[45]

Nevertheless, it should be noted that Kant's attitude towards universal practical philosophy is not entirely negative. In fact, his inclusion of a brief discussion of it in GMS seems intended not merely as a criticism of it (though it is certainly that), but also as an attempt to warn his readers not to confuse his project with the Wolffian one. Indeed, since his lectures on ethics used Baumgarten as a text, Kant included universal practical philosophy as one of the basic divisions of these lectures. And at one point he justifies this inclusion on the grounds that it furnishes a preparation for the metaphysics of morals or *metaphysica pura*, which he characterizes as the first part of moral philosophy (the second being moral anthropology) (MM 2: 29: 599; 226). Moreover, in his own *Metaphysics of Morals*, Kant retained the heading "Philosophia

---

[44] See Wolff (1963, 47). In the same section, however, Wolff also notes that practical philosophy, particularly ethics, likewise borrows principles from metaphysics, especially ontology and natural theology. For the distinction between rational and empirical psychology in the Wolffian system see note 33.

[45] Lest one wonder whether there is really a significant difference between grounding moral principles in an analysis of volition as such and in the universal concept of a rational being as such, it must be kept in mind that the latter is understood in modal terms and applies (counterfactually) to any conceivable rational being. Moreover, we have seen that Meier explicitly rejects any such scope extension on the grounds of our lack of knowledge of non-human rational beings. Thus, by "volition as such" the Wolffians understood merely human volition considered in abstraction from its particular ends.

Practica Universalis" for section III of his Introduction, which he also entitled "Preliminary Concepts of the Metaphysics of Morals" (MS 6: 221; 376). There, as in the much earlier lectures, Kant's point seems to have been that universal practical philosophy should be seen as a prolegomenon to or preparation for practical philosophy rather than as its foundational element. The latter, as already noted, can be provided only by a critique of (pure) practical reason.

II

We have seen Kant's critique of universal practical philosophy consists essentially in the charge that, because of its focus on volition in general rather than on pure will, it failed to provide an adequate philosophical foundation for morality. But in criticizing the foundation it purports to provide, Kant implicitly credited it with at least attempting to do something that he regarded as necessary for both moral theory and practice, namely, supplying a philosophical foundation for morality in a set of first principles. By contrast, Kant's quarrel with popular moral philosophy, which assumes a much more prominent role in the argument of GMS, turns on the latter's eschewing the need for anything like a metaphysical foundation of moral theory, preferring instead an appeal to common sense and experience.

Although he is not mentioned by name in GMS, it is generally recognized that Kant's highly critical remarks regarding popular moral philosophy are aimed primarily at Christian Garve, specifically at Garve's translation with commentary of Cicero's *De officiis*, which first appeared in 1783.[46] The major external evidence for this is a series of letters from Hamann to various friends in the winter and spring of 1784, in which Hamann chronicles Kant's work during this period on what became GMS and its connection with his interest in Garve's *Cicero*. According to Hamann, Kant's project began as an "*Antikritik*" against Garve, which, though motivated by the latter's review of the first *Critique* (to be discussed below), was directed against his work on Cicero, and evolved into "*einem Prodromo zur Moral*" [a forerunner to ethics], which, though no longer merely a critique of Garve's *Cicero*, was still related to it.[47] We shall also see that there is considerable internal evidence that Kant had *De officiis* in mind in his analysis of the concept of a good will at the beginning of GMS 1. Given Kant's longstanding interest in Cicero and the importance generally attributed to Cicero's writings at the time, this, of itself, need not lead one to conclude that Kant was influenced by Garve rather

[46] Garve (1792a and 1792b). The references are to the fourth edition, which retains the pagination of the original edition.

[47] The letters are: Letter 729 to Johann Gottfried Herder, February 18, 1784, Hamann (1965, 141): Letter 732 to Johann Friedrich Hartknoch, March 14, 1784, Hamann (1965, 131); Letter 733 to Johann George Scheffner, March 15, 1784, Hamann (1965, 134); Letter 736 to Johann Georg Müller, April 30, 1784, Hamann (1965, 141); Letter 738 to Johann Gottfried Herder, May 2, 1784, Hamann (1965, 147). I am indebted to Manfred Kuehn for these references. For a detailed account of the influence of Garve's *Cicero* on GMS, see Gibert (1994). For a brief but highly useful account of the role of the influence of Garve on the composition of GMS, see Kuehn (2001a, esp. 277–84, and 2001b, 270–78).

than directly by Cicero.[48] But in view of some of the language that Kant uses, which suggests Garve's translation, together with what we have already seen about Kant's interest in Garve's *Cicero*, this conclusion is difficult to avoid.[49]

The discussion of this section is divided into three parts. The first briefly surveys the historical background of Kant's concern with Garve's work. The second considers their dispute regarding the place of popularity in philosophy, particularly moral philosophy. The third analyzes Garve's methodology and some of the central tenets of his moral philosophy, as expressed in his translation of and commentary on *De Officiis* to which Kant responded in GMS.

(A) The historical background of Kant's response to Garve

In order to understand the factors underlying Kant's concern with Garve's *Cicero*, we must begin with the harsh critique of Kant's theoretical philosophy contained in the notorious "Göttingen review" of the first edition of the first *Critique*. Originally written by Garve, this review was heavily edited by J. G. H. Feder and published anonymously in January 1782.[50] Kant regarded this review, which attributed to him a crude form of idealism, as involving not merely honest misunderstanding, but a willful distortion of his views. Accordingly, he wrote a scathing response, which he included in an appendix to the *Prolegomena*, at the end of which he issued a challenge to its author to identify himself (Pro 4: 379–80; 166).

Garve responded in a letter to Kant of July 13, 1783, in which he acknowledged authorship, but excused himself from full responsibility on the grounds that the published version had been amended without his knowledge (Br 10: 328–35; 191–95).[51] Although Garve was justified in claiming that his review had been substantially altered and given a tone that was lacking in his generally respectful version, the basic line of criticism regarding Kant's idealism was already expressed by Garve.[52] Moreover, there are two aspects of his original review that are worthy of note, because they help to explain Kant's concern with Garve's *Cicero* and the extent of the critical

---

[48] On the importance of Cicero's *De officiis* for Kant and other philosophers of the time, see DesJardins (1967, 237–42). DesJardins also notes, however, that Garve's translation is the only version of the work that Kant owned.

[49] This must be distinguished from the stronger and far more controversial thesis, initially expressed by Reich (1939b, 446–63) that Kant's various formulations of the categorical imperative in GMS 2 are to be seen as attempts by Kant to rehabilitate in his own terms three Stoic moral principles that were emphasized by Garve. Although, like many, I am highly skeptical of this thesis, I shall here set that question aside on the grounds that such a rehabilitation project, if it were indeed Kant's, would have no direct bearing on his critique of popular moral philosophy, which is our present concern.

[50] Both the originally published review and Garve's unedited version have been translated by Sassen (2000, 53–77).

[51] Garve did not, however, tell Kant that the person responsible for these changes was J. G. Feder, who was editor of the *Den Göttischen Anzeigen von gelehrten Sachen*, in which the review appeared.

[52] For a discussion of the nature and extent of Feder's revisions, see Beiser (1987, 172–77).

attention paid in GMS to popular moral philosophy, of which Garve was the leading representative.[53]

The first of these aspects is Garve's three-paragraph discussion of the Canon, of which Kant could not have been aware prior to seeing the original review, since there is no hint of it in Feder's version.[54] In order to appreciate the importance that this discussion would have had for Kant, we must keep in mind that his original plan, as spelled out in the Architectonic, called for the *Critique of Pure Reason* to provide the foundation for both a metaphysics of nature and the long-projected metaphysics of morals. And since the Canon is the only place in the first *Critique* where Kant deals explicitly with practical philosophy, it is there that we must look for the foundation that Kant thought that he had provided for the latter.

The situation is complicated, however, by the fact that in the Canon Kant stipulates that all the interests of reason (speculative as well as practical) are expressed in three great questions: "**What can I know?**" "**What can I do?**" and "**What may I hope?**" (KrV A805/B833).[55] Moreover, Kant states that the second of these, which alone is entirely practical, is not itself a fit subject for the *Critique*, since it is not transcendental. This leaves the third question, which Kant reformulates as: "If I do what I should, what may I then hope?", which he characterizes as both theoretical and practical (ibid.). It therefore appears that Kant assumed that the foundation of moral philosophy is provided by the answer to the theoretical-practical question: what may I hope for under the condition that I have done what morality requires?

A striking feature of this formulation of the issue is Kant's apparent unconcern with what seems to be the most obvious question to ask regarding the foundations of morality, namely, the validity of moral demands. In sharp contrast to the position he will adopt in GMS, Kant dismisses this worry on the grounds that he assumes "that there really are moral laws, which determine completely *a priori* . . . the action and omission . . . of a rational being in general, and that these laws command absolutely (not hypothetically under the presupposition of other empirical ends), and are thus necessary in every respect." In short, he assumes that there is such a thing as the categorical imperative and the specific duties that are derived from it. And, in support of this, Kant appeals "not only to the proofs of the most enlightened moralists but also to the moral judgment of every human being, if he will distinctly think such a law"

---

[53] For an account of the contemporary importance of Garve, see Muller (1905, esp. 3–12, 18–20).

[54] Garve's original version of the review was published in the *Allgemeine deutsche Bibliothek*, supplement to vols. 37–52 (1783) 838–62.

[55] Elsewhere, in his account of philosophy in the "cosmopolitan," as contrasted with the "scholastic" sense, Kant adds a fourth question: "*What is man?*" He assigns this question to anthropology and suggests that this encompasses all of philosophy, since the first three questions relate to the last (JL 9: 25; 538). As he generally does in texts after 1781, Kant assigns the third question, "*What may I hope?*", to religion, with no suggestion that this involves the foundation of morals. An additional noteworthy feature of this text is that Kant assigns the first question, "*What can I know?*", to metaphysics rather than to epistemology. Kant expresses a similar view in a letter to Carl Friedrich Stäudlin, dated May 4, 1793, which he sent together with a copy of his just published *Religion* (see Br. 11: 429; 458).

(KrV A807/B835). Thus, whatever fundamental problems Kant thought must be addressed in order to put morality on a firm footing, it is clear that he did not include a skepticism regarding the genuineness of duties among them.

Before turning to the question of what Kant thought was required for the foundation of morality that is supposedly provided by the Canon, it will be useful to consider two constraints that were placed on this foundational aim by Kant's larger critical project. First, in spite of his appeal to the *a priori* nature of moral principles, Kant explicitly excluded moral theory from the domain of transcendental philosophy.[56] Second, Kant limited the business of the *Critique* to transcendental philosophy.[57] It follows from this that, if the *Critique* is to provide the foundation for moral philosophy, it must do so on the basis of something that lies outside the domain of the latter narrowly construed. And the only viable candidates for this are the postulates of God and immortality, since they provide the warrant for moral hope.[58]

We saw in the previous chapter that, since the object of hope is happiness, Kant's attempted grounding of morality in the Canon has a eudaemonistic dimension. But we also saw that Kant endeavored to mitigate this, by distinguishing between happiness [*Glückseligkeit*] and the worthiness to be happy [*Glückswürdigkeit*]. By connecting morality with the latter rather than the former, Kant apparently hoped to preserve the purity of morality, while acknowledging its connection with happiness in the idea of the highest good. Moreover, morality, so construed, has its foundation in the first *Critique*, insofar as the latter gives the theoretical ideas of God and the soul an essential practical function as conditions of the attainment of the highest good, which is itself understood as a condition in which happiness is distributed in accordance with one's worthiness of it (KrV A810/B839). Unlike theoretical proofs, however, Kant does not purport to demonstrate that God exists and that there is a future life, but merely to establish a right to believe in them on moral grounds.

Since it is evident that, when viewed from the point of view of GMS and Kant's later writings in moral philosophy, this account of morality, as grounded in a warranted hope in the attainment of happiness in proportion to one's worthiness of it, is both eudaemonistic and heteronomous, it is puzzling how Kant could have thought at the time that it was sufficient. I believe that there are three reasons for this optimism, which Garve may inadvertently have played a role in undermining.[59]

---

[56] See KrV A14–15/B28–29.

[57] See KrV A805/B833.

[58] Even though in the first *Critique* Kant regarded freedom, together with God and immortality or, more properly, the soul, as a transcendental idea, he explicitly excludes it from the list of postulates, since morality requires merely practical, as opposed to transcendental freedom, and the former is warranted by experience (KrV A805/B831). This stands in considerable tension with some of Kant's other accounts of practical freedom. For my discussion of this issue, see Allison (1990, esp. 59–66).

[59] The last point is sheer speculation on my part, since there is no evidence indicating that Garve played a positive role in the development of Kant's moral theory between 1781 and 1785. Nevertheless, in light of some of the considerations introduced below and later in this work, it is not implausible suspect that Kant's reflections on Garve, including both his review of the first *Critique* and his commentary on Cicero, played

The first is the already mentioned distinction between the desire for happiness *per se* and the desire to be worthy of it. Presumably, Kant thought that this distinction was itself sufficient to preserve the purity of morals from its corruption by eudaemonism, since it is the latter, rather than the former, at which the virtuous person supposedly aims. Unfortunately, however, by proceeding in this manner, Kant neglected the fact that the only reasonable answer to the question of why one should desire to be worthy of happiness is that such worthiness somehow makes its attainment more likely, if not guaranteed, which leads to what might be described as a second-order eudaemonism.

The second is that Kant was not yet in possession of the idea of the autonomy of the will, which, simply put, is the seemingly paradoxical thesis that only a law that the will imposes upon itself can be unconditionally binding.[60] Accordingly, the fact that this account of morality locates its ground in something lying outside the will, namely, happiness to the extent to which one is worthy of it, would not then have been recognized as a problem by Kant. Indeed, as one commentator has noted, the "discovery" of the principle of autonomy "marks a decisive turn in the development of Kant's thought" and is comparable to the Copernican revolution in his theoretical philosophy.[61]

The third reason, which was alluded to in the previous chapter, is that Kant thought that the fundamental problem regarding the foundation of morality concerned the moral incentive or the *principium executionis*, rather than the *principium diiudicationis*, which we have seen he here regarded as unproblematic. Like Hume, Kant held that to be valid moral claims must motivate; but unlike Hume, who concluded from this that morality must be grounded in sentiment rather than reason, once Kant settled in the 1770s on the view that morality is grounded in reason, this became non-negotiable and the task was to explain, pace Hume and other sentimentalists, how purely rational principles could have motivational force. Kant's answer, circa 1781, was that they attain such force through the postulates, which provide rational grounds for the belief that happiness will be rewarded (whether in this life or beyond) in proportion to one's worthiness of it. That this was Kant's view at the time is evident from many texts, including the passage from the Canon cited in the previous chapter: "[W]ithout a God and a world that is now not visible to us but is hoped for, the majestic ideas of morality are, to be sure, objects of approbation and admiration but not incentives for resolve and realization" (KrV A813/B841).[62]

---

some part in leading Kant to develop his principle of autonomy, which became the distinctive feature of his moral theory.

[60] Kant's complex account of autonomy and its contrast with heteronomy will be a central topic in Chapter 9.

[61] Carnois (1987, 45).

[62] Other places in which Kant claims that the postulates of God and immortality are necessary to have an incentive to be moral include KrV A589/B617, A634/B662, A811/B839, *Ethik* 48, 40; 49, 41; 65, 54. In ML 1 28: 289, Kant connects the moral incentive specifically with the postulation of immortality. The most extensive discussion of the difference between Kant's moral theory in the Canon and other writings stemming from the time of the publication of the first edition is by Guéroult (1954, 331–57).

The question therefore becomes what Garve had to say in his review regarding the Canon and it is noteworthy that, in spite of its brevity, Garve's account focuses on the very points that would have been of chief interest to Kant. Thus, in commenting upon Kant's distinction between happiness and the worthiness to be happy and his prioritization of the latter, Garve remarks, with an apparent air of irony, that Kant's claims that we recognize a certain conduct as absolutely worthy of happiness and that this worthiness, rather than happiness itself, is the final purpose of nature, "will both be less evident to many readers than some of the propositions that the author's critique has rejected."[63] And, with regard to the postulation of God and immortality, Garve writes, supposedly expressing Kant's view:

What we cannot know on speculative grounds reason enjoins us to believe because it provides us with a priori certain and necessary rules of conduct. These rules, however, could not be true, or could at least not be motivating powers of our will, if there were no God and no afterlife, that is, if there were no intelligible creator of the world and no state in which blessedness and desert are always together.[64]

By the propositions that Kant's critique had rejected and that would seem more plausible to many readers Garve meant the doctrines of rational psychology, cosmology, and theology that Kant criticized in the Dialectic. Thus, Garve, in effect, claimed that these rejected doctrines of traditional metaphysics have a greater credibility than the proposition that the end dictated by morality is to become worthy of happiness rather than the attainment of happiness. It is not difficult to imagine that Kant would not have been pleased by this claim.

Furthermore, Kant did not maintain in the Canon (or any place else for that matter) that the worthiness to be happy is the final purpose of *nature*. To be sure, Kant does refer to a systematic union of nature and freedom, the sensible and intelligible worlds, as a moral ideal, which is explicitly modeled on the Leibnizian idea of a harmony between the realms of nature and grace, and which, under the direction of a supreme intelligence, involves a state of affairs in which happiness (which pertains to nature) is rewarded in precise proportion to the worthiness of it.[65] But this amounts to the thesis that the purposiveness of nature, considered in light of the practical idea of the highest good and under the direction of a most perfect and rational primordial being, consists in the distribution of happiness according to one's worthiness of it (KrV A814/B843), which is quite distinct from the view that nature's end or purpose is to produce beings that are worthy of happiness. Such worthiness, in contrast to happiness itself, is not something that can be produced by nature, since it must be self-wrought.

Garve's paragraph concerning the postulates would probably have afforded less cause for offense on Kant's part, since, with one exception, it provides a fairly accurate report

---

[63] Garve (2000, 73).

[64] Ibid.

[65] See KrV A815–16/843–44.

of his views at the time. The exception, which Garve immediately qualifies, is the suggestion that for Kant moral rules would not be *true* (my emphasis), if there were no God and afterlife. While we have seen that in the Canon Kant does maintain that a belief in God and immortality is necessary to give these rules motivating force, he explicitly denies that God is the ground of moral laws themselves. As he there put it in agreement with Wolffian anti-voluntarism, "So far as practical reason has the right to lead us, we will not hold actions to be obligatory because they are God's commands, but will rather regard them as divine commands because we are internally obligated to them" (KrV A819/B847). Insofar, then, as he took pains to distinguish between the ground and incentive for morality, Kant would have had reason for regarding Garve's seemingly innocent and brief discussion of the Canon as containing a serious distortion of his views.

(B) The principle of popularity

As previously noted, by "popularity" is here understood general comprehensibility, or at least comprehensibility by the literate portion of the public, rather than wide public acceptance. As such, it is concerned with the mode of presentation of a philosophical doctrine rather than its content; though we shall see that it has implications for what can count as a proper content. That philosophy should be made more popular in this sense was a common theme in the *Aufklärung*.[66] With respect to Kant, the demand was clearly expressed by Garve in his review, where, lamenting the obscurity of Kant's philosophical terminology, he remarks that "It [the teachings of the *Critique*] must be translatable ... into a more common language, though perhaps with some loss of precision."[67]

Garve reiterated this sentiment in his previously mentioned letter to Kant. After admitting his part in the Göttingen review, he there tells Kant that he "believed that it be possible to render more easily comprehensible (to readers not wholly unaccustomed to reflection) the truths that are supposed to bring about important reforms in philosophy." And he further remarks that it is still his opinion that Kant's "whole system, if it is really to become useful, must be expressed in a popular manner, and if it contains truth then it can be expressed" (Br 10: 331; 193). In short, for Garve general comprehensibility is a criterion of the truth of a philosophical doctrine or system.

Considering the implications of this for the *Critique*, Kant's response is mild, reflecting his personal respect for Garve. Rather than directly challenging Garve's view, he simply notes that the criticism of a lack of popularity in his work is one "that can in fact be made of every philosophical writing, if it is not to conceal what is probably nonsense [*Unsinn*] under a haze of apparent cleverness." And he adds (referring to the *Critique*) that "such popularity cannot be attempted in studies of such high abstraction" (Br 10: 339; 197). The natural retort to this by a defender of

---

[66] In the following discussion I make considerable use of Petrus (1994, 280–302).
[67] Garve (2000, 60).

the popularity principle is to say that this is a good reason for abandoning such studies as useless. Kant does not take up this possible challenge directly in the letter; instead, he discusses some of the central themes in the *Critique* and exhorts Garve to take another look at the work as a whole. But he does address it indirectly in a note referring to the transcendental deduction of the categories, where he both insists on the overriding importance of such a deduction and challenges anyone to accomplish it in "an easier, more popular fashion" (Br 10: 339; 197).

Overall, Kant's treatment of the question of popularity in the writings of the critical period exhibits a certain ambivalence. This ambivalence does not concern the articulation and justification of first principles. On this issue, Kant unwaveringly affirms that scholastic precision is required; it concerns rather the potential for popularization of the system as a whole, once its first principles are in place. For the most part, Kant seems to acknowledge the possibility, indeed the desirability, of such popularity, as long as it is not sought at the beginning. Thus, he writes with respect to moral theory:

This descent [*Herablassung*] to popular concepts [*Volksbegriffen*] is certainly very laudable, if the ascent to principles of pure reason has already occurred and been brought to complete satisfaction, and that would mean first *grounding* the doctrine of morals on metaphysics, and afterwards, once it stands firm, providing *access* to it through popularity. But it is the height of absurdity to want to humor popularity in the first investigation, upon which all correctness of principles depends. (GMS 4: 409_{20-26})[68]

In the same context, Kant contrasts a "true *philosophical popularity*," which is supposedly rare and difficult, with the kind achieved by the popular moral philosophers. According to his caustic description, proponents of this kind of popularity renounce all well-grounded insight, producing only "a disgusting mishmash [*Mischmasch*] of patched together observations and half-reasoned principles." Against this, Kant speaks of the need "to gain the right to be popular," which is accomplished only through the acquisition of determinate insight (GMS 4: $409_{29}-10_2$).

At times, however, Kant seems to rule out popularity completely as a desideratum, or even a possibility, at least as far as the *Critique* is concerned. Thus, in the Preface to the second edition, he baldly states that a critique of pure reason "can never become popular, but also has no need of being so" (Bxxxiv).[69] And, ten years later, in response to Garve's claim that every philosophical system must be capable of being made popular, he writes:

I gladly admit this with the exception only of the systematic critique of the faculty of reason itself, along with all that can be established only by means of it; for this has to do with the distinction of the sensible in our cognition from that which is supersensible but yet belongs to reason. This can

---

[68] See Pro 4: 261; 58 for a parallel statement regarding popularity in the theoretical domain.

[69] In the Preface to the first edition, Kant adopts a somewhat more sanguine attitude towards achieving popularity (in the sense of general comprehensibility) for the *Critique*. Apparently viewing the latter as requiring the extensive use of examples and illustrations, he rejects this on the grounds of prolixity rather than principle; though he also acknowledges that this work could never be made suitable for popular use (Axviii).

never become popular—no formal metaphysics can—although its results can be made quite illuminating for the healthy reason (of an unwitting metaphysician). Popularity (common language) is out of the question here; on the contrary, scholastic *precision* must be insisted upon, even if this is censured as hair-splitting (since it is the *language of the schools*); for only by this means can precipitate reason be brought to understand itself, before making its dogmatic assertions. (MS 6: 206; 366)

Kant's ambivalence regarding popularity is nicely illustrated by his treatment of the topic in the *Jäsche Logic*. Referring explicitly to logic rather than to a transcendental critique, Kant draws a distinction between two manners of exposition [*Vortrag*]: the *scholastic* and the *popular*. In the former, the rules of logic are presented "*in their universality or in abstracto*"; while in the latter they are presented "in the particular or *in concreto*." In light of this contrast, Kant makes two claims: (1) that only the scholastic procedure is appropriate for those who wish to treat the cognition of logical rules as a science, while the popular suffices for those "who do not study logic as a science but only want to use it to enlighten their understanding"; (2) that the former is the foundation for the latter, "for the only one who could expound something in a popular way is one who could also expound it more thoroughly" (JL 9: 19; 533–34). Since anything might be expounded in a popular manner, Kant clearly meant expounded adequately, that is, in a way that does not distort or obfuscate the principles of the science, even if it leaves them ungrounded. Presumably, this would be equivalent to the "true popularity" of which Kant speaks in GMS.

This leaves unanswered the question of whether every science is capable of attaining such popularity. Although Kant does not explicitly address this question, he does introduce a further distinction between *exposition* and *method*, which bears upon it. His main point is that, while there may be a certain variability in the manner of exposition (scholastic or popular), there is none with regard to method, by which Kant understands "the way to cognize completely a certain object, to whose cognition the method is applied." Since this is derived from the nature of the science and its object, it is an order of thought that cannot be altered (JL 9: 19; 534). This suggests that the method requisite for a science imposes certain constraints on the manner of exposition possible for that science. Thus, if scholastic precision, thoroughness of argumentation, and the introduction of new distinctions or of a new manner of understanding old distinctions (such as that between the sensible and the supersensible) are ineliminable features of that science, then a popular mode of presentation is impossible with respect to that science. And this is what Kant believed held of the *Critique*.

Nevertheless, a metaphysics of morals is not a transcendental critique. On the contrary, since Kant held that everyone is equipped with such a metaphysics in the sense that the basic principles of morality are contained in the common human reason, it would seem to be the ideal candidate for a popular exposition. But, then, everything turns on whether a moral theory attains what Kant considers true popularity rather than the "mishmash" of which he accuses popular moral philosophy. And this means that the real dispute concerns the method rather than the mode of presentation of popular moral philosophy as Kant understood it.

(C) The methodology and content of popular moral philosophy as contained in Garve's remarks to his translation of Cicero's De officiis

There is much in the remarks that Garve added to his translation of *De officiis* that would have given Kant impetus to consider writing what Hamann initially described as an "*Antikritik*" and to include a critique of Garve's views in his revised project, which eventually became GMS. Such a critique would be directed at two closely related aspects of Garve's position: one methodological and the other substantive. The former is Garve's assumption that morality must be grounded in an empirical account of human nature; the latter is his uncompromising eudaemonism. Since these views were virtual commonplaces of the moral philosophy of the *Aufklärung*, the fact that Kant attacked them does not, of itself, establish that Garve was his specific target; just as it was earlier noted that the fact that Kant appears to have directed some of his remarks in GMS 1 against Cicero does not prove that they were actually aimed at Garve's *Cicero*. As already suggested, however, I believe that when this is combined with the information provided by Hamann, Garve's treatment of Kant's discussion of the highest good in the Canon, and the fact that Kant's critique of these views takes the form of a critique of *popular* moral philosophy, the case for viewing Garve as Kant's main target in GMS seems compelling.[70]

Since, after Aristotle, Cicero was perhaps the most articulate classical spokesperson for these views, it is not surprising that Garve turned to him as a means for expressing his own thoughts on the topic and his use of Cicero is an excellent illustration of the issues involved. Although he was prepared to subject his translation and commentary to scholarly judgment, Garve made it clear that the audience he primarily had in mind was composed of those who are not familiar with the Latin text; and his goal was to acquaint these readers with the philosophical nuggets contained in *De officiis*.[71] While it would not be accurate to say that he treats Cicero as a contemporary, he does present him as a clear, if not terribly original, expositor of a *philosophia perennis*, which, with Garve's help, can be made to speak directly to a contemporary audience in a way that largely accords with sound common sense and moral experience.

In this context, it is also noteworthy that, in spite of his own empiricist proclivities, Garve pointed to a strong parallel between the Ciceronian and the Wolffian projects. For example, he suggested that Cicero's *De finibus* stands to *De officiis* as the Wolffian universal practical philosophy stand to ethics proper [*Ethik*]. The former work is

---

[70] The contrary view is expressed by Wood, who is highly skeptical of any significant influence of Garve's *Cicero* on Kant. See Wood (2006b, 361–65).

[71] Garve (1792a xiii–xiv).

concerned with the doctrine of the highest good, which Garve presented as dealing with the general ground of obligation and the essence of virtue; while the latter provides a systematic account of the various duties and virtues that are ultimately derived from the highest good.[72] And, in commenting on the relationship between these two works, Garve remarked that the first, which he did not translate, is the locus of most of the obscurities in Cicero's account.[73]

However, precisely because of their foundational role in the Ciceronian scheme, Garve could not ignore completely the doctrines and conceptions connected with the highest good in *De finibus*. In fact, he described the latter work as a "treatise on the moral nature of human beings" and suggested that whoever wishes to determine the nature of the (human) good must first investigate "the first incentives of our desires" [*die ersten Triebfedern unsrer Begierden*], from which the grounds of morality can be uncovered.[74] The basic idea is that if we wish to determine which actions are best, we must examine human nature (including its main incentives) in order to discover which actions and the satisfaction of which desires best accord with our nature and therefore our happiness. Thus, the identification of moral goodness or virtue with happiness is made explicit from the beginning.

That Cicero likewise affirmed this identification is already apparent from the structure of *De officiis*, which is divided into three books. The first is concerned with the morally good or honorable [*honestum*]. Cicero believed that every relationship and station in life brought with it its own set of duties; but following the classical view, he also held that there were four cardinal virtues from which the others are derived through modifications of circumstances. The second book deals with the nature of the expedient or useful [*utile*]. The third book is concerned with possible conflicts between the *honestum* and the *utile*. Following the Stoic identification of virtue and true happiness, Cicero denies the possibility of any such conflict and the same view is endorsed by Garve.

Although the last point is clearly the one most antithetical to Kant and lies at the heart of his dismissive treatment of popular moral philosophy, I shall focus the present discussion mainly on issues regarding the cardinal virtues, together with some of the problems, which were recognized by Garve and assumed central importance for Kant, concerning the nature–freedom problem, insofar as it arises from the view that moral virtues are grounded in human nature.

According to Cicero, who made no claim to originality, the four cardinal virtues are prudence [*prudentia*] or wisdom [*sapientia*], justice [*iustitia*], courage [*fortitudo*], and temperance [*temperentia*] or moderation [*modestia*], which Garve, following Cicero, links directly with four characteristics of human nature: curiosity, sociability, magnanimity, and a sense of order.[75] The question with which Garve

---

[72] Garve (1792a xiii–xiv), 8.   [73] Ibid., 8, 30.   [74] Ibid., 8.
[75] See Cicero (1893, I v. Loeb 17–19); Garve (1792b, 44–55).

was concerned is whether this classification of virtues is arbitrary or grounded in human nature.

Garve argues for the latter; but, as he frequently did, he begins his defense of Cicero's classification by playing the devil's advocate. Appealing to a Wolffian model of the mind, according to which the classification would be viewed as arbitrary, he suggests that there are fundamentally two types of operations of the soul, namely, thought and desire, from which he concluded that there are only two species of perfection, which must function as the source of all the virtues. As Garve put it, echoing the Wolffian view rather than his own, if a mind correctly thinks and correctly wills, it is doing precisely what, according to its nature, it ought to be doing.[76] Moreover, since volition (on the Wolffian view) is based on the mind's insights regarding the best alternatives, it seems that at the end of the day moral virtue is reducible to cognitive perfection. Otherwise expressed, rather than there being four cardinal virtues, reflection on the nature of the soul suggests that there is only one: prudence or *Klugheit*. For example, a person who clearly understands what she is and what other persons are cannot but act justly. Similarly, the correct knowledge of what is really dangerous and what is harmless constitutes human courage; while the correct evaluation of the objects of one's desires makes one temperate.[77]

Garve admits that this reductive argument seems persuasive as long as one treats the matter as a bit of conceptual analysis; but he denies that it accords with the facts, introducing several arguments in support of this claim of which I shall consider two. The first turns on the claim that the cognition, which (again on the Wolffian view) is supposedly the ground of every virtue, often already presupposes the virtue it is assumed to ground. For example, Garve claims that whoever looks upon the possible loss of life or a substantial good as not so great a danger that it could prevent him from doing his duty, must already have felt a certain firmness or strength of soul before he could acquire this sublime concept.[78] And, continuing the same line of argument, Garve adds that certain dispositions of the soul serve as the cause of the acquisition of certain concepts, just as the latter can be the cause of the strengthening of these dispositions.[79] He therefore concludes (contrary to the Wolffian intellectualistic view) that all the virtues should be regarded as resulting from a certain mixture of natural disposition and acquired insight.

Garve's second argument takes the analysis in an even more naturalistic direction by affirming a strong connection between virtues and temperament. Garve saw this as supporting the classical view against the arbitrariness charge on the grounds that a division of virtues that is based upon perceived differences in temperament can hardly be dismissed as arbitrary. And, in support of this thesis, Garve points out that there are people who by nature are courageous and intrepid [*muthig und kühn*], others who are

---

[76] Garve (1792b, 45).   [77] Ibid.   [78] Ibid., 46.   [79] Ibid.

sagacious, still others who are honest and kind-hearted [*ehrlich und gutherzig*], and yet others with a tranquil spirit. His basic point is that these qualities of mind indicate fundamental predispositions [*Grundanlagen*], which morality [*die Moral*] can develop but not create. Moreover, in support of their status as fundamental predispositions, Garve points to the fact that they manifest themselves in the earliest years; while, in apparent conflict with the classical doctrine of the unity of the virtues, he notes that these predispositions must be distinct from one another because they are often found separately.[80]

Garve was well aware, however, that this naturalistic, dispositional analysis of the virtues created a fresh and far deeper problem than the initial one regarding their classical division. The problem is that, while qualities such as intelligence, strength (both physical and psychological), as well as various capacities, may be objects of admiration, they are not considered objects of moral praise, unless it is assumed that their possession is somehow up to the individual rather than something with which the individual is endowed by nature. And the same applies, *mutatis mutandis*, to negative qualities or vices. In language that will resonate with Kant, Garve points out that there seems to be a need to distinguish between virtues, on the one hand, and "gifts of nature" [*Naturgaben*] or talents, on the other.[81]

Although Garve regards the problem as insoluble because of its connection with the likewise irresolvable problem of freedom, he did not believe that this undermines the classical division of the virtues or, more generally, the conception of virtue itself. Rather, on Garve's view, we must simply learn to live with the aporia built into this conception; otherwise, he, in effect, argues, we will succumb to the danger of throwing out the baby with the bath water. Specifically, this means recognizing that, while some virtues seem to involve a greater degree of voluntariness [*Freywilligkeit*] than others, for example, temperance and neighborly love, as compared with prudence and greatness of soul, all human virtues contain a mixture of natural innate capacities and predispositions, on the one hand, and something voluntary or up to the subject, on the other. As he puts it in a formula, which again points to a sharp contrast with Kant's radical nature–freedom separation, "[I]n every virtue nature and the diligence [*Fleiss*] of human beings are joined with each other."[82]

In support of the first part of this thesis, Garve argues that there must be something innate in every human virtue or predisposition; for if this were not already there, it would be impossible to produce it (human virtue would have to be conceived as a kind of creation *ex nihilo*).[83] The argument for the second part consists essentially in pointing out that an innate capacity or predisposition is not sufficient to constitute a virtue in the sense of a possible object of moral praise. The latter requires that the innate feature (the talent or gift of nature) be developed and put to a proper use. This is the work of human diligence and is what is properly up to us.[84]

---

[80] Garve (1792b, 45), 46–47.   [81] Ibid., 51, 54, 226.   [82] Ibid., 53.
[83] Ibid., 54.   [84] Ibid., 54–55.

The result of Garve's analysis is an aporetic situation according to which we are forced to acknowledge that every virtue is in part a gift of nature and in part up to us, though we are incapable, in any given situation, of drawing a precise boundary between them. But rather than concluding on a skeptical note, Garve claims, in a manner reminiscent of Kant's claims regarding the moral benefit of the unavailability of any theoretical proof of the existence of God or immortality, that this is actually beneficial to morality, specifically to our moral judgments regarding our selves and others. With respect to ourselves, the point seems to be that this awareness brings with it a much needed sense of humility, which prevents us from arrogantly assuming that we are totally responsible for our virtues. With respect to others, it tends to moderate the harshness of our judgments, thereby mitigating our negative reactive attitudes. In short, the recognition of the ambiguity of our moral situation tends to make us more tolerant and nuanced than we might otherwise be.[85]

The importance that Garve attributed to this issue is reflected in the fact that he returns to it in an appendix to his remarks. Since much of what he says here, which consists in a series of observations, repeats, albeit in somewhat different terms, the line of argument advanced in the main text, I do not propose to discuss the details of this new account. It will be useful, however, to take a brief look at the last of these observations for the light that it sheds on the difference between Garve's view and Kant's.

Garve affirms that, in the case of actual human actions, it is impossible to separate the component that is due to diligence from that which is a product of nature and, more to the point, he suggests that the attempt to do this courts the danger of "deforming virtue itself" [*die Tugend selbst zu verunstalten*].[86] Although Garve does not explain what he means by this, given his previous account, the point seems to be that, if one attempts to "denature" virtue by denying it any intrinsic connection with the dispositional bases of the self, that is, with one's propensities and predispositions, one destroys its human quality, making it into (to revert to the language used earlier) a creation *ex nihilo*. And he further suggests that it was for this reason that the ancients (including Cicero), avoided this tangle of metaphysical issues and characterized everything that is praiseworthy, that ennobles and embellishes human nature with the term "virtue."[87]

Since Kant's response to many of the points that Garve raises, particularly those regarding the freedom–nature issue, are central to the understanding of GMS, I shall reserve discussion of them for subsequent chapters. For the present, my concern is merely to note the major respects in which Garve's work on Cicero fits the unflattering

---

[85] Ibid., 53–54.   [86] Ibid., 235.   [87] Ibid.

picture of popular moral philosophy that Kant provides. The first of these is its empiricism, which undermines the possibility of the kind of *a priori* moral theory that Kant thought necessary. As we have seen, Kant insists not only upon the need to separate the pure or *a priori* aspect of morality from everything empirical (moral anthropology), but also that the former alone is essential to morality. The second is the eudaemonism of popular moral philosophy, which is a constant refrain that is epitomized in Cicero's denial (endorsed by Garve) of even the possibility of a conflict between virtue and expediency.

Although these two features of popular moral philosophy are clearly compatible, they also appear to be logically independent. Thus, one might very well argue that experience offers all too many examples of virtue going unrewarded and immoral conduct proving to be highly advantageous to the perpetrator. Moreover, Cicero argues (and he is here followed by Garve) not merely that there are in fact no such conflicts, but that it is impossible for there to be any, which hardly sounds like an empirical claim.

Cicero's justification for the latter claim is to be found in his analysis of human nature, which underlies this thesis and is itself supposedly empirically grounded. Following Stoic principles, Cicero argues in *De officiis* III that to act dishonorably or unrighteously is to act contrary to one's nature and that such an act can never be to one's true advantage. According to Garve's loose rendering of a typical passage:

To take away from someone something that is his, and through harming and oppressing him further one's own advantage, – conflicts with our nature more than poverty, pain, or any other evil, which concerns our body or outer condition.[88]

In spite of his deep sympathy with certain elements of Stoic thought, it is not difficult to appreciate why Kant was displeased with the use to which it was put by Garve. As already noted in connection with the analysis of universal practical philosophy, the concept of nature (like that of perfection) and the Stoic dictum that one should live according to nature are simply too ambiguous to serve as moral principles. And, for reasons already noted, we can see why, from Kant's point of view, Garve's attempt to improve upon Cicero by avoiding sharp distinctions and the metaphysical issues underlying them, appealing instead to psychological considerations, made matters even worse. Indeed, for Kant, this made a step beyond the eclectic empiricism and

---

[88] Garve's German rendering of the opening lines of *De officiis* III, v reads: "*Einem andern etwas von dem Seinigen entziehen, und durch den Schaden und die Bedrückung desselben, seine eigne Vortheile befördern, - streitet mehr mit unserer Natur, als Armuth, Schmerz, oder irgend ein andres Uebel, welches unser Körper, oder unserm äusseren Zustand betreffen kann.*" Garve (1792a, 181).

eudaemonism of popular moral philosophy into metaphysics necessary, not, to be sure, a theoretical metaphysics regarding nature, but a metaphysics of morals in which moral principles are derived from the concept of a rational agent in general rather than from the empirical concept of human nature.[89]

[89] Although discussing the matter would take us well beyond the boundaries of a commentary on GMS, it must at least be noted that Kant's polemic with Garve did not end with this work. It was revived by Garve's later critique of Kant's moral theory in his *Versuche über verschiedene Gegenstände aus der Moral, Literatur und dem gesellschaftlichen Leben* [*Essays on Various Topics from Morals and Literature*] (1792), which focused on the second *Critique* rather than GMS, particularly on Kant's accounts of the highest good and moral motivation. Kant responded to this in the first part of his 1793 essay: "On the Common Saying: That may be Correct in Theory, but it is of no Use in Practice," a text which is of considerable importance for the understanding of Kant's moral theory, particularly with respect to issues regarding the relationship between virtue and happiness. Moreover, this essay was not Garve's last discussion of Kant's moral theory; for there is a lengthy account of it in Garve (1798, 183–394), a work which he dedicated to Kant. Kant acknowledged receiving this work in a letter dated September 21, 1798, in which, after commiserating with Garve regarding his physical problems and noting his own, he laments his lack of progress on his projected "Transition from the metaphysical foundations of natural science to physics," the lack of which presumably left a "gap" in the critical system. This work, which was never finished, became the centerpiece of what has been called Kant's "Opus Postumum." With regard to the disagreement between the two philosophers, the most relevant portion of the letter is Kant's reference to a footnote on page 339 of Garve's work, which Kant noted having come across while "skimming" it. In the note, Garve suggests that it was the investigation of the questions of the existence of God and the immortality of the soul that first set Kant on the path to the critical philosophy. In response, Kant avers that it was not the existence of God and immortality but rather the antinomy of pure reason that "first aroused me from my dogmatic slumber and drove me to the critique of pure reason itself, in order to resolve the scandal of ostensible contradiction of reason with itself" (Br 12: 257–58; 552). As far as the substantive content of Garve's last treatment of Kant is concerned, the part dealing with moral theory contains the following four objections: (1) that Kant starts from unproven presuppositions and develops his ideas according to postulated goals, (2) that his rational law lacks motivational force, (3) that he ends by reuniting virtue and happiness after all, in contradiction to his own theory, and that the moral law lacks content. Of these, only the last seems to be new. Moreover, as Zweig also points out in an editorial note to Kant's letter, Kant responds explicitly to the first objection in a passage contained in the "Opus Postumum," where he writes: "To Garve. My principles are not taken from a certain, previously extracted purpose, for example, what is best for everybody, but simply because that is the way it must be without any conditions. It is in no way the assumption of a principle" (OP 21: 47879). (This material is taken from Zweig [1999, 552n], who apparently based it on the editorial comments of Rudolf Reicke [Br. 13: 486–87].) For useful discussions of the relationship between the Kant of *Theory and Practice* and Garve, see Timmermann (2007b, 167–82) and Ludwig (2007, 183–93).

PART II

GMS 1

3

The Good Will

The second part of this commentary deals with GMS 1, which Kant entitles "*Transition from Common Rational Moral Cognition to Philosophical Moral Cognition.*" Unlike the transitions that occur in GMS 2 and 3, which involve, respectively, the replacement of one philosophical standpoint by another (popular moral philosophy by a metaphysics of morals) and one level of philosophical discourse by another (a metaphysics of morals by a critique of pure practical reason), that of GMS 1 may be described as a movement in place, since its argument consists in a clarification or making explicit of what is supposedly implicit in a shared, pre-philosophical, understanding of morality. Accordingly, Kant quite properly views his approach in this section as Socratic, even though it takes the form of a conceptual analysis rather than a dialogue. The ultimate goal of this analysis is to uncover the supreme principle of morality, which is allegedly presupposed in the moral judgments of what Kant terms "common rational moral cognition."

The examination of GMS 1 consists of three chapters, the first of which (this chapter) is devoted to the first thirteen paragraphs of the text (GMS 4: 393_1–99_{34}). These paragraphs deal with three topics: (1) an account of the good will and the unique status that Kant assigns to it; (2) a teleological reflection, which is intended to support Kant's claim about a good will and its unique status; and (3) an analysis of acting from duty, the aim of which is to clarify the concept of a good will under human conditions. Accordingly, the present chapter is divided into three parts, one dealing with each of these topics.

I

Kant's account begins with the famous pronouncement that, "It is not possible to think of anything in the world, or indeed out of it, that can be held to be good without limitation [*Einschränkung*] except a **good will**" (GMS 4: 393_{5-8}). The emphasis here is to be placed on the phrase "not possible to think," since this indicates that Kant's point is not simply that as a matter of fact we can find nothing that is good without limitation except a good will, but that we cannot even conceive of the possibility of such a thing. Although the apparent intent behind Kant's extension of this claim to anything "out of" the world is to allude to the thesis that the concept of a good will is normative for a perfect or holy will as well as for ours, it might also be taken to refer to other possible worlds, where the claim about the unique goodness of a good will must likewise be assumed to hold.

Kant supports this thesis by systematically surveying other goods, which he divides into "gifts of nature" [*Naturgaben*] and "gifts of fortune" [*Glücksgaben*]. The former are subdivided into what Kant terms "*talents* of the mind" [*Talente des Geistes*], which encompass intellectual qualities such as understanding, wit, and judgment, and "qualities of *temperament*," which include courage, resoluteness, and persistence. As examples of the latter, Kant lists power, wealth, honor, health, and happiness, defined as an entire well-being and contentment with one's condition. While acknowledging these to be in many respects good, Kant denies that they are good in all respects or without limitation. On the contrary, he claims that they can become extremely evil and pernicious [*schädlich*], if the will which makes use of them is not itself good. And, in the case of happiness, he adds:

A rational impartial spectator can take no delight in the contemplation of the uninterrupted well-being of a being adorned with no trace of a good and pure will, and so a good will seems to be the indispensable condition of even the worthiness to be happy. (GMS 4: 393$_{18-24}$)

In the next paragraph, Kant considers other qualities, which might be conducive to a good will in the sense that they make its task easier, and are genuine objects of esteem, yet still have no "inner unconditioned worth" and cannot be regarded as "absolutely good" [*schlecthin gut*]. As before, this is because their goodness and estimability depend upon whether their owner also possesses a good will. In this context, Kant refers to three of the virtues recognized by the ancients: moderation in the affects and passions, self-control, and calm deliberation [*nüchterne Überlegung*].[1] With respect to these, Kant remarks that, though they may seem to constitute part of the inner worth of a person (at least they did to the ancients), "they lack much to be declared good without limitation." Once again, this is because "without the principles of a good will they can become extremely evil." Kant illustrates this by referring to the cold-bloodedness of a scoundrel, which not only makes him far more dangerous but more abominable than he would be without it (GMS 4: 394$_{6-12}$).

Kant completes his paean to the good will in the third paragraph with a preliminary account of what its unlimited, unconditioned, or absolute goodness (which are here

---

[1] Schönecker and Wood (2004, 44n8) note that Kant's list includes three of the four cardinal virtues, which they describe as temperance or moderation, courage, prudence, and justice. Although the list of cardinal virtues differs from thinker to thinker, it is worthy of note that only the first three of these are on Cicero's list. Nevertheless, Kant's discussion of courage as a quality of temperament is close to Cicero's, for whom courage is not one of the cardinal virtues because in imperfect men it is commonly found together with violent passions. See Cicero (1893, 64–66).

taken as equivalent) and its supreme worth consists in.[2] With respect to the first point, Kant states that a good will is good though its volition [*das Wollen*], rather than through its efficacy in bringing about an intended end. With respect to the second, Kant claims that such a will is to be estimated as having a far higher worth than anything that could be brought about by the will in response to inclination. Finally, at the beginning of the next paragraph, Kant refers to such a will as having "absolute worth" [*absoluten Werthe*] (GMS 4: 394$_{32}$).

Since the fact that a good will is good without limitation does not entail that it has absolute worth, Kant is here making two distinct points about a good will. The former expressions refer to the *kind* of goodness it possesses, while the latter refers to its value or *degree* of goodness. These claims are logically distinct because there is nothing to prevent something that is good without limitation from lacking absolute worth.[3] In the remainder of the paragraph, Kant reinforces both points, without distinguishing between them; though he does add two significant provisos. First, he notes that, even if, due to "the disfavor of fate or the meager endowment of a stepmotherly nature," this will were totally unable to attain its chosen ends, this would not subtract from its value. Second, after emphasizing that the goodness of the will consists in its actually willing, that is, striving with all its capacity to attain this end, as opposed to merely wishing for it to come about, he insists that attaining its ends would not add to its value.[4]

Kant expresses this dual thesis by means of an analogy with a precious jewel. In the first case (lack of success), he suggests that the good will would "shine like a jewel for itself as something that has its full worth in itself"; while in the second (success in attaining its ends), it would provide only "its setting, as it were, which would make it easier to handle in ordinary commerce or to attract the attention of those who are not sufficiently expert, but not to recommend it to experts and determine its worth" (GMS 4: 394$_{25-31}$). In the words of Allen Wood, Kant here affirms both the "non-diminishability" and the "nonincreasability thesis" with respect to the good will.[5]

Although in this initial discussion of the concept of a good will Kant is ostensibly expressing what he takes to be the generally accepted opinion, there is ample evidence from his lectures and *Nachlass* that he shared this view. For example, in a lecture from the time of the composition of GMS, he is quoted as saying that, "Everyone knows [*Es weiss jedermann*] that nothing in the world is absolutely good, without limitation, save a

---

[2] Kant himself implicitly equates being good without limitation with being absolutely good at GMS 4: 394$_3$. Schönecker and Wood (2004, 42n4) argue for the equivalence of "*ohne Einschrankung*" ["without limitation"] and "*unbedingt*" ["unconditioned"] in this context.

[3] It has long been noted in the literature that intrinsic goodness does not uniquely apply to a good will, since other goods, notably happiness, share this feature. Recently, however, Wood has pointed out that what he refers to as the "higher worth thesis" is logically independent of the "good without limitation thesis" and its equivalents. See Wood (2006a, 29–31).

[4] The distinction between willing and wishing as two manifestations of the faculty of desire is noted by Kant at MS 6: 213; 374–75.

[5] Wood (2006a, 28).

good will, and that this good will sets the limit to everything and for that reason is then good without limitation" (MM2 29: 607; 231).[6] But while the ultimate goal of GMS 1 is to derive the supreme principle of morality from an analysis of this concept, it would be a mistake to regard the latter as something like an axiom or first principle in Kant's moral theory. Rather, its function is essentially expository or heuristic; the intent being to show that this concept (together with its principle) is implicit in "naturally healthy understanding, which does not need to be taught but rather only [in Socratic fashion] to be brought to light" (GMS 4: 397$_{2-4}$). Indeed, we shall see in the third part of this chapter that Kant uses the concept of a good will primarily as an entrée for the concept of duty, which later plays the central role in his derivation of the supreme principle of morality and which he claims "contains that of a good will, though under certain subjective limitations and hindrances" (GMS 4: 397$_{7-8}$).

For the present, however, further comment is in order regarding certain features of Kant's preliminary account of a good will that remain highly controversial. As we have seen, according to Kant's analysis, not only is a good will good without limitation, and, indeed the only conceivable candidate for such an attribution, but it is the condition of the value of all other goods, the goodness of which depend upon the use to which they are put by the will. If the latter is the case, it follows that the good will is the *only* thing that could be good without limitation, since, *ex hypothesi*, the goodness of everything else is conditioned by it. But then the question becomes whether Kant has shown that a good will is, in fact, the condition of the goodness of *all* other goods. Assuming that he has shown that it is the condition of the previously mentioned classes of goods, namely, the gifts of nature and fortune, the virtues affirmed by the ancients, and happiness, it still remains to be seen whether one can generalize from this to make a claim about all goods other than a good will.

It is likely that Kant did not worry about this because he assumed that all other goods could be brought under one of these categories, particularly the indeterminate number of merely instrumental goods that are valued by individuals as means to (or essential ingredients in) their happiness. But since it might still be thought that Kant moves too quickly here, it should prove instructive to consider the status of some commonly prized goods that are not on his list, namely, knowledge, the creation and appreciation of beauty, and pleasure, the last of which has been and continues to be viewed by some philosophers as the sole good.

As far as knowledge is concerned, apart from the fact that it obviously can be misused (for, example, the evil scientist, who uses his knowledge in the service of morally bad ends), which precludes it from being good under all conditions, we have Kant's own testimony to the effect that he did not regard it as unconditionally good. As Kant wrote it in an oft-cited fragment in which he pays homage to Rousseau:

---

[6] See also MPC 27: 259; 53; R6890 19: 194–95; R6914 19: 204; R7206 19: 284; R7216 19: 287–88; R7217 19: 288; R7254 19: 295; R1020 15: 456; R1175 15: 519.

I am myself by inclination an investigator. I feel a complete thirst for knowledge and an eager unrest to go further in it as well as satisfaction at every acquisition. There was a time when I believed that this alone could constitute the honor of mankind, and I had contempt for the rabble who know nothing. *Rousseau* brought me around. (BB 20: 44; 7)[7]

Although we have no similarly eloquent testimony regarding the merely conditioned goodness of the creation and appreciation of beauty, later in GMS Kant does briefly touch upon the matter in connection with his distinction between price [*Preis*] and dignity [*Würde*] as two species of value. Within the former category Kant distinguishes between a "market price" [*Marktpreis*], which is attributed to whatever satisfies human need, and an "affective price" [*Affektionspreis*], which applies to what is pleasing to taste (GMS 4: 434_{36}–35_3); but the main point is that the latter as well as the former have merely a relative value, whereas what has dignity, namely, "morality and humanity, insofar as it is capable of morality," is elevated above all price (GMS 4: 435_{6-9}).

Moreover, as Paton points out, there can be little doubt that neither Kant nor the common understanding of morality in whose name he is speaking, would think it a good thing that Nero fiddled while Rome burned, regardless of the beauty of the music that he produced.[8] In response, it might be objected that that the situations are nonetheless perfectly symmetrical, since the lack of goodness of the complex situation does not detract from the goodness of either the evil scientist's knowledge or the beauty of Nero's music, just as the failure of the good will to attain its chosen ends does not detract from its goodness. This response neglects, however, a significant asymmetry; for in the case of both the evil scientist and Nero the ground of disapproval is itself moral and, as such, is concerned precisely with the lack of any hint of a good will.[9]

Finally, it is easy to see why Kant would not regard pleasure as unconditionally good. To begin with, pleasure in the suffering of others would hardly be judged a good thing by anyone save a sadist or perhaps an extremely hardheaded act utilitarian Moreover, even in non-moral contexts, it is often noted that pleasure, or at least the absence of pain, may lead one to ignore a pathological condition, which can become the source of great physical harm. Accordingly, the case for the claim that these goods are not good without limitation is compelling, which I believe to be sufficient to place the burden of proof on those who deny that the good will is the only thing that is good in this manner.

Another feature of Kant's account that calls for comment is his anomalous treatment of happiness. This stems from the fact that, as an intrinsic good, happiness differs from the other limited goods in that it seemingly cannot lose its goodness by being badly

---

[7] This passage is cited for the same purpose by Paton (1958, 42).

[8] Paton (1958, 39).

[9] A version of this objection is formulated by Ameriks (1989, 46–47), who believes that it constitutes a problem for the claim of the unique goodness of a good will, if the latter is understood as the particular intention of an agent in acting from duty in a specific situation. Although I agree with Ameriks in preferring what he terms the "whole character" reading of the good will, I believe that the asymmetry about which he worries holds even on the latter view of the good will.

used. In fact, it does not appear to make sense to think of it as badly used, since it does not make sense to regard it as used at all. To be sure, Kant attempts, somewhat halfheartedly, to treat happiness in the same way as he treats the other allegedly limited or conditioned goods, suggesting that, apart from being conjoined with a good will, which would limit its effect on the mind [Gemüt], even this could become bad by producing arrogance [Übermut] rather than simply courage [Mut] (GMS 4: 393$_{15-16}$). But even though he here presents it almost in the form of an afterthought, it seems clear that Kant's main reason for denying that happiness is good without limitation is not that it can become evil or pernicious without the controlling influence of a good will, but, rather, that happiness in someone without a trace of a good will could never be approved by an impartial observer.

Kant also makes it clear in the previously cited passage that the reason why an impartial observer could not approve of the happiness of someone without a good will is that such an observer could not endorse a condition of happiness apart from the worthiness of it. In light of what we have seen in the preceding chapter, this reiteration of the distinction between happiness and the worthiness of it can be seen not only as a general response to eudaemonism, but also to Garve's snide remark in his review of the first *Critique* that this distinction will be less evident to many readers of the *Critique* than the propositions of speculative metaphysics that Kant attacked in the Dialectic. For Kant, the distinction between happiness and the worthiness of it and the proposition that the former should not approved without the latter is not only more evident than those fallacious propositions, it is also implicitly acknowledged by the ordinary human understanding to which both he and Garve appeal.

It is therefore important to keep in mind that the lack of a proportional distribution of happiness in accordance with the worthiness of it would be lamented by Kant's impartial observer, who can be regarded as an idealized version of the ordinary human understanding. Moreover, even though Kant claims that the good will is the sole good without limitation, he does not equate it with the *complete* good. As one would expect, the latter is identified with the highest good, understood as the allotment of happiness in proportion to virtue. Although Kant does note in passing that the good will may not be the single and entire good (GMS 4: 396$_{24-25}$), he does not explicitly draw the contrast in GMS.[10] He does do so, however, in a roughly contemporaneous lecture, where he reportedly claimed:

[A] good will is simply good without limitation, for itself alone, in every respect and under all circumstances. It is the only thing that is good without other conditions, but it is also not completely good. A thing can be unconditioned and still not complete ... It does not yet constitute the whole of goodness. The highest good is unconditionally good, and also constitutes

---

[10] In fact, at one point Kant identifies the highest good with the good will (GMS 4: 396$_{25}$), and at another point with God (GMS 4: 409$_1$). But this merely means that he is not here using the term in a technical sense, not that he did not already have the concept, since we have seen that the latter is already present in the first *Critique*.

the whole of goodness. Were there a being in the world, such that his good will frequently led to his ruin, his good will would shine all the brighter. But the possession of virtue is not yet the whole of goodness. . . .Virtue is the greatest worth of our person, but our state [Zustand] must also be worth wishing for. The greatest worth of one's state is happiness. So virtue combined with happiness is the highest good. Virtue is the condition under which I am worthy of happiness; but that is not yet the highest good . . . (MM2 29: 599–600; 227).[11]

The distinction between being good without limitation and being the complete (or whole) good is essential not only for understanding Kant's moral theology, but also for the proper interpretation of the opening paragraphs of GMS. In order to appreciate this, we need to note that at least one of the worries posed by Kant's account of the unique value of the good will is that by separating the goodness of such a will so radically from its results, it leaves the impression that the only thing that counts *from a moral point of view* is the willing, which seems to conflict with the basic intuitions about morality that Kant purports to be articulating.[12]

The above-mentioned distinction suggests, however, that Kant's account need not be read as having such untoward consequences, since it provides a model for seeing how a total situation involving a good will might be deemed morally better or worse, in the sense of having different degrees of completeness or perfection, even though the goodness of the willing itself can be neither increased nor diminished. In other words, just as a world in which happiness is attained proportionally to virtue is morally preferable to one in which it is not, so a situation in which a good will is not prevented by a "stepmotherly nature" or the force of circumstances from attaining its intended results is not simply better in some indeterminate sense, but *morally* superior (has a greater degree of moral perfection) than one in which it is prevented, even though the goodness of the will itself remains the same in both sets of circumstances.

This still leaves us with two fundamental questions regarding a good will: one concerns the locus of its unlimited goodness, the other its identity, that is, the referent of the expression "good will." With regard to the former, we have already seen that its goodness is to be found in the principles underlying its volitions and we shall explore this further in the final section of this and subsequent chapters; but for the present something must be said regarding the second. As it is commonly discussed in the literature, the issue is whether a good will is to be identified with the specific intentions of an agent in a particular act or the agent's character.[13] Otherwise expressed, the issue

---

[11] As before, I have slightly modified the Heath translation.

[12] The problem was already discussed by Garve (1792b, 14–21) from the point of view of Stoic ethical theory and its conception of the perfect virtue of the sage. There the worry is that since virtue in its entirety is located in the disposition of the agent, neither the nature of the act itself nor success in its execution affects its moral worth, which Garve seems to have thought violates common sense.

[13] For a thorough and illuminating discussion of the issue see Ameriks (1989, 45–65). Actually, Ameriks distinguishes between three lines of interpretation, which he terms the "particular intention," the "general capacity," and the "whole character" views; but since the second of these refers to the question of the status of rational beings as ends in themselves, I do not consider it as offering a serious reading of Kant's account of the

is whether the goodness of a good will is to be understood as an occurrent condition or as a dispositional trait.[14]

Inasmuch as Kant will link his conception of a good will with that of moral worth and the latter concept refers to the motivation or intention underlying particular actions, some interpreters understand the Kantian good will in the former way.[15] But apart from the philosophical difficulties that this view involves, it does not square very well with the text.[16] In fact, early in his account of a good will, Kant explicitly identifies it with character (GMS 4: 393$_{14}$) and he repeats this identification later (GMS 4: 398$_{37}$). Moreover, in the passage from the nearly contemporaneous lecture cited above, Kant seems to equate a good will with a virtuous one; and while we sometimes speak of virtuous actions, virtue itself is clearly a character trait and therefore a dispositional property, which is manifest in particular acts. Finally, referring again to the passage from the lecture, it seems reasonable to assume that the condition under which one is worthy of happiness, which is presumably the possession of a good will, is an underlying disposition rather than an episodically occurring condition. Accordingly, the textual evidence for the view that at the time of GMS Kant identified a good will with a good overall character seems compelling.[17]

If this is correct, the next task is to determine what Kant meant by "character" [*Charakter*] and the main text in which we must look for an answer is the *Anthropology*.[18] With regard to the character of a person, Kant there distinguishes between two senses in which the term is to be understood.[19] One is a person's *Sinnesart*, which Kant equates with temperament and which may be rendered in

---

good will in GMS 1. Thus, using Ameriks terminology, the live options are the particular intention and the whole character interpretations.

[14] This way of expressing the point was suggested by one of the anonymous reviewers of my manuscript.

[15] In addition to Paton, Ameriks includes Wood and Robert Louden in this camp. See Ameriks (1989, 50–51).

[16] As Ameriks note, the main difficulty is understanding why the intention expressed in a particular action should trump all the other features of the context of the action, as it supposedly must do if it is equated with a good will. See Ameriks (1989, 46–51). But since I do not think that this represents Kant's view, I shall not attempt to deal with the problem.

[17] This understanding of a good will is argued for forcefully by Ameriks (1989) and seems to have become the accepted view. A recent expression of this view, which cites Ameriks, is by Timmerman (2007a, 17). I have limited this reading to GMS and contemporaneous texts, however, because in his later writings Kant identifies virtue with a person's *strength* of character in acting from good maxims and states that a good will can coexist with the lack of virtue (MS 6: 408; 535), indeed with radical evil (RGV 6: 29; 77). By contrast, in the earlier literature, a good will is sometimes simply identified with a virtuous one without noting any of the difficulties and complications that this identification involves. See, for example, Ross (1954, 11) and Harbison (1980, 47–59). I have discussed this matter in Allison (1990, 158–61).

[18] Although Kant only published his *Anthropology* in 1798, it is based on lectures which he gave regularly. Moreover, the conception of character which I here attribute to Kant, if not the precise wording, is present in the version of the lectures that he gave at the time of the composition and publication of GMS (winter 1784–85). See AM 25: 384–92.

[19] In the *Anthropology* Kant also discusses the character of the sexes, of various peoples and of the human species as a whole (see A 7: 285; 384). It is, however, only the character of a person that is relevant to our concerns.

English as "manner" or "way of feeling" (A 7: 285; 384). The other is a person's *Denkungsart*, which is usually translated as "manner" or "way of thinking" and sometimes by "attitude" or "cast of mind." At one point, Kant characterizes the latter as "that property of the will by which the subject binds himself to definite practical principles that he has prescribed to himself irrevocably by his own reason" (A 7: 292; 389–90).[20] More generally, it might be described as a general orientation of the will with regard to the moral law, which is based on freely adopted principles rather than sentiment. Indeed, Kant's emphasis is on the latter, since a character in the sense of *Denkungsart* is something that rational agents must acquire for themselves.[21]

Since Kant regarded a good *Sinnesart* or temperament as a gift of nature, it obviously cannot be the sense of "character" that is identified with a good will. But since he also recognized that a *Denkungsart* might be grounded in morally evil principles, it is not the case that we can simply identify a good will with a *Denkungsart* as such.[22] Nevertheless, I believe that it can be identified with a good *Denkungsart*, by which is understood one that is firmly committed to morally good principles.[23] We shall see that this commitment can be expressed in two ways, depending on whether a proposed course of action is regarded as morally required. In that case, a good *Denkungsart* is one that is predisposed, as the result of a free resolve, to regard the obligatory nature of an act as a sufficient reason to perform it, regardless of any possibly conflicting interests that the agent may have. In other words, the agent is predisposed to act from duty alone. In other cases, where a proposed course of action is motivated by the agent's personal ends and ultimately the desire for happiness, an agent with a good *Denkungsart* makes sure that the proposed course of action is morally permissible before deciding upon it. In these cases, then, conformity to the moral law is a necessary condition or *sine qua non* of the volition of an agent with a good *Denkungsart*.

It does not follow from this, however, that we must understand by a good will under human conditions one that *always* acts in this fashion, which is why I have described a good *Denkungsart* as a general orientation of the will and used language such as "predisposed" to characterize its mode of behavior. Although it cannot be claimed that Kant is clear on this matter, he does on occasion distinguish between a good will

---

[20] In this passage Kant is referring explicitly to "character" [*Charakter*], understood in the honorific sense, according to which not every subject may be said to have a character; but the context indicates that he means by this a *Denkungsart*. Moreover at AM 25: 1385 Kant equates character "in the strictest sense" with a *Denkungsart*. Nevertheless, I do not believe that this should be taken to mean that only some subjects have a *Denkungsart*, since Kant seems committed to the view that every rational being has a *Denkungsart*, though only in some of them does it acquire the firmness that warrants referring to it as a character in the honorific sense. See A7: 294; 392.

[21] Ibid., 293; 390, 294; 392.

[22] At one point Kant remarks that the principles to which a person of character is committed "may sometimes...be false and incorrect" (A 7: 292; 390); and citing the example of Sulla he also notes that even an evil character can arose a kind of admiration through his firm maxims (A 7: 293; 391).

[23] Another term that Kant uses, which seems to function as a virtual synonym for *Denkungsart* is *Gesinnung*, which is usually translated as "disposition." Thus, a good will could also be understood as a good *Gesinnung*. I discuss the latter concept, which plays a large role in *Religion*, in Allison (1990, 136–45).

simpliciter and an absolutely [*schlecterdings*] good will, which at one point he defines as one that cannot be evil (GMS 4: 437_{6-7}).[24] This suggests that Kant recognizes the possibility that a human good will or, more generally, that of a finite rational agent could on occasion perform immoral actions and *a fortiori* actions that only contingently accord with moral requirements without totally losing its goodness. Moreover, we can understand this if we keep in mind that having a good will is a function of character and that it is perfectly possible for some one to act "out of character," for example, when one is momentarily carried away by an affect [*Affekt*].[25] We shall examine the core Kantian notions of acting from duty and moral worth in the final section of this chapter; but before turning to that topic we must consider the teleological reflections that Kant introduces in support of his thesis that a good will is the only thing that is good without limitation.

II

Kant's four-paragraph venture into teleology (GMS 4: 394_{32}–96_{37}), which separates his initial discussion of a good will from the remainder of GMS 1, is a source of considerable perplexity. The ostensive reason for its presence is that, in spite of its alleged agreement with common human reason, Kant thinks that "there is something so strange in the idea of the absolute worth of a mere will, without any consideration of utility in its estimation" that it might well arouse the suspicion of stemming from "a high flown fantasy" (GMS 4: 394_{32-37}). This calls to mind Kant's frequently expressed worry that morality might be a mere "phantom of the brain," which is only addressed in GMS 3. What is different here and the major source of the perplexity is that Kant frames the worry in teleological terms. Specifically, the worry is that "nature might have been falsely understood in the aim it had in assigning reason to govern our will" (GMS 4: 394_{37}–95_1), which, according to Kant, is to provide the requisite preconditions for the production of a good will, namely, practical reason.

By formulating the worry in this way, Kant makes it clear that a good will must be regarded as a product of reason. Although this is implicit in Kant's initial account, a reader of the opening paragraphs might still be left with the impression that the

---

[24] It must be admitted, however, that there is a certain ambiguity in Kant's use of the expression "an absolutely good will." Sometimes he equates it with a holy will, which precludes assigning it to a finite agent (GMS 4: 439_{29-30}), whereas elsewhere he states that the principle governing such a will must be a categorical imperative (GMS 4: 444_{28-29}), which entails that it must be attributed to a finite rational agent. He also speaks of a will that is absolutely and without limitation good (GMS 402_3), where "absolutely" seems to be equivalent to good without limitation, which would apply to every good will.

[25] Kant contrasts affects and passions. By the former he understands a feeling of pleasure or displeasure in a subject's present state that blocks the reflection through which the subject could decide on the basis of reason whether or not to act on this feeling. By contrast, a passion for Kant is an inclination that can be conquered only with great difficulty, if at all by the subject's reason (A 7: 251; 352–54). Elsewhere Kant says that an affect can coexist with the best will, which cannot be said of a passion (MS 6: 408; 535). Although as far as I can tell Kant nowhere provides a list of the factors that could prevent a subject with a good will from behaving properly, it seems clear that being under the temporary sway of an affect would loom large on such a list.

unlimited goodness of a good will is a function of having the proper sentiments. One outcome of what I shall call Kant's "teleological interlude" is that it blocks any such reading and places the focus on the role of reason in determining the will, that is, on reason as *practical*.

I believe, however, that the chief function of this interlude is, polemical, which is to say that its main targets are the Wolffians and the views of Garve as expressed in his *Cicero*. The relevance of the former is obvious, since Wolff is notorious for interpreting Leibniz's doctrine that this is the best of all possible worlds in a strongly anthropocentric and eudaemonistic fashion, according to which the arrangement of nature is seen primarily as intended to maximize human happiness.[26] But though it is less obvious, I believe, in essential agreement with Klaus Reich, that Kant's teleological reflections must also be seen as part of his response to Garve.[27] As Reich points out, the fourth chapter of the first book of *De officiis* affirms precisely the view that Kant challenges, namely, the thesis that nature's purpose in giving reason to human beings was to endow the species with superior means of self-preservation and the capacity for higher forms of well-being than were available to non-rational beings.

Cicero begins the chapter by affirming that every living thing has been endowed by nature with the instinct of self-preservation, which takes the form of an avoidance of what appears harmful and securing the necessities of life. And he adds to this list of universally shared aspects of the instinct of self-preservation the mating instinct and an innate concern for the welfare of offspring. The remainder of the chapter considers the advantages that humans possess over the beasts in virtue of the possession of reason, which, like the above-mentioned instincts, is regarded as a gift of nature. Cicero breaks these advantages down into basically three kinds: (1) an ability to learn from the past and to anticipate the future, which presumably is highly advantageous for self-preservation and well-being; (2) through making possible the power of speech, reason also makes social life possible, which brings with it a wider sphere of interests, concerns, and refined emotions; (3) a capacity to seek the truth, which Cicero regards as the most important of all. In short, Cicero's point is that the possession of reason makes possible a distinctly human form of existence, which, among other things, involves the appreciation of beauty, of the orderliness of the universe, and a sense of rectitude.[28]

Kant would have no quarrel with either Cicero's thesis that the possession of reason is required for the capacities that he lists or that these are good things to have. His quarrel is rather with the implicit assumption that these goods, which (apart from the last) have already been shown to be only good in a limited sense, can trump the unlimited goodness of a good will. Underlying the dispute are the unstated teleological

---

[26] See Beck (1969a, 273–74).

[27] See Reich (1939b, 450–51). I do not, however, accept Reich's further contention that, here as elsewhere, Kant employs what Reich calls Kant's "cosmopolitan maxim," which is really a version of the principle of charity, to provide a sympathetic reading of Cicero's teaching (op. cit., 451). Rather, my view is that Kant is providing a critique and its target is more Garve's use of Cicero than the actual views of Cicero.

[28] Cicero (1893, 12–16).

premises that nature has a purpose in giving reason to a species of natural beings and that this purpose is to be determined by a consideration of the highest form of goodness of which a natural being equipped with reason is capable.

Although Kant shares these premises with the Wolffians, Garve, and many other enlightenment thinkers, his account of the unique goodness of the good will leads him to take them in a radically different direction. Kant begins his discussion with a statement of the teleological principle on which his account is based: "In the natural predispositions of an organized being, i.e., one disposed purposively for life, we take it as a principle that no instrument [*Werkzeug*] is to be found in it for any end except that which is the most suitable to and appropriate for it" (GMS 4: 395$_{4-7}$). Following Christoph Horn, I shall refer to this as the "principle of suitability."[29]

Armed with this principle, Kant uses it to test the assumption that nature's purpose for a being with reason and will, that is, a reason that is practical, is happiness.[30] In other words, practical reason on this view is regarded as an instrument for the production and maintenance of the happiness of the creatures possessing it. Kant curtly dismisses this view on the grounds that reason is ill-equipped for this purpose, which could be accomplished far more expeditiously by instinct. In short, if happiness, which, perhaps under the influence of Garve's *Cicero*, Kant here defines in terms of *preservation* [*Erhaltung*] and *welfare* [*Wohlergehen*] rather than in his usual fashion as complete satisfaction with one's whole existence, were nature's aim for humankind, it would not have chosen the most efficient means, which would constitute a direct contradiction to the principle of suitability.[31]

Kant further suggests that if reason were granted to such a "favored creature," that is, one who instinctively and infallibly pursues its true welfare, "it would not serve as a guide to action, but only to enable it to contemplate the happy predisposition of its nature, to admire it, to rejoice in it and to render it thankful to the beneficent cause of it" (GMS 4: 395$_{17-20}$). Although Kant may have been speaking here with tongue in cheek, we shall see that the distinction between reason and will and the possibility that a rational being might have a reason that is *not* practical are serious issues that emerge in GMS 3 in connection with Kant's endeavor to ground the moral law and categorical imperative.

In the third paragraph of his teleological interlude, Kant turns from a consideration of a narrowly instrumental view of reason as a means for preserving one's life and the maintenance of one's well-being to a consideration of a cultivated reason as itself the chief source of satisfaction. It is here that Kant addresses the historical Cicero, who was, in effect, appealing to the Aristotelian view that the life of the mind is inherently the most satisfactory form of life, at least for those fortunate enough to be capable

---

[29] See Horn (2006, 46).

[30] As we shall see, Kant identifies the will with practical reason at GMS 4: 412$_{29-30}$.

[31] In IAG Kant asserts that an organ that is of no use and an arrangement that does not achieve its purpose "are contradictions in the teleological theory of nature" (8: 18).

of it.[32] Echoing Rousseau and other cultural pessimists, Kant arrives at the decidedly non-Aristotelian conclusion that those who endeavor to live such a life not only fail to attain true contentment, but, if they are honest with themselves, must admit to a certain misology, a "hatred of reason" [*Hass der Vernunft*] (GMS 4: 395$_{33}$). Allegedly, this is because after weighing in the balance all the advantages supposedly gained through the theoretical use of reason one invariably comes to the realization that, from the point of view of personal happiness, they come to nothing (GMS 4: 395$_{33}$–96$_1$).

Kant also suggests, however, that this has beneficial aspects, since it leads one to envy rather than despise the ordinary, non-enlightened human beings, who supposedly live closer to instinct. Finally, by way initiating a transition to the claim that moral goodness rather than happiness (whether sensual or intellectual) is the true end of nature in giving human beings a reason that is capable of governing the will, Kant suggests that the judgment of these misologists, who are at bottom disappointed lovers, is not really ungrateful toward the "world's government" [*Weltregierung*], since it is grounded in the idea of another, higher aim of existence, for which reason has been given (GMS 4: 396$_{10–13}$).

The fourth and final paragraph of the interlude links the discussion with the concept of a good will by equating the latter with this higher aim. The argument consists of three steps, supplemented by some final reflections on the good will as the condition of worthiness to be happy, which gesture toward, without mentioning, the doctrine of the highest good.[33] Leaving aside these final reflections, which really add nothing new, the central argument of the paragraph proceeds as follows:

(1) It has been shown that reason is not sufficiently effective in directing the will to the satisfaction of all our needs—indeed, it serves to multiply them—and this satisfaction could be more reliably secured by an innate instinct (GMS 4: 396$_{14–18}$).

(2) But reason has been imparted to us (presumably by nature) as a practical faculty, that is, one that *ought* to influence the will (GMS 4: 396$_{18–20}$).

(3) Since practical reason must have been given to us for *some* purpose for which it is ideally suited (otherwise it would violate the principle of suitability), the true vocation of reason must be to produce a will that is good in itself, and not merely as a means to some other end (GMS 4: 396$_{20–24}$).

It is obvious that each step is open to criticism and therefore that the argument as a whole is far from compelling. In particular, the principle of suitability on which the argument turns, is simply assumed and not argued for. Thus, while it may have some

---

[32] See Cicero (1893, 18–22).

[33] As already noted, Kant here identifies a good will with the highest good, while acknowledging that it may not be the single and entire good (GMS 4: 396$_{24–26}$), which echoes the view expressed in the ethics lectures.

force against the Wolffians and Garve, who presumably would accept this principle in some form, it offers no answer to anyone who might deign to question it.

Moreover, even accepting the teleological framework in which the argument is cast, there appears to be a serious problem with the third and crucial step. Simply put, it seems to involve a *non sequitur* of a kind that is all too familiar in Kant, since it apparently neglects alternative possibilities. This is because Kant moves directly from the rejection of the thesis that nature's aim in giving humankind a reason capable of guiding conduct, rather than trusting merely to instinct, is to enhance its capacity to attain happiness to the assertion that nature's aim in equipping us with practical reason was to make it possible for us to attain a good will. Kant does not suggest that we should think of nature as actually providing us with a good will, since that would make such goodness into a gift of nature. Rather, we are to assume that, by providing us with practical reason, nature gives us the capacity to acquire such a will for ourselves—what we do with this capacity being up to us. But this still leaves us with the question of why these should be the only alternatives worth considering. Assuming (for the sake of argument) that nature is purposive and that this purposiveness extends to equipping human beings with a faculty of reason that has the capacity to direct conduct, why should happiness and the attainment of a good will be the only conceivable candidates for nature's end in this largess?

What gives this question a certain urgency is the fact that Kant himself had offered an alternative answer in his essay, "The Idea of Universal History with a Cosmopolitan Aim," which he had published one year before GMS (1784) and which one can therefore assume that he had in mind when composing this teleological interlude. Specifically, Kant there argues that nature's end with respect to the human race is the establishment of a civil society based on republican institutions and lawful external relations between nation states. In a word, nature's end is political rather than moral; and far from being unique to this essay, this is the view that Kant consistently maintained in his historical-teleological writings.[34]

Although this difference is significant and the generic problem of neglected alternatives remains in place, I do not think that this warrants charging Kant with offering a teleology in GMS that stands in blatant contradiction with the one contained in this essay and therefore with neglecting an alternative that he had himself proposed a short time earlier. First, the fact that in "The Idea of Universal History" the teleology that Kant sketches is explicitly historical and, as such, is concerned with the future development of humankind, whereas that in GMS is non-historical, can be accounted for on the grounds that a venture into a philosophy of history would not accord with the sharply limited aims of GMS, namely, the setting forth and establishment of the supreme principle of morality. Accordingly, it seems perfectly possible to view these two accounts as complementary rather than as contradictory.

---

[34] These include, but are not limited to, §83 of the third *Critique* (KU 5: 429–34; 297–301) and Kant's most systematic and best known treatment of the topic: *Toward Perpetual Peace* (1795).

Second, both texts assume essentially the same teleological principle; for corresponding to the principle of suitability in GMS is the principle that "All natural predispositions of a creature are determined sometime [*einmal*] to develop themselves completely and purposively" (IAG 8: 18; 109). To be sure, this differs from the principle of suitability in that it refers to the future development of natural predispositions rather than their present function; but once again this reflects the historical dimension of "The Idea of Universal History," which, for understandable reasons, is not present in GMS.

Third, they both firmly reject the widely shared enlightenment view that nature's end with regard to humankind is the attainment of happiness and affirm instead the quintessentially Kantian view that what matters most is not what nature does for us ("gifts of nature"), but what we as rational beings with wills can do for ourselves. As Kant puts it in the essay,

Nature has willed that the human being should produce everything that goes beyond the mechanical arrangement of his animal existence entirely out of himself, and participate in no other happiness or perfection than that which he has procured for himself free from instinct through his own reason. (IAG 8: 19, 110).

Finally, and more speculatively, in the same essay Kant seems to gesture vaguely toward the idea of a future trans-political goal for humankind, for which nature supposedly prepares they way by means of the mechanism of "unsociable sociability."[35] He does so by suggesting at one point that the creation of a federation of nation states, the supposed goal of the historical process, would correspond roughly to the half-way point in the development of humanity (IAG 8: 26; 116). Although Kant does not indicate what he thinks (or hopes) will occur in this second half of this developmental process, which he evidently viewed as lying in a distant future, it seems reasonable to assume that he had in mind a progress in morality, which, expressed in terms of GMS, could be seen as something like the collective attainment of a good will.[36]

If this reading is correct, it would provide further support for the view that there is a deep connection between the teleology of "The Idea of Universal History" and that of GMS, one which transcends the differences already noted. But there is no need to argue for that here, since all that is required is to show that that the two accounts are

[35] For an excellent analysis of the concept of unsocial sociability and its centrality to Kant's anthropological thought, see Wood (1999, esp. 213–15 and 273–75; and 2009, 112–28).

[36] Although he does not put it in this way, this reading of Kant's obscure remark regarding the attainment of a confederation of nation states marking only the half-way point in the development of humanity has been suggested by Wood (1991, 341). Wood also points out that this accords with the distinction that Kant draws in the third *Critique* between nature's "ultimate end" [*letzter Zweck*], which Kant there defines as culture and which is something that nature can goad humankind (largely through the mechanism of unsociable sociability) to attain, and the "final end" [*Endzweck*] of humanity, which is the attainment of the highest good. Perhaps of greater relevance is Kant's conception of an ethical commonwealth [*ethischen gemeinen Wesens*] in *Religion*, which he envisions as a future historical condition in which humanity is governed by moral rather than merely juridical laws. Admittedly, however, there is no direct evidence that Kant had such a conception in mind at the time of writing GMS.

compatible, which I think they clearly are. Thus, I shall conclude the discussion of Kant's teleological interlude by reiterating what I take to be the main reason for its inclusion in the text besides the one that Kant explicitly assigned to it, which was to remove the air of paradox attached to the thesis that a good will is the only thing in the world (or out of it) that is good without limitation. As already indicated, I regard its presence as due mainly to polemical considerations and, more specifically, as directed against the Wolffian and especially the Garvean views on the relationship between morality and happiness.

Admittedly, there is no direct evidence for this, since Kant's teleological interlude contains no reference to either the Wolffian teleology or the views of Garve and Cicero. I have tried to show, however, that there is considerable indirect evidence, particularly with respect to Garve's *Cicero*. Moreover, I submit that if, as is usually done, one ignores this aspect of Kant's account, it is difficult to resist dismissing this interlude as at best an unnecessary appendage and at worst an additional source of obscurity; whereas if one reads it in light of Kant's polemical concerns, its presence in the text no longer seems mysterious, even if its argumentation remains less than compelling.

III

After completing his teleological interlude, Kant turns in the next five paragraphs (GMS 4: 397_1–99_{34}) to an account of the notion of acting from duty, ostensibly as a means to clarify further that of a good will. His central claim is that the concept of duty "contains that of a good will, though under certain subjective limitations and hindrances, which far from concealing it and making it unrecognizable, bring it out by contrast and make it shine forth all the more brightly" (GMS 4: $397_{7–10}$). In other words, the good will is the broader concept or genus of which a will whose goodness is conditioned by these subjective limitations and hindrances and is therefore subject to duty is a species.

The other species is that of a perfect or holy will. Since, *ex hypothesi*, such a will is free from these limitations and hindrances, which is a consequence of its being unencumbered with a sensuous nature, it follows the dictates of the moral law by its very nature, without need for constraint. And since there are only duties when there is need for constraint, one cannot speak of duties with regard to a holy will.[37] But since the human will (and that of all finite rational agents) is encumbered with a sensuous nature, and as such must be constrained to follow the dictates of morality, these dictates always take the form of duties for it.

Although Kant's aim in these paragraphs is supposedly to analyze what is involved in acting from duty and to show why such action is the expression of a good will under human conditions, he complicates matters and provides ammunition for his critics in at

---

[37] See GMS 4: $414_{1–10}$.

least two ways. One is by discussing acting from duty prior to providing a definition of duty.[38] The other is by introducing, without sufficient preparation, the concept of moral worth, which is a value attributed to action from duty and to such action alone.[39] The former can easily be explained on the basis of Kant's analytic method, according to which definitions in philosophy come only at the end.[40] But the latter raises a problem that must be dealt with, since it underlies many misinterpretations of Kant's view.

The basic problem is that the concept of a good will refers to a disposition, whereas moral worth applies to something occurrent; and this calls for an account of how the two concepts are supposed to relate to one another. Some interpreters try to finesse the problem by understanding a good will in light of the concept of moral worth as referring to particular intentions, thereby taking it as referring to something occurrent.[41] But we have seen that this approach fails, because the concept of a good will, understood as a good *Denkungsart*, is clearly a dispositional concept.

Alternatively, one might think that the problem can be dealt with by defining a good will under human conditions as one that acts from duty, as the result of which all of its actions possess moral worth. Unfortunately, this will not do either. To begin with, not every action that an agent with a good will performs need be done from duty. On the contrary, it has already been noted that many, if not most of the actions of such an agent are directed at private ends, not involving obligation, and this does not detract from the goodness of the agent's will, as long as a reflection indicating the permissibility of the proposed course of action precedes the act. Moreover, it was also noted that it is not necessary that a finite rational agent must always follow the dictates of morality in order to be credited with a good will, since goodness is a matter of the agent's overall character and, as such, is compatible with an occasional lapse, particularly those that result from a momentary affect such as anger, as long as the latter does not degenerate into the passion of hatred.[42]

While these considerations show that having a good will cannot be regarded as a sufficient condition of acting from duty, they leave open the possibility that it could be a necessary condition. In other words, though not every (or even most) of the volitions of an agent with a good will have moral worth, no volitions of an agent without a good will could have such worth. I believe that this best expresses Kant's never clearly articulated position on the matter, at least on the assumption that by a good will is understood a good *Denkungsart*, and I shall present an argument for this in the next chapter. For the present, however, I shall confine myself to the text, devoting the

---

[38] Kant later defines "duty" as "the necessity of an action from respect for the law" (GMS 4: 400_{18-19}). As such, it presupposes the concepts of law and respect, neither of which has been introduced at the present stage of the argument.

[39] Its first appearance is at GMS 4: 398_{14}.

[40] See U 2: 276–78; 248–50.

[41] See note 15.

[42] See A 7: 252; 354.

remainder of the chapter to an analysis of Kant's discussion of acting from duty and moral worth in the paragraphs with which we are presently concerned.

Kant's strategy in these paragraphs is to canvass various scenarios, until he arrives at those that would supposedly be recognized by common human reason as instances of acting from duty and to which a special kind of value (moral worth) would be assigned. He begins by quickly eliminating those that are already recognized as contrary to duty. Although he acknowledges that such actions might prove useful for certain purposes, Kant denies that the question of their being done from duty can even arise (GMS 4: 397₁₁₋₁₅). Against this, it is sometimes objected that one might mistakenly believe that one was acting dutifully, in which case one would (subjectively speaking) be motivated by the thought of duty, while (objectively speaking) acting contrary to duty.[43] And, in this context, it is also pointed out that, while in GMS Kant seems to hold that common human reason has no difficulty in recognizing duties, he acknowledges elsewhere the possibility of error in this matter.[44]

The issue turns on the interpretation of the phrase "already recognized" [schon . . . erkannt]. The recognition that a possible course of action is contrary to duty [pflichtwi-drig] might be attributed either to an idealized observer or to the agent. If it is the former, then the problem remains, since what is recognized as contrary to duty by such an observer might not be recognized as such by the agent. But if it is the latter, then it is clear that someone who recognizes that a certain course of action is contrary to duty cannot perform that action from a sense of duty. Although the text does not speak clearly in favor of the latter reading, it is compatible with it and makes much better sense of Kant's argument.[45]

A different kind of case, which Kant's also thinks requires little comment because it would be readily recognized as being without moral import, is that of a person who, though acting in complete conformity with duty, is motivated neither by a sense of duty nor an immediate inclination, but acts purely on the basis of prudential calculation. Kant's example is a shopkeeper who, having no immediate inclination to treat his customers honestly, such as a sympathetic concern for their well-being, nonetheless does so from an interest in maximizing his long-term profit. In short, he is someone for whom "honesty is the best policy," rather than a matter of either principle or a kind-hearted sentiment. Inasmuch as he does consistently treat his customers honestly, this shopkeeper's behavior is in accordance with duty; but since it is based entirely on a morally irrelevant prudential calculation, it has no genuine moral worth. Accordingly, while it is certainly a good thing that this shopkeeper treats

---

[43] See, for example, Kerstein (2002, 96–97).

[44] Among the places where Kant appears to allow room for an erroneous moral judgment are his treatment of conscience in the *Doctrine of Virtue*, where he admits that one can err in one's "objective judgment as to whether something is a duty or not" (MS 6: 401; 529) and in the *Anthropology*, where he acknowledges the possibility that the principles adopted by a person of character "might occasionally be mistaken and imperfect" (A7: 292; 390).

[45] In the recent literature this solution has been suggested, Kerstein (2002, 97–98), and Baron (2006, 73).

his customers honestly, it is generally recognized that he is not a good person because of the reason underlying his outwardly honest behavior.[46]

In the same Kant context, suggests that, while it is easy to determine whether an action is performed from duty rather than from a self-seeking purpose [selbstsüchtiger Absicht] when there is no immediate inclination favoring the action, it becomes much more difficult to make this determination when there is such an inclination (GMS 4: 397_{19-21}). Kant also notes in passing that this difficulty would apply in the case of the shopkeeper, if rather than naked self-interest, he was motivated by a feeling such as love for his customers (GMS 4: 397_{27-30}), that is, if his behavior stemmed from what might be termed a good Sinnesart. These seemingly parenthetical suggestions are puzzling in two respects. First, given Kant's sharp contrast between duty and inclination, it is not clear why the presence of an immediate inclination should make it more difficult to determine whether the action was performed from duty. Second, in view of Kant's skepticism regarding the possibility of determining the true motivation of an act, it likewise not clear how one could confidently determine the true motive in either case.[47]

I believe that the solution to both puzzles requires the recognition that Kant misstates his true position. In the case of the first puzzle, this misstatement is fairly blatant. Rather than asserting that it is more difficult to determine whether an action is from duty or self-interest when there is also an immediate inclination for the same course of action, Kant should have said that under this condition it is more difficult to determine the moral worth of the action. This is because actions motivated by an immediate inclination share a common feature with those from duty, namely, they are undertaken for their own sake rather than, as in the case of the prudent shopkeeper, for the sake of some extrinsic end. Moreover, the solution to the second puzzle follows from that of the first; for this indicates that rather than being a matter of the relative ease or difficulty in determining an agent's motivation, Kant is making an axiological point regarding the comparative difficulty of distinguishing the moral value of actions performed from a sense of duty from those motivated by an inclination such as love or sympathetic feeling.[48]

The latter also accords with common intuitions, inasmuch as most people (including many philosophers in both Kant's time and our own) would tend to regard both the

---

[46] I am here equating a "good person" with "one with a good will."

[47] It should be noted, however, that Kant only introduced the issue of motivational skepticism in GMS 2. See GMS 4: 407_{1-15}. I shall return to this issue in the next chapter in connection with the analysis of Kant's account of maxims.

[48] This analysis is influenced by Baron's (2006, 75–76) , who likewise insists that Kant is not to be read as making a claim about the relative difficulty of distinguishing between different types of motivation. The difference is that, whereas she takes Kant's point to be about "differentiating concepts," on my view, this cannot be the whole story, since the concept of an act motivated by an immediate inclination is as distinct from one motivated by duty as the latter is from one motivated by self-interest. Rather, the difficulty concerns the relative assessment of moral value. That is why I characterize it as an axiological rather than a conceptual difficulty.

shopkeeper who deals honestly with his customers from a genuine affection for them and the one who does so from duty as good persons, whereas few would regard the one who does this solely out of calculating self-interest in this way. This is also reflected in the fact that, apart from a few highly heterodox moralists, such as Mandeville, Helvétius, and LaMettrie, naked self-interest is generally rejected as a source of an authentically moral motivation, while many thinkers, for example, the British sentimentalists from Shaftesbury through Smith, not to mention present-day "virtue ethicists," hold that a proper sentiment is the appropriate moral motive. Thus, Kant's concern is to show that, despite initial appearances, there is a decisive difference in moral import between actions motivated by immediate or direct inclinations such as love or sympathetic feeling and those motivated by duty, and that only the latter possess genuine moral worth.

This is the main task of the next three paragraphs (10–12), where Kant examines the motivational issue in connection with two generally recognized duties: self-preservation and beneficence, and one somewhat odd one: securing one's own happiness, which Kant considers an indirect duty. Like any dutiful actions, these can be performed for a number of reasons and Kant's concern is to specify the conditions under which actions that accord with these duties may be regarded as having moral worth.

Kant's treatment of self-preservation is relatively straightforward. His point is that precisely because most people have a direct inclination to preserve their lives, the great care that they take in this regard may be in accordance with duty but has no moral significance because it is not *from duty* or, as Kant also puts it, their "maxim has no moral content" (GMS 4: 397_{36}–98_1). This is contrasted with a situation in which the normal love of life has been lost through adverse circumstances, yet the unhappy person, who actually wishes for death, nonetheless preserves his life without loving it, from duty rather than from either fear or inclination. Under those conditions, Kant suggests "his maxim [of life preserving behavior] first has moral content" (GMS 4: 398_7). In other words, Kant is contrasting two situations in which an agent's actions accord with the duty to preserve his life. In one of them, when he is simply acting on the basis of inclination, his maxim has no moral content; while in the other, where this inclination is lacking, it does have such content. Presumably because the inclination to preserve one's life is viewed as an innate natural drive, which is not dependent on the choice of the agent, the claim that the maxim to preserve oneself, insofar as it is based on this inclination, is without moral content is relatively non-controversial. But, of course, to deny that a maxim has moral content is not to say that it is immoral.[49]

Kant's treatment of beneficence is much more complex and controversial. He begins by stating:

---

[49] The notion of moral content is an important but generally neglected aspect of Kant's account, which I shall discuss in Chapter 5.

To be beneficent, where one can, is a duty, and besides this there are many souls who are so sympathetically attuned that, even without any other motive of vanity or self-interest, they find an inner satisfaction in spreading joy around them and can take delight in the contentment of others, insofar as it is their work. But I assert that in such a case an action of this kind, however dutiful [*pflichtmässig*] it may be, has nevertheless no true moral worth, but is on the same footing with other inclinations, e.g., the inclination to honor, which when it fortuitously [*glücklicherweise*] encounters something that in fact serves the common interest and is in conformity with duty, and thus worthy of honor [*ehrenwert*], deserves praise and encouragement, but not esteem [*Hochschätzung*]; for the maxim lacks moral content, namely doing such actions not from inclination but *from duty*. (GMS 4: 398$_{8-21}$)

Assuming that Kant's intent is to present an example of a mode of behavior that many would regard (albeit incorrectly) as worthy of the highest moral praise, he unnecessarily muddies the waters by stipulating that the sympathetically attuned agents to whom he refers take delight in spreading joy "insofar as it is their work." This suggests that what motivates them is not so much a disinterested concern with the well-being of others, as it is being the source of this well-being (and perhaps even being recognized as such), which dulls somewhat the contrast with the blatantly self-interested shopkeeper.

Nevertheless, a careful consideration of the passage as a whole suggests that Kant's aim is two-fold. On the one hand, he intends to contrast the behavior of the sympathetically attuned benefactors with that of both the cold and calculating shop-keeper and those who preserve their lives from self-love by suggesting that the former deserve praise and encouragement, which, presumably, one would not say of the latter.[50] On the other hand, and this is Kant's main point, in denying that the conduct of these sympathetically attuned agents is worthy of esteem, he indicates that the moral status of their beneficent deeds is qualitatively distinct from those of someone who acts beneficently from duty.

It also seems clear that Kant wants to emphasize that the reason for this is that the behavior of these sympathetically attuned agents only "fortuitously" accords with duty. In part, this means that sympathetically motivated beneficence can lead to morally prohibited conduct. To cite the example used by Barbara Herman, a person of sympathetic temperament sees someone struggling late at night with a heavy burden outside a museum. Being sympathetic by nature, her inclination would be to help the person struggling with the burden, thereby inadvertently becoming a collaborator in an art theft.[51] In fact, sympathetic action can not only violate duty to others; it can also violate a duty to oneself, as, for example, if unconstrained giving to those who seem needy leads one to neglect one's own true needs. In short, even though beneficence is a duty, when not governed by moral principles, it can lead to conduct that is contrary to

---

[50] This is not to say that one would either blame the shopkeeper for or discourage him from treating his customers honestly; but if any praise is called for, it would only be for his business acumen.

[51] Herman (1993, 3–4).

duty, which explains why its agreement with the dictates of morality is merely fortuitous.[52]

As the comparison with the inclination to honor indicates, however, this is not the whole story; for even when actions motivated by sympathetic feelings do (fortuitously) produce results that accord with duty, Kant denies that they posses genuine moral worth. This is because in such cases the performance of the dutiful action is contingent upon the presence and efficacy of the sympathetic feeling or some other functionally equivalent *Sinnesart*, such as the love of honor. Accordingly, there are two distinct ways in which the conformity to duty of inclination-based actions is contingent: first, in not violating some duty and, second, in the appropriate *Sinnesart* being present and effective.

Once again, however, this does not mean that Kant holds that inclination-based dutiful actions are unworthy, disreputable, or indicative of a *bad* will, since he acknowledges that they deserve "praise and encouragement." The point is rather that he denies that they are worthy of the highest moral accolade, esteem, which requires that the action be from duty. In fact, Kant later claimed that we have an indirect duty to cultivate our sympathetic feelings, since the more sensitive we become to the needs of others, the better able we will be to practice the duty of beneficence (MS 6: 457; 575–76). Consequently, the distinction between actions that deserve merely praise and encouragement because they are based on inclination and those that are worthy of esteem because they are motivated by the idea of duty is crucial for Kant.[53]

---

[52] That being motivated by a sentiment of beneficence can lead to acts that are contrary to duty is also indicative of the fact that beneficence is an imperfect duty. As we shall see, one of the problems with Kant's oversimplified account in GMS 1 is that he does not appeal to the distinction between perfect and imperfect duty, first introducing it in GMS 2.

[53] There is an interesting contrast on this point between the views of Kant and Adam Smith. The corresponding distinction in Smith is between virtue and mere propriety, which he describes as "between those qualities and actions which deserve to be admired and celebrated, and those which simply deserve to be approved of." See Smith (1982, 25). Although this parallels Kant's distinction between actions that deserve praise and encouragement and those that merit esteem, his ranking is the reverse of Kant's. Thus, while, as a result of his dark view of human nature, Smith maintains that, as a matter of fact, a sense of duty is almost always necessary to motivate human beings to do the right thing, it has the status for him, much as it did for Hume, of what would today be called a "default motive," which comes into play only when the proper sentiment is lacking. Accordingly, Smith held that, as unexceptional, actions motivated by a sense of duty deserve to be approved and even merit some "applause," whereas truly virtuous actions are exceptional, and, for that reason, worthy of admiration. According to Smith, "As in the common degree of the intellectual qualities, there is no ability; so in the common degree of the moral, there is no virtue. Virtue is excellence, something uncommonly great and beautiful, which rises far above what is vulgar and ordinary" (op. cit., 25). Here the contrast with Kant could not be greater, since for him all that morality requires of us is no more than simple duty, which in Smith's terms reduces to mere propriety. As Kant puts it in a passage that seems as if it had been written with Smith in mind, "To teach only *admiration* [*bewundern*] for virtuous actions, however great a sacrifice these may have cost, falls short of the right spirit that ought to support the apprentice's feeling for the moral good. For however virtuous someone is, all the good that he can ever perform is still his simple duty" (RGV 6: 48–49; 93). Clearly, the "right spirit" for Kant is a sense of duty. For an informative discussion of the relationship between Kant and Smith and Kant's knowledge of the latter's work, see Fleischacker (1991, esp. 249–52).

In the remainder of the paragraph devoted to beneficence, Kant sketches two hypothetical scenarios in which beneficent action would both possess genuine moral worth, and thus be worthy of esteem, rather than merely praise and encouragement, and this worthiness would be evident. The first features an example of the sympathetically attuned soul or friend of humanity, in whom, as the result of personal misfortune, all sympathetic concern for the fate of others has been eradicated. Then, and only then, Kant claims, when "he tears himself out of this deadly insensibility" and, lacking any inclination, performs the action solely from duty, does his action for the first time have genuine moral worth (GMS 398_{20-27}).

In commenting on this passage, Herman points out that Kant is here contrasting the moral status of the beneficent action of the same individual in two different psychological states: one in which a beneficent impulse or inclination is still present and another in which it has been lost. Accordingly, on her reading, with which I concur, Kant's point is merely that the actions of *this particular individual* only attain moral worth when the duty motive takes the place of inclination, which is quite different from claiming that moral worth in general requires the absence of inclination.[54] I shall return to this point in the next chapter in connection with an analysis of Schiller's famous objection to Kant's moral psychology.

In the second scenario, we are invited to imagine a very different person, one who rather than having lost a sympathetic feeling for humankind never had one and, though an honest man, is by temperament cold and indifferent toward the suffering of others. About such a person Kant asks rhetorically, "would he not still find within himself a source to give himself a far higher worth than that which a good natured temperament might have?" To which he answers, "By all means! Just there begins the worth of character, which is moral and the highest without any comparison, namely, that he is beneficent, not from inclination, but from duty" (GMS 4: $398_{34}–99_2$).

Unless it was for the sake of systematic completeness (a perfect duty to others [honest dealing]; a perfect duty to oneself [self-preservation]; an imperfect duty to others [beneficence]; and an indirect duty [securing one's own happiness]), it is difficult to fathom the function of the last example.[55] Here Kant emphasizes that human beings have by nature the most powerful inclination to seek happiness, since the idea of it consists in the satisfaction of the sum of all inclinations. This suggests that the idea of a duty to seek or preserve one's happiness would be otiose, which is how Kant generally

---

[54] Herman (1981, 378–79). See also Baron (2006, 81).

[55] Even the assumption of a desire for systematic completeness does not fully explain Kant's inclusion of this example, since we shall see that, when Kant appeals to different classes of duty in GMS 2 in his endeavor to illustrate the operation of the categorical imperative, he chooses examples of perfect and imperfect duties to self and others; ignoring any discussion of an indirect duty. In fact, the notion of an indirect duty does not have a systematic place in Kant's ethical theory; though he does claim that we have an indirect duty to promote (or at least not neglect) our own happiness in all three of his major writings in ethical theory. In addition to the present passage, see KpV 5: 93; 214–15, and MS 6: 388; 519–20). I discuss this matter in connection with Kant's claim regarding an indirect duty to develop sympathetic feelings in Allison (1996, 121–23).

viewed the matter.[56] Nevertheless, he suggests that a moral dimension is involved, because the indeterminate nature of the idea of happiness can easily lead one to act for the sake of an immediate good that is to one's long-term detriment, which, in turn, might put one in a situation in which one was open to temptation to violate genuine duties. For example, someone who throws away all his money on a foolish business venture might find himself in a situation in which he was tempted to steal or commit other crimes in order to recoup his losses. But the actual example that Kant gives, namely, someone who suffering from gout decides to indulge in a rich meal, points in a different direction. Of such a person Kant writes:

[I]f the universal inclination to happiness did not determine his will, if for him at least, health did not count as so necessary in his reckoning, then, as in all other cases, there still remains a law, namely to promote his happiness not from inclination but from duty, and then his conduct has for the first genuine moral worth. (GMS 4: 399$_{21-26}$)

It is, to say the least, odd to speak of promoting happiness, the very idea of which consists of the satisfaction of the sum of one's inclinations, not from inclination, but from duty. And, in the case of the gout sufferer, it is difficult to see what duties his dangerous indulgence would tempt him to violate, save perhaps the prohibitions against suicide or gluttony. It seems possible to make sense out of what Kant is getting at here, however, if we take him to be referring not to the promotion or preservation of happiness as expressed in this idea, but merely simple prudence. In other words, even though prudence *per se* is not a duty for Kant, I think that he may be read as claiming that there is something like a duty to act prudently in cases in which failing to doing so would forseeably have harmful consequences, whether or not these consequences lead to the violation of genuine duties. But even granting prudential conduct the status of a quasi duty, it remains difficult to see why Kant would attribute "genuine moral worth" to such conduct, since, *ex hypothesi*, there is no genuine duty by the thought of which it could be said to be motivated. One could, of course, say that it is the duty of self-preservation that is at issue; but in that case the example collapses into the first.

Although Kant's account of these cases is deeply suggestive and has generated endless discussion in the literature, due largely to the analytic-regressive nature of his procedure, it is also radically incomplete and raises many more questions than it answers. Chief among these is whether acting from duty is compatible with also having an inclination or, more generally, a non-moral incentive to perform the dutiful act, which led to the classical objection of Schiller and a host of attempts to respond to it. Accordingly, this will be a central concern of the next chapter, which begins with an analysis of Kant's conception of maxims and their role in the exercise of rational agency on which his whole account is ultimately based.

---

[56] See, for example, MS 6: 387; 519, where Kant denies that one's own happiness, as contrasted with the happiness of others, is an end that it is also a duty.

4

Maxims and Moral Worth Redux

The present chapter is concerned with the major unanswered questions left by the accounts of a good will and moral worth in the preceding chapter. Since Kant's entire account, including his discussion of a good will, is based on his conception of maxims, the first part of this chapter will provide an analysis of this core Kantian conception. In light of this, the second part will revisit Kant's account of moral worth sketched in the preceding chapter, focusing on Friedrich Schiller's classical objection. After discussing some of the important responses to this objection offered in the literature, I shall provide my own response, which is based on what I term Kant's "incorporation thesis."

I

Although Kant refers to maxims early in his account of acting from duty (GMS 4: 397_{36}), he only defines the term in two footnotes long after he had already made significant use of it. In the first of the definitions, which is attached to his definition of duty in GMS 1, Kant writes:

A *maxim* is the subjective principle of volition; the objective principle (i.e., that which would serve all rational beings also subjectively as a practical principle, if reason had full control over the faculty of desire) is the practical law. (GMS 4: 400_{34-37})

In the second reference, which occurs in connection with his account of imperatives as objective practical principles in GMS 2, Kant writes somewhat more expansively:

A *maxim* is the subjective principle for action and must be distinguished from the *objective principle*, namely the practical law. The former contains the practical rule that reason determines according to the conditions of the subject (often its ignorance, or even its inclinations), and is thus the principle according to which the subject *acts*; but the law is the objective principle, valid for every rational being, and the principle according to which it *ought to act*, i.e., an imperative. (GMS 4: 420_{36}–21_{30})

It is clear from both definitions that maxims are subjective principles of practical reason. As *subjective*, they are principles on which an agent actually acts, as contrasted with objective principles or practical laws, which are those on which an agent *ought* to act and would act if perfectly rational. Moreover, as *principles*, maxims are general rules or policies, which specify action-types under certain conditions, rather than particular actions or intentions. Kant subsequently underscores this point by noting that all maxims have the form of universality (GMS 4: 436₁₅). Since maxims are subjective principles, this obviously must be understood as a subjective universality governing the choices of the agent whose maxim it is; but we shall see in later chapters that this provides the justification for the application of the universalizability test to maxims, which is intended to determine whether they can *also* be assigned an objective universality, that is, can be willed as universal laws. In addition, as principles, maxims have an authoritative or normative status for the agents whose maxims they are, providing "subjectively valid" reasons, that is, reasons that serve to justify an action for an agent. Finally, as *products of practical reason*, maxims are freely adopted by agents rather than either possessed from birth in the manner of an instinct or passively acquired in the course of experience in the manner of a Humean habit. Properly speaking, one does not simply have a maxim, one makes it one's maxim, which, as an act of spontaneity, is imputable to the agent.

In the second *Critique*, Kant further notes that maxims presuppose interests and interests rest on incentives [*Triebfedern*] (KpV 5: 79; 204).[1] The situation is complicated, however, by the fact that Kant defines the latter term differently in the two works. In GMS, Kant contrasts "*Triebfeder*" and "*Bewegungsgrund*," both of which could be rendered in English by the multi-faceted term "motive"; though many translators reserve this term for the latter, using "incentive" to render the former. In any event, Kant here defines an incentive [*Triebfeder*] as "the subjective ground of desire" and a motive [*Bewegungsgrund*] as the "objective ground of volition" (GMS 4: 427₂₆₋₂₇). Since an incentive, so understood, is inherently subjective, reflecting an agent's contingent desires, there could be no such thing as an incentive to obey the moral law, which as an objective principle of practical reason serves as a motive in the sense of a *Bewegungsgrund*.

By contrast, in the second *Critique*, Kant defines an incentive as "the subjective determining ground of the will of a being whose reason does not by its nature necessarily conform to the objective law" (KpV 5: 72; 198). According to Beck, it is the "conative or dynamic factor in volition," whereas the objective determining ground is the rule or principle governing the action.[2] Although this seems similar to the account in GMS, the difference is that Kant now speaks of the moral law, which is the objective determining ground of the will, as being "subjectively sufficient," in

---

[1] Kant here underscores the inseparability of these three notions, noting that all three are applicable only to finite rational beings: "For they all presuppose a limitation of the nature of a being, in that the subjective constitution of its choice does not of itself accord with the objective law of practical reason; they presuppose a need to be impelled to activity by something because an internal obstacle is opposed to it." And he adds that this cannot be said of the divine will (KpV 5: 79; 204). Although Kant does not discuss the matter, it may be assumed that he would not deny that ends should be assigned to the divine will, since the concept of an end is inseparable from the concept of a will. The point is rather that the ends of a divine will are set necessarily by pure reason, without any need for a subjective interest as the determinant of these ends.

[2] Beck (1960, 216).

which case it itself serves as an incentive. In fact, a fundamental thesis of the second *Critique* is that respect for the law is the moral incentive. We shall see in the next chapter that Kant provides a similar, albeit much sketchier account of respect in GMS 1, which does not invoke the language of incentives, though it does connect respect with the associated notion of an interest.

In GMS, Kant defines an interest as "the dependence of a contingently determinable will on principles of reason" (GMS 4: $413n_{26-28}$); while in the second *Critique* he defines it as "an incentive of the will insofar as it is *represented by reason*" (KpV 5: 79; 204). Both suggest that an interest is an incentive that is endorsed by practical reason as worthy of being acted upon. To have an incentive to x is to have a reason to x, but it is not yet to have an interest in $x$ing. For example, I might have a desire to eat an ice cream cone, which gives me an incentive to buy one; yet I still might not have an interest in making the purchase, if, for example, I were lactose intolerant and knew that eating the ice cream would lead to unpleasant consequences. Accordingly, for Kant one does not simply have interests, rather one *takes* an interest in something, which requires an exercise of practical reason.

Interests, so construed, are the source of ends, which are chosen by an agent on the basis of interests; but to take an interest in $x$ing is not yet to include it among one's ends. The latter requires an open-ended commitment to pursue that interest with some degree of regularity, a commitment that rests on a value assigned to the pursuit of that interest in one's overall life plan. For example, I take an interest in film noir, but I would not include viewing specimens of this genre among my ends, since it does not in any sense give direction to my life, and I am perfectly content to act on this interest intermittently, when there are no more pressing or competing interests involved. Moreover, ends, and through them interests, are embedded in our maxims, which are basically principles dictating the pursuit of a specific end in a determinate manner and under certain conditions.

In light of these considerations, a maxim may be schematically rendered as a principle of the form: "When in S-type situations, perform A-type actions in order to attain end E."[3] Let us assume that I make it my maxim to exercise regularly in order to maintain my health. S-type situations are those in which some form of exercise is a viable activity and A-type actions are the various forms of exercise in which I might engage. Unlike a resolution to do fifty pushups every morning, a maxim to exercise regularly leaves one with a certain leeway regarding the choice of the form of exercise; its extent, and its frequency. Correlatively, health maintenance is the end embedded in the maxim and it obviously reflects an interest in maintaining one's health. Leaving aside moral considerations, lacking this or some other interest in exercising (say to keep

---

[3] For a similar account, see Korsgaard (1996, 58). I have characterized this account as provisional because it does not address the question of whether an agent's incentive should be included in the maxim. In the next section of this chapter, I shall argue, contra Wood, that it should be.

my wife from constantly reminding me how out of shape I am), I would not make this my end and therefore not adopt the maxim.

Finally, in view of the analysis of a good will as a good *Denkungsart* offered in the preceding chapter, a word is in order regarding a topic that Kant treats only in passing and that is seldom broached in the literature, at least in these terms, namely the relationship between an agent's maxims and its *Denkungsart*.[4] Inasmuch as it consists in a "way of thinking," a maxim might itself be described as a *Denkungsart*.[5] But while Kant seems to assume that a rational agent can have any number of maxims, reflecting its diverse ends and interests, it presumably can have only a single *Denkungsart* (at least at any one time).[6] Thus, I believe that a *Denkungsart* can also be described as a higher order or "meta-maxim," which, as already noted, expresses a general orientation of the will and which, as such, guides agents in their selection of the more specific maxims on which they actually act.

Moreover, I think that this understanding of the relationship between maxims and *Denkungsarten* helps us to see why, on Kant's view, a good *Denkungsart* is a necessary (though not a sufficient) condition for agent's actions having moral worth. There are two points to be made here. The first is that is that in order for an act to have moral worth it does not suffice that on a particular occasion the duty motive happens to "win out" over an inclination to act contrary to duty.[7] For example, though he could use the money, a professor resists a $1000 bribe to give a passing grade to a student whose work has been unsatisfactory. Clearly, the professor has done the right thing, but one would not for that reason alone attribute moral worth to this act. It is also necessary to assume that the professor would have acted in the same way had circumstances been different; say the bribe was $10,000 instead of only $1000.[8] In other words, in order to assign moral worth to an act, it must be assumed that it was non-contingently dutiful, that is,

---

[4] For example, in the version of Kant's anthropology lectures that is contemporaneous with GMS, Kant says of the character of a human being (understood as its *Denkungsart*) that it "rests on the rule [*Herrschaft*] of maxims" and he goes on to add that "the character could therefore also be defined as the determination of the will [*Willkür*] of a human being through enduring and recognizable maxims" (AM 25: 1385).

[5] In fact, we shall see that in his discussion of the fourth example of the application of FLN (that of the individual who refuses to help others in need), Kant refers to the agent's *Denkungsart* rather than to a maxim (GMS 4: 423₂₃). Kant uses the term *Denkungsart* only two other times in GMS (426₁₃ and 435₂₅). In the first, it refers to the slack or even base way of thinking that Kant attributes to popular moral philosophy in the search for the supreme principle of morality. In the second, it refers to the way of thinking manifested in those who act from respect for the law.

[6] The qualification "at any one time" is intended to express the fact that Kant held open the possibility of a change of *Denkungsart* (or *Gesinnung*) through a radical conversion or reorientation of the will. See RGV 6: 46–49, 71–74; 91–93, 11–15.

[7] As will become clear in the second part of this chapter, the expression "win out," indeed, any language that suggests that motivation for Kant is a matter of relative psychological force is inappropriate. I am using it in this context, however, to avoid unnecessary complications.

[8] Actually, the issue is somewhat more complex than this suggests; for, as Herman has argued, it is not *always* the case that one would deny moral worth to an act simply because it is assumed that under radically different circumstances person might have acted differently. See Herman (1981, 369). Nevertheless, Herman also has denied that she holds that counterfactual considerations are *never* relevant to the determination of moral worth. I discuss this issue in more detail in Allison (1990, 114–16, and 266).

that its performance was not simply a function of contingent circumstances.[9] But the latter assumption presupposes that the act is an expression of the agent's underlying *Denkungsart* or *Gesinnung*; for it is only on the basis of such an assumption that the non-contingency claim is warranted.[10]

The second point is that rational agents do not select their maxims willy-nilly; rather, they reflect a general orientation of the will, that is, a *Denkungsart*. Accordingly, while agents lacking a good will, such as Kant's scoundrel, might very well perform actions from a sense of duty, these actions are not "from duty" in Kant's sense and therefore are not proper candidates for the assignment of moral worth. Consider the stereotypical Mafia don, who, while generally ruthless, is intensely loyal to certain associates. Although we can imagine such a person as prepared to make great personal sacrifices, say going to prison, rather than betraying a loyalty, one would not say that his conduct, however heroic, has genuine moral worth in Kant's sense, because his course of action is really an exception to his general mode of behavior. In fact, his real maxim might be characterized as something like: "I shall be absolutely ruthless, except when it concerns my associates and close relations," which is hardly indicative of a good *Denkungsart*.

Apart from the claims of the preceding three paragraphs, most of this is relatively non-controversial. The problems begin when we push the analysis a step further and ask whether maxims must be consciously adopted by an agent through something like an inner act of commitment, e.g., "I henceforth make it my maxim to *x*," and whether in acting on a maxim the agent must be explicitly aware of it. The above example of a maxim to exercise regularly fits this model, since adopting a regular program of exercise is something that one deliberately chooses to do with a specific goal in mind. And so does Kant's characterization of maxims as self-imposed principles, as well as his view that maxims are the proper objects of moral deliberation and assessment. At the same time, however, it is sometimes thought to be a consequence of this view that most agents will have few, if any, maxims and that much of what we regard as morally assessable behavior, including but not limited to "sins of omission," does not fall under a maxim, since it is performed unreflectively. Moreover, it might be argued that, if this turned out to be the case, the consequences would be dire not only for Kant's moral theory, but also his conception of rational agency, inasmuch as the latter appears to equate genuine intentional action, in contrast with mere behavior, with action based on a maxim.

I shall deal with these problems in two steps. The first introduces a distinction between two forms of self-consciousness, which I term reflexive and reflective.

---

[9] This point is emphasized by Timmermann (2007a, 27), who attributes to Kant what he terms the "principle of non-contingence." According to Timmermann, Kant had already affirmed this principle in the Preface, when he wrote that "it is not enough that [an action] conform to the moral law, but it must also happen *for the sake of this law* [*um desselben willen geschehen*]; otherwise that conformity is only contingent and precarious" (GMS 4: 390₄₋₆).

[10] In my discussion of this issue in Allison (1990) I generally used the term "*Gesinnung*." For a discussion of the relation between "*Denkungsart*" and "*Gesinnung*" see Chapter 3 note 23.

Although not explicitly drawn by Kant, I take this distinction to be implicit in both his account of cognition and his conception of rational agency. The second step consists in the application of this distinction to three functions of maxims in Kant's thought, which have usefully been distinguished by Talbot Brewer: in moral deliberation, in moral assessment, and in Kant's theory of rational agency.[11]

(1) *Reflexive and reflective self-consciousness*: By reflexive self-consciousness I understand the first-order awareness that is built into any conscious activity and is a condition of engaging in that activity. By contrast, reflective self-consciousness is a second-order awareness that arises through taking a first-order consciousness as its object.[12] Within Kant's theoretical philosophy, the former is the consciousness that pertains to the apperceptive I. Inasmuch as (discursive) cognition for Kant consists in representing to oneself a synthesis of sensory data by bringing it under a concept in a judgment, which might also be schematically depicted as taking an x as F, such cognition is impossible apart from a reflexive self-awareness.[13] Moreover, since this act of "taking as" is spontaneous in the sense that it is something that the subject does for itself rather than something it finds itself causally determined to do (as in the case of association), this consciousness can also be called a consciousness of spontaneity.

Kant's term for this second form of self-consciousness is "attention" [*Aufmerksamkeit/attentio*]. In the first *Critique*, it makes a cameo appearance in the second edition in connection with Kant's inter-related accounts of inner sense, self-affection, and empirical self-knowledge (B156–57n). The basic idea is that by attending to its representations, through the conceptual unification of which it represents to itself external objects, consciousness makes these representations into themselves objects of inner sense.[14]

Allowing for the difference between a theoretical and a practical use of reason, a similar story applies in the practical domain. We have already seen that for Kant a *Denkungsart*, an interest, and a maxim are all, in the above-mentioned sense, products of the spontaneity of the agent and that this is the ground of their imputability. And since each involves the use of reason, albeit in an evaluative or practical rather than a theoretical manner, I cannot adopt them without a reflexive awareness of what I am

---

[11] Brewer (2002, 541). Most of what follows in the remainder of this part of the chapter can be seen as an attempt to respond to the worries regarding Kantian maxims raised by Brewer in this paper. This response has also been influenced by Fricke (2008, 125–35).

[12] In some ways this parallels the distinction drawn by Sartre and others within the phenomenological tradition between a "non-thetic" and a "thetic" or, equivalently, a "non-positional" and a "positional" self-consciousness. See Sartre (1957, esp. 31–60). Roughly speaking, this corresponds to a distinction between a form of conscious in which the self is aware of what it is doing, but not of itself as doing it, and one in which it is explicitly aware of itself as the subject engaged in the activity. Otherwise expressed, in the first case the I is not positioned within such consciousness as an object (as "a me"), whereas in the second case it is.

[13] For a more detailed discussion of this topic see Allison (1996, 53–66).

[14] Kant provides more expansive discussions of attention in different contexts at various places in the *Anthropology*. See A 7: 131–32, 161, 163, 208; 242–43, 272, 274, 314. My fullest discussion of this topic is in Allison (1983, 268–71).

doing. Again, this awareness is built into the activity itself and, indeed, into any intentional action.

Continuing the parallelism with cognition, a reflective practical self-awareness would, like its cognitive counterpart, involve an explicit becoming conscious of what I have done or propose to do.[15] In the case of a *Denkungsart*, an interest, or an ordinary intentional action, it seems evident not only that a reflective awareness is not a necessary condition of attributing it to an agent, but that such reflection seldom occurs. Thus, even though one's *Denkungsart* underlies and informs all expressions of one's rational agency, only a deeply reflective person would even attempt to acquire a *reflective* grasp of it; though a *reflexive* awareness of it must be present, if it is to guide one's action. Similarly, in the case of an interest, it is usually only when one finds that pursuing it leads one into a difficult situation that one stops to reflect upon it and to ask oneself why (and how) one initially acquired it, and perhaps whether one should (for moral or prudential reasons) abandon it. But, again, just as one cannot have an interest without taking it as such, so one cannot have it without being reflexively aware of it as one's interest. And, *mutatis mutandis*, much the same can be said of an intentional action, since one cannot intend something without being aware that one is doings so; though this hardly requires that one makes one's intending into an object of reflection. This brings us, then, to maxims and, as already noted, I shall address the issue of whether they require a reflective self-consciousness by considering each of the three functions of maxims distinguished by Brewer.

(2) The three functions of maxims

(a) *In moral deliberation*: Moral deliberation is a prospective activity concerned with the determination of whether a proposed course of action is morally required, prohibited, or permissible. Since for Kant such deliberation takes the form of an examination of the maxim under which the proposed course of action is subsumed, it seems evident that it requires that the deliberator have a reflective, not merely a reflexive, awareness of the maxim being considered. In other words, in order to test a maxim for its universalizability it is necessary that the agent have in mind an explicitly formulated maxim fitting the schema described above. Indeed, the centrality given to moral deliberation in GMS and the featured role that maxims play in this deliberation no doubt help to reinforce the impression that for Kant having and acting on maxims requires a reflective awareness of them by an agent.

(b) *In moral assessment*: At first glance it might seem that much the same could be said about the retrospective activity of moral assessment. Since the proper objects of moral assessment for Kant are an agent's maxims rather than particular acts falling under them,

---

[15] I am assuming that a reflective awareness of what I am presently doing, that is, of the very act in which I am currently engaged is impossible, since it is only after the fact that I can reflect upon my engagement. Accordingly, such reflection is possible only with respect to what I have done or what I propose to do in the future. In the former case it is assessment and in the latter deliberation.

and since one must be aware of something in order to assess it, it seems to follow that such assessment, whether it be of oneself or another agent, presupposes something like a reflective awareness of the maxims being assessed.

Setting aside the fact that we obviously have no direct access to the maxims of others, which limits our assessment to their overt actions and what can be inferred from them, there are two complications involved in applying the reflective awareness model to the assessment of maxims. The first is Kant's agnosticism regarding the determination of one's own motivation, which was alluded to in the preceding chapter. As Kant puts it at one point,

[I]t is absolutely impossible to determine with complete certainty through experience a single case in which the maxim of an otherwise dutiful action has rested merely on moral grounds and on the representation of duty. Indeed, it is sometimes the case that with the most penetrating self-examination we find nothing besides the moral ground of duty that could have been powerful enough to move us to this or that good action and to so great a sacrifice; but from this it cannot be concluded with certainty that it was not actually some covert impulse of self-love, under the mere pretense of that idea, that was the real determining cause of the will; for we like to flatter ourselves by the false presumption of a nobler motive, though in fact we are never able, even through the most strenuous self-examination, to get entirely behind the covert incentives, because when we are talking about moral worth, what counts are not the actions, which one sees, but their inner principles, which one does not see. (GMS 4: 407_{1-16})[16]

For present purposes, the main question posed by this passage is its compatibility with the reflective awareness required by Kantian morality. Although the necessity of such awareness is not thematized in GMS, it is elsewhere by Kant. For example, in view of our strong propensity for self-deception, Kant maintained that the "**First Command** of all Duties to Oneself" is to "'*know* (scrutinize, fathom) *yourself*,' not in terms of your natural perfection . . . but rather in terms of your moral perfection in relation to your duty," by which he understands the purity or lack thereof of one's motivation. As Kant puts it in a parenthetical remark at the end of his discussion of this

---

[16] This thesis of Kant was later criticized by Garve, who concluded from the impossibility of attaining certainty about acting completely unselfishly that Kant's moral theory is guilty of the absurdity of imposing a demand on human beings (for moral purity) of which no one can be assured of having met. See Garve (1967, 135–36). Kant responded by conceding that no one can be certain of performing his duty completely unselfishly, but claims that this is beside the point. This is because one can be aware that one ought to perform one's duty unselfishly, from which it follows (by ought implies can) that one can. And he further claims that if, as a result of a rigorous self-examination one can find no cooperating motive but instead self-denial with regard to many motives opposed to the idea of duty, one can become aware of having a maxim of striving for such purity, which, in turn, suffices for the observance of duty (TP 8: 284–85; 286–87). Similarly, at MS 6: 447; 567 Kant appeals to the unattainableness of knowledge of the purity of one's moral disposition as justification for classifying the duty to seek moral perfection as imperfect. I discuss this in Allison (1990, 176–79).

duty, "Only the descent into the hell of self-cognition can pave the way to godliness" (MS 6: 441; 562).[17]

I do not think that there is any conflict here, however, since Kant's agnosticism regarding motivation is highly restricted. First, it is limited to the question of purity, that is, to whether one acted from duty alone or some inclination was also at work. Second, it precludes only the attainment of absolute certainty and therefore allows for a high degree of probability on the matter, which in the case of evident impurity approaches full certainty. In other words, while one might self-deceptively take oneself to have acted solely from duty, when there is some impulse of self-love at work, it does not seem plausible to assume that one could really be acting from duty, when reflection indicates clearly that the motive was self-love. Third, Kant's reference to the necessity of descending into the "hell of self-cognition" provides ample evidence of the extent to which he thought a reflective awareness of one's motivation is possible; for if this self-cognition yielded only meager or highly questionable results, it could hardly be described as a hell.

The second problem involved in the application of the reflective awareness model to moral assessment is that we commonly include under the category of genuine and morally assessable actions many which do not appear to be subsumable under any maxim. Whereas the first worry concerns the identification of maxims under which an action is performed, the second involves genuine actions that do not appear to fall under *any* maxim. Although this is a broad category, I shall at present limit myself to those which might be thought of as "spur of the moment" or "out of character," since these seem the most directly germane to the question of moral assessability. I shall say a few words about the larger category, which encompasses all non-reflective actions, below in connection with a preliminary consideration of the role of maxims in Kant's conception of rational agency.

To begin with, the classes of spur of the moment (or impulsive) and out of character actions are not equivalent, since an agent without firm principles might characteristically act in a seemingly impulsive (non-reflective) manner and, conversely, an agent whose mode of behavior is usually fairly predictable might, on a particular occasion, act in an uncharacteristic way, even after a good deal of reflection. But since these frequently overlap, I shall consider an example that fits both descriptions. It is a variant of Kant's own famous example of a person who considers making it his maxim to make a false promise to repay a loan when he finds himself in dire financial straits. While in Kant's use of this example, which will be discussed in later chapters, we are asked to consider an agent who contemplates adopting this as a general policy and in this spirit raises the question of its morality, in the present case we are considering an agent who may never have contemplated such an action before, but decides to do so at this time because he feels that his situation is desperate and can see no other way to obtain the

---

[17] Also relevant here is Kant's view that the "inner lie" is the worst form of lie (MS 6: 430–31; 553–54).

needed funds. This can be viewed either as a spur of the moment decision, perhaps prompted by the fact that the agent just happens to run into an acquaintance, who is known to be likely to make the loan, or as the result of considerable deliberation; but in either case, the question arises regarding the maxim (if any) under which this act of deceitful promising falls.

Let us first consider the case of a spur of the moment decision, made without any prior deliberation. First of all, it is a *decision*, that is, a choice made by the agent. And even though the alternatives confronting the agent may be grim, say starvation for himself and his family, or severe repercussions from the failure to repay a loan made under duress, they are still alternatives that might have been chosen.[18] Second, the agent must be reflexively aware of what he is doing; otherwise the act could not be regarded as resulting from a decision and imputed to the agent. Third, it must be based on a reason, which justifies the choice in the eyes of the agent as in some sense good (which includes being the lesser of evils). Finally, since reasons as such are universal, in making this decision, the agent is implicitly committed to the view that the same choice would be justified in other relevantly similar occasions.

We shall see in subsequent chapters that the universality of reasons principle is usually appealed to in attempt to show that if an agent regards a rule of action as reasonable for him, he is committed to regarding it as reasonable for all other agents in relevantly similar circumstances. The present point is merely that the same principle holds for a single agent. In other words, if I regard a course of action as warranted for me in given circumstance, which I do in the very act of choosing it, then, quite apart from any reflective awareness on my part, I rationally commit myself to the principle that acting in that way in relevantly similar circumstances is in some sense good. The suggestion, then, is that being rationally committed to this principle (by the principle of the universality of reasons) is sufficient to attribute this principle to the agent as a maxim.

Moreover, if this is correct, it is equally applicable to an agent who does reflect on the proposed course of action and decides that, while it would be unacceptable as a general policy, it is warranted by the exigent circumstances in which she finds herself. Although such an agent might insist that she is not committed to a general policy of making false promises regarding the repayment of loans and has no intention of ever doing it again, she is committed by the universality of reasons to the *principle* that such action is warranted in relevantly similar circumstances, should they arise.[19] And this,

---

[18] The view of a maxim as a criterion of choice [*Auswahlkriterium*] by which every responsible agent orients her practical reflection is advocated by Fricke (2008, esp. 128–33), as a way of making plausible the thesis that maxims are involved in all practical reflection.

[19] Kant himself treats an agent similar to the one discussed here under the rubric of someone who makes an exception for himself to the categorical imperative, while still acknowledging its general validity (see GMS 4: 424₁₅₋₃₈). At present, however, I am not considering the case of someone who is trying to justify to herself violating a duty, but merely the sense in which such an agent is acting on a maxim. For Kant, of course, the maxim cannot be *to violate* the categorical imperative, though it, in fact, does do so.

I submit, is sufficient to attribute the maxim of making false promises *in these circumstances* to the agent. In short, at least for the purpose of assessment, the attribution of a maxim to an agent is not a function of what an agent is explicitly committed to, or would acknowledge being committed to, but what the agent is *rationally* committed to (by the universality of reasons) in virtue acting for the reason she does.

(c) *Maxims and rational agency*: The worry, which figures prominently in Brewer's account, concerns the general category of non-reflective actions, by which he understands those which "have [not] been preceded by anything resembling conscious deliberation" and for which, even retrospectively, one might not be able to specify the reason one performed it.[20] More specifically, the worry is that the lack of prior deliberation and the subsequent inability to identify the reason for one's action suggest that the action was not based on a maxim, which, in turn, threatens to undermine a central tenet of Kant's theory of action, which, according to Brewer, is that the difference between genuine actions and mere events, such as "sneezes, tremblings, twitches, and involuntary blinks," is that the former fall under a maxim while the latter do not.[21] Since, as already noted, Kant only sketches his views concerning the nature of agency (which is as close as he comes to providing a theory of action in the contemporary sense) in GMS 2, it is impossible to pursue the topic adequately at this point. Nevertheless, I believe that the basic points made above apply here as well.

Let us consider briefly Brewer's own example of a non-reflective action, which does not appear to fall under a maxim, at least as he perceives maxims to be understood by Kant himself and contemporary Kantians.[22] In Brewer's account, he finds himself picking up the phone late at night to call some nearly forgotten friend, without any prior deliberation or a clear intention in mind.[23] This is obviously intended as an example of a spur of the moment action, which we are all conscious of having performed many times, often without being clear regarding the reason why we did it. Brewer takes this example to show that "agents are not always able to articulate what exactly they see in their own actions that makes these actions worth performing." And he further suggests that, if this is correct and one still wishes to maintain the thesis that all actions are performed on maxims, it presents a Kantian with something of a dilemma: one must admit either that "the realm of actions is much less expansive

---

[20] Brewer (2002, 545).

[21] Ibid.

[22] In fairness to Brewer, it must be kept in mind that his project is not to deny that actions, such as the one he describes, fall under maxims, but to offer an original interpretation of maxims in which they do. At the heart of this endeavor is the construal of maxims as "evaluative outlooks" which, as such, have "a striking structural similarity to desires," with the latter understood in the manner of T. M. Scanlon, as proto-inferential outlooks. See Brewer (2002, 554). Although there is much with which I am sympathetic in this provocative and suggestive paper, particularly the need to provide an account of maxims which recognizes their partial opacity, I have attempted to argue that the resources for providing such an account of maxims are provided by Kant himself, a thesis which Brewer seems to resist, if not explicitly reject.

[23] Brewer (2002, 544–45).

than we ordinarily think, or maxims are not always consciously accessible to those whose maxims they are."[24]

Since we have seen that, at least where acting from duty is concerned, Kant himself explicitly acknowledged the second alternative, there should be no difficulty in opting for this horn of the dilemma. Accordingly, the question is why the existence of a certain undeniable opacity regarding the reasons for one's actions should be thought to create a problem for Kant. In offering this as a possible reason, Brewer seems to be suggesting that, in order to bring an action, such as his late night phone call, under a maxim, it is necessary (at least on what he takes to be the view of Kant and many contemporary Kantians) to assume that the agent is fully conscious of the reason for his action and is explicitly following a rule of the form: whenever I find myself in an S-type situation (say feeling bored, or desiring to speak to a friend) I shall perform an A-type action (calling that friend) regardless of the hour. And, of course, it is highly implausible to assume that agents always (or even often) have some such principles in mind.

Nevertheless, it is evident from Kant's doubts regarding the possibility of attaining full certainty regarding the ultimate reasons for one's dutiful actions that it is also implausible to attribute such a view to him. Rather, as I have argued above, all that is required to attribute a maxim to an agent is that the agent be reflexively aware of what he is doing and that this act is based on a reason; for given the principle of the universality of reasons, it follows that the agent is rationally committed to the principle that the course of action chosen is the correct and, as such, would be warranted in all relevantly similar situations. Granted, the partial opacity remains; but from the point of view of a theory of rational agency (as contrasted with an account of moral delibera-tion), what is crucial is that an intentional action be regarded as based on *some* maxim (understood as a rational commitment to a principle of action), even though there may not always be complete certainty regarding the nature of this maxim. Moreover, though it might seem to be both strange and un-Kantian to suggest that an agent could act on a maxim of which the agent himself is not reflectively aware, such a view has deep roots in Kant's account of radical evil and the role therein of self-deception.[25]

II

Although there are any number of variations, at bottom there are two fundamental lines of objection to Kant's account of moral worth. One concerns his privileging of the duty-motive over sentiment as expressing a higher moral value. While earlier moral theorists, such as Hume and Smith subordinated the duty-motive to sentiment, they acknowledged its existence and necessity as a default motive in those cases where the

---

[24] Brewer (2002, 544–45), 545.
[25] I discuss this topic in Allison (1990, 146–61).

proper sentiment is lacking.[26] In recent times, however, the denigration of the duty-motive has taken a more radical form. In this new form, the duty-motive is not simply given a subordinate place in the taxonomy of moral goodness, but is dismissed as morally repugnant and alienating. Since a consideration of the issues posed by this line of attack would take us considerably beyond the scope of a commentary on GMS, I shall not attempt to address them here directly; though I believe that much of what has already been said and what will be said in the next chapter in connection with Kant's definition of duty is germane to the topic.[27] Instead, the focus of the remainder of this chapter will be on the second major line of objection, which was epitomized by Schiller. Rather than questioning either the primacy or moral appropriateness of the duty-motive, this line of objection claims that Kant errs in excluding sentiment from any positive role in morality. Schiller's objection is epitomized in the oft-cited verses, which take the form of a caricature of Kant's account:

> Gladly I serve my friends, but alas I do it with pleasure.
> Hence I am plagued with doubt that I am not a virtuous person.
> To this the answer is given:
> Surely, your only resource is to try to despise them entirely,
> And then with aversion do what your duty enjoins you.[28]

The twin assumptions underlying these mocking verses are that Kant's examples imply that acting from duty requires either the lack of any inclination that might lead one, independently of the voice of duty, to do what is required or an actual disinclination or aversion to doing so, and that this is totally at variance with our intuitions regarding moral goodness. In what follows, I shall attempt to provide a defense of Kant against the Schillerian objection and its many reincarnations by first surveying and critically examining some of the major responses found in the literature and then sketching my own view.

(A) The method of isolation response

An essential feature of the Kantian response to the Schillerian objection has been formulated by Paton, who notes that in the examples discussed in the preceding chapter Kant is practicing what Paton terms the "method of isolation."[29] In other words, rather than claiming (as Schiller's verses suggest) that acting from duty requires either the absence of any inclination to do what duty requires (apathy) or a disinclination (aversion), Kant is simply using these scenarios to illustrate situations in which the moral worth of the dutiful actions and the difference between acting from duty and

---

[26] For my discussion of Smith's view and its relation to Kant's, see Chapter 3 note 52.

[27] I have discussed some of these issues, particularly in connection with the Kant-critique of Bernard Williams, in Allison (1990, 191–97). For an excellent analysis and critique of contemporary denigrators of the moral significance of acting from duty, see Baron (1984 and 1995, 117–45).

[28] This version is taken from Paton (1958, 48).

[29] Ibid., 47.

from inclination are most evident. As we have seen, Herman has taken this response a step further, pointing out that in the first of the two scenarios regarding beneficence Kant is comparing the moral value of the beneficent actions of the *same individual* in two different psychological states rather than, as the objection assumes, making a general claim to the effect that the absence of an inclination to pursue the course of action that duty requires is a necessary condition for an action to possess moral worth. Otherwise expressed, Kant's point, according to Herman, is that it is the act of *this agent* that first acquires moral worth when the non-moral incentive disappears, not that of *any* agent.

Even granting this, however, all is not clear sailing for the Kantian view; for a full response to the Schillerian objection seems to require showing that an agent could (and should) act from duty, even when that agent has an inclination to do what is morally required. And since the plausibility of this thesis is far from evident, it is incumbent upon a defender of the Kantian view either to defend its plausibility or show that, contrary to appearances, Kant is not committed to it.

(B)   The over-determination thesis

One version of the first alternative has been advanced by proponents of the so-called "over-determination thesis," which holds that dutiful actions can be motivated by *both* a sense of duty *and* an inclination and still possess moral worth. What is required is simply that the duty-motive is present and that it would have sufficed to produce the action, if other motives had not been present, even though these other motives would also have sufficed absent the duty-motive. Richard Henson, the major proponent of this view, uses as an example Kant's own activity as a university lecturer. Assuming that Kant both enjoyed lecturing and recognized a duty to lecture, Henson's point is that Kant's enjoyment of this activity does not lessen its moral worth, as long as it was done from a sense of duty, as well as the expected enjoyment. Henson acknowledges that this does not reflect Kant's actual teaching in GMS, where he attributes what he terms a "battle citation" model of moral worth to Kant, which essentially amounts to the view that Schiller ridicules; but he suggests that it is compatible with what Kant says in the *Metaphysics of Morals*, where he allegedly adopted a "fitness report" model, which allows for over-determination in this sense.[30]

The strength of this response is that it captures what we have seen to be a central feature of Kant's account of moral worth, namely, that in order to be a candidate for the attribution of moral worth it is necessary to assume that the agent would have acted from duty even if circumstances had been different, which in this case means that the inclination favoring the dutiful action had not been present. It accomplishes this by placing the stress on the sufficiency of the duty-motive, if alone. Unfortunately, however, this strength is outweighed by the fact that it reflects

---

[30] Henson (1979).

a decidedly non-Kantian, empiricist view of agency, in which actions are seen as the causal consequences of desires, impulses or passions. As Wood puts it, citing Marcia Baron, "The motive of duty is...seen as one of these [desires, impulses or passions], tugging at us along with other inclinations and producing actions by something like a parallelogram of psychic forces."[31]

(C) Wood on acting from duty, the good will, and moral worth

Building his case largely on the implausibility of attributing anything like the above view to Kant and the thesis that for Kant "acting from duty is possible only where rational self-constraint is required, hence where there is no incentive other than duty,"[32] Wood constructs a highly complex and sophisticated version of the second of the above-mentioned response to Schiller's objection. He begins by distinguishing between two possible strategies for answering the objection, which are basically equivalent to those noted above: "(a) we can deny that a will can be good only when it acts from duty, or (b) we can assert that it is possible to act from duty even where there are no temptations to act contrary to duty and nonmoral motives to act in conformity with duty."[33] Wood affirms the former partly on the basis of what he takes to be "compelling" textual reasons and partly on the basis of the alleged untenability of the latter. In short, he maintains that while a will that acts from duty is certainly good, it does not follow that *only* such a will is good, since acting from duty is not a necessary condition of having a good will.

For the reasons given in the preceding chapter, I believe that Wood is correct in denying that acting from duty is a necessary condition of having a good will. I further believe, however, that he is to be faulted for not considering the converse of this proposition, namely, that having a good will, understood as a good *Denkungsart*, is a necessary condition of the possibility of acting from duty. In fact, I shall argue below that, far from recognizing that the possession of a good will is a necessary condition of acting from duty, Wood's account implies that such action is incompatible with the possession of a good will. And for this reason I find his account of acting from duty in some ways closer to the views of Hume and Smith, for whom duty functions as a default motive, than it is to Kant's. The difference, which keeps Wood within the Kantian orbit, is that he retains the thesis that only actions from duty merit esteem as opposed to mere praise and encouragement.[34] But the question is whether this attribution of a higher value to actions from duty makes sense, if duty is in effect a default motive, divorced from an underlying good will.

---

[31] Wood (1999, 33). The reference is to Baron (1995, 188–93). Wood makes a similar point in (2006a, 35n).
[32] Wood (1999, 31).
[33] Ibid., 33.
[34] Ibid., 27.

What is essential here is Wood's account of the conditions under which acting from duty is necessary or even possible. On his reading, these reduce to situations in which the agent is either disinclined to do what duty requires, or at least has no inclination to do so, that is, when there is either aversion or apathy to moral demands. In all other cases, such as Kant's examples of those who act beneficently from a sympathetic disposition, and even the prudentially honest shopkeeper, Wood insists that the will may be no less good than one that is motivated by duty.[35] I have serious doubts about this; but setting these doubts aside, one might wonder whether an agent who has either aversion or apathy to moral demands could be said to have a good will in Kant's sense. And if not, as I suspect to be the case, and if, as Wood maintains, these are the *only* conditions under which acting from duty is possible, it is difficult to avoid the conclusion that only an agent *without a good will* could act from duty!

The claim is not that Wood himself endorses such a view; on the contrary, it is evident that he does not.[36] It is rather that this is the conclusion to which his analysis inevitably leads. Moreover, I believe that the source of Wood's difficulty is that he draws an erroneous conclusion from a correct premise. The correct premise is that acting from duty requires rational self-constraint and that where there is no need for the latter, there is no place for the former. Where Wood goes astray is in limiting the need for such constraint to conditions of aversion or apathy. Apart from the conclusion to which it leads, there are three problems with this view. The first and most fundamental is that it ignores Kant's thesis that no matter how good their temperament, or even how virtuous their character, human, indeed all finite rational beings, are *never* beyond the need for such constraint, because they are always subject to temptation to act contrary to duty.[37] Kant generally characterizes this temptation as a propensity to prioritize self-interest over the dictates of duty; but, as the examples of the sympathetic person who unwittingly aids a thief or who in giving to the needy ignores his own true needs show, this can occur even when the inclination is not self-directed.[38]

Second, Wood's reading is incompatible with an essential feature of Kant's account of a good will, which Wood himself emphasizes, namely, that "the good will is different from such things as a fortunate temperament and possessed of an essentially higher value."[39] The problem here is that both the cleverness of the shopkeeper, which enables him to recognize that scrupulous honesty is in his long-term best interest, and the sympathetic nature of those who are naturally disposed to act beneficently fall

---

[35] Wood (1999, 31), 34–35.

[36] For example, Wood states that "the good will does not always act from duty, nor do all acts of the good will have this special moral worth" (1999, 27), which implies that the good will *sometimes* acts from duty and that *some* of its acts have moral worth.

[37] Wood is not only aware of this feature of Kant's view on this matter, he calls attention to it in his excellent discussion of lost innocence and moral goodness. See (1999, 45–47). Strangely, however, he appears to take this as confirming rather than conflicting with his thesis about the limited scope of the duty-motive.

[38] Although Kant does not make this point explicitly in GMS, he does in his account of respect as the unique moral incentive in the second *Critique*. See, for example, KpV 5: 84.

[39] Wood (1999, 27).

under the category of "gifts of nature," the former being a "talent of the mind" and the latter a "quality of temperament." Accordingly, if Wood is willing to attribute a good will to such subjects, it is difficult to see how he can avoid acknowledging that a good will can be a function of gifts of nature rather than, as Kant clearly holds, a *Denkungsart* governed by moral principles, which is precisely what cannot be regarded as a gift of nature.

Third, Wood ignores the distinction, which has gained some currency in the literature, between two senses in which we can view duty as a motive: (1) as a directly motivating factor and (2) as an underlying commitment to do what morality requires.[40] In effect, Wood recognizes only the first of these senses, which is usually operative in the case of perfect duties, such as the duty not to lie. Indeed, Wood's narrow understanding of the role of the duty-motive appears to underlie his view that the idea of duty has no place in the case of non-obligatory actions, not to mention cases of imperfect duty, where the obligation is to adopt a maxim rather than, except in rare circumstances, to perform a particular act. This overlooks, however, the possibility that in the case of non-obligatory actions undertaken in pursuit of one's happiness, the idea of duty functions, at least for the person with a good will, as a "filter," which rules out certain courses of action as impermissible; whereas in the case of imperfect duties it functions as a regulative principle in the form of an underlying commitment to perform the duty in question, when the occasion is perceived to warrant it.[41]

This still leaves us, however, with Wood's charge against the more traditional readings, namely, that they require accepting the allegedly absurd view that one can act from duty, even when one would happily do what duty requires.[42] For if this is truly absurd, we are led unavoidably to something like Wood's tight restrictions on the conditions under which acting from duty is possible, regardless of how deleterious this may be for Kant's accounts of the good will and moral worth. Wood's rejection of the possibility of acting from duty in instances where the agent has an inclination to perform a dutiful act turns entirely, however, on the assumption that it presupposes a conception of over-determination that is both un-Kantian and inherently implausible. And though I agree with Wood's rejection of this conception of over-determination, I believe that he is too hasty in jumping from this to the rejection of the possibility of

---

[40] The distinction between two senses in which the idea of duty can motivate appears to have initially been drawn by Herman (1981), in order to find a role for the duty-motive in the determination of permissible but not obligatory acts. On her reading, duty, as the directly motivating factor, is termed a "primary motive," whereas in filtering out impermissible actions it functions as a "secondary motive." Subsequently, Baron (1995, esp. 129–33) has gone beyond this by arguing that what Herman calls a secondary motive, but which she understands as an underlying commitment to morality, construed in accord with the model of a Kantian regulative idea, functions also in the case of imperfect duties.

[41] This formulation reflects the language of Herman and Baron respectively. See the preceding note.

[42] Here it is essential to distinguish between gladly doing one's duty because one has an inclination to perform the very act that is morally required and gladly doing what duty requires because it is a duty. The latter is what Schiller called an "inclination to duty" and regarded as the highest stage of morality. Kant rejected this as incoherent, on the grounds that duty requires constraint. For my discussion of this, see Allison (1990, 183–84).

acting from duty when one also has an inclination to do what duty requires. But since Wood does an excellent job of defining the issue, I shall deal with it in the terms that he proposes. The question, as he sees it, is: "Does the ground or incentive from which the subject adopts its maxims also belong to these maxims as part of their content?"[43]

The relevance of this seemingly arcane question stems from Wood's belief that those who think that a good will for human beings belongs only to subjects who act from duty are committed to answering it in the affirmative, while those who (like him) think that it "includes some subjects who do not act from duty" will answer it in the negative.[44] This is because he thinks that on the latter view, it would be possible for the two shopkeepers to adopt the same maxim (say of treating all customers honestly) from different incentives (say duty and prudence) and for both of them to exhibit a good will.[45] By contrast, if one thinks that a good will belongs only to those who act from duty, then one is committed to including the incentive in the maxim. On this view, if two shopkeepers shared the policy of treating all their customers honestly, but one did so from duty and the other from prudence (or immediate inclination), they would really have different maxims and therefore could not both be said to have a good will.

In pursuing Wood's question, let us consider again Kant's prudent shopkeeper in light of the analysis of maxims sketched in the first part of this chapter. According to this analysis, "treat all customers honestly" is an incomplete description of his maxim, since it omits the end for which this maxim was adopted namely, maximizing his profit. In other words, honesty is chosen by this shopkeeper because it was judged to be the best means for attaining his chosen end. Moreover, this end presupposes an interest in getting rich, which, in turn, provides him with the incentive to treat his customers honestly. Thus, the actual maxim of this shopkeeper may be more adequately characterized as: "Always treat one's customers honestly in order to maximize profit." Consider, by contrast, the case of the moral shopkeeper. His maxim likewise involves treating his customers honestly; but this again is an incomplete description, since it omits the end, which in this case might be described in Kantian terms as respecting the status of his customers as persons. Thus, a more complete description of this

---

[43]   Wood (2006a, 33). This appears to reflect a later development of Wood's view, which is not found in Wood (1999). I am assuming that he regards it as consistent with his earlier account.

[44]   Ibid.

[45]   Although he is not terribly clear on this point, I take Wood's reasoning to be roughly as follows: (1) *ex hypothesi*, the shopkeeper who acts from duty exhibits a good will; (2) also *ex hypothesi*, a good will is a function of the agent's maxim; (3) but it is assumed that the two shopkeepers act on the same maxim; (4) therefore, the shopkeeper who is prudentially motivated must also have or exhibit a good will. In addition to the apparent conflation of the occurrent and the dispositional conceptions of a good will, the main problem with this line of reasoning is that it can easily be converted into a *reductio* of the view it purports to defend. Thus, one might argue that since (1) a good will is a function of the agent's maxims; and (2) the two shopkeepers have different motives [*Bewegungsgründe*] for treating their customers honestly; (3) but the motive, that is, the reason why the action-type is endorsed, must be part of the maxim, since it specifies the condition under which the agent proposes to engage in such activity; (4) therefore, the two shopkeepers must be acting on different maxims.

shopkeeper's maxim would be something like: "Always treat my customers honestly in order to respect their moral status as persons."[46]

Do these two very different shopkeepers share the same maxim? Clearly not according to the account given in the first part of this chapter, which was based upon Kant's own characterization of maxims and their connections with interests and incentives. Also relevant to this issue is the notion of a maxim having "moral content," which Kant denies of the maxim of both those who endeavor to preserve their lives from an immediate inclination and those who act beneficently because they are "sympathetically attuned," but attributes to that of a person, who, having lost his love for life, nonetheless endeavors to preserve it from a sense of duty. Unless one wishes to deny that a maxim's moral content is part of the maxim, it seems evident that whatever this content turns out to be, it must be included in the maxim. But Kant explicitly informs us that the maxim of the person who preserves his life in spite of not loving it has moral content when and only when he does so from duty rather than inclination or fear (GMS 4: 398$_7$), and that the maxims of those who act beneficently only because they are sympathetically attuned lack such content because they act from inclination rather than from duty (GMS 4: 398$_{18-19}$). Thus, pace Wood, it seems that an examination of the text offers strong support for the view that Kant held that the incentive (whether it be a sense of duty or an inclination) is, indeed, part of the maxim, since it is determinative of whether or not the latter has a moral content.

Although Wood suggests that those who (in his view erroneously) maintain that the ground or incentive belongs to a maxim as part of its content also tend to assume that human beings have a good will only insofar as they act from duty, I do not propose to draw this conclusion. On the contrary, as already noted, I am in full agreement with Wood's contention that subjects with a good will do not always act from duty. Rather, as was also already noted, what I do wish to claim is that having a good will is a necessary condition of acting from duty. This is because, as far as I can see, a good *Denkungsart* is the only conceivable source of the moral incentive, which we both agree is incorporated into the maxim in those cases in which a subject acts from duty.

Moreover, we have seen that a major reason why acting from duty presupposes a good *Denkungsart* is that the conformity of an action possessing moral worth with duty cannot be a function of circumstances and that its attribution to a good *Denkungsart* avoids this by licensing the assumption that the agent would have acted in a similar fashion under different circumstances. In our initial discussion of this issue, the different circumstance was understood as one in which the non-moral incentive for performing a dutiful act was no longer present; but the same considerations apply when the non-moral incentive is present. In other words, if an agent with a good *Denkungsart* can act from duty absent a non-moral incentive, that agent must also be able to do so when this incentive is present. Otherwise, the agreement of the act with moral requirements

---

[46] For the purpose of this discussion, I am assuming an explicit awareness of the maxim on the agent's part and bracketing the issues regarding the partial opaqueness of maxims discussed in the first part of this chapter.

would be merely contingent, which is incompatible with the attribution to it of genuine moral worth. And it follows from this that either (a) one must dismiss as incoherent the whole notion of acting from duty, a move which many moral philosophers would be happy to make, but which is presumably not open to Wood, since it would involve abandoning the position he is trying to defend, or (b) it must be acknowledged that acting from duty is compatible with the presence of a non-moral incentive to perform the very same act that is morally required.[47]

Obviously, this does not constitute a defense of Kant's conception of moral worth as a value reserved for acts from duty alone. Any such defense would have to rest ultimately on Kant's claim that it reflects a shared, pre-philosophical understanding of morality; and it must also be kept in mind that at this point Kant is leaving open the possibility that morality might be nothing more than a phantom of the brain. The aim of the above reflection is rather to show that *if* one assumes that such acts are possible, then one must also assume that it is possible to act from duty alone, even if one also has a non-moral incentive to perform the dutiful act. And my further claim, to which I shall devote the rest of this chapter, is that Kant's explanation of this possibility is to be found in his incorporation thesis, from which it follows that this thesis is also the key to the Kantian response to the Schillerian objection.

(D) Agency and the incorporation thesis

In Kant's canonical formulation, the thesis states:

[F]reedom of the power of choice [*Willkür*] has the characteristic, entirely peculiar to it, that it cannot be determined to action through any incentive *except so far as the human being has incorporated it into his maxim* (has made it into the universal rule for himself, according to which he wills to conduct himself); only in this way can an incentive, whatever it may be, coexist with the absolute spontaneity of the power of choice of freedom). (RGV 6: 24; 73)

Although Kant only formulated this thesis in *Religion*, there is strong evidence that he was committed to its basic idea prior to GMS.[48] In fact, it is presupposed by Kant's fundamental idea, discussed at the beginning of this chapter, that we do not simply have maxims, but we make something our maxim, where this making is understood as an act of spontaneity imputable to the subject. And closely connected with this is another idea, which was discussed in connection with maxims, namely, that having an incentive or desire does not of itself provide a reason to act, as it does on the standard Humean and related views. It becomes one only if it is incorporated or taken up into a

---

[47] I am here assuming that Wood wishes to defend the core Kantian notion that acts from duty possess a unique value, which merits esteem rather than merely encouragement and approval and that he only rejects the equation of such acts with those of a good will, which would effectively make acting from duty a sufficient condition of having a good will.

[48] This evidence includes passages from the first *Critique*, various versions of the lectures on metaphysics and *Reflexionen*. For my references to and discussion of some of these texts, see Allison (1990, 38–39 and 1996, 131–32).

maxim, which means being brought under a principle of action, which licenses (at least from the point of view of the agent) pursuing the end dictated by this incentive.

This does not mean that inclinations are of no import or play no motivational role for Kant. The point is rather that their role is to provide the raw data for volition and they only become reasons to act when they are taken as such (incorporated into a maxim) by the agent. Moreover, as is often the case in Kant, this closely parallels his account of cognition, where sensory intuitions are the raw data and only become cognitions of an object when brought under concepts. And from this two consequences follow, which are directly germane to our present concerns: (1) every maxim includes an incentive, which is the ground of its adoption as part of its "deep structure," even if it is not explicitly mentioned in the formulation of the maxim and one cannot attain complete certainty regarding its nature; and (2) one can have an inclination or desire to x, choose to x, or, equivalently, act on a maxim to pursue x as an end (under suitable conditions) and still not act from x. In other words, one can act *with* but not *from* an inclination, in which case the inclination does not serve as an incentive in the sense of an *operative* reason to act.

Since I believe that the first point has been sufficiently established, I shall devote the remainder of the chapter to a defense of the second. This defense will consist of three steps. In the first, I draw a sharp line between the incorporation thesis and the conception of over-determination, which shares with it the premise that one can act from duty even when there is also a non-moral incentive to perform the dutiful act. In the second, I attempt to answer an objection raised by Marcia Baron, which bears directly on the issue before us, namely, that while it is easy to understand how an agent might refuse to incorporate an incentive into her maxim insofar as she also rejects the course of action prompted by that incentive, it is much more difficult to understand how an agent could refuse to incorporate an incentive while still acting as she would if she had acted from that incentive. Finally, I shall try to show how the incorporation thesis is the key to Kant's response to the Schillerian objection.

(1) *Incorporation and over-determination*: To begin with, it is crucial not to conflate the incorporation thesis with the conception of over-determination, which we have seen was appealed to by Henson in an endeavor to explain how an action could be from both duty and inclination, but was rejected by Wood on the grounds that it foists upon Kant an implausible view of motivation. As already noted, I agree with Wood on this score, but I differ from him in affirming that the incorporation thesis allows for this possibility.[49] The key point is that this thesis regards the will not as being *determined* [*bestimmt*], but as having *determining grounds* [*Bestimmungsgründe*], which are reasons to

---

[49] Although Wood claims to accept the incorporation thesis as the key to understanding Kant's conception of rational agency, he evidently does not see its relevance to this issue. See Wood (1999, 51–53, 73).

act, not psychological causes.[50] And while it would clearly be absurd to say that *a* was caused to act by *x* (even assuming that *x* is only a partial cause) but did not act (even in part) from *x*, it seems perfectly intelligible to say that an agent had a reason to act in a certain way, but acted for another reason, even though the resulting action was the same as it would have been if the agent had acted for the first reason.

Let us consider once again the shopkeeper, this time envisaged as possessing a good will. Being an astute businessman, which is presumably not incompatible with having a good will, this shopkeeper, like Kant's prudential one, realizes that treating his customers honestly is the best policy, but that is not why he chooses to adopt that policy. Rather, he does it simply because he recognizes that it is the right thing to do. Clearly, the choice of such a shopkeeper is not over-determined, because the profitability of always treating his customers honestly is not even a partial determining ground of his will, since, *ex hypothesi*, he would have treated his customers in precisely the same manner had the prudential calculus come out differently.

This should not be taken, however, to imply that a choice for Kant can have only a single determining ground. On the contrary, there is no reason why two or more incentives cannot be incorporated into a single maxim providing a set of jointly sufficient conditions for an action.[51] Consider a variant of Henson's example: I make it my maxim to accept invitations to lecture when and only when (a) the honorarium is sufficient; (b) the invitation stems from a prestigious university or conference; and (c) the trip is not overly lengthy and taxing. Assuming that this is my maxim with respect to lecturing, one would not say that my choice to accept an invitation (should one meeting these conditions be proffered) was over-determined, since it would not be determined (in a causal sense) at all; it is rather *multi-conditioned*.

In fact, Kant even allows for the possibility of multi-conditioned maxims in which duty is one of the conditions. At least he suggests as much, when he remarks that it is "hazardous to let any other incentive (such as that of advantage) so much as cooperate [*mitwirken*] *alongside* the moral law" (KpV 5: 72; 198). And later he insists that all empirical incentives "must without exception be separated from the supreme moral principle and never be incorporated [*einverleibt*] with it as a condition, since this would destroy all moral worth" (KpV 5: 93; 215). Moreover, we can easily see why he would say this by considering a maxim that would incorporate both the moral law and an empirical incentive bearing on one's own happiness. Let us, for example, attempt to incorporate the incentives of the two shopkeepers into a single maxim. Presumably, it would be something like: "I shall treat my customers honestly because it is the morally correct thing to do, as long as doing so is compatible with the maximization of my

---

[50] See GMS 4: 401_{13}, 460_{31}, 462_8.

[51] Baron (1995, 151ff.) draws a useful distinction between over-determined and hybrid actions. The former are those in which either motive, if alone, would suffice; the latter are those in which two or more motives are required to produce the action. What I have described above corresponds to the latter. As Baron also points out, however, the important point is that neither species of action can possess moral worth for Kant.

profits." The trouble with such a maxim is obvious: it makes the performance of duty contingent upon extra-moral considerations, which makes the maxim morally but not psychologically, impossible. Indeed, maxims of this type are all too common.[52]

(2) *Not acting from an inclination, but as the inclination directs*: As we have seen, the incorporation thesis allows space for having an inclination and not acting from it. One simply does not incorporate the inclination or, more precisely, the incentive based upon it, into one's maxim. But while this seems to make good sense when an agent acts in a way that is contrary to that inclination—say resisting an inclination to drink beer and watch a football game on TV in order to go out for a brisk walk—it seems more problematic when the course of the action chosen is the same as the one to which following the inclination would have led.

Thus, Baron, who raises this problem, asks pointedly, "Does it make sense to suppose that we can refrain from acting from an inclination without refusing to act as the inclination directs?"[53] And, in an attempt to highlight the problem, she offers the example of a person who intends to cause someone pain by telling her something that is true and that this person would probably want to be informed about, for example, that her husband is having an affair. According to Baron, the only way that this malicious person could refrain from acting on her desire (to cause pain) is to give up the proposed course of action prompted by that desire.[54]

In order to deal with the issue, it is necessary to rephrase Baron's example in the appropriate Kantian terminology. To begin with, it is once again essential to distinguish between inclinations (or incentives) and interests, both of which fall under the umbrella term "desire." In GMS, Kant defines an inclination [*Neigung*] as "[t]he dependence of the faculty of desire [*Beghrungsvermögens*] on sensations," and he adds that the presence of an inclination always indicates a need (GMS 4: 4: 413n$_{26-27}$). Eschewing complexities arising from the contrast between immediate and mediate inclinations and other distinctions that Kant draws within the category of inclination, the term (taken in the broad sense) refers to any stimulus to action that stems entirely from our sensuous nature. We have seen that in the same note Kant defines an interest (in contrast to an inclination) as "the dependence of a contingently determinable will on principles of reason." And though the previous contrast was between an interest and an incentive, rather than an inclination, the same point applies, namely, that an interest is a product of practical reason. Accordingly, the malicious person in Baron's example does not simply *have an inclination* to harm the person to whom she plans to provide the unpleasant information, she *takes an interest* in doing so and makes this her end, to which conveying the unpleasant news is intended as the means. Moreover, when the

---

[52] Kant associates such maxims with impurity, which represents the second of the three grades of the propensity to evil (RGV 6: 30; 77–78).

[53] Baron (1993, 432).

[54] It must be noted that Baron is herself a staunch supporter of the Kantian position, including the conception of acting from duty. Thus, she has offered this objection in the spirit of a devil's advocate seeking clarification rather than as a critic of Kant and it is in this spirit that I attempt to address it.

scenario that Baron offers is described in these terms, it appears in a somewhat different light. Specifically, it becomes a matter of abandoning the end (inflicting pain), while still retaining the intended means (conveying the unpleasant news). Clearly, this is absurd; but the absurdity has nothing to do with the incorporation thesis.

It is also important to note that for Kant the scenario that Baron worries about, namely, having an inclination and acting *as* that inclination prescribes, but not *from* that inclination, arises only when there is also an overriding non-inclination-based reason prescribing the same course of action. This is the precise opposite of the situation Baron describes, however, where it is assumed that the inclination provides the *only* reason for acting in that manner. In an effort to clarify the matter, let us return yet again to our shopkeeper, this time Kant's original, prudentially minded version, who treats his customers honestly only because he deems it in his best interest. Let us also suppose, however, that he has experienced a "moral conversion," as a result of which he comes to the realization that, while in the past he had kept to the "letter of the law," because he saw that it was to his advantage to do so, he had ignored its "spirit." Accordingly, he sincerely resolves in the future to strive to follow the spirit as well. Presumably, apart from some possible changes in the way he greets his customers, say asking about their health, their family, and the like (which we can easily imagine having been part of his past behavior, as a matter of "customer relations"), there is no change in his overt behavior, since he continues to treat his customers honestly.

Nevertheless, *something* has changed, since, as already noted, this "born again" shopkeeper does this for very different reasons, which for Kant indicates the presence of a different *Denkungsart*. Moreover, assuming that he continues to want to make money and to realize that this dictates a policy of treating his customers honestly, his original incentive remains; but it is now subordinated to a higher, purely moral one.[55] Expressed in Baron's terms, this shopkeeper has an inclination to make money, acts *as* this inclination dictates, but not *from* that inclination.

This suggests the need to distinguish the way in which the incorporation thesis applies when the incentive is to act in a way that is contrary to the dictates of morality and when it fortuitously accords with these dictates. In the former case, it is simply a matter of refusing to incorporate the incentive into one's maxim; whereas in the latter case incorporation requires subordinating the incentive to moral requirements, such that if a conflict between the inclination-based incentive and these requirements should arise, the agent would be prepared to set the former aside. At the risk of multiplying theses beyond necessity, one might term this the "subordination thesis"; but the main point is that it is really an aspect of the incorporation thesis.

We have also seen that the incorporation thesis is concerned with maxims, whereas what Baron provides is a particular intention. But while we cannot infer a maxim from

---

[55] In *Religion*, Kant argues that since both the moral incentive and the incentive of happiness or self-love are ineradicable, the difference between a morally good and a morally evil person depends on which is subordinated to which. See RGV 6: 32–39; 79–85.

a particular intention, since the latter might fall under a number of different maxims, it seems reasonable to assume that the maxim on which Baron's agent acts (perhaps without reflective awareness) is something like the following: "In order to inflict pain on people whom I dislike, while avoiding blame, I shall make use of means which are generally deemed morally permissible, but which in certain circumstances can cause harm." Setting aside the morality of this maxim, the point is that one cannot retain the maxim while rejecting its underlying incentive (causing pain without opening oneself up to blame), since it would no longer be the same maxim. What is misleading in the scenario that Baron provides is the implicit separation of the incorporation of an incentive into a maxim from the adoption of the maxim. It is not, as her scenario suggests, that one first adopts a maxim and then casts about for the appropriate incentive to incorporate into it; it is rather that in adopting a maxim one at the same time incorporates an incentive into it, since, as we have already seen, an incentive is part of the deep structure of a maxim, even if it is not always made explicit.[56]

(3) *The incorporation thesis as the response to the Schillerian objection*: We have seen that the objection comes down to the charge that Kant's view, at least as expressed in the examples given in GMS 1, is that one cannot act from duty or possess a good will (these are generally not distinguished by those who affirm this objection[57]), if one has an inclination or some other non-moral based reason to perform a dutiful act. And it is further assumed by the critic that this amounts to a *reductio* of Kant's moral psychology, particularly if, as Kant maintains, this view is intended to express a shared understanding of morality.

We have also seen that one strategy for dealing with this problem involves an appeal to the conception of over-determination and that this was rejected on the grounds that it assumes an implausible and non-Kantian view of agency. Beyond responding to Baron's objection, not very much has been offered in defense of the plausibility of the incorporation thesis, which is the proposed alternative to over-determination. Nevertheless, it should at least be evident that this thesis provides the conceptual space that allows for the possibility of speaking of acting *with* an inclination but *from* duty.

---

[56] In my initial reply to Baron on this point I suggested, among other things, that she saw the incorporation thesis as a two-step process: first selecting a maxim and then incorporating an incentive into it (Allison, 1996, 119). In the published version of her reply, Baron rejected the suggestion that this was her view and says instead: "I am imagining, rather, that I might have a maxim that would be permissible were it not for the nasty incentive (or the relation between the incentive and the proposed action) and I am asking: Is it part of my freedom that I can 'revise' the maxim by jettisoning the incentive, replacing it by another? Or can I say 'No' to the incentive only by saying 'No' to the entire plan of action" (Baron, 1993, 441 n5). The problem here is the same as the one noted in connection with the discussion of Wood, namely, the confusion that arises when one attempts to separate maxims from incentives. Accordingly, the impossibility of keeping (in a "revised" form) the maxim while changing the incentive is a matter of logic rather than a restriction on freedom. Freedom is involved in selecting a maxim *cum* incentive.

[57] In his own formulation, Schiller speaks of being "a virtuous person," which, apart from a definition of "virtue," preserves this ambiguity.

Moreover, this is precisely what is required to respond to the Schillerian objection; for the whole force of this objection stems from the assumption that such action is impossible. We shall revisit the incorporation thesis and the issue of its plausibility in the fourth part of this commentary in connection with a consideration of Kant's account of freedom in GMS 3; but our next concern is with the remaining portion of GMS 1.

5

Kant's Three Propositions, the Supreme Principle of Morality, and the Need for Moral Philosophy

The subject matter of this chapter is GMS 4: 399_{25}–405_{35}, which encompasses the last eight paragraphs of GMS 1. It involves the consideration of three issues. The first is the three propositions, which presumably follow from the analysis of the concept of a good will under human conditions. The second is the formulation of the supreme principle of morality, which is supposedly latent in ordinary human reason and can be derived from these three propositions. The third, which serves as a bridge to GMS 2, is the apparent tension between Kant's claim that the supreme principle of morality is contained in ordinary human reason and his insistence on the necessity of a metaphysics of morals.

I

After completing his analysis of the conditions under which an action has moral worth, or its maxim moral content, Kant abruptly remarks that,

> The second proposition is: An action from duty has its moral worth *not in the purpose [Absicht]*, which should thereby be achieved, but in the maxim, according to which it was decided upon, and thus does not depend upon the actuality of the object of the action, but rather merely on the *principle of the volition*, in accordance with which the action is done, without regard for any object of the faculty of desire. (GMS 4: 4: 399_{35}–400_3)

In the next paragraph, Kant informs the reader that the third proposition, which he regards as a consequence of the first two, is that *"duty is the necessity of an action from respect [Achtung] for the law"* (GMS 4: 400_{17-18}). Although the latter two propositions are important and require analysis, the first question that must be dealt with is the identity of the first proposition, which Kant never expressly formulates, but which he evidently assumed could be readily inferred from his preceding account.

(A) Kant's first proposition

Allowing for minor variations, the standard view is that this unformulated proposition states that an action has moral worth if and only if it is performed from duty alone.[1] This is the most natural reading, since this thesis seems be the main import of the argument of the preceding paragraphs and it makes for a smooth transition to the introduction of the second proposition, which is concerned with the source of moral worth. Nevertheless, this reading has sometimes been called into question, usually on the grounds that it does not appear to be compatible with Kant's claim that the third proposition is a consequence of the first two. One line of interpretation, which has been advocated by Duncan and others, is to identify the first proposition with the first sentence of GMS 1.[2] But since such a reading cannot even begin to explain the connection between this proposition and the other two, not to mention how the third follows from the first two, it has been widely rejected. In the recent literature three interpreters (Jürg Freudiger, Dieter Schönecker, and Jens Timmermann), who reject both Duncan's and the standard reading on the grounds that they fail explain how the third follows from the first two, have offered alternatives, which they claim meet this condition. I shall briefly consider each of them and then offer my own proposal, which is close but not equivalent to the standard view.

(1) *Freudiger's proposal*: According to Freudiger, Kant's third proposition combines the subjective and objective aspects of acting from duty. Consequently, on his reading the missing first proposition states simply that "Duty presupposes subjective motivation"; the second that "Duty presupposes an *a priori* principle as determining the action"; and the third that "Duty presupposes respect as the *a priori* principle."[3] In addition to the fact that the first proposition on this reading is extremely vague and fails to distinguish the Kantian position from many others, while the second and third propositions are not precisely the same as Kant provides, in order to have the third proposition follow from the first two, Freudiger's reconstruction requires the importation of a supplemental premise to the effect that respect is the only subjective motive that allows for an *a priori* principle to determine the action.[4] And since the main objection against the standard reading is precisely that it requires additional premises in order to make the third proposition follow from the first two, it is difficult to see how Freudiger's proposal marks an improvement over the standard reading.

---

[1] See, for example, Aune (1979, 9ff.); Beck (1969b, 16); Hill and Zweig (2002, 199, 267 n21; 18–19); Paton (1956, 18–19); and Wolff (1973, 65f.).

[2] See Duncan (1957, 59). Along with Duncan, Schönecker lists Liddell (1970, 40f.) and Marshall (1989, 186).

[3] Freudiger (1993, 77–79).

[4] Ibid., 79.

(2) *Schönecker's proposal*: According to Schönecker, Kant's first proposition is that, "An action from duty is an action from respect for the moral law."[5] In partial agreement with Freudiger, Schönecker affirms that the first proposition deals with the subjective moment of acting from duty, the second with its objective moment, and the third combines them, which makes it easy to see how the third proposition is a consequence of the first two. But whereas Freudiger sees the introduction of respect as resulting from the importation of an additional premise, Schönecker sees this as affirmed already in the first proposition.

The obvious problem with this proposal is that the first mention of "respect" is in the third proposition (GMS 4: 400_{19}) and the concept is explicated in a long footnote attached to Kant's analysis of this proposition (GMS 4: 401_{17-40}). Schönecker is aware of this and in justification for his proposal argues that paragraphs nine through thirteen all deal with the first proposition and that the latter cannot be identified with any particular claim contained in these paragraphs, but rather must be identified with "the abstract quintessence of his [Kant's] thoughts about the 'subjective moment' of the concept of duty, which, when analyzed, turns out to be respect."[6]

Although Schönecker is correct in regarding respect as the concept underlying Kant's account of moral motivation, it does not follow from this that we should construe Kant's first proposition as referring to it. The problem is not only that the concept is not, in fact, introduced in these paragraphs, but that it *could not be*. Since, as Schönecker notes, the concept of respect presupposes the concept of a practical law and *that* concept is only introduced in paragraph fourteen (under the guise of a "principle of the will"), it makes no textual sense to read it into the earlier paragraphs. Rather, it seems more reasonable to say that these paragraphs prepare the way for the introduction of the concept of respect, which, presumably, could also be said of the first proposition, whatever it turns out to be.

(3) *Timmermann's proposal*: On Timmermann's reading, the first proposition should be taken as asserting that "An action that coincides with duty has moral worth if and only if its maxim produces it by necessity, even without or contrary to inclination."[7] Like most commentators who reject the standard view, Timmermann's motivation is to provide a reading in which the third proposition can be seen as combining elements of the first two. According to him, the first proposition contributes the element of necessity, which is featured in the third proposition, but not contained in it on the standard reading.

[5] See Schönecker (2001, 94). A similar view is expressed in Schönecker and Wood (2004, 61–77); but since Wood indicates in a footnote to his translation (2002, 15 n23) that he accepts the traditional reading of the first proposition, I assume that he has either changed his mind or is not in agreement with his co-commentator on this point.

[6] Schönecker (2001, 92).

[7] Timmermann (2007a, 26).

Timmermann's proposal differs sharply from both Freudiger's and Schönecker's in viewing necessity rather than motivation or, more generally, the "subjective moment" of a good will, as the topic of the first proposition. Underlying this proposal is an appeal to what Timmerman refers to as the "principle of non-contingence," according to which the attribution of moral worth to an act is incompatible with it being the outcome of contingent factors, such as a non-moral incentive to perform the act or external circumstances.[8]

Although we have already seen that this principle plays a key role in Kant's account of moral worth and helps to explain why having a good *Denkungsart* is a necessary condition of acting from duty, Timmermann's proposal is questionable in two respects. First, it is doubtful that non-contingence is equivalent to the sense of necessity affirmed in the third proposition. Second, I shall argue below that, rather than being Kant's first proposition, this principle of non-contingence provides the basis on which the latter is affirmed.

(4) *An alternative proposal*: Since the question of the identity of the first proposition is hermeneutical rather than philosophical in nature, addressing it calls for hermeneutical assumptions. Clearly, the underlying assumption shared by the revisionist interpreters discussed above is that the first proposition must be such that, together with the second, it yields the third. Inasmuch as Kant explicitly claims this regarding his third proposition, this assumption is eminently reasonable, particularly if, as these interpreters generally avoid doing, "as a consequence of" [*als Folgerung aus*] is not taken in a rigorous logical sense.

There is, however, another, equally reasonable, hermeneutical assumption, which is made by those who advocate the standard reading of the first proposition, namely, that, if at all possible, the unexpressed first proposition should be identified with something that Kant actually says, even if not in precisely the same terms, in paragraphs nine through thirteen, rather than with something that he presupposes without stating or that must be read back into the text on the basis of what Kant says later in order to generate the desired connection with the third proposition. With this in mind, I shall give priority to the latter assumption. Accordingly, I shall first attempt to derive the first proposition from what Kant actually says in these paragraphs and, then, after considering the third proposition, turn to the question of how (if at all) it might be seen as a consequence of the first two.

To begin with, there is another expression that Kant uses almost as frequently in these paragraphs as "moral worth," but has received much less attention, namely, "moral content."[9] Although these expressions are closely related, they differ in that

---

[8] Timmermann (2007a, 26), 40.

[9] In these paragraphs, Kant mentions "*moralischen Gehalt*" at GMS 4: 397_{36}–98_1 and 398_7 and "*sittlichen Gehalt*" at GMS 4: 398_{14}. He mentions *moralischen* or *sittlichen Wert* (sometimes with the modification "*wahren*" or "*echten*") at GMS 4: 398_{14} and $_{27}$ and 399_{26}. The expression also appears twice in paragraph fourteen, which contains the second proposition, and which is undoubtedly one of the chief reasons for

"moral worth" is applied to actions, while "moral content" is attributed explicitly to maxims. Kant tells us both that a maxim lacks moral content when the course of action it proposes is chosen on the basis of inclination (or fear) and that it possesses such content when the reason for adopting it is that the course of action it prescribes is a duty (GMS 4: 398_{7-20}). In light of this, and keeping in mind that Kant's concern in these paragraphs is with the goodness-making property of a good will under human conditions, my proposal is that Kant's missing first proposition be expressed as follows: "A good will under human conditions is one whose maxims have moral content," by which is understood one for which the dutifulness of a course of action is contained in (incorporated into) its maxim as a condition of its adoption. To be sure, Kant does not formulate this proposition in so many words, but it is clearly implicit in his account.

Although both this and the standard reading meet the criterion of expressing something that Kant actually says or clearly implies in the paragraphs under consideration, I believe that this proposal has several things in its favor. First, inasmuch as a good will is defined by Kant in terms of the character of the agent to whom it belongs and this character is equated with the agent's *Denkungsart*, this goodness is more appropriately linked to the content of an agent's maxims, which presumably reflects the agent's *Denkungsart*, than to an agent's actions, the goodness of which is itself a function of the content of the agent's underlying maxim.

Second, it is the possession (or lack) of a moral content that determines whether a maxim meets the non-contingency condition, which is rightly emphasized by Timmermann. This requires that the perceived rightness or dutifulness of the course of action proposed in the maxim be the reason for that choice, since any other reason from "I have a strong inclination to x" to "It is God's will that I x" would effectively make the agreement of this course of action with the requirements of morality contingent or, in Kant's terms, "fortuitous."

Finally, interpreting Kant's first proposition as concerned with the moral content of maxims rather than the moral worth of particular actions makes it easier to explain the point introduced in the last chapter, namely, that the duty-motive can function as a condition for the adoption of a maxim in two distinct ways: (1) as a sufficient condition, in the sense of being the directly motivating factor or (2) as a necessary background condition, which consists in an underlying commitment to do what morality requires. As already noted, the former is operative in the case of perfect duties, which are duties to perform or, more often, omit performing tokens of certain action-types; the latter is operative both in the case of imperfect duties, which are duties to pursue certain ends rather than, except in rare circumstances, to perform particular acts, and in cases of non-obligatory but permissible acts, where an agent with a good will is acting for the sake of her own happiness, while still being guided by moral

including it in the first. In addition, Kant also refers to a "*Wert des Charakters*," which is equated with moral worth and deemed the highest (GMS 4: $398_{37}-99_1$).

principles. The point is simply that the idea of dutifulness can be incorporated into a maxim in either of these two ways, each of which gives the maxim moral content. Otherwise expressed, this enables us to understand how an agent may act "under the idea of duty," as it were, without acting directly *from* duty, which is something for which the first proposition on the standard reading cannot account.

(B) Kant's second proposition

As already noted, Kant's second proposition states that, "An action from duty has its moral worth *not in the purpose*, which should thereby be achieved, but in the maxim, according to which it was decided upon, and thus does not depend upon the actuality of the object of the action, but rather merely on the *principle of the volition*, in accordance with which the action is done, without regard for any object of the faculty of desire." It should also be noted, however, that this is Kant's second edition formulation of the proposition, which is generally regarded as authoritative. In the first edition version, the clause referring to the maxim according to which the dutiful action has been decided upon is not present.[10] This has the effect of making the connection between the negative portion of the proposition (the source of moral worth not lying in the purpose of the action) and its positive portion (locating the source in the principle of volition) more direct, which was presumably Kant's intent.[11] But, as formulated, this omits the crucial point that a principle of volition can only function as such for Kant insofar as it is incorporated into a maxim. This is rectified in the revised version, which therefore brings out the connection between the moral worth of an action and the moral content of its maxim, which was discussed above.[12]

In his explanation of this proposition, Kant makes it clear that he is adopting his usual strategy of arguing by elimination and that he bases this elimination on the results of the preceding argument. It is assumed that there are two possible grounds for the moral worth of an action: the objective or state of affairs at which it aims and the principle of volition underlying the choice of this objective. But since the former has been ruled out on the grounds that no intended aim or objective could give an action an unconditioned worth, we are left with the latter as the only conceivable alternative.

---

[10] This is noted by Schönecker and Wood (2004, 79 n47).

[11] This is evidenced by Kant's use of *Sperrdrucken*. Here it should be noted that when the clause containing the reference to the maxim is added in the second edition, the emphasis remains on "principle of volition" rather than "maxim."

[12] The fact that Kant paid sufficient attention to the text to revise the formulation of the second proposition in the second edition makes it even more puzzling how he could overlook his glaring omission of an explicit formulation of the first. There seem to be only two possible explanations: (1) that it is a matter of sheer carelessness on Kant's part—although this is rendered somewhat less plausible by his careful attention to the second proposition it remains a possibility; (2) he thought that the identity of the first proposition was so evident as not to require specification. The latter speaks in favor of the standard reading; but I believe it to be compatible with my alternative, which, as noted, may be viewed as a variant of the standard reading. In any event, it is certainly the case that the subsequent controversy regarding the identity of the first proposition shows that it is not as evident as Kant may have assumed it to be and that he should have rectified the situation in his revised version.

Although it is formulated in terms of actions possessing moral worth, this typically quick Kantian argument calls to mind the earlier discussion of the good will. Expressed in these terms, it amounts to an important supplement to the latter. Whereas Kant initially had emphasized that the goodness of a good will is not a function of what it accomplishes, he now adds the more problematic thesis that it is also not a function of its intentions, as praiseworthy as these may be (for example, taking proper care of one's health or helping those in need), but of the reason or principle on the basis of which one has these intentions.

Underlying this argument is the core Kantian thesis that the selection of ends is up to us and therefore that the locus of absolute value, if there be such, can lie only in the principle of volition, on the basis of which these ends and the actions that stem from them in particular circumstances are chosen. If our ends were set for us by nature (or nurture), rather than freely chosen, then nothing, including our volition, could be of absolute value; for in that case the latter would be conditioned by gifts of nature (or fortune), which, as we have already seen, do not have unconditioned worth.[13] Like all the arguments of GMS 1 and 2, this one is conditional, inasmuch as it proceeds on the assumption that morality is not a "phantom of the brain," which it would necessarily be for Kant, if there were nothing of absolute value.

The role of the second proposition in the overall argument emerges with Kant's attempt to clarify the nature of this principle of volition. Up to this point, we know only that it is the source of a maxim's moral content, which, as such, must be connected with the dutifulness of the course of action projected in the maxim, and that only actions stemming from a maxim with this content possess moral worth and merit esteem, though other actions and their underlying maxims, may deserve praise and encouragement. As a first step in the endeavor to specify this principle, Kant characterizes the situation of the will, insofar as it is governed by it:

for the will stands between its *a priori* principle, which is formal, and its incentive [*Triebfeder*] *a posteriori*, which is material, as at a crossroads; and since it still must be determined by something, it must be determined through the formal principle of volition as such, if an action occurs from duty, since every material principle has been withdrawn from it. (GMS 4: 400_{10-16})

What is striking in this passage is the characterization of the principle of volition as both *a priori* and formal. As is usually the case in Kant, these notions are closely related and in this instance both are intended as consequences of the preceding analysis.[14] Moreover,

---

[13] I include nurture as well as nature and gifts of fortune as well as gifts of nature in order to encompass the view that an agent's character in the Kantian sense of *Denkungsart*, which encompasses what that agent values and the ends that she sets for herself, might be viewed as largely a product of training and habituation. Although Kant does not really deal with this issue in GMS, it is a central concern in the *Doctrine of Virtue*, where he insists that setting an end is always an act of freedom. See MS 6: 384–85; 516–17, and 395; 526. This does not mean that nature (one's innate temperament) and nurture (one's environment and training) do not influence the choice of one's ends, but merely that their influence is not causally determinative.

[14] In the first *Critique*, the (*a priori*) pure concepts of the understanding are "forms of the thought of an object in general," while *a priori* or pure intuitions are "forms of sensibility." At one point Kant notes that he

for this reason both must be understood merely in the negative sense as non-empirical and non-material respectively. To say that the principle of volition is *a priori* is to say that it is *not* based on an incentive, which, as already noted, Kant views in GMS as stemming from inclination. In other words, if the principle of volition that supposedly governs the will were based on an incentive provided by our sensuous nature, it would itself have to be *a posteriori*, since it would rest upon a prior knowledge of this incentive. Consequently, the principle must be formal because all "material," that is, all determinate ends or objectives that might be provided for it by the faculty of desire have been ruled out. At this point in the argument, then, the principle is formal by default, which means that we have no real sense of what this formality involves.

(C) Kant's third proposition

In addition to informing us that it is a consequence of the two preceding propositions, Kant tells us that he would express this proposition as "[D]*uty is the necessity of an action from respect for the law*" (GMS 4: 400_{18-19}). Although Kant does not call attention to the matter, it seems likely that he intended this as a correction of the definition of duty that he attributed to Wolff and Baumgarten in his lectures, namely, "the necessity of an action according to the greatest and most important grounds of motivation" (MM 2 29: 598; 226). As Kant makes clear in his discussion of this definition and as one might expect from what we have already seen in Chapter 2, Kant's quarrel with the Wolff–Baumgarten conception of duty concerns its appeal to the deliberately vague expression "the greatest and most important grounds of motivation" [*der grössten und wichtigsten Bewegungs Gründe*]. From Kant's point of view, this leaves it open whether these grounds are from reason or inclination. As such, it ignores what is essential to morality, which, for Kant, is a consequence of the fact that this account of duty pertains to universal practical philosophy rather than moral philosophy or ethics proper.

Whether or not it was Kant's intent, the third proposition can be read as an attempt to remove the lacunae in the Wolff–Baumgarten account by introducing the concept of respect (which does not appear in the lecture) as the subjective motivating ground or the *principium executionis*, with the still not specified practical law serving as the objective ground of the will or its *principium diiudicationis*. In any event, Kant's argument for his complex proposition turns on an ambiguity in the notion of respect, which I shall attempt to clarify by introducing a distinction between "spectator-respect" and "agent-respect."[15]

---

prefers the expression "*formal* idealism" to characterize his transcendental idealism because it brings out the contrast with "*material* idealism," which doubts or denies the existence of external things (KrV B518–19n). Here "*formal*" refers to the *a priori* conditions (sensible and conceptual) of cognition.

[15]   There is a also a third sense of respect as something owed to rational agents as ends in themselves, having intrinsic worth or dignity. This might be termed a second-person conception of respect. We shall consider this conception in Chapter 8 in connection with the so-called "Formula of Humanity" (FH) of the categorical imperative. It should also be noted that it plays a large role in the *Doctrine of Virtue*, where Kant speaks of duties of respect (MS 6: 642–48; 579–83).

The former is a third-person and involuntary "pro-attitude" directed toward persons whose behavior exhibits moral qualities to a high degree. As Kant puts it in the second *Critique*, "*Respect* [in this sense] is a *tribute* that we cannot refuse to pay to merit, whether we want to or not; we may indeed withhold it outwardly but we still cannot help feeling it inwardly" (KpV 5: 77; 202). As such, spectator-respect presupposes a consciousness of the moral law as the supreme norm and is akin to the already discussed esteem [*Hochschätzung*], which is paid only to actions from duty, as contrasted with praise and encouragement, which may be directed toward actions motivated by generally approved sentiments such as sympathetic feeling rather than by the recognition of their dutifulness.[16] Accordingly, respect in this sense is not directly motivating, though it may (and should) motivate indirectly by providing a moral exemplar.[17] By contrast, agent-respect, as a first-person response, which is inseparable from the consciousness of standing under the moral law, is directly motivating for Kant, which is what enables it to serve as the *principium executionis*.

Kant's argument is caught up in this ambiguity because it moves, without calling attention to the fact, from spectator to agent-respect. Thus, Kant begins by contrasting the things that one might like, approve of, or even love on the basis of inclination, which includes *products* of the will, with an object of respect, which is always the *activity* of a will [my emphases] (GMS 4: 400_{19-25}). This is spectator-respect. But Kant then continues: "Only that which is connected with my will as ground, but never as effect, what does not serve my inclination, but outweighs it, or at least excludes it entirely from consideration in making a choice, thus only the mere law for itself can be an object of respect and hence a command" (GMS 4: 400_{25-29}). As the reference to "*my* will" and "*my* inclination" [my emphases] indicate, Kant is now making a first-person claim, not, to be sure, about himself, but about *any* agent who becomes conscious of standing under a still not specified practical law. His point is that the peculiar feeling (agent-respect) is a direct consequence of the consciousness of this law as a law for oneself and hence as an unconditionally binding command.

Kant could have smoothed the transition from spectator to agent-respect by noting that the objects of the former are actions that express or, given his agnosticism regarding ultimate motivating grounds, that are taken as expressing agent-respect as their motivating ground. Setting that aside, however, Kant's main point is that actions from duty (if there be such) may also be described as actions from respect for the law. This is because:

[A]n action from duty is supposed to abstract entirely from the influence of inclination and with it every object of the will, thus nothing remains to determine the will except objectively the *law* and subjectively *pure respect* for this practical law, hence the maxim of complying with such a law, even when it infringes on all my inclinations. (GMS 4: $400_{29}-401_2$)

---

[16] In the second *Critique*, however, Kant does say that, strictly, speaking, respect is paid always to the law and only to the person, who serves as an exemplar of the law (KpV 5: 78; 203).

[17] On this point, see especially KpV 5: 77–78; 202–3.

As in the second proposition, we have an argument by elimination, in which it is again assumed that every conceivable inclination and its object has been precluded as a possible determining ground of a will that supposedly acts from duty. This time, however, the "principle of volition," which was previously characterized merely as "formal" and "*a priori*" and which serves as the objective determining ground or *principium diudicationis* of a will that acts from duty, is further described as "the law," thereby underscoring its normative character; while respect is introduced as the subjective determining ground or motive [*Bewegungsgrund*] for obeying the law, that is, as the *principium executionis*. Nevertheless, much as was the case in the second proposition, where "formal" and "*a priori*" seemed to have merely negative connotations, here the term "respect" appears to be little more than a place-holder for whatever non-inclination-based motivational factor is operative in action from duty.

Kant attempts to provide content to the notion of respect as *Bewegungsgrund* in a footnote, which we shall examine below. But first it is necessary to consider the concluding clause in the passage cited above, where Kant suggests that acting from respect for the law involves adopting a maxim of complying with the law, even when doing so conflicts with what one is inclined to do. This is because if one excludes all inclination-based motivation, respect is the only motivating force or incentive left. Accordingly, the law and respect for it constitute respectively the objective and subjective aspects of the moral content of the maxim of an agent who acts from duty. Moreover, these are not separable; for respect can be directed at nothing except the law, while the law only binds insofar as respect provides the ground of the incorporation of it into one's maxim as the norm governing one's volition.

The second paragraph that is ostensibly devoted to the third proposition may be more properly viewed as a conclusion to the entire discussion up to this point. In addition to issuing the important reminder that the highest and unconditioned good can be found only in the will of a rational being, Kant there points out that "the pre-eminent good, which we call moral," occurs only when the determining ground of the agent's will is the "*representation of the law* in itself" (GMS 4: 401_{10-14}). By referring to the *representation* of the law, rather than simply the law, as the determining ground of the will of a rational agent, Kant underscores his core contention that the exercise of rational agency must be viewed as a free, self-conscious act, in which the agent recognizes the principle on which she acts as her principle and therefore as normative for her.[18]

Since the reference to respect occurs in the preceding paragraph rather than the one presently under consideration, it seems puzzling that Kant attaches a footnote

---

[18] It may also be regarded as an anticipation of Kant's claim that the distinguishing feature of rational beings is their capacity to act "*according to the representation* of laws" (GMS 4: 412_{26-27}), which will be a major theme in subsequent chapters.

discussing respect to it rather than to its predecessor.[19] But regardless of its location in the text, this note is crucial for understanding Kant's position in GMS and became the basis for a central chapter in the second *Critique*.[20] Accordingly, I shall first cite it in full and then discuss its salient points. For ease of reference I have numbered each of the sentences.

(1) One could accuse me of seeking refuge behind the word *respect* in an obscure feeling rather than giving a distinct reply to the question through a concept of reason. (2) But even though respect is a feeling, it is not one *received* through influence, but a feeling that is self-produced [*selbstgewirktes*] by a concept of reason and therefore specifically different from all feelings of the first kind, which may be reduced to inclination or fear. (3) What I immediately recognize as a law for me, I recognize with respect, which signifies merely the consciousness of the *subordination* of my will to a law, without the mediation of other influences on my sense. (4) The immediate determination of the will through the law and the consciousness of it is called *respect*, so that this is regarded as the *effect* of the law on the subject and not as its *cause*. (5) Actually, respect is the representation of a worth that infringes upon my self-love. (6) Therefore, it is something that is considered neither as object of inclination nor fear, though at the same time it has something analogous to both. (7) The *object* of respect is thus solely the *law*, and indeed that which we *impose* [*auferlegen*] upon *ourselves* and yet as necessary in itself. (8) As law we are subject to it without asking self-love for its permission; as imposed upon us by ourselves it is still a consequence of our will, and in the first respect it has an analogy with fear, in the second with inclination. (9) All respect for a person is actually only respect for the law (of righteousness, etc.) of which the person gives us the example. (10) Because we also regard the enhancement of our talents as a duty, we represent to ourselves a person with talents also, as it were, as an *example of a law* (through practice to become similar to him in this) and that constitutes our respect. (11) All so-called moral *interest* consists solely in respect for the law. (GMS 4: 401n$_{17-40}$)

---

[19] This might be because Kant had already attached a note defining "maxim" to that paragraph and did not wish to attach two important notes to the same paragraph. But, as already suggested, it would have been more natural for Kant to have attached his maxim note to the passage where the term first appears, namely, GMS 4: 397$_{36}$–98$_1$.

[20] This is chapter 3 of the *Analytic of Pure Practical Reason*: "On the Incentives of Pure Practical Reason" (KpV 5: 71–89; 198–211). Although the brief account in GMS contains essentially the same view that Kant there presents in a more developed form, there are several differences that are worthy of note. First, the second *Critique* offers a much more nuanced moral psychology. Whereas in the note in GMS Kant simply juxtaposes respect and self-love, in the second *Critique* he distinguishes between self-love [*Selbstliebe*] or selfishness [*Eigenliebe*] and self-satisfaction [*Wohgefallens*] or self-conceit [*Eigendünkel*] and claims that the consciousness of the law has a distinct effect on each (KpV 5: 75–76; 201). Second, though in both texts Kant insists that respect has both a negative and a positive side, in GMS he compared them with fear and inclination respectively (emphasizing that there is only an analogy rather than an identity), in the second *Critique* he describes the negative side of respect as pain and connects it with humiliation, while the positive side is distinguished sharply from pleasure and connected with self-approbation [*Selbstbilligung*] (KpV 5: 76, 80–1; 201–2; 204–5). Finally, in the second *Critique* Kant adds the claim, not found explicitly in GMS, that both sides of this feeling can be cognized *a priori* as the necessary consequences of the effect of the consciousness of the moral law on sensuously affected rational agents (KpV 5: 79; 204). I discuss Kant's concept of respect in Allison (1990, 120–28).

(1) Kant begins by acknowledging that his introduction of the concept of respect might appear as a purely *ad hoc* solution to the problem of how the representation or consciousness of the law (which at this point has been described only as an *a priori* and formal principle) could serve as the determining ground of the will. And Kant seems to have regarded the fact that he here appeals to an "obscure feeling" rather than to a "concept of reason" as particularly problematic. Although Kant does not explain what he means by the latter, the context makes it reasonable to assume that he was referring to some sort of conceptually articulated reason (for example, the principle of happiness) rather than to an idea of reason in the technical Kantian sense.

(2) Kant provides the first step of his answer in the second sentence, where, while acknowledging that respect is a feeling, he insists upon its uniqueness, which stems from the fact that it is "self-produced by a concept of reason" [*Vernunftbegriff*]. By characterizing the feeling in this way, Kant is explicitly linking its genesis with the spontaneity of reason rather than, as with all other feelings, the receptivity of our sensuous nature. Here the "concept of reason" clearly refers to the not yet specified moral law, which is itself an idea of reason for Kant. Naturally, rational agents could not have this (or any) feeling, if they did not also have a sensuous nature; but for Kant respect is the only feeling that does not stem entirely from this nature, since it is dependent on a reason that is practical in the sense that it can, of itself, determine the will.

(3) The third sentence begins Kant's positive characterization of respect by focusing on its first-person, normative character. What is immediately recognized as a law for oneself is recognized with respect, which signifies merely the consciousness of the subordination of one's will to a law. What is important here is that it is recognized as being a law *for oneself*, that is, as having normative force. As the last clause indicates, "immediately" does not mean without any reflective activity, but without the consideration of any sensuous influences.

(4) The fourth sentence contains a partial reiteration of the central claim of the third; but it adds the significant point that respect is to be regarded as the *effect* of the law on the subject rather than its *cause*. Kant is here rejecting the view of moral sense theorists and other sentimentalists that feeling is the ground (cause) of the normative force that we assign to certain moral principles, and arguing instead that such feeling is the consequence (effect) of our consciousness of the normative status that a moral principle possesses independently of any feeling.

(5) The fifth sentence interjects the conception of value or worth into the account and contrasts the worth assigned to the object of respect with that stemming from self-love, understood as a propensity to value whatever one takes to be conducive to one's happiness. The claim that respect is the representation of a value that "infringes upon

self-love" means that it trumps all values associated with the latter, without totally negating these values, since they provide legitimate reasons to act when they do not conflict with moral requirements.

(6) In the sixth sentence, Kant suggests that, while respect is neither a matter of inclination nor of fear (these having already been ruled out in virtue of their grounding in our sensuous nature), it has something analogous to both. Kant does not explain this analogy and in the account of the second *Critique* he replaces it with the seemingly more apt analogy with pain, connected with humiliation, as the negative aspect of the feeling and self-approbation, which Kant distinguishes sharply from pleasure, as its positive aspect (KpV 5: 76, 80–81; 201, 205).[21]

(7) Although the expression is not used, by characterizing the object of respect, namely, the law, as both self-imposed and necessary in itself, the seventh sentence implicitly introduces the central Kantian notion of autonomy, which is first referred to as such in GMS 2. To say that the law is "necessary in itself" is to say that its dictates are intrinsically necessary, apart from any non-moral ends or interests that an agent might have. We shall see that a fundamental task of Kant's moral theory is to demonstrate the seemingly paradoxical thesis that a moral principle can only be necessary in the requisite sense, if it is also self-imposed.

(8) Without spelling out what it involves, the eighth sentence affirms a connection between the two aspects of autonomy noted in the preceding sentence (self-imposition and necessity (*auto* and *nomos*) and the analogy between the feeling of respect and inclination and fear noted in the sixth. In order to make any sense of this cryptic remark, however, it is necessary to read it in light of the richer account in the second *Critique*.

(9–10) Kant here makes the transition from agent-respect, which has been the topic under consideration up to this point, to spectator-respect. Kant also points out that, while the object of respect is always the law, spectator-respect is directed at an agent who is taken to exemplify the law in her conduct.

(11) In the final sentence, Kant cryptically connects respect with what he terms "so-called moral interest." The basic idea is that respect for the law produces an interest in obeying it. The qualification "so-called" appears intended as an implicit critique of those moral theorists who locate the source of this interest in anything other than respect. We shall see in Chapter 9 that Kant is casting a wide net, which encompasses all moral theories that do not acknowledge the grounding of morality in the autonomy of the will, that is, all forms of heteronomy.

Our remaining concern in this section is with the vexing question of how to understand Kant's claim that the third proposition is a consequence of the first

---

[21] I analyze Kant's treatment of respect in the second *Critique* in Allison (1990, 120–28).

two (GMS 4: 400₁₆). We have seen that it is primarily this problem that has led some commentators to reject the standard interpretation of the unformulated first proposition, namely, that an action has moral worth if and only if it is from duty alone. Without addressing that issue, I offered as a candidate for the first proposition the thesis that a good will under human conditions is one whose maxims have moral content, by which is understood that the idea of duty is incorporated into the maxim, either as the directly motivating factor or as an underlying commitment to the not yet formulated moral law as the guiding normative principle. Accordingly, our present task is to consider whether, on this understanding of the first proposition, the third may be viewed as a consequence of the first two.

Here everything turns on how one understands "consequence of" [*Folgerung aus*] and there seem to be two possible models: (a) the deductive model, where the first and second propositions are premises from which the third is a logical consequence; or (b) the combinatory model, in which the third proposition is viewed as a combination or synthesis of the first two.[22] The first seems to be a non-starter and to my knowledge no interpreter has advocated it. By contrast, the second model appears more promising and is endorsed, albeit in different ways, by all three of the previously discussed revisionary readings. As we have seen, for Freudiger and Schönecker the first proposition affirms the subjective aspect of acting from duty, the second affirms the objective aspect, and the third the combination of the two; while according to Timmermann the first proposition emphasizes the element of necessity, the second the law, and the third reverence or respect, which supposedly "completes the definition of duty."[23] We have also seen, however, that all of these reconstructions seem strained and in some cases involve importing into Kant's propositions claims that are not found at the place in the text to which they are assigned.

Basically, I agree with all three of the revisionary readings that the combinatory model is the appropriate one for interpreting Kant's claim and with Freudiger and Schönecker that the best way of understanding this is to regard the first and second propositions as providing respectively the subjective and objective aspects of such action, which are then combined in the third proposition: "[D]uty is the necessity of an action from respect for the law." Assuming this framework, my proposal amounts to the suggestion that the attribution to a maxim of a moral content is this subjective aspect and what makes it subjective is simply that maxims for Kant are by definition subjective

---

[22] A possible third alternative has been suggested by Wood, who rejecting the deductive model, states that it is more likely that Kant "means merely that (3) is a consistent extension of (1) and (2) or lies a bit further along the same path of thinking down which he has been directing us with (1) and (2)." Wood (1999, 43). Such a reading, however, strains the interpretation of "consequence of" and after making this suggestion Wood seems to advocate the combinatory model.

[23] See Timmermann (2007a, 40). Like Paton, Timmermann translates "*Achtung*" as "reverence" rather than "respect."

principles on the basis of which finite rational beings actually act. Moreover, as I have already argued, it has the advantage over the other revisionary proposals in that it corresponds to something that Kant actually says in the relevant portion of the text, which is certainly a hermeneutical desideratum.

Granted, this also applies to the standard view, which identifies the first proposition with the claim that an action has moral worth if and only if it is performed from duty alone. In addition, one might argue that the same considerations support the view that this corresponds to the subjective factor, thereby resolving the apparent difficulty that this proposition is unable to explain how the third could be regarding as a consequence of the first two. But in response to this objection I would simply point to the previously noted advantages of my proposal over the standard view, as well as the fact that the notion of moral content prepares the way for the introduction of respect in a way that moral worth cannot do. In fact, what we learn in the course of Kant's analysis is that respect for the law just is the moral content, which motivates actions possessing moral worth. Thus, while I acknowledge that my case for the identity of the mysterious first proposition is not iron clad, I believe that, all things considered, it is more plausible than any of the alternatives found in the literature.

II

Having shown that a good will under human conditions is one that acts from duty and that duty is to be understood as "the necessity of an action from respect for the law," the next obvious question concerns the nature of this law. Up to this point, we have learned only that it must be formal and a priori, in the negative sense of not being material (having as its content any ends stemming from the faculty of desire) and not being derived from experience (what an agent in fact desires). But we have yet to acquire any positive information about its nature. Kant attempts to deal with this issue in paragraphs seventeen and eighteen. In the first of these, he provides his long awaited derivation of this law and in the second he illustrates its functioning by means of the example of false promising. These, then, provide the subject matter of the present section. I shall begin with an analysis of Kant's derivation of the law. In view of its intrinsic importance and the controversial nature of Kant's cryptic account, I shall once again cite the paragraph in full, numbering its sentences for ease of reference, and then comment upon its various components.

(1) But what kind of a law can it be, the representation of which must determine the will even without regard to the expected result, in order that it can be considered good absolutely and without limitation? (2) Since I have robbed the will of all impulses, which could arise from obedience to any particular law [*irgend eines Gesetzes*], nothing remains which could serve the will as its principle except the conformity of the action with universal law as such, that is, I ought never to proceed [*verfahren*] other than in such a way *that I could also will that my maxim should become a universal law.* (3) Here it is only the mere conformity to law as such (without grounding it in some law determining certain actions) that serves the will as its principle and must so serve it, if

duty is not to be everywhere an empty delusion and chimerical concept; common human reason completely agrees with this in its practical judgments and has the above-mentioned principle always before its eyes. (GMS 4: 402_{1-15})

In the first sentence, Kant poses the problem concerning the nature of the law, the representation of which must determine the will, if it is to be considered good absolutely and without limitation.[24] As such, it points back to the opening paragraphs of GMS 1. But since the *representation* of a law (as contrasted with a law itself[25]) determines the will in the sense of providing it with a sufficient reason to act apart from any regard for a projected result, just in case the will acts from (is motivated by) respect for that law, the question Kant is addressing here might also be formulated as: what must be the nature of a law such that a will could be motivated to act from respect for it? And, inasmuch as Kant moves in GMS 1 from a consideration of what motivates a good will to the nature of the normative principle governing it, his answer to this question constitutes the culmination of what has been termed his "motivational analysis."[26]

The second sentence contains the derivation of the sought for law. The first clause, in which Kant states that he has "robbed the will of all impulses which could arise from obedience to any particular law," is a statement of where things stand as a result of the preceding motivational analysis. Here Kant's reasoning seems to be that the prior exclusion of all motivating grounds for obeying a law stemming from impulse (inclination) entails that no particular law could serve as the principle of such a will. This is because any such law, regardless of its content, *has a content*, which means that it presupposes some end as the ground of its normativity. But since we have seen that no such end could be good without qualification, it cannot provide a norm for a will that is good in the specified sense. And since it is assumed that a good will must be governed by *some* law, it follows that the only remaining candidate for the normative principle for a good will is the conformity of its maxims with universal law as such.[27]

---

[24] It was noted in Chapter 3 that Kant at times distinguishes between a good will *simpliciter* and an absolutely [*schlecterdings*] good will and that sometimes, but not always, he identifies the latter with a holy will. But since in the present case "absolutely" is paired with "without limitation" and the latter is the defining feature of the goodness of a good will as such, and Kant is clearly here concerned with a good will under human conditions, I take it that here the function of the term is purely rhetorical. Accordingly, I do not believe that it plays any role in the derivation of the supreme principle of morality.

[25] Kant's locution here seems to anticipate his important thesis in GMS 2 that, "Everything in nature works according to laws. Only a rational being has the capacity to act according to the representation of laws, that is, according to principles, or has a will" (GMS 4: 412_{26-28}). I shall discuss this thesis in the next and subsequent chapters.

[26] The expression is used by Korsgaard (1996, 47). A similar account of Kant's strategy is provided by Schönecker and Wood (2004, 91). Unlike Korsgaard, however, they argue that Kant's strategy here is unsuccessful, since it (allegedly) does not follow from the fact that the motive (respect) cannot involve the attainment of a subjective end that this must be a property of the law itself. As a counter-example, they offer the possibility of conceiving of the moral law as a supernatural law of God. But it seems clear that for Kant the mere fact that a law is believed to stem from God cannot make it an object of respect, unless it is already assumed that what God wills must conform to a moral norm that is independent of his will.

[27] At GMS 4: $446\,7_{15-21}$ Kant argues, on the basis of the premise that a will is a kind of causality, that a will as such (not merely) a good will, must be law-governed. I shall discuss this issue in Chapter 10.

In evaluating Kant's derivation, it is essential to keep in mind the previous analysis of the concept of a good will. It was claimed that by a good will is to be understood a good *Denkungsart*, which, in turn, may be characterized as a general orientation of the will with respect to the moral law. As we have seen, a *Denkungsart* with this orientation is one for which the law is recognized as the supreme norm, which, as such, governs both what is morally required and what is permissible. With respect to the latter, the law provides a necessary but not a sufficient condition of acting, since an interest in performing the permissible (but non-obligatory) act is also required. With respect to the former, conformity to the law is both a necessary and a sufficient condition of its performance, which means that an agent with a good *Denkungsart* does what the moral law requires simply because it requires it. Otherwise, its conformity to the law would be merely contingent, which is incompatible with the character of a good will. And, as I shall argue below, a proper understanding of the use to which Kant puts this concept of a good will in the derivation of the supreme principle of morality as its principle is the key to dealing with the notorious "gap problem" in Kant's derivation.

This problem does not arise, however, in connection with what we have considered up to this point, namely, the principle that the conformity of a maxim with universal law as such is the law out of respect for which a good will under human conditions acts. Rather, it stems from Kant's subsequent gloss on this principle: "*I ought never to act except in such a way that I could also will that my maxim should become a universal law.*"[28] The problem is that the gloss appears to say considerably more than the principle it glosses, since the requirement that my maxim conform to universal law does not seem to entail that I must be able to will that it *be* a universal law. Moreover, since similar considerations are thought to apply to the argument in GMS 2, where Kant claims that the content of a categorical imperative (what it enjoins) can be derived from the analysis of the concept of such an imperative, this has seemed to many critics to point to a fundamental difficulty at the heart of Kant's moral theory.

Although the moral principle at which Kant arrives in GMS 1 is essentially equivalent to the so-called formula of universal law or FUL that he subsequently derives from the concept of a categorical imperative (GMS 4: 420_{24}–21_9) and a similar worry about "gappiness" is often thought to arise in both cases, I believe that it is a mistake simply to lump them together. For one thing, it must be noted that there are three, not merely two, derivations of FUL, or close approximations thereof, in GMS: the two mentioned above and one at the beginning of GMS 3.[29] For another, each of these derivations proceeds by the analysis of a different concept. In GMS 1, the *analysandum* is the concept of a good will under human conditions; in GMS 2, it is the concept of a categorical imperative; and in GMS 3, it is the negative concept of freedom.

---

[28] I describe this as a gloss because Kant's introduction of it with "that is" [*d.i.*] indicates that he takes it to be a clarification of the principle of conformity to universal law as such rather than a distinct claim. In some English translations this point is obfuscated by the fact that the gloss is presented as a distinct sentence.

[29] This is also noted by Schönecker and Wood (2004, 90 n59 and 93).

Accordingly, even though it will inevitably involve some repetition, particularly in the case of the first two derivations, I believe that these differences in the *analysanda* require that each of these derivations be considered in its own terms. Thus, I shall here focus solely on the passage immediately before us, saving an analysis of the other derivations for subsequent chapters.[30]

According to Aune, who has provided the most extensive treatment of the issue, the gap problem stems from the fact that the two principles which Kant allegedly regarded as equivalent, namely, "Conform your actions to universal law" and "Act only on that maxim through which you can at the same time will that it should become a universal law" differ with respect to "practical import," which makes it difficult to accept the thesis that they are different versions of the same principle.[31] By claiming that these principles differ in practical import, Aune means that the former is not action guiding in a meaningful way, since, like "Be authentic," it does not appear to enjoin or prohibit any particular course of action; whereas the latter at least purports to do so. Accordingly, this line of objection is close in spirit, if not in form, to Kant's previously discussed charge that Baumgarten's version of the moral principle ("*fac bonum, omitte malum*") is tautologous, as well as the notorious Hegelian emptiness charge raised against the categorical imperative.[32]

As far as Aune's analysis is concerned, the essential point is that the first of the two principles that he attributes to Kant is not affirmed by Kant in the form that Aune suggests. Rather than characterizing the principle as "conform to universal law as such," which is in the imperative mood and therefore must be understood prescriptively, Kant twice formulates it as "conformity to universal law as such," which, since it is in the indicative mood, must be understood descriptively. And, as the text also indicates, what it describes is the nature of the principle governing a will that is presumed to be good without limitation. Hence, the gap, if there is one, is not located in the move from a vacuous prescriptive principle to a contentful one, but from a descriptive to a prescriptive principle. This should not be taken, however to mean that the gap in question is the familiar one of a move from an "is" to an "ought," where the former is understood in Humean fashion as a statement of empirical fact. Clearly, the claim that by a good will is meant one whose maxims conform to universal law as such

---

[30] The fact that Kant provides three derivations of the categorical imperative in GMS and that each proceeds on the basis of a different *analysandum* seems to have been overlooked by those who have dealt with the so-called "gap problem." This includes Aune (1979, 28–34); Kerstein (2002); Rickless (2004); Köhl (2006), and Allison (1996, 143–54). In the last-mentioned essay, I had assumed with Aune that there was a genuine gap in Kant's analysis and attempted to deal with it in a systematic fashion, using the derivation in the second *Critique*, which appeals to transcendental freedom, as the key to its resolution. My present treatment of the issue differs from the earlier one both in denying that there is a gap that needs to be filled by importing extraneous premises and in abandoning the global approach and considering each of the arguments in GMS in its own terms.

[31] These two principles are formulated in this way by Aune (1979, 29–30).

[32] Although he does not refer to Aune, the connection with the Hegelian objection is noted by Wood (1990, 161–64).

is not an empirical claim about the behavior of wills (or agents) that are regarded as especially good. Rather, like all the central theses of GMS 1, it is a conceptual claim regarding the nature of the principle governing a will that is good without limitation, which is derived from the concept of such a will by a lengthy process involving most of the preceding propositions of GMS 1.

Moreover, understanding Kant's principle descriptively is not incompatible with the previously noted point that a good will under human conditions, that is, a good *Denkungsart*, does not always act "in character."[33] These claims would be incompatible, if the principle of conformity to universal law were taken to describe the behavior of an actual good human will, since it has been acknowledged that it cannot be maintained that such a will (if, indeed, it exists) always acts in conformity with its character; but there is no incompatibility, if, as I believe to be the case, what it describes is the principle governing such a will considered qua good or insofar as it is good. Otherwise expressed, Kant is making a descriptive claim about the *concept* of a good will, considered as such, which would supposedly hold even if this concept were never completely instantiated.

If this is correct, then the task is to understand the move from the descriptive "conformity with universal law as such" to the manifestly prescriptive "Act only on that maxim through which you can at the same time will that it should become a universal law," which amounts to a formulation of the categorical imperative. Critics, including Aune, are correct to point out that Kant moves precipitously from one to the other and that some explanation of this move is required; but I think that a careful consideration of the text and its underlying argumentation both provides this explanation and answers the objection that Kant's account is vitiated by a gap such as Aune and other critics maintain.

The key lies in the inclusion of maxims in the prescriptive claim, which Kant misleadingly presents as a simple gloss on the descriptive one for which he argues in the first and the bulk of the second sentence. Simply put, maxims provide the necessary content to the seemingly empty notion of conformity to universal law as such and in so doing also introduce prescriptivity into Kant's account. They do this by indicating that this conformity is a requirement placed on an agent's maxims, which brings with it prescriptivity because these maxims, even those of agents with a good will under human conditions, do not as such conform with universal law. Rather, maxims, as subjective principles, express an agent's personal ends and interests, which if they conform to universal law do so only contingently. We have seen, however, that in order to avoid this contingency the maxims of an agent with a good will must not merely conform to universal law, they must be adopted *because they conform* or, more

---

[33] See Chapter 3, section I. A worry that a descriptive understanding of Kant's principle is incompatible with the fact that Kant is referring to a good will under human conditions and that such a will does not necessarily act as it ought to act was voiced by one of my readers for OUP. What follows is an attempt to respond to this worry.

precisely, only on the condition that they conform.[34] And since finite agents have a sensuous as well as a rational nature, and since the former is the source of ends and interests that are perfectly legitimate insofar as they conform to the requirements of the latter, it follows that the task for a good will under human conditions is to incorporate the principle of conformity to universal law as such into its maxims in such a way that the former serves as a restricting or limiting condition on the latter. Moreover, this is just what the principle that one should never act in such a way except that one could *also will* [my emphasis] that one's maxim should become a universal law specifies.[35]

It follows from this that the prescriptive principle at which Kant arrives is at bottom a test of the permissibility of the maxims that are submitted to it rather than, as is sometimes assumed, as self-standing duty-generator. To be sure, it is not totally useless in the latter regard, since it does seem to be a source of negative duties to reject maxims that fail to conform to this principle and therefore to omit actions based upon such maxims. But we shall see in the subsequent discussion of the categorical imperative in its most familiar formulation that even this is limited.[36] Nevertheless, though this will likewise require further discussion in subsequent chapters, I think that this goes a long way toward responding to the familiar emptiness charge; for even if it merely rules out certain maxims and courses of action, Kant's principle has normative force in a way that principles such as Baumgarten's *fac bonum, omitte malum* do not. Moreover, this is because it is grounded in a conception of the will as having a power of self-determination according to principles of reason for which the Wolffian universal practical philosophy has no place.[37]

Prior to the semi-colon, the third and final sentence reiterates the point that "the mere conformity to law as such" must serve the will as its principle. But rather than connecting this principle with a good will, as he had done at the beginning of the

---

[34] The non-contingency requirement is here crucial. On Aune's analysis, Kant needs a principle to the effect that a maxim conforms to universal law just in case that maxim can include itself as a universal law. And he denies this on the grounds that a maxim might very well conform to universal law without being able to include itself as a universal law. See Aune (1979, 88). Aune neglects, however, to note that any such conformity would be merely contingent and therefore not indicative of a good will.

[35] It is essential to emphasize "also will" [*auch wollen*] because it underscores the point that the will invariably incorporates other ends or incentives into its maxims besides conformity to universal law as such, and that what is at issue is the compatibility of the former with the latter. We shall see that in his official derivation of the categorical imperative Kant uses the phrase "at the same time will" [*zugleich wollen*], but these come to the same thing.

[36] To anticipate, what is strictly ruled out are courses of action on impermissible maxims, not courses of action *per se*.

[37] Dealing with Hegel's objections would be a far more complicated matter with which I shall not engage in here, since it would require a detailed discussion of Hegelian texts. But I at least wish to note that, at the end of his lengthy discussion of reason [*Vernunft*] in the *Phenomenology*, Hegel addresses Kant's view of the categorical imperative, without referring to him by name, by distinguishing between the function of reason in generating and in testing laws The latter, which I take it is intended to correspond to the Kantian view, is rejected on the grounds that the universality requirement is a tautology, which is precisely the objection that Kant raises against the Wolffians. See Hegel (1977, 256–59). As far as I can see, however, Hegel does not provide much of an argument for this objection and he seems to view the issue as testing putative laws for their normativity rather than maxims expressing the subjective ends of an agent for their permissibility.

paragraph, Kant now claims that this is necessary "if duty is not to be everywhere an empty delusion and chimerical concept." This formulation and its many variants is a common theme in the first two parts of GMS, reflecting the important methodological point that Kant is there concerned with determining the nature of the supreme principle of morality rather than establishing its reality. Accordingly, all of Kant's claims about this principle in these parts of the work are conditional and to be understood with this caveat.

Finally, in the concluding clause of the third sentence, Kant remarks that his analysis is in complete agreement with "ordinary human reason" and that the latter "has the above-mentioned principle always before its eyes." It is in order to support this claim that Kant considers in the next paragraph the case of false promising, which reappears in a slightly altered form in GMS 2. He begins by distinguishing sharply between the questions of the prudence and of the morality of such a practice. His point is that, whereas the prudential question may be extremely complex, involving any number of variables, the moral question is quite simple. To answer it "in the shortest and yet infallible [*untrügliche*] manner" one need only ask oneself: "Would I really be content if my maxim (of getting out of difficulty through an untruthful promise) should hold as a universal law (for myself as well as for others), and could I really say to myself that anyone may make an untruthful promise when he finds himself in a difficulty that he cannot get out of in any other way?" (GMS 4: 403$_{5-9}$). Not surprisingly, Kant's answer is no, because, while I can will the lie, I cannot will a universal law to lie:

For according to such a law there would actually be no promises, because it would futile to avow my will regarding my future actions to others who would not believe this avowal or, if they rashly did so, would repay me with the same coin; hence my maxim, as soon as it was made into a universal law, must destroy itself. (GMS 4: 403$_{12-17}$)

This passage suggests one of the familiar criticisms of Kant's categorical imperative, namely, that in spite of his protestation that the principle of morality should not be concerned with consequences, at the end of the day Kant's theory amounts to a form of consequentialism, specifically a "rule consequentialism," since it appears to appeal to the cessation of the institution of promising as the unacceptable consequence of the universalization of a principle permitting false promising. Once again, I shall reserve consideration of some of the issues posed by this line of objection for later. For the present, I wish simply to point out that the problem with the universalization of the maxim of permitting false promising is not that it would spell the end of the institution of promising (that might not necessarily be a bad thing, or at least Kant has not given us any reason to assume that it would be); it is rather that this would be incompatible with the end that the agent had in mind in incorporating this procedure into his maxim, namely, using false promising as a means for avoiding difficulties. That is why Kant claims that the maxim, if made into a universal law, must destroy itself.

III

After completing his account of how the principle of morality is in the possession of ordinary human reason, Kant poses the following rhetorical question:

Would it therefore not be more advisable in moral things to remain with the judgment of common reason and bring in philosophy at most only in order to exhibit the system of morals all the more completely and comprehensibly, and likewise its rules in a manner that is more suitable for their use (but still more for disputation), but not in order to bring common human understanding out of its happy simplicity, in its practical aspect, and through philosophy to set it on a new path of investigation and instruction? (GMS 4: 404$_{28-36}$)

The last two paragraphs of GMS 1 are devoted to Kant's answer to this rhetorical question. But before turning to a consideration of these paragraphs, it will be useful to ponder for a moment the significance of the question itself. This significance stems largely from the tension between what Kant has said in the preceding paragraphs regarding common human reason's capacity to proceed in moral matters without having to rely on philosophy and what he had already said in the Preface and will proceed to argue further in the opening paragraphs of GMS 2 concerning the absolute indispensability for both moral theory and practice of a metaphysics of morals. Although neither Kant's question nor his preceding remarks that give rise to it bear directly on the former aspect of the alleged indispensability of such a metaphysics, they are certainly germane to the latter. Indeed, these remarks seem, at least at first glance, to stand in direct contradiction with Kant's indispensability thesis, which, in turn, calls into question the import of his project in GMS as a whole.

Kant's response to this question and therefore his defense of the indispensability thesis turns on the introduction of a distinction between two possible uses that common human reason might make of philosophy in the practical domain: (1) as a science from which one can derive moral instruction and (2) as a means "to provide access and durability [*Eingang und Dauerhaftigkeit*] for its precepts" (GMS 4: 405$_{4-5}$). Kant's point is that, while the first use has been ruled out by his preceding remarks, since they have shown that the precepts in question are those of common human reason rather than philosophy, the second has not. Moreover, Kant begins his answer to his rhetorical question by suggesting that the latter use of philosophy is rendered necessary by the fact that "innocence," by which he apparently means the pre-reflective moral condition of common human reason, is "easily seduced" (GMS 4: 405$_{1-2}$).

As Kant goes on to explain, the "seducer" lies within human nature itself, specifically, in the needs and inclinations, whose collective satisfaction is termed "happiness," and which constitutes "a powerful counterweight [*ein mächtiges Gegengewicht*]" to the commands of duty issued by reason (GMS 4: 405$_{5-9}$). In spite of Kant's mechanistic terminology, it is clear that he does not mean to suggest that the voice of reason is simply overwhelmed by the superior force of our needs and inclinations. After all, the governing metaphor of the entire discussion is seduction, which requires the willing acquiescence of its victim. Otherwise expressed, the "seduction" consists in needs and inclinations providing spurious, but seemingly legitimate reasons for ignoring or at least mitigating the strictness of the uncompromising demands of duty.

Kant reinforces the point that the issue concerns competing reasons to act rather than a conflict between reason and sensibility by introducing the idea of a "*natural* dialectic." As Kant describes this dialectic, it consists in

a propensity [*Hang*] to rationalize [*vernünfteln*] against those strict laws of duty, and to raise doubt concerning their validity, or at least their purity and strictness, and, where possible, to make them more into accord with our wishes and inclinations, i.e., to corrupt their ground and to deprive them of their entire dignity [*Würde*], something which not even common reason can in the end call good. (405_{13-19})

Although from the way in which Kant introduces the problem one might have expected something like an antinomy between the claims of duty and inclination, what Kant presents under the label "natural dialectic" hardly takes the form of an antinomy and he does not characterize it as such. It is rather a dialectic of practical reason in the sense that empirically conditioned practical reason creates the deceptive illusion of usurping the proper place of pure practical reason.[38] A striking feature of this dialectic, however, is its virtual equivalence to what Kant subsequently described as a "propensity to evil" (RGV 6: 29–33; 76–79). And equally striking is the fact that, whereas in the later work Kant characterizes this propensity as inextirpable and therefore as something that can be struggled against but never completely overcome, in the seemingly more optimistic mood of GMS he suggests that an antidote for it is to be found in philosophy.

This is the theme of the final paragraph of the section, where affirming a parallelism between the theoretical and the practical uses of reason, Kant locates the requisite antidote not simply in philosophy, or, as one might expect at this point, a metaphysics of morals, but in a "complete critique of our reason" (GMS 4: 405_{34-35}). Kant begins his case for the need for such a critique by asserting that common human reason finds itself impelled on purely practical grounds to leave its home terrain and take a step into practical philosophy "in order to receive information and clear direction regarding the source of its principle and its correct determination in contrast with maxims based on need and inclination" Such information, Kant continues, is necessary, in order for common human reason to escape from its perplexity regarding the claims of both sides and therefore to "avoid being deprived of all genuine ethical principles through the ambiguity into which it easily falls" (GMS 4: 405_{24-30}). And from this Kant concludes that even common human practical reason, "when it cultivates itself" [*wenn sie sich*

---

[38] On this point see Beck (1960, 240 n7).

kultiviert] finds itself enmeshed in a dialectic, which, as noted above, can only be put to rest by a complete critique of reason (GMS 4: 405₃₀₋₃₅).

It is difficult to avoid concluding from this not only that Kant's assertion of the need for a critique to resolve the dialectical situation in which common human reason finds itself in its cultivated state is highly artificial, but also that it is in tension with central tenets of GMS. Beginning with the latter point, we have seen that when Kant discusses the need for moral philosophy in the Preface and again in GMS 2 he explicitly mentions a metaphysics of morals, understood as a pure or *a priori* moral philosophy, which serves as a bulwark against the threat of eudaemonism, rather than a critique. Although it is true that he also asserts that only a critique can provide an adequate foundation for such a metaphysics, he refers explicitly to a critique of pure practical reason rather than a "complete critique of reason," which certainly suggests one that encompasses both theoretical and practical reason. Moreover, in at least apparent contradiction with the passage presently under consideration, we have seen that he also says that such a critique is not as necessary in the practical as in the speculative use of reason because in the latter it is "entirely dialectical," whereas in the former it "can readily be brought to a great correctness and completeness" (GMS 4: 391₂₁₋₂₄). Finally, while Kant explicitly makes a transition to a critique of pure practical reason in GMS 3, this critique is devoted to grounding the categorical imperative rather to the concerns referred to in the last paragraph of GMS 1.

In fact, the two concerns that Kant points to as requiring a turn to philosophy on the part of common human reason, namely, establishing the source and providing the correct determination of its fundamental moral principle, are properly tasks for a metaphysics of morals, as Kant conceived it at the time. More specifically, chief among the tasks of such a metaphysics are to show that this principle is grounded in the very concept of a rational agent as such and to specify its formula (or formulas), which is presumably what Kant means by providing a correct determination of the principle. The latter is the central concern of GMS 2 and both are clearly beyond the capacity of common human reason as Kant conceived it. Accordingly, if in GMS 1 Kant assumed the role of a Socrates, serving in a maieutic manner to make common human reason aware of its principle, in GMS 2 he will function more as an Aristotle bringing coherence and completeness to the moral views of this same reason.

Why, then, does Kant call for a critique of reason rather than a metaphysics of morals, especially since the latter would have the added benefit of making possible a smooth transition to GMS 2? The answer appears to lie in Kant's characterization of the plight of common human reason as involving a "natural dialectic." Since it is a cardinal tenet of the critical philosophy that a dialectic requires a critique, the antidote to this particular dialectic must likewise lie in a critique. But herein lies the main source of the artificiality of Kant's account; for it is not clear that what he describes as a "natural dialectic" counts as a dialectic in the requisite sense. To be sure, it has one of the essential features of such a dialectic, namely, specious reasoning with the semblance of truth. At the same time, however, it lacks the seeming compellingness of the dialectical reasoning that Kant exposed in the first *Critique*, a compellingness that was due to the fact that it was rooted in the necessary, yet illusory, transcendental ideas. Moreover, since empirically conditioned practical reason is not itself dialectical, if there were a genuine dialectic at work here, it is difficult to see how it could consist in anything other than an antinomy between pure and empirically conditioned practical reason. But we have already noted that Kant does not characterize this conflict as an antinomy.[39]

Nevertheless, setting aside the artificiality of the appeal to either a natural dialectic or an antinomy, Kant's account of the plight of common human reason does provide the basis for a critique, if not one precisely of the kind that he appears to have proposed. Expressed in Kantian terminology, this could be described as a critique of the pretensions of an empirically conditioned practical reason in the service of the needs and inclination, when it seeks to assert its authority over practical reason as such, which includes pure practical reason.[40] The aim of this critique would be to demonstrate that, when it proceeds in this manner, empirical practical reason oversteps its proper boundaries by endeavoring to obfuscate the difference between it and pure practical reason. Not coincidentally, this also constitutes the Kantian charge against eudaemonism in all its forms, but particularly popular moral philosophy. Accordingly, read in this way, the final two paragraphs of GMS 1 may be taken as providing a transition to the topics of GMS 2 after all.

---

[39] It should be noted that, apart from the first *Critique*, a dialectic for Kant is always equated with an antinomy. For example, there are no paralogisms of pure practical reason, of aesthetic, or of teleological judgment. In the third *Critique* Kant does refer to an "ideal of beauty" (KU 5: 232–36; 116–20), but this is part of the Analytic of the Beautiful not the Dialectic.

[40] This corresponds to the first two theorems of the second *Critique*, where Kant mounts a similar critique of empirically conditioned practical reason (KpV 5: 21–26; 155–60).

PART III

GMS 2

6

Rational Agency and Imperatives

This is the first of four chapters dealing with the complex argument of GMS 2. As its title ("*Transition from popular moral philosophy to the metaphysics of morals*") indicates, this section commences with a critique of popular moral philosophy and proceeds to the exposition of the categorical imperative. As such, it is concerned with the first of the two tasks that Kant assigns to the work, namely, the search for the supreme principle of morality. But since we have seen that GMS 1 was likewise concerned with this task and culminated in a formulation of this principle, which is in all essentials equivalent to the initial formulation provided in GMS 2, this is not sufficient to account for the presence of the latter section in the work. As was noted in the Introduction, the problem is that, given Kant's own account of his task, the question naturally arises: why did Kant not proceed directly from GMS 1 to GMS 3, bypassing completely GMS 2. Although this would have resulted in a much shorter and less interesting work, it presumably would have sufficed to accomplish the systematic task that Kant assigned to the work as a whole.

This question admits of two answers. The first and most obvious is that it is only in GMS 2 that Kant introduces the principle of autonomy, which, as the culmination of the regressive argument of GMS 2, might be said to set the agenda for GMS 3. But while it is true that Kant's attempt to ground the categorical imperative in GMS 3 relies crucially on the assumption of the autonomy of the will, the fact that in the second *Critique* he derives autonomy directly from the analysis of this imperative, without the lengthy detour that he took in GMS, indicates that this answer is insufficient.[1]

I believe that the second and most important reason lies in the previously discussed claim regarding the modal status of whatever is to count as the supreme principle of morality, that is, its absolute necessity. That a principle has this status cannot be established by showing that it is implicit in, or presupposed by, common rational moral cognition, which is all that Kant claims to have shown in GMS 1. This is because such a result is perfectly compatible with the possibility that this principle is grounded in human nature or, as Kant puts it at one point, in "a particular direction of human reason" (GMS 4: 425_{20-21}), which would preclude the candidate-principle

---

[1] See KpV 5: 33; 166.

from possessing the requisite modal status. Demonstrating that the supreme principle of morality, now identified with the categorical imperative, has this status is therefore the central positive task of GMS 2.[2] And following the meta-ethical prescription specified in Chapter 1, Kant attempts to do this by deriving it from an analysis of the concept of a rational agent as such or, more precisely, the concept of a finite rational agent.

The situation is further complicated, however, by the fact that Kant does not stop with the initial derivation of the categorical imperative in its supposedly canonical form as the "Formula of Universal Law" (FUL). Instead, he proceeds to derive at least three formulas for (or formulations of) what he insists is a single categorical imperative: the Formula of the Law of Nature (FLN), the Formula of Humanity as an End in Itself (FH), and the Formula of Autonomy (FA) and its variant the Formula of the Realm of Ends (FRE).[3] Moreover, this raises the same question *within* GMS that we have just seen arises regarding GMS 2 as a whole, namely, what systematic purpose is served by the introduction of the additional formulas? Otherwise expressed, why could Kant not move directly from the derivation of FUL as *the* categorical imperative to GMS 3, thereby circumventing the lengthy and confusing account of these additional formulas? Once again, one might reply that Kant needed this to introduce his pivotal concept of autonomy; but, as already noted, his much more compact discussion in the second *Critique* shows that the introduction of further formulas was not required to achieve that end.[4]

Although it is only dealt with explicitly in Chapter 9, the answer to this question provides the organizing principle of the four chapters dealing with GMS 2. To anticipate, it will be argued that the various formulas express different stages in the complete construction of concept of the categorical imperative and that these stages

---

[2] The negative task is the critique of popular moral philosophy from which a transition to the metaphysics of morals is supposedly made in GMS 2. This is to be found primarily in the opening portion (GMS 4: 406_5–12_{25}) and the transition from FLN to FH 426_7–27_{18}). But having already discussed the main elements of this critique in Chapters 1 and 2, I shall not go over that ground again. Accordingly, the analysis will begin at the point at which Kant first articulates his conception of rational agency (GMS 4: 412_{26}), which is the true starting point of the positive or constructive portion of the argument.

[3] The number of formulas for the categorical imperative that Kant provides remains a subject of some dispute. In maintaining that there are only three formulas (properly speaking), I am following Kant's explicit statement on the topic (GMS 4: 436_{8-9}). In spite of this, Guyer (1998, 216 and 228–34) maintains that there are four, while Paton (1958, 129–32) famously insisted that there are five. The appearance of five is suggested by the fact that both the first and third come in two forms. More recently, Adrian Piper has claimed that there are thirty-two formulations of the fundamental principle of morality in GMS. See Piper (1997, 263). But the fundamental principle of morality cannot be identified with the categorical imperative and, as she notes, only four of these are in the imperative mood.

[4] The issue of the presence in GMS 2 of the additional formulas was posed in a sharp form by Duncan (1957). I shall discuss Duncan's views on this topic in some detail in Chapter 9. At present, I wish only to add that one cannot claim that Kant needed at least the formula of autonomy in order to arrive at the principle, since, as we shall also see in Chapter 9, the formula is not equivalent to the principle of the autonomy of the will, which Kant does need and which is found in the second *Critique* without any reference to the formula.

correspond to stages in a progressive analysis of the concept of a finite rational agent. On this reading, Kant remains true to his meta-ethical procedure; but the process of constructing the complete concept of the categorical imperative is complicated by the fact that the concept of finite rational agency, in which this concept is grounded, is itself complex, consisting of distinct layers, which Kant progressively uncovers, each of which is connected with a specific formula of the categorical imperative.

The present chapter is divided into three parts. The first examines Kant's generic analysis of rational agency, the distinction between perfectly and imperfectly rational agents, the connection between the latter species of agents and imperatives, and the distinction between hypothetical and categorical imperatives. The second analyzes Kant's account of the possibility of a hypothetical imperative as an "analytical-practical proposition" (GMS 4: 419$_{4-5}$). The third notes the peculiar difficulties that Kant found in accounting for the possibility of a categorical imperative, difficulties which led him to postpone a consideration of the issue until GMS 3, and analyzes Kant's treatment of the task that he undertook in its stead: the derivation of the categorical imperative from an analysis of the concept of such an imperative.

I

Kant's analysis of rational agency begins with the famous claim that,

Every thing in nature works according to laws. Only a rational being has the capacity to act *according to the representation* of laws, that is, according to principles, or a *will*. Since reason is required for the derivation of actions from laws, the will is nothing other than practical reason. (GMS 4: 412$_{26-30}$)

The first question posed by this passage concerns the nature of the laws according to the representation of which rational beings or, more properly, agents, act.[5] Inasmuch as by "laws" in the first sentence Kant means laws of nature, it might be thought that the term has the same meaning in the second sentence as well. On this view, the defining feature of rational agents is that they act according to their representation of laws of nature, as opposed simply to acting according to these laws themselves.[6] Although this has the advantages of being based on a literal reading of the text and attributing a consistent sense to "law" in these two sentences, it makes it impossible to understand

---

[5] Although the text says "has the capacity to act" [*Vermögen zu handlen*] rather than simply act, I take Kant's view to be that insofar as rational beings actually act, that is perform what could be called an action [*Handlung*], which is something that can be imputed, they do so according to their representation of laws. This is suggested by the contrast with every thing in nature, which Kant says "works" [not acts] according to laws. Accordingly, in what follows I shall usually omit reference to a capacity to act and speak simply of acting. In theoretical contexts, however, Kant uses "*Handlung*" in a broader sense, which does not involve reference to choice. See, for example, KrV A204–5/B249–50.

[6] Such a reading has been advocated by Cramer (1972, 168n). For a useful survey of the literature on this point to which the present discussion is indebted see Laberge (1989).

the argument based upon this account of rational agency, the ultimate goal of which is the formulation of the moral law in its imperatival form. Moreover, while it is certainly true that rational agents sometimes act according to their representation of laws of nature, for example, when one endeavors to decide whether a particular course of action is physically possible, dangerous, or the like, this could hardly be viewed as the defining feature of rational agency.

Since the *terminus ad quem* of Kant's analysis is the formulation of the categorical imperative, a more likely candidate for the laws according to the representation of which rational agents supposedly act would be moral laws.[7] This reading finds further support in the fact that Kant's official view is that among practical principles only the categorical imperative (or moral law) counts as a practical *law*.[8] As the ensuing discussion makes clear, however, this reading is too narrow; for in spite of his official view Kant here uses the term "laws" in a broad sense as equivalent to objective practical principles, which include instrumentally as well as morally practical principles.[9]

A third possibility is to identify the practical laws in question with maxims. In addition to capturing the notion of acting on principles, which is Kant's gloss on acting according to the representation of laws, this reading appears to leave room for a more unified and broader view of rational agency. And since maxims are freely adopted by agents, this reading has the virtue of placing practical spontaneity or freedom at the heart of Kant's account.[10] Unfortunately, however, this likewise raises several exegetical difficulties. (1) Kant repeatedly contrasts laws as objective practical principles with maxims as subjective ones.[11] (2) He links maxims, together with interests and incentives specifically with finite, imperfectly rational agents, whereas the characterization of rational agency presently under consideration presumably applies to rational agency in general, which encompasses the infinite (a perfect or holy will) as well as the finite variety.[12] (3) Kant speaks of rational agents acting according to their *representation* of

---

[7]   This is the view of Duncan (1957, 103).

[8]   See GMS 4: 420$_{3-6}$ and KpV 5: 5: 20; 154. In both texts Kant regards other (non-moral) practical principles as "practical precepts" [*praktische Vorschriften*] rather than laws.

[9]   In order to avoid unnecessary complications and to capture the actual progress of Kant's argument, I am using "instrumentally practical" and "instrumental reason" in a broad sense to encompass both instrumental reasoning in the narrow sense (means–end reasoning) and prudential or what Kant also terms "pragmatic" reasoning, which as concerned with the attainment of happiness involves the choice of certain ends as well as means. This distinction will become relevant when Kant introduces the distinction between two types of hypothetical imperative, which govern these two forms of reasoning.

[10]   Such a reading was adopted by Paton (1958, 80–81), Bittner (1974), and Allison (1990, 86).

[11]   Kant does, however, on occasion refer to "subjective laws," which he identifies with maxims (see, for example, *Ethik*, 52: 43; P 9: 481; 469).

[12]   See KpV 5: 79; 204. As Laberge (1989, 88) points out, however, Kant is not completely consistent on this point, since elsewhere in the second *Critique* he says of a holy will that it is incapable of any maxim conflicting with the moral law (KpV 5: 32; 165), which implies that such a will may be thought of as acting on maxims.

laws and it seems awkward to speak of acting according to the representation of maxims rather than simply according to or on the basis of them.[13]

Given the framework in which Kant's analysis operates, this leaves us with objective practical principles (both moral and instrumental) as the most viable candidates for the "laws" referred to in the second sentence.[14] By characterizing these principles as "objective" Kant means that they are valid for every rational being as such (GMS 4: 413_{24}). They are contrasted with maxims or subjective principles, which are valid only for the agent who adopts them. As valid for every rational being, these principles apply to a holy or perfectly rational as well as to finite, imperfectly rational agents.[15] The difference is that with respect to the former they are descriptive laws, characterizing the *modus operandi* of such agents, while with respect to the latter they are prescriptive laws expressed in imperatival form.[16] In the latter case, these principles (both moral and instrumental) are intimately related to maxims; since they prescribe the norms according to which finite rational agents *ought to* (but do not always) choose their maxims and actions. I shall return to this topic below.

---

[13] This last objection is also noted by Laberge (1989, 87–88), but he points out that it can be easily countered by transforming "representation of laws" into "laws represented," the point being that it is intelligible to speak of an agent as acting in accordance with the representation (consciousness) of its maxims. As we saw in Chapter 3, however, this (reflective) consciousness is not a necessary condition of acting under a maxim.

[14] Recent commentators who affirm this reading include Timmermann (2007a, 60) and Willaschek (2006, 125).

[15] By attempting to characterize rational agency in perfectly general terms referring to both moral and instrumental practical rationality and connecting it with principles that apply to both holy and finite wills, Kant might be thought guilty of precisely the same error of which he accused the universal practical philosophy of the Wolffians. In fact, this objection has been raised by Bittner (1989, 21). Moreover, while not putting it in the form of an objection, Laberge has insisted that, because of its generality, the Kantian text currently under consideration must be assigned to universal practical philosophy, which he links closely with popular moral philosophy, rather than to a metaphysics of morals, which, in turn, leads him to challenge the view (to which I adhere) that this text marks the beginning of the transition from popular moral philosophy to the metaphysics of morals. See Laberge (1980 and 1989). I believe, however, that this line of interpretation, whether it is viewed as critique or simply as exegesis, misses the essential points of difference to which Kant alludes in the Preface and were discussed in Chapter 2. To begin with, while it is true that Kant, like the Wolffians, begins with a consideration of agency or volition in general, he makes a decisive break with the Wolffian program with the sharp distinction between the two types of practical principles and, with respect to finite rational agents, their corresponding manners of constraint. In the case of moral principles, it is the latter that opens up the conceptual space for the notion of a "pure will," that is, one whose motivating ground lies in an *a priori* principle that is totally independent of inclination, which, as we have seen, Kant charges the Wolffians with ignoring. Moreover, Kant could charge the Wolffians with not being universal enough, since we have also seen that they limit their analysis to the *human* will, not considering the will of other finite rational agents. This explains their reliance upon empirical psychological principles, which Kant eschews.

[16] It might seem strange to think of a holy will as concerned with a mere instrumental rationality, which is why the expression "perfectly rational" here seems more appropriate. Nevertheless, if we think of God as creator and providential governor of the universe, we must also regard him as having ends and choosing the best conceivable means to these ends. A problem remains, however, regarding pragmatic principles or principles of prudence, which, as concerned with the furtherance or attainment of one's own happiness, are difficult (to say the least) to attribute to a divine being. For a discussion of this point, see Timmermann (2007a, 62–63, n27).

The second question posed by the above-cited passage is the meaning and import of its claim that, in contrast to every thing in nature, rational agents act according to their *representation* of laws rather than merely according to laws. In order to understand this claim, it is useful to consider it against the backdrop of Kant's distinction between an *arbitrium brutum* and an *arbitrium liberum*, which he drew in his in his lectures on ethics and was first discussed in Chapter 2, and then in Chapter 4 in connection with the incorporation thesis. With regard to the first, we saw that the distinction between the two species of *arbitria*, which resembles but is distinct from Baumgarten's distinction between an *arbitrium sensitivum* and an *arbitrium liberum*, is intended to contrast two radically distinct forms of necessitation: pathological and practical.[17] The former, which pertains to the *arbitrium brutum*, is causally determinative and therefore leaves no room for choice. The latter, by contrast, does leave room for choice, since even though the human will is pathologically, that is, sensuously affected, it is not pathologically determined. What the formulation in terms of the distinction between working (or occurring) according to laws and the representation of laws effectively does is to subsume the notion of an *arbitrium brutum* under the generic label "every thing in nature," thereby further accentuating the uniqueness in the scheme of things of rational beings.

For its part, the incorporation thesis provides the conceptual underpinning for both distinctions and therefore for Kant's coextensive conceptions of free will and rational agency. Seen in light of this thesis, we can understand acting according to one's *representation* of laws to consist in an agent taking or recognizing a law (in the broad sense of an objective practical principle) as normative for him because it is normative for every other rational agent in relevantly similar circumstances or, more simply, because it is a law (again in the broad sense). In other words, to act according to one's representation of laws is to act in light of recognized norms, which Kant equates with acting on principles; though in the case of finite rational agents this does not guarantee obedience to the laws or principles in question.

The above-cited passage also indicates that to be governed by laws in this sense is what it means to have a will, which Kant here identifies with practical reason. Again, this identification applies to rational agents in general; whereas talk of practical reason determining (or failing to determine) the will applies only to the finite variety. Kant attempts to clarify the matter by distinguishing between two ways in which reason can determine the will: invariably [*unausbleiblich*] or not invariably. In the first case, actions that are recognized as "objectively necessary," that is, as dictated by reason, are also "subjectively necessary," which means that there are no countervailing incentives that might lead an agent to act contrary to them (GMS 4: 412_{30-34}). The will of such an

---

[17] For the radical difference between the Kantian and Baumgartian views, which is partially masked by their terminological similarity, see Chapter 2, note 37.

agent is perfectly good or holy (GMS 414_{1-8}).[18] In the second case, this invariability is lacking, because the will is subject to various incentives, which may run counter to what in the eyes of reason is deemed objectively necessary. Consequently, for such a will what is objectively necessary is subjectively contingent. As such, it is subject to constraint or *necessitation* [*Nötigung*], which Kant characterizes as "the relation of objective laws to a will which is not thoroughly good" (GMS 4: 413_{4-6}).

Since the human and indeed every conceivable finite will falls into the latter category, it is subject to necessitation. Kant explains what this involves in a one-sentence paragraph containing two stipulative definitions:

The representation of an objective principle, insofar as it is necessitating for a will is called a command (of reason) and the formula of the command is called [an] *imperative*. (GMS 4: 413_{9-11})

As Kant proceeds to make clear in the next paragraph, the defining feature of a command of reason is that it is directed at something that is regarded as good (though not necessarily morally good) on the basis of objective grounds of reason, that is, on grounds that are valid for every rational being. As such, the good is distinguished from the agreeable, which is determined by subjective causes (sensations) rather than objective grounds of reason. Although this might appear to suggest that nothing agreeable could also be deemed good, this is clearly not Kant's view. His point is rather that the agreeable is not considered good simply qua being agreeable, since many agreeable things (e.g., a juicy steak for someone suffering from gout) could be quite harmful and, conversely, many disagreeable things good. When endorsed by reason, however, something agreeable (e.g., the same steak for a healthy and hungry carnivore) is deemed good, though, again, not morally good.[19]

In view of complications that will emerge later, Kant's characterization of an imperative as the *formula* of a command rather than simply as a command calls for comment. The German "*Formel*," like its English counterpart, is a rendering of the Latin "*formula*" and it can signify, among other things, "norm," "rule," and "formula-tion."[20] Although in various places Kant uses this term in all of these senses and others as well, we shall see that, at least with regard to moral principles, the primary sense in which he uses it is the mathematical, where a formula serves as a rule for solving a problem. Nevertheless, in the present context, where Kant is considering the generic concept of an imperative and has not yet introduced the categorical-hypothetical distinction, it seems reasonable to take the term as equivalent to "formulation."

---

[18] In GMS this applies only to the divine will; whereas elsewhere Kant refers in passing to the concept of a finite holy being, understood as one which could never be tempted to violate duty (MS 6: 383; 515). In GMS, however, Kant refers at one point to an "absolutely good will," understood as one that can never be evil (GMS 4: 437_{6-8}).

[19] Kant's fullest accounts of the relation between the good and the agreeable are in KpV5: 58; 186 and KU 5: 205–9; 91–94.

[20] I am here following Schönecker and Wood (2004, 125).

In other words, an imperative is the formula of a command of reason in the sense of being its verbal expression or articulation. Moreover, basically the same may be said about Kant's comment two paragraphs later that "imperatives are only formulas expressing the relation of objective laws of volition in general to the will of this or that rational being, e.g., to the human will" (GMS 4: 414$_{8-11}$). As the latter passage indicates, an imperative does not differ from a practical law or objective principle of reason in its content but in its mood or illocutionary force.

The introduction of the concept of an imperative as the form that practical principles governing finite rational agents take prepares the way for the now classical distinction between a hypothetical and a categorical imperative. Given Kant's distinction between categorical and hypothetical judgments in his table of judgment forms in the first *Critique* (KrV A70/B95), it is tempting to interpret his distinction between the two types of imperative in light of it. As has often been pointed out, however, the latter distinction has nothing to do with grammatical (or logical) form, since a moral imperative can be expressed in a hypothetical form and a non-moral one in a categorical form. Rather, as Kant understands the distinction, it is adverbial in nature; it concerns *how* an imperative commands rather than *what* it commands.[21] As Kant puts it, "all imperatives command either hypothetically or categorically" (GMS 4: 414$_{12-13}$). To command hypothetically is to command under a condition, which is some actual or possible end of an agent. To command categorically or unconditionally is to command independently of any such end. Moreover, these two ways of commanding are correlated with two senses of the good: the good as a means to something else and that which is good *in itself* (GMS 4: 414$_{22-24}$).

This distinction between the two ways in which an imperative can command underscores two central features of Kant's account. The first is that end-setting is an essential feature of rational agency. With the partial exception of happiness (to be discussed further below), rational agents do not simply have ends given to them by nature, they make something their end through an act of freedom. Kant only makes this connection between agency and end-setting explicit with his derivation of the second formula of the categorical imperative (GMS 4: 427$_{19-24}$); but it is already implicit in his foundational claim that all such agents act on the basis of their representation of laws. The basic point is that these laws or, more precisely, principles, guide finite rational agents in their adoption of maxims, which themselves always involve setting an end and choosing the appropriate means to this end.[22] The second essential

---

[21] On this point, see Beck (1965, 178) and among more recent treatments Ludwig (2006, 141–42).

[22] My suggestion that "principles" is more appropriate than "laws" here, in spite of Kant's characterization of rational agency, is based upon the fact that Kant connects the notion of a *practical* law explicitly with a categorical imperative, while characterizing the rules embedded in hypothetical imperatives as principles rather than laws on the ground that what is necessary for the attainment of a discretionary aim is itself contingent (GMS 4: 420$_{3-11}$).

feature is, as already noted, that a categorical imperative, if there is one, would command independently of any of an agent's pre-given ends.[23]

II

After drawing the contrast between hypothetical and categorical imperatives, Kant poses the predictable question: "How are all these imperatives possible?" (GMS 4: 417_3). As Kant makes clear, he is here raising a conceptual rather than a psychological question and what requires explanation is how to conceive the constraint or necessitation imposed upon volition by an imperative. Otherwise expressed, the problem is for any imperative that commands x, to explain why (on what rational grounds) one *ought* to x. To supply these grounds is to account for the possibility of the imperative in question. We shall see in the next section that there are peculiar difficulties involved in doing this in the case of the categorical imperative; but our present concern is mainly with hypothetical imperatives, where this difficulty allegedly does not arise.

To begin with, though all hypothetical imperatives are directives to will something deemed necessary as a means to a presupposed end, Kant distinguishes between two kinds of hypothetical imperative, which turns on the nature of the ends involved: arbitrary ends, which are based on an agent's contingent ends at a particular time, and happiness, which is a necessary and therefore non-arbitrary natural end. This distinction reflects two peculiarities of Kant's conception of happiness as an end. First, unlike other ends, happiness is one that we necessarily have as finite beings with a sensuous as well as a rational nature, since it is supposedly given to us by nature (GMS 4: 415_{28-33} and 430_{19}).[24] Second, also unlike other ends, it is indeterminate in the sense that it is essentially a place-holder for the satisfaction of the sum-total of an agent's desires (GMS 4: 418_{1-4}).[25] Inasmuch as happiness on Kant's view is an end that one cannot simply abandon, the imperative to will the means necessary to attain it, might seem to be categorical in nature. What makes it merely hypothetical is its indeterminacy, which means that agents largely define it for themselves. As a result, principles dictating the

---

[23] We shall see, however, that Kant does not view this as incompatible with the view that the categorical imperative can itself be the source of ends.

[24] Although Kant is not terribly clear on this point, the basic idea behind the unique status given to happiness as a natural and necessary end seems to be that, in addition to a reason that is practical, finite rational agents, like other sensuously affected but not rational beings, that is, animals, have a "faculty of desire" [*Begehrungsvermögen*], which Kant defines as "the faculty to be, by means of one's representations, the cause of these representations" (MS 6: 211; 373). (For similar definitions see also KrV 5: 9n, 144; KU 5: 178n, 65; A7: 251, 353). And since such beings have a sensuous as well as a rational nature, the former is the source of desires, which, as inherent in this nature, are ineliminable and, within the limits prescribed by the categorical imperative, legitimately demand satisfaction. Accordingly, Kant consistently and strenuously rejects the view that morality requires the abandonment of the pursuit of happiness, insisting instead that it requires its subordination to moral requirements, when there is a conflict between the two. Perhaps Kant's clearest statement on this point is in his response to Garve, who had accused him of holding just such a view. See TP 8: 278–79; 281–82.

[25] See also KpV 5: 25; 159.

means for the attainment of happiness lack necessity and therefore full imperatival status, a point which Kant makes by characterizing them as "*counsels* of prudence" (GMS 4: 416_{19}).

In an effort to introduce a systematic ordering into his account of imperatives, Kant characterizes the various imperatives in terms of the functions of modality from his table of the logical functions of judgment in the first *Critique*. Thus, he suggests that the first kind commands *problematically* (since the end involved is arbitrary); the second *assertorically* (since the end is willed by all finite rational agents); and the third *apodictically* (since it commands independently of any end and therefore unconditionally) (GMS 4: 415_{1-4}). The first two correspond to the two types of hypothetical imperative distinguished above and the third to the categorical imperative. Kant also characterizes hypothetical imperatives of the first type of as both "imperatives of skill" and as "technical imperatives," and notes that they abstract from the morality of the end and apply only to the use of means to attain it (GMS 4: 415_{13-15}). In addition to "*counsels* of prudence" Kant terms hypothetical imperatives of the second type "pragmatic," which he connects closely with prudence (GMS 4: 417_1 and note$_{32-37}$); while he calls the third or categorical imperative the "imperative of morality" (GMS 4: 416_{13-14}).[26]

Since it seems evident that Kant introduced the concept of a hypothetical imperative primarily as a means to highlight the uniqueness of the categorical imperative and the peculiar difficulty in grounding it rather than as part of an attempt to present a self-standing systematic account of instrumental reasoning, I do not intend to examine his account in great detail.[27] Nevertheless, this account does raise a number of important questions of which I shall discuss four. The first concerns the analyticity of the proposition which allegedly grounds hypothetical imperatives of all types.[28] The

---

[26] It should be noted, however, that Kant later rejected this tripartite taxonomy of imperatives. Thus, in a footnote to his account of the conception of a "technic of nature" [*Technik der Natur*], in the first Introduction to the third *Critique*, Kant acknowledges having erred in GMS in calling imperatives of skill problematic, since the notion of commanding problematically involves a contradiction in terms. Instead, he states that he wishes them to be called *technical* imperatives. Kant further claims that, even though pragmatic imperatives (those concerning happiness) presuppose an actual and subjectively necessary end, they should be subsumed under technical imperatives on the grounds that prudence is nothing other than "the skill of a being to use for one's intentions free human beings and among these even the natural dispositions and inclinations in oneself" (FI 20: 200; 7). In the end, then, Kant seems to have affirmed a binary classification of imperatives, where the crucial point is that the categorical imperative commands unconditionally and all others under some condition. Moreover, in his latest systematic treatment of the topic, Kant gives clear expression to the binary view, dividing all imperatives into categorical or unconditional and technical or conditional (MS 6: 222; 377).

[27] For an insightful discussion of this topic, see O'Neill (1989, 89–94), where she argues, persuasively that the principle of the hypothetical imperative, which I term GP, is merely one, though perhaps the most important one, of "a family of Principles of Rational Intending" (op. cit., 91). Another virtue of O'Neill's brief discussion is that she uses her discussion of the hypothetical imperative and its principle to introduce the idea of a contradiction in the will, which is clearly the key to understanding the categorical imperative.

[28] Kant claims that "The imperatives of prudence would likewise be analytic and in complete agreement with those of skill, if only it were so easy to give a determinate concept of happiness. For here, as there, it would be said: whoever wills the end also wills (necessarily in accordance with reason) the sole means to it that are in his control" (GMS 4: $417_{27}-18_1$).

second is how it grounds such imperatives. The third is whether the imperatives it grounds are themselves analytic. The fourth is whether we may speak of a generic hypothetical imperative, corresponding to the categorical imperative, or merely of an indefinite number of hypothetical imperatives.

(A) The grounding principle and its analyticity

According to Kant, all hypothetical imperatives are grounded in the analytic principle: "Whoever wills the end, also wills (insofar as reason has decisive influence on his action) the means that are indispensably necessary to it that are in his power" (GMS 4: 417_{8-10}). Because of its function, I shall henceforth refer to this as the grounding principle (GP). The first point to be made is that GP does not contain any reference to an "ought." Instead, it describes the behavior of an agent who wills an end and for whom "reason has decisive influence on his action." As such, it is descriptive rather than prescriptive. I shall return to the latter point below.

The second point is that, rather than declaring *tout court* that GP is analytic, Kant specifies that it is analytic only "as far as volition is concerned" (GMS 4: 417_{10-11}). As his subsequent explanation indicates, Kant means by this that it is based on an analysis of what is contained in the thought of willing an end. According to Kant, this involves conceiving of oneself as a causal agent; and the claim is that one cannot conceive of oneself as such without also conceiving of oneself as using the necessary means to bring about the object of volition, that is, the desired end (GMS 4: 417_{11-14}). Kant clearly intended this to be taken as a tautology and he provides his clearest expression of the tautologous nature of the claim, when he notes that "to represent something as an effect possible though me in a certain way and to represent myself, in regard to it, as acting in the same way are one and the same" (GMS 4: 417_{24-26}).

The third feature of GP that calls for comment is its parenthetical qualifying clause: "insofar as reason has decisive influence on his action." This suggests that, far from denying that, as a matter of either psychological fact or logic, one could will an end without also willing the necessary means, he is merely denying that one could do so insofar as one's volition is governed by reason. Moreover, this accords with our experience that people all too often appear to do precisely that, as well as with Kant's underlying thesis that for finite rational agents what is objectively necessary is subjectively contingent.

The problem, however, is that, since there is supposedly a contradiction in the very concept of willing an end without also willing the necessary means, it is difficult to see what bearing reason having (or lacking) a decisive influence has on the matter. One could claim that reason would prevent one from engaging in such an inherently futile project in the first place; but this does not appear to create conceptual space for the possibility of an agent for whom reason did not have decisive influence actually *willing* an end without willing the requisite means.

In attempting to deal with this problem, I shall begin with a consideration of what Kant understood by reason having (or failing to have) decisive influence [*entscheidenden*

Einfluss] on the will. Although Kant does not elaborate, there appear to be two possibilities. The first and most obvious is that reason controls impulses to act in ways that run counter to its dictates. Such a scenario is most familiar in the moral context, when there is a conflict between duty and inclination; but it also occurs in purely prudential situations. In such cases, reason failing to have decisive influence would typically involve agents subordinating their long-term interests to the attainment of present gratification, which might have deleterious consequences. And since agents supposedly cannot abandon their long-term interest (happiness), since the pursuit of it is built into their nature, this appears to fit the description of a case in which the agent wills the end but not the necessary means to that end.

The second possibility is epistemic: an agent does not know the requisite means but endeavors to pursue an end anyway. For example, I attempt to perform a certain operation on my computer with only the vaguest idea of what is required. As a result, I waste several hours trying various possibilities, until I give up in disgust. This, too, might be viewed as a case of willing the end without willing the requisite means because reason did not exercise a decisive influence; though in this case reason's influence would have led me not to will the end until I knew what was required to accomplish it.

In considering the mathematical problem of bisecting a line, Kant introduces two further conditions on the analyticity of GP, when he notes that, even though mathematics teaches this through synthetic propositions, it is an analytic proposition that "if I know that the specified effect could occur only through such an action, if I fully [*vollständig*] will the effect, I would also will the action that is required for it" (GMS 4: 417_{21-23}). These conditions are: (1) that the agent must have knowledge that the end in question could not be attained apart from a particular course of action; and (2) that the agent must fully or completely [*vollständig*] will the end. As already noted, if an agent lacked knowledge of the requisite means to a given end, that agent could still be said to will that end without also willing the means. And, as also noted, this might likewise be considered a case of reason not having decisive influence.[29]

The really interesting condition, however, is the second, which again Kant does not bother to explain. Nevertheless, it seems reasonable to assume that by willing an end, but not willing it fully or completely, is to be understood as a situation in which an agent makes something less than a full commitment to the end in question. Here the agent presumably must take *some* steps toward realizing this end; otherwise it would be a matter of merely wishing for or desiring, which require no action on the agent's part, rather than willing the end.[30] But it is also not only possible, but all too common, for an agent to do less than is required actually to attain the end. For example, I make the proverbial New Year's resolution to lose weight and improve my overall physical

---

[29] This epistemic reading of reason's failure to have a decisive influence is suggested by Ludwig (2006, 149).

[30] On the distinction between wishing and willing, see Chapter 3, note 4.

condition through a regular exercise program. After reflecting on my age and condition, I decide that the best form of exercise would be on a stationary bike. To this end, I purchase such a bike, resolutely install it in my bedroom, and begin a program of exercise. But, as invariably happens, after a few weeks I find myself using it with increasingly less regularity, discovering reasons such as my busy schedule, fatigue, and the like not to use it on a given day. I do not simply stop using the bike altogether, since that would mean abandoning the end; rather, I use it much less frequently and with little benefit. In such a case, I may be said to have willed the end but not *fully* willed it. And it may also be said that reason did not exert a *decisive* influence on my will, where "decisive" means sufficient to resist the temptations to abandon the course that reason prescribes.

If the preceding is correct, it puts us in a position to formulate somewhat more precisely the complex analytical proposition, which supposedly grounds all hypothetical imperatives, namely, "If A fully wills E and knows that M is indispensably necessary for E and M is in its power, then A will M." I shall call this GP_1. It differs from Kant's GP in that the reason exerting decisive influence condition drops out on this formulation, since its force is captured by the fully willing the end and knowledge of the indispensably necessary means conditions.[31]

Finally, it should not be objected, as is sometimes done, that hypothetical propositions cannot be analytic for Kant because his official criterion for analyticity, namely, the predicate being contained in the concept of the subject, is applicable only to categorical propositions. As Kant makes clear in the *Prolegomena*, the distinction between analytic and synthetic judgments concerns their content rather than their logical form (Pro 4: 266; 62). Accordingly, propositions in the hypothetical form can be analytic: for example, "If the soul is material, it is extended."[32]

(B) The relationship between GP_1 and hypothetical imperatives

Simply put, the problem is to explain how a proposition containing an ought-operator can be derived from or grounded in one (GP_1) that does not.[33] The proposed solution, which, like most such endeavors, is an attempt to provide Kant with an argument that he never bothered to develop, consists of two main steps. The first is to note that, even though it is not prescriptive, GP_1 is normative. This is essential because it makes it possible for this principle to ground prescriptions without itself being prescriptive.

---

[31] It should also be noted that by the "indispensably necessary means" is to be understood merely the necessary set of causal conditions, that is, the *conditio sine qua non*, not the (in some respect) optimal means. For a number of reasons (including moral ones) an agent might not choose what, from the point of view of sheer efficiency, is the optimal means to a given end, yet still fully will the end. The point is noted by Seel (1989, 154). I believe that Seel expresses the matter somewhat misleadingly, however, when he contrasts the *conditio sine qua non* with the *sufficient* condition. Clearly, for Kant, if an agent fully wills an end that agent also wills the means sufficient to produce it; though these need not be the optimal means.

[32] I discuss this issue in Allison (2004, 90–91). The fullest discussion of this issue in the literature, particularly with regard to its bearing on practical propositions, is by Patzig (1966).

[33] The problem is concisely expressed in these terms by Seel (1989, 166–67).

We have already encountered the difference between normativity and prescriptivity in the preceding chapter in connection with the derivation of the principle of morality in GMS 1 and we shall return to it in the last section of the present chapter in the analysis of the derivation of the categorical imperative in GMS 2. For present purposes, the essential point is that normativity in the practical domain applies to what is deemed good or bad, whereas prescriptivity applies to what one ought or ought not to do. Since what one ought to do is always what is deemed good and what one ought not to do is what is deemed bad, it is usually assumed that these overlap; what is normative in every case providing the grounds for a prescription. For Kant, however, the situation is more complicated, since his conception of a perfectly good or holy will is clearly normative, inasmuch as it concerns what is good in the highest respect, but it is also descriptive rather than prescriptive, since it describes how such a will necessarily acts (according to the moral law) rather than prescribing how it ought to act in order to be perfectly good or holy. Accordingly, for Kant there can be normativity without prescriptivity, though not the converse.

The present suggestion is simply that normativity without prescriptivity is also found outside the moral domain. In particular, it seems reasonable to assign a normative status to GP_1 with regard to instrumental rationality, even though, lacking the inclusion of an ought, it is not prescriptive. In fact, as the analogue of the normative yet descriptive moral law, in contrast to the prescriptive categorical imperative, GP_1 may be regarded as the formula for an absolutely good (rational) will in the instrumental sense.[34]

Even granting this, however, a second step is required in order to account for the presence and function of the ought-operator in imperatives grounded in GP_1. Although the most natural approach is to view this "ought" and the necessitation of the will it expresses as imposed upon an agent from without in the manner of a legal statute, the problem is that, like GP_1, legal statutes do not contain an "ought" or its equivalent. For example, the law dictates that everyone *must* stop at a red light; it does not say that they *ought* to stop, which in the context would suggest something weaker than a command, perhaps more like a recommendation.[35] The "ought" or necessitation arises not from the law itself but from the agents in their self-conscious relation to the law. In this sense, then, it could be claimed that even hypothetical imperatives presuppose something like autonomy or at least the necessity for a rational endorsement. We have also seen that this is built into the notion of acting according to one's representation of laws.

---

[34] Assuming that a perfectly rational or holy being would also be omniscient and omnipotent, the fully wills, knowledge of means, and the means being in the agent's power requirements would be redundant. Consequently, the principle could be formulated simply as "If A wills E and M is indispensably necessary for E, then A will M." We need not here be concerned, however, with this subtlety.

[35] During the time in which I lived there, it was a standing joke in the Boston area that Boston drivers view traffic regulations as "recommendations" rather than laws that must be obeyed. From what I gather, things have not changed since I left the area.

It follows from this that, in order to understand the "ought" embedded in hypothetical imperatives, which is what is required in order to account for their possibility, we must approach the matter from the standpoint of a finite rational agent, who is its addressee.[36] This is necessary because every ought-proposition (whether hypothetical or categorical) is addressed to such an agent. But since we are presently concerned only with hypothetical imperatives, we must consider what is required in order for such agents to become or, more precisely, to take themselves as addressees of such an imperative. And when viewed in this way, the answer seems obvious. Rather than being directly imposed upon an agent by the law, the "ought" is introduced by an agent posing the question: "What should I do?" Since we are concerned with hypothetical imperatives, it must be assumed that the question is motivated by the agent's desire for some end (E) and that what is being asked is how to proceed in order to attain this end. In other words, the agent is asking about the means required for E, which means that GP_1 is already presupposed in the question; otherwise the question (at least in this form) would have no sense.[37]

Finally, this indicates that, given GP_1, the necessitation on the agent to M stems ultimately from the agent wanting E, together with the fact that the agent knows (or believes) that M is indispensably necessary for E. Moreover, if this is correct, the agent's bit of instrumentally practical reasoning could best be expressed as: "*Since* I want E and M is the indispensably necessary means to E, I *must* M." The point of substituting "since" for "if" in the schematic rendering is to underscore the locus of the necessitation on the agent's will; while the substitution of "must" for "ought" gives expression to this necessity. If the agent were simply to think, "If I were to will E, I would also have to will M," there would no constraint or necessitation, merely the consideration of a hypothetical theoretical proposition regarding a means–end relation. Although this leaves the agent free to abandon the pursuit of E on either moral or prudential grounds, which would then free the agent from the constraint, this has no bearing on the presence of the necessitation under the condition that the agent wills E, which is what a hypothetical imperative expresses.[38]

---

[36] In approaching the issue from the point of view of the addressee of a hypothetical imperative I have been influenced by the paper of McCarthy (1979). I differ from McCarthy, however, who was himself influenced by Patzig (1966), in rejecting his thesis that practical propositions, which express necessitation, are reducible, via the concept of necessitation, to theoretical propositions which do not (op. cit. 387 and 391 n28). On my reading, rather than being reducible to theoretical propositions, practical propositions make an ineliminable appeal to a normative principle, which in the case of those expressing hypothetical imperatives is GP_1.

[37] The parenthetical phrase "at least in this form" is intended to indicate that the question might also be taken in a moral sense, in which case the agent's desire for some end would not be the determining factor.

[38] For this reason I question the view expressed by Hill (1992, 24) that, properly construed, what he terms "the hypothetical imperative" should be stated as presenting the agent with an option: "Take the necessary means or else give up the end." To acknowledge that one can free oneself from the necessitation imposed by a hypothetical imperative by abandoning the end is not to say that the option of abandoning the end should be built into the imperative. In addition, it appears that an imperative formulated in these disjunctive terms would be categorical rather than hypothetical. The first part of this criticism has also been expressed by

(C) Are hypothetical imperatives analytic?

Does the fact that their principle (GP_1) is analytic entail that the imperatives themselves are analytic? This question arises because, even though on more than one occasion Kant characterizes hypothetical imperatives as analytic, there appear to be at least two reasons for thinking that they cannot be.[39] The first is semantic: since imperatives are not propositions, it is difficult to see how they (whether hypothetical or categorical) could be *either* analytic *or* synthetic. The second is suggested by the above analysis of hypothetical imperatives Since in addition to the analytic GP_1, we have seen that these imperatives presuppose factual information concerning both the addressee's desires and the means required to satisfy them, it would seem that, if they are anything they must be synthetic. Accordingly, so the argument goes, Kant's remarks concerning the analyticity of hypothetical imperatives must either be taken in a very loose sense or viewed as referring only to GP_1.[40]

In order to deal with the first of these objections, we must consider what Kant meant when he referred to such imperatives as analytic. An examination of the text indicates that what Kant actually regarded as analytic are practical propositions corresponding to the imperatives, rather than the imperatives themselves, considered as commands. Thus, in contrasting the imperative of prudence with that of skill, Kant notes that the former would be an "analytic-practical proposition," if only the means to happiness could be specified with certainty (GMS 4: 419_{3-5}). This implies that the imperative of skill is such a proposition and that the imperative of prudence is only prevented from being one by its anomalous nature, which actually prevents it from being a genuine imperative at all. Similarly, Kant refers to the categorical imperative as a "synthetic-practical proposition *a priori*" (GMS 4: 420_{14}). All of this strongly suggests that by a practical proposition Kant understands one that contains an "ought," or its equivalent, which makes it action guiding or prescriptive. Consequently, propositions of the form: "You ought to x" or "If you want y, you ought to x" would count as imperatives in Kant's sense, even though they have propositional form and are not, grammatically speaking commands.[41] Moreover, it is their propositional form that enables these "imperatives" to be either analytic or synthetic, which can be made explicit by expressing them in the "It is the case that you (or one) ought to . . ." mode.

Assuming that when Kant characterized hypothetical imperatives as analytic, he had in mind such practical propositions, which qua propositions could be either analytic or synthetic, the next question is why, given their already noted empirical conditions, he claimed that they were analytic. The short answer is that, as practical, they are analytic only "as far as volition is concerned." From this point of view, which is that of the

---

Timmermann (2007a, 70), who remarks that, "It is not the purpose of a hypothetical or any other kind of imperative to 'leave us options.'"

[39] Kant characterizes hypothetical imperatives as analytic at GMS 4: 4: 417_{27}–18_1; 419_{3-4}; 419_{8-10}.

[40] This is basically the view of Beck (1960, 87).

[41] They become commands when expressed in the imperatival mood, e.g., "x" or "Do x."

addressee, what is analytic is the proposition: "*Since* I want E and know (or believe) that M is indispensably necessary for attaining E, I *must* M." In other words, given an agent's desire for E and knowledge (or belief) that M is the indispensably necessary means for E, it follows analytically (by means of GP$_1$) *for* A that A must M. Moreover, keeping in mind that for Kant to explain the possibility of an imperative is to account for the necessitation of the will it expresses, we can see why he regarded this task as relatively easy in the case of hypothetical imperatives. Since the volition of an end is presupposed and the principle (GP$_1$), which describes what rational agents must do to attain their ends (whatever they may be) is analytic, nothing further is required to account for the possibility of such imperatives.

(D) Is there a generic hypothetical imperative?

The issue has been posed in its sharpest form by Thomas Hill, who argues that, in addition to an indefinite number of specific hypothetical imperatives, there is something called "the hypothetical imperative," which is the counterpart of "the single categorical imperative." According to Hill, this principle, states that, "*If a person wills an end and certain means are necessary to achieve that end and are within his power, then he ought to will those means.*"[42] Although Hill acknowledges that Kant never formulated this principle in so many words, he points out that he does refer to "the imperative which commands the willing of the means to him who wills the end" as a principle presupposed by imperatives of both skill and prudence (GMS 4: 419$_{8-10}$).[43] Moreover, at one point Kant remarks that, "*The* [my emphasis] hypothetical imperative . . . says only that the action is good for some *possible* or *actual* aim" (GMS 4: 414$_{32-33}$). And he also speaks of *the* technical imperative and *the* pragmatic imperative [my emphases], which are contrasted with the moral imperative (GMS 4: 416$_{29}$–17$_2$). Thus, in addition to the symmetry it gives to Kant's account of practical reason, there seems to be some textual support for Hill's thesis that Kant is committed to a generic hypothetical imperative.

The problem, however, is that Kant's reason for insisting that there is a single categorical imperative does not appear to apply to hypothetical imperatives. This is because the categorical imperative always enjoins the same thing, namely, act only on maxims which you can at the same time will to be universal laws. Accordingly, it abstracts completely from an agent's ends, which is the reason for its singleness. In response, one might point out that "the hypothetical imperative" likewise abstracts from the particular ends that an agent has and requires only that, whatever they may be, the agent choose the indispensable means to these ends. But this ignores a significant difference, namely, that in the case of hypothetical imperatives the specific end is the decisive determinate of what one should do; whereas the categorical imperative purports to require or prohibit actions (or maxims) independently of the ends that an

---

[42] Hill (1992, 17–18). See also Rawls (2000, 220–21).
[43] Hill (1992, 18).

agent may have.[44] And since this end is the source of their necessitation, hypothetical imperatives have a particularity that is lacking in categorical imperatives such as "Do not lie." All things considered, then, it does not seem necessary, or even particularly useful, to attribute a generic hypothetical imperative to Kant. To be sure, both Kant's own GP and its variant GP_1 are single and this may be what Hill and others who believe in a generic hypothetical have in mind; but, as I have argued above, neither is an imperative.

III

We have seen that at the basis of Kant's account of rational agency is the thesis that the defining feature of rational agents is that, unlike every non-rational being, such agents act according to their representation of laws, understood as objective practical principles, rather than merely according to laws (of nature). We also saw that, in the case of finite rational agents, who do not automatically follow the course of action dictated by reason (what is objectively necessary is subjectively contingent), this representation of law imposes a necessitation or constraint on the will of the agent, which, since it stems from the agent's representation of the law rather than the law itself and, as such, involves an act of taking or incorporation on the part of the agent, is to be distinguished from a causal necessity. Finally, we saw that for such agents this constraint or necessitation takes the form of an imperative, from which Kant concludes that to account for the possibility of an imperative is to explain the grounds of this constraint.

Kant found no difficulty in accounting for the possibility of hypothetical imperatives, since the source of their necessitation can be traced to an agent's volition of an end. Since A wills E and knows (or believes) that M is a necessary condition for E and M is in A's power, A must take itself to be necessitated to will M, which, again, is to be distinguished from being causally determined to M. By contrast, the great difficulty in accounting for the possibility of a categorical imperative (if there is one) stems from the fact that, *ex hypothesi*, there is no presupposed end upon which the necessitation it expresses could be based. And by applying his analytic–synthetic distinction to the contrast between the two types of imperative, Kant claimed that, while a hypothetical imperative is "an analytic-practical proposition" (GMS 4: 419_{4-5}), a categorical imperative would be "a synthetic-practical proposition *a priori*" (GMS 4: 420_{14}). As Kant puts the issue in a note intended to explain the latter claim,

I connect the deed with the will *a priori*, without a presupposed condition from any inclination, therefore necessarily (though only objectively, i.e., under the idea of a reason, which would have complete control over all subjective motives [*Bewegursachen*]). This is therefore a practical

---

[44] The second objection against a generic hypothetical imperative corresponding to the categorical imperative has been made in somewhat different forms by Patzig (1966, 251–52) and McCarthy (1979, 386–87). These writers were not, however, responding to Hill, since Patzig's paper was published seven years before the initial publication of Hill's, while McCarthy makes no reference to Hill.

proposition that does not derive the volition of an action analytically from another volition already presupposed (for we have no such perfect will), but is immediately connected with the concept of the will of a rational being as something that is not contained in it. (GMS 4: 420$_{29-35}$)

In considering this note, it is essential to keep in mind that the as yet unspecified categorical imperative is a *practical* proposition. For present purposes, this means two things: (1) that the proposition concerns volition; and (2) that it is a statement of what *ought* to be the case rather than of what is (or necessarily is) the case. These features are shared by all imperatives, qua propositions. A categorical imperative would differ from a hypothetical imperative in that the necessitation of the will it expresses is *not grounded in* a presupposed volition, i.e., the willing of some end. This is both the ground of its categoricality (the unconditioned nature of its command) and, presumably, the locus of its syntheticity.

At this point, however, where Kant's concern is to develop the concept of a categorical imperative rather than to establish its reality, its alleged syntheticity can be understood only in negative terms. Strictly speaking, the most that Kant is entitled to claim at this juncture is that the practical proposition expressing such an imperative could not be analytic, at least not in the way in which those expressing hypothetical imperatives are analytic, which means that the move from this to its syntheticity is based entirely on the underlying assumption of the exhaustiveness and exclusivity of the analytic–synthetic distinction.[45] In short, if the imperative is not analytic, it must be synthetic, since Kant allows no conceptual space for anything possessing propositional form, including practical principles, that is neither analytic nor synthetic.

In spite of Kant's seemingly unquestioned reliance upon this assumption, it is not obvious that it applies, at least not without significant qualifications, beyond the sphere of theoretical judgments, which was its original home.[46] In fact, much of what Kant says on the subject suggests that he is offering a practical analogue rather than a strict equivalent to the theoretical synthetic *a priori*, in which the predicate is not contained in the concept of the subject, but is necessarily connected with it in a judgment. For, as Kant makes clear in the note, what serves as the predicate is not a concept but a *deed* (the course of action required or prohibited by a categorical imperative) and its connection with the subject (the concept of the will of a rational being) is not grounded in the relation of both to an *a priori* intuition, as it would have to be in a synthetic *a priori* theoretical judgment. In fact, we shall see that when Kant returns to

---

[45] Although Kant does not make this explicit in GMS, he does in the third *Critique*, where he endeavors to explain the even more problematic claim that the principle of taste is synthetic *a priori*, even though it is normative for feeling rather than cognition. As he there puts it, judgments of taste are synthetic because "they go beyond the concept and even the intuition of the object and add to that as a predicate something that is not even a cognition at all, namely the feeling of pleasure (or displeasure)" (KU 5: 288; 169). I discuss this issue in Allison (2001b, 167, 172–75, and 178).

[46] Although it is itself a deeply controversial matter, I shall not here consider objections to Kant's analytic–synthetic distinction as such and the problem of the synthetic *a priori* in the theoretical domain, since it is beyond the scope of this work. For the most recent statement of my views on this topic, see Allison (2004, 89–96 and 2005, 343–59).

the issue of the synthetic *a priori* nature of the categorical imperative in the context of its deduction, he indicates that the comparison with the way in which theoretical judgments relate concepts to intuitions is only rough or approximate rather than precise, which suggests that Kant is offering an analogy rather than a strict equivalence between the theoretical and the practical synthetic *a priori*.[47]

We shall revisit the question of the synthetic *a priori* status of both the categorical imperative and the moral law in connection with the analysis of their deductions, but the point that I wish to emphasize at present is that the issue with which Kant is here concerned, namely, the peculiar difficulties involved in accounting for the possibility of a categorical imperative, can be readily understood without reference to the problem of the synthetic *a priori*. Simply put, the task is to account for the possibility of a constraint on the will that is not a function of some presupposed end or object of volition. This is essential because, if Kant has shown anything in the portion of the text considered so far in this chapter, it is that any end-conditioned constraint could yield merely a hypothetical imperative. Otherwise expressed, if there is a categorical imperative, it must be one in which its imperatival status is not grounded in some presupposed end.

A further complication and potential source of confusion in Kant's explanatory note is his elliptical and parenthetical reminder of the fact that finite rational beings such as ourselves "have no such perfect will." The statement itself is non-problematic, since we presumably already know that a perfect will or, more precisely, a perfectly rational will, would be one for which what is objectively necessary is also subjectively necessary, because there are no sensuous impulses to interfere with the dictates of reason and that this does not apply to beings like ourselves. What is problematic, or at least puzzling, is the point of this reminder, particularly since it is located in a sentence, the main point of which is presumably to show why a categorical imperative does not, like a hypothetical imperative, "derive the volition of an action analytically from another volition already presupposed." Kant's syntax suggests that the point is that if, *per impossibile*, we had such a perfect will, a categorical imperative would be analytic.[48] Clearly, however, this cannot be what Kant meant, since we have seen that for beings with such a will there could be no imperatives. The point rather seems to be that for a perfect will the connection between its volition and the course of action, which for finite rational agents is required by a categorical imperative, would be analytic. In other words, it is an analytic truth that a perfect will would do whatever the moral law requires, because the thought of its failure to do so contradicts the concept of such a will.[49] And from this it evidently follows that, lacking a perfect will, finite rational

---

[47] See GMS 4: 454$_{6-19}$.

[48] This is reminiscent of but distinct from Kant's later claim that. "[I]f freedom of the will is presupposed, morality, together with its principle follows from it, through mere analysis of its concept" (GMS 4: 447$_{8-9}$), which I have dubbed the "the reciprocity thesis." I shall discuss this thesis in Chapter 10.

[49] This does not mean, however, that the moral law is itself analytic. This is an important issue that I shall take up in Chapter 10.

beings do not, by their very nature, automatically do what the moral law requires, which is why they are subject to constraint or necessitation. But the question remains: why should Kant refer to the distinction between the two species of rational agent in a sentence, the apparent purpose of which is to clarify the distinction between the two kinds of imperative to which only one of these species is subject?

In any event, Kant concludes from this that accounting for the possibility of a categorical imperative does not fall within the purview of a metaphysics of morals, which, at least as he construes it in GMS, is basically an essay in conceptual analysis. That undertaking must be reserved for a critique of pure practical reason, the basic features of which Kant provides in GMS 3.[50] Nevertheless, Kant also thought that there was a preliminary, yet essential task that did pertain to a metaphysics of morals, so construed, namely, to provide the "formula" for the categorical imperative, by which he understood the proposition expressing what such an imperative would enjoin (GMS 4: 420_{18-20}). Kant thought that this task fell within the purview of a metaphysics of morals because it could be accomplished by means an analysis of the concept of such an imperative, quite apart from the question of its possibility.[51] This analysis, which contains the derivation of the formula of the categorical imperative, proceeds as follows:

If I think a *hypothetical* imperative in general, I do not know in advance what it will contain until I am given the condition. But if I think a *categorical* imperative, then I know immediately what it contains. For since besides the law, the imperative contains only the necessity that the maxim should conform with this law, while this law contains no condition to which it is restricted, nothing is left with which the maxim of action is to conform but the universality of law as such, and this conformity alone is what the imperative actually represents as necessary.

There is therefore only a single categorical imperative and it is this: *Act only according to that maxim through which you can at the same time will that it become a universal law.* (GMS 4: 420_{24}–21_8)

Since Kant here arrives at substantially the same result as he did in GMS 1 by a somewhat different route, it is possible to be fairly brief. The crucial point is that, even though these derivations arrive at essentially the same result and employ a similar strategy (an argument by elimination), they start from quite different places and therefore constitute two logically distinct arguments. In an effort to clarify the issue, I shall briefly review the result of the previous analysis and then contrast it with the present argument.

We saw that the derivation in GMS 1 was the culmination of a motivational analysis based on the concept of a good will under human conditions. At issue was what

---

[50] See GMS 4: 444_{35}–45_{15}. I say "the basic features" of a critique of pure practical reason," rather than a complete critique, because we have seen that in the Preface Kant excused himself from the task of providing such a critique on the grounds that it would require establishing the unity of speculative and practical reason, a task which is not directly germane to the limited project of the *Groundwork* (GMS 4: 391_{20-31}).

[51] See GMS 4: 426_{25-30}.

principle could determine this will such that it would be deemed unconditionally good from the standpoint of an enlightened common rational moral cognition. The first step was to show that it must be determined by respect for law; but since it was further argued that no particular law could furnish the principle of a will governed by respect for law, nothing remained as its determining ground except the conformity of its actions with universal law as such. Consequently, this conformity was claimed to be the principle governing the volition of an unconditionally good will, which Kant glossed as the principle: "*I ought never to act except in such a way that I could also will that my maxim should become a universal law*" (4: 402₇–₉).

We also saw, however, that a problem was posed by this gloss, since it appeared to involve an unexplained and seemingly unwarranted move from the apparently vacuous requirement to conform one's actions to universal law as such, that is, to law qua law, to a supposedly contentful prescription. This raised the specter of a gap that threatened to undermine Kant's derivation of the supreme principle of morality by means of his motivational analysis.

The proposed response to this worry over gappiness turned on two points. One was an appeal to the motivational nature of Kant's analysis, which appears to have been ignored by the critics who raised the gappiness objection. The basic point was that the actions of an absolutely good will must not only conform to universal law as such, they must also be performed or, better, their underlying maxims adopted, *because they conformed*, which means that such conformity must provide the reason for adopting, or at least a sufficient reason for rejecting, maxims that fail to conform to universal law as such.[52] Otherwise, the conformity would be a purely contingent matter, having no moral import.

The other was that the idea of conformity to universal law is not itself a prescription (in which case it would be vacuous), but is a description of the principle governing the volitions of a will considered as good without limitation. Prescriptivity, it was argued, only enters the story when this idea is connected with the will of a finite rational agent equipped with maxims embodying its own non-moral interests, and it consists in the requirement that all such agents incorporate the principle of conformity to universal law as such into their maxims as the supreme limiting condition of their adoption. On this reading, there is no fatal gap in Kant's argument and no derivation of a contentful principle from a vacuous one, because the content is provided by the agent's pre-given maxims.

Since the derivation of the categorical imperative in GMS 2 is based on an analysis of the concept of such an imperative rather than that of a good will, the course of the argument cannot be precisely the same. Thus, we cannot attempt to remove the gappiness, which still seems to lie in the move from the requirement to conform to

---

[52] We have seen that conformity to universal law is not, of itself, a sufficient reason to adopt non-obligatory but permissible maxims. Lack of such conformity is, however, a sufficient condition for rejecting such maxims.

universal law as such to the full-blooded categorical imperative, in precisely the same manner. Nevertheless, I believe that, once again, Kant provides us with sufficient materials for the task.

These materials are largely, though not entirely, contained in Kant's account in the first paragraph of his analysis of the content of such an imperative. They are:

(1) *The law*: This is the source of the constraint on volition. Every imperative presupposes a law, at least in the weak sense of an objectively valid practical principle. This is because without a law there could be no necessity and without necessity (or, better, necessitation) no imperative. The law underlying a categorical imperative, which is the kind of law with which we are presently concerned, would dictate an unconditional constraint on volition.

(2) *The necessity that the maxim conform to this law*: This necessity expresses the relation between the law and the maxim of the agent to whom the imperative is addressed. This is the reciprocal of the first point; for just as there can be no necessity without a law, so there can be no law without necessity. In the case of a categorical imperative, this necessity would be absolute in the sense that it holds in all possible worlds containing finite rational agents, regardless of the ends that such agents have set for themselves.

(3) *The elimination of any determinate content from the law, conformity to which is commanded in the imperative*: This is the decisive step in distinguishing the categorical from a hypothetical imperative. The basic point is that the inclusion of any determinate content in the law, that is, some end or object that the law requires us to pursue, would render the imperative merely hypothetical or conditional, since the normative force of the law would be a function of the desirability of this end to an agent.

(4) *The result of the elimination of determinate content*: If the preceding is the essential negative step in Kant's derivation, eliminating in one fell swoop the pretensions of all determinate laws to be *the* categorical imperative, this is its positive counterpart.[53] The main point is that the elimination of all determinate content from the law, conformity to which is thought in the concept of a categorical imperative, does not leave us with nothing. Rather, it leaves us with the idea of conformity to universal law as such or, more simply, lawfulness.

(5) *The conclusion*: What the concept of a categorical imperative represents as necessary is just the conformity to universal law as such, that is, conformity to the *idea* of lawfulness or universality.

Of the elements of Kant's derivation of the categorical imperative cited above, the one that calls for further comment at this point is the fourth, since it is here that

---

[53] It is important to keep in mind that Kant is here concerned with formulating *the* categorical imperative, understood as the supreme principle of morality. Obviously, particular categorical imperatives, e.g., "Do not lie," have a determinate content, but they presuppose the categorical imperative.

something new is interjected into the discussion. This is the ubiquitous Kantian distinction between form and matter, which is here applied both to practical laws and the maxims that are tested in light of these laws. I maintain that this distinction is here used, even though it is not mentioned, because it provides the vehicle by means of which Kant concludes that something significant remains when one removes all determinate content or matter from the concept of a law, namely, its form, which is simply the thought of lawfulness as such.[54] Moreover, this thought reduces to universality because that is the property common to every law (theoretical or practical, descriptive or prescriptive, empirical or *a priori*) and therefore what alone remains, if one abstracts from the matter or content of a law.

Kant's underlying and deeply controversial assumption is that the mere form of a principle, apart from its matter, can be normative, that is legislative, indeed for this very matter.[55] In order to understand this assumption, which is the key to Kant's derivation of the categorical imperative from the concept of such an imperative, it is useful to consider it in light of the form–matter distinction as it is operative in the "critical philosophy" as a whole. But since this is a large topic, the full treatment of which would require a book in its own right, I can here merely provide a brief sketch of what I take to be the basic elements of Kant's view.[56]

In essential agreement with the Aristotelian tradition, Kant defined matter as the "determinable in general" [*das Bestimmbare überhaupt*] and form as its "determination" [*Bestimmung*] (KrV A266/B322).[57] As Kant recognized, this definition gives matter a logical priority over form, since the concept of form is applicable only when there is something *to be formed*, that is, a matter. But while not denying this conceptual point, Kant radically transforms the traditional understanding of their relation by considering it in light of his qualitative separation of sensibility and understanding. On Kant's view, this separation leads to a transformation of the traditional understanding of the matter–form relation, at least with respect to cognition, because he maintained that this relation is to be found in the domain of each of these cognitive faculties and that in each case it assumes the form of the relation between something conditioned (the matter) to its condition (the form).[58] Thus, there are forms of sensibility (space and

---

[54] Kant set the stage for this earlier in GMS 2, when he remarks that a categorical, in contrast to a hypothetical imperative, concerns the form rather than the matter of an action (MS 4: 416$_{10-11}$).

[55] In the second *Critique*, Kant refers to the lawgiving or legislative [*gesetzgebende*] form of maxims (KpV 5: 28; 162). Again, I am assuming that this applies to all practical principles, not simply to maxims.

[56] For a systematic and critical treatment of the topic, see Pippin (1982).

[57] These definitions are contained in the chapter on the "Amphiboly of Concepts of Reflection," which is primarily directed against Leibnizian intellectualism. Here matter and form are regarded as one of four concept-pairs, the others being identity and difference, agreement and opposition, inner and outer, which supposedly underlie all reflection, that is, acts of comparison by the understanding. In his account, Kant seems to privilege the matter–form contrast, stating that these concepts "ground all other reflection, so inseparably are they bound up with every use of the understanding" (KrV A266/B322).

[58] Kant appears to maintain in his discussion of the "Amphiboly of Concepts of Reflection" that, if, like both Leibniz and Locke, one fails to recognize the radical distinction between sensibility and understanding as cognitive faculties, one is unavoidably led to equate matter with the sensible content of experience and form

time), which are the conditions under which sensible data (the matter) are given to the mind in experience and forms of understanding (pure concepts), which are conditions under which objects (the matter) can be thought by the understanding. Since a condition is logically prior to what it conditions, this effectively reverses the traditional understanding of the matter–form relation by making form *epistemically*, though *not ontologically*, prior to matter. Kant's explanation of this, which cannot be pursued here, consists in the dual thesis that the forms (of both sensibility and understanding) are *a priori* contributions of the mind, while the matter is given *a posteriori*, which leads directly to Kant's "formal idealism."[59]

Kant's derivation of the categorical imperative may be seen as resting on an analogous move. Whereas for traditional moral theories, the matter, that is, the end or object of a moral principle is primary and its form, that is, its lawful or normative status, is a consequence of and therefore presupposes this matter, Kant once again reverses the order of priority.[60] For him it is the bare idea of lawfulness that does the normative work and the matter of a practical principle (presumably a maxim) is judged in terms of its conformity (or lack thereof) to this idea. The difference is that, whereas in the theoretical domain, the form is the condition of the *cognizability* of the matter, in the practical it is the condition of its *permissibility*. At least this must be the case if there is a categorical imperative, which at this point remains in doubt.

So far, then, the analysis of the concept of a categorical imperative has led to the conclusion that if there is such an imperative, it must be grounded in the idea of the conformity of the maxims of a finite rational agent to universal law as such. In the subsequent one-sentence paragraph, Kant concludes from this that there is only a single categorical imperative, meaning thereby that there is only one putative imperative that could command unconditionally, namely, "*Act only according to that maxim through which you can at the same time will that it become a universal law.*"

Even though it now takes the form of a complete sentence (indeed a separate paragraph) rather than merely a clause tacked on to a sentence referring to the idea of such conformity, this recalls the worry about gappiness considered in the preceding chapter. As before, the worry is that Kant seems to derive a presumably contentful prescription (the categorical imperative as described above) solely from the seemingly vacuous idea of bare conformity to universal law as such. But also as before, this worry is misguided, since Kant is not engaged in the futile project of deriving a contentful

---

with its intellectual component, which then functions merely to bring clarity and distinctness to what is sensibly given. From this point of view, which Kant regarded as shared by both rationalists and empiricists, it is evident that matter is logically prior to form. Moreover, in this context, Kant also suggests that this view would be correct if appearances (sensibly given objects) were things were things in themselves (see KrV A267–68/B322–24). I discuss the issues involved here in Allison (2004, esp. 27–32).

[59] Kant refers to his transcendental idealism as "formal" at Pro 4: 375, 162–63 and KrV B519. Again, for my interpretation of this idealism, see Allison (2004).

[60] We shall see in Chapter 9 that the view attributed to traditional moral theories is equivalent to heteronomy and Kant's reversal to autonomy.

prescription from a vacuous principle, which, as we have seen, was precisely the objection he raised against the Wolffian procedure. Instead, he is formulating the only possible categorical imperative on the basis of a prior analysis of the concept of such an imperative, which showed that this concept contained nothing more than the bare idea of conformity to universal law as such. And, of course, the concept of an imperative is not itself an imperative, which is to say it is not prescriptive.

As we have already seen, in order to generate an imperative from this idea, it is necessary to provide an addressee, more specifically, a finite rational agent equipped with maxims expressing the agent's subjective ends and interests. As was the case in the first derivation, these maxims provide the content that is subjected in the imperative to the conformity to universal law as such principle. The difference is that, in the first case, the result was arrived at by reflection on what could motivate a will that was unconditionally good; while here it is reached by means of an analysis of what could be commanded unconditionally. But we should not be surprised to find that for Kant these come to much the same thing; for only something that is unconditionally required could motivate (be the determining ground of) a will that was un-conditionally good and, conversely, only a will whose determining ground was an unconditionally binding law could be deemed unconditionally good.

The contrast between the concept of a categorical imperative and the imperative itself is best approached in terms of the previously considered conception of a formula. We have seen that Kant defines imperatives (including both the categorical and hypothetical varieties) as "formulas expressing the relation of objective laws of volition in general to the will of this or that rational being, e.g., to the human will" (GMS 4: 414_{8-11}), from which it was concluded that an imperative does not differ from a practical law or objective principle of reason in its content but, rather, in its mood or illocutionary force. Assuming that, in the case of the categorical imperative, the practical law or objective principle of reason, which we have seen is a descriptive rather than a prescriptive principle, is conformity to universal law as such, then "*Act only according to that maxim through which you can at the same time will that it become a universal law*" may be seen as its formula, since it expresses the relation between the law and the will of a finite rational agent equipped with its maxims based on the agent's private interests.

It seems evident that the term "formula" should here be taken in its mathematical sense, where it serves as a rule for solving a problem. The problem is to explain how the law applies to a finite rational agent and the answer is in the form of the categorical imperative, as specified above. In other words, the way in which such an agent conforms to this law is by acting only according to maxims which the agent could at the same time will to be universal laws. Still otherwise expressed, the maxims of such an agent conform to universal law just in case the agent can also will these maxims as universal laws. This is the function of the qualifier "at the same time" [*zugleich*], which makes it clear that what is at stake is the compatibility of the content of an agent's actual maxim with the thought of the *same maxim* as a universal law.

Finally, I believe that it is in light of this that we must interpret Kant's oft-cited remark in a note contained in the Preface to the second *Critique*, where in response to a critical review of GMS by Johann Friedrich Flatt, who had objected that Kant had not provided a new principle of morality but merely a new formula, he replies:

[W]hoever knows what a *formula* means to a mathematician, which determines quite precisely what is to be done to solve a problem and does not let him miss it, it will not take a formula that does this with respect to all duty in general as something that is insignificant and can be dispensed with. (KpV 5: 9n; 143)[61]

I take Kant's point to be that the idea of conformity to universal law as such, like the supreme value of a good will, is implicit in ordinary rational moral cognition and that what the categorical imperative does is to provide a formula in the sense of a procedure for applying it. In the next chapter we shall be concerned with this application through an analysis of Kant's notorious set of examples; but before turning to that it may be useful to present the results of this chapter in summary form, which can be expressed in the following eight propositions:

(1) Rational agents act according to their representation of laws.

(2) For finite rational agents, with a sensuous as well as a rational nature, what is objectively necessary (according to the represented law) is subjectively contingent.

(3) Consequently, for such agents what is represented as a law assumes a prescriptive-imperatival form, that is, it imposes a constraint upon the will.

(4) If some condition (end of the agent) is presupposed, then the constraint or necessitation, which is expressed in the imperative, is merely conditional and what the law represents as necessary is the choice of a certain means to that end.

(5) If, on the other hand, there is a categorical (unconditional) imperative, its constraint or prescriptive force would have to be independent of any of an agent's ends.

(6) Consequently, the content of such an imperative could include only the thought of conformity to universal law as such, that is, to the idea of lawfulness regarded as an unconditioned norm.

(7) But a maxim of a finite rational agent conforms to universal law as such, if and only if that agent could also will it (with its embedded interests) as a universal law.

(8) Therefore, a categorical imperative would require that an agent adopt only maxims which that agent could at the same time will as universal laws.

---

[61] See also EF 8: 348n; 321; and VEF 23: 157–58.

7

The Universal Law (FUL) and the Law of Nature (FLN)

The previous chapter began with a consideration of Kant's characterization of rational agency as a capacity to act according to the representation of laws or on principles and culminated in an analysis of Kant's derivation of the content of the categorical imperative (FUL) from an analysis of the concept of such an imperative. The present chapter commences at the point at which the previous one ended and is concerned with three topics: (1) the move from FUL to FLN, (2) Kant's account of the application of FLN to examples of the various types of duty, (3) an analysis of the numerous counter-examples, both false positives and false negatives, which have been alleged in the literature to arise regarding the application of FLN to the case of false promising. Although each of Kant's illustrations of the application of FLN has been subject to a host of criticisms, I shall focus mainly on those to false promising, because it is presented by Kant as a violation of a perfect duty to others, which is arguably the most fundamental type of duty, since it concerns claims of justice and right.

I

In the two paragraphs immediately following the formulation of the categorical imperative, Kant makes two important claims that underlie much of the controversy surrounding his account of this imperative, not only in GMS 2, but in his moral theory as a whole. The first is the claim that,

[I]f from this single imperative all imperatives of duty can be derived [*abgeleitet*] as from their principle, then even though it remains undecided whether what we call duty is as such an empty concept we can at least designate what we think thereby and what this concept means. (GMS 4: 421$_{9-13}$)

The crucial interpretive issue here is the meaning of "*abgeleitet.*" Does Kant mean by this that the test of his formulation, if not the reality, of the categorical imperative, is whether it can be shown to be the source of all (or even a significant subset) of generally recognized duties, or does he have something weaker in mind? Although

I shall return to this question below in considering Kant's account of this principle at work, we have already seen from the analysis of its derivations that its application presupposes the presence of a maxim that an agent subsumes under the maxim to test its permissibility or moral possibility.

The second claim, which is the immediate object of our attention, is that,

Because the universality of law, in accordance with which effects occur, constitutes what is properly called *nature* in the most general sense (with regard to form), that is, the existence of things insofar as it is determined in accordance with universal laws, so the universal imperative of duty could also be stated as follows: *so act as if the maxim of your action were to become through your will a* **universal law of nature**. (GMS 4: 421$_{14-20}$)

Underlying this passage is a distinction that Kant drew in the first *Critique* and the *Prolegomena* between two ways of conceiving nature: formally and materially. Nature, considered in the first way, is the existence of things in accordance with universal laws; considered in the second way, it is the sum-total of appearances.[1] The claim, which Kant makes without any attempt at argument, is that the concept of nature in the first sense may be used to express the conformity to universal law thought in the categorical imperative. This yields FLN and immediately raises two questions. (1) How can the idea of conformity to laws of *nature* represent the idea of conformity to laws of a completely different type, specifically, laws of *freedom*? (2) Assuming that this mode of representation is possible, what function does it serve?

Although Kant does not address these questions directly in GMS, he does do so in a brief but important section of the second *Critique* entitled "Of the Typic of Pure Practical Judgment" (KpV 5: 67–71; 194–98). As the reference to judgment rather than reason indicates, Kant saw the issue as the practical analogue of the schematism problem discussed in the first *Critique*. In both cases, the concern is with the power of judgment [*Urteilskraft*], understood as the capacity to subsume given particulars under rules.[2] In the first *Critique*, these rules are concepts of the understanding, particularly pure concepts, and the problem of subsumption is generated by the complete lack of homogeneity between the latter and sensibly given particulars. Given this lack of homogeneity, Kant reasons that, in order to be able to subsume the latter under the former and thus exercise the theoretical power of judgment, there is need for some "third thing," a mediating representation, which is in one respect sensible and another intellectual, and which provides the commonality requisite for such subsumption. Kant terms this mediating representation a "transcendental schema"

---

[1] See KrV A418–19/B446 note; Pro: 4: 295–96; 90–91, 318; 110–11.

[2] In the Introductions to the third *Critique*, Kant introduces a distinction between the determinative and the reflective powers of judgment. In the exercise of the former, the universal is given and the function of judgment is to subsume a particular under it. In the exercise of the latter, the particular is given and the function of judgment is to find the universal under which it falls (FI 20: 211; 15, and KU 5: 179; 66–67). In the case of practical (moral) judgment, it is primarily the determinative function that is involved, since the universal (the moral law) is assumed to be given and the question is whether a particular maxim or course of action can be subsumed under it.

and he equates these schemata with "transcendental determinations of time," that is, with universal formal features of things and events qua temporal. I have argued elsewhere that these schemata may be regarded as translations into temporal terms of the rules thought in a purely intellectual manner in the pure concepts of the under-standing.[3]

As Kant points out, the possibility of "pure practical judgment," that is, judgment involving the subsumption of cases under the categorical imperative, cannot be accounted for in the same way as the theoretical judgments involving the application of the categories to objects of possible experience. Since this imperative is a product of reason rather than the understanding, which, as such, cannot be brought into an analogous relation to the sensibly given, a strict parallel to the solution proposed by the doctrine of the schematism in the first *Critique* is not available. Nevertheless, inasmuch as it embodies the key idea of universality, Kant suggests that the concept of a natural law can serve as a "type" [*Typus*] or model (as opposed to a schema) for the imperative (KpV 5: 69; 196). In other words, in spite of its radically different genealo-gy, for purposes of practical judgment, we can consider a universalized maxim as if it were a law of nature and by this means judge its conformity (or lack thereof) with the imperative.[4] Indeed, according to Kant, not only can we do this, we *must*, if we are to apply the moral law to particular cases; for this is the only way in which we can bring the law, as a product of pure practical reason, to bear on such cases. Moreover, Kant notes that this yields the following rule of judgment: "Ask yourself whether, if the action you propose were to take place by a law of nature of which you yourself were a part, you could indeed regard it as possible through your will" (KpV 5: 69; 196).

Although it takes the form of a rule of practical judgment rather than an imperative, this is logically equivalent to FLN in GMS. In both cases, the operative question is whether a proposed course of action is one that an agent could endorse as a law of a nature of which the agent is a part, with the idea of being a law of nature expressing the universalizability requirement built into the categorical imperative. Kant further claims that "Everyone does, in fact, appraise actions as morally good or evil by this rule"; and he endeavors to illustrate this by appealing to three of the four examples used in GMS 2. In each case, one is supposed to ask, "if you belonged to such an order of things [one which allowed deception when it was believed to be to one's advantage, shortening one's life when one is weary of it, and complete indifference to the needs of others] would you be in it with the assent of your will?" (KpV 5: 69; 196).

---

[3] See Allison (2004, 202–28).

[4] Although Kant refers to the moral law rather than the categorical imperative in the "Typic," presumably in order to accentuate the parallelism with laws of nature, his formulation of the moral law in the second *Critique*, referred to as the "Fundamental Law of Pure Practical Reason," is actually of the categorical imperative. See (KpV 5: 30; 164). We shall return to the question of the relationship between the moral law and the categorical imperative in connection with the analysis of the argument of GMS 3.

A perplexing feature of this discussion is the precise function that Kant assigns to the stipulated rule of practical judgment. Kant's claim that it is used to appraise actions as morally good or evil indicates that he viewed it as determining duties (what is morally good) as well as mere permissibility (what is not morally evil). Later in the same paragraph, however, Kant claims that, "If the maxim of the action is not so constituted that it can stand the test as to the form of a law of nature in general, then it is morally impossible" (ibid.). This suggests that the rule has the lesser but still significant task of serving as a test of the moral possibility (permissibility) of maxims, that is, as a kind of moral filter, ruling out maxims that fail the universalizability test and letting pass those that do not. This is a lesser task because, while a maxim or action that is morally impossible is evil, it is not the case that one that is morally possible is, for that reason, also morally good.

Inasmuch as this rule of judgment is logically equivalent to FLN, it is not surprising that the same ambiguity attaches to Kant's account of the latter in GMS 2. On the one hand, there is the previously cited claim that "all imperatives of duty," that is, all imperatives specifying particular duties, can be "derived" from FLN as their principle, which strongly suggests that the latter is intended to serve as a self-standing source of duties.[5] On the other hand, we shall see that, even though Kant organizes his examples in terms of the traditional classification of duties into perfect and imperfect, self-regarding and other regarding, which suggests that he is concerned to show that FLN can generate duties of each type, his actual discussion of these examples indicates that his intent is rather to show how FLN is fruitful in ruling out maxims that violate each of these duty-types as impermissible or morally impossible.

Against this it cannot be objected that, if successful, this line of argument would suffice to establish duties, at least indirectly, because if a course of action is shown to be contrary to duty, it follows that we have a duty to perform (or omit) its opposite. Although this line of argument seems most plausible in the case of negative or perfect duties, such as the prohibition against suicide, we shall see that even here FLN is too weak for this purpose, since it is used to test particular maxims. As such, the most that it can show is the impermissibility of a course of action *under a given maxim*; and inasmuch as the same course of action might be chosen on the basis of a number of different maxims, FLN cannot rule out a course of action *tout court*, as would be required to ground a negative or perfect duty.

This limitation is even more apparent with regard to imperfect or positive duties, which are duties to adopt a particular maxim, for example, beneficence, rather than

---

[5] In addition, there is the disputed passage, which follows immediately upon Kant's discussion of the four examples, in which he remarks that, "[T]hese are some of the many actual duties, or at least what we take to be duties, whose division [*Abteilung*] clearly meets the eye" (GMS 4: 423$_{36}$–24$_1$). Because of Kant's use of "*abgeleitet*" at GMS 4: 421$_{10}$, as well as stylistic considerations, some editors, e.g., Cassirer, have apparently taken *Abteilung* [division or classification] as a misprint for *Ableitung* [derivation] and this reading has been incorporated into most of the standard English translations (e.g., Beck, Paton, Ellington, Gregor, and Zweig), which supports the view that Kant is, in fact, concerned here with the derivation of duties. For a useful discussion of the issue with a defense of the original terminology, see Wood (2006a, 40–41, editorial note 52).

(except in extreme circumstances) to perform a particular act This is because it is one
thing to show that a maxim of non-beneficence cannot be willed without contradiction as a universal law of nature and quite another to show that we have a duty to adopt
a maxim of beneficence. Since these are contraries rather than contradictories, the
denial of the former does not entail the affirmation of the latter.[6] Accordingly, any set
of duties that could be derived from FLN would be remarkably thin and uninteresting.
In fact, when Kant does attempt to derive a system of duties in the *Doctrine of Virtue*,
FLN does not appear and universalizability is assigned a very limited role, entering
directly only into the derivation of the duty of beneficence.[7]

Accordingly, in spite of the ambiguity of the text, I believe that these considerations,
taken together with the analyses in the preceding two chapters of Kant's actual
derivations of the categorical imperative, strongly suggest that FLN is best seen as a
test of moral permissibility, which, as such, has only an indirect bearing on the
determination of specific duties.[8] But though this appears to be the standard reading
it calls for some defense, since it has not gone unchallenged. In fact, it has been argued
both that this reading is too strong and that it is too weak.

Prominent among those who take the former view are Barbara Herman and Mark
Timmons. Appealing largely to the notorious counter-examples to Kant's account of
the universalization process (to be discussed in the third part of this chapter) and the
closely associated problem of determining the proper description of the maxim to be
subjected to this procedure, they (and others) have concluded that the latter is not
capable of serving as a viable test for permissibility, not to mention for the derivation of
duties. But still interested in finding work for FUL or FLN, they have constructed

---

[6] See Wood (1999, 100), who argues this point against Herman.

[7] See MS 6: 452–54; 571–73.

[8] Since Kant refers to the universalizability requirement as the "canon of moral judgment" (GMS 4: 424$_3$),
the point could also be made in terms of contrast between a canon and an organon to which Kant appeals in
the first *Critique*. Although Kant does not offer a formal definition of "organon," the way in which he uses
the term indicates that he understood it in the classical sense as a tool or instrument for the acquisition of
knowledge, which in this case means synthetic *a priori* knowledge. Thus, he states that an organon of pure
reason, assuming that one is possible, "would be a sum-total of those principles in accordance with which all
pure *a priori* cognitions can be acquired and actually brought about" (KrV A11/B25). In the same context, he
also remarks that a critique of pure reason is "a preparation, if possible, for an organon, and, if this cannot be
accomplished, then at least for a canon, in accordance with which the complete system of the philosophy of
pure reason . . . can . . . at least some day be exhibited" (KrV A12/B26). And later, explicitly contrasting an
organon with a canon, he states that "general logic, which is merely a **canon** for judging, has been used as if it
were an organon for the actual production of at least the semblance of objective assertions, and thus in fact it
has thereby been misused" (KrV A61/B85). Finally, at the beginning of his chapter on "The canon of pure
reason," Kant states that, "The greatest and perhaps only utility of all philosophy of pure reason is . . . only
negative, namely that it does not serve for expansion, as an organon, but rather, as a discipline, serves for a
determination of the boundaries, and instead of discovering truth it has only the silent merit of guarding
against errors" (KrV A795/B823). These texts suggest that, even though Kant's distinction between canon
and organon is not completely firm, providing a canon is always conceived as a more modest task than
supplying an organon. For a discussion of the different senses that Kant assigns to the term "canon," see
Wood (2008, 71–72).

revisionary readings, which attempt to avoid rather than address the problems generated by these counter-examples.[9]

The claim that limiting FLN (or, as he prefers, FUL) to the purely negative task of ruling out certain maxims as impermissible is too weak to capture Kant's intent and that it must be viewed not merely as a test of permissibility, but as self-sufficient source of obligations, specifically fundamental duties of justice and beneficence, has been argued recently by Stephen Engstrom.[10] Engstrom grounds his interpretation of the categorical imperative in a systematic account of practical cognition and judgment, which, as such, is centered more on the second *Critique* than GMS. At the heart of his account lies a two-fold thesis: (1) that morality for Kant is to be understood as a type of cognition, specifically, a practical cognition, which differs from its theoretical counterpart in that it aims at bringing about rather than merely comprehending its object, the good;[11] (2) that like its theoretical counterpart, practical cognition lays claim to a two-fold universal validity, which following a hint in the third *Critique*, Engstrom refers to as objective and subjective.[12]

According to Engstrom, the objective side of the universal validity of practical cognition serves to distinguish judgments of the good from the agreeable and consists in the assumption that what I judge to be good for me, I must also judge to be good for every other agent in relevantly similar circumstances.[13] Correlatively, the subjective side of the universal validity of practical judgments is that every other rational agent equipped with the same information would share in my judgment of the good, that is, they would agree that it would be good that x was done, not simply that it would be good for me.[14] On Engstrom's reading, this bears on the universality test involved in the application of the categorical imperative in that both aspects of universality are assumed. In other words, when I ask whether my maxim is possible as a universal law, I am not merely asking whether I can consistently will it as such, but also whether it is one which *any* rational agent could find acceptable as a universal law. And, by building both senses of universality into the first formulation of the categorical imperative, Engstrom mounts arguments for both perfect duties of "natural justice" or prohibitions

---

[9] See Herman (1993, esp. 145–48) and Timmons (2006, esp. 160). According to Herman, who resists a deontological reading of Kant's ethics, seeing it instead as rooted in the supreme value of rational agency, duties are reduced to "moral presumptions," which, as such, are capable of being overridden. And from this point of view, she regards the function of the CI-procedure to be to provide the pre-deliberative moral knowledge, which is the source of the content of moral judgment and sets the terms for moral deliberation. Timmons shares Herman's worries about the capacity of FLN (or FUL) either to generate duties or to provide a viable test of permissibility and offers what he terms a *"formal constraint"* interpretation of FUL and FL. According to this interpretation, rather than serving as rules that are themselves sufficient for a moral decision procedure, these formulas provide a set of formal constraints on the content of moral reasons.

[10] See Engstrom (2009, esp. 174–75 n9), where he criticizes my reading together with Wood's and Korsgaard's on this point.

[11] Ibid., 6–7 and passim.

[12] Ibid., 111–22 and passim. The passage from the third *Critique* is at KU 5: 214–15; 99–100.

[13] Ibid., 115–17; 122–26.

[14] Ibid., 116, 122–26.

on "assaults on the freedom and property of others" (GMS 4: 430₃₋₄), which includes but is much broader than Kant's own example of a lying promise to repay a debt and an imperfect duty of beneficence.[15] Finally, by appealing to subjective universality as a constitutive feature of practical judgments, Engstrom argues for the equivalence of the first and second formulations.

Since I intend to take up some of the issues posed by Engstrom's analysis below in connection with a discussion of Kant's examples, I shall not comment further on them at this point. For the present, it must suffice to note that my disagreement with Engstrom is more methodological than substantive. More specifically, while I agree with his core contention that the categorical imperative involves both types of universality, I do not believe that FLN, considered in its own terms, involves the subjective side of universality as he understands it.[16] To be sure, the latter could be read into it, if it is interpreted in light of what comes later in GMS 2 or what Kant says about the categorical imperative elsewhere; but I believe that this approach does not accord with the methodology of GMS 2, where, as already noted, I view Kant as attempting to provide the complete construction of the concept of the categorical imperative by means of a series of progressively deeper reflections on the nature of rational agency.

II

Kant's statement of FLN is followed by an "enumeration [*herzählen*] of some duties," which are presented according to what he describes as the usual classification of duties to ourselves and to other human beings and perfect and imperfect duties (GMS 4: 421₂₁₋₂₃). As he indicates in a note attached to this passage, Kant proposes to reserve a systematic taxonomy of duties for a future metaphysics of morals. Accordingly, the present division is considered merely discretionary [*beliebig*], that is, as a convenient device for ordering his examples. In the same note, Kant states that he understands by a perfect duty one which "permits no exception to the advantage of inclination" and that his division, which he does not attempt to defend, differs from that of the schools in that it includes perfect internal as well as external duties (GMS 4: 421n₃₁₋₃₈).[17]

After concluding his enumeration, Kant further remarks that maxims of actions that violate perfect or strict duties are such that they cannot even be *thought* without

---

[15] See Engstrom (2009, esp. 174–75 n9, 188–215).

[16] My disagreement with Engstrom and O'Neill, whose account his closely mirrors, is epitomized in the distinction I shall draw between an inter-subjective and an intra-subjective universality, which differs from Engstrom's contrast between an objective and a subjective universality. We shall see that this disagreement is closely related to the weight (or lack thereof) that we assign to FLN in applying the categorical imperative.

[17] Although he does not call attention to the fact, Kant's taxonomy also differs from the traditional one in not recognizing any duties to God. This is pointed out by Timmermann (2007a, 79).

contradiction as a universal law of nature, while in the case of imperfect (here termed "wide or meritorious") duties, it is merely impossible to will them without contradiction as a universal law of nature (GMS 4: 424$_{8-14}$). These are generally referred to in the literature as the "contradiction in conception" and the "contradiction in will" tests and I shall consider them with respect to each of the examples they are intended to cover.

Before proceeding to Kant's examples, however, it will be useful to note four points about his procedure. First, in each case Kant assumes that the reader will grant that the course of action being contemplated is a violation of a generally recognized duty. Second, in each case Kant makes sure to point out that the agent who is applying the test is proceeding conscientiously. In other words, in spite of his self-interest the agent is also concerned with the morality of the proposed course of action, and it is from this perspective that he raises the question of the universalizability of his maxim. Third, for this reason the maxim that the agent is considering adopting is the one on which he would perform the action (or omission) in question, not one which might be concocted after the fact in order to provide a veneer of justification. Finally, although in each case the universalized maxim will turn out to involve a contradiction (either in conception or will), prior to the test for its universalizability the maxim which the agent is considering adopting has a certain *prima facie* justificatory force for that agent.

(1) *Suicide*: As a putative duty to oneself, the prohibition against suicide does not seem suitable for the universalizability test, as it is usually understood.[18] Since the latter involves conceiving (or willing) a world in which there is a law dictating that everyone act in a certain way, it is difficult to see how the universalization of the maxim that Kant ascribes to the agent contemplating suicide, namely, "From self-love, I make it my principle to shorten my life, if its longer duration threatens more ill than it promises agreeableness" (GMS 4: 422$_{5-8}$) involves a contradiction. A world in which there was a law of nature specifying that everyone act on this maxim would be significantly depopulated, but there is no contradiction in that. In fact, Kant does not attempt to mount such an argument. Rather, on this view, the law of nature that would be generated by the universalization of this maxim is a teleological one. Hence, the contradiction that would supposedly emerge has been aptly termed a "teleological contradiction."[19] In Kant's account, the agent contemplating suicide asks whether the

---

[18] The point is noted by Timmermann (2007a, 80).

[19] As far as I can tell, the expression "teleological contradiction" was first used by Korsgaard (1996, esp. 87–92). What she calls the "simple view" of such a contradiction is one that "emerges when an action or instinct is used in a way that is inconsistent with its natural purpose, or is not used in a way that its natural purpose calls for" (op. cit., 87). It might also be described as an instance of contra-purposiveness, which, as such, presupposes that something (e.g., an entity, faculty, instinct, process, organ, predisposition, inclination) has an identifiable natural purpose, but behaves in a way or leads to results that are contrary to this purpose. As such, it is not a contradiction in anything like a logical sense.

above-mentioned principle of self-love could become a universal law of nature. And the answer Kant provides is that,

One soon sees that a nature whose law it was to destroy life through the same sensation [*Empfindung*] whose proper function [*Bestimmung*] is to impel the furtherance of life would contradict itself, and thus could not subsist as nature; hence that maxim could not possibly hold as a universal law of nature and, consequently, entirely contradicts the supreme principle of all duty. (GMS 4: 422$_{7-14}$)

One of the few truly non-contentious claims in Kant scholarship and interpretation is that this argument is unsuccessful. Indeed, even Paton, who emphasized the centrality of teleological considerations to Kant's ethics, acknowledged that this is the weakest of Kant's arguments.[20] Moreover, we shall see, when discussing Kant's treatment of suicide under FH, that it also differs markedly from his analysis of it elsewhere. Setting that aside for the present, however, there are at least four major difficulties with this argument. First, since the law that would arise from the universalization of the maxim is teleological, the suicide case differs from Kant's other examples in that it cannot be intelligibly formulated in terms of FUL, which is presumably why commentators who gloss over the distinction between FUL and FLN can find virtually nothing to say about it. Second, without totally eschewing teleology, one might question the necessity of regarding the furtherance (or even the preservation) of life as nature's purpose in equipping humankind and other animal species with an instinct of self-love. Admittedly, such a view seems reasonable on the strong teleological assumption that *every* organ, faculty, etc., has a determinate purpose; and we have seen that Kant espouses this assumption in GMS 1 and elsewhere. Nevertheless, it seems odd that such a strong assumption would be required to determine the impermissibility of taking one's life under the conditions described. Third, even assuming that the enhancement of life is the purpose underlying the instinct of self-love, it remains unclear why this fact should enter into the considerations of someone contemplating the morality of suicide. Unlike the other examples, the end at issue here is *nature's* not the agent's, which invites the question: why should an agent, particularly one in the dismal psychological

---

[20]   Paton (1958, 154). Paton's general thesis is that the laws of nature with which Kant is concerned in his account of FLN are in each case teleological rather than causal laws. This is because the maxims under consideration are maxims of action and action, as such, is essentially purposive. Accordingly, the test on Paton's reading is whether a given maxim harmonizes with a systematic harmony of ends (op. cit., 150–51). It does not follow, however, from the fact that action is purposive either that the putative laws in question must be teleological or that FLN should be viewed as testing for a harmony of ends. With regard to the first point, unless one assumes that all psychological laws are teleological, there is no difficulty in regarding the laws at issue, at least in the second and fourth example, as straightforwardly causal laws of human behavior. Admittedly, the situation is complicated by the fact that Kant denies the possibility of psychological laws; but that does not affect the present issue, since what is involved is merely a thought experiment in which one considers a certain principle of behavior *as if* it were a law of nature. With regard the second point, we shall see in Chapter 9 that the notion of a systematic harmony of ends is operative in connection with the formula of a realm of ends (FRE) rather than FLN.

state Kant describes, worry about *nature's* ends?[21] Finally, since whatever nature's intent may be, from the agent's point of view, which is presumably the one to be taken in moral deliberation in general and self-regarding duties in particular, agreeableness is not seen as a means to the enhancement of life, but as the condition under which one is willing to endure it. Although this is a position to which Kant is deeply opposed, the present point is only that this argument does not show why it is morally objectionable.

(2) *False promising*: This is by far the most widely discussed of Kant's examples, largely because it brings out most of the issues that are deemed central to his universalizability test. It concerns an agent who is driven by circumstances to feel the need to borrow a sum of money under false pretenses, promising to pay it back, while knowing that he will be unable to do so. The agent is depicted as conflicted. On the one hand, he wants to make the false promise, since he sees it as the only way in which he will be able to acquire the needed sum; while, on the other hand, "he has conscience enough to ask himself: Is it not impermissible and contrary to duty to get out of distress in such a way?" (GMS 4: 422_{19-20}). In short, the perceived need is not seen by the agent as itself providing a sufficient (justifying) reason to act in this manner.

In this context, the agent is depicted as conducting a thought experiment in order to determine the moral permissibility of what he feels compelled by circumstances to do. To increase the psychological plausibility of the scenario Kant is describing, we might view the agent as recognizing the validity of a general rule to the effect that such a course of action is morally wrong, while still wondering whether an exception might be made in his case due to the exigencies of his circumstances.[22] In any event, the first step is to specify the maxim on which he would be acting, if he decided on this course of action. As Kant describes it, the maxim is: "If I believe myself to be in financial distress, I will borrow money and promise to pay it back; although I know that this will never happen" (GMS 4: 422_{22-23}). Applying FLN, the question becomes whether the agent could, without contradiction, will this maxim as a universal law of nature. And, not surprisingly, the answer is negative:

For the universality of a law that anyone, who believes himself to be in need, could promise whatever he pleases with the intention of not keeping it would make the promise and the end one might have in it itself impossible, since no one would believe what is promised him, but would laugh at all such expressions as vain pretenses. (GMS 4: 422_{31-36})

---

[21] One possible explanation for Kant's curious line of argument at this point is that he is directing an *ad hominem* attack on the Stoics, who both affirmed the moral principle "Live according to nature" and justified suicide for the Stoic sage. Although this does not lead to anything like a "contradiction in conception," it at least helps to understand why Kant would discuss suicide under FLN.

[22] This would accord with Kant's claim, to be discussed below, that when we violate a duty, we do not will that our maxim should become a universal law; rather we recognize that the law holds generally and merely make an exception for ourselves (GMS 4: 424_{15-20}).

One of the major questions posed by Kant's examples is the nature of the contradiction that supposedly emerges when an impermissible maxim is regarded as a universal law of nature. We have seen that the alleged contradiction in the universalization of the suicide maxim is best described as teleological, since it is not logical and seems to involve violating a teleological rather than a causal law. In the present case, however, which, like the suicide example, supposedly involves a contradiction in conception, that is, in the mere conception of the maxim as a universal law of nature, it does seem possible to speak of a logical contradiction. Such a contradiction would consist in willing both *a* and *not-a* at the same time. Applying this schema to false promising, it would mean willing both that there are promises (since one intends to profit by making one) and that there would not be promises (since a promise that no one would believe would not count as a promise).[23] Clearly, in order to generate the contradiction, it must be assumed that the promisee is aware of the "law" regarding the making of promises without the intention of keeping them; otherwise the no one would believe them condition would not obtain.

In the more recent literature, however, an alternative interpretation of the contradiction has emerged and gained fairly wide acceptance. This has been termed by Korsgaard, who is its most explicit, but by no means its only advocate, "the practical contraction interpretation."[24] The contraction is practical because it involves a contradiction between an agent's end in making false promises (profiting from them) and the state of affairs that would result if this were made into a human law of human nature (the end could not be attained because promises would not be believed). Like the logical contradiction interpretation, this depends crucially on the assumption that the promisees are aware of the "law" and for that reason promises would no longer be believed. The key difference is that, rather than simply rendering impossible the institution of promising, what it renders unattainable is the agent's end in adopting the maxim. This would yield a genuine contradiction (of a practical sort) because the agent would be willing both the end and a state of affairs that would make it unattainable.

Although the textual evidence is ambiguous, I think that several considerations speak in favor of the practical contradiction interpretation. First, it better accords with the way in which the issue is posed, namely, as one in which an agent with a particular end in view (in this case acquiring needed funds) is reflecting on the permissibility or moral possibility of using certain means (making a lying promise to repay a loan) in order to attain that end. And the agent's question is whether he could,

---

[23]   See Korsgaard (1996, 81–82) and Wood (1999, 87–89). Defenders of this reading include Kemp (1969, 236–38). For a modified version of the logical contradiction reading, which he refers to as the "Causal-Law Theory," and which he offers in response to an early version of what has subsequently come to be termed the "practical contradiction interpretation" by Onora O'Neill, see Timmons (1984). A distinctive feature of Timmons' reading is that the logical impossibility characterizes the system of nature as a whole, considered as a causal system.

[24]   Korsgaard (1996, 92–94).

without contradiction, will his maxim as a universal law of nature. In other words, the locus of the contradiction is in the *will*, not in nature, even though it is illustrated by considering the universalized maxim, as if it were a law of nature. And that I believe is why in the above-cited passage Kant points out that a universal law based on the maxim would render impossible not only the promise, which is the point emphasized by proponents of the logical contradiction interpretation, but also "the end one might have" in making the lying promise.[25]

Second, the practical contradiction interpretation does a better job of capturing our moral intuitions about what is wrong with false promising of this sort, namely, making an exception for oneself from a policy that one assumes to be followed by others. Third, it more closely corresponds to the kind of contradiction that Kant locates in the third and fourth examples. Since we have already seen that neither is capable of making sense of the anomalous suicide example, there is no prospect of finding a single kind of contradiction that is applicable to all four of Kant's examples. Nevertheless, there is something to be said for an interpretation that is arguably applicable to three of the four examples, as contrasted with one that is plausibly applicable only to one.

Fourth, it yields a form of contradiction that is specifically applicable to the *practical* use of reason, which, since the concern is with volition, is presumably what we should expect. Similarly, it suggests a greater continuity with the kind of contradiction involved in the violation of a hypothetical imperative. In both cases, it is a matter of what can be rationally intended (willed). The difference is that in the latter case the contradiction is located in the intention itself (attaining the end without willing the necessary means); whereas here it is the intention qua universal law that generates the contradiction.

Fifth, the practical contradiction interpretation is suggested by the derivation of the content of the categorical imperative from an analysis of its concept. As we saw in the preceding two chapters, the conformity to universal law requirement takes the form of a demand that the content of an agent's maxim be compatible with the putative law produced by its universalization. Accordingly, in the present case, which involves a contradiction in conception, the essential point is that the end embedded in the maxim be compatible with the thought of the *same maxim* as a universal law. And the failure to meet this requirement yields a practical rather than a logical contradiction.[26]

(3) *Failing to develop one's talents*: Kant considers the cultivation of one's talents an imperfect duty to oneself, which means that a maxim advocating their neglect, that is, a maxim of slothfulness, would lead to a contradiction in the will rather than in conception. That such a maxim would not lead to a contradiction in conception is obvious, since, as Kant points out with reference to the South Sea Islanders, given

---

[25] For a similar point see GMS 4: 403$_{16-17}$ and KpV 5: 27–28; 161.

[26] The second, third, and fourth of these considerations are central to Korsgaard's argument for the practical contradiction interpretation. See Korsgaard (1996, 92–94, 101–2).

favorable circumstances, a nature could subsist in which human beings devoted all their energies to enjoyment. Accordingly, the question becomes why one could not *will* such a seemingly blissful state of affairs as a universal law of nature, which, Kant suggests, might take the form of an instinct implanted in us by nature. Kant's answer is that such a volition is impossible because "as a rational being he [the hypothetical agent contemplating adopting a maxim of neglecting his talents or capacities] necessarily wills that all the capacities in him should be developed, because they are useful and given to him for all kinds of possible aims" (GMS 4: 423$_{13-16}$).

It seems possible to distinguish two lines of argument at work in Kant's treatment of this example. One, which is largely implicit, is teleological in nature and points to a parallel with the argument for the prohibition of suicide. This line of argument is suggested by Kant's characterization of the talents or capacities that the slothfully inclined individual does not want to bother cultivating as "fortunate natural predispositions" [*glücklichen Naturanlagen*] or, as he also terms them, echoing the introductory account of a good will, "gifts of nature." By emphasizing nature as the source of these gifts, one might tease out a teleological contradiction analogous to the one to which Kant appealed in his discussion of suicide. The difference would be that, as a violation of a merely imperfect duty, slothfulness would involve ignoring rather than acting directly against something given to us by nature, which would explain why it could be conceived, if not willed, without contradiction as a universal law of nature. But, in addition to being based on strong and highly questionable teleological assumptions, a difficulty which it shares with the anti-suicide argument, this reading leaves it unclear why a maxim of slothfulness could not be willed as a universal law of nature.[27]

The other, which appears to be the dominant line of argument, appeals to a practical rather than a teleological contradiction. As such, it avoids, or at least mitigates, these difficulties, though it runs into problems of its own. The main problem on this reading is to avoid reducing it to a matter of prudence, involving a violation of merely a hypothetical rather than the categorical imperative. After all, unless one is fortunate enough to live in a South Seas paradise (and perhaps even then) it would seem only prudent to develop at least some of one's capacities in order to be able to deal with future contingencies. Thus, prudentially construed, the argument would be that a maxim of neglecting to develop one's capacities in order to maximize the agreeableness of one's present condition might be seen as a case of willing an end (an agreeable life)

---

[27] The teleological dimension of Kant's argument is emphasized by Timmermann (2007a, 83–84), though by referring to Kant's critique of Baumgarten's claim that the perfection of one's talents is a duty to oneself (MPC 27: 363–64; 140), he also argues that Kant changed his view on the matter in GMS. At most, however, Kant's criticism applies to Baumgarten's argument for the development of particular talents and not of the capacities of which Kant also speaks in GMS. In this respect, Kant's argument is not directed so much at Baumgarten's claim that we have such duties, as it is against the perfectionist reasoning on the basis of which Baumgarten argued for them. Instead, Kant suggests that such duties are grounded in the essential ends of humanity, which anticipates the argument of FH.

without willing what seems to be an essential means to this end, namely, capacities sufficiently developed to ensure its maintenance. This would involve a practical contradiction, albeit one that has nothing to do with universalization.

Following O'Neill, Korsgaard, and Herman, I believe that the key to understanding Kant's argument in this (as well as the next) example, in a way that distinguishes it from prudential reasoning governed by a hypothetical imperative, is to introduce the conception of ends that are essential to one's finite rational agency.[28] Such ends reflect what Kant terms our "true needs."[29] The point is that, in contrast to arbitrary ends, which we can always abandon, if the cost of pursuing them is deemed too great, such ends cannot be abandoned without forsaking our rational agency, which entails by the principle of hypothetical reasoning that the perceived necessary means to these ends cannot be abandoned either.

Arguably, one of these indispensable needs is the capacity to set ends, since this is constitutive of agency. But inasmuch as the successful exercise of this capacity requires the development of certain talents, it follows that a will which made it its maxim not to cultivate any of the latter (a kind of principled slothfulness) would be in contradiction with itself, if made into a universal law. Unlike the practical contradiction in the universalized maxim of the deceitful promiser, however, where the contradiction is between the end embedded in the maxim (acquiring the needed funds) and the universalized policy of making deceitful promises, here the contradiction is between two of the agent's ends: the arbitrary end of ensuring an existence of maximal agreeableness and the non-arbitrary and essential end of preserving and enhancing his end-setting capacity. Even assuming its premises regarding agency and essential ends, this argument is of limited force; since it does not require the development of any particular talent or of any to a particular degree. Indeed, though this is controversial, I do not think that it even requires the adoption a maxim of the cultivation of one's talents; rather, it merely precludes, as morally impermissible, a maxim of their complete neglect.[30]

(4) *Non-beneficence*: Unlike his other examples, rather than ascribing a maxim to a hypothetical agent, Kant attributes a "*Denkungsart*," which we have seen can be rendered as a way of thinking, caste of mind, or even attitude. Although Kant is quite vague, this *Denkungsart* seems to amount to the adherence to the dictum "I am not my brother's keeper" or, alternatively, "Live and let live." In any event, the agent who thinks in this way neither wishes ill of nor envies others for their good fortune; he

---

[28] See O'Neill (1989, 98–101); Korsgaard (1996, 96–97); and Herman (1993, 52–62).

[29] MS 6: 393.524. The passage is referred to by Herman (1993, 55).

[30] Here I disagree with Timmermann, who asserts that a positive duty can be derived from this negative criterion on the grounds that, "If a maxim cannot be sustained as a universal law, one must adopt the opposite attitude" (2007a, 85). As I have argued above in agreement with Wood, this does not follow because the maxims are contraries rather than contradictories, which leaves logical space for adopting neither maxim.

is merely unwilling to contribute to their welfare when they are in need. Kant points out that there is no contradiction in conceiving such a *Denkungsart* as a law of (human) nature, since the human race could still subsist. Indeed, with some rather heavy-handed irony, he suggests that such a state of affairs would be preferable to one in which people constantly chatter about benevolent actions, even occasionally perform them, but also cheat when possible, steal, or otherwise infringe on human rights. Nevertheless, Kant denies that one could will that such a principle hold as a universal law of nature:

> For a will that resolved upon this would be in contradiction with itself, since many cases could arise in which he [the agent entertaining this *Denkungsart*] needs the love and sympathetic participation of others and where, through such a law of nature arising from his own will, he would rob himself of all hope of the assistance that he wishes for himself. (GMS 4: 423$_{31-35}$)

Like the previous example, this one rests crucially on the assumption that there are some ends that a finite rational agent cannot abandon because they belong essentially to the will. Otherwise, it would be open to an agent to reject any offer of assistance from others on the grounds that he places ultimate value on his independence, for the sake of which he is willing to sacrifice any potential benefits that could only be attained with the help of others. The rejoinder is that among the ends of a finite rational agent that require the aid of others to attain or preserve, are some that, at least under some circumstances, an agent cannot abandon without abandoning necessary conditions for the preservation and enhancement of his agency: for example, basic sustenance. Accordingly, if this *Denkungsart* is regarded as a universal law, it would yield a practical contradiction in the will of the agent, since such an agent would be committed to willing at the same time both that no one help those in need and that others be willing to help him when he is in dire need. Indeed, it might be argued that even the would-be Stoic stands in need of at least the negative assistance of others (being left alone), which is a direct consequence of our social nature. Once again, however, the most that this line of argument can show is that it is morally impermissible to adopt a policy of non-beneficence, not that we have a positive duty of beneficence.

III

Although all four of Kant's illustrations of the application of FLN are deeply controversial and have been and continue to be the subject of heated criticism from a variety of perspectives, the case of false promising has shown itself to be particularly susceptible to the perennially popular philosophical move of refutation by counter-example. And since these counter-examples call into question not merely the particular case of false promising, but Kant's analysis of the whole category of perfect duties to others, which lies at the heart of any deontic moral theory, they threaten the viability of the categorical imperative, at least in the form of FLN. For this reason, then, I shall devote the remainder of this chapter to a consideration of representative sample of these counter-examples, which come in two forms: false positives and false negatives. Inasmuch as an underlying assumption of those critics who stress these counter-examples is that virtually any course of action can be made to pass the universalizability test, dealing with the issue will involve revisiting the initial account of maxims sketched in the first part of Chapter 4, supplemented by a portion of Kant's account in the second *Critique*, which goes beyond what he says on the matter in GMS.

(A) False positives

These come in two types: those that are based on attributing to an agent a highly specific maxim, on the basis of which a proposed course of action could be made to pass the universalizability test, and those that are not. I shall here consider each in turn, arguing that, while the former can be dealt with fairly easily by a careful consideration of the maxim in question, the latter cannot and therefore constitute a real challenge to FLN, considered as a self-standing and sufficient canon for moral judging.

(1) *False positives involving "strange maxims" and "weird agents"*: While hardly unique to him, examples of this type are emphasized by Wood.[31] His own example, which is designed to show that any maxim can pass the universalizability test, if it is made sufficiently specific, is that of an agent in need of money, who decides to borrow it at a certain time, with no intention of repayment, from an acquaintance named Hildreth Milton Flitcraft. On Wood's construal, the agent's maxim is to borrow money without intending to pay it back, but only from people named Hildreth Milton Flitcraft and only on Tuesdays in August.[32] The underlying assumption is that the specificity of the maxim evades the contradiction in conception test, since if made into a universal law it would not undermine the whole institution of promising, on the viability of which the agent's proposed course of action depends.

There are two things to be said with respect to counter-examples of this type. First, in spite of their restrictions, which are obviously designed simply to evade FLN, such maxims do not in fact succeed in their intended task. This is because increasing the specificity of the maxim has the unintended consequence of narrowing the scope of its universalization, without evading the universalizability requirement itself. Thus, if the agent's maxim really is to profit by promising falsely only under a specific set of conditions, then its being made into a universal law of nature would still be inherently self-defeating *under these same conditions*.[33] In other words, however generally gullible he might be, under such a law of nature, Hildreth Milton Flitcraft would not believe

---

[31] Wood (1999, 103).

[32] Ibid. A similar example and analysis is provided by Timmons (2006, 176–77). The maxim can, of course, be further specified, virtually *ad infinitum*.

[33] Although I am here assuming the practical contradiction interpretation, I believe that the same result would follow, *mutatis mutandis*, on the logical contradiction interpretation as well.

promises to repay loans, at least not on Tuesdays in August. In response it might be argued that this assumes that poor Flitcraft is aware of this law, since if he were not, he would have no reason not to continue lending. This is true, but beside the point; for it overlooks the already noted fact that the thought experiment assumes from the beginning that all those involved, including the promisee, are aware of this law.

The second and more intractable problem concerns precisely what is to be tested for its universalizability. As many have pointed out, the same course of action, say telling a lie or making a false promise, could fall under a variety of descriptions, some of which allow for and others appear to exclude universalization. Accordingly, it seems that the results of applying FLN depend crucially on which description is chosen and there is therefore need for some procedure, which Kant allegedly does not supply, to determine which description, is appropriate in each case. To cite Ross' example, an act of lying to a would-be murderer might be described, among other ways, simply as telling a lie, telling a lie to a would-be murderer in order to save a life, or doing what circumstances require to save a life. In the first case it would clearly fail the universalizability test; while in the second and third it would arguably pass.[34]

I shall return to this issue below in connection with a consideration of some false negatives. For the present, I wish merely to underscore the point that FLN is conceived by Kant as a test of the permissibility of maxims and concerns the maxim on the basis of which an agent is actually contemplating a course of action, not, as Ross seems to have assumed, an action or even, as Wood intimates, an intention, which is more particular than a maxim. Thus, returning to Wood's example, his hypothetical agent's specific intention in making a deceitful promise may have been merely to obtain surreptitiously a certain sum from a particular individual (selected as the victim); but this is quite distinct from the maxim or general policy of which the former is an expression.[35] Presumably, the maxim, which provides a subjective justification for the agent's endeavor to realize his particular intention, would be something like: "Whenever I am need of funds and find someone who is likely to be deceived by a false promise to repay a loan, I shall make such a promise, knowing that I shall never repay it."

This differs from Kant's own example in two respects, only one of which is relevant. The one that is not relevant is the qualification that the person of whom the loan is requested (e.g., Wood's Flitcraft) is deemed likely to make the loan. This is not relevant because it is a purely prudential consideration, which is already built into the maxim and does not bear on the universalizability issue. Simply put, quite apart from moral considerations, it is reasonable to seek loans from those who are likely to make them, presumably because they have the resources and are more apt trust you. The second difference, which may be of some relevance, is that in Kant's example we are assuming

---

[34] Ross (1954, 32–33). I have modified Ross' account to include the third alternative, which he does not consider. In the recent literature, Ross' objection has been reiterated by Timmons (2006, 163, 176, 180).

[35] The distinction between an underlying maxim and a specific intention is emphasized by O'Neill (1989, 97). It should also be noted here that Wood explicitly refers to the agent's intentions (1999, 103), thereby implicitly equating maxims and intensions.

that the promiser is a conscientious individual, who is in dire straits and strongly tempted to make the false promise, but still asks if it is permissible. In Wood's example, by contrast, there appears to be no worry about the morality of the act, but simply of concocting a way to evade the scope of FLN. Would, for example, Wood's hypothetical agent feel any compunctions about making his deceitful request, if the potential mark's name were Mary Elizabeth Weatherby and it was a Monday in July? One thinks not.

(2) *Other false positives*: In addition to those false positives that arise through concocting highly restricted maxims on which few, if any rational agents would actually act, there are many that do not. Moreover, while these come in various forms, both the prevalence and the moral significance of those involving acts of violence and coercion—what Herman has colorfully described as maxims of "murder and mayhem"—makes it reasonable to focus on them.[36] Adopting a distinction drawn by Rawls between two kinds of rule, Korsgaard characterizes these problematic cases as involving "natural" as contrasted with "conventional actions."[37] The distinction rests on the principle that acts such as false promising depend for their possibility on the existence of "institutions" or conventions such as promising. Accordingly, a contradiction arises when one wills both the practice and a state of affairs in which the practice is no longer possible. Since this does not occur in the case of so-called natural actions, which include acts of violence and coercion, they pose a special challenge for FLN.

A case in point is a maxim formulated by Korsgaard on the basis of a suggestion by Paul Dietrichson, namely, to kill babies whose crying at night prevents one from sleeping.[38] Although obviously immoral, a maxim of disposing of babies who disturb one's sleep simply in order to facilitate one's sleeping does not seem to generate a contradiction (either logical or practical), if considered as a universal law of nature. And it would be easy to construct many other examples of a similar nature. For instance, one which my students enjoyed: "I shall murder professors who demand a lot of work and give low grades." If this were a law of nature, the professoriate would be somewhat smaller and more "student friendly"; but far from finding it contradictory, many would see this as a desirable state of affairs.

There appear to be three strategies for dealing with this type of counter-example in the literature, none of which is completely successful. One is Korsgaard's, who admits that a subset of manifestly immoral natural actions is not captured by FLN, which in her terms means that their universalization does not yield a practical contradiction, while insisting that there is also a subset that does. On her view, the decisive feature of natural actions that are subject to this test is that the agent's intent in committing the murder (or other violent act) is to secure some other end, for example, a desirable job (one which someone would, as the saying goes, "kill for"). Her point, which seems to be offered primarily as an argument for the superiority of the practical over the logical

---

[36] See Herman (1993, 113–31).   [37] Korsgaard (1996, 84–87).   [38] Ibid., 82.

contradiction interpretation, is that inseparable from the desirability of this end is a certain degree of security in its possession. Accordingly, one could not, without contradiction, will both the end and a means that would make possession of this end inherently insecure.[39] Presumably, one might extend this line of argument to cover examples such as Dietrichson's on the grounds that a universal law to that effect might prevent one from surviving infancy. As Korsgaard herself admits, however, even if we accept this line of argument, it does not cover all natural actions. For example, it leaves out murder (or other malicious acts) motivated by hatred or revenge, to which one might add, among other things, violent crimes committed for the sheer thrill of it, where the danger or insecurity is part of what makes the course of action desirable to an agent who is so inclined.

A second strategy, which was suggested by Dietrichson and developed by Herman, is to admit that maxims of violence pass the contradiction in conception test, but insist that they fail the contradiction in will test. In other words, the universalization can be conceived but not willed as a universal law of nature, which brings them within the scope of FLN.[40] According to Herman, the main point that brings maxims of violence (murder and mayhem), such as convenience killings, under the contradiction in will test is the principle that rational agents cannot will a world in which their agency imposes no moral restrictions on the actions of others, from which it follows that a maxim of violence of this kind cannot be willed (though it can be conceived) as a law of nature.[41]

Inasmuch as Herman's analysis is part of a longer argument to the effect that Kantian morality is fundamentally concerned with distinguishing correct and incorrect valuation of rational agency rather than establishing a deontological system, it cannot be dealt with here.[42] For present purposes, what is important is that, as she readily acknowledges, given Kant's correlation of the contradiction in conception test with strict or perfect duties and the contradiction in will test with wide or imperfect ones (GMS 4: 424_{10-14}), this move has the paradoxical consequence of relegating the most heinous crimes to the category of violations of wide or imperfect duties, which, according to Kant, demonstrate a lack of virtue rather than positive evil and/or a violation of rights.[43] But, surely, for Kant and virtually all moral theorists, if anything is a strict or perfect duty, it is the prohibition of such acts; so that if FLN is only capable of dealing with them by treating them as failing under the broader contradiction in will test, there is something radically amiss with FLN.[44] Thus, whatever the merits of

---

[39] Ibid., 98–99.

[40] See Dietrichson (1969, 188–89) and Herman (1993, 113–31).

[41] Herman (1993, esp. 119–25).

[42] The spirit of Herman's approach is nicely expressed by the title of the concluding chapter of her book: "Leaving Deontology Behind" (1993, 208–30).

[43] The point is argued by Korsgaard in response to Dietrichson. See Korsgaard (1996, 84).

[44] Not surprisingly, this point is emphasized by critics of FLN (or FUL) as a self-sufficient canon of moral judgment. See Wood (1999, 97–101) and Timmons (2006, 173–74). Responding to Herman, their specific target is what Wood calls the "correspondence thesis," that is, the thesis that the two types of contradiction

Herman's reconstruction of Kantian ethics, it is clear that it cannot stand as a reading of the text; for rightly or wrongly, it is evident that Kant regarded the action-types in question as violations of strict and perfect duties and the contradiction in conception test as applying to them.[45]

A third strategy is that of O'Neill, which has recently been reaffirmed in somewhat different terms by Engstrom. Rejecting the approach of those who endeavor to restrict the contradiction in conception test to actions-types that presuppose practices (such as false promising), O'Neill argues that maxims of brute violence and coercion fail this test because they "undercut the agency of those whom they victimize."[46] Her point is that maxims that lead to such results cannot even be conceived, much less willed, as universal laws, because, save perhaps for masochists, rational agents cannot endorse courses of action that effectively undermine their agency.[47] Accordingly, O'Neill takes the universalizability condition as limiting permissible maxims to those that are universally endorsable. Even though his focus is more on the violations of rights than violence, we have seen that substantially the same thesis has been expressed by Engstrom, through his insistence that the universalizability test requires that maxims be both subjectively and objectively universalizable, where the former means essentially that they must be maxims that all rational agents could endorse.

Although I take the intuition behind this reading to be fundamentally correct, since it expresses the universalizability requirement at the deepest level at which Kant understood it, namely, one involving the conception of rational agents as autonomous legislators in a realm of ends, I do not find it plausible to tease this thick notion of universalizability out of FLN. In fact, it is noteworthy that in her later work O'Neill completely ignores FLN and the problems it raises regarding counter-examples, focusing instead entirely on FUL;[48] while Engstrom interprets FLN in an idiosyncratic and, in my judgment, unconvincing manner.[49]

---

correspond to the two classes of duty. Their assumption, which seems reasonable, is that if FLN is not capable of yielding a viable basis for distinguishing between these classes of duty, its import is seriously compromised.

[45] We shall see in the next chapter that, in his discussion of FH, Kant includes attacks on the freedom and property of others, together with false promising under the category of perfect duties to others (GMS 4: 430_{3-4}).

[46] O'Neill (1989, 133).

[47] Ibid., 132–33.

[48] I distinguish between the O'Neill of 1989 and of 1975, because in the earlier work she did pay close attention to FLN. Following Kant's account in the second *Critique* of the law of nature as a typic, she there focused explicitly on its application, introducing the conception of the "*universalized typified counterpart*" (or UTC) to refer to the maxim universalized as a law of nature (1975, 61–63). Moreover, in anticipation of the practical contradiction interpretation later developed by Korsgaard, she emphasized that what is tested is "whether the agent can consistently *simultaneously* hold his maxim and will its UTC" (op. cit., 69), which is quite different from the question of whether the maxim is universally endorsable.

[49] In his interpretation of FLN, Engstrom contends that by "laws of nature" Kant means "laws of our *rational* nature," which he identifies with humanity; and from there it is but a short step to the view that being able to will one's maxim as a universal law of nature is equivalent to being able to will it as one that would be valid for (in the sense of endorsable by) all rational agents. See Engstrom (2009, 161–64). In support of this reading, he argues that the laws must be such that their efficacy depends upon their being known as such by

These considerations indicate the need to introduce a distinction between two senses of universalizability, which differs from the one drawn by Engstrom. I shall call them intra- and inter-subjective universalizability. The former is the sense of universalizability required by FLN. It is *intra*-subjective because it concerns the compatibility of an agent's maxim with the *same maxim* considered as a universal law. This sense of universalizability is most clearly operative in Korsgaard's practical contradiction reading, but it appears to underlie the logical contradiction interpretation as well. The latter is the sense of universalizability appealed to by O'Neill and it corresponds to Engstrom's subjective universalizability. It is *inter*-subjective because it requires the endorsability of one's maxim by all other rational agents.

If this is correct, the great problem in understanding Kant's derivation or complete construction of the concept of the categorical imperative is to see how (or if) he is able to proceed from the former to the latter conception of universalizability. Addressing this problem will be a central concern of Chapter 9; but for now we must consider a new set of objections to FLN based on an apparent plethora of false negatives.

(B) False negatives

These are maxims that everyone would agree to be morally unobjectionable, but that appear to violate FLN. If false positives pose a challenge to the sufficiency of FLN, false negatives pose one to its necessity. The latter include, but are not limited to, what Herman has termed "timing" or "coordination" maxims: for example, I shall save money by shopping in this year's after-Christmas sales for next year's presents; or I shall play tennis on Sunday mornings at 10:00 a.m., because others are likely to be in church and the courts will be less crowded.[50] In the first case, the problem is that if everyone acted in this way the practice of Christmas sales would die out, which would prevent the agent from profiting from the practice. Similarly, in the second case, if everyone chose to skip church in order to play tennis at that time, the policy would become self-defeating, thereby apparently violating the practical contradiction test.[51] In neither case, however, does there appear to be anything morally wrong with the

---

the beings to which they apply. Although we have seen that this is correct (otherwise there would be no contradiction), it does not follow from this that they must be laws of rational nature in the sense suggested by Engstrom. All that is required is that the agents with respect to whom the actions falling under the law apply be conscious of the law. For example, we have seen that in the case of false promising, the promisee is assumed to be a rational agent who is aware of the (putative) "law" of human nature that people attempt to borrow money with no intention of paying it back. Moreover, Engstrom's reading glosses over the fact that the contradiction in non-universalizable maxims under FLN is between the universalized maxim and the end that the agent attempts to achieve through acting on the maxim.

[50] See Herman (1993, 138).

[51] A distinctive feature of Herman's analysis (1993, 140–43) is that she views these counter-examples as applying only to the practical contradiction interpretation. Although she thinks that the logical contradiction avoids this problem, she suggests that it involves difficulties of its own.

maxim. Although both maxims involve taking advantage of the behavior of others for one's own benefit, in neither case does it seem to be an *unfair* advantage, which would be the source of its immorality.

Wood reiterates the tennis example and adds two more of own, which are likewise borrowed from others: (1) "I will buy a clockwork train, but never sell one." (2) "When the Dow-Jones average reaches the next thousand, I will sell all my stocks."[52] And, as Wood points out, it is not difficult to imagine many more. For example, I shall arrive early (or late) to beat the crowd, avoid traffic delays, etc. There is no need to increase the list or examine them in detail, however, for underlying them all is the same seemingly indisputable principle, which can be formally expressed as: For any course of action x, the mere fact that if everyone x-d, either I could not succeed in attaining the end that I have in x-ing (the practical contradiction test) or x-ing would become impossible (the logical contradiction test) does not of itself make x-ing morally wrong, because it does not point to a morally salient fact.

It must be admitted that if this line of criticism holds, it would be devastating for FLN, if not for Kant's moral theory as a whole. But, as even its proponents acknowledge, these counter-examples can be addressed simply by reformulating the maxim held up to the universalizability test. For example, Herman notes, "[T]he 'tennis at 10:00' maxim could be replaced by a maxim of playing tennis when the courts are least likely to be used. And so on."[53] Nevertheless, in spite of the apparent ease of defusing the force of the false negatives in this way, Herman and other proponents of this line of objection resist this strategy on the grounds that it creates a host of new difficulties. In particular, it poses the problem of determining the relevant level of description, which not only seems to introduce an unwanted element of arbitrariness into the "CI procedure," but also to raise the specter, already suggested by Ross, that one and the same act might be morally permissible (or even obligatory) under one description and immoral under another.[54]

Although the worries over arbitrariness and the proper level of description are legitimate, I believe that critics have been too hasty in rejecting an approach that involves a closer examination of the Kantian conception of a maxim. For at bottom, the issue is not whether maxims, such as those proposed, which seemingly yield false negatives, can be replaced by others which do not; it is rather whether the former are proper maxims at all in the Kantian sense. I shall argue that they are not and that the familiar false negatives result from a failure to distinguish carefully between maxims, specific intentions and practical rules, which fall under maxims without themselves being maxims. Admittedly, this line of argument does not suffice to preclude the very

---

[52] Wood (1999, 105). Unlike Herman, Wood maintains that both the practical and logical contradiction readings founder on false negatives.

[53] Herman (1993, 139).

[54] Ibid., 142–43; and Wood (1999, 106–7).

possibility of genuine false negatives, but it does shift the burden of proof to those who insist upon them and their critical import.

By focusing on Kant's definitions in GMS, we have already learned several important things about Kantian maxims. (1) They are subjective practical principles, on which an agent actually acts, as contrasted with objective principles or practical laws, which are principles on which they *ought* to act and would act if they were perfectly rational. (2) As *subjective*, they presuppose particular ends and interests of an agent. (3) As *principles*, maxims are general rules or policies, which specify action-types under certain conditions, rather than particular actions. Accordingly, there are always a number of different ways in which one can act on a particular maxim, in contrast to rigid rules [*Vorsätze*], such as starting each day with fifty pushups, which leave little or no room for practical judgment. (4) As *products of practical reason*, maxims are consciously adopted by an agent; that is, one does not simply have maxims, one makes something one's maxim and, in so doing, assigns it a normative status, at least with respect to oneself. (5) A maxim may be schematically rendered as a practical principle of the form: When in S-type situations, perform A-type actions in order to attain end E.

To these we now add one further and crucial point, which is brought out by Kant's discussion of maxims in the second *Critique*. Kant there begins by defining practical principles as "propositions that contain a general determination of the will having under it several practical rules." Maxims are then defined as the subset of those principles that are subjective in the sense that "the condition is regarded by the subject as holding only for his will" (KpV 5: 19; 153). Presumably, by the "condition" Kant here understands the agent's incentive for adopting the maxim. So far, this corresponds to the definitions in GMS; but Kant proceeds to go further by adding that, as general determinations of the will, maxims have (or can have) under them a number of practical rules. As Otfried Höffe, who has emphasized the importance of this definition of maxims for the interpretation of Kant's universalizability test, points out, the claim that different practical rules fall under a maxim is ambiguous, since it could mean either that these rules are to be seen as deductive consequences of a maxim or that a maxim provides the normative criterion for the rules, which are determined by a judgment that is attendant to particular circumstances. Although the former is suggested by the traditional (logical) conception of a maxim as the "*propositio maxima*," Höffe argues convincingly that it is the second view that Kant has in mind.[55]

In light of this, let us reconsider some of the putative maxims which allegedly yield false negatives. To begin with, it is obvious that Herman's playing tennis on Sunday mornings at 10:00 a.m., because others are likely to be in church and the courts will be less crowded, is not a maxim. Rather, it is merely a rule or *Vorsatz*, because, like starting

---

[55] Höffe (1979, 92).

each day with fifty pushups, it leaves no space for practical judgment. More precisely, it is the outcome of a practical judgment, combined with its justifying ground. Moreover, the justification for choosing that particular time stems entirely from the contingency that in the agent's neighborhood potential tennis players happen to attend church at 10:00 on Sunday mornings. If she lived in a predominantly Jewish, Muslim, or secular neighborhood, she would doubtless choose a different time; but I do not believe that one would wish to say that she would therefore be acting on a different maxim.

Somewhat less obviously, Herman's proposed more general alternative, namely, play tennis whenever the courts are less likely to be used, though it evades the false negative worry, is not a proper maxim either. This is because the specific reference to tennis precludes it from counting as a *general determination of the will*. The latter need not include a reference to tennis but would include the end for the sake of which the agent engages in this activity. As such, it would allow room for judgment in the sense that tennis could be replaced by some other activity, which would fulfill the same function, without changing the general determination of the will. For example, let us assume that the agent plays tennis on Sunday mornings (or at whatever other time is most convenient) because, for the sake of her health and overall well-being, she wishes to engage in some regular form of physical exercise, which she finds enjoyable. Her maxim would then be something like: "For the sake of my well-being, I shall engage regularly in a form of physical exercise that I enjoy." Let us further assume that our Sunday tennis player becomes too old to play tennis up to her former standards, or simply loses interest in the game, and decides to take up golf instead. Would we want to say that she has adopted a different maxim? Although this point is certainly debatable, I believe that the answer is still negative, since the general determination of her will remains unchanged.

Finally, consider the "I will buy a clockwork train, but never sell one" example. Its universalization would yield a law to the effect that everyone would buy such items and no one would sell them. This would create a situation in which no one could purchase clockwork trains. Since there is obviously no logical contradiction in this, the contradiction rendering it a false negative would have to be practical. Admittedly, such a state of affairs would make our agent's endeavor self-defeating, since there would be no possibility of augmenting his collection. Nevertheless, this is beside the point, since, as described, the agent's procedure is not a proper maxim, because it expresses a particular intention rather than a general determination of the will, which would provide a reason for the course of action.[56]

The predictable response to this line of defense is that it is arbitrary. Although maxims may express general determinations of the will, these determinations, or lasting

---

[56] For similar reasons Aune likewise denies that this example is a genuine maxim. See Aune (1979, 122–23).

policies, come in various grades of generality.[57] Accordingly, so the objection goes, it is impossible to draw the distinction between maxims (or more general) and rules (or less general) determinations of the will in a sharp way, which means that the problem of the appropriate description remains. In addition, it might be pointed out that Kant himself did not seem to have been concerned with either determining the appropriate level of generality or with drawing a distinction between maxims and rules in his examination of sample maxims in GMS, since we have seen that these maxims come in various degrees of generality.

I shall take the second point first, since it can be dealt with briefly. Although it is true that Kant is extremely casual in his discussion of maxims in GMS and does not refer to the maxim–rule distinction, this is readily understandable in light of his limited intentions in this work. As already noted, his concern is to illustrate the applicability of FLN by examining some generally accepted duties, through a consideration of the maxim on the basis of which agents, who are considering acting contrary to that duty, may be thought likely to act. Accordingly, from this point of view, there is no need for Kant to consider the maxim–rule distinction, or even to concern himself with the problem of false negatives (or positives). But inasmuch as Kant did draw the maxim–rule distinction in the second *Critique* and connected the former with general determinations of the will, it seems appropriate to appeal to it in an effort to determine whether Kant provides the resources to deal with objections raised by present-day critics.

A response to the first and most important of these objections requires a further consideration of the sense of generality operative in the expression "general determination of the will." The key point is that one practical principle is not more general than another in the relevant sense in virtue of covering more cases or being applicable to more agents, but in virtue of its greater explanatory and justificatory power. And since maxims are subjective principles of action these come to much the same thing. In other words, the reasons that explain why I adopt a policy of x-ing under certain conditions are also those which justify x-ing under these conditions *for me* (though not necessarily from an objective point of view).

In light of this, let us revisit Herman's cryptic tennis at 10:00 on Sunday mornings example. Like the *Vorsatz*, do fifty pushups every morning, this does not include its reason or explanatory ground. Herman's alternative, namely, play tennis whenever the courts are less likely to be used, does better in this regard, since it provides a rationale

---

[57] According to Beck (1960, 78), by a "general determination of the will" Kant understands a lasting policy or settled disposition, that is, a freely chosen propensity to act in certain ways under certain conditions. Characterizing the policy as lasting is intended to indicate that it has a definite, non-trivial temporal extent, but not that it necessarily amounts to a "life rule" [*Lebensregel*] as is affirmed by Höffe (1979) and Bittner (1974). I have criticized the equation of maxims with *Lebensregeln*, as well as the related but somewhat distinct view of them by O'Neill, in Allison (1990, 191–94). In other respects, however, my present account is closer to theirs than that of my early work, where I was not directly concerned with issues involving the application of the categorical imperative.

for the time chosen and leaves room for choosing another time if that proves to be more practicable. Thus, it both explains and justifies the decision to play at 10:00 on Sunday mornings; and in so doing it makes explicit what is merely implicit in the more cryptic formulation.

As we have seen, however, this is still not a *general determination of the will* in the relevant sense, because it embodies a specific intention (playing tennis). Accordingly, we arrive at the truly general determination by going one step further, enquiring into the agent's rationale for playing tennis at all, that is, for forming this specific intention.[58] And while there are any number of possible rationales for this, we have assumed in our initial discussion of Herman's example that she played tennis because she was interested in maintaining her overall well-being and to that end chose a course of regular exercise that she found enjoyable. Clearly, given her end, if the latter condition had not been met, she would have chosen some other form of exercise; but, as already noted, this has no bearing on the general determination of her will and, therefore, would not involve a change of maxim.

Nevertheless, this is still not the end of the story. Inasmuch as maxims for Kant are themselves adopted by agents on the basis of reasons, it follows that we can also enquire into the grounds for their adoption. Indeed, we have seen that this is precisely the question that arises when the concern is with the determination of moral worth or content of a maxim, as opposed merely to its permissibility. And this might seem to raise the specter of an explanatory regress (indefinite, if not infinite), which reintroduces the worry about the arbitrariness of the decision regarding the specific determination of the will to be subjected to the universalizability test, particularly if, as seems to be the case, some pass the universalizability test, while others, proposing the same course of action, do not.

Fortunately, the threat of such a regress is blocked by the nature of the grounds underlying the adoption of a maxim, as contrasted with a more determinate rule that stands under a maxim. As we have seen, these grounds are found in the agent's interests (themselves products of practical reason) that are embedded in the maxim. In the present case, the central interest underlying the agent's adoption of the maxim is to maintain her well-being. This, together with the belief, arrived at through instrumental reasoning, that engaging in a regular program of exercise is the optimal means to attain that end and that the regularity is best maintained by choosing a form of exercise that she finds enjoyable and can perform at a reasonably high level provide the sufficient explanatory and justificatory grounds for the adoption of this maxim by this agent.

---

[58] Although she is addressing a different problem, namely, the plausibility of the claim (to which Kant seems committed) that every intentional action falls under a maxim, rather than that of the arbitrariness of the attribution of a particular maxim, Fricke (2008, 125–35) offers a substantially similar solution, when she suggests that a maxim is the subjective principle or rule of action that contains the criterion of choice [*Auswahlkriterium*].

We can, of course, pursue the explanatory quest a step further and ask why the agent chooses to maintain her well-being; but at this point only two possible answers are available on a Kantian account, namely, self-love and a sense of duty, neither of which has a further explanatory ground.[59] More to the present point, however, it is precisely because maxims, so construed, contain these grounds that they are the appropriate subject of a universalizability test; for the whole purpose of such a test is to determine whether these grounds can withstand their own universalization.

(C) Some final thoughts on FLN and its alleged counter-examples

Our consideration of the counter-examples to Kant's account of the application of FLN to the category of perfect duty to others that are prominent in the literature has led to a somewhat mixed result. Assuming with Korsgaard and many others that the contradiction in conception that is supposedly found in maxims that violate such duties is best interpreted as practical, that is, that such maxims are inherently self-defeating or, alternatively, that they fail to possess an intra-subjective universalizability, we saw that, though FLN could readily handle many of the allegedly false positives, there is at least one subset of these, namely, those that Herman named maxims of "murder and mayhem," that appear to survive intact.[60] Moreover, given the manifest immorality of the action-types falling under these maxims, we also saw that this is not a minor problem, which might be dealt with by tinkering with Kant's distinction between a contradiction in conception and a contradiction in will, but one that threatens the core of Kant's moral theory.

As far as false negatives are concerned, we have seen that their claims to be genuine counter-examples turns on one's interpretation of Kant's view of maxims; and by appealing to Kant's accounts of maxims in both GMS and the second *Critique* it was argued that those that are usually cited in the literature are not genuine counter-examples because they are not based on genuine maxims.[61] But even assuming the correctness of my analysis, an obvious limitation of this approach is that it leaves open the possibility of finding other false negatives, which means that the most that I can claim to have accomplished with regard to this class of counter-example is to have shifted the burden of proof to the critic, who must provide ones that accord with

---

[59] We shall see that in GMS 3 Kant argues that the impossibility of explaining freedom brings with it the impossibility of explaining why an agent takes an interest in morality. Similarly, in *Religion*, Kant insists on the inexplicability of radical evil, understood as a propensity to subordinate moral considerations to self-love.

[60] By focusing on the practical contradiction interpretation of Kant's test, I do not mean to suggest that these false positives would fare better under the logical contradiction interpretation. The point is rather that I view the former as the best characterization of Kant's position.

[61] An alternative strategy for dealing with false negatives, which was initially suggested by T. S. Scanlon, has been developed by Pogge (1998, esp. 189–96). According to Pogge, the universalizability test is understood to refer to the permissibility of maxims. On this reading, the idea is that a certain maxim must be universally available to be acted on, which does not entail that everyone must act on it. Although this move does appear to avoid false negatives of the sort that have worried so many commentators, I do not see how it is reconcilable with FLN; for while there may be permissive moral principles, I do not think that any sense can be made of the notion of a permissive law of nature.

Kant's conception of a maxim. But though I am skeptical about the prospects of finding such counter-examples, this still leaves us with our main problem, which seems of itself sufficient to undermine the pretensions of FLN to provide an adequate test of permissibility, namely, the above mentioned maxims of murder and mayhem.

We shall see in the next chapter that Kant provides a new and seemingly more effective way of dealing with such maxims in terms of FH. But before turning to that we must consider a paragraph that might be regarded as an appendix to Kant's account of FLN, in which he addresses the question of how rational agents could act on maxims that they recognize violate this principle (GMS 4: 424$_{15-37}$). Kant's question is not a psychological one concerning motivation, since that, at least in his eyes, is obvious: what leads rational agents to violate the categorical imperative is that they allow the claims of inclination to trump the demands of morality. And Kant does not appeal to some version of weakness of will to account for this, since it is assumed that the violator is a rational agent capable not only of knowing but of doing what is right. His concern is rather with the rationale for this in the eyes of the agent, that is, with a first-person or subjective justification, since an objective one in this case would be impossible.

Such justification is required by Kant's conception of rational agency, which, as we have seen, maintains that rational agents act according to their representation of law, or on principle. Accordingly, the problem could be described as explaining how agents, who act on principle, could justify to themselves acting in ways that are contrary to what they acknowledge to be the supreme normative principle. Simply put, Kant's explanation is that in such cases agents do not challenge the principle itself; rather they attempt, in their own eyes, to make an exception for themselves for the sake of inclination. Although this may be seen as a further development of the line of thought that Kant introduced at the end of GMS 1 in connection with his reference to a "natural dialectic," the existence of which was appealed to in order to justify the need for moral philosophy, the import of the present discussion is somewhat different. As Kant puts it, it shows that "we actually recognize the validity of the categorical imperative and (with due respect for it) allow ourselves only a few exceptions, which are, as it seems to us, insignificant and forced upon us" (GMS 4: 424$_{35-37}$). In other words, FLN is honored even in its breach, which is perhaps the clearest illustration of the role that it plays in the judgment of ordinary human reason for Kant.

8

The Formula of Humanity (FH)

This chapter is concerned with Kant's argument for and application of his second formulation of the categorical imperative, the "formula of humanity" or FH, and is divided into five parts. The first discusses Kant's claim that the categorical imperative presupposes the existence of something that is an end in itself. The second lays out Kant's taxonomy of ends. The third deals with the exegetical question of the meaning of "humanity" [*Menschheit*] in the claim that humanity is an end in itself. The fourth analyzes Kant's argument for the claim that humanity has such a status and the derivation of FH from this result. Finally, the fifth examines Kant's application of FH to the same examples that were used to illustrate FLN.

I

After five transitional paragraphs in which he reminds the reader of what has (and has not yet) been established, reprises the argument for the necessity of a metaphysics of morals, and underscores the error of attempting to ground morality in human nature or, more generally, experience (GMS 4: 425_1–27_{19}), Kant begins the move to FH by enriching his initial account of rational agency. Kant had initially characterized rational agents as beings with the capacity to act according to their representation of laws and equated this capacity with the possession of a will or practical reason. He now restates the point in somewhat different terms, defining "the will is a capacity to determine itself to act *in conformity with* [*gemäss*] the representation of certain laws," to which he adds that "what serves the will as the objective ground of its self-determination is the *end*" (GMS4: 427_{19-23}).[1] The latter provides us with a second essential feature of rational agency, namely, its intentionality or end-directedness. Kant did not hold that having ends is unique to rational beings, since we have seen that he

---

[1] Although the language is somewhat different, reflecting the different context in which it occurs, I take this to be in essential agreement with the "transcendental" definition of "end" [*Zweck*] that Kant provides in the third *Critique*: "an end is the object of a concept insofar as the former is considered as the cause of the former (the real ground of its possibility" (KU 5: 220; 105). By "transcendental" Kant here means perfectly general in the sense of abstracting from everything empirical.

was willing to apply teleological considerations to all organic beings and even to nature as a whole. What is unique to rational agents is that they set for themselves their own ends, rather than (except in the special case of happiness) having them provided by nature.

Kant's intent is to link this feature of rational agency with a formulation of the categorical imperative and this linkage is affirmed in the following passage:

> But suppose that there were something *whose existence in itself* had an absolute worth, which, as an end in itself could be a ground of determinate laws; then in it and only in it would lie the ground of a possible categorical imperative, i.e., of a practical law. (GMS 4: 428$_{3-6}$)

While leaving open the questions of whether there is something that is an end in itself and whose existence has an absolute worth and whether there is a categorical imperative, Kant here affirms that they reciprocally imply each other. In other words, the existence of something that could be regarded as an end itself is both a necessary and sufficient condition of the possibility of a categorical imperative.[2] Although a good deal of work would be necessary to clarify the point (including an account of what is understood by "end in itself"), the idea that the existence of something that is an end in itself is a *sufficient* condition of the possibility of a categorical imperative seems relatively unproblematic, since, arguably, entities with this status (if they exist) could be the source of unconditioned commands. This does not appear to be true, however, of the claim that the existence of ends in themselves is also a *necessary* condition of this possibility. In fact, Kant's emphasis on the purely formal nature of the categorical imperative and his insistence that any principle grounded in a presupposed end could have merely a conditioned status might seem incompatible with this claim.

Nevertheless, it is a core Kantian principle, long antedating GMS, that the concept of moral obligation presupposes an end that is necessary in itself.[3] Moreover, we shall see that Kant's denial that ends can ground the categorical imperative is limited to ends that are to be affected or brought about and that the end that Kant has in mind, namely, humanity or rational nature as end in itself, is not of that sort. But before turning to a consideration of Kant's distinction between different sorts of end and their relation to the categorical imperative, I shall attempt to sketch what I take to be the line of argument underlying Kant's claim that the categorical imperative presupposes an end. It runs as follows:

---

[2] I take this to be the force of Kant's statement that "in it [something that is an end in itself] and only in it would lie the ground of a possible categorical imperative." To say that the ground of a possible categorical imperative lies in something that is an end in itself is to say that the latter is a sufficient condition of the former; while to say that this ground lies *only* in it is to say that it is a necessary condition.

[3] See U 2: 298–99; 272–73. The passage is noted by Wood (1999, 114).

(1) Since ends are the sources of reasons to act, if an agent has no end in view, then that agent would have no reason to act.[4]

(2) But any imperative presupposes that there are reasons to act and a categorical imperative presupposes that these reasons are valid for all rational agents, which entails that they must be independent of any interests that are not shared by every conceivable rational agent.

(3) This entails that there must be an end that is likewise independent of any such interests; otherwise it would not be universally valid.

(4) Such an end, by definition, would be an end in itself.

(5) Therefore, if there is a categorical imperative, there must be something that exists as an end in itself.

As noted above, this argument does not purport to show either that there is a categorical imperative or that there exists anything which might be regarded as an end in itself. It likewise does not purport to show either that this end in itself is to be identified with humanity or rational nature or that the existence of the latter has absolute worth. I believe that it does show, however, that the existence of *something* with end in itself status is a necessary (as well as a sufficient) condition of a categorical imperative, which was the point at issue.

Against this, it might still be objected that, since it appears to ground morality in a pre-given value that is independent of the will, the dependence of the existence of a categorical imperative on the existence something with the status of an end in itself is incompatible with the autonomy of the will and, indeed, with the prioritizing of the right over the good, which since Rawls has often been considered a defining feature of the Kantian view.[5] Although this raises a number of complex issues, which will be discussed at various points in this chapter, for the present it must suffice to point out that the ends that are presupposed by the categorical imperative are only ends in a negative sense, that is, sources of constraint on the acts that one can permissibly perform. Moreover, as such, they presuppose the categorical imperative, which imposes this constraint on the will of finite rational agents, who are themselves the ends in question. In other words, it is not that being human or having a rational nature has an independent value, which is the source of an obligation to treat beings with these qualities with respect; it is rather that the categorical imperative bestows this

---

[4] I consider the thesis that ends are the sources of reasons to act, which is the essential premise of this argument, to be implicit in Kant's account of the connection between rational agency and ends at GMS 4: 427_{19-23}. Moreover, I do not think that there is any incompatibility between this and Kant's claim in both GMS 1 and the second *Critique* that the moral law itself provides an incentive and therefore a reason to act; for, as the second formula indicates, it only does so by providing an end, namely, humanity. I am indebted to Oliver Sensen for pointing out this possible source of objection.

[5] This line of objection has been forcefully argued by Sensen (2009, 317–18 and 2010, 103–4). I discuss the relation between Rawlsian prioritization of the right over the good and Kant in the Introduction.

value upon them by enjoining us to treat such beings with respect, which turns out to mean not using them merely as means to one's own ends.[6]

II

Assuming, then, that the categorical imperative presupposes the existence of something that is an end in itself, Kant's first task is to establish that humanity (understood as a place-holder for finite rational agency) is the required end. Since Kant's strategy for achieving this is the familiar one of canvassing the various sorts of end and then arguing by elimination that humanity alone fills the bill, we shall begin by examining Kant's taxonomy of ends.

(A) Objective and subjective ends

According to Kant, an objective end is one that is "given through mere reason" (GMS 4: 427$_{23}$). This means that the reason for its adoption is not based on inclination or any merely subjective preference, but on reasons that are valid for all rational agents. Conversely, subjective ends depend on inclination, and since different agents have different inclinations, such ends are not based on reasons that are valid for all rational agents. Kant accounts for this distinction by appealing to the previously discussed contrast between a *Bewegungsgrund* [motive] and a *Triebfeder* [incentive]. An objective end would be based on the former, which Kant defines as the "objective ground of volition," and a subjective one on the latter, which he defines as "the subjective ground of desire, that is, inclination" (GMS 4: 427$_{26-27}$).

The contrast between objective and subjective ends might seem puzzling, inasmuch as Kant's generic definition of an end as the "objective ground of the will's self-determination" suggests that all ends must be objective. The explanation lies in a distinction between two senses of "objective," which Kant fails to draw explicitly, but which is implicit in his account. I shall term them *objective$_1$* and *objective$_2$*. The former pertains to all ends, even subjective ones, insofar as they are sources of reasons to act, which, qua reasons, are universal and, as such, objectively valid. The latter, by contrast, are the subset of these that are given by pure reason and, as such, are valid for all rational agents, regardless of their inclinations. If any end is required for a categorical imperative, it would be an objective$_2$ end; but we shall see that the situation is complicated by the fact that such an end can be related to the categorical imperative in two distinct ways.

(B) Formal and material practical principles and their corresponding ends

Immediately after distinguishing between subjective and objective ends, Kant introduces a distinction between formal and material practical principles, which he

---

[6] It will be argued below that the ground for this lies in the fact that beings with a rational nature or humanity have the capacity for morality, that is, the capacity to recognize and obey the categorical imperative.

connects, at least in part, with the former distinction. We are told that a formal practical principle abstracts from all *subjective* [my emphasis] ends, whereas a material one is based on these very ends (GMS 4: 427$_{30-32}$). Although Kant does not say so explicitly, this implies that a formal principle does not abstract from objective ends or, more precisely, from objective$_2$ ends.

Kant introduces the notion of value into his account by noting that all material ends, which he identifies with ends that rational agents propose as effects of their discretionary action [*Handlung nach Belieben*] (GMS 4: 427$_{33-34}$), are merely relative, because their value is entirely a function of the agent's desires.[7] As such, they can provide the ground only for hypothetical imperatives. Again, Kant is implying, but not explicitly claiming, that objective$_2$ ends would have a non-relative or absolute value, that is, one that is independent of any desires or inclinations of agents and that could therefore ground the categorical imperative.

In the next and previously cited paragraph, Kant refers to an unspecified something, whose existence in itself has an absolute worth. While it is evident that this "something" is an objective$_2$ end, it remains unclear at this point whether it must be more than that, namely, a particular kind of objective$_2$ end. In order to appreciate the issue, it is necessary to keep in mind that the function of the sought-for end is to ground the categorical imperative and that this is distinct from being grounded in or required by such an imperative. It is easy see that objective$_2$ ends fall into the latter category, since, *ex hypothesi*, they are given by pure reason, but it is still not clear that any fall into the former.

Consider the good will. Although a paradigm case of something whose existence in itself has absolute worth or unconditioned value, it cannot plausibly be claimed to ground the categorical imperative; for the simple reason that it presupposes and, with the exception of a perfect or holy will, is itself defined in terms of it.[8] Moreover, the same can be said of the two obligatory ends (one's own perfection and the happiness of others), on the basis of which Kant later structured his doctrine of virtue.[9] As ends, the pursuit of which are morally required of all finite rational agents, they are both objective$_{2,}$ but they cannot be viewed as sources of the categorical imperative, since their status as morally required ends is a consequence of this imperative.

(C) Ends to be effected and self-standing ends

Kant introduces this distinction at GMS 4: 437$_{25-27}$ and it reflects the ambiguity of both the English term "end" and the German "*Zweck*." Although they usually refer to some purpose or aim to be achieved, they can also refer to something that already exists

---

[7] By "discretionary action" I take Kant to be referring to an action that is not obligatory.

[8] I take this to be the main reason for rejecting the thesis of Dean (2006) that humanity is to be identified with a good will. I shall take up other aspects of Dean's views in the next section.

[9] See MS 6: 384–88; 516–20. Presumably, a good will would be one that is committed to the end oft moral perfection, the pursuit of which falls under the end of one's own perfection.

and that constitutes a limit. Kant here terms the former an "end to be effected" [*ein zu bewirkender Zweck*] and the latter a "self-standing end" [*selbstständiger Zweck*]. The former is the familiar sense of "end" that is built into every maxim and constitutes the goal of every intentional action. What makes the latter an end is that it is likewise a source of reasons to act or, more often, to refrain from acting. In Kant's terms, this qualifies it as an objective ground of the will's self-determination, which is just his definition of an end.

The relevance of this distinction is that it makes it possible to specify just what kind of end is capable of grounding the categorical imperative. To begin with, it is evident from what we have just seen that it could not be an end to be effected, since any such end (even the good will) presupposes a reason to bring it about. Less obviously, however, it is also the case that not every self-standing end is capable of grounding the categorical imperative. For example, when people doff their hats to their country's flag they usually have no end to be effected in mind, but they nonetheless act for the sake of an end, namely, the revered object to which a symbolic value is attached.[10] But even though flags or other revered objects count as self-standing ends, they cannot ground a categorical imperative, because they are not valued for reasons that hold for all rational agents, that is to say, they are not objective$_2$ ends. Moreover, we can see from this that any end capable of grounding a categorical imperative must meet two distinct conditions: (1) it must be objective$_2$; and (2) it must be self-standing. Presumably, both conditions are met in what Kant describes as "something *whose existence in itself* [has] an absolute worth."

III

After defining the conditions that an end capable of grounding a categorical imperative must meet, Kant writes:

Now I say that the human being [*der Mensch*] and in general every rational being *exists* as end in itself, *not merely as means* for the discretionary use of this or that will, but must in all his actions, whether directed to himself or also to other rational beings, always be regarded *at the same time* [*zugleich*] as an end. (GMS 4: 428$_{7-11}$)

In light of the above stipulative claim, this section is devoted to the questions of what Kant understands by "the human being" and "humanity" and in virtue of what property he assigns to their referents the status of being an end in itself. Although there is general agreement that Kant uses these terms to refer to rational agents rather than to either individual human beings or the species, there is a decided lack of unanimity concerning the properties or capacities in virtue of which rational agents are deemed ends in them themselves A survey of the literature reveals three competing views: (1) Kant regards all minimally rational agents as ends in themselves in virtue of

---

[10] The example is borrowed from Wood (1998, 165–87).

their capacity to set ends; (2) Kant attributes this status only to agents with a good will; (3) Kant regards as ends in themselves all rational agents with a capacity for morality.[11] After criticizing the first two options, I shall argue for the third.

(A) Rational agents and the capacity to set ends

It is a prevalent view in the literature that "humanity," as it is used in GMS, refers to every minimally rational agent and that what qualifies every such agent to be an end in itself is a capacity to set ends, quite apart from the morality (or lack thereof) of these ends. This view receives its most direct support from Kant's statement that "Rational nature distinguishes itself from the rest [of nature] in that it sets itself an end" (GMS 4: 437$_{21-22}$). The most prominent proponents of this view are Korsgaard and Wood, who offer slightly different versions of it and emphasize different texts in supporting it. Accordingly, I shall consider the textual evidence to which each of them appeal in support of their reading. But before proceeding, it must be noted that the question of what Kant means by "humanity" is complicated by the fact that his accounts in various writings involve two distinct contrasts: with "animality" [*Tierheit*], on the one hand, and with "personality" [*Personalität*], on the other. Although both Korsgaard and Wood cite passages from both groups, Korsgaard appears to emphasize the former and Wood the latter.

(1) *Korsgaard's view.* In arguing for her thesis that the capacity to set ends is both the defining feature of rational agency and the ground for regarding rational agents as ends in themselves, Korsgaard provides what she takes to be both primary and supplementary textual evidence. I shall focus on the former.[12]

Although she does not characterize it as such, the first piece of evidence that Korsgaard cites is Kant's claim that "The capacity to set oneself an end—any end whatsoever—is what characterizes humanity (as distinguished from animality)" (MS 6: 392; 522).[13] This is as clear and unambiguous a statement as one could wish regarding the distinction between humanity and animality. Not only does Kant locate the distinguishing feature of humanity vis-à-vis animality in a capacity to set ends rather than merely in the possession of reason, understood as a cognitive capacity, he also explicitly affirms that this encompasses *all* ends, not merely those that are morally required.

Korsgaard finds additional support for her interpretation in Kant's teleological argument in GMS 1. At first glance, this seems an odd text to cite, since its main import is to argue that we should assume that reason was given to us in order to make it possible to attain a good will rather than happiness; but she takes the account of

---

[11] I am following Dean's characterization of the exegetical options. See Dean (2006, 17–33).

[12] Korsgaard's supplementary evidence consists of passages from the "Methodology of the Teleological Power of Judgment" at the end of the third *Critique*, which she takes as confirming her central thesis that rational choice is the source of objective value and the locus of absolute or unconditioned worth. See Korsgaard (1996, 128–31).

[13] Ibid., 110.

happiness that Kant provides as showing that for him reason has the task of choosing the ends required for happiness and not merely the means to ends that are set by nature.[14]

In support of her reading, Korsgaard also refers to Kant's playful account of the opening chapters of Genesis in the "Conjectural beginning of human history." Here the point is that the transition from animality to humanity and therefore the first step in a lengthy process of development, which eventually leads to morality, begins with the replacement of instinct by reason. As she puts it,

[T]here can be no question that in this essay Kant thinks of all human ends as being partially "set" by the operations of reason. They may be objects of desire or inclination, but it is reason that is responsible for the unique human characteristic of having non-instinctual desires.[15]

Korsgaard's final main piece of evidence is Kant's distinction in *Religion* between the predispositions to humanity and personality. Since this plays a central role in Wood's interpretation, I shall reserve further discussion of it for the analysis of his views. For the present, it must suffice to note that Korsgaard takes Kant's account of reason in connection with the predisposition to humanity to be in accord with the account given in his historical essays.[16]

(2) *Wood's view*: Wood likewise takes Kant to understand by "humanity" a capacity to set ends based on reason rather than a specifically moral capacity; though he broadens this to include related rational capacities. As he puts it, "The capacity to set ends through reason holds together the set of capacities constituting our humanity."[17] For Wood, however, the central text supporting this proposition is the one that is last on Korsgaard's list, namely, Kant's discussion in *Religion* of the three predispositions [*Anlagen*] to good in human nature: to "animality," to "humanity," and to "personality" (RGV 6: 26–28; 74–76). Accordingly, unlike Korsgaard, Wood contrasts the predisposition to humanity with the predisposition to personality, as well as with animality.[18] And since the former is explicitly a predisposition to morality, this forces him to deal with the question, which was largely glossed over by Korsgaard, of why Kant grounds the status of rational agents as ends in themselves in humanity rather than personality.

In order to address this question, we must consider briefly Kant's account of the predisposition to humanity, which according to Wood encompasses "all our rational capacities having no specific reference to morality."[19] In Kant's own characterization, this predisposition "can be brought under the general title of a self-love which is

---

[14] Ibid., 111–12.   [15] Ibid., 113.   [16] Ibid., 113–14.   [17] Wood (1999, 119).

[18] Admittedly, this is not completely fair to Korsgaard, since she does state that, "Humanity, completed and perfected, becomes personality." See Korsgaard (1996, 114). But this suggests that that there is a gradual transition from the capacities associated with humanity, that is to say culture, to morality, which I do not believe to be Kant's view. In addition, it naturally suggests the question: why should the status of being an end in itself not be reserved for perfected humanity?

[19] Wood (1999, 118).

physical and yet involves comparison (for which reason is required)," and the latter is necessary because "it is only in comparison with others that one judges oneself happy or unhappy" (RGV 6: 27; 75). In other words, what Kant finds to be distinctively human is a form of self-love, which involves a sense of self-worth, where this worth is measured by comparison with the worth of others.[20] To feel oneself superior to others, in whatever terms the comparison is being drawn, is to be happy; while to feel oneself inferior is to be unhappy. Presumably, such self-love requires reason in two respects: first, because any comparison must be based on a criterion, the selection of which requires a use of reason; and second, because gaining superiority, whether real or perceived, requires some sort of rational plan.

Here and elsewhere, Kant displays a certain ambivalence toward this predisposition.[21] On the one hand, he sees it as the root of culture, which Kant viewed as a civilizing process and in the third *Critique* characterized as the ultimate purpose of nature with regard to human kind.[22] Indeed, as Wood points out, the predisposition to humanity presupposes "a kind of freedom, namely, the ability to resist the immediate coercion of desires and impulses," which is a necessary (though not a sufficient) condition for morality.[23] On the other hand, Kant also suggests that this predisposition is the source of "diabolical vices," such as envy, ingratitude, and *Schadenfreude* (RGV 6: 27; 75). The latter point gives urgency to the above-mentioned question of why Kant appears to privilege the predisposition to humanity over personality.

Wood offers two reasons for this privileging, neither of which is completely satisfactory. The first is that the categorical imperative requires preserving and respecting rational nature in all of its functions, not merely in its moral function.[24] Although this is correct, it is beside the point; for the issue is not what the categorical imperative requires, but in virtue of what property or capacity does humanity attain the status of an end in itself. That all of the functions of such a being deserve respect is a consequence of

---

[20] This is contrasted with a "physical and merely *mechanical*" form of self-love, for which reason is not required and which can be attributed to animals and to the predisposition to animality in human nature. This form of self-love is manifested in the desire for self-preservation and the propagation of the species, which encompasses both sex and the preservation of the offspring. Oddly, Kant also includes under the predisposition to animality a social drive for community with other human beings. Presumably, Kant included it here rather than its more natural home, the predisposition to humanity, because he deemed it as instinctual rather than as based on reason (see RGV 6: 27; 75).

[21] Kant's ambivalence regarding the predisposition to humanity goes hand in hand with his ambivalence towards the culture-critique mounted by Rousseau in his "Second Discourse" (Rousseau, 1964, 101–228). In this essay, which deeply influenced Kant, Rousseau presents the course of civilization as involving the corruption of human beings as they were in an original "pure state of nature," where they were guided by instinct rather than reason. While Kant, particularly in his essays in the philosophy of history and the third *Critique*, shared Rousseau's views that the civilizing process began with the replacement of instinct by reason and that this inevitably led to inequality, corruption, and all of the vices connected with the development of society, Kant connected this with an historical teleology through which social conflict rooted in competition and spurred on by humankind's unsociable sociability will lead eventually to a positive outcome.

[22] See KU 5: 429–34; 297–301.

[23] Wood (1999, 119).

[24] Ibid., 120.

the status of such a being as an end in itself and therefore cannot be used to account for this status.

Wood's second reason suffers from a similar difficulty. He claims correctly that, "[I]t follows necessarily from the role played by the concept of an end in itself in grounding the categorical imperative that rational beings cannot be ends in themselves only insofar as they are virtuous or obedient to moral laws."[25] And Wood also correctly notes that the reason for this is that a categorical imperative is supposed to be *necessarily* binding on all rational beings. Indeed, if, as Kant maintains, this imperative addresses rational agents as such, and is grounded in the very concept of such an agent, it must also govern the treatment of every rational agent, since any agent who did not stand under this imperative, that is, who was not a being with regard to whom other agents have the obligation to treat as an end in itself, would likewise not have any obligations to these beings, which is contrary to the hypothesis. Nevertheless, this is again beside the point; for the present question is not whether end in itself status is applicable only to virtuous agents (that will be the next view to be considered), but whether the possession of a predisposition to humanity (as contrasted with personality) is sufficient for assigning this status. In rejecting the latter, Wood appears to conflate possessing the predisposition to personality with being virtuous. But inasmuch as the possession of the predisposition involves merely being conscious of standing under moral laws, not necessarily obeying them, it does not follow from the fact that being virtuous is not a condition of being an end in itself that having the predisposition to personality is not.

In conclusion, then, neither Korsgaard nor Wood succeed in making the case for their claim that for Kant the status of humanity as an end in itself is grounded solely in the capacity to set ends. At the same time, however, it must be admitted that unclarity on Kant's part is in some measure responsible for the situation. Kant does identify humanity with rational nature and claim that its defining characteristic is the capacity to ends of all kinds, not merely morally required or even permissible ones. And he does attribute an end in itself status to humanity, which suggests that it is because of the capacity to set ends that humanity has this status. But in spite of what Kant's account may suggest, it does not follow that a capacity to set ends is a *sufficient* condition for being an end in itself.

(B) Humanity as end in itself and the good will

The view that the humanity to which Kant assigns the status of end in itself is attributed only to rational agents with a good will, rather than to all minimally rational agents, has been argued by Richard Dean.[26] Although Dean's interpretation is deeply counter-intuitive and involves major difficulties, some of which will be discussed below, it has the virtues of addressing a significant problem in Kant's text and of avoiding what is especially problematic in the alternative considered above, namely, the separation of

---

[25] Ibid.
[26] See Dean (2006).

"humanity" and "end in itself" from anything specifically involving morality. While one might wonder why the mere capacity to set ends should confer a special status and dignity on rational beings, regardless of how this capacity is used, no such worry arises in the case of beings with a good will.

Dean provides two arguments for his reading: (1) a direct argument from an analysis of Kant's concept of value, particularly as it is manifested in GMS; and (2) an examination of the texts. But since the latter is concerned more with challenging alternative readings rather than directly supporting his own, I shall concentrate on the former. Dean's central argument turns on the similarities between Kant's accounts of the concept of a good will and of an end in itself. Although this is often viewed as a source of embarrassment, since it seems to commit Kant to the implausible view that we have duties only to those with a good will, Dean grabs the bull by the horns and argues for their identity.[27] Appealing to Kant's definitions and discussions of these concepts, he advances two premises:

(P$_1$)   If x has value independent of inclinations . . . , then x must be an end in itself.[28]

(P$_2$)   If x is valuable in all possible circumstances . . . , then x must be good without qualification.[29]

By supplementing these conditional premises with the claim that humanity has value in all possible circumstances, the equivalence of humanity and a good will supposedly follows. This is because Kant had previously argued that only a good will is good in all possible circumstances. Given this, Dean claims that, since something is good in all possible circumstances if and only if its value is independent of inclination, and since, *ex hypothesi*, the latter holds of an end in itself, it follows that humanity, insofar as it is regarded as an end in itself, is identical to a good will.[30] In other words, since Kant claims of both a good will and humanity (as an end in itself) that it is the only thing "in the world, or indeed . . . outside it" that is good without limitation, it follows that

---

[27]   Ibid., esp. 92–95. It should be noted that part of Dean's strategy involves deflating the requirements for having a good will. To this end, he defines it as "the will of a being who is committed to acting morally, who gives priority to moral principles rather than acting simply to satisfy her own desires, inclinations, impulses, or sentiments" (op. cit., 24). His point is that, since a good will, so defined, is not rare, the identification of beings with a good will and those that are ends in themselves does not lead to a moral elitism regarding those to whom we have duties. But even if one grants that Dean's account avoids the danger of a moral elitism regarding the *objects* of morality (those with regard to whom we have duties), it leads to paradoxical consequences concerning the *subjects* of morality (those who supposedly are obligated). For if having a good will is a necessary condition of attaining this status, it follows that those who lack it are not morally obligated. At one point (op. cit., 81), Dean appears to address this worry by claiming that those without a good will are obligated to strive to attain it. But while this may represent Kant's view, it is of no help here; for the question then becomes: why rational agents, who, *ex hypothesi*, lack humanity and therefore are not ends in themselves because they lack a good will, are so obligated?

[28]   Dean (2006, 38). The omitted portion in this and the following proposition refers to dignity, which Dean himself acknowledges is not essential to the argument.

[29]   Ibid., 39.

[30]   Ibid., 39–40.

in order to avoid attributing to Kant a fundamental inconsistency, it is necessary to identify humanity (as an end in itself) with a good will.[31]

An unargued premise in Dean's account is the identification of being *valuable* with being *good*; from which it follows that if something is deemed unconditionally valuable, it must likewise be considered unconditionally good and vice versa. Although this conclusion seems warranted, it actually rests on a conflation of two modes of evaluation, which is correlated with the two types of end distinguished previously, that is, between an end to be effected and a self-standing end. We saw that ends of the latter type, which include humanity, are ends in the negative sense of being entities that must never be acted against or disrespected. In other words, they pose a limiting condition on the will rather than providing it with a goal to be pursued. While it is good (morally required) to respect and sometimes to further such ends and bad (morally prohibited) to fail to do so, it would be strange to characterize ends in this sense as themselves good, since, unlike the good will, they are not among the objects of practical reason.[32]

Moreover, the very fact that a good will is an end to be effected makes it of the wrong logical type to ground a categorical imperative. As already noted, this is because its status as an end presupposes such an imperative as the source of the reasons to strive for its realization. Accordingly, it cannot also be claimed to ground the categorical imperative in the sense of being a condition of its possibility. And since Kant apparently assigns such a task to the concept of an end in itself, it follows that the concept of a good will cannot be regarded as equivalent to that of an end in itself.

(C) Humanity and the capacity for morality

The third view to be considered is that it is the capacity for morality that grounds the distinct status and worth that Kant assigns to humanity. This capacity involves both the consciousness of standing under moral laws and the capacity to obey them, but is compatible with these laws not being obeyed. Given the difficulties with the first two alternatives, this has obvious virtues as a fallback position, perhaps as an account of what Kant *should* have said; but I shall argue that an examination of the texts strongly suggest that it is the view he actually held.[33]

Since Kant uses "humanity" in a number of different contexts, each of which involves a different shade of meaning, I shall limit my consideration to those places in which he connects it with the status of being an end in itself, which, as such, possesses a dignity or inner worth that is incommensurate with any price. What is to be

---

[31] Ibid., 40.

[32] At KpV 5: 58; 186, Kant claims that the only objects of practical reason are the good and the evil [*Böse*]. By an "object of practical reason" I take Kant to understand an objective, that is, a state of affairs to be brought about or, in the language of GMS, an end to be effected.

[33] I also take this to be the view that many commentators (not including Korsgaard and Wood) implicitly attribute to Kant, often without treating the matter thematically. Dean (2006, 64–90) includes in this category Hill, Herman, and O'Neill. Another strong proponent of this view, to whom Dean does not refer, is Rawls (2000, esp. 158–60).

determined are the grounds on which Kant makes these claims about humanity. In one such passage Kant writes:

Now morality [*Moralität*] is the condition under which alone a rational being can be an end in itself, because only through it is it possible to be a legislative member in the realm of ends. Thus it is morality [*Sittlichkeit*] and humanity, insofar as it is capable of it, that alone has dignity. (GMS 4: 435$_{5-9}$)[34]

Although the claim that being a legislative member in the realm of ends is the condition under which a rational being can be an end in itself might suggest the good will reading, this is counterbalanced by the claim that it is humanity, *insofar as it is capable of morality*, that has dignity. Moreover, if, as seems reasonable, one understands by a legislative member in the realm of ends simply a being who has autonomy, then this too is perfectly compatible with the capacity reading, since having autonomy is merely a necessary and not also a sufficient condition of moral goodness.

The same view is also to be found in the second *Critique*, where it is connected with the notion of personality and membership in an intelligible world. Immediately after his famous paean to duty, Kant first notes that it is nothing other than personality, understood negatively as freedom and independence from the mechanism of nature and positively as a capacity for being subject to laws given by their own reason, that is, autonomy, that elevates human beings above the sensible world and makes them members of an intelligible order of things and thereby subject to morality (KpV 5: 87; 219). And he continues in the next paragraph,

The moral law is holy (inviolable). A human being is indeed unholy enough, but the *humanity* in his person must be holy in him. In the whole of creation everything one wants and over which he has any power can also be used *merely as a means*; a human being alone, and with him every rational creature, is an end in itself: by virtue of the autonomy of his freedom he is the subject of the moral law, which is holy. (KpV 5: 87; 210)

Finally, in his discussion of servility [*Kriecherei*] in the *Metaphysics of Morals* Kant both denies that it is merely the capacity to set ends that is the source of the unique worth of humanity and reiterates the thesis that the source of this worth lies in being subject to morality. He does the former by stating that, in comparison with animals,

Although a human being has, in his understanding, something more than they and can set himself ends, even this gives him only an *extrinsic* value ... that is to say, it gives one man a higher value than another, that is, a *price* as a commodity in exchange with these animals as things, though he still has a lower value than the universal medium of exchange, money, the value of which can therefore be called preeminent (*pretium eminens*). (MS 6: 434; 557)

---

[34] Unlike Hegel, Kant tended to regard "*Moralität*" and "*Sittlichkeit*" as synonyms.

And, with regard to the latter, he writes:

> But a human being regarded as a *person*, that is, as the subject of a morally practical reason, is exalted above any price; for as a person (*homo noumenon*) he is not to be valued merely as a means to the ends of others or even his own ends, but as an end in itself, that is, he possesses a *dignity* (an absolute inner worth) by which he extracts *respect* for himself from all other rational beings in the world. (MS 6: 434–35; 557)

Although major interpretive issues can seldom be decided by a single text, the first of these passages appears to provide a fairly decisive refutation of the Korsgaard–Wood thesis that it is the capacity to set ends that accounts for the unique status and value of humanity. While Kant here states that this capacity, together with the possession of understanding with which it is inseparably linked, differentiates human and other rational beings from reasonless animals and gives them a higher value in the sense of price, he denies that it gives them a qualitatively distinct kind of value.

In addition to reiterating the thesis that it is qua subject of morality or, as Kant here puts it, "of a morally practical reason," that we (and other rational beings) count as persons and have a dignity rather than merely a price, the second passage characterizes a person as "homo noumenon." This is not to be taken as a metaphysical thesis about the "noumenal" nature of persons, but rather as an indication that autonomy and imputability are not empirical properties or capacities of rational agents, but qualities that we assign to them insofar as we conceive of them as persons or, equivalently, as subjects or addressees of morally practical reason.[35]

For an understanding of what Kant means by "person" and "personality," however, perhaps the most important text is the following:

> A *person* is a subject whose actions can be *imputed* to him. *Moral* personality is therefore nothing other than the freedom of a rational being under moral laws (whereas psychological personality is merely the ability to be conscious of one's identity in different conditions of one's existence). From this it follows that a person is subject to no other laws than those he gives to himself (either alone or at least in accord with others). (MS 6: 223; 378)

Two points in this passage call for comment. The first is the contrast between moral and psychological personality. The latter, which is the sense of "personality" at issue in the Third Paralogism in the first *Critique*, is basically equivalent to personal identity, construed in a Lockean sense.[36] By contrast, moral personality is understood as freedom

---

[35] Kant uses the expression "*homo noumenon*" in the *Metaphysics of Morals*, often contrasting it with "*homo phaenomenon.*" The contrast is between human beings considered as persons or subjects of morality, and as merely natural beings. This usage abstracts from, but does not deny, the physical properties of phenomenal human beings. See, for example, MS 6: 239; 317, 295; 442, 335; 476, 418; 544, 423; 547, 430; 533, 434; 557, and VMS 23: 257 and 398.

[36] See KrV A361–66 and B408. In the *Anthropology* Kant states that what makes a human being into a person is the capacity to have the "I" in his representations, that is, self-consciousness, and that it is through the unity of consciousness through the changes he undergoes that he is one and the same person. In the same context, Kant also suggests that this is the source of the dignity that humans possess vis-à-vis animals and the

under laws, which involves imputability and autonomy (a person being subject to no laws other than those she gives to herself). The second point is that "moral personality" is defined in terms of "being *under* moral laws" [my emphasis] rather than as obeying them. At this point, this should be no surprise; but given the virtual synonymony of "personality" and "humanity," it provides additional confirmation for the thesis that it is the *capacity* for morality that grounds the unique status and value of humanity.

Before concluding this defense of the capacity for morality reading of the special status that Kant assigns to humanity, it is necessary to respond to the criticism of this reading advanced by Dean, which basically boils down to the thesis that it is absurd to attribute a higher value to a capacity than to its realization. As he puts it,

It is conceptually bizarre and possibly even incoherent, to place a higher value on an unrealized capacity than on the thing itself. To claim that the capacity of morality has the highest possible value is to embrace just this sort of conceptual perversity.[37]

If this is what the capacity reading maintained, Dean would be correct. But it is not committed to the absurd view that it is somehow better merely to have the capacity to be moral than actually to be moral. As was already indicated in discussing Dean's identification of a good will with an end in itself, the issue is not what is better or best, but what is the *condition* of treating humanity in our own person and others as an end in itself having dignity. And that this condition is the capacity for morality in no way conflicts with Kant's view that the good will is the only unconditioned good.

IV

We have seen that, after claiming that the possibility of a categorical imperative rests on the existence of something that is an end in itself and whose existence has an absolute worth, without further ado, Kant writes:

Now I say that the human being and in general every rational being *exists* as an end in itself, *not merely as means* for the discretionary use of this or that will, but must in all his actions, whether directed to himself or also to other rational beings, always be regarded *at the same time* as an end. (GMS 4: 428$_{7-11}$)

In the previous section, we began an analysis of this pivotal claim by trying to determine the property or capacity in virtue of which Kant claims that a human being exists as an end in itself. And, after examining the major interpretive options, it was concluded that it was in virtue of possessing a capacity for morality. The next logical step would be to demonstrate that human and, more generally, rational agents, actually

---

right to do with them as they see fit (A 7: 127; 239). Inasmuch as Kant here characterizes the ground of the unique value of humanity entirely in terms of a theoretical capacity, his account differs from that found in his various writings in moral philosophy.

[37] Dean (2006, 87).

have this capacity, which, on Kant's analysis, turns out to be autonomy. But since Kant has not yet introduced the concept of autonomy and since, even if he had, demonstrating that rational agents possess it does not fall within the scope of a metaphysics of morals, Kant cannot proceed in this way. Instead, he uses the thesis that rational agents are to be regarded as ends in themselves as a means for deriving a new formulation of the categorical imperative. His intent is to show that *if* there is a categorical imperative, it may be expressed in terms of the formula of humanity: "*So act that you use humanity in your own person as well as in the person of any other, always at the same time as end and never merely as means*" (GMS 4: 429_{10-13}).

The present section analyzes this derivation, which occupies two paragraphs of the text (GMS 4: 428_7–29_{13}). The first begins with the bald assertion cited above and the second ends with the presentation of the formula. Kant's derivation is complicated, however, by the fact that FH presupposes that humanity, both in our own selves and others, exists as an end in itself. But inasmuch as Kant is not yet in a position to demonstrate this, since that would require stepping outside the domain of a metaphyics of morals, Kant's problem is to construct a viable argument within these self-imposed methodological constraints.

Seen in this light, it is clear that the only route available to Kant is to demonstrate not merely that we necessarily must regard rational agents in this way, but that we have good reason (which falls short of proof) for doing so, beyond it being necessary for morality. In what follows, I shall assume this to be Kant's procedure and attempt to formulate the argument underlying it. It consists of two steps, each of which is contained in one of the paragraphs. The first assumes that the possibility of a categorical imperative presupposes the existence of *something* as an end in itself and argues by elimination that rational agents are the only viable candidates for that status. The second argues that we have good reasons to regard rational agents as ends in themselves. These reasons fall short of proof because Kant is forced to rely on a premise that he is not yet in position to establish, which makes the overall argument conditional in a two-fold sense. First, it presupposes the existence of the categorical imperative in order to argue for a particular formulation of it. Second, Kant helps himself to a premise regarding the nature of rational agency, which he is not yet in position to justify and which he provisionally characterizes as a "postulate."

(A) Humanity as an end in itself and the possibility of a categorical imperative

After stating that humans and, indeed, all rational agents, exist as ends in themselves, Kant proceeds to eliminate various other potential candidates for this status, namely, objects of inclination, the inclinations themselves, and non-rational natural entities. The first consists of ends to be effected, the second provides the motivating grounds for effecting such ends, while the third encompasses self-standing ends that are not products of human activity. After briefly considering Kant's rejection of the claims of each of these for end in itself status, we shall examine his appeal to rational beings, under the title of "persons," who presumably have at least a *prima facie* claim to such status.

(1) *Objects of inclination*: The denial of end in itself status or unconditioned worth to such objects is relatively non-controversial.[38] As Kant puts it, "All objects of inclinations have only a conditioned worth; for if the inclinations and the needs grounded on them did not exist, their object would have no worth" (GMS 4: 428_{12-14}). Expressed in the language of ends, if making x my end were based on an inclination, then x would be merely a "relative" or "material end," since its status as an end would be contingent on the fact that I happen to have an inclination for it.[39]

(2) *The inclination themselves*: Although inclinations are not the sort of things that one would regard as ends, except perhaps in the special case where one might endeavor to develop a liking for something, say broccoli, because it is supposedly nutritious, Kant includes them among his targets for elimination on the grounds that they are the source of needs and therefore of ends that presuppose needs. Kant goes beyond a simple elimination, however, by claiming notoriously that "inclinations . . . are so far from having an absolute worth, so as to make one wish to have them, that it must rather be the universal wish of every rational being to be entirely free from them" (GMS 4: 428_{15-18}).[40] The general response to this is that this global disparagement of inclination goes too far, since some inclinations, for example, a sympathetic feeling for those in need, are undoubtedly good things, even if they are not unconditionally good. Moreover, it is customary to cite Kant's own quite different, assessment of inclinations in *Religion*, where he claims that,

> *Considered in themselves* natural inclinations are *good*, i.e., not reprehensible, and to want to extirpate them would not only be futile but harmful and blameworthy as well; we must rather only curb them, so that they will not wear each other out but will instead be harmonized into a whole called happiness. (RGV 6: 58; 102)

It seems evident that this represents Kant's considered view on the matter. In addition to the indirect moral benefit provided by some inclinations, this passage reminds us that the (harmonious) satisfaction of inclination constitutes happiness for

---

[38] I have characterized this argument as *relatively* non-controversial because it has been criticized by Kerstein (2006, 204). He objects to it on the grounds that a critic might claim that Kant got things backwards. According to Kerstein, rather than it being the case that something is good because we desire it, we should say that we desire it because it is good. Although this is correct, it is misguided as an objection to Kant. As both Korsgaard and Wood point out, the value of *all* ends, even inclination-based ones, is an *objective* matter, since it is a product of reason (see Korsgaard, 1996, 114–17 and Wood, 1999, 127–30). In other words, rather than claiming that some things (objects of inclination) are good simply because we desire them, Kant maintains that, even in these cases, we desire things because we deem them good, though the reasons for this may be agent-relative.

[39] As Dean points out (2006, 118), Kant presents his argument by elimination in terms of value, denying that objects of inclination could have an unconditioned worth; but the point can also be made in terms of ends.

[40] For a similar statement, see KpV 5: 118; 235.

Kant. But happiness for Kant is not only a non-relinquishable natural end, but, when proportioned to morality, an essential component of the highest good. And since to wish to be free of inclinations is to wish to be incapable of happiness, this is clearly not a view that Kant would endorse. Moreover, the present argument does not rely on this extreme claim, since the need to curb inclinations is sufficient to undermine their claim for unconditioned worth.

(3) *Things*: Kant lumps together all natural and non-rational beings under the label "things" [*Sachen*] and claims that they have only a relative value as means. Since this includes the entire non-human animal kingdom, and since the ends for which they serve as means prominently include the inclination-based (objective$_1$) ends of human beings, it is not surprising that many Kantians, not to mention moral philosophers of non-Kantian orientations, find this claim unsettling, if not repugnant.[41] But since an examination of this claim would involve a venture into normative ethics that lies well beyond the meta-ethical framework of GMS, it cannot be undertaken here. Thus, it must suffice to note that, far from granting a moral permission to treat animals in any manner that one wishes, Kant affirmed that we have obligations to treat them humanely. What is distinctive about Kant's position regarding the treatment of animals is merely that he does not regard these obligations as duties, strictly speaking, *to animals*.[42] Rather, Kant maintains that we have duties to ourselves with *regard to* [*in Ansehung*] animals, which, by means of an "amphiboly in moral concepts of reflection," we mistakenly take as a duty *to* [*gegen*] them (MS 6: 442; 563).[43]

(4) *Rational beings*: The fourth and final type of entity that Kant considers in his quest to find something that may be said to exist as an end in itself are rational beings and he suggests that their possession of this status is indicated by the fact that they are called "persons." Nevertheless, at least two problems remain. One is the familiar problem of neglected alternatives. Kant has argued, in effect, that rational beings, considered as persons, are the only conceivable candidates for end in itself status, but that claim rests on the premise that he has excluded all the alternatives. Thus, it seems reasonable to ask how Kant can be sure that he has really done so.[44]

---

[41] Typical of the Kantian response is the remark of O'Neill, who writes: "The sharp distinction Kant draws between persons and things is not convincing. The intermediate possibilities often perplex us. Are infants and animals, the senile and the comatose, things or persons? Provided that we respect other persons, may we use all inanimate objects as mere means—including works of art, deserts and wildernesses, the earth itself? Despite his insistence that ethics is for *finite* rational beings, Kant fails to address the full implications of finitude" (1989, 138 n11). Although the status of infants, the senile, the comatose (and the insane) may be problematic, given Kant's rigid thing–person dichotomy, the classification of all non-rational animals as things is clear.

[42] I say duties "strictly speaking" because in his lectures Kant suggests that we have analogues of duties to animals insofar as animal actions are analogues of human actions (MPC 27: 459–60; 212–13, and MSV 27: 710; 434–35).

[43] For a useful discussion of this topic from a contemporary Kantian perspective, see Wood (1999, 101–5).

[44] This objection has been raised by Kerstein (2006, 204), who poses the issue in terms of absolute goodness and suggests, as a possible neglected alternative, a state of affairs in which all rational agents are happy. Although Kerstein is correct to note that Kant does not consider this possibility here, it is clear from his

Although arguments by elimination involve an unavoidable indeterminacy, I believe that Kant can provide a plausible answer that is based partly on his account of ends and partly on his conception of a rational being. Setting aside inclinations, which, as noted above, are not usually considered ends, we have seen that Kant recognizes two ontologically distinct types of end: ends to be effected or brought about and self-standing ends. At least for the purpose of the present argument, Kant seems to assume that inclination-based ends encompass the complete class of the former. We have seen that this is not strictly true, since Kant recognizes non-inclination-based ends of the first type, for example, the good will and the two ends that are also duties of the *Doctrine of Virtue*; but the situation can be easily rectified to accommodate these. All that is needed is to point out that the latter are not ends in themselves (objective$_2$ ends) *in the required sense*, since their status as ends presupposes and therefore cannot ground a categorical imperative.

This leaves us with self-standing ends, which is a somewhat trickier matter. Here, I take the essential point to be the connection between rationality and self-consciousness, which Kant builds into his concept of a person. Simply put, only a being that is an end *for itself*, which requires self-consciousness, can lay claim to being an end *in itself*. Perhaps Kant's clearest statement of this, which also underscores the connection between self-consciousness and personality, is at the very beginning of the *Anthropology*, where he writes:

The fact that the human being can have the "I" in his representations raises him infinitely above all other living things on earth. Because of this he is a *person*, and by virtue of the unity of consciousness through all that happens to him, one and the same person—i.e., through rank and dignity an entirely different thing [*Wesen*] from things [*Sachen*], with which one can do as one likes. (A 7: 127; 239)[45]

I shall return to this crucial point below in connection with an analysis of the second step in Kant's argument. But first it is necessary to note the second of the two problems with the first step. It concerns the grounds for Kant's claim that rational beings are persons and therefore objective ends in the sense that no other end can be set in their place to which they would serve merely as means. Although if what was said above is correct, Kant could have mounted an argument for this claim, the only supporting reason he provides at this juncture is that, if one were to deny it, "nothing at all of *absolute worth* would be encountered; but if all worth were conditioned, hence contingent, then no supreme practical principle for reason could be encountered anywhere" (GMS 4: 428$_{29-33}$). In effect, then, at this point Kant is content to claim that the price

account of the good will that he did not regard happiness *per se* as an unconditioned good. Admittedly, this does not resolve the issue, since it might still be supposed that with a little ingenuity it is possible to provide other candidates; but it at least places the burden of proof on the critic.

[45] Since this passage is from the *Anthropology*, it is not surprising that it refers specifically to human beings; but it is clear that the point is applicable to rational beings as such.

of denying personhood or personality to rational agents is a moral nihilism, which leaves open the whole question of whether such nihilism might not be justified.[46]

(B) The warrant for regarding rational beings as ends in themselves

Kant begins the second paragraph of his derivation of FH by reiterating what is at stake. To this end, he reminds us that, if there is such an imperative, "it must be one such that from the representation of that which is necessarily an end for everyone, because it is an *end in itself*, it constitutes an *objective* principle of the will" (GMS 428_{35}–29_2). In other words, such an imperative must be regarded as necessarily an end for everyone, which is only possible if it is taken as an end in itself. From this, together with the argument by elimination in the preceding paragraph, Kant concludes that the ground of this still sought for principle is "*Rational nature exists as an end in itself*" (GMS 4: 429_{2-3}). This remains, however, a bare assertion and stands in need of further argument. Kant attempts to provide this argument in two steps, each of which consists of a single sentence.

(1) "The human being necessarily represents his own existence in this way; so far it is therefore a *subjective* principle of human actions" (GMS 4: 429_{3-5}). As Wood notes, this is the crucial premise and its brevity makes its interpretation particularly precarious.[47] Beginning with what is relatively clear, Kant's locution indicates that his intent is not to argue that the principle "rational nature exists as an end in itself" is a *merely subjective* principle, but, rather, to argue that it is *at the very least* a subjective principle. Due to the inclusion of the element of necessity, it is also clear that Kant is not presenting this principle as an empirical generalization regarding how human beings tend to value themselves. Instead, Kant's principle seems to involve a claim about the essential nature of rational agency and the task is to determine exactly what this is supposed to be.

I believe that the key to understanding Kant's claim lies in the above-mentioned connection between rational agency, personhood (or personality), and self-consciousness. In an effort to spell this out, I shall briefly revisit the question of what is involved in setting an end. First, we have seen that only rational beings have the capacity to set ends. To this we can now add that this capacity is dependent upon the possession of self-consciousness. The reason for this is simply that one cannot set an end without knowing that one is doing so.

Second, in setting an end I am making it *my* end. This does not mean that the end must be selfish, since I can and (according to the categorical imperative) should adopt unselfish ends, such as furthering the happiness of others. It is rather that any end that I could conceivably have is mine, not merely in the trivial sense that it is defined as such, but in the more substantive sense that I am both the one who set the end and the

---

[46] I use the expression "moral nihilism" here in order to underscore the fact that Kant's point is that if there were no entities to which the label "person" could legitimately be attached, there would be no specifically moral values.

[47] Wood (1999, 125).

one *for whom* it is an end. As Kant himself put it, while I can be constrained by others to perform actions that are means to their ends, "I can never be constrained by others *to have an end*; only I myself can *make* something my end" (MS 6: 381; 513).

Third, if Wood is correct (and I believe he is) in claiming that, "In the broadest sense . . . an end is anything *for the sake of which* we act (or refrain from acting)," then in setting any end, I must necessarily also regard myself as an end.[48] This follows from the fact that I am the one for whom the end is set. And, as Wood also notes, in regarding myself as the being for whom an end is set, I am also attributing a certain worth to myself. Accordingly, the questions become: what kind of end must I regard myself as being in the act of setting any particular end and what sort of worth must I attribute to myself?

Since it is clear that I do not regard myself as an end to be effected (I cannot literally bring myself into existence, though I can endeavor to change my condition), if I consider myself as an end, it must be as a self-standing one. We have seen, however, that the concept of a self-standing end is not equivalent to that of an end in itself, since some such ends, for example, a national flag, are only valued as ends, that is, as things for the sake of which we act or refrain from acting in a certain way, because of their relation to something else, which is the source of their value. Thus, we are led to ask: why must I consider the self-standing end that I take myself to be also as an end in itself?

This is obviously the crucial question and, equally obviously, the answer depends on how the latter notion is understood. And if, as seems appropriate, we base our interpretation on how Kant takes the expression "in itself" in his formulation and application of FH, it appears that its force is to preclude treating the end in question "merely as means," which is equivalent to "as nothing more than as a means to a further end." In other words, to take oneself as an end in itself is just to take oneself as one who cannot be regarded as nothing more than a means to some further end, but whose status as an end must always be respected, even when one is being used as a means.

If this is what considering myself as an end in itself involves, it follows that I must necessarily regard myself in this way in my capacity as the one for whom an end is set, because the failure to do so would involve a contradiction. The contradiction consists in the fact that in the same act I would be regarding myself as both setting an end and as not setting one, since, *ex hypothesi*, my "end" would be nothing more than a means to the end of another. Clearly, I can *make* the ends of others my ends, in the sense that I can endeavor to help them realize their ends, but that is quite different from regarding my ends as nothing more than the ends of another; for in that case they would no longer be my ends.

This brings us to the question of value or worth, which has two aspects: one regarding the end and the other the end-setter. With regard to the former, it is often

---

[48] Wood (1999, 125), 116.

noted that, in making something my end, I necessarily regard it as good.[49] Moreover, as a rational agent, I base my assessment on reasons, which I regard as valid for all rational agents. In the case of inclination-based ends, however, the scope of these reasons is limited to those who share my inclination and are in relevantly similar circumstances. Thus, if my end were to enjoy a meal in a fine Thai restaurant, I would not deem it good for someone who is allergic to peanuts. This, then, would be what Kant calls a "subjective end" or, in the language introduced earlier, it would be objective$_1$. And from this it follows that all such ends have merely a relative worth.

As is clear from the argument by elimination, it also follows that if unconditioned worth is to be found anywhere, it must be in the end-setter rather than in the end that is set. But the problem is complicated by the fact that the end-setter must likewise be considered under two aspects: as the agent who sets the end and as the one for whom the end is set, even though both pertain to one and the same agent, who is a person in the forementioned logical sense. Accordingly, it is necessary to determine under which aspect such worth is supposedly assigned by Kant.

Although to my knowledge the issue has never been framed in quite this way, the prevailing view appears to be that the former aspect is the locus of unconditioned worth, on the grounds that the setting of objective ends is the ultimate source of value. As Wood, summarizing the argument on this interpretation puts it, the key step consists in "the inference from the objective goodness of our ends to the unconditional goodness (as an end in itself) of the rational capacity to set ends, on the grounds that it is the source of this goodness."[50]

While there is no quarrel with Wood's claim that rational nature is the ultimate value for Kant, there is room for disagreement regarding his location of this value in the capacity to set ends, as well as his interpretation of the argument presently under consideration. Having already dealt at some length with the first point, I shall not return to it. As far as the second is concerned, I must admit that I fail to see the regressive argument from conditioned to condition that both he and Korsgaard find in the text.[51] Granted, given the cryptic nature of Kant's argument, *any* interpretation is bound to be somewhat conjectural. Nevertheless, I maintain that better sense can be made of it, if we attribute unconditioned worth to the person qua that for whom the end is set rather than to the person qua setter of the end.

First of all, this accords with the preceding analysis of what leads rational agents necessarily to regard themselves as ends in themselves, that is, with the subjective

---

[49] See, for example, Korsgaard (1996, 114–19) and Wood (1999, 127–32).

[50] Wood (1999, 129). Although there are differences in the way in which she develops her interpretation, fundamentally the same thesis is affirmed by Korsgaard (1996, esp. 119–24).

[51] Here I am in agreement with Kerstein (2006, esp. 210). For the view that Kant is here presenting a "regressive argument" that moves from conditioned to its condition, see Korsgaard (1996, esp. 119–25) and Wood (1999, 127).

necessity of this self-conception. If that is correct, then, given the correlation between end in itself status and unconditioned worth, one would expect that it is in virtue of being that for whom ends are set that rational agents necessarily take themselves as having unconditioned worth. Furthermore, it seems clear that in setting an end, I am also implicitly assigning *some* worth to myself as that for whom the end is set. Finally, this worth must be viewed as unconditioned, not because, like the good will, it is considered good without limitation, or even good at all, but because there is literally nothing by which the worth of that for whom the end is set could be conditioned.

Against this it might be objected that one's self-worth is conditioned by the value of the ends that one sets. Thus, if through reflection I come to regard the ends that I have set for myself as impractical, trivial, selfish or, even worse, evil, this will inevitably lessen my sense of self-worth. Moreover, in support of this one could cite Kant's account of respect for the law as the moral incentive in the second *Critique*. According to Kant, the recognition of the failure to live up to the dictates of the law has the effect of "striking down self-conceit," thereby producing a feeling of humiliation. Indeed, at one point he states that, absent agreement with the moral law, a person's opinion of his self-worth is "reduced to nothing" (KpV 5: 78; 203). How, then, can one claim that for Kant a person's self-worth is unconditioned?

This objection misconstrues the point at issue. The claim is not that for Kant every person's sense of self-worth or self-esteem is unconditioned. Even apart from moral considerations, that would be an absurd bit of empirical psychology. It is rather merely a certain kind of self-worth, namely, that which pertains to a person qua the one for whom ends are set, that is unconditioned, because, as noted above, there is nothing by which it could be conditioned. It is also, I submit, only a person, so considered, to whom Kant attributes a dignity [*Würde*], that is, a worth that is incommensurate with any price (GMS 4: 434$_{31}$–35$_{28}$)

Moreover, this points to the need to assume an irreducible duality within the self, which stems from the nature of self-consciousness and here takes the form of a distinction between the self qua end-setter and the self qua that for whom ends are set. Perhaps the most familiar phenomenon that seems to presuppose such a duality is self-deception, which also plays a central role in Kant's account of evil.[52] Any explanation of self-deception and its possibility requires a distinction between the self qua deceiver and the self qua deceived, even though both must be regarded as aspects of a single self. The same duality also seems to underlie common expressions such as "I let myself down," "I cannot live with myself," "I am ashamed of myself," etc. These all express negative self-relations, which like the conception of self-consciousness or personality that underlies them (and their positive counterparts), presuppose a two-fold self: one is the self *of whom* one is ashamed, the other the self *who* is ashamed. The worth of the former is conditioned and relative to the latter; whereas the worth of the latter

---

[52] For my discussion of this topic, see Allison (1990, esp. 158–61).

self, as end in itself, is unconditioned.[53] As Nietzsche nicely put it, "Whoever despises himself still esteems the despiser within himself."[54]

(2) The aim of the preceding account was to show why Kant held that it is subjectively necessary for the self to attribute a unique worth to itself qua that for whom ends are set, or, in the case of Nietzsche, the self who makes the valuations and for whom the valuations are made. The next step is to determine whether this is something more than a subjective necessity, perhaps a strange psychological quirk. Kant claims that it is something more in the following passage:

> But every other rational being necessarily represents his own existence in this way as a consequence of the same rational ground as is valid for me; therefore it is at the same time an *objective* principle, from which, as a supreme practical ground, all laws of the will must be capable of being derived. (GMS 4: 429₅₋₉)

This statement is likewise open to a variety of interpretations. Essential to any interpretation, however, is the note that Kant attaches to it, in which he writes: "This proposition I here set forth as a postulate. In the last section one will find the grounds for it" (GMS 4: 429₃₅₋₃₆). Since the last section to which Kant refers is GMS 3, this means that he is at present making a claim within the framework of a metaphysics of morals that has a provisional status, which can only be vindicated through a critique of pure practical reason. And since Kant attaches the asterisk to the phrase "the same rational ground as is valid for me," this suggests that what is here being postulated, or provisionally assumed, is the *objective* validity of my conception of myself as an end in itself, together with all that this entails.[55] Accordingly, like Kant, we shall here take this for granted and explore what supposedly follow from it.

The text indicates that Kant affirms two consequences, the second of which follows from the first. The first is a change in both the epistemic status and scope of a person's self-conception as an end in itself. In other words, because of the postulate I may now consider my self-conception as objectively rather than merely subjectively valid, that is, as holding not merely for myself, but for all rational agents in the sense that they are rationally constrained to acknowledge it. The second is the formulation of the sought-for principle of morality (FH) on the basis of this result. At this point, each of these

---

[53] The idea here is that to think of the worth of the latter self as conditioned requires assuming another self for the sake of whom it exists, which presumably could only be God. But for the self to conceive of itself in this way would involve conceiving itself as something like a means for God's ends. Although this may express the view of some religious thinkers, it is incompatible with the Kantian conception of the self as an end in itself, not to mention as autonomous.

[54] Nietzsche (1955, 75). The passage is cited by Wood (1999, 162).

[55] Wood (1999, 131–32) suggests that what is postulated is transcendental freedom. I concur; but would add that the emphasis should be placed on the positive conception of freedom as autonomy, rather than the negative conception of causal independence. The point is that the former involves not merely the capacity to set ends (Wood's view), but the capacity for morality, that is, a predisposition to personality, not simply to humanity.

consequences can be dealt with expeditiously and I shall consider the former here and the latter below.

The confusing thing about the first point concerns the role of the postulate, since Kant's cryptic statement creates the impression that he is taking back with one hand what he has given with the other, namely, objective validity to the self's conception of itself as an end in itself. Nevertheless, I believe that we can understand what Kant is getting at by considering how the argument might proceed without this postulate. Presumably, the most it could show is that, inasmuch as it is subjectively necessary for me to conceive my existence in this way, it is also subjectively necessary for other rational agents to conceive theirs in the same manner. But even setting aside the problematic nature of such a claim, this result would have no normative import; for the fact that all rational agents, including myself, regard themselves as ends in themselves, no more obligates me to treat them as such, than the fact that someone believes he is Napoleon obligates me to treat him as such.

If this is correct, then the function of the postulate is to make possible the introduction of normativity into the discussion, which is necessary if it is to lead to the formulation of a moral principle. Moreover, it does this in two steps. The first is to convert the subjective necessity of conceiving myself as an end in itself into an objective one and therefore a right. The second is to extend this right to all rational agents, which brings with it a corresponding obligation on the part of all rational agents to recognize this right and to act accordingly. Taken together they yield a universalization argument to the effect that the same rational ground (the postulate) that licenses me to regard myself as an end in itself also warrants all other rational agents to regard themselves in the same way.[56] And since this concerns a right or warrant to be regarded in a certain way it has normative import.

(3) "*So act that you use humanity, whether in your own person or in the person of any other, always at the same time as an end, never merely as means*" (GMS 4: 429_{10-12}). This is FH, the moral principle or formula, which Kant derives immediately from the preceding considerations. In fact, it is the direct translation into imperatival terms of the principle that rational nature exists as an end in itself. Simply put, the claim is that if this is how rational nature, whether in oneself or others, rightly regards itself, then this is how it ought to be treated. And since to consider something as end in itself just is to consider it as not being merely the means to some further end, it follows that this is also how it should be treated, which is what the formula claims.[57]

We shall examine below how Kant applies this formula to particular cases; but first a word is in order regarding the inclusion of the term "humanity" in the formula, even

[56] Korsgaard (1996, 123) likewise attributes a universalization argument to Kant at this point; though hers is based on the premise that rational choice involves a value conferring status, which one cannot claim for oneself without also attributing it to others.

[57] It is essential to keep in mind that the argument is from a premise about how rational agents necessarily regard themselves to a conclusion about how they ought to be treated, rather than from a metaphysical premise about their inherent nature. The latter would lead to a heteronomous moral realism.

though it does not appear in the argument leading up to it. Inasmuch as the term that Kant does use in the preceding argument, namely, "rational nature" is synonymous with "humanity," there is no real problem here. In fact, Kant could easily have used the former term in the formula. Nevertheless, the terminological shift is noteworthy in that it suggests that a richer conception of rational agency is at work in the second formulation than in the first. At least this is the case if, as I have argued, "humanity" be understood as involving a capacity for morality rather than merely the capacity to set ends, which might be regarded as a minimal condition for the attribution of rational agency. Moreover, this suggests the intriguing possibility that some of the problems discovered in the analysis of the application of FLN in the preceding chapter might be dealt with more successfully by means of FH. I shall explore this possibility in the following section.

V

Although Kant uses the same examples to illustrate FH as he did with FLN, we shall see that in the first two examples he expands his analysis to cover other cases based on the same principle. He likewise again structures his discussion on the basis of the distinctions between the objects of obligation (duties to oneself and duties to others) and the nature of the obligation (perfect and imperfect). Without apprising the reader of the fact, however, Kant introduces new terminology: referring to perfect or strict duties as "necessary" or "owed" [*schuldige*], and imperfect or wide duties as "contingent" or "meritorious" [*verdienstlichen*]. But since Kant apparently regarded these terms as synonyms, we can ignore this complication.[58]

Of greater interest are the issues regarding the relative import of the two formulas. For some commentators, who are dissatisfied with the formalism of FUL and FLN, FH offers a fresh start, one which seemingly makes possible grounding morality in a substantive value (rational nature) rather than in abstract principles. While not going quite this far, Wood strongly favors FH, not only because it brings into focus what Kantian morality is really about, namely, respect for persons, but also because he views it as far superior in illustrating the application of the categorical imperative. As he remarks at one point, "it would be impossible to overestimate the importance of FH for applying the principle of morality."[59] Moreover, in support of this he points out that in the *Metaphysics of Morals*, where Kant's concern is to derive a system of duties, FH plays a dominant role; while FLN and talk about universalizing maxims is almost entirely absent.[60]

---

[58] On this point see Gregor (1963, 97).

[59] Wood (1999, 141).

[60] Ibid., 138–39. The point is also noted by Korsgaard (1996, 124). My view is that the discrepancy between Kant's claim about the formulas in GMS and his procedure in the *Metaphysics of Morals* can be explained in terms of his different concerns in the two works. Whereas in the latter work it is with the derivation of duties, in the former it is with the nature of moral judgment or appraisal. And since the former

It can also be objected, however, that FH suffers from limitations of its own, which make it ill suited to serve as the supreme principle of morality. Although this may be expressed in a number of ways, the basic problem is that it appears to lack just what FLN supposedly provides, namely, a decision procedure. Instead, FH seems more like an exhortation than a practical guide. Wood himself compares it to the Sermon on the Mount and other utopian visions; while Ross assigns it an essentially homiletic value as a means to edification rather than enlightenment.[61] Nevertheless, Kant's discussion of his examples in terms of FH is of considerable interest, since it highlights features of his position that appear problematic when examined through the prism of FLN alone.

(1) *Suicide*: As in the examples falling under FLN, Kant begins with an agent's question concerning the moral permissibility of the contemplated course of action. But rather than asking whether the maxim could be conceived as a universal law of nature, the agent asks whether the contemplated action "could subsist [*bestehen*] together with the idea [*Idee*] of humanity as an *end in itself*" (GMS 4: 429$_{16-18}$). Accordingly, it remains a matter of consistency; but rather than consistent willing, what is required is compatibility with an idea. Kant denies that such compatibility would obtain in a case of suicide on the grounds that a person who destroys himself in order to escape a "burdensome condition [*beschwerlichen Zustande*], is using himself merely as a means for the preservation of a bearable [*erträglichen*] condition for the remainder of his life" (GMS 4: 429$_{18-20}$). But, in explaining what is wrong with treating oneself merely as a means, Kant simply asserts that, "The human being is not a thing, hence something that can be used *merely* as a means, but in all his actions always must be considered as an end in itself" (GMS 4: 429$_{20-23}$). And from this he concludes that "I cannot dispose of the human being in my own person, so as to maim, corrupt, or kill him" (GMS 4: 429$_{23-25}$).

The vagueness of the language that Kant uses to characterize the motivation for suicide (escaping from a "burdensome condition") suggests that he is using it as a place-holder for any discretionary end, which conceivably could run the gamut from avoiding prolonged and excruciating pain to simple boredom.[62] The essential question, however, is why taking your life for any such reason should be viewed as a matter of using your person merely as a means. Kant here seems to be proceeding under the assumption that to fail to respect humanity in your own person is, *eo ipso*, to treat it merely as a means. But while it is certainly arguable that suicide under the stipulated condition could be seen as a failure to respect humanity in oneself, it is less clear that it should be characterized as a case of using oneself merely as a means. We shall see that in

---

involves testing prospective maxims for their conformity or compatibility with moral requirements, it is not difficult to see why Kant would favor FLN.

[61] See Wood (1999, 139) and Ross (1954, 53). In a similar vein, Wolff (1973, 176) claims that FH fails to provide a substantive moral criterion.

[62] In the *Metaphysics of Morals* Kant uses the expression "discretionary end" [*beliebigen Zweck*] to describe the motivation of a would-be suicide (MS 6: 423; 547).

the case of false promising one is using another merely as a means to one's own end; but how can one use or treat *oneself* merely as a means? As a means to what end?

The answer suggested by the text and generally accepted in the literature is that the would-be suicide is using his humanity, that is, his rational nature, as a means for the creation and preservation of a tolerable condition (however that be defined), which does seem to be Kant's position in GMS. Moreover, if by "humanity" is understood an agent's non-moral rational capacities or, more specifically, the capacity to set ends and create values, it could be argued that these capacities are being used merely as a means to create and maintain a tolerable condition. Thus, Korsgaard, who adopts this reading, argues that what is wrong with suicide, considered under FH, is that a rational being is using herself as a mere means to a relative or conditioned end (the preservation of a tolerable condition). And she adds that this involves a genuine contradiction, as opposed to a case of misevaluation, because "the relative end must get its value from the thing that is being destroyed for its sake."[63]

Nevertheless, I neither find this line of argument persuasive nor believe that it expresses Kant's considered view on the matter. To begin with, I fail to find a contradiction here, even if we accept Korsgaard's premise that all value for Kant is the product of rational choice. Let us assume that the person in question has freely determined that the maintenance of a certain "quality of life," which might include the absence of extreme pain and the preservation of one's mental faculties, constitute conditions without which life is not worth living. One might still argue, as Kant clearly does, that the absence of one or more of these conditions would not justify taking one's own life; but it is difficult to see why the decision to take one's own life in such a situation would constitute a contradiction of the sort that Korsgaard maintains. Simply put, if the self is the source of all value, then it is also the source of its own value and, as such, is free to determine the conditions under which it deems life worth living.

Furthermore, I have argued earlier that it is a mistake to identify "humanity" with the non-moral features of rational agency. Indeed, the point is nicely illustrated by Kant's account of the prohibition of suicide in the *Metaphysics of Morals*, where the argument turns on the status of a human being as a person, understood in the moral rather than the psychological sense, that is, as a being with the capacity to obey the categorical imperative. Accordingly, the contradiction that Kant there finds is in the idea that such a being might have a moral authorization to withdraw from obligation, which would be to act as if no authorization were needed. As Kant there puts it, "To annihilate the subject of morality in one's own person is to root out the existence of morality itself from the world, as far as one can, even though morality is an end in itself" (MS 6: 423; 547). In other words, Kant is envisioning a would-be suicide as someone who is assuming something like a right to take his own life, which as such would stem from his own moral agency, even though doing so would involve

---

[63] Korsgaard (1996, 126).

annihilating this very agency. This might be viewed as a kind of contradiction (a right to do away with rights); but the main points are that in committing suicide one is disowning one's personality and that by "humanity" or "personality" Kant understands a capacity for morality, not merely the capacity to set ends.

Returning to the GMS account, there are three additional points worth noting. First, like the argument under FLN, the one under FH does not purport to rule out suicide *per se*, but only suicide for the sake of escaping some situation that the agent regards as personally intolerable. Thus, it leaves open the broader question of whether there are *any* conditions under which suicide is justifiable.[64] Second, as already noted, the key premise on which the argument turns, namely, that "The human being is not a thing, hence something that can be used merely as a means, but in all his actions always must be considered as an end in itself," is simply asserted, presumably on the grounds that it had already been established, albeit tentatively via the postulate, in the preceding argument. In any event, the application of FH appeals to a substantive principle, which contrasts with FLN, where the formula was derived, via typification, from the concept of the categorical imperative. Finally, unlike the discussion of suicide under FLN, that under FH indicates that, in addition to suicide, the argument is intended to apply to other, less extreme, forms of self-destructive behavior such as maiming and damaging oneself.[65]

(2) *False promising*: As in the illustration of FLN, this is offered as an example of a necessary or owed [*schuldige*] duty to others, that is, a strict duty to which others have a right to demand compliance. Unlike the discussion under FLN, however, Kant is not here concerned with the putative false promiser's maxim. His point is rather that, regardless of the maxim, the false promiser is treating the promisee merely as a means, by which is understood using another human being in such a way that the end of one's action cannot be shared by the one being used as a means. Conversely, one avoids using another *merely* as means to one's own ends when the other is able to endorse the end

---

[64] Kant does consider the broader question in light of the Stoics' approval of suicide, at least in the case of the sage, in the *Metaphysics of Morals* and various versions of his lectures on ethics. For example, he considers the case of Cato, who committed suicide in order to save his honor, and he seems to have regarded it as the exception that proves the rule (MPC 27 370–71; 145). Perhaps the most revealing of Kant's discussions of the topic, however, is in the Vigilantius version of 1794, where he discusses the example of a man who is bitten by a rabid dog and takes his own life in order to avoid infecting others. Whereas in the *Metaphysics of Morals* Kant includes this among the casuistical questions (MS 6: 623–24; 548), in the lecture he suggests that, rather than taking his own life, the unfortunate person could have considered having himself tied up at the appropriate time to prevent him from harming others; and he further remarks that a remedy for the bite of a mad dog had recently been found through administering oil to the victim internally and anointing him completely on the outside (MSV 27: 603; 346).

[65] Kant remarks parenthetically that he is here passing over a closer determination of this principle, which would encompass questions like the permissibility of the amputation of limbs to sustain oneself or of putting one's life in danger to sustain it on the grounds that they belong to actual moral theory [*eigentlichen Moral*] (GMS 4: 429_{25–28}). Kant discusses other forms of self-destruction in more detail in the *Metaphysics of Morals*, where he describes acts such as maiming oneself by extracting a tooth to sell or give to another, or having oneself castrated in order to make a better living as a singer as instances of "partially murdering oneself" [*partialen Selbstmorde*] (MS 6: 423; 547).

embodied in the action. Kant further suggests that the false promiser immediately sees [*sofort einsehen*] that he is using the promisee merely as a means (GMS 4: 429₃₀₋₃₃) and that this illicit treatment is even more evident in attacks on the freedom and property of others, which he characterizes as a violation of the rights of those who are treated in this way (GMS 4: 430₄₋₉).

The latter point is of particular interest, since it suggests that, at least with regard to strict duties to others, FH has considerably more power than FLN. We have seen, for example, that certain kinds of "false positive," specifically those that involve maxims of violence and coercion, appear to conform to FLN, even though they are manifestly immoral. But it is clear that these cases involve an attack on the freedom (if not the property) of others and that they treat those whom they attack as mere means. Similarly, if not quite so obviously, it could be argued that certain of the "false negatives," such as the so-called "timing maxims," which appear to fail the universalizability test, turn out to be perfectly innocent under FH, because, though they treat others as means, they do not treat them merely as such. This raises the crucial issue of the equivalence of the formulas, but I shall postpone a further discussion of this issue until the next chapter, where we shall have all of Kant's formulas and his account of the relationship between them before us.

In the meantime, a word is called for regarding the note that Kant attaches to his discussion of strict duties to others (GMS 4: 430₃₁₋₃₇). Kant's intent in the note is to convince the reader that, despite superficial similarities, the categorical imperative or, more precisely, FH, is not to be equated with the so-called "Golden Rule," which he here formulates partially and in negative terms as: "*quod tibi non* vis *fieri, etc.*" [what you do not want others to do to you, etc.]. Kant characterizes this familiar principle as trivial [*triviale*]; yet he also states, without any explanation, that it is derived from the categorical imperative. His main point, however, is that, unlike the categorical imperative, it cannot be the source of duties, which he attempts to illustrate by systematically eliminating duties to oneself of all kinds and duties of kindness or beneficence and strict duties (of justice) to others. The exclusion of the first two are obvious and do not require comment; but the third is interesting and somewhat contentious. Here Kant's point against the normative import of the principle is that a criminal might appeal to it before a judge who is about to sentence him. In his commentary on GMS, Timmermann finds Kant's putative counter-example to be artificial. According to Timmermann, the judge could respond to the criminal that he (the judge) would have to be treated in the same way as he will treat the criminal, if he were guilty of the crime for which the criminal is being sentenced.[66] Although this is true, it is beside the point: for such a response is not possible on the basis of the Golden Rule, which I take it is Kant's point in the example. Finally, it should be noted that Kant provides a hint of what he understood by the claim that the principle can be derived from the categorical

---

[66] Timmermann (2007a, 100).

imperative, which appears to give it *some* normative import, in a lecture where he suggests that it is one of the moral principles that apply in a realm of ends and that it refers to duties to others (MM2: 29: 610–11; 234).[67]

(3) *Neglecting one's talents*: According to Kant, the cultivation of one's talents (rational capacities) is a contingent or meritorious duty to oneself. Unlike the two considered so far, it is also a positive duty. Kant's "derivation" of this duty from FH, which, like the other examples, appears to be more of an illustration of how it can be understood in light of FH than a strict derivation, consists of three steps. First, Kant raises the stakes by indicating that it is not enough that an action not conflict with [*widerstreite*] humanity in one's own person, it must also *harmonize with it* [*dazu zusammenstimmen*] (GMS 4: 430_{11-13}). Second, he makes the strong teleological claim that in humanity there are predispositions to greater perfection, which are among the ends of nature with regard to humanity in our subject (GMS 4: 430_{13-15}). Finally, he observes that the neglect of these predispositions might be compatible with the preservation of humanity in our person as an end in itself, but not with its furtherance or enhancement [*Beförderung*] (GMS 4: 430_{15-17}).

As a positive duty, Kant's treatment of the duty to cultivate one's talents differs from the negative duty to oneself (the prohibition of suicide) in that it contains no reference to treating oneself merely as a means, which was a problematic feature of the latter. On the contrary, the problem with the failure to cultivate one's talents is supposedly that it fails to make use of the means that nature has provided us for self-improvement. But whereas the treatment of suicide under FH seemed preferable to its treatment under FLN, largely because it avoids the strong teleological assumptions on which the latter is based, in this case the situation is reversed. Although we saw that teleological considerations were not completely absent in the treatment of this duty under FLN, they played a subordinate role in the guise of "gifts of nature;" whereas here they occupy center stage. But the final and most important problem, which also concerns Kant's next example, is the appearance of the seemingly new requirement, not merely to avoid treating humanity in ourselves and others as something less than an end in itself, but also somehow to further or promote it. This is a problem because Kant characterizes an end in itself as an end in the negative sense, that is, as something not to be acted against, which, as such, functions as a limitation on what we can permissibly do, rather than as an end to be effected.

It is therefore surprising to find Wood maintaining that the argument under FH is superior to the one under FLN, because it shows why a rational being would necessarily will that all his talents be developed, whereas the latter does not.[68] In response, I have three points to make. First, if, as Wood claims, Kant's account succeeds in this task, it only does so on the basis of the substantive and here unargued teleological premise that nature's purpose in giving us these talents is that we develop

---

[67] This is noted by Timmermann (2007a, 100, n101).
[68] Wood (1999, 149).

them so as to be better able to attain the ends that we set for ourselves. Second, the fact (if it is a fact) that these talents were given to us by nature for that purpose does not, on the Kantian theory, entail that we have a duty to develop them; though it would for teleological theories such as those of the Stoics and the Wolffians. Finally, we have seen that in the *Metaphysics of Morals* Kant maintains that ethical duties, or duties of virtue, which encompass all non-juridical duties, including the duty to cultivate one's talents, are not derivable from the categorical imperative alone (under any formula), but from a synthetic *a priori* principle, which is itself supposedly derived from the categorical imperative. Kant may not have been clear about the need for a subordinate synthetic *a priori* principle for the application of the categorical imperative to human beings and the derivation of particular duties in 1785; but his treatment of sample duties in GMS is perfectly compatible with this, since, as has been noted on several occasions, Kant is not there in the business of deriving duties. Wood himself emphasizes this in his highly critical treatment of FLN; but he seems to have overlooked it when discussing FH.

(4) *Non-beneficence*: Kant presents the duty to help others in need as a wide or meritorious duty to others, which means that others cannot claim a right to such aid. In explaining this duty in terms of FH, Kant first reaffirms the familiar thesis that the natural end of all human beings is their own happiness (GMS 4: 430_{18-19}). He then draws a distinction, which was implicit in the previous example, between a negative and a positive agreement with the conception of humanity as an end in itself. A policy of neither helping nor interfering with others' pursuit of their happiness meets the negative test, which amounts to not treating others merely as means, but not the positive one, which requires an agreement with humanity as an end in itself. The latter requires that everyone endeavor, to the extent possible, to further the ends of others (GMS 4: 430_{19-24}). And from this Kant concludes that "the ends of a subject who is an end in itself must as far as possible also be *my* ends, if that representation is to have its *full* effect on me" (GMS 4: 430_{24-27}).

The basic problem posed by this example is the same as the last: how can the essentially negative concept of an end in itself yield positive duties (whether to oneself or to others)? Kant attempts to clarify the situation by distinguishing between a negative and positive agreement with the requirement to treat human beings as ends in themselves, which was implicit in the previous example. Presumably, the former consists in not treating human beings merely as means, while the latter requires fully respecting their status as ends in themselves. But even granting this distinction, it remains unclear why the latter should require going as far as making, to the extent possible, the ends of others one's own, as contrasted, say, with the occasional performance of acts of kindness.[69]

---

[69] The situation is complicated by the fact that Kant is inconsistent in his accounts of beneficence, sometimes construing it as the duty to make the permissible ends of others one's own and sometimes as the duty to help others in distress. On this point see Eisenberg (1966, 255–69).

This is essentially the same problem that was noted in the discussion of this duty under FLN, where it was argued that the most that could be shown was the impermissibility of adopting a maxim of non-beneficence, that is, of principled indifference to the well-being of others, rather than the necessity of adopting a maxim of active beneficence. Moreover, the moral of the story is the same as it was with regard to the duty to cultivate one's talents, namely, the need to appeal to the distinct principle of duties of virtue in order to derive positive duties. And, as noted above, even if Kant recognized the need for such a principle in 1785 (which is not clear), there was no need to appeal to it in GMS, because his concern in this work was to establish the categorical imperative as the fundamental principle of morality, not, except for illustrative purposes, to derive duties from it.

Nevertheless, Wood once again argues for the superiority of Kant's treatment of this duty under FH to that under FLN. His claim is that in the latter case Kant's argument "requires some possibly controversial empirical assumptions about what is rational given the facts of human vulnerability and interdependence," whereas "FH enables us to provide a less questionable argument."[70] We have seen that Kant's argument under FLN does rely on the assumption that there are some ends that a finite rational being cannot abandon because they belong essentially to the will, as necessary conditions of the preservation and enhancement of rational agency. Although this assumption may be controversial, it is not clear that it is empirical, and I fail to see why it is more problematic than Kant's strong teleological premise in the preceding example with which Wood does not appear to find any difficulty.

Finally, I question Wood's claim for the superiority of the derivation of beneficence under FH. This claim seems to be based on the premise that "The reason it would be impossible to will that others not help me is that their refusal would show contempt for my humanity, which I must regard as an end in itself."[71] In other words, I cannot will that others show contempt for or disrespect my humanity. Once again, this seems correct, but beside the point. For the same self-reliant and prosperous individual to whom Wood and many others appeal as a counter-example to Kant's thesis under FLN might claim that he does, indeed, want others to respect his humanity, but that this can best be done by leaving him alone, just as he respects their humanity by doing the same with them. In short, it is not at all clear that Kant's treatment of the wide duties to self and others is any more (or less) successful under FH than his treatment of them under FLN.

---

[70] Wood (1999, 150).
[71] Ibid.

9

Autonomy, Heteronomy, and Constructing the Categorical Imperative

It was suggested that the organizing principle of GMS 2, indeed its veritable *raison d'être*, is to provide a complete construction of the concept of the categorical imperative on the basis of a progressive analysis of the concept of a finite rational agent. By such a construction is understood an account of the necessary and sufficient conditions of its possibility.[1] According to Kant, there are three conditions that a categorical imperative must meet. (1) It must have a strictly universal form. (2) It must presuppose something of absolute value. (3) It must command unconditionally.[2] Not coincidentally, each of these requirements is supplied by one of the formulas. FLN supplies the moment of universality, modeled on the conception of a law of nature. FH rests on the assumption that there is something of absolute value, namely, rational nature or humanity, which, as an end in itself, provides a limiting condition on the pursuit of private ends and the means to attain them. Finally, the formula of autonomy (FA) gives the imperative its unconditional status; for we shall see that Kant maintained that only a law that is self-imposed can command unconditionally, that is, apart from any interest or incentive that an agent may have to follow its dictates. Since these are individually necessary and jointly sufficient conditions of the possibility of the categorical imperative, we can say, using Kant's terminology, that they provide its "complete determination." Moreover, I believe that this explains why Kant insists that there are only three formulas for the categorical imperative, in spite of the fact that he appears to provide more.[3]

It was further suggested that this procedure was rooted in Kant's fundamental meta-ethical thesis that the supreme principle of morality (whatever it turned out to be) must

---

[1] It must be kept in mind that, strictly speaking, we are talking about the concept of such an imperative. The conditions of its actuality are dealt with in GMS 3.

[2] Although she does not put it this way, the point is suggested by Baker (1988, 399–400).

[3] On this point see Chapter 6, note 3.

be grounded in the concept of a rational agent as such and, insofar as it takes an imperatival form, in the concept of a *finite* rational agent as such. In the preceding three chapters, we have analyzed the first two stages of this construction, which led to two formulations of this imperative. First, starting with a conception of rational agents as beings with the capacity to act according to their representation of laws or on principles, we arrived, by means of an analysis of the concept of a categorical imperative, at FUL, which, in order to be applied, took the typified form of FLN. Then, after thickening the conception of rational agency to include its end-directedness or intentionality, we saw that this led to a second formulation of the categorical imperative (FH), which featured this end-directedness and argued from it to the status of such agents as ends in themselves. Our present concern is with the third and final stage of this process and the conclusions that Kant draws from it. This will take the form of a commentary on the remainder of GMS 2 (4: 430_{28}–45_{15}). Apart from the discussion of autonomy, which must be central to any interpretation of GMS, this portion of the text is often dismissed as containing little that adds to the argument. In my view, however, it has an essential unifying function, tying together the various strands of argument found in the earlier portions of GMS 2. Accordingly, I shall treat it in more detail than is usually thought necessary.

The starting point of the discussion will be Kant's concept of autonomy, which will be considered both as the third and final step in the development of his conception of rational agency and, in the guise of FA, the third formula of the categorical imperative, which completes the construction of the concept of this imperative. We shall then explore Kant's account of the relationship between the formulas and the highly controversial issue of their equivalence (or lack thereof). Finally, we shall discuss Kant's contrast of autonomy and heteronomy as a pair of all-inclusive and mutually exclusive meta-ethical principles and his claim that all moral theories except his own are based on the latter.

I

After completing the application of FH to the examples of the four types of duty and reminding us that the preceding principle, that is, the proposition that every rational agent is an end in itself, "is the supreme limiting condition of every person's freedom of action" (GMS 4: 430_{28}–31_2), Kant moves abruptly to autonomy.[4] Unfortunately, this move is something less than a model of clarity. The general point is clear enough, namely, that autonomy is a consequence of the combination of the preceding two

---

[4] The belated appearance of autonomy, in spite of its systematic significance, is due to the analytic or regressive nature of Kant's procedure, according to which the most important elements come last.

principles. What is unclear is precisely how the combination is supposed to work. In an endeavor to explain this, Kant writes:

The ground of all practical legislation lies *objectively in the rule* and in the form of universality, which (according to the first principle) makes it capable of being a law (perhaps even [*allenfalls*] a law of nature), subjectively, however, it lies in the *end*; but the subject of all ends is every rational being as an end in itself (according to the second principle): from this now follows our third practical principle of the will, as the supreme condition of its agreement with universal practical reason, the idea *of the will of every rational being as a will giving universal law.* (GMS 4: 431₉₋₁₈)

That the objective ground of practical legislation lies in the law and the subjective ground in the end are familiar themes, which have emerged from the consideration of FLN and FH; but by themselves they neither appear to entail any additional principle nor enable us to understand why this principle is the supreme condition of the agreement of the will with universal practical reason. I shall address each of these issues in turn.

With regard to the first, the key point lies in the notion that rational being (or humanity) as an end in itself is the "subject of all ends." The latter expression, like its counterpart the "subject of morality," is ambiguous, because it can refer either to those for whom ends exist, that is, to rational beings qua end-setters, or to the objects of those ends, namely, the same rational beings qua self-standing ends. Moreover, each of these, when combined with the notion of universal law, as expressed in the first formula, provide a route to autonomy.

If "the subject of all ends" is taken in the first sense, then in testing my maxim for its universalizability, I must take into account the fact that the domain of those with respect to whom my maxim is being considered as a possible universal law is the totality of end-setters. Accordingly, to claim from this point of view that my maxim is universalizable is to say that the end I am endeavoring to attain through my action, as well as the means through which I intend to attain it, are universally endorsable. Correlatively, if "the subject of all ends" is taken in the second sense, then the point is that the universe of rational agents constitutes a limiting condition on both the ends that I set for myself and the means that I select to attain them, which really comes to the same thing as the first sense.

Although "the idea *of the will of every rational being as a will giving universal law*" may seem to be simply a restatement of FLN, there has been a significant change in the understanding of universalizability. This was previously alluded to in terms of the distinction between an intra- and inter-subjective universalizability, which I shall henceforth refer to respectively as universalizability$_1$ and universalizability$_2$. We have seen that the former is the sense of universalizability at work in the application of FLN and that it is intra-subjective because it concerns the compatibility of an agent's maxim with the *same maxim* considered as a universal law. As a direct result of the introduction of the conception of rational beings as ends in themselves, however, it has been supplanted by an inter-subjective sense of universalizability (universalizability$_2$), which is expressed in the idea of the will of every rational agent as legislating universal law. This is an inter-subjective universalizability because it requires that a maxim be universally endorsable, that is, endorsable as consistent with universal law by every rational agent. Clearly, every maxim that is universalizable in the second sense is also universalizable in the first; but we shall see that the converse does not appear to hold and that this underlies the issue of the equivalence of the various formulas.

For the present, however, the crucial point is that it is the fact that the law which the will gives to itself is universalizable$_2$ that provides the key to understanding why Kant claims that the principle of autonomy is the "supreme condition of the agreement of the will with universal practical reason." In explaining the significance that he assigns to this principle, Kant notes that, according to it, "the will is not merely subject to the law, but subject in such a way that it must also be regarded as *giving the law to itself*, and just because of this as subject to the law (of which it can consider itself as author)" (GMS 4: 431$_{21-24}$).

At first glance, the idea that the will is only subject to the law because it is also its author suggests a radical amoralism; for if moral requirements are self-imposed, they would appear to lack any authority beyond what the agent gives to them. And since this authority can easily be withdrawn, it seems to follow that these requirements lack any obligatory force. Such a construal of Kantian autonomy is blocked, however, by the fact that an autonomous agent is legislating not merely for himself, but universally, which, as a result of the status of all rational agents as ends in themselves, entails that his maxims must be universally endorsable.[5]

The reason why Kant insists that only a self-imposed law could serve as a categorical imperative is his view that morality requires not merely that one's maxims conform to the law, but also that they be adopted from respect for it. His claim is that this is conceivable only if the moral law is regarded as self-imposed; for it is only under this condition that the agent can dispense with the need for some non-moral incentive to obey its dictates, which would undermine its categorical status. In other words, if some non-moral interest must be presupposed in order to have an incentive to obey moral requirements, then the necessitation expressed in these requirements is conditional and the imperative is merely hypothetical. Kant further claims that this point is made explicit in the third formula, which he here characterizes as "the idea of the will of every rational being as *a will which makes universal law*" (GMS 4: 432$_{3-4}$).

Since this formula is not in imperatival form, it is not immediately obvious that it can be regarded as an expression of the categorical imperative. Nevertheless, this can be easily rectified by citing what appears to be the canonical formulation of the principle of autonomy: "Choose only to act in such a way that the maxims of your choice are at

---

[5] In other words, critics who raise the arbitrariness or "anything goes" charge against Kant's conception of autonomy neglect the line of reasoning through which he arrived at it. For an alternative defense of Kant against this common objection, which is based on the view that Kantian autonomy is best understood as modeled on the idea of political sovereignty, see Reath (2006, 122–24, 137–45).

the same time comprehended with it in the same volition as universal law" (GMS 4: 440_{18-20}). In other words, the formula of autonomy requires that we choose under the idea of autonomy and what Kant must show is that this way of viewing obligation brings to the fore the independence from interest that is implicit in the concept of the categorical imperative. Kant endeavors to accomplish this by means of the following argument, which has a *reductio* form:

> For if we think of such a will [one which makes universal law], then although a will *that stands under laws* may still be bound to this law by means of some interest, a will that is itself the supreme lawgiver could not, as such, possibly depend upon any interest; for such a dependent will would itself need yet another law that would limit the interest of its self-love to the condition of a validity for universal law. (GMS 4: 432_{5-11})

One of the difficulties posed by this passage is understanding the notion of the will as "supreme lawgiver." If a will is thought to function in this way simply in virtue of the fact that it makes its own maxims, then the conclusion that a will, considered as such, could not possibly depend on any interest is obviously false. Things look considerably different, however, if we take the law to refer to whatever is universalizable$_2$; for there could be no extra-moral incentive, that is, no incentive or, in the language of GMS, *Bewegungsgrund*, other than the law itself, to submit one's maxims to that requirement.

Another problem is the obscurity of Kant's suggestion that if the will were dependent on interest, it would need another law to "limit the interest of its self-love to the condition of a validity for universal law." This can be understood, however, if we take Kant to be not only ruling out self-interest as the ground of the maxims of a will functioning as supreme lawgiver, but also indicating that self-interested actions would be "lawful," if they are compatible with a universal$_2$ law. In other words, although self-interest cannot ground a categorical imperative, self-interested action is morally permissible, subject to the condition that it does not conflict with universal$_2$ laws.

Finally, a will that gives the law to itself independently of interest has autonomy, which Kant now defines as "the property of the will to be a law to itself (independently of every property of the objects of volition)" (GMS 4: 440_{16-18}). With this Kant introduces a third feature of autonomy. Not only is it the source of a distinct formula of the categorical imperative (FA), which by combining the conception of rational beings as ends in themselves with the idea of conformity to universal law leads to a new and deeper understanding of the universalizability requirement (universal endorsability or universalizability$_2$), and the "supreme condition of the agreement of the will with universal practical reason," it is also a property of the will. Moreover, it is considered qua property of the will that autonomy constitutes the third and final stage in Kant's progressive account of the concept of rational agency in GMS 2. For we now have learned not only that rational agents have the capacity to act according to their representation of laws and that their actions are end-directed or intentional, but also that they have the capacity to legislate to themselves independently of any of the ends that might be suggested to them by their sensuous nature, a capacity which is not entailed by the previous characterizations of rational agency.

We shall revisit the conception of autonomy in all three of its guises and analyze the contrast that Kant draws between autonomy and heteronomy later in this chapter. Our immediate concern, however, is with the connection that Kant affirms in the following passage between autonomy and the concept of a realm of ends:

> The concept of every rational being as one who must regard itself as making universal law through all the maxims of its will in order to judge itself and its actions from this point of view, leads to a very fruitful concept that is attached to it, namely that *of a realm of ends* [*eines Reichs der Zwecke*]. (GMS 4: 433$_{12-16}$).[6]

It seems reasonably clear from this and other texts that Kant regarded the realm of ends as an idea on the basis of which one can frame for oneself the conception of autonomous agency.[7] In other words, to conceive of oneself as an autonomous agent is just to consider oneself as a lawgiving member of a realm of ends, that is, as legislating universally for oneself and other autonomous agents, who, as such, are also ends in themselves. In order to appreciate this, however, it is necessary to understand what Kant meant by a "realm of ends." Kant's definition is stipulative and proceeds in two steps: first defining "realm" in general and then specifying the distinguishing feature of a realm of ends. Kant stipulates that by a realm he understands "a systematic union [*Verbindung*] of different rational beings under common laws" (GMS 4: 433$_{17-18}$). The key term here is "systematic," which has teleological connotations, suggesting a unification in which the various members are not merely compatible but harmonious with one another and mutually supportive.[8] Applying this conception to ends, a realm of ends would be a systematic unification in which the members are ends in themselves.

The situation is complicated, however, by the fact that such a realm includes not only the systematic union of rational beings as ends in themselves, but also the personal or private ends of these beings. As such, it includes two radically different types of end. Moreover, adding to the confusion, Kant contends that we arrive at the notion of a realm of ends by abstracting from both the personal differences between rational beings and the content of their private ends (GMS 4: 433$_{19-21}$). The problem is to understand how the idea of a realm of ends can include the private ends of the rational beings

---

[6] Although there is general agreement that "realm" is the more natural rendering of "*Reich*," there is considerable divergence on the question of whether in Kant's use of the term it should be rendered as "kingdom" or "realm." Among the English translators, Abbott, Ellington, Gregor, Paton, Timmermann, and Zweig opt for the former, Beck and Wood for the latter. Strong support for the former reading is provided by Kant's obvious allusions to the biblical notion of the "Kingdom of God," Augustine, and Leibniz. Moreover, Kant himself explicitly relates the notion to the views of Augustine and Leibniz in MM 29: 629; 246. Nevertheless, I have opted for the latter, largely because of Kant's definition of "*Reich*," to be discussed below. For a useful discussion of the issue with a consideration of the arguments on both sides see Paton (1958, 187–88).

[7] See MM 29: 629; 246.

[8] This is noted by Wood (1999, 166).

thought in it, if, *ex hypothesi*, it is formed by abstracting from the content of these very ends.

The answer lies in distinguishing between the *fact* that rational beings have private ends and the *content* of these ends. Inasmuch as the realm of ends contains finite rational agents for whom happiness is a necessary end, these agents necessarily have private ends, which express the manner in which they conceive their happiness. And since it is precisely these private ends that differentiate such agents, the idea of their systematic union must include these ends; otherwise there would be nothing to unify. But while the idea of a realm of ends must include the assumption that these agents have such ends, it cannot include the ends that they actually have; for, as Kant argued in the second *Critique*, these ends often conflict, and when they do not, they constitute merely a contingent agreement that cannot ground a moral principle.[9] Accordingly, in forming the idea of a realm of ends we must first distinguish between the existence of private ends, which is necessary, and the actual content of these ends, which is contingent; and, second, abstract from the latter but not the former. Otherwise expressed, the idea of a realm of ends includes rational agents with private ends, but it does not assume that they have any such ends in particular. Rather, it requires that whatever these ends may be, they conform to universal$_2$ law, which means that they should harmonize with one another.[10]

Kant further claims that the realm of ends is possible according to the "above principles" [*obigen Principien*] (GMS 4: 433$_{25}$), by which he presumably meant the previous formulas of the categorical imperative. In the next paragraph, however, Kant links this realm specifically with FH, suggesting that it could be brought about if everyone would treat themselves and others "*never merely as means*, but always at *the same time as an end in itself*" (GMS 4: 433$_{27-28}$). Kant admits that such a state of affairs is only an ideal (GMS 4: 433$_{32}$); but the fact that he also claimed that it is possible according to categorical principles and later states that it would be brought about if everyone scrupulously obeyed this imperative (GMS 4: 438$_{29-32}$), indicates that he viewed it as an ideal that could be realized (or at least approached asymptotically).[11]

An additional complication arises from an ambiguity in Kant's conception of a realm of ends; for despite characterizing this realm as an ideal, he also speaks of rational agents as members of such a realm. In fact, Kant distinguishes between two types of member: ordinary members and its *supreme head* [*Oberhaupt*]. As ends in themselves, both make universal$_2$ law. The difference is that, whereas ordinary members not only make laws

---

[9] See also KpV 5: 25–26; 159–60.

[10] The best known contemporary version of this principle is Rawls' conception of the "original position" (choice under a presumed "veil of ignorance"). Rawls explicitly acknowledges the Kantian roots of this principle by characterizing it as "a procedural interpretation of Kant's conception of autonomy and the categorical imperative." See Rawls (1971, 256).

[11] Kant's position here seems quite close to the conception of a moral world, understood as one in which there is full conformity with all moral laws, which he articulated in the first *Critique* (KrV A808/B836). It might also be compared with the idea of an "ethical community" [*ethischen gemeinen Wesens*], to which Kant appealed in *Religion* and which he viewed as the goal of an historical process (RGV 6: 98–109; 133–41).

through their maxims, they are also subject to them, Kant suggests that the supreme head is not subject to the will of the others (GMS 4: 432$_{34-37}$). Although not incorrect, the latter point seems to be a misstatement; for on Kant's view it is an essential feature of *all* autonomous agents that they are not subject to the will of another, which entails that this cannot be used to distinguish the *supreme head* from the ordinary members of a putative realm of ends.[12] It is clear from what follows, however, that Kant's real point is that the supreme head, as a fully independent being, unburdened by needs or limitations of any sort, is not subject to any constraint, while finite rational agents, who constitute the class of ordinary members, are so subject.

Finally, Kant completes his discussion of the realm of ends by revisiting the question of value. His thesis, for which we have been largely prepared by his earlier discussions of the topic, is that,

In the realm of ends everything has either a *PRICE* or a *DIGNITY*. Whatever has a price can be replaced by something else as its *equivalent*; whereas what is elevated above any price, and hence allows for no equivalent, has a dignity. (GMS 4: 434$_{31-34}$)

At first it might seem strange to find Kant locating things or states of affairs with a mere price or relative value in the realm of ends. The puzzle disappears, however, if we keep in mind that this realm includes not merely autonomous rational agents, but also their private ends. Accordingly, it is to these ends, and the means necessary to attain them, that a value in the sense of a price is attached. Kant distinguishes between two types of price, which he characterizes as a "market price" [*Marktpreis*] and an "affective price" [*Affectionspreis*]. The former refers to those things that satisfy inclinations and needs; the latter to those things that provide an aesthetic satisfaction that is independent of any need. Kant ignores the issue of the comparative value of these two kinds of "goods" and instead contrasts both with the sole condition under which something can be an end in itself, to which he attributes an intrinsic value or inner worth (GMS 4: 434$_{35}$–35$_4$).

Two aspects of this passage and the ensuing discussion of value and dignity (GMS 4: 435$_5$–36$_7$) require comment. The first is Kant's inclusion of aesthetic satisfaction under the category of price or relative value. This indicates that Kant did not equate inner or intrinsic worth with non-instrumental value; otherwise, he would have been forced to include aesthetic satisfaction, which already in 1785 Kant regarded as disinterested, among the intrinsic goods. The second is a lack of clarity on Kant's part concerning the conditions under which rational agents are assigned a value that is incommensurate with any price.

In a passage cited in the previous chapter, Kant remarks that "morality and humanity, insofar as it is capable of it, is what alone has dignity" (GMS 4: 435$_{7-8}$), where dignity appears to be equivalent to unconditioned worth. In my initial discussion of this passage, I argued that it was in virtue of a *capacity* for morality rather than its

---

[12] The point is noted by Timmermann (2007a, 107).

actualization that rational beings are regarded as having such worth. It might seem, however, that this is called into question by what Kant says in the present context.[13] For example, in what appears to be an attempt to explicate the above-cited statement, Kant remarks that, while qualities such as skill and diligence in work have a market price and others such as wit, lively imagination, and humor have an affective price, "fidelity in promising, benevolence from principle (not from instinct) have an inner worth" (GMS 4: 435_{9-12}). Moreover, continuing in this moralistic vein, Kant maintains that neither nature nor art have anything to put in place of these principles, because their value stems not from their utility but from the disposition [*Gesinnung*], which they reflect and which is an object of immediate respect, quite apart from the success of the actions stemming from it. And, finally, Kant concludes by attributing a dignity to the *Denkungsart* that is manifested in such principled volitions (GMS 4: 435_{13-28}).

Although Kant does not use the expression, it is clear that the qualities, disposition, and principles to which he refers are those that are constitutive of a good will. But whereas in his initial discussion of the good will Kant's aim was to show that its status as the only thing (in the world or out of it) that is good without limitation is latent in common rational moral cognition, his present concern is to account for the unique value and status assigned to such a will. Thus, Kant begins the final paragraph of his discussion of the topic of value by asking: "[W]hat is it that justifies the morally good disposition or virtue in making such high claims?" (GMS 4: 435_{29-30}); and his answer is that the autonomy of the will is the "ground of the dignity of the human and every rational nature" (GMS 4: 436_{6-7}).

Between the question and the answer Kant provides his justification for the latter, which, simply put, is that the value of a morally good *Denkungsart* is not a function of either its given nature or what it is able to accomplish, but, rather, of the fact that it is self-wrought, a product of the agent's own making of universal law. And if this is true, it follows that a dignity or intrinsic worth must be attributed not only to the agent's *Denkungsart* or good will, but also to that in virtue of which the latter is possible, namely, the agent's autonomy. As already argued in the previous chapter, the condition of the possibility of the goodness of a good will does not lose its status simply because it fails to attain the goodness that is assumed to be within its power.

II

This section is concerned with Kant's account of the relations between the various formulas of the categorical imperative in the four paragraphs that follow upon his initial

---

[13] Such a view is expressed by Timmerman (2007a, 114), who takes Kant to be maintaining that what distinguishes us qualitatively from merely natural beings and gives us dignity is not autonomy as such, but "*successful* autonomous legislation in moral action." This is essentially the same as the view of Dean discussed in the preceding chapter.

discussion of autonomy and its connection with the idea of a realm of ends (GMS 4: 436_8–37_4). Kant begins by informing the reader that, "The three forementioned ways of representing the principle of morality are fundamentally only so many formulas of the very same law, one of which unites the other two in itself [*deren die eine die anderen zwei von selbst in sich vereignt*]" (GMS 4: 436_{8-10}).[14] As we shall see, the "three forementioned ways" are FLN (not FUL), FH, and FA/FRE. This sentence, however, contains two distinct claims that call for separate treatment. The first is that these formulas are all expressions of the same law or principle, which I shall call the singularity thesis. The second is that one of them unites in itself the other two. I shall discuss the singularity thesis below; but since Kant only spells out what he means by the second claim subsequently, before turning to that it will be necessary to consider another important claim that Kant makes in the next sentence, which concerns the nature of the difference between these formulas. These, then, constitute the subject matter of the first two of the four sub-divisions of this section. The remaining two concern the claim that these formulas are expressions of the form, matter, and complete determination of the categorical imperative, which defines their mutual relations, and Kant's introduction, seemingly out of the blue, of the so-called "universal formula" (UF).

(A) The singularity thesis

This thesis concerns the categorical imperative, which was first formulated at GMS 4: 421_{6-8} and has hitherto been referred to as FUL. We have seen that Kant characterized this imperative as "only a single one"; so the present statement reinforces his thesis that there can be only a single fundamental or first principle of morality. Kant's clearest statement of this thesis is in his lectures on ethics, where, in criticizing Baumgarten's various moral principles, Kant is reported as stating that "Where there are already many principles in ethics, there is certainly none, for there can be only one true principle" (MPC 27: 266; 59).[15] Since the true principle of morality for Kant is the categorical imperative, this means that he is committed to the view that there is either a single categorical imperative or none at all. It also suggests that in affirming the singularity thesis Kant is warning the reader that the three formulas designated above are not to be taken as self-standing, independent moral principles, but as variant formulations of the single categorical imperative. We shall see that, in addition to the challenge to the singularity thesis provided by the apparent non-equivalence of the results obtained by

---

[14]   There is a significant disagreement amongst the English translators regarding the proper rendering of "*deren die eine.*" Grammatically, it can be rendered either as "one of which" or "any one of which" [unites the other two in itself]. Of the eight English translations I have consulted (Abbott, Beck, Ellington, Gregor, Paton, Timmermann, Wood, and Zweig), four of them (Abbott, Beck, Gregor, and Zweig) take Kant to be affirming the latter; two (Ellington and Paton) preserve the ambiguity; while Timmermann and Wood render it as unambiguously claiming the former. For a discussion of the philological issue, see Timmermann (2007a, 110–11 and notes 122 and 125).

[15]   This passage is referred to by Timmermann (2007a, 110).

applying the different formulas to the same maxims, some of what Kant says in the paragraphs discussed in this section casts further doubt on this thesis.

(B) The nature of the difference between the formulas

Despite insisting that the three formulas are merely different ways of representing the same moral principle rather than themselves independent principles, Kant notes that,

> [T]here is yet a difference between them, which is to be sure subjectively rather than objectively-practical [*die zwar eher subjectiv als objectiv-praktisch ist*], namely, that of bringing an idea of reason nearer to intuition (according to a certain analogy) and thereby to feeling. (GMS 4: 436_{10-13})[16]

This sentence contains an essential part of Kant's attempt to explain how the presence of three distinct formulas is compatible with the singularity thesis. Clearly, this could not be the case if there were an objective difference between the formulas, since this would mean that they are distinct moral principles, which if they happened to yield the same results in particular cases, would be a matter of sheer contingency. This would not follow, however, if they differed merely subjectively, that is, in the manner in which they bring an idea of reason (presumably, the *same idea*) nearer to intuition and by this means to feeling.

The most obscure portion of this sentence is the parenthetical remark that the various formulas bring an idea of reason nearer to intuition "according to a certain analogy." The necessity for an appeal to analogy stems from a fundamental tenet of Kant's thought, which is reiterated in all three *Critiques*, namely, that ideas of reason, as contrasted with concepts of the understanding, cannot be brought to intuition or, in Kant's technical terms, "schematized." In discussing the relation between FUL and FLN in Chapter 7, we saw that Kant dealt with this problem in the second *Critique* by characterizing the latter as a "typic" of the former, by which he understood a model or symbolic representation on the basis of which we can apply the former to particular maxims in moral deliberation. In the present case, Kant is expressing the same thought, albeit in somewhat different terms, and applying it to all three formulas, not simply to FLN. But since the term that Kant uses here instead of "typic" is "analogy," it is necessary to determine how this is to be understood.

Although Kant uses the term in a number of different senses, it is evident that it is here used to refer to the manner in which we can legitimately think about supersensible objects, which, *ex hypothesi*, cannot be directly cognized.[17] It is with this in mind

---

[16] Once again, there is a significant difference among the translators, this time concerning "*eher.*" This can be translated either as "rather than," in which case Kant is claiming that the difference between the formulas is subjectively rather than objectively practical, or as "more . . . than," in which case Kant is claiming that the difference between the formulas is more subjectively than objectively practical, which suggests that it is, at least in part, also objectively practical. Abbott, Ellington, Gregor, Paton, and Timmermann opt for the former alternative, Beck, Wood, and Zweig for the latter. My own view is that the text requires the former reading, since I cannot see how the latter can be made consistent with the singularity thesis.

[17] Prominent among the other senses in which Kant uses the term "analogy" is the logical sense, in which it is contrasted with "induction." See JL 9: 133n; 626. He also uses it in the first *Critique* to refer both to the set

that Kant elsewhere characterized *"cognition according* to analogy" as based on "a perfect similarity between two relations in wholly dissimilar things," as contrasted with "an imperfect similarity between two things," which, Kant suggests, is how the term is usually understood (Pro 4: 357–58; 146–47). The basic idea is that the relation between two known things is viewed as similar to that between a third known thing and the supersensible object that is to be thought by means of the analogy. To cite one of Kant's examples, a child's welfare stands to parental love as the welfare of humankind as a whole stands to divine love (Pro 4: 358n; 147).

With this example of an analogy Kant intended to make both a negative and positive point. The former is that we have no grounds to assume that divine love is similar in kind to human parental love, albeit infinitely greater in extent and degree. The latter is that, despite our total and ineliminable ignorance regarding the supersensible, we may attribute certain properties to God, provided we know what we are doing, that is, that we are not literally predicating love (or any other property) of the divine, but merely exercising a permission to use this (or some other appropriate) analogy to reflect on God's relation to the world for the purpose of either the practical use of reason or its regulative use with respect to the thought of experience as a whole.[18]

A somewhat similar line of thought is at work in Kant's account of the relationship between the categorical imperative and its distinct formulas. The essential point is that each formula represents the single categorical imperative on the basis of a different analogy, which supposedly ensures that their differences are subjectively rather than objectively practical. We have already seen this at work in connection with FUL and FLN. Even though the former appeals to a prescriptive law of freedom and the latter to a descriptive law of nature, the fact that they share the underlying generic idea of lawfulness makes it possible to use the latter as a model in applying the categorical imperative by asking whether a maxim could subsist with itself qua law of nature.

The application of this procedure to the remaining formulas, however, appears to be more problematic. The problem with FH is that it does not seem to involve any such analogy with the categorical imperative and it appears neither to have nor (unlike FLN) to be a typic. Moreover, while FRE may be viewed as something like a typic of FA, it is a purely intellectual representation, which, as such, itself seems to stand in need of a symbol or typic.

---

of principles designated by that name (the "Analogies of Experience") and the general relation between category and schema that applies to all the principles. For my discussion of the latter use, see Allison (2004, 225–28).

[18] It appears that this discussion of analogy is directed explicitly against Hume's famous critique of the appeal to analogy in the attempt to determine the nature of God in his *Dialogues concerning Natural Religion.* Kant agrees with Hume that the appeal to analogy cannot yield a determinate cognition of the Deity, while defending its use, if undertaken with the appropriate critical strictures. In fact, he describes his use of analogy as "the true middle way between the dogmatism that Hume fought and the scepticism he wanted to introduce" (Pro 4: 360; 149).

I believe that the best way to make sense out of Kant's position on this matter is by appealing to his conception of a realm of ends as a realm of nature, which will be discussed further below. For the present, the point is that it is precisely by conceiving a realm of ends in this way that it becomes possible to use it as a model in terms of which one can conceive of oneself as an autonomous lawgiver in a realm of ends. This also helps to bring out the contrast with FLN; for rather than asking oneself whether one's maxim could subsist with itself as a universal law of nature, the question that the agent now asks is whether her action could be part of a realm of ends, considered as a realm of nature, which presumably would be one in which the ends of rational agents mutually harmonize. In other words, whereas the first analogy is between the requirements of the categorical imperative and a nature governed by causal laws, the second is between these requirements and nature as embodying a teleological order. And since the basis for this distinction lies in the introduction of the concept of a rational agent as an end in itself, one could perhaps claim that the idea of such an order serves as a typic for FH as well.

(C) Form, matter, and complete determination

After describing the manner in which the three formulas differ, despite being formulations of the "very same law," Kant turns to the question of their mutual relation. It is in this context that he claims that one of these formulas unites within itself the other two, which he bases on the premise that every maxim has a form, a matter (or end), and a complete determination. He further claims that this involves a progression, which he likens to that within the category of quantity, from unity to plurality to allness or totality (GMS 4: 436_{7-28}).

Since the first two formulas, which Kant connects with essential features of maxims (their possession of both a form and a matter), go over ground that has already been covered, they do not require extensive further treatment. Nevertheless, it is noteworthy that when Kant initially introduced these formulas he grounded them in a reflection on the nature of a moral law and only subsequently applied them to maxims. Now, however, Kant, argues that every maxim has the form of universality, from which he concludes that in this respect the formula for the moral imperative is expressed as "Maxims must be chosen, as if they could hold as universal laws of nature" (GMS 4: 436_{23-25}).[19] In view of its reference to laws of nature, this is equivalent to FLN (not FUL). Similarly, Kant claims that every maxim has a matter [*Materie*], which

---

[19] Although Kant does not mention the fact, the universality that he here affirms must be subjective. This is because Kant refers explicitly to *all* maxims, which include those that are not universalizable in the objective sense, that is, not capable of including themselves as a universal law. Moreover, we have seen that every maxim is universal for Kant in the sense that it is a general rule for an action-type under certain conditions. Similarly, when he says that every maxim has a matter or an end he is not limiting this to those that respect rational nature in oneself and others as an end in itself.

he equates with an end and derives from this the formula: "[A] rational being, as an end according to its nature, and hence as an end in itself, must in every maxim serve as the limiting condition of all merely relative and arbitrary ends" (GMS 4: 436$_{29-32}$).

In addition to the apparent disappearance of FUL (to be discussed below), the perplexing feature of Kant's review of the formulas concerns the third, which here appears in the guise of FRE rather than FA, and which he relates to the idea of a complete determination [*vollständige Bestimmung*].[20] Although Kant suggests that, like form and matter, this applies to every maxim taken individually, it is far from obvious how this is to be understood. Paton suggests that it means simply that every maxim has both a form and a matter.[21] This would explain how the third formula combines the other two, but at the cost of trivializing Kant's claim.

Kant's point seems rather to be that complete determination is something that happens to a maxim, when it harmonizes with both the agent's other maxims and the (presumably) lawful maxims of all (conceivable) rational agents through the application of the substantive principle that "all maxims from one's own legislation ought to harmonize into a possible realm of ends as a realm of nature" (GMS 4: 436$_{24-26}$). In a note attached to this passage, Kant remarks:

Teleology considers nature as a realm of ends, morality a possible realm of ends as a realm of nature. There the realm of ends is a theoretical idea for the explanation of what exists. Here it is a practical idea for bringing about what does not exist, but what can become actual through our deeds and omissions, and what we are to bring about in accordance precisely with this idea. (GMS 4: 436$_{32-36}$)

This indicates that the idea of a realm of ends, as a realm of nature, is a practical idea (or symbol thereof), which FRE makes perspicacious and which expresses the ideal at which morality aims. As such, it not only goes beyond FLN and FH, taken individually, it also unites them, not in the mechanical and trivial way suggested by Paton, but, rather, by making explicit what is merely implicit in each of them. Moreover, for the same reasons, the comparison between the progression in these formulas and that which occurs in the categories of quantity (from unity, to plurality, to allness or totality) likewise obtains, since, as is the case with each of the triadic sets of categories, the third constitutes a synthetic unity composed of the elements provided by the first two.[22]

---

[20]   In his discussion of the Ideal of Pure Reason in the first *Critique*, Kant makes considerable use of the principle of thoroughgoing determination [*durchgängige Bestimmung*], which is a metaphysical principle that holds that "Among all possible predicates of things, insofar as they are compared with their opposites, one must apply to it" (KrV A571/B579). Despite the obvious verbal similarity, it is not clear how this relates to the notion of complete determination to which Kant appeals in GMS.

[21]   Paton (1956, 140).

[22]   KrV B110. See also KU 5: 197n; 82–83.

(D) The universal formula

After completing his account of the relationship between the three formulas and the categorical imperative, Kant complicates matters further by suddenly introducing what seems to be a new, previously unmentioned, formula. He does this by remarking that,

[O]ne does better in moral appraisal [*Beurtheilung*] always to proceed according to the strict method and put at its basis the universal formula of the categorical imperative: *Act according to that maxim which can at the same time make itself into a universal law.* But if at the same time one wishes to obtain access [*Eingang*] for the moral law, it is very useful to take one and the same action through the three named concepts in order thereby, as far as possible, to bring it [the action] nearer to intuition. (GMS 4: 436$_{28}$–37$_4$)

This passage marks the only appearance of the expression "universal formula" and, apart from its identification, the main issues it poses are the role that Kant assigns to it as the preferred formula for moral appraisal and its relation to the three formulas of the categorical imperative that Kant officially designates as such, namely, FLN, FH, and FA. Since Kant has already characterized FUL as the single categorical imperative and since its wording seems close to that of FUL, it has been widely assumed that the universal formula, or UF, is logically equivalent to FUL. This consensus view has been challenged, however, by Wood, who contends that FA, rather than FUL, represents Kant's universal formula and is therefore the one required by the "strict method."

Wood's reason for the latter claim is not, as one might expect, that FA supplies a more reliable criterion for testing maxims than FUL, since he tends to play down, if not totally reject, this whole way of looking at the categorical imperative. Rather, his point is that the problem of appraising maxims in light of the categorical imperative is essentially one of avoiding having one's moral reflections "degenerate into comfortable and corrupt rationalizations," which presumably requires an austere version of the principle, as contrasted with one that is nearer to intuition. As Wood puts it, "Kant's point . . . is not one about *a priori* laws but about human psychology."[23]

While it cannot be gainsaid that Kant had such a concern, the text supports neither Wood's claim that this explains Kant's preference for the more austere formula nor his identification of the latter with FA rather than FUL. First, FUL is at least as "austere" as FA, which is precisely why many critics deny its usefulness as a practical principle. Second, Kant could hardly have thought that bringing the actions (or maxims) to be appraised in terms of the categorical imperative and the imperative itself nearer to intuition would exacerbate the danger to which Wood alludes. Otherwise, he would not have claimed that the usefulness of the various formulas consists precisely in their capacity to do this.

---

[23] Wood (1999, 190).

Nevertheless, I believe that there is something to Wood's suggestion, even though it is not exactly what he had in mind.[24] The point is that FA has a stronger claim than FUL and its counterpart (FLN) to be the preferred formula in moral appraisal because, in contrast to these, it requires universalizabilty$_2$. We have seen that the latter is grounded in the conception of rational agents as ends in themselves and that this is why it can require the universal endorsability of an agent's maxims (the idea being that any maxim that treats a rational agent merely as a means would, for that very reason, not be universally endorsable). Since FH does not explicitly appeal to a universaliz-ability requirement, it is not built into this formula. It does, however, become explicit in FA, which we have seen is presented by Kant as the product of the union of FLN and FH.

For this reason, I think it is unfortunate that Kant failed to reconsider his examples of the various types of duty under FA. Instead, he excused himself from the task on the grounds of its redundancy, suggesting that the results would be the same as in the first two formulas (GMS 4: 432$_{35-37}$). Kant apparently meant by this that all four of his examples would yield the same results, since maxims of suicide, false promising, slothfulness, and non-benefice would be ruled out under FA as they were under FLN and FH. Although this may be true, the interesting question, which Kant side-steps, is whether they would be ruled out *for the same reasons*. It is this that I find doubtful. Once again, it is one thing to reject a maxim on the grounds that it cannot coexist with itself as a universal law and quite another to reject it on the grounds that it could not be universally endorsable. By failing to apply the formula of autonomy to his previous examples (or to fresh ones for that matter), Kant gives the impression that he did not recognize any significant difference.

Acknowledging this difference does not, however, suffice to warrant the identifica-tion of UF with FA rather than FUL. Indeed, it seems reasonable to assume that, if Kant had intended to identify UF with any of the three designated formulas, he would have said so. But I also do not think that we should conclude from this that UF must be identified with FUL as the default position. Rather, I take Kant's position to be more complex, since there are senses in which UF may be both identified with and distinguished from *both* FUL *and* FA.

At first glance, the way in which Kant presents these formulas seems to favor the view that UF is logically equivalent to FUL. The former requires that one "*Act only according to that maxim through which you can at the same time will that it become a universal law*"; whereas the latter tells us to "*Act according to that maxim which can at the same time make itself into a universal law.*" There are two differences between these formulas, only one of which is significant. The first and insignificant one is the presence of "only" in FUL and its absence from UF. This as insignificant because "only" is redundant. Regardless of how the universalizability requirement is understood, it is obvious that

---

[24] My present view of the matter differs significantly from my earlier discussion of Wood's equation of the universal formula with the formula of autonomy. For the earlier view, see Allison (2001a).

we are required to act *only* on such maxims. The second and significant difference is that FUL requires us to act only on maxims that we can, at the same time, *will* as universal laws; whereas UF requires us to act only on maxims that we can, at the same time, *make* into universal laws.

This is also the difference noted by Wood and it constitutes a substantial part of his case for equating UF with FA rather than FUL. According to Wood, being able to will one's maxim as a universal law applies to an agent's maxims taken in isolation and provides, at best, merely a test for their permissibility; whereas being able to make one's maxims into universal laws is concerned with these maxims taken collectively and requires not merely that they be consistent with themselves in the sense that each can be willed without contradiction, but also (and primarily) that they harmonize with each other in the sense that they constitute a consistent whole.[25]

Although I agree with the importance that Wood attributes to the distinction between being able to will and being able to make one's maxims into universal laws, I disagree with his interpretation of it. That one's maxims harmonize with each other is a requirement of coherent willing; but it has nothing specifically to do with morality, since it applies to a successful criminal as well as to a person with good will. Rather, as previously indicated, I think it makes better sense to take the harmonization require-ment to apply to the wills of all rational agents. In other words, what is required of finite rational agents is that they proceed on the assumption that they are making laws for all such agents (including themselves), which is just what it means to consider oneself as a lawmaking member of a realm of ends.

Nevertheless, one might still ask, why not bite the bullet and simply identify UF with FA? The answer is that FA and UF are not formulas of the categorical imperative in the same sense and at the same level, which means that their identifica-tion would involve a type/token confusion. We have already seen in Chapter 6 that Kant uses the term "formula" in a number of ways, which are largely context dependent. Thus, in introducing the concept of an imperative (whether categorical or hypothetical) he characterized it as the "formula of the command" (GMS 4: 413_{10-11}), where "formula" means simply the verbal formulation of the command. In the moral context, in which we presently find ourselves, the operative contrast is between a principle and its formula. It is in this sense that Kant speaks of FLN, FH, and FA/FRE as three formulas of the single categorical imperative, which is itself the fundamental principle of morality (the moral law) expressed or formulated in the imperatival mood.

Inasmuch as Kant also regarded this formulation of the fundamental principle of morality in the imperatival mood, that is, the categorical imperative, as itself a formula, namely, FUL, this suggests that the three above-mentioned formulas are formulas of a formula, which seems incoherent.[26] Any aura of paradox or incoherence can be

---

[25] Wood (1999, 187–90).

[26] The problem is noted by Timmermann (2007a, 104 n108). He does not, however, consider the ambiguity of the term "formula" in Kant.

avoided, however, by distinguishing between first- and second-order formulas. On this view, FLN, FH, and FA/FRE are first-order formulas, which are applied directly to maxims, whereas FUL is a second-order formula or "meta-formula," which underlies and is expressed by these first-order formulas.

Assuming that some such distinction is in order, our question becomes: what are we to say of UF? Kant obviously regarded it as a formula, since he explicitly characterizes it as such; but the fact that he insists that there are three formulas of the categorical imperative and he does not include UF among them suggests that it must be a second-order formula. But if this is the case, how are we to understand its relation to FUL? We have seen that the standard view is to equate UF with FUL. However, in addition to the fact that this leaves it inexplicable why Kant would muddy the waters by introducing a new formula, rather than simply saying (as he is often taken to have held) that FUL should be used in moral appraisal and the subsidiary formulas used to bring it nearer to intuition, we have also seen that UF differs from FUL in one non-trivial respect, namely, the difference between being able to *will* maxims that could qualify as universal laws and being able to *make* maxims with this property. And if this were not enough, there is the puzzle about why Kant would suddenly declare that a formula, which is presumably logically equivalent to FUL, should be used in moral appraisal, when immediately after introducing FUL, Kant shifts to FLN (its typic) in order to test maxims for their permissibility!

We shall revisit these issues in more detail the next section of this chapter. For the present, it must suffice to note that I believe that the best way to make sense of all of this is to consider it in light of the previously enunciated thesis that Kant's overriding aim in GMS 2 is to provide a complete construction of the concept of the categorical imperative. We have seen that Kant regarded FUL as expressing the content of the concept of this imperative; but it is only the concept of the imperative in skeletal form. Before this imperative can be applied, it must be fleshed out, a task which is supposedly accomplished through the three formulas, which provide it with a determinate form (FLN), a content (FH), and a complete determination (FA/FRE). Moreover, if this is the case, it indicates that, like the universalizability requirement, FUL is ambiguous, since it can refer to the formula either in its initial form in which it is derived directly from the concept of the categorical imperative or its fully developed or constructed form in which it is equivalent to UF. I shall call the former FUL_1 and the latter FUL_2 and shall argue that this distinction, which like the distinction between the two senses of universalizability is not explicitly drawn by Kant, provides the key to dealing with the equivalence issue.

III

In the four paragraphs immediately following his account of the relationship between the formulas, Kant provides a recapitulation of the entire argument up to this point from the concept of a good will to autonomy ($GMS4$: 437_5–40_{13}). But since the only really new element in these paragraphs is Kant's brief, incomplete, and often neglected discussion of the issue of the equivalence of the formulas, this will be the concern of the present section. The discussion is divided into two parts. In the first, I attempt to spell out how my underlying interpretive thesis offers a framework in terms of which the issue of equivalence can be approached and then apply this to Kant's own brief discussion of the issue. In the second, I contrast my approach to the issue with that of O'Neill.

(A) The equivalency problem and a proposal for its solution

Setting aside the additional complexity provided by UF, the first question to be asked is how we are to understand the claim that the three designated formulas are equivalent, which seems to be required by the singularity thesis. In response, it might be argued that it follows immediately from the hypothesis that the three formulas are steps in the construction of the complete concept of the categorical imperative that they are expressions of the "very same law" and in this respect, at least, must be regarded as equivalent. Otherwise, they could not be involved in the construction of the *same concept*. Taken by itself, however, this sense of sameness is too weak. For example, one might say that FLN, FH, and FA are expressions of the same law in the sense in which youth, maturity, and old age are stages in the life of the same person, in which case there is no reason to assume that the application of each formula to similar cases would yield uniformly consistent results.

What is needed, then, is to show that the formulas are at least extensionally equivalent, which means that they yield the same results for the same cases.[27] But while it is evident that Kant intended to affirm this, the results attained so far render this claim highly problematic.[28] In addition to the problem caused by the apparent counter-examples to FLN (the false positives), which are readily rejected by FH, an extensional equivalence seems difficult to reconcile with Kant's claims that the three formulas provide respectively the form, matter, and complete determination of the categorical imperative and that there is an analogy between these formulas and the progression within the category of quantity from unity to plurality to allness or totality.[29] Moreover, the claim that FLN and FA appeal to different senses of universalizability (an intra- and an inter-subjective conception) seems only to exacerbate the problem; for it is difficult to see how two formulas, which appeal to these two different senses of universalizability, could be extensionally equivalent. Accordingly, we seem driven to a view such as Wood's, who summarily dismisses any claim of equivalence, asserting instead that the later formulas are "less inadequate than the

---

[27] To claim that they are also intensionally equivalent is to say that they not only yield the same results, but that they do so for the same reasons. O'Neill (1989, 131) maintains that they are equivalent in both senses.

[28] I take this to be implied by Kant's claim that the difference between the formulas is "subjectively *rather than* [my emphasis] objectively practical" (GMS 4: 436_{10-11}), as well as by his decision not to consider his examples under the formula of autonomy because it would be redundant.

[29] The latter point is emphasized by Wood (1999, 185).

earlier ones" and that "The Groundwork's search for the supreme principle of morality should be seen as ending only when we grasp the moral law as a 'system of formulas'."[30]

Nevertheless, it also seems clear that, inasmuch as it effectively denies the singularity thesis in any serious sense, such a view should be accepted only as a last resort by anyone who is sympathetic to Kant's account of the categorical imperative. The essential point is nicely put by O'Neill, when she notes that, "If the claim of equivalence cannot be sustained, the argument of the *Groundwork*, and more generally of Kant's ethics, is deeply disappointing."[31] We thus seem to find ourselves at an impasse. On the one hand, Kant's ethical theory requires the singularity thesis and the latter seems to require at least the extensional equivalence of the formulas; while, on the other hand, Kant's account of the relationship between the formulas make it difficult to see how this equivalence can be maintained.

In spite of the difficulties involved, I think that the complete construction interpretation of Kant's project in GMS 2, taken together with some of the points made at the end of the previous section, offer the best hope for sustaining the extensional equivalence of the formulas and therefore the singleness of the categorical imperative. The main reason for this is that it allows for the possibility of considering FUL in two ways: as it initially emerges from Kant's analysis of the concept of a categorical imperative and as it is fully constructed in the course of GMS 2. In the preceding section, I expressed this duality by distinguishing between FUL_1 and FUL_2; the point being that some such distinction is necessary, if one is to affirm an extensional equivalence. The equivalence that this makes possible, however, is not only, or even primarily, between these formulas themselves, but also between each of them and the completely constructed categorical imperative (FUL_2 or UF).

As often the case in Kant, a Leibnizian analogy is useful here. Leibniz was fond of illustrating his perspectivalism by comparing the universe to a city, which is perceived by the various monads from their distinctive points of view.[32] His point was that, just as different views of a city represent the same city from different points of view, so each monad represents the same universe from a different point of view. Applying this to Kant, one could say that there is only a single categorical imperative (or supreme principle of morality), which each of the three formulas represents from a distinctive point of view (that of form, matter, and complete determination). And just as the various representations of the universe for Leibniz are equivalent (they represent the same universe) without being identical, so, as expressions of the single categorical imperative, the three formulas are (extensionally) equivalent without being identical.

---

[30] The latter point is emphasized by Wood (1999, 185), 183.

[31] O'Neill (1989, 127).

[32] Leibniz (1989, 220).

With this as our model, let us consider the forementioned passage from his recapitulation in which Kant appears to affirm the equivalence of FUL and FH. He there writes:

The principle [*Princip*]: act with reference to every rational being (to yourself and others) so that in your maxim it holds at the same time as an end in itself, is at bottom the same [*im Grunde einerlei*] as the basic principle [*Grundsatz*]: act on a maxim that at the same time contains in itself its own universal validity for every rational being. For to say that in the use of means to any end I ought to limit my maxim to the condition of its universal validity, as a law for every subject, is tantamount to saying that the subject of ends, i.e., the rational being itself, must be made the basis of all maxims of action, never merely as a means, but as the supreme limiting condition in the use of all means, i.e., always at the same time as an end. (GMS 4: 437_{33}–38_7)

Kant's claim that the *Princip*, which is clearly equivalent to FH, and the *Grundsatz* are "at bottom the same" passes muster only if the latter is understood as FUL_2 or its equivalent UF. This is because taking the *Grundsatz* to refer either to FUL_1 or FLN (the only two other viable candidates) does not yield the desired equivalence. In the first case, it is because this skeletal, unconstructed formula does not involve a determinate sense of universalizability, which is why Kant insisted that its application requires an appeal to FLN as its typic. In the second, it is because the sense of universalizability that FLN involves (universalizability$_1$) does not entail universal endorsability, which is what FH requires. If we identify the *Grundsatz* with FUL_2 or UF, however, the equivalence claim does hold; for a maxim that "contains in itself its own universal validity for every rational being" is, by definition, one that every rational being could endorse, whereas a maxim that prescribed treating even one rational being merely as a means and not also (at the same time) as an end would, for that very reason, not be universally endorsable.[33] In other words, universal endorsability and treating rational beings as ends and never merely as means reciprocally imply one another. Moreover, we have seen that this is precisely the sense of universalizability affirmed by FUL_2 or UF.

It should also be noted that this change in the conception of universalizability, which is brought about through the complete construction of the concept of the categorical imperative, does not lead to the abandonment of an appeal to a law or order of nature as a typic for conceiving the universalizability requirement. It is rather that it takes a new form: as a teleological rather than a straightforwardly causal law. This is evident from Kant's account of the complete determination of the categorical imperative, where he appeals to the principle that "all maxims from one's own lawgiving ought to harmonize into a possible realm of ends as a realm of nature" (GMS 4: 436_{24-26}). As was suggested when first discussing this text, it provides a model or analogy for

---

[33] More precisely, it would not be endorsable under the assumption that no rational being could, qua rational, consent to be used *merely* as a means. The intent is to rule out cases of "brainwashing" or other procedures which might bypass the agency of the being who is used merely as a means.

conceiving oneself as an autonomous lawgiver in a realm of ends. As such, it is comparable to FLN in that it preserves the core Kantian idea of the need for some sensible correlate in order to represent, however indirectly or symbolically, ideas of reason. It differs from FLN, however, in that rather than asking whether one's maxim could subsist with itself as a universal law of nature, the question is whether the end embodied in one's maxim and the means chosen to attain it could harmonize with the ends of all rational agents.[34] Accordingly, this involves a reconceptualization of nature as embodying a teleological rather than merely a mechanistic causal order, which is reflected in Kant's previously cited claim that "Teleology considers nature as a realm of ends, morality a possible realm of ends as a realm of nature" (GMS 4: 436$_{32-33}$).

In the third *Critique*, the conception of nature as a realm of ends, which here functions merely as a typic or analogy, the function of which is to help bring the idea of universal endorsability "nearer to intuition," is linked to the reflective power of judgment, which enables it to play an essential systematic role in effecting a transition from the domain of nature to that of freedom (morality). But since this is a large topic and not germane to the limited project of GMS, I shall not attempt to deal with it here.[35] Instead, I shall conclude the discussion of the equivalence problem by contrasting O'Neill's treatment of the problem with the one offered here.

(B) O'Neill on the equivalence issue

O'Neill is the staunchest proponent of the equivalence thesis, arguing for both the extensional and intensional equivalence of the formulas.[36] Eschewing the problems arising from Kant's account of the relationship between the formulas, which was the major source of the puzzle considered in the first part of this section, her discussion focuses squarely on the threat to equivalence that is posed by the apparent counter-examples to the first formulation (false positives involving maxims of coercion, cruelty, or wanton violence). As we have seen, the apparent immunity of maxims of this type to the contradiction in conception test has led some interpreters to adopt the desperate expedient of appealing to the contradiction in will test to handle them. In other words, while admitting that such maxims can be *conceived* without contradiction as universal laws of (human) nature, they also insist that they cannot be *willed* as such, which has the counter-intuitive consequence that some of the most heinous acts conceivable are classified as violations of broad or imperfect duties rather than of strict or perfect ones.

---

[34] In some respects, this accords with Paton's view, who, as previously noted, appeals to the notion of teleological laws as the key to understanding Kant's examples under FLN. See Paton (1956, esp. 148–52). The main difference is that, for reasons already given, I deny that the notion of a teleological law (or a teleological contradiction) is operative at the initial stage of Kant's construction of the concept of the categorical imperative.

[35] The significance of this transition, which makes possible the conception of nature as amenable to our moral requirements, is that it allows us to conceive of these requirements as realizable in the natural (phenomenal) world. For my discussion of this topic and its importance for Kant's moral theory, see Allison (2001b, 195-218).

[36] O'Neill (1989, 131).

And we also saw that an interpreter as sensitive to this problem as Korsgaard is only able to avoid this consequence by sharply limiting the class of so-called "natural actions" that fall under FLN.

In contrast to these strategies, as well as the one sketched in the preceding section, O'Neill's is straightforward, comprehensive, and elegant. It consists essentially in claiming that of itself FUL rules out maxims of violence or coercion on the grounds that "they undercut the agency of those whom they victimize."[37] And since the same obviously holds of FH, it follows that the two formulas yield the same results for essentially the same reason, which means that they are both extensionally and intensionally equivalent. More specifically, O'Neill maintains that both FUL and FH ask an agent's question "What ought I to do?," albeit from a different perspective. As she puts it,

FUL addresses the question from the perspective of agents who acknowledge that others too are agents, and enjoins them to shun principles that could not be adopted by others, that is, that could not be universal laws. FEI [FH] addresses the agent's question from the perspective of agent's who acknowledge that action affects others and enjoins them to avoid damaging others' capacities to act.[38]

O'Neill is certainly correct in emphasizing that the two formulas ask an agent's question from two different perspectives and that each assumes a world in which there are other rational agents who are affected by our actions. She is also correct in noting both that maxims of the type under consideration effectively undercut the agency of those whom they victimize and that no rational agent (or at least no sane one) could endorse a course of action that undercut her agency. The problem with her account, which also applies to that of many other commentators, is that she completely ignores FLN, thereby regarding what Kant says about it as if he were referring to the FUL of which the former serves as its typic or application-condition.[39] Moreover, if one sticks to the Kantian text, which uses FLN (rather than FUL) to examine maxims and lists FLN (again rather than FUL) among the three formulas of the categorical imperative, then things are not as clear-cut as O'Neill's account suggests.

To begin with, although FLN and FH both ask the agent's question, they understand this agency in subtly different ways, which reflect the different levels in the analysis of rational agency with which the two formulas are connected. Moreover, this opens up the possibility of different answers to the question, depending on the different conceptions of rational agency that are at work. Since FLN is correlated with Kant's initial characterization of rational agents as beings with a capacity to act according to

---

[37] Ibid., 133.

[38] Ibid., 128–29. O'Neill uses "FEI" to express what I refer to as "FH."

[39] Although, as previously noted (see p. 195 note 48), in her first book O'Neill focused considerable attention on FLN, she did not there deal with the equivalency issue.

their representation of laws, the universalizability test presumably applies to rational agents so considered. Considered under FH, however, these same beings are also regarded as ends in themselves, who, as such, are never to be treated merely as means. And under FA/FRE they are considered not merely as rational agents *simpliciter*, but as *autonomous* agents, who, as such, must be able to endorse the principles on the basis of which an addressee of the categorical imperative acts. Although the latter is an essential ingredient in Kant's moral theory and fully worked out conception of rational agency, it cannot be included in deliberation under FLN, since it has yet to be "constructed."

Accordingly, while in the case of false promising, under FLN it is necessary to assume that the promisee is a rational agent in the first or "thin" sense, since only such a being could be the addressee of a promise; there are as yet no grounds in place for also assuming that the addressee is a rational agent in the "thick" sense of being an end in itself. Moreover, if this is the case, it follows that the universalizability required concerns merely the relation between a maxim to itself qua universal law, that is, universalizability$_1$, which I have argued is best expressed by the practical contradiction test as described by Korsgaard.

In conclusion, then, while I believe that O'Neill is on the right track, particularly with her insistence on the importance of there being a single categorical imperative (in contrast to Wood's view that Kant offers us nothing more than a "system of formulas"), I also believe that by ignoring FLN and the peculiar problems that it raises, she has made things somewhat too easy for herself; for when FLN is recognized as one of the three formulas, as it explicitly is by Kant, the equivalence for which she argues is not to be found. And, this again, is why I think that something like the complete construction reading holds out the best prospect for dealing with the equivalency issue, and therefore for defending Kant's claim that there is a single categorical imperative.

IV

The subject matter of this section is the concluding portion of GMS 2 (GMS 4: 440$_{14}$–45$_{15}$), which is concerned primarily with the contrast between autonomy and heteronomy. Kant divides his discussion into three parts, to which he gives the headings: "*The autonomy of the will as the supreme principle of morality*" (440$_{15-33}$); "*The heteronomy of the will as the source of all spurious [unächten] principles of morality*" (441$_{1-24}$); and "*Division of all possible principles of morality from the assumed fundamental concept of heteronomy*" (441$_{25}$–45$_{15}$). But since the first two parts are intended as complementary, it will be convenient to consider them together; and since the last paragraph of the section constitutes a transition to the problematic of GMS 3, it calls for a brief consideration. Accordingly, the discussion will be divided into three parts: (A) an analysis of the competing claims of autonomy and heteronomy to provide the supreme principle of morality; (B) an examination of Kant's taxonomy of the various forms of heteronomy; and (C) a glance at Kant's transitional paragraph.

(A) Autonomy and heteronomy as claimants for the title "supreme principle of morality"

Kant's central concern at this point is to show that morality is possible, if and only if it is grounded in the principle of autonomy; and since by morality Kant understands the common conception thereof, which he claims to have shown presupposes the categorical imperative, the question is which of these principles is capable of accounting for the possibility of such an imperative. Kant's argument closely parallels the indirect argument for transcendental idealism that he mounts in connection with the resolution of "The Antinomy of Pure Reason" in first *Critique*. Starting with the assumption that transcendental idealism and transcendental realism constitute two all-inclusive and mutually exclusive meta-philosophical standpoints, Kant there argues that the contradictions of reason with itself, which emerged in the four anti-nomial conflicts, are irresolvable if we assume the standpoint of transcendental realism, but disappear if we accept transcendental idealism.[40] Just as it was crucial to Kant's first *Critique* argument that all opposing philosophical positions, no matter how diverse their metaphysical and epistemological theories, can be shown to fall under the umbrella term "transcendental realism," so we shall see that it is equally crucial for Kant's project in GMS that all opposing moral theories fall, in virtue of their fundamental principle, under the label "heteronomy." But since Kant begins with a discussion of autonomy and describes heteronomy in essentially negative terms by contrasting it with autonomy, we shall likewise begin with a return visit to autonomy.

(1) *The principle of autonomy*: In our initial discussion of autonomy, we saw that Kant introduced it as the third practical principle of the will (the first two being universality and the conception of an end in itself) and claimed that it is the supreme condition of the agreement of the will with universal practical reason. The idea was that only a self-imposed or legislated principle could serve as a categorical imperative, because only such a principle could prescribe unconditionally. We further saw that Kant characterizes autonomy in three distinct ways: (1) as the principle of morality; (2) as itself a formula of the categorical imperative; and (3) as a property of the will. Our present concern is with the first and third senses and the connection between them. Although Kant does not put the matter quite so straightforwardly, the essential point is that it is qua property of the will (not qua one of the three formulas) that autonomy serves as the supreme principle of morality.

As we have seen, Kant defines autonomy, qua property, as "the property [*Beschaffenheit*] of the will to be a law to itself (independently of every property belonging to the objects of volition)" (GMS 4: 440_{16-18}). Since prior to introducing autonomy in the process of constructing the concepts of the categorical imperative and rational

---

[40] For my account of the contrast between transcendental idealism and transcendental realism and analysis of the indirect argument, see Allison (2004, 20–49 and 388–95).

agency in GMS 2, Kant had claimed that rational agents are self-determiners in the sense that they determine themselves to act on the basis of self-imposed maxims in pursuit of freely selected ends, it is evident that the essential aspect of this definition lies in its parenthetical clause, which indicates that it is not simply that the will is law to itself, but that it is so "*independently of every property belonging to the objects of volition*" [my emphasis]. By "object of volition" Kant understands an objective or possible state of affairs that is to be brought about intentionally through the agency of the subject, because it is viewed by the subject as in some sense good. Accordingly, to say that the will has the property of autonomy is to say that it has the capacity to bind or determine itself to act or refrain from acting independently of any such object. We have seen that it is in virtue of this capacity that autonomy is the supreme condition of the agreement of the will with universal practical reason and it is in virtue of the same capacity that it is the supreme condition of morality.

There are, however, two further points to be made before we can turn from autonomy to heteronomy. The first is that autonomy is not the supreme principle of morality in the same sense as the categorical imperative. The latter is the supreme principle in the straightforward sense that it constitutes the norm on the basis of which the moral status of particular maxims is determined. Obviously, without such a norm there could be no such thing as morality, since moral claims are inherently normative. Reverting to the terminology that Kant used in his earlier lectures, the categorical imperative is the *principium diiudicationis*. Autonomy, by contrast, is the supreme principle of morality in the very different sense that it alone accounts for the binding-ness or unconditioned authority of the imperative.[41]

The second point is that, even if Kant's claims regarding autonomy are correct, they are insufficient to establish the thesis that it is the supreme principle of morality in the above-mentioned sense. The problem is not that we do not yet know whether morality is anything more than a phantom of the brain; it is rather that the most that this argument can show is that morality (as grounded in the categorical imperative) is possible, *if* we attribute the property of autonomy to the will. But this still leaves open the possibility that other meta-ethical principles might do the job equally well or better. Thus, we find ourselves once again caught up in the familiar Kantian argument pattern, where the goal is to show that x is possible if and only if y, and the latter is established by eliminating all conceivable non-ys. Or, more precisely, we are caught up in the variant of that pattern in which there is only one conceivable non-y (heterono-my), which requires that all competing views be brought under that label. As noted above, this corresponds to the pattern in the first *Critique*, where Kant appealed to the contrast between transcendental realism and transcendental idealism.

---

[41] As such, autonomy also cannot be identified with the *principium executionis*, since Kant assigns that task to respect as the moral incentive or *Bewegungsgrund*. But as the source of the authority of the law and therefore the ground of the respect that we have for it, it is closely related to the latter.

(2) *The principle of heteronomy*: If the above analysis of Kant's procedure is correct, his account of heteronomy must establish two things, both of which are implicit in his characterization of it "*as the source of all spurious [unächten] principles of morality.*" The first is that on the assumption of heteronomy a categorical imperative is inconceivable. The second is that all conceivable non-autonomy-based moral theories must be regarded as forms of heteronomy. Together, they would establish the *only if* portion of Kant's argument, which is logically equivalent to showing that autonomy is a necessary condition of the possibility of morality.

Given Kant's account of the categorical imperative and his characterization of heteronomy, the first of these goals is easily established. According to Kant, we have heteronomy whenever "the will does not give itself the law, but the object through its relation to the will gives the law to it" (GMS 4: 441_{7-8}). Since on this account of agency, it is the end or object of desire that is the source of the necessitation to act, it is evident that all imperatives would be hypothetical, which is just Kant's point (GMS 4: 441_{8-11}).

This shows that the key issue is the second, namely, whether all non-autonomy-based moral theories can be regarded as species of heteronomy, so described; or, alternatively, whether "heteronomy" can be regarded as something like a natural kind term that encompasses all ethical theories that lie on the non-autonomy side of a meta-ethical fault line. We shall see in the next section that Kant was keenly aware of this issue and attempted to deal with it by providing a supposedly exhaustive taxonomy of the varieties of heteronomy. But before turning to that we must consider the objection that heteronomy, as Kant describes it, really applies to only one particular slice of the domain of non-autonomy-based moral theories and that Kant is therefore guilty of trying to force diverse theories or principles into a one-size-fits-all mold.

The issue turns on the interpretation of the phrase: "the object through its relation to the will gives the law to it." On a widely accepted interpretation of this phrase and related passages in the second *Critique*, by an object giving the law to the will is to be understood the view that it is the expectation of satisfaction through the attainment of this object that provides the incentive that determines the will. And since this satisfaction is understood as the attainment of pleasure or the avoidance of pain, this means that on Kant's account all non-moral motivation is hedonistic, which effectively makes the contrast between autonomy and heteronomy arbitrary and far from exhaustive.[42] In other words, on this reading, Kant is only led to the view that autonomy is the sole principle of morality by his extremely limited conception of the alternatives, which is itself a consequence of his impoverished empirical psychology.

---

[42] This objection seems to be traceable to T. H. Green. See Green (2003, 182). More recent versions of the thesis that Kant is a hedonist regarding non-moral motivation have been raised, with appeal to Green, by Irwin (1984, 39–41); Meerbote (1984, 66–67); and Wood (1984, 83). The fullest response to this interpretation and the criticism it yields is by Reath (2006, 33–66). Much of what I say here on the topic is influenced by this important paper.

In responding to this objection, the first thing to note is that it ignores an important distinction that Kant draws between two ways in which the relation between the object and the will to which it supposedly gives the law can be understood: as resting either on inclination or on "representations of reason" [*Vorstellungen der Vernunft*] (GMS 4: 441$_{9-10}$). At best, this line of objection is applicable only to the first of these two forms of heteronomy, in which some inclination for an object, which is traceable to our sensuous nature, is required in order to determine the will. It does not apply to the second form, wherein representations of reason, which have nothing directly to do with our sensuous nature and therefore with feelings of pleasure and pain, provide the means for determining the will. Although at this point Kant does not explain what he means by "representations of reason," we later learn that he is referring to the concept of perfection, which we have seen to be the fundamental principle of the Stoic and Wolffian moral theories.

Moreover further consideration indicates that the psychological hedonism charge cannot even be leveled at the form of heteronomy in which a relation to a sensuous inclination is necessary for an object to determine the will. This is because for Kant the relation between inclination and the feelings of pleasure and pain is causal rather than intentional. In other words, while it is the case that inclinations, which are habitual desires, invariably have sensations of pleasure or pain as part of their causal histories, it does not follow that the experience of tokens of the pleasant sensation or the avoidance of tokens of the unpleasant one is the end at which one aims in acting from that inclination.

Consider, for example, Kant's "friend of man" or naturally sympathetic person of GMS 1. As we have seen, though acting from inclination rather than duty, the intended end of his beneficent actions is the well-being of others rather than his own. Although he would not help others in need unless doing so gave him satisfaction, which is what makes his course of action heteronomous, his end is truly the satisfaction of the needs of others and not his own needs. Accordingly, if by psychological hedonism is understood the view that the end at which all intentional action aims is the maximization of one's own pleasure or the minimization of one's own of pain, then in appealing to this example, which is also a clear instance of heteronomy, Kant is not proceeding as a psychological hedonist.[43]

Perhaps the most important point to keep in mind, however, in endeavoring to understand Kant's anti-heteronomy argument is that both autonomy and heteronomy (at least as Kant understands the latter here) reflect a conception of rational agency in

---

[43] It should be noted that most of the passages that have been taken as evidence of Kant's psychological hedonism with regard to non-moral motivation are taken from the second *Critique*, particularly the first and second theorems, where Kant discusses "material practical principles," that is, those which presuppose an object of the faculty of desire as the determining ground of the will, which he claims all fall under the general principle of self-love or one's own happiness (KpV 5: 21–26; 155–60). Since I am attempting to write a commentary on GMS rather than the second *Critique*, I cannot here discuss these texts; but I endorse Reath's analysis of them, where he argues for a non-hedonistic interpretation. See Reath (2006, 40–48).

which agents act according to their representation of laws or on principles, as contrasted with merely acting in accordance with natural laws. In other words, the difference between autonomy and heteronomy is not so much a metaphysical one, according to which only autonomous agents are genuinely agents, while heteronomous ones are at best mere automata, but a practical one, concerning possible sources of reasons to act.[44]

In order to clarify this point, let us consider briefly what heteronomous agency looks like on the Kantian picture. Although, by definition, a heteronomous agent lacks autonomy, it would possess all the other capacities that Kant associates with rational agency. Thus, it would be a "self-determiner" in the minimal sense discussed above, according to which it would select its own ends and act on the basis of maxims that possess a subjective universality in the sense that the agent must acknowledge their validity for any agents who share these interests (or ends) and find themselves in relevantly similar circumstances. Consequently, such an agent would be subject to hypothetical imperatives governing the selection of means for its self-chosen ends. It would not, however, be subject to any principle that the agent could regard as *unconditionally* binding, since the bindingness of any principle would be a consequence of some interest of the agent that underlies the adoption of that principle. In short, it would lack the capacity to recognize a categorical imperative; not in the intellectual sense of being incapable of grasping its concept, but in the practical sense of being unable to acknowledge its unconditional bindingness.

This points to the centrality of the concept of an interest in Kant's account. We have seen that for Kant only rational agents can have interests, as opposed to desires, since an interest requires a certain endorsement of a desire by reason. And we have also seen that these interests are the sources of reasons to act and, as such, conditions of the bindingness of a course of action. This holds on both the autonomy and the heteronomy-based accounts. The difference lies in the nature of interests of which agents are capable on the two views. We shall see that Kant held that the possibility of obedience to the categorical imperative presupposes a pure "moral interest," which is the correlate of a pure will and pertains only to autonomous agency. By contrast, from the standpoint of heteronomy, all volition must stem ultimately from some pre-given interest, which entails that it can give rise only to hypothetical imperatives. In other words, implicitly at least, all such theories have the form: "I ought to do something

---

[44] Admittedly, Kant is not consistent on this matter, since we shall see that in most of his uses of the term in GMS 3, he does seem to equate "heteronomy" with causality according to laws of nature, which is contrasted with genuine agency. (Yet see GMS 4: 460₂₅.) Moreover, there are two passages in the second *Critique* that suggest that only autonomous agency, and therefore morally good behavior, exhibits genuine agency. See KpV 5: 33; 166 and 43; 174. More generally, the notion that the object gives the law to the will suggests a causal picture and underlies the still prevalent but deeply mistaken view that Kant held that we are free only when we act from duty. I shall have more to say on this topic in the succeeding chapters, when we consider Kant's conception of freedom; for the present it must suffice to note that "dependence" on laws of nature need not be regarded as a causal dependence. On the contrary, it is better understood as a dependence on nature (including one's own sensible nature) as a source of reasons to act.

because I will something else" (GMS 4: 441_{10-11}). Or, as Kant puts it somewhat more expansively,

> Whenever an object of the will must be assumed as the ground for prescribing the rule determining the will, there the rule is nothing but heteronomy; the imperative is conditioned, namely: *if* or *because* one wills this object, one ought to act thus or thus; consequently, it can never command morally, that is, categorically. (GMS 4: 444_{1-5})[45]

Although developing this theme would take us well beyond the scope of the present work, I feel that it would be amiss not to at least mention that Kant's anti-heteronomy, pro-autonomy argument as sketched above constitutes a striking anticipation of his more famous depiction of the so-called "Copernican hypothesis," which he described some two years later in the preface to the second edition of the first *Critique* (KrV B xvi–xix). In fact, I believe it fair to say that they are the meta-epistemological and meta-ethical counterparts of each other. Thus, just as it is impossible to account for the possibility of *a priori* knowledge, if one assumes that cognition must conform to objects, so, too, one cannot explain the possibility of a categorical imperative, that is, an *a priori* practical principle with the requisite universality and necessity, if one assumes that an object (of the will) must be the source of the (moral) law. And just as *a priori* cognition is possible, if we assume that objects must conform to the *a priori* conditions of our cognition of them, so, too, a categorical imperative is possible, if we assume that the will is the source of the law that it is obligated to obey.[46]

(B) Kant's taxonomy of the forms of heteronomy

Kant not only argues for the inadequacy of any heteronomy-based moral theory, he also provides what he claims to be an exhaustive inventory of such theories. Echoing a remark in the Preface to the first edition of the first *Critique*, in which he suggests that the critical path on which he will proceed is the only one left (Axii), Kant reflects that, "Here as elsewhere in its pure use, as long as it lacks a critique, human reason tries every possible incorrect way before it succeeds in finding the single true one" (GMS 4: 441_{29-31}).[47] Kant arrives at his classification of heteronomous moral theories by first dividing them into two main types: the empirical and the rational and then further dividing each of these into two sub-types.

Kant claims that those theories that are based on empirical principles are drawn from the principle of happiness, and are built upon either physical or moral feeling. The former encompasses the various forms of hedonism and the latter refers to moral sense or sentimentalist theories. Rational moral theories, according to Kant, are all based on the principle of perfection; but here, too, he finds room for a further distinction

---

[45] For a parallel version of this argument see KpV 5: 33; 166.

[46] This analogy is noted by Carnois (1987, 45).

[47] The parallel is noted by Wood in a note attached to his translation of the *Groundwork* (2002, 59 n99). In the theoretical domain Kant characterizes the incorrect paths as dogmatism and skepticism.

between those that are built upon the rational concept of perfection as a possible effect of our will and those that are built upon the concept of an existing perfection (the will of God) as the determining ground of our will (GMS 4: 441_{32}–42_5).[48]

In spite of regarding all these positions as incorrect, Kant ranked them in terms of their relative suitability as moral principles. Not surprisingly, he claimed that all empirical principles are inadequate on the familiar grounds that they are incapable of accounting for the universality and necessity that a categorical imperative requires. Also not surprisingly, he regarded the principle of *one's own happiness*, which he apparently equated with physical feeling, as the most objectionable, since it is not only false but utterly perverts the moral incentive. By contrast, even though Kant regarded sentimentalist theories as superficial and fanciful (insofar as they appeal to the existence of a special moral sense), he gave them credit for at least recognizing the immediate satisfaction and esteem felt for virtue (GMS 4: 442_6–43_2). In short, though heteronomous and based on our sensuous nature, such theories are explicitly anti-hedonistic, which once again undercuts the view that all such theories are grounded in a hedonistic psychology.

For this reason, however, it is surprising that Kant includes sentimentalist theories under the principle of happiness. But seemingly aware of the paradoxical nature of this classification, he deals with it in a note, which makes specific reference to Hutcheson, who is the only philosopher to whom he refers by name in his taxonomy.[49] Kant writes:

I count the principle of moral feeling under happiness, because every empirical interest promises to contribute to our well-being through the agreeableness which something affords, whether this happens immediately and without regard to [one's own] advantage or with regard to the latter. One must likewise, with *Hutcheson*, count the principle of sympathetic participation in the happiness of others under the same moral sense assumed by him. (GMS 4: 442_{32-36})

---

[48] Here Kant seems to have simply assumed rather than to have argued for the completeness of his inventory. In his subsequent treatment of the topic in the second *Critique*, however, Kant argues explicitly for the completeness of his list, even claiming that this is made visually evident by being presented in tabular form (KpV 5: 39–41; 172–73). Moreover, the principles of division are different, which appears to be consequence of the fact that Kant there frames the issue in terms of the contrast between material and formal determining grounds of the will, with the idea being that the elimination of all conceivable forms of the former (which are equivalent to forms of heteronomy) leaves the latter (which is equivalent to autonomy) by default. And instead of dividing all erroneous moral principles into the empirical and the rational, which are then subdivided in the manner noted, Kant provides an overlapping distinction between objective and subjective material determining grounds of the will, on the one hand, and internal and external grounds, on the other. Finally, the class of subjective and external determining grounds, under which Kant includes principles based on education (for which he cites Montaigne) and those based on the civil constitution (for which he cites Mandeville) have no parallel in the GMS taxonomy. Kant also had constructed taxonomies of erroneous moral theories in earlier texts, which antedate the autonomy–heteronomy contrast. Examples of these include R 6631 and 6637 (19: 118–19 and 121–22) and *Ethik* 14–17; 12–15. For a discussion of this issue see Beck (1960, 103–8).

[49] This, again, differs from the taxonomy of the second *Critique*, in which each position is linked with a specific philosopher or school.

Inasmuch as Kant both explicitly distinguishes between the principle of happiness *simpliciter* and *one's own* happiness and credits moral sense theories with recognizing that virtue is esteemed for its own sake, he is not misrepresenting Hutcheson, with whose views he was quite familiar, as an egoist or hedonist. Kant's point is rather the more subtle one that, by basing judgments of moral value on a sense of the immediate or disinterested agreeableness of certain actions to either the agent or the spectator, Hutcheson, and presumably other sentimentalists, grounded such judgments in a contingent feature of human nature, namely, that we are so constituted as to find certain courses of action as either agreeable or disagreeable. And, presumably, it is because it is a matter of a feeling of agreeableness that Kant lists the moral sense principle under happiness, though not one's own happiness, since what one finds agreeable (or disagreeable) according to such theories is the condition of someone else rather than one's own.[50]

With regard to the rational principles of morality, both of which are based on the concept of perfection, Kant states his clear preference for the ontological concept (the Wolffian view) over the theological concept, by which he apparently understands the divine command theory of Crusius.[51] This is because even though the former is empty and, as we have seen, supposedly leads to tautologous claims, it avoids both the crude circularity that is characteristic of the latter (we need a concept of goodness in order to determine that God's will is supremely good and therefore ought to be obeyed) and the concept of the divine will that we would be left with, if we endeavor to avoid this circularity, namely, one that is totally amoral and, as such, completely incapable of providing a foundation for morality (GMS 4: 443_{3-19}). Kant completes his critical survey of the various forms of heteronomy by remarking that if he were forced to choose between the moral sense and the ontological perfection views, he would opt for the latter, because, even though it cannot decide anything, it at least locates the question of the ultimate ground of morality in the "court of pure reason," where it supposedly belongs (GMS 4: 443_{20-28}).

In light of the attention that Kant devotes to what he terms "popular moral philosophy" in GMS 2, which I have identified primarily with the views of Garve, one might wonder why neither is assigned a distinct place in what is supposedly an exhaustive account of the possible forms of heteronomy. The answer is not that Kant did not regard popular moral philosophy in general and the views of Garve in particular as heteronomous, since he obviously did. It lies rather in the unprincipled eclecticism, which Kant evidently found to be the worst feature of popular moral philosophy. In other words, as "a disgusting mishmash [*Mischmasch*] of patched together observations

---

[50] If this reading of Kant's position in GMS is correct, then there appears to be a significant difference between it and his later view, expressed in the second *Critique*, that "All material [heteronomous] practical principles as such are, without exception of one and the same kind and come under the general principle of self-love or one's own happiness" (KpV 5: 22; 155). I discuss this issue in Allison (1990, 102–3).

[51] Crusius is explicitly mentioned in the second *Critique*, along with other (unnamed) "theological moralists for whom moral principles are rooted in the will of God" (KpV 5: 40; 172).

and half-reasoned principles" (GMS 4: 409_{29}–10_2), the latter does not constitute a coherent philosophical position, which would merit inclusion in Kant's taxonomy.[52]

(C) The transition to GMS 3

After completing his critique of heteronomy and taxonomy of its various forms, Kant devotes the final paragraph of GMS 2 to a statement of the problem to be dealt with in GMS 3. Referring to the categorical imperative, he reflects that "*How such a synthetic practical proposition a priori is possible* and why it is necessary, is a problem that cannot be resolved within the bounds of the metaphysics of morals"; and he further notes that up to this point he has made no attempt to establish its truth (GMS 4: 444_{35}–45_1). Instead, Kant re-emphasizes the analytic nature of his procedure in this and the preceding section, according to which an analysis of the generally accepted concept of morality has led to the conclusion that the autonomy of the will lies at its foundation. Accordingly, for all that we have learned about the *concept* [my emphasis] of morality, the possibility remains open that morality itself is "merely a chimerical idea without truth" (GMS 4: 445_6). And Kant further suggests that the demonstration that the latter is not the case "requires a *possible synthetic use of pure practical reason*, upon which we cannot venture without a prior *critique* of this rational faculty itself" (GMS4: $445_{11–13}$).

We shall revisit portions of this text in the next chapter; but the only thing that calls for comment at this point is the italicized phrase, which is deeply ambiguous. The problem concerns the meaning to be attached to a "synthetic use of pure practical reason." Perhaps the most natural reading is to understand by this its use in grounding the categorical imperative through its deduction, which is contrasted with the "analytic use" operative in the first two parts of the work.[53] This makes little sense, however, for at least two reasons. First, it is not the case that for Kant a critique of the practical faculty of reason is required *before* one can provide a deduction of the categorical imperative. As we shall see in the following chapters, it is rather that this deduction is the essential element of this critique. Second, and most important, neither the analytic method operative in GMS 1 and 2 nor the synthetic method of GMS 3 can be said to involve a use of *practical* reason. Practical reason is the *object* of these investigations, *not the means* by which they are carried out. Accordingly, I think that by the synthetic use of pure practical reason is to be understood its use in determining the will, which is required if there is to be such a thing as a categorical imperative. As such, it is to be contrasted not with the use of reason in connection with the analytic or regressive method, but with its practical use in forming and imposing hypothetical imperatives.

---

[52] The point could also be made by noting that Kant's taxonomy is of heteronomous *principles*, whereas the problem with popular moral philosophy for Kant is that it is without a governing principle.

[53] This appears to be the way in which it was understood by Paton, who thereby objects to Kant's claim. See Paton (1956, 141).

PART IV

GMS 3

10

The Moral Law, the Categorical Imperative, and the Reciprocity Thesis

By the end of GMS 2, with the introduction of the principle of autonomy as the supreme principle of morality and its contrast with heteronomy as the underlying principle of all spurious moral theories, that is, all theories except his own, Kant had completed the first of the two tasks that he assigned himself, namely, to search for and formulate the supreme principle of morality as it is found in common human reason. We have seen that Kant characterized his procedure in the first two parts as analytic or regressive. In GMS 1, starting with the concept of a good will, which is presumed by common human reason to be the only thing that is good without limitation, Kant arrived at a version of the categorical imperative as the principle on which a good will under human conditions would act. Correlatively, in GMS 2, Kant took as his starting point the concept of a rational being or agent as such; and after deriving the content of the categorical imperative (FUL) from an analysis of the concept of such an imperative, understood as the form in which an unconditional practical law (the moral law) would address a finite rational agent as such, he devoted the remainder of this section to articulating various formulations of this imperative, arriving eventually at the principle of autonomy as the supreme principle of morality.

Throughout his account Kant took pains to remind the reader that this analytic procedure left open the question of whether morality was something real rather than a "chimerical idea" (GMS 4: 445_6) or a "phantom of the brain" [*Hirngespinnst*] (GMS 4: 407_{17} and 445_8). It was also noted, however, that a peculiar feature of Kant's procedure is that he did not regard the correctness of his analysis of morality as a similarly open question. Rather, Kant took it for granted that *if* morality is to be something more than a chimerical idea or phantom of the brain, it *must* have the form and be based on the principles that he attributes to it.

GMS 3 is devoted to the second of the tasks assigned to the work as a whole, namely, to establish the objective validity or reality of the principle of morality by means of a deduction.[1] Although Kant does not refer to his deduction in GMS 3 as "transcendental," since he tended to reserve that term for theoretical concepts and principles, it has the same function, which can be characterized as exorcizing a specter.[2] As suggested above, the specter is that morality might be nothing more than a chimerical idea or phantom of the brain. Clearly, if GMS is to fulfill its systematic function of providing a foundation for the projected metaphysics of morals, it must show that any such worry is unfounded.

In essence, then, this constitutes the subject matter of this and the two following chapters. The present chapter focuses on the introduction to the problem and is divided into two parts. The first begins with a consideration of the identity of the proposition or propositions for which Kant purports to provide a deduction. It argues that these include the moral law as well the categorical imperative, since, contrary to what is sometimes maintained, both are synthetic a priori. The second part is concerned with the argument of the first three paragraphs of the text (GMS 4: 446_7–472_{25}), to which Kant gave the heading: "*The concept of freedom is the key to the explanation of the autonomy of the will.*" This section contains what I have termed Kant's "reciprocity thesis," namely, that "a free will and a will under moral laws are one and the same thing [*einerlei*]" (GMS 4: 447_{6-7}). In addition to analyzing this thesis and defending Kant's argument for it, I shall contrast my understanding of it with Dieter Schönecker's and offer a response to the frequently voiced objection that, by defining a free will as one that is under moral laws, this thesis makes it impossible for Kant to account for the imputability of either morally evil or good actions.

I

Although it is evident that Kant's ultimate goal in GMS 3 is to provide a deduction of the categorical imperative and that this requires demonstrating its unconditional bindingness for all finite rational agents, there are at least two competing accounts in the literature regarding how Kant sets about doing this. Moreover, the difference between these accounts turns largely on the weight and status that is assigned to the

---

[1] Here, as elsewhere, Kant's use of terminology is fluid. Usually he uses "reality" [*Realität*] to refer to the relation between a concept and its object (does the object instantiate or fall under the concept?) and validity to characterize the normative status of a principle (its genuineness or legitimacy). Thus, the question regarding freedom is almost always put in terms of its "objective reality," which Kant claims to have established from a practical point of view (see, for example, GMS 4: 455_{25}, as well as numerous passages in the second *Critique*); while he tends to frame the question concerning the moral law and/or categorical imperative in terms of its validity (see, for example, GMS 4: 424_{30-31}, 425_{31}, 449_{29}, 460_{25}–61_3). At times, however, Kant also refers to the reality of the principle of morality (see, for example, 425_{15}, 449_{26}, and KpV 5: 47 176–77). Since at GMS 4: 449_{24-30} Kant seems to treat these as equivalent, I shall here follow him in this regard.

[2] I analyze Kant's transcendental deductions in the first *Critique* and the Introduction to the third as attempts to exorcize the specters of transcendental and empirical chaos respectively, by which I understand a fundamental incoherence in experience at the transcendental and empirical levels. See Allison (1990, 38 and 2004, 160).

moral law, as distinct from the categorical imperative. The dispute does not concern the question of whether Kant distinguishes between them, since it is obvious that he does; it concerns rather how he understands the relation between the two and, more specifically, whether the only deduction contained in the text is of the categorical imperative or whether it also contains a deduction of the moral law. For ease of reference, I shall refer to them as the single deduction and the double deduction readings respectively.

In the recent literature, the single deduction reading has been most forcefully articulated by Schönecker, who bases his interpretation on two main points. The first is a privileging of part four of GMS 3, which addresses the question: "*How is a categorical imperative possible?*" (GMS 3: 453_{16}–55_9). Since Kant there clearly equates his argument showing how a categorical imperative is possible with its deduction, while apparently treating the three preceding sections as "preparatory" and devoting the succeeding section to methodological reflections on the boundary of practical philosophy, it has seemed to Schönecker and others that this constitutes the heart of the argument of GMS 3. Accordingly, by showing how a categorical imperative is possible, Kant has completed the positive task of GMS. The second point is the view that for Kant the moral law or supreme principle of morality, insofar as it is distinct from the categorical imperative, does not require a deduction because it is an analytic proposition. In support of this, Schönecker appeals to Kant's claim that, "[I]f freedom of the will is presupposed, morality, together with its principle follows from it, through mere analysis of its concept" (GMS 4: 447_{8-9}) and similar texts.[3] Schönecker refers to this as "*Kant's Analytizitätsthese.*"

The double deduction reading, which I favor, finds textual support in the fact that Kant mentions the term "deduction" three times in GMS 3 and each time it seems to have a different referent. The second of these is located in the third and final paragraph of the section dealing with the possibility of a categorical imperative and clearly indicates that accounting for this possibility is the job of a deduction (GMS 4: 454_{20}). But in its first appearance the term refers to the concept of freedom and Kant suggests that what is needed is a deduction of this concept "from pure practical reason," which, he adds, will also account for the possibility of the categorical imperative (GMS 4: 447_{22-23}). Moreover, in its final appearance, Kant refers to "our deduction of the supreme principle of morality" (GMS 4: 463_{21-22}), an expression that he usually uses as equivalent to the moral law rather than the categorical imperative.

Since Kant linked the deduction of freedom directly with his account of the possibility of the categorical imperative, he might not have thought of the first two of the above-mentioned deductions as distinct. But, in spite of his notorious carelessness in particular cases, we have seen that it is essential for Kant to distinguish between the moral law and the categorical imperative. The former is a descriptive

---

[3] See Schönecker (1999, esp. 153–95 and 2006, esp. 302–8).

principle, which depicts the *modus operandi* of either a perfectly rational agent or an imperfectly rational one, considered merely qua rational, that is, in abstraction from whatever ends or interests that such an agent might have in view of its sensuous nature. The latter is a prescriptive principle, which applies only to finite or imperfectly rational agents. Inasmuch as the moral law is a descriptive principle, its deduction cannot speak to its bindingness or obligatory force. Rather, the task of such a deduction would be to establish the validity of this law for all rational beings with a will. I shall argue that this deduction is an essential precondition for the deduction of the bindingness for beings like ourselves of the categorical imperative; but for the present I shall content myself with trying to show that the moral law, like the categorical imperative, is a synthetic *a priori* proposition.

The first step is to identify the proposition that Kant characterizes as the moral law. References to the moral law in GMS are fairly sparse; but the most important of these is in Kant's discussion of the interest attached to the idea of morality, where he explicitly equates it with the principle of the autonomy of the will and calls attention to the problem of an apparent circularity in the argument. He there writes: "[I]t seems as if in the idea of freedom we actually presupposed the moral law, namely the principle of the autonomy of the will itself, and could not by itself prove its reality [*Realität*] and objective necessity" (GMS 4: 449$_{24-27}$).[4]

Apart from posing the problem of a circle, which will be discussed in the next chapter, this passage is important in two respects. First, it provides an unambiguous characterization of the moral law. Second, and equally important, it shows that Kant recognized a problem in establishing the validity of the moral law, which he would not have acknowledged if he had regarded it as an analytic principle.[5] Operating on the basis of this assumption and with the aim of determining whether the moral law for Kant is analytic or synthetic, I shall consider three passages bearing on this topic. Although the first two might seem to support the view that the moral law is analytic and the third, which appears to affirm its syntheticity, has been the subject of considerable debate, I shall argue that the first two are perfectly compatible with the view that the moral law is synthetic and that the third, which proves to be decisive, must be read as affirming this.

The first passage constitutes Kant's explanation for his characterization of the autonomy of the will as the supreme principle of morality. He writes:

Autonomy of the will is the property of the will to be a law to itself (independently of every property of the objects of volition). The principle of autonomy is therefore: not to choose to act except in such a way that the maxims of your choice are at the same time comprehended with it

---

[4] Other places where the expression "moral law" (either "*moralischen Gesetz*" or "*sittlichen Gesetz*") is to be found in GMS include: 389$_{24}$, 390$_5$, 410$_{27}$, 437$_1$, 450$_{16-17}$, 453$_{5-6}$, and 461$_{11-13}$.

[5] Unfortunately, Kant muddies the waters in the remainder of the sentence and the rest of the paragraph, when he equates the principle with its imperatival form and poses the problem of an incentive, which is not applicable to the moral law as such (see GMS 4: 449$_{27}$–50$_2$).

in the same volition as universal law. That this practical rule is an imperative, i.e., the will of every rational being is necessarily bound to it as a condition, cannot be proven by mere analysis of the concepts contained in it, because it is a synthetic proposition; one would have to go beyond the cognition of objects and to a critique of the subject, i.e., of pure practical reason, for this synthetic proposition, which commands apodictically, must be able to be cognized completely *a priori*; but this enterprise is not the concern of the present section. Nevertheless, that the specified [*gedachtes*] principle of autonomy is the sole principle of morality may well be shown through the mere analysis of the concepts of morality. For one finds thereby that its principle must be a categorical imperative, but this commands nothing more or less than precisely this autonomy. (GMS 4: 440$_{16-32}$)

Since the first two sentences were already discussed in the preceding chapter, they require little further comment. Suffice it to note that the first sentence refers to autonomy qua property of the will and the second to it in its role as a formula of the categorical imperative. The third sentence speaks to the synthetic *a priori* character of the imperative or, more precisely, of the practical proposition that affirms that the will of every rational being is necessarily bound by the principle of autonomy, and notes that justifying the latter assertion is not the task of the present section (GMS 2). Hence, it is silent on the question of the syntheticity of the moral law in its non-imperatival form, which is likewise to be identified with the principle of autonomy.

For present purposes, however, the main interest of the passage lies in its last two sentences. At the heart of the matter is an ambiguity in the phrase: "the mere analysis of the concepts of morality." Although an analysis of concepts for Kant usually results in an analytic judgment, and this is clearly what Kant had in mind in the initial reference to an analysis of the concepts contained in the principle of autonomy, I take Kant to be referring here instead to the conceptual analysis that is operative in the application of the analytic or regressive method of the first two parts of GMS. So construed, Kant's point is that it is the analysis of the conception of morality pertaining to common human reason (not the concept of autonomy itself) that has led to the claim that autonomy is the supreme principle of morality.

Kant emphasizes that this analysis does not establish the bindingness of this principle because the predicate expressing this bindingness is not contained in the concept of autonomy. This does not speak, however, to the question of whether the principle of autonomy itself is analytic or synthetic. Moreover, this cannot be decided by the claim that its status as the sole principle of morals can be established by "the mere analysis of the concepts of morality"; for we have already seen that it does not follow from the fact that a principle is arrived at by a regressive or analytic procedure that it is itself analytic.[6]

---

[6] This is the locus of my major disagreement with McCarthy (1976). Although he correctly emphasizes the importance of not confusing Kant's analytic method with analytic judgments, McCarthy nonetheless claims that all the steps in Kant's analytic arguments in GMS 1 and 2 are themselves analytic. His reasoning is that since Kant's analytic argument cannot appeal to intuition and since it is only by means of the latter (whether empirical or pure) that the various steps in a regressive argument composed of synthetic propositions can be established, that the steps in Kant's regressive argument in GMS from the concept of a good will to the

And when, in the last sentence, Kant endeavors to justify the claim of the preceding one, he is merely reiterating the results of his regressive account of the conditions of the possibility of morality, not claiming (or even implying) that the propositions "the principle of morality must be a categorical imperative" or "the categorical imperative requires nothing more or less than autonomy" are analytic.

The second text, a portion of which was likewise cited in the previous chapter, forms part of the transition from GMS 2 to GMS 3. Kant there writes,

> The absolutely good will, whose principle must be a categorical imperative, will therefore, undetermined with respect to all objects, contain merely the *form of volition* [*Wollens*] as such, and indeed as autonomy, i.e., the suitability of the maxim of every good will to make itself into a universal law is itself the sole law that the will of every rational being imposes on itself, without grounding it in any incentive or interest.
>
> *How such a synthetic practical proposition a priori is possible* and why it is necessary, is a problem whose solution does not lie within the bounds of the metaphysics of morals, also we have here not asserted its truth, much less claimed to have a proof of it in our power. We have only shown through the development of the generally accepted concept of morality: that it is unavoidably connected with or rather grounded on an [*eine*] autonomy of the will. (GMS 4: 444_{35}–45_5)

There are two relatively clear features of this dense bit of text. The first is that, even though Kant had previously defined an absolutely good will as one that cannot become evil (GMS 4: 437_{6-7}), he cannot here be taken as identifying it with a holy will; for he says that the principle of this will must be a categorical imperative and Kant is consistent in denying that a holy will is subject to imperatives. Accordingly, it seems that by an "absolutely good will" Kant must mean the will of a finite rational being, considered qua acting in obedience to the categorical imperative.[7] The second is that the proposition that a will, so considered, cannot become evil is analytic, since its denial would contradict the concept of such a will.

---

principle of autonomy must all be analytic, from which it follows that the principle itself (as the conclusion of an analytic or regressive argument) must be analytic. I think that this analysis is wrong on three grounds. First, it is based entirely on Kant's account of theoretical cognition and ignores whatever modifications of the understanding of the analytic–synthetic distinction are required to apply it to the practical domain. Second, it is not clear that it holds even in the theoretical domain. Consider, for example, Kant's analysis of mathematical reasoning according to which a synthetic *a priori* conclusion can follow deductively (in accordance with the principle of contradiction) as long as the initial premise of the demonstration is synthetic *a priori* (see KrV B14). Accordingly, if the first premise of Kant's reductive argument, i.e., that the good will is the highest value recognized by common human reason, is synthetic, then even if the proposition that the principle of autonomy is the supreme principle of morality were supposedly intended to follow from this by a chain of analytic judgments (which seems highly unlikely), it would still follow that the principle of autonomy is synthetic. Finally, even though Kant's regressive method is one of conceptual analysis, this does mean that it consists solely (or even primarily of an analysis of what is contained in a concept. Instead, I think that Kant's procedure in GMS 1 and 2 may be more properly described as an analysis of a *conception*, namely morality, as it is viewed by common human reason, rather than of a *concept* composed of a determinate number of marks. Moreover, we have seen that Kant's standard move in these sections is to look for what is *presupposed by* rather than what is *thought in* this conception of morality; and it is not at all clear that claims of the form "A presupposes B" or "B is a necessary condition of A" must be considered analytic.

7   The point is clearly made by Paton (1958, 201).

What remains obscure, however, is the identity of the synthetic *a priori* proposition to which Kant refers in the first sentence of the second paragraph. If one focuses on the characterization of the principle of an absolutely good will as the categorical imperative, one is naturally led to identify the proposition with this imperative. But if, as also seems reasonable, one identifies the synthetic *a priori* proposition with the propositional content of the preceding single sentence paragraph as a whole, one arrives at a somewhat different result. For the main point that Kant seems to be making there is that the law governing an absolutely good will concerns merely the form of its volition or willing as such, that is, the suitability of its maxims to serve as universal laws. Accordingly, on this reading, the synthetic *a priori* proposition to which Kant refers is not the categorical imperative *per se*, but the principle of autonomy considered as describing the *modus operandi* of an absolutely good will. And this, as I have already indicated, could be equated with the moral law.

Although the obscurity of the text makes any interpretation hazardous, I suspect that Kant wanted to make both points.[8] That is to say, the synthetic *a priori* practical proposition to which Kant refers at the beginning of the second paragraph may be described either as the moral law or as the categorical imperative. I further suspect that the reason for Kant's lack of clarity on this point stems from the fact that the moral law and the categorical imperative share the same content and differ only with regard to mood. And even though the law expressed in both its moods is synthetic *a priori*, each requires a distinct justification or deduction. In the case of the former, it is merely a matter of establishing a necessity claim, where necessity is equivalent to universal validity; whereas in the case of the latter, it requires establishing a *necessitation* of the will by this universally valid principle. As Kant indicates, however, at this point he is not interested in establishing either, which perhaps provides a further reason for the ambiguity of his account.

In the third passage Kant writes:

If, therefore, freedom of the will is presupposed, morality together with its principle, follows from it through mere analysis of its concept [of freedom]. Nevertheless, the latter [the principle of morality] is always a synthetic proposition: an absolutely good will is that whose maxim can always contain itself, considered as a universal law, for through the analysis of the concept of an absolutely good will that property of the maxim cannot be found. (GMS 4: 447$_{9-14}$)

The first sentence refers to the first part of the reciprocity thesis and will be discussed further in the second part of this chapter. Our immediate interest in it is limited to the fact that it has been taken as affirming that the moral law (the principle of morality), as contrasted with the categorical imperative, is analytic. This, in turn, leads to an apparent contradiction with the second sentence, which on the most natural reading, which takes "the latter" [*das letztere*] to refer back to the "principle of morality" in the previous sentence, maintains that it is synthetic.

---

[8] This reading is suggested, but not explicitly endorsed, by Paton (1958, 201).

To begin with, I believe that it is a mistake to read the first sentence as implying that the moral law is analytic. Simply put, it does not follow from the fact that morality together with its principle (the moral law or the principle of autonomy) follows from an analysis of the concept of freedom that the moral law itself is analytic. The reciprocity thesis also maintains that if the moral law is assumed, freedom of the will follows from an analysis of the concept of such a law; but I doubt very much that one would infer from this that for Kant the proposition that rational agents have a free will is analytic. The proposition expressing the moral law or principle of autonomy as the descriptive law of an absolutely good will would be analytic, if it could be derived from the analysis of the concept of such a will (as contrasted with the concept of freedom); but this is precisely what Kant denies in the second sentence.

Although this analysis of the first sentence removes the worry that it is contradicted by the second; it still leaves us with the problem that the second sentence appears to be incompatible with Kant's analytic or regressive argument of GMS 1 and 2, where he is taken to have argued that the moral law or principle of autonomy is, in fact, derived from the concept of a good (if not an absolutely good) will. Indeed, faced with this apparent contradiction, some commentators have claimed that Kant here made a slip and misstated his real position.[9]

An alternative reading has been proposed by Schönecker, who shares the view that the moral law is analytic, but wishes to avoid attributing such a gross slip to Kant. According to Schönecker, "the latter" [*das letztere*] refers forward to the passage after the colon rather than backward to the subject of the preceding sentence and thus should be rendered "the following"; while the contrasting conjunction "Nevertheless" [*Indessen*] serves to juxtapose the analyticity of the connection between freedom of the will and the principle of morality affirmed in the first sentence with the syntheticity of the proposition following the colon, which Kant states cannot be derived analytically from the concept of an absolutely good will.[10] And since his reading of GMS 3 as a whole rests on the premise that the categorical imperative is the only synthetic *a priori* principle at issue, Schönecker identifies Kant's characterization of the maxim of an absolutely good will as a statement of the categorical imperative rather than of the moral law.

As far as the first alternative is concerned, it must be granted that it is possible that Kant misstated his view when he claimed that the principle of morality (in its non-imperatival form) is synthetic rather than analytic. Nevertheless, attributing this to sheer carelessness on Kant's part seems highly implausible, particularly given the importance of the matter for him and the fact that he failed to correct his misstatement in the second edition of GMS, for which he did make a number of changes.

---

[9] This view was initially and most forcefully expressed by McCarthy (1976, 576), who argued for the need of a textual emendation. More recently, it has been seconded by Milz (1998, 190 n9). Korsgaard (1996, 75 n56) and Timmerman (2007a, 124 n19) express a similar view in a more tentative manner.

[10] Schönecker (1999, 166–67; 2006, 306–7).

Moreover, this implausibility is increased if one considers the structure of the passage as a whole. To begin with, as Schönecker correctly points out, by starting the second sentence with "Nevertheless" Kant is indicating a contrast with the analytic connection between freedom and morality and its principle (autonomy or the moral law) that is affirmed in the first. Presumably, if Kant had wished to claim that the connection between this principle and the concept of an absolutely good will was analytic as well, he would not have begun the sentence in this way.[11] Instead, he would have said something like "And it is also the case that...".

Although Schönecker's reading has the virtue of taking the text seriously, I think that he forces an unnatural and unconvincing reading on it in order to make it conform to his view. The most natural reading, which, ironically, is assumed by those who hold that Kant must have misstated his view, is to take "the latter" to refer back to the principle of morality mentioned in the first sentence. In fact, this is implicitly acknowledged by Schönecker, who suggests that the referent of the pronoun is "perplexing" [verwirrend].[12]

Moreover, the phrase which Schönecker characterizes as a statement of the categorical imperative ("an absolutely good will is that whose maxim can always contain itself considered as a universal law") is clearly descriptive rather than prescriptive, a point which, despite his emphasis on the descriptive nature of the moral law, he passes over in silence. And, finally, in order to make the passage fit his interpretation, Schönecker is forced to attribute to Kant a puzzling ambiguity in his account of an absolutely good will. Whereas he maintains (and I believe correctly) that Kant elsewhere understood by an absolutely good will either the will of a perfectly rational being or the will of a sensibly affected rational being, considered merely qua rational, Schönecker insists that in the passage currently under consideration Kant cannot mean such a will, since it would stand under the moral law but not the categorical imperative.[13] Rather, according to Schönecker, Kant here (but not elsewhere) understands by an absolutely good will simply one that is good without restriction, which corresponds to Kant's initial characterization of a good will *simpliciter*.[14]

Apart from underscoring the difficulty of interpreting the text, the chief lesson to be derived from this venture into the hermeneutical thicket is that in order to preserve the integrity of the text (not having Kant saying the opposite of what he meant to say), it is necessary to take Kant at his word, when he asserts that "an absolutely good will is that

---

[11] This point is recognized by Schönecker (2006, 306–7); but he concludes from this that in the latter (synthetic) proposition Kant is referring to the categorical imperative. I can find no support for this reading other than that his interpretation of GMS 3 requires it.

[12] Schönecker (1999, 166).

[13] For his account of an absolutely good will apart from this passage, see Schönecker (1999, 160).

[14] Ibid., 167. See also Schönecker (2006, 307).

whose maxim can always contain itself considered as a universal law" is synthetic.[15] Moreover, I believe that the reasons that have led commentators to resist this straightforward reading are less than compelling. As we have seen, this resistance is motivated mainly by three considerations: (1) the assumption that the conditional proposition: "If... freedom of the will is presupposed, morality, together with its principle, follows through mere analysis of its concept" entails that the principle of morality is itself analytic; (2) a puzzlement regarding Kant's justification of the syntheticity of this principle; and (3) an antecedent conviction that the sole synthetic *a priori* practical proposition with which Kant is concerned in GMS 3 is the categorical imperative.

Having already addressed the first point, there is no need to say anything further about it here; though I shall return to it later in the chapter. With regard to the second point, Kant is correct in denying that the principle of autonomy or the moral law can be derived from (in the sense of contained in) the concept of an absolutely good will. For all that is contained or thought in this concept, however obscurely, is that the goodness of such a will is unrestricted or unconditioned; and, as Kant points out, this does not tell us that the maxims of such a will necessarily have the property of containing themselves when considered as universal laws. To be sure, in the analytic or regressive portion of the argument, the principle of autonomy and, indeed, the categorical imperative are supposedly derived from (in the sense of discovered by) a regress from the concept of a good will (not an *absolutely* good will) and, more generally, from the conception of morality adhered to by common human reason. But, as already noted, this is a matter of uncovering presuppositions, which is quite different from explicating what is already thought in a concept.

As for the third point, a common, though largely unexpressed, assumption of those who insist upon the analyticity of the moral law, as distinct from the categorical imperative, is that, since the syntheticity of the latter is a consequence of the fact that it contains a claim of bindingness or prescriptivity, which cannot be derived from an analysis of its concept, and since this feature is lacking in the moral law as a descriptive law of an absolutely good will, that the latter must be analytic. It is easy to see, however, that this inference is fallacious; for it hardly follows from the fact that the moral law is descriptive rather than prescriptive that it must be analytic. Indeed, if this were the case, it would also follow that the *a priori* laws of nature (both the transcendental laws of the *Critique* and the metaphysical ones of MAN) are analytic, which is a proposition that few Kant interpreters would accept.[16]

---

[15] According to Beck (1960, 122) this principle expresses the moral law (as distinct from the categorical imperative) and I concur.

[16] Such a view has been maintained by some Kant commentators, albeit more as an account of what should have said than of what he actually maintained. Examples of this are C. I. Lewis (1947, 161–62) and Bennett (1966, esp. 4–14).

Finally, lest it be objected that a purely descriptive law would lack practical import or normativity, it must be kept in mind that Kant did not equate the normative with the prescriptive. We have already seen this in connection with the analysis of FUL, where the idea of conformity to universal law was seen to be normative, though not, as such, prescriptive. But the clearest illustration of this point is Kant's conception of a holy will. To say that a will is holy is to say that it is absolutely good, which is surely a normative claim if anything is; but, as we have also seen, with respect to such a will the moral law (or principle of autonomy) functions purely descriptively.

Accordingly, I conclude that, even though in describing the aims of GMS 3, Kant emphasized the question: "*How is a categorical imperative possible?*" and regarded the explanation of this possibility as a deduction, which is concerned with the possibility of a synthetic *a priori* cognition, this by no means precludes the possibility that he was also concerned with the deduction of a second synthetic *a priori* proposition, namely, the moral law. We have seen that, unlike the deduction of the categorical imperative, this deduction cannot purport to establish the bindingness of this law; since this applies only to imperatives. But this does not preclude a deduction of the principle of autonomy as a descriptive law characterizing the behavior of a perfectly rational being or of any finite rational agent, considered qua purely rational. Indeed, I shall argue in the next chapter not only that Kant attempts such a deduction (its success being another matter), but also that it is a necessary preliminary to the deduction of the categorical imperative.[17] Our immediate concern, however, is with the first section of GMS 3.

II

Kant's heading for the first section of GMS 3 reads: "*The concept of freedom is the key to the explanation of the autonomy of the will.*" Since Kant had concluded the regressive portion of his argument by claiming that autonomy is the supreme principle of morality, it is only to be expected that GMS 3 would be concerned with justifying the ascription of autonomy to the will of rational agents. And it is hardly surprising that Kant would claim that the concept of freedom provides the key to this endeavor, since it is already clear from the account of autonomy in GMS 2 that freedom is a necessary condition of its possibility.

What is surprising, however, is Kant's claim that freedom is not merely a necessary, but also a sufficient condition of autonomy and therefore of morality as viewed by common human reason and as analyzed in GMS 2. Although Kant does not state it in so many words, this is what he effectively maintains, when he states that "a free will and a will under moral laws are one and the same" (GMS 4: 447$_{5-6}$). And the same can be said of a previously cited passage, where he writes that, "If . . . freedom of the will is

---

[17] The point is nicely put by Paton (1958, 199), "Kant attempts to justify the principle *as a moral law* and only thereby to justify it *as a categorical imperative.*"

presupposed, morality, together with its principle, follows through mere analysis of its concept" (GMS 4: 447$_{8-10}$). Moreover, in the second *Critique* Kant reiterates this, claiming that "freedom and unconditional practical law reciprocally imply each other" (KpV 5: 29; 162), and that "it [the moral law] would be analytic if the freedom of the will were presupposed" (KrV 5: 31; 164).[18]

Because of the first passage from the second *Critique* cited above, I have termed this the reciprocity thesis and an examination of this thesis, the argument that Kant provides for it, and its role in the overall argument of GMS 3 will be the main concerns of this section of the present chapter. The discussion is divided into three parts: (A) an examination of Kant's argument for this thesis; (B) a comparison of the reciprocity thesis with its counterpart in Schönecker, which he terms "*Kants Analytizitätsthese*"; (C) some reflections on the compatibility of the reciprocity thesis with the possibility of imputation.

(A) Kant's argument for the reciprocity thesis

Kant begins GMS 3 with a fresh definition of the will. Initially, he had defined the will simply as practical reason (GMS 4: 4: 412$_{29-30}$), but he now characterizes it as "a species of causality of living beings insofar as they are rational" (GMS 446$_{7-8}$). In addition to the reference to living beings, which presumably precludes any with a holy or divine will, the significant new feature of this definition is the introduction of causality.[19] A will is not only attributed solely to rational beings, it is also understood as a causal power possessed by such beings or, better, a power that such beings are presumed to possess. Moreover, this conception of the will provides the basis for introducing the concept of freedom, which is characterized as one of two conceivable types of causality. Specifically, it is the type of causality that has the property [*Eigenschaft*] of being effective "independently of alien [*fremden*] causes *determining it.*" As such, it is contrasted with "*natural necessity,*" which is the type of causality attributed to all non-rational beings and is described as the property of being determined to act through the influence of alien causes (GMS 4: 446$_{8-12}$).

The expression "alien causes" calls for some comment. As Kant understands it, it refers not merely to external causes in the usual sense, that is, to entities or events external to the agent, which exert a causal influence on the agent, but also to "inner" causes that might be located in the antecedent state of the agent, for example, occurrent desires and dispositions. The latter point is crucial to Kant because it marks his main difference from the Leibnizian view, which he elsewhere characterizes as a "wretched subterfuge" and the "freedom of a turnspit," since it recognizes only a "comparative" concept of freedom in which the causes of "free" actions are located in the antecedent

---

[18] I shall return to the last of these passages in connection with an analysis of Schönecker's interpretation.

[19] In the second *Critique*, Kant defines "life" as "the faculty of a being to act in accordance with laws of the faculty of desire" (KpV 5: 10n; 144).

state of the agent.[20] It is to distance himself from this doctrine, which admits only a "relative spontaneity" or "*spontaneitas secundum quid*," that, as we shall see below, Kant insists that genuine freedom requires *absolute* spontaneity. For the moment, however, it suffices to note that Kant recognizes two conceivable species of efficient causality: freedom and natural necessity, or, as he characterizes the latter in the first *Critique*, "causality according to nature."[21]

With these definitions in place, Kant begins his argument for the reciprocity thesis by noting that his initial characterization of freedom in terms of an independence from determination by alien causes is merely negative and, as such, incapable of yielding any insight into its nature. Since freedom is defined as a kind of causality, what is necessary is a positive characterization of it, which would explain what it means to be determined by a "non-alien cause." Kant addresses this question by considering the nature of the law that could govern the activity of any agent with such freedom and the reciprocity thesis affirms that it must be the moral law (here understood as the principle of autonomy). The argument for this thesis goes as follows:

(1) Since the concept of causality brings with it that of *laws* according to which through something that we call cause, something else, namely, the consequence [*Folge*] must be posited [*gesetzt*]: so freedom, even though it is not a property of the will according to natural laws, is not for that reason entirely lawless, but must rather be a causality according to immutable laws, but of a particular kind; for otherwise a free will would be a non-entity [*Unding*]. (2) Natural necessity was a heteronomy of efficient causes; for every effect [*Wirkung*] was possible only in accordance with the law that something else determined the efficient cause to causality; what else can freedom of the will be than autonomy, i.e., the property of the will of being a law to itself? (3) But the proposition: the will is in all its actions a law to itself signifies only the principle, to act on no other maxim than that which also can have as object itself as universal law. (4) This, however, is precisely the formula of the categorical imperative and the principle of morality: therefore a free will and a will under moral laws are one and the same. (GMS 4: 446$_{15}$–47$_7$)

The argument of this passage can be broken down into four steps, corresponding to its four sentences. Following the usual procedure, I have numbered these steps in the text for ease of reference. It has roughly the following form: (1) As a kind of causality, a free will must be law-governed. (2) As free, it cannot be governed by laws of nature, since these presuppose natural necessity; consequently, it must be governed by self-imposed laws, that is, it must be autonomous. (3) Autonomy is equivalent to the principle of autonomy, which is, in turn, equivalent to the moral law. (4) Therefore, by a free will is understood a will under moral laws.

The first two steps of this reconstruction basically parallel Kant's argument; but since I find that major problems arise with the move from two to three, I shall abandon Kant's pattern in order to underscore some of the problems that he glosses over and to

---

[20] See KpV 5: 96–98; 216–18 and ML$_1$.28: 267; 80. For my discussion of the topic, see Allison (1990, 59–64, 2006, 382–85).

[21] See KrV A532–41/B560–69.

mount a defense of the reciprocity thesis that is responsive to these problems. This reconstruction/defense will consist of five steps and include an analysis of Kant's argument for this thesis in the second *Critique*.

(1) *Freedom as a kind of causality*: Kant's first step is to affirm the connection between freedom and law, which he does by defining freedom as a kind of causality. The latter point is problematic because by "freedom" (negatively defined) Kant understands what he elsewhere refers to as "transcendental freedom," that is, "absolute spontaneity" or the capacity of an agent to begin a state "**from itself**," which might be regarded as incompatible with the view that a free will is law-governed. In the first *Critique*, Kant characterized freedom, so construed, both as a pure transcendental idea and as a cosmological concept (KrV A533/B561). By the former, Kant meant that it neither borrows anything from experience nor can have as an object anything given in experience. By the latter, Kant connected this idea to the cosmological question taken up in the Third Antinomy: whether the conception of the world as a whole (the totality of appearances) requires for its completion the assumption of a first (uncaused) cause.[22]

Although the familiar concept of a first cause does not seem to have anything directly to do with the concept of freedom of the will, Kant forges a connection between them by noting that the practical concept of freedom, which refers to the latter, is grounded in this transcendental idea and that this is the source of the notorious difficulties in the latter concept (KrV A533/B561).[23] Kant meant by this that the conception of free will, like the cosmological conception, involves the idea of an absolute spontaneity; though in this case the spontaneity is understood as a capacity to act independently of determination by sensuous impulses, which Kant regards as the putative causal factors to which opponents of freedom of the will typically appeal as the determining grounds of choice.[24] In response, Kant distinguishes between being pathologically (or sensuously) **affected** and being pathologically **determined** (KrV A534/B562). His central contention is that we must affirm the former but deny the latter of finite rational beings, if we are to attribute to them a free will.

At the same time, however, Kant refuses to equate not being pathologically deter-mined with not being determined at all. Rather, since the notion of causality is

---

[22] I discuss the cosmological issue posed in the Third Antinomy in Allison (2004, 376–84).

[23] See also KrV A448/B476.

[24] One might think that by limiting the relevant causal factors to psychological ones, Kant is undermining his claim for the need for absolute spontaneity and therefore transcendental freedom, particularly since in the metaphysical lectures of the 1770s he had contrasted an absolute with a merely comparative conception of freedom, connecting the former with rational and the latter with empirical psychology. On this point, see Ameriks (2003, 164). I shall explain why I do not believe this to be the case in Chapter 12. It must be admitted, however, that I am here glossing over a number of contentious issues regarding Kant's views on the relation between transcendental and practical freedom and the sense of freedom required for morality, which are emphasized by Ameriks, on the grounds that the reciprocity thesis presupposes transcendental freedom. For my views on these issues, see Allison (1990, 54–70).

inseparable from that of law and freedom is, by definition, a kind of causality, a free will must be determined (in the sense of governed) by law, though not by the kind of law according to which natural occurrences are determined (laws of nature). Kant had already prepared the grounds for this move with his initial characterization of rational beings as having the capacity to determine themselves to act according to their representation of laws, understood as acting on the basis of principles rather than merely responding to stimuli. Moreover, this suggests that, when Kant states that a lawless will is a non-entity, he has in mind one that is not governed by a rule or principle of *any sort*, even if it be something like the "principle" of always acting on the basis of one's strongest desire; or always do the first thing that comes to one's mind. Here Kant is in agreement with the Leibnizians in their insistence that free actions must have a sufficient reason, which accounts for their law-governedness; though he differs from them in denying that this reason must be traced to an antecedent state of the agent.

(2) *Kant's equivocations regarding "autonomy" and "heteronomy"*: Assuming that a free will must be governed by *some* law, Kant's second step is to provide this law. He begins by identifying the natural necessity that is opposed to the causality of freedom with heteronomy, which, in view of the dichotomy between autonomy and heteronomy presented at the end of GMS 2, leads directly to the identification of the law of free causality with autonomy: "the property of the will of being a law to itself."

At first glance, this claim seems plausible; for if we are to think of a free will in the sense indicated by Kant as law-governed, it would have to be governed by a law that the will imposes on itself, which is the literal meaning of "autonomy." Moreover, this fits the description of a non-alien cause. Closer consideration, however, suggests that the argument is deeply problematic, because the conclusion that Kant wishes to draw is stronger than the premises warrant.

To begin with, if the preceding reconstruction of the implicit argument for the impossibility of a lawless will is correct, it establishes the necessary law-governedness of a free will in only a weak sense. What seems to be required is merely that volition be grounded in a representation of law, which is a condition that can be met by any maxim. And since a will that acts on the basis of maxims that are self-imposed but reflect the subjective interests of an agent is presumably not a "nonentity," it remains unclear how an appeal to the necessary law-governedness of a free will is capable of yielding the reciprocity thesis as Kant understands it. Otherwise expressed, the problem is that Kant needs to show that a free will is governed by a *necessary law*, but the most that the argument seems capable of showing is that a free will is necessarily governed by *some* (non-alien) "law," for which it seems that even a maxim, as a "subjective law," would suffice.[25]

---

[25] Kant is cited as characterizing maxims as "subjective laws" in *Ethik* 52; 43.

Unfortunately, the characterization of the law of a free will as autonomy only exacerbates the problem, because Kant arrives at this conclusion by means of a blatant equivocation involving both "autonomy" and "heteronomy." We have seen that, when Kant drew this contrast near the end of GMS 2, it was in the form of a distinction between two all-inclusive and mutually exclusive meta-ethical principles, which speak to two different ways in which practical laws, that is, first-order principles, could exert authority on the will of a rational agent. According to heteronomy-based theories, some object of volition must be presupposed in order to give the law to the will. But, and this is the crucial point, "giving the law to the will" is understood as imbuing the principle on which it acts with authority or normative force, not as causally determining it. Conversely, according to the principle of autonomy, the will serves as a law to itself, by which is understood that it is the source of its own authority or normativity. In short, the contrast between heteronomy and autonomy, as Kant presents it in GMS 2, is between two views of the source of the authority or normative force of the principles on which rational agents act. And Kant's core claim is that only autonomy is capable of accounting for the possibility of a categorical imperative.

In the passage currently before us, however, Kant takes the contrast between heteronomy and autonomy to be between two incompatible conceptions of causality. According to the former, the actions of rational agents are regarded as mere events or bits of behavior necessitated by antecedent causes. According to the latter, they are genuine actions, in which an agent is self-determined according to the law of its own will. As in the first version of the contrast, the denial of heteronomy entails autonomy, since they are viewed as contradictories; but the problem is that this only entails the sense of autonomy that is contrasted with heteronomy understood as necessity according to laws of nature, and this is quite distinct from the *moral* autonomy affirmed in the reciprocity thesis. In other words, Kant's argument linking freedom negatively defined (independence from alien causes) with autonomy, turns on an equivocal use of both "autonomy" and "heteronomy." I shall call the two senses of "autonomy" that Kant conflates autonomy$_1$ (moral autonomy) and autonomy$_2$ (free agency in general) respectively, and of "heteronomy" heteronomy$_1$ (a meta-ethical principle) and heteronomy$_2$ (causal determinism). Applying this terminology, we can say that the problem is that Kant effectively takes the negation of heteronomy$_2$ to entail autonomy$_1$; whereas the only conclusion that he is entitled to draw from this negation is the non-specifically moral autonomy$_2$.[26]

(3) *The reciprocity thesis in the second Critique*: Inasmuch as Kant's argument in GMS appears to turn on the conflation described above, it may prove useful to consider his argument for the reciprocity thesis in the second *Critique*, since it avoids this conflation. This thesis there constitutes the culmination of the first six propositions of the Analytic

---

[26] The objection in roughly the latter form has been raised by Bittner (1983, 119–34) and Prauss (1983, esp. 19–61).

and it leads directly to the formulation of the "fundamental law of pure practical reason" in the seventh. Starting with the definition of a practical law as an objective and universally valid practical principle (§1), Kant first excludes all material practical principles, that is, all principles that presuppose an object or matter of the faculty of desire, as possible candidates for a practical law, on the grounds that all such principles are empirical (§2); from this he concludes, by appealing to the form–matter dichotomy, that, (§4) "If a rational being is to think of his maxims as practical universal laws, he can think of them only as principles that contain the determining ground of the will not by their matter but only by their form" (KpV 5: 27; 160).[27] In short, Kant argues by elimination that only a formal principle could count as a practical law.

Kant moves from this to the reciprocity thesis by posing two complementary problems. The first is based on the supposition that "the mere lawgiving [*gesetzgebende*] form of maxims is the only sufficient determining ground of a will," and the problem is "to find the constitution [*Beschaffenheit*] of a will that is determinable by it alone" (KpV 5: 28; 162). The second assumes that the will is free and the problem is "to find the law that is alone competent to determine it necessarily" (KpV 5: 29; 162). In response to the first problem, Kant claims that only a free will (in the transcendental sense) could have its determining ground (sufficient reason to act) in the mere form of its maxims. Moreover, since we have seen that a practical law must concern the form of an agent's maxims, it follows that having a free will is a necessary condition of standing under a practical law. In response to the second problem, Kant argues (1) that since a free will (by definition) must be independent of all "empirical conditions," which includes the "material" element of practical principles, but (2) must nonetheless be "determinable" (presumably according to some law), it follows that (3) "the lawgiving form, insofar as it is contained in the maxim, is the only thing that can constitute a determining ground of the [free] will." And, combining these solutions, Kant concludes in the previously cited passage at the very beginning of the remark attached to §6, that "freedom and unconditional practical law reciprocally imply each other" (KpV 5: 29; 162).[28]

Although it shares the premise that a free will must in some sense be law-governed and arrives at a logically equivalent conclusion, this argument is quite distinct from the one in GMS. Moreover, in addition to the fact that it avoids the forementioned conflation, there at are least two respects in which it constitutes a clear improvement over the latter. First, by focusing on the contrast between the matter and form of a maxim, Kant poses the issue within the framework of his underlying account of

---

[27] §3, which includes a corollary and two remarks (KpV 5: 22–26; 155–60), is devoted to Kant's controversial thesis that all material practical principles are based ultimately on the principle of self-love or one's own happiness. This is an additional argument for their unsuitability as moral principles; but it need not be considered here, since it is not directly relevant to the reciprocity thesis.

[28] For a closely related version of this argument, see MSV 27: 501; 267–68.

rational agency. Second, it corresponds to what I believe Kant was trying to say (or at least should have been trying to say) in his GMS account in terms of the autonomy–heteronomy contrast. This is because the defining feature of heteronomy-based moral theories of all stripes is that they seek the source of the authority or normative force of whatever law or moral principle to which they subscribe in some object of volition, which, translated into the terms of Kant's account of rational agency, is equated with the matter of a maxim. And, as noted above, this means that this matter is the ultimate source of reasons to act, not that it causally necessitates the action.

Nevertheless, the problem remains; albeit in a new form. Whereas in GMS the source of the difficulty lay in an equivocal use of "autonomy," which was driven by a similarly equivocal use of the complementary term "heteronomy," it now lies in a slide in Kant's understanding of "form" and "formal." As noted above, operating with the form–matter contrast, Kant initially concluded that any practical law must be formal in the sense that it abstracts from the matter of a practical principle. In posing the first of the two problems, however, Kant assumes, without further argument, that any candidate for practical law status must be formal in the seemingly quite different sense that it has "lawgiving form," by which Kant evidently meant suitability as a universal law.

(4) *A defense of the reciprocity thesis*: In partial defense of Kant, it can be argued that the lawgiving nature of this form is implicit from the beginning. Since it is assumed that a free will must be subject to some law and since any matter or object of the will has been excluded as a potential source of this law, there is nothing left beside the form of the maxim, from which it follows that this form must be the source, which is to say that it must be lawgiving. Even if one accepts the terms in which Kant frames the issue, however, this is only a partial defense, because there is a sense in which the form of *every maxim* may be described as lawgiving. As we have seen, for Kant every maxim (like every concept) has the form of universality (albeit a merely subjective universality that applies only to the agent whose maxim it is), and this form has normative force for the agent in the sense that it is a principle specifying how the agent should act whenever a certain set of conditions obtains. Accordingly, it requires further argumentation to show why the maxims of a transcendentally free agent must involve universality and lawgiving in the stronger (objective) sense on which Kant insists.

The argument for this stronger claim turns on two key points: (1) the radical nature of the concept of freedom that Kant is here assuming and (2) the requirement that the maxims of a rational agent not only justify the actions of the agent, but must themselves be justifiable.[29] Together they yield the conclusion that justification goes all the way up, which rules out rational egoism and similar heteronomous or "material" principles as the ultimate determining grounds of a free will. It is not that agents cannot act on

---

[29] For earlier formulations of this argument see Allison (1990, 207–12, 1996, 285–91).

such principles; it is rather that actions based on such principles cannot be justified for rational agents who are assumed to be free in the transcendental sense.

At the heart of the matter is the connection between transcendental freedom, rational justification, and the incorporation thesis. We have seen that in GMS Kant initially defines such freedom negatively as independence from determination by alien causes, whereas in the first *Critique* he characterized this independence in positive terms as an absolute spontaneity. We further saw that, considered in relation to the will of a rational being, this independence is understood primarily in relation to sensuous impulses. Although finite rational agents are not free from such impulses or, more generally, from any incentives stemming from their sensuous natures, they are free from necessitation or causal determination by them, which means that a free agent retains the capacity to act independently of and even contrary to any sensuous incentive.

According to this conception, freedom of the will amounts to a capacity for self-determination, where the "self" is identified with the rational nature of the agent, and the model for conceiving (though not explaining) this capacity is provided by the incorporation thesis. As we have seen, this thesis maintains that an impulse, inclination, or desire does not of itself constitute a sufficient reason to act, but only becomes such by being taken up or "incorporated" into a maxim, which, as an act of spontaneity of the subject, presupposes that the subject is free in the transcendental sense.

The relevance of this to our present concern consists in the fact that the incorporation thesis enables us to understand the connection between transcendental freedom and rational agency. This connection has two closely related aspects. The first is that such freedom blocks certain familiar kinds of justification, for example, those based on any incentive stemming from an agent's sensuous nature. If, qua transcendentally free agent, I act on the basis of such an incentive, it is I, not nature in me, that is the source of this behavior, since it results from incorporating this incentive into my maxim as providing a sufficient reason for the action.

The second aspect of the connection between the incorporation thesis and rational justification is that it extends the justification requirement to the first principles or fundamental maxims on the basis of which agents act. It was this with in mind that I suggested earlier that for Kant rational justification goes all the way up. Even though Kant only explicitly deals with the issue in *Religion* in connection with his account of radical evil, where he locates the ground of evil in the adoption of a fundamental maxim to subordinate the moral incentive to that of self-love or one's own happiness, I believe that it is already implicit in GMS and is essential to the interpretation and defense of the reciprocity thesis.[30]

---

[30] For Kant's account of radical evil, see RGV 6: 29–39; 76–85. I have discussed this conception on several occasions, the most recent being Allison (2002).

This analysis can be readily applied to the familiar figure of the rational egoist. As rational, this egoist recognizes, within limits, the need for justification or, in other words, that actions ought to be based on good reasons. Accordingly, such an egoist would reject courses of action that seem to yield satisfaction, if he judges that their long-term consequences are likely to prove deleterious to himself. In short, the rational egoist respects the normativity of prudential reasoning. But at this point he draws the line; for him the question of the justification of his highest principle, namely, self-interest, cannot arise, since it constitutes the supreme norm on the basis of which all his choices are made. For him, like modern-day decision theorists, who assume that all principles of rational choice are relative to individual preferences and, as such, are uncriticizable by reason, the justificatory buck stops here.[31]

This is, however, what the hypothesis of transcendental freedom denies. Precisely because all such preferences and subjective principles are assumed to be products of the practical reason of a transcendentally free agent, they are criticizable by this very reason. Accordingly, the task is to uncover the objective principle of reason on the basis of which these preferences and subjective principles are to be judged.

Before considering the nature of this principle, which for Kant is obviously the moral law, it must be noted that in order to be rationally justified the subjective principles of a transcendentally free agent must not only conform to an objective principle of reason, they must be adopted *because* they conform. This follows from the combination of transcendental freedom and the rationality requirement. First, as transcendentally free, an agent has the capacity to abstract from all empirically conditioned incentives and adopt a principle or course of conduct solely on the grounds of its conformity with principles of reason. Second, much as in the case of the analysis of moral worth, if an agent adopts principles that happen to conform with the moral law, but not because of this conformity, then this conformity is a purely contingent matter and, as such, does not constitute a rational justification of the choice. This is because such justification is concerned not merely with the choice (including the choice of principles), but also with the reasons for it, which must themselves stem from a principle. In short, the choice of a correct principle for the wrong reasons, say following the moral law because one believes that it will maximize happiness, is not merely without moral worth, it is also not rationally justified.

(5) *Completing the argument: the moral law as the law of freedom*: Even granting this, however, it still leaves us with the task of providing the argument for the identification of the needed objective principle of reason with the moral law, which, since we are here concerned with finite rational agents, takes the form of the categorical imperative. Fortunately, given the results of our previous analysis, this task should not be unduly daunting. The argument, which I take to be implicit in Kant's account, has the familiar "if and only if" form, which is to say that, as the reciprocity thesis maintains,

---

[31] The point is nicely put by Hill (1998, 254).

conformity to the moral law (or an unconditional practical law) is both a sufficient and a necessary condition of the justification of the maxims or subjective principles of a rational agent.

The first or *if* portion of the argument is unproblematic. What stronger justification could there be for one's adoption of a maxim than its being required by an unconditional practical law? If a rule of action is deemed "right" for all rational agents, whatever their interests or desires, then clearly it is right for me. Again, if my reason for *x*-ing is that it is dictated by such a law, then I have all the justification I could conceivably need for *x*-ing. This is not to deny that there could be grave difficulties, which Kant may have underestimated, in determining exactly what such a law requires in a given instance. But this has no bearing on the present point, which is merely that if a maxim can be shown to meet this requirement, there can be no logical space for any further questions about the justification of adopting and acting on the basis of it.

The claim that conformity to the moral law is also a *necessary* condition for the justification of a maxim appears to be somewhat more problematic. The problem is not that there are a plethora of other candidates, since we have already ruled out all heteronomous or material practical principles on the grounds that they are only conditionally valid. It is rather that it might seem that this requirement is too stringent, since it appears to imply that a maxim is rationally justifiable only if it is adopted because it is judged by the agent to be required by the moral law. And if this were Kant's view, it would be problematic, since it entails that only actions from duty are justifiable, thereby excluding all morally permissible but not obligatory actions. Nevertheless, this problem can be dealt with by recalling that in GMS Kant treats the categorical imperative primarily as a test for the permissibility of maxims and actions, which leaves the agent free to choose among morally permissible courses of action on the basis of self-interest.

If successful, the argument sketched above shows that a non-contingent conformity to the moral law is both a sufficient and a necessary condition of the justification of the maxims of a transcendentally free rational agent. And since it is assumed that the agents in question are both transcendentally free and rational (in the sense that they act according to their representation of laws or on principles), it follows that transcendental freedom and the moral law reciprocally imply one another; or, as Kant puts it in GMS, that "a free will and a will under moral laws are one and the same."

Clearly, however, this argument does not show either that we must attribute transcendental freedom to every conceivable rational being with a will or that finite rational beings stand under the categorical imperative. An examination of Kant's attempt to establish these claims will be the concern of the next two chapters. But before turning to these weighty and difficult issues, there remains some unfinished business regarding the interpretation of the reciprocity thesis itself.

(B) The reciprocity thesis and the Analytizitätsthese

Schönecker terms what I call the reciprocity thesis "*Kants Analytizitätsthese*" or "Kant's thesis of analyticity"; and he takes it to refer to Kant's claims that "a free will and a will under moral laws are one and the same" (GMS 4: 447_{6-7}) and that "if freedom of the will is presupposed, morality, together with its principle follows from it by mere analysis of its concept" (GMS 4: 447_{8-9}). But since, despite some broad areas of agreement, we offer significantly different readings of the text, I feel that I cannot leave the topic without noting these differences.

I shall begin with a consideration of the differences in the characterization of the thesis that we both attribute to Kant: reciprocity thesis or *Analytizitätsthese*? Although he does not make the point explicitly, Schönecker seems to assume that the two claims cited above regarding the relation between freedom and the moral law are logically equivalent and therefore that his *Analytizitätsthese* and my reciprocity thesis completely overlap.[32] In fact, however, they are not equivalent; for to say that a free will and a will under the moral law are the same is to say more than that if freedom of the will is presupposed, morality and its principle follow from an analysis of the concept of freedom. It is also to affirm the converse, namely, that if morality is presupposed the concept of freedom follows analytically. In short, it affirms a bi-conditional or strict reciprocity (which is why I have termed it the reciprocity thesis), whereas the *Analytizitätsthese* affirms merely a simple, one-way conditional. Accordingly, the latter corresponds merely to the first half of the reciprocity thesis.

Closely related to this and likewise reflected in Schönecker's terminology is the question of the analyticity of the moral law (as distinct from the categorical imperative). A central feature of Schönecker's account is the claim that the *Analytizitätsthese* is a thesis about the analyticity of the moral law in its descriptive (non-imperatival) form. As he puts it at one point, explicitly attributing the claim to Kant: "With regard to perfectly rational and free beings the moral law is not a synthetic, but an *analytic* proposition."[33] Not only did Kant not in fact make such a claim, but in my judgment he could not have done so without undermining his understanding of the analytic–synthetic distinction; for he explicitly denied that *the same proposition* could be analytic in one case and synthetic in another.[34] What is analytic for Kant are the conditional:

---

[32] See Schönecker (1999, 153–95, 2006, esp. 302–8).

[33] Schönecker (2006, 303).

[34] The question of whether synthetic judgments can be made analytic by adding predicates to the subject concept of the judgment was initially posed by Kant's contemporary critic J. G. Maass, who affirmed the possibility of doing this as a means of trivializing Kant's distinction. The Kantian response, which was provided by J. G. Schultz, is contained in his review of the second volume of Eberhard's *Philosophisches Magazin*, in which Maass' essay appeared. According to Schultz, whose response may have been directed by Kant, such a procedure would involve substituting one judgment for another expressed by the same sentence rather than converting a synthetic judgment into one that is analytic. Since adding the predicate "perfectly rational" to the subject concept "rational being" (or agent) would fall under this description, Kant could not have endorsed the *Analytizitätsthese* as Schönecker interprets it. The definitive modern treatment of this issue is by Beck (1965, 74–91). Making substantial use of Beck's analysis, I discuss the issue in Allison (1973, 65–67).

"if freedom then the moral law" and the proposition that a perfectly rational agent or an imperfectly rational one, considered as acting in a purely rational manner, would always act morally. Moreover, I suspect that the conflation of these analytic propositions with the claim that the moral law itself is analytic plays a large role in Schönecker's *Analytizitätsthese*.[35]

Further support for this reading is provided by a passage in the second *Critique*, which appeals to the second half of the reciprocity thesis and at first glance seems to support Schönecker's view. It occurs in the context of Kant's discussion of the moral law, or the consciousness thereof, as a "fact of reason," where he writes: "[I]t [the moral law] would be analytic if freedom of the will were presupposed" (KpV 5: 31; 164). To begin with, for the reason noted above, Kant would not wish to claim that that the addition of the presupposition of freedom (or of anything else for that matter) could convert a synthetic proposition into one that is analytic. Accordingly, I believe that Kant is best read as claiming that *if* freedom were presupposed, the moral law would follow analytically, which is to say that one cannot both affirm freedom and deny the moral law. Although this affirms a relation of logical implication between the two propositions, it no more entails that the proposition expressing the moral law is analytic than the propositions that "God is omniscient" and "God knows that $7+5=12$" entails that "$7+5=12$" is analytic.

Inasmuch as the use of the second half of the reciprocity thesis is prominent in the second *Critique* and both Schönecker and I are concerned with interpreting GMS, this might not seem to have any direct bearing on our interpretations of the latter work. I believe that it has a significant indirect bearing, however, because it points to the systematic import that Kant attributes to the reciprocity thesis in his overall meta-ethical project. More specifically, since I view this thesis as underlying the structure of the argument in both works, I attribute to its first part an essential, albeit preliminary role in the argument of GMS 3. For Schönecker, by contrast, in spite of the considerable attention that he devotes to it, the sole function that he assigns to the *Analytizitätsthese* appears to be to underscore the problematic of the deduction in GMS 3, which is that the bindingness of the categorical imperative cannot be derived directly from an analysis of the presupposition of freedom. Otherwise expressed, for him the task of the *Analytizitätsthese* is to define the problem; while on my reading the reciprocity thesis is the first step in the solution.[36]

Schönecker's view of the function of this thesis is a direct consequence of his interpretation of the proof-structure of GMS 3. As already noted, for him everything turns on the deduction of the categorical imperative as binding on the wills of finite

---

[35] For example, at one point he states that all that what he terms the *Analytizitätsthese* really claims is that "A perfectly rational and free will always wills morally." Schönecker (2006, 304).

[36] At one point he states that section one of GMS 3, which contains the *Analytizitätsthese*, formulates the task of the deduction. See Schönecker (1999, 410).

beings with both a rational and a sensuous nature. This synthetic *a priori* practical proposition, and this alone, constitutes the object of the deduction. In light of this exegetical assumption, Schönecker rejects any reading in which a substantive conclusion is reached prior to Kant's response to the question: "*How is a categorical imperative possible?*" In particular, there is no special problem in grounding the moral law, given the presupposition of freedom, since the *Analytizitätsthese* apparently maintains not merely that it follows analytically from the presupposition of freedom (which would suggest the need for a deduction or justification of the latter), but that it is itself an analytic proposition.

I agree with Schönecker that the first part of the reciprocity thesis does not entail that a free will as such is subject to the categorical imperative, as contrasted with standing under the moral law. And I likewise agree that this prevents Kant from arguing directly from the need to presuppose freedom (which he does in the second section of GMS 3) to the bindingness of the categorical imperative for finite rational agents. To establish the latter, some further step (or steps) beyond the necessity of presupposing freedom is required.

Nevertheless, I think that Schönecker goes too far when he claims that: "A free will is . . . a will under the principle of morality, but not under the categorical imperative; that is the thesis."[37] Presumably, the "thesis" referred to here is the *Analytizitätsthese*; and if all that is meant by this is that this thesis claims only that a free will, as such, is under the moral law and does not *also* maintain that it is bound by the categorical imperative then all that Schönecker can be accused of is a certain lack of clarity of expression. But it cannot be maintained that this thesis *denies* that a free will is under the categorical imperative, since that would foreclose the possibility of any deduction of the latter based on the supposition of freedom. Rather, granting that a perfectly rational or holy will is not subject to the categorical imperative because it is not subject to *any* imperatives, it remains an open question whether imperfectly rational beings are bound by the categorical imperative (assuming that they have a free will).

(C)   The reciprocity thesis and the problem of imputation

The final issue before us in this chapter is a classical objection to the reciprocity thesis that comes in two parts. The first is the claim that by defining a free will positively as one with the property of autonomy, Kant effectively attributes all non-morally motivated actions to "alien causes," which means that they are not imputable. The second is that the thesis make it difficult to see how even morally motivated actions are imputable. For if, as is commonly assumed by libertarians, a capacity to do otherwise is a necessary condition of imputation and if, as Kant seems to suggest, a free will is governed by the moral law in a manner analogous to the way in which natural

---

[37]   Schönecker (1999, 163). See also Schönecker (2006, 303).

phenomena are governed by laws of nature, it seems that a free will could no more violate the moral law than a falling body could violate the law of gravity.[38]

Like any classical or near classical objection to a philosophical thesis, no matter how misguided, the one sketched above has some basis in the text. In particular, there are at least two aspects of Kant's account of the reciprocity thesis that seem to fuel it. One is the claim that free actions, like natural events, must be subject to a necessary law; the other is Kant's characterization of the causality of natural occurrences as "a heteronomy of efficient causes." The former seems to entail that a free will obeys the moral law in a manner that is comparable to the way in which natural occurrences obey the laws of nature and the latter that, as heteronomous, actions of a rational being that are not governed by the moral law, that is, any morally indifferent or evil actions, must be causally necessary and, as such, not imputable.[39]

One strategy for responding to this line of objection is to admit that it applies to GMS, while denying that it is applicable to the more nuanced conception of freedom that Kant developed in his later writings.[40] But since such a strategy requires rejecting the reciprocity thesis and with it the entire argument of both GMS 3, as well as the Analytic of the second *Critique*, I believe that it should be adopted only as a last resort. I also believe that it is not necessary to pay this price, since, despite the unfortunate way in which Kant sometimes expresses himself, the major elements of his "late" theory of freedom are implicitly at work in GMS and that these suffice to dismiss this line of objection.[41]

---

[38] The above is intended as a generic version of a line of objection that has been formulated in a number of different ways. It can be traced back at least to Reinhold, who objected to Kant's identification of the will with practical reason and freedom in the positive sense with autonomy on the grounds that it makes it inconceivable how one could freely violate the moral law. In order to account for this possibility, Reinhold suggested (1975a, 252–74) that freedom be defined as a capacity for self-determination, either in accordance with or contrary to the law. Kant responded by appealing to the *Wille–Willkür* distinction (MS 6: 226–27; 380–81) to which Reinhold replied with a critique of that distinction (1975b, 310–24). I discuss Reinhold's objection and Kant's response in Allison (1990, 133–35). The best known version of the objection in Anglo-American philosophy is by Sidgwick (2005, 181–87), who, ignoring the *Wille–Willkür* distinction, attributed two incompatible conceptions of freedom to Kant: one in which freedom is equated with rationality (also called "Good" or "Rational Freedom"), the other in which it is equated with the capacity for free choice (also called "Neutral" or "Moral Freedom"). According to Sidgwick, the sense of freedom to which Kant appeals in the reciprocity thesis involves a conflation of both senses. More recently, a subtle and detailed discussion of the issue in terms of the problem of non-moral action, which includes a critique of Reinhold's formulation of the objection, has been provided by Prauss (1983, 60–115, esp. 83–89.).

[39] The former is affirmed by Prauss (1983, 60–115) and the latter by Ross (1954, 71).

[40] See, for example, Silber (1960, esp. lxxx–cxlii) and Hill (1998, 254–55).

[41] It seems reasonable to speak of two radical changes in Kant's conception of freedom. The first is his abandonment of the Wolffian view in the 1770s and its replacement with the conception of transcendental freedom as an absolute spontaneity. The second is his adoption of the principle of autonomy in 1784–85. I believe that subsequent changes, which are manifest in the writings of the 1790s, reflect Kant's somewhat different concerns in his later writings rather than a radical change in his conception of freedom. Whereas in both GMS and the second *Critique*, freedom was considered almost entirely from the limited perspective of its relation to the moral law and categorical imperative, in the later writings it was considered from the broader perspective of moral evil, virtue, vice, and the choice of ends, topics that were dealt with only in an incidental manner, if it all, in the works of the 1780s.

The two essential elements of this "late" theory are the incorporation thesis and the *Wille–Willkür* distinction. I have made systematic use of the incorporation thesis, which is an aspect of his conception of freedom that Kant only fully articulated in *Religion*, because I consider it as implicit in the conception of free agency to which Kant appealed already in the first *Critique*. But since it might seem more dubious to impose the *Wille–Willkür* distinction on the argument of GMS, I have hitherto refrained from attempting to do so.[42] Nevertheless, in order to address the objection currently before us, a brief look at this distinction and its relation to Kant's account of the will in GMS appears to be called for.

Although Kant uses the *Wille–Willkür* distinction in *Religion*, he first draws it explicitly in the Introduction to the *Metaphysics of Morals*, where he presents it in two different places (6: 213–14; 374–75, and 226–27; 380–81). In the first of these, Kant attempts to move from a general account of the faculty of desire, which may also be attributed to animals, to an analysis of human volition, which stems from what Kant terms a "faculty of desire according to concepts."[43] In the second, he is concerned exclusively with the nature and grounds of human volition or rational agency. In both places, Kant identifies *Wille* with practical reason, as he does in GMS; but in the second he adds significantly that "Laws proceed from the will [*Wille*], *maxims* from choice [*Willkür*]." In general, it seems fair to say that for Kant *Wille* and *Willkür* refer to two distinct aspects of a single faculty of volition, which differ with respect to function. The function of the former is legislative; while that of the latter is executive (executing or obeying the laws stemming from the former). But since Kant also uses "*Wille*" to refer to this faculty as a whole, we need to distinguish between a broad and a narrow sense of the term: the former referring to the faculty as a whole and the latter to one of its two aspects with its specific function.[44]

For present purposes, two aspects of this distinction are of crucial importance. One is the connection of *Willkür* with maxims. We have seen that maxims are made by agents through a spontaneous exercise of choice guided (but not causally determined) by practical reason; and given what has already been said about maxims, it seems evident that Kant's account of them presupposes something like the *Wille–Willkür* distinction, even though no such distinction is explicitly drawn in GMS. Second, it is equally evident that this distinction is closely intertwined with the incorporation thesis; for, again, it is through the spontaneity of *Willkür*, presumably guided by practical reason (*Wille*), that incentives are incorporated into maxims. Otherwise expressed, the entire account of rational agency in GMS, including the definition of rational beings as those with the capacity to act according to the representation of laws, rests upon the

---

[42] The term "*Willkür*" occurs only twice in GMS (428_{24} and 451_2; in the former case Wood translates it as "arbitrary choice" and in the latter simply as "choice"). It appears frequently in the second *Critique*, where Kant seems to use it as a synonym for "*Wille*" (on this point, see Beck, 1960, 75n).

[43] For an account of what Kant understands by a faculty of desire, see Chapter 6, note 24.

[44] For a fuller discussion of this distinction and its relation to Kant's theory of freedom, see Allison (1990, 129–36).

conception of a spontaneous power of choice, which is governed by practical reason. And this indicates that, rather than being a radical innovation of the late Kant, the *Wille–Willkür* distinction makes explicit what is already implicit in GMS. Thus, if, as I believe to be the case, this distinction and the incorporation thesis suffice to dismiss this line of objection, then it cannot be raised against the reciprocity thesis. On the contrary, this objection arises from the failure to consider that this thesis is anchored in a conception of rational agency that runs throughout GMS as a whole.

With regard to the second part of the objection (the imputability of morally good actions), it is crucial to keep in mind that Kant does not define a free will in terms of a capacity to do otherwise. Rather, he understands it negatively as independence from determination by alien causes and positively as autonomy, that is, as a capacity to obey laws stemming from one's own practical reason. In the case of finite rational agents, who have a sensuous as well as a rational nature, the latter involves a capacity to resist the pull of incentives arising from their sensuous nature, which, owing to their imperfection, is not always exercised. But it is in the capacity to obey the dictates of pure practical reason, not our frequent and all too human failure to exercise this capacity, that Kant locates the essence of freedom.[45] Moreover, as is frequently pointed out, in the case of God or a perfectly rational being, there is (for Kant at least) no thought of a capacity to do otherwise; yet this is recognized as the highest form of freedom.

A related worry about the relation between the reciprocity thesis and imputation, which has been emphasized by Schönecker, is that the moral law, as distinct from the categorical imperative, is a descriptive rather than a prescriptive law. And while it is easy to understand how a free agent might violate a prescription, it seems to involve a contradiction to maintain that an agent (free or otherwise) could violate a genuinely descriptive law.[46]

I have two points to make in response to this worry. First, the reciprocity thesis asserts an identity between a free will and a will that *stands under* moral laws not between a free will and one that *obeys them*. Thus, what is being described is a will for which this law functions as the supreme norm on the basis of which its choices must be justified. And only a being who is under the moral law, that is, for whom the law is normative, has the "capacity" to disobey it. Schönecker endeavors to rebut this response by stressing that the reciprocity thesis (his *Analytizitätsthese*) applies only to either a perfectly rational being without a sensuous nature or to imperfectly rational beings with a sensuous as well as a rational nature, but considered in abstraction from their sensuous nature. Since the existence of a sensuous nature is for Kant a necessary

---

[45] See especially KpV 5: 29–30; 162–64: MS 6: 226–27; 380–81. The second of these passages contains Kant's reply to Reinhold regarding this matter. See note 42.

[46] I say "a genuinely descriptive law" to distinguish it from one that describes how some things behaves usually or for the most part. Obviously, there is no particular problem in understanding how something might violate such a "law."

(though not a sufficient condition) of violating the moral law, it follows that a free will, so characterized, cannot fail to obey it.[47] But, as Schönecker himself admits, it hardly follows from this that the flesh and blood person, with a sensuous as well as a rational nature, necessarily follows it.[48]

Second, we have already seen that a descriptive practical principle can be normative for Kant. Admittedly, Kant seems to deny this in the first *Critique*, when he contrasts laws of nature, which specify what necessarily happens, with laws of freedom, which dictate what *ought* to happen, even if it never does.[49] And this may have misled some critics into believing that, by treating the moral law as a descriptive law, Kant is effectively undermining the distinction between laws of nature and laws of freedom. But Kant's use of this language should be seen as an example of his failure to distinguish sharply between practical laws and imperatives, rather than as a denial of the normativity or even the very existence of the former. Otherwise, we could not claim that a perfectly rational or holy will is either good or free. And since the moral law is normative in the sense that it formulates the law of a morally good will, it justifies as well as explains the actions of the agents whose volition it describes, which, in turn, suffices to preserve the distinction between a (descriptive) moral and a natural law.

---

[47] The emphasis here should be placed on the fact that possession of a sensuous nature is *not a sufficient condition* of moral evil. This is the central theme of Kant's account of radical evil in *Religion*. For my analysis of this see Allison (1990, 146–61, 1996, 169–82, and 2002, 337–48).

[48] See Schönecker (1999, esp. 188–94). He notes that in GMS Kant fails to address the problem of moral evil and I agree; but I also think that this failure is irrelevant to the reciprocity thesis.

[49] See KrV A547–48/B575–76; A802–3/B830–31.

11

The Presupposition of Freedom, the Circle, and the Two Standpoints

In the third and final paragraph of the first section of GMS 3, after having shown that a free will and a will under moral laws are one and the same, Kant reflects on what remains to be done in order to establish that morality is not merely a chimerical idea or phantom of the brain. The essential point is that, despite having argued that if freedom of the will is presupposed, morality, together with its principle, follows from freedom by the mere analysis of its concept, Kant insists that the moral law is a synthetic *a priori* proposition. And since this means that the validity of this law cannot be established by the analysis of the concept of an absolutely good will, there is need for some "third thing" to connect the law with the concept of such a will. Kant asserts that the *positive* concept of freedom, that is, autonomy, "provides this third thing" and he suggests that the latter "cannot, as in the case of physical causes, be the nature of the world of sense (in the concept of which the concepts of something as cause, in relation to something as effect come together)" (GMS 4: 447_{17-20}). Although Kant's terminology strongly suggests that by this third thing to which freedom points us he understands the intelligible world, he does not assert it at this point. Instead, he indicates that more preparation is required, before we are in a position to comprehend "the deduction of the concept of freedom from pure practical reason, and with it the possibility of a categorical imperative" (GMS 4: 447_{24-25}).

The present chapter is concerned with this further preparation. It covers the second and third sections of GMS 3 and is divided into three parts. The first is devoted to section two, to which Kant gives the heading: "*Freedom must be presupposed as a property of the will of all rational beings*" (GMS 4: 447_{26-27}). The last two deal with section three, to which Kant gives the somewhat misleading heading: "*Of the interest that attaches to the idea of morality*" (GMS 4: 448_{23-24}). This is misleading because the focal point of this section is not the concept of a pure moral interest, but an apparent circle, which Kant believes can only be avoided by introducing the idea of an intelligible world. The discussion of this section is divided into two parts because Kant's argument is itself so divided. In the first part (the subject matter of the second part of this chapter), Kant suggests that the analysis up to this point has led to an apparent *cul de sac* in the form of a circle. In the second part (the subject matter of the third part of this chapter), Kant argues that the distinction between the sensible and intelligible worlds, considered as two standpoints, provides the only way out of this circle. Moreover, by avoiding the circle in this manner, Kant at the same time provides a deduction of both the presupposition of freedom and the moral law, which is the final and essential step in preparing the way for the deduction of the categorical imperative.

I

As its heading indicates, the aim of the second section of GMS 3 is to demonstrate the necessity of presupposing freedom. Because of its brevity and importance, I shall cite it in full and then comment on its various steps, which I have once again numbered for ease of reference.

(1) It is not enough that, on whatever ground, we ascribe freedom to our will, if we do not also have sufficient grounds to attribute it to all rational beings as well. (2) For since morality serves as a law for us only insofar as we are *rational beings*, it must also be valid for all rational beings, and since it must be derived merely from the property of freedom, freedom must also be proven as a property of the will of all rational beings; and it does not suffice to derive it from certain supposed experiences of human nature (though this is absolutely impossible and can only be established *a priori*); rather, one must prove it as belonging universally to the activity of rational beings endowed with a will. (3) Now I say: Every being that cannot act otherwise than *under the idea of freedom*, is just for that reason actually free in a practical respect, i.e., all laws that are inseparably bound up with freedom hold for it, just as if its will had also been declared free in itself, and in a way that is valid for theoretical philosophy. (4) Now I assert: that we necessarily must also lend the idea of freedom to every rational being that has a will, under which it alone acts. (5) For in such a being we think a reason that is practical, i.e., has causality with regard to its objects. (6) Now one cannot possibly think of a reason that, in its own consciousness, would receive direction [*eine Lenkung*] from elsewhere with regard to its judgments; for then the subject would not ascribe the determination of its judgment to reason, but to an impulse. (7) It must regard itself as the author of its principles, independently of alien influences; consequently it must, as practical reason, or as the will of a rational being, be regarded by itself as free; i.e., the will of a rational being can be a will of its own only under the idea of freedom, and must therefore for practical purposes be attributed to all rational beings. (GMS 4: 447_{28}–48_{22})

Although Kant's avowed aim in this paragraph is to demonstrate the necessity of presupposing freedom, and he is quite emphatic in GMS and, indeed, all of the writings of the critical period, that the reality of freedom cannot be proven by a theoretical or speculative use of reason, he speaks (again somewhat misleadingly) in the second sentences of the need to *prove* [*beweisen*] that rational beings have a free will.[1]

---

[1]   A quite different view has been advanced by Ameriks, who claims that at the time of GMS Kant was still committed to the speculative proof of absolute (transcendental) freedom, which he had expressed in his metaphysical lectures of the 1770s. According to Ameriks, Kant's seemingly modest claims regarding being free in a practical respect, attributing freedom for practical purposes, and showing the necessity of acting

Nevertheless, this terminological anomaly can safely be ignored, since nothing is lost if we replace the language of "proof" with that of "presupposition," which is the term that Kant uses in the heading of the section. As Kant's account makes clear, the point of the first two sentences is not to insist that, in order to account for the possibility of morality, it is necessary to prove that the will is free; it is rather to underscore the necessity of extending the scope of the attribution of freedom to all rational beings with a will. This necessity follows from the combination of the underlying methodological assumption of GMS and the reciprocity thesis. As we have seen, the assumption is that, inasmuch as morality expresses a law for every rational being as such, its principle "must be bound up (fully *a priori*) with the concept of the will of a rational being as such" (GMS 4: 426_{24-25}). And since the reciprocity thesis maintains that freedom is the property of the will from which subjection to moral requirements is derived, it follows that the legitimization of morality depends crucially on the connection of freedom with the will of every rational being.

In steps three and four, Kant makes two stipulative claims, the second of which presumably finds its support in the last three sentences The first of these stipulations is that every being that cannot act other than under the idea of freedom is, for that reason, really free in a practical respect, which Kant glosses as meaning that such a being is subject to whatever practical principles it would be subject to if the will could be demonstrated to be free by a theoretical use of reason. The practical principle at issue is obviously the moral law. Given the reciprocity thesis, this would enable Kant to assert that this law is valid for every being that cannot act other than under the idea of freedom. Moreover, in a note attached to this sentence, Kant remarks that he is linking this claim to the *idea of freedom*, rather than to its reality, in order to avoid having to provide a theoretical proof of freedom (GMS 4: 448_{28-35}).

The second stipulative claim is that we must necessarily apply the idea of freedom to every rational being as an idea under which it alone can act. In his metaphysical lectures, Kant made essentially the same point by claiming that, "Freedom is a mere idea and to act in conformity with this idea is what it means to be free in the practical sense," to which he adds some lines later that "freedom is practically necessary—man must therefore act according to an idea of freedom and he cannot act otherwise" (Met M 29: 898; 265). If both of these claims, which Kant introduces by the stipulative

---

under the idea of freedom do not reflect his rejection of this speculative proof, but merely his belief that certain peculiarities of this proof led Kant to regard it as merely practically sufficient. See Ameriks (2003, esp. 163–75). Although it is true that Kant affirmed a speculative proof in the metaphysical lectures (and *Reflexionen*) of the 1770s in connection with his account of rational psychology, I can find no convincing evidence that he remained committed to it in the first *Critique*, not to mention GMS. Rather, I believe that Kant is to be taken at his word when claims to be concerned to ground the *presupposition* of freedom, by which I understand the practical use of the transcendental idea. Moreover, it should be kept in mind that when Kant speaks of a deduction of the concept of freedom it is "from pure *practical* [my emphasis] reason." This is relevant because it seems reasonable to assume that Kant did not regard practical reason (pure or otherwise) as yielding a speculative proof.

phrases "Now I say" and "Now I assert," hold, it follows that every rational being with a will, stands under the moral law in virtue of being free in a practical respect.

Since it is evident from the first claim that to be free in a practical respect is to act, or at least to have the capacity to act, under the idea of freedom, it is essential to understand what Kant means by this and his grounds for attributing this capacity to all rational beings with a will. To begin with, freedom, as Kant here understands it, is a transcendental idea, the content of which is an absolute spontaneity. As such, freedom is a thought that rational beings bring to the conception of themselves (and others) as agents, not a fact or property that might be discovered through introspection or some other form of enquiry. And from this it follows that it likewise cannot be refuted by an appeal to experience. In short, for Kant the free will problem cannot be resolved at the empirical level, but is instead a conceptual issue, which in Kant's terminology means that it is transcendental rather than physiological.[2]

The question remains, however: what exactly is involved in acting under the idea of freedom? There seem to be two possible answers. One is that one must believe (though cannot know) that one is free.[3] The other is that one must act *as if* one were free, without necessarily having the belief. And since the former is rendered implausible by the fact, frequently noted by determinists of various stripes, that they find no more difficulty engaging in deliberation about what to do than libertarians and that in so doing they have no need to give up their belief that determinism is true, acting *as if* one were free appears to be the default position.[4]

Although the Kantian view may be characterized in these terms, great care must be taken, if one is to avoid a radical misunderstanding, since, the expression "as if," like its

---

[2] See KrV A448/B476 and A535/B503.

[3] Although some have interpreted Kant in this way (e.g., Ross, 1954, 68), it seems clear that he would not characterize the claim that we can act only under the idea of freedom as a matter of holding a belief. Kant distinguishes between different kinds of belief, just as he does between different kinds of freedom. In the first *Critique*, he calls the kind that is relevant to our present concerns "moral belief" and its objects are God and a future life, regarded as necessary conditions of the attainability of the highest good (KrV A828/B856). Accordingly, freedom is not here included among the objects of belief. Admittedly, it seems to be viewed in this way in the second *Critique*, where it is listed together with God and a future life as a postulate of pure practical reason (KpV5: 132; 246). But it must be kept in mind that the freedom that Kant there treats as a postulate is not the freedom under the idea of which he claims that we can alone act in GMS. *That* conception of freedom (transcendental freedom) was given a deduction from the moral law in the Analytic of Practical Reason and it would have been bizarre for Kant to have treated as a postulate in the Dialectic the same conception for which he had provided a deduction in the Analytic. Rather, the kind of freedom that Kant treats as a postulate is the freedom or, better, the capacity to do whatever is necessary to attain the highest good. In a word, it is freedom as autocracy rather than as autonomy. For discussions of this issue, see Beck (1960, 207–8) and Carnois (1987, 116–21).

[4] An influential present-day spokesperson for this view is Daniel Dennett, who argues that, because of the epistemic openness of the future, determinism leaves ample "elbow room" for deliberation. Dennett further maintains that the reason for the mistaken belief that determinism excludes any space for deliberation is its conflation with fatalism. Whereas determinism maintains that everything that happens is the necessary consequence of antecedent causal conditions, fatalism is the view that something will happen regardless of what else happens, including what an agent may choose. See Dennett (1984, 101–30). I discuss the relationship between Dennett's views and Kant's in Allison (1997).

German counterpart "*als ob,*" is highly ambiguous and can be taken in a number of senses, both fictive and non-fictive.[5] Specifically, what must be avoided is the infamous fictive reading of Hans Vaihinger, who treated Kant as the philosopher of *as if*.[6] Vaihinger not only claimed that for Kant ideas of reason are fictions adopted for purely heuristic purposes, but also that this theory of fictions, particularly as it bears on conceptions such as freedom and human dignity, marks "the high water-mark of his [Kant's] critical philosophy" and, indeed, any human thought. "Only a few, only an élite," Vaihinger remarks with rhetoric reminiscent of Nietzsche, "can continue to breathe at all at this altitude: the vast majority need a different, a less rarified atmosphere."[7]

A consideration of what Kant actually says, however, indicates that the atmosphere to which Vaihinger refers is too rarified even for Kant.[8] To be sure, in the Appendix to the Dialectic of the first *Critique*, Kant uses the expression "*als ob*" with respect to the ideas of the soul, the world, and God, in order to underscore their merely regulative status (KrV A684–86/B712–14). Moreover, in the Doctrine of Method, Kant even refers parenthetically to the transcendental ideas as "heuristic fictions" (KrV A771/B799), which seems to provide direct confirmation for Vaihinger's reading.[9] Nevertheless, I believe it would be a mistake to characterize these ideas as fictions in Vaihinger's sense.

There are two main reasons for this. First, in his deduction of the ideas of reason, Kant insists that these ideas are not arbitrarily invented concepts or empty thought entities, but necessary products of reason to which he attributes a certain objective validity, which necessitates providing them with a transcendental deduction.[10] Second, Kant is agnostic rather than dogmatically negative regarding the existence of entities

---

[5] For an analysis of the various senses in which the German expression "*als ob*" is used, as well as its uses in Kant, see Adickes (1927, 15–43).

[6] See Vaihinger (1935). The most influential critic of Vaihinger's reading was Adickes, who provided a detailed and devastating critique of it. See Adickes (1927). While I am in complete agreement with Adickes regarding the negative part of his account, that is, his rejection of Vaihinger's view that Kantian ideas and other basic conceptions are all to be taken as heuristic fictions, I have some problems with the view that he puts in its place, namely, a full-fledged metaphysical realism. According to Adickes, Kant was certain regarding the absolute (transcendental) reality of things in themselves, God, immortality, and freedom and questioned only the possibility of demonstrating their reality. On my reading, this would make Kant a transcendental realist *malgré lui*. Although after Adickes' critique, most Kant interpreters have tended to shy away from appealing to Vaihinger's fictionalist interpretation, one who has not is Eva Schaper, who has attempted to rehabilitate and even to extend, albeit not uncritically, key elements of Vaihinger's reading. See Schaper (1966 and 1979, 118–32).

[7] Vaihinger (1935, 293).

[8] In commenting on this astonishing statement of Vaihinger, Adickes remarks sarcastically that the only one who lives in this rarified atmosphere is Vaihinger himself. See Adickes (1927, 170).

[9] Kant also uses the term "heuristic" [*heuristisch*] three times in the Dialectic of the first *Critique*: KrV A616/B644, A663/B691, and A671/B699, in all of which it is closely related to the merely regulative function of the idea in question.

[10] For my analysis of this deduction, see Allison (2004; 437–48). My interest here is not in defending this deduction, but simply in pointing out that the very attempt to provide one indicates the inadequacy of Vaihinger's reading.

corresponding to these ideas.[11] His view is that claims about such entities should be taken problematically, which means that instead of denying them a real existence, as a consistent fictionalist supposedly would do, Kant simply abstracts from the question of whether objects corresponding to these ideas are possible.

Similar considerations apply to Vaihinger's treatment of Kant's account of freedom and the moral law in GMS 3.[12] Focusing on the fact that Kant explicitly treats freedom as an idea and appeals to the necessity of acting under it, Vaihinger regards this idea, like its theoretical counterparts, as a fiction.[13] In this spirit, he takes Kant's claim that freedom must be presupposed as a property of the will of all rational beings as equivalent to "'look upon as','assign to', 'ascribe to', in short=imagine" it as such a property, even though we know that there really is no such property.[14] And, in support of this, he maintains that "'presuppose' does not denote an hypothesis but a fiction."[15]

Vaihinger was correct in denying that "presuppose" [*voraussetzen*] in the sense in which Kant uses it in connection with the idea of freedom, is to be understood as making an hypothesis, since that would open it up to empirical disconfirmation; but he was wrong to conclude from this that it must be merely a fiction. Rather, freedom, like the other transcendental ideas, expresses a conceptual necessity. In its theoretical function, it is to provide explanatory closure through the idea of a first cause or unconditioned condition. In its practical function, with which we are here concerned, it is to regulate the conception of ourselves as rational agents, that is, as centers of thought and action. And for this reason it is also constitutive in its practical function, not of some putative object—the self—but of one's conception of oneself as a rational agent.

Moreover, so construed, the idea of freedom has normative force. To act in conformity with it is to place oneself in the logical space of (practical) reasons, thereby subjecting oneself to norms of both a moral and prudential sort. That is why Kant insists on the necessity of this idea and why any purely heuristic reading of Kant's claim, which would give it a merely pragmatic grounding, is inadequate. The point is simply that the idea of freedom is inseparable from the conception of oneself as a deliberator— engaged in a process of deciding a proposed course of action. As Kant might have put it, we can deliberate only under the idea of freedom, not because this is the way our

---

[11] See, for example, KrV A673/B701.

[12] Actually, the *reductio* of Vaihinger's reading of Kant's moral philosophy lies in his claim that, because of its reliance on ideas, "all morality is based on fictions" (1935, 291). Such a claim about morality itself is perfectly coherent and has been maintained by Nietzsche, among others. But it is one thing to make such a claim about morality and quite another to attribute it to Kant. For we have seen that Kant's concern in GMS 3 is precisely to show that morality is *not* a mere phantom of the brain, that is, a fiction. Accordingly, if we accept Vaihinger's reading, we must not only conclude that Kant failed to accomplish what he set out to do, which is quite possible, but that he somehow failed to see that, if successful, the argument of GMS 3 would establish the precise opposite of what it is was supposed to show!

[13] Ibid., 290.   [14] Ibid., 289.   [15] Ibid., 290.

mind works or because doing so is the best way to deliberate successfully, but because it is only under this presupposition that deliberation and therefore the exercise of rational agency is conceivable. From this perspective, theoretical belief about freedom of the will, or the lack thereof, simply do not enter into consideration, which is why Kant claims that the presupposition of freedom holds only in a "practical respect."[16]

Returning to the text, the final three sentences supposedly provide the justification for Kant's second assertion, namely, that "we necessarily must also lend the idea of freedom to every rational being that has a will, under which it alone acts." The first step (sentence 5) consists in the reminder that to attribute a will to an agent is to attribute to it practical reason, that is, a reason that has causality with respect to its objects. In the final two sentences, Kant connects the idea of freedom first with the exercise of theoretical and then with practical reason.

This connection with theoretical reason or, more precisely, the understanding, is based on the conception of the latter that Kant provides in the first *Critique*. According to this conception, which I have termed the "discursivity thesis," cognition consists in the application of concepts to sensory data given in intuition in an act of judgment.[17] For present purposes, the key element of this is Kant's characterization of the understanding as spontaneous.[18] In previous work, I have attempted to illustrate this conception of the spontaneity of the understanding in judging by proposing that we consider a judgment as an act of "taking as."[19] In the simplest case, an indeterminate something$=x$ is taken as an F; in more complex cases, Fx is qualified by further "determinations" or predicates, for example, Fx is G; while in still more complex cases, distinct "takings" (categorical judgments) are combined in a single higher-order "taking" (hypothetical and disjunctive judgments). There are two essential points here: (1) that cognition requires more than the mere reception of sensory data, it also requires the active taking up and unification of these data, in a concept; and (2) that this activity is not arbitrary, but rule-governed, with the rules being supplied by concepts and ultimately by the pure concepts of the understanding and their schemata.

In the text currently before us, Kant makes basically the same point in a roundabout and somewhat infelicitous manner, stating that, "[O]ne cannot possibly think of a reason that, in its own consciousness, would receive direction from elsewhere with regard to its judgments; for then the subject would not ascribe the determination of its judgment to reason, but to an impulse." By stating that "one cannot possibly think of a reason" operating in the manner described, Kant indicates that he is affirming

---

[16] Kant expressed himself more clearly on the matter in 1783 when he wrote: "[T]he practical concept of freedom has nothing to do with the speculative concept, which is abandoned entirely to the metaphysicians. For I can be quite indifferent as to the object of my state in which I am now to act; I ask only what I have to do, and then freedom is a necessary practical presupposition and an idea under which alone I can regard commands of reason as valid" (RSV 8: 13; 10).

[17] For my analysis of the discursivity thesis, see Allison (2004, 12–16 and passim).

[18] See, for example, KrV A51/B75, A69/B93, A126, B129–30, B150.

[19] See Allison (1990, 36–38; 1996, 98–104 and 132–33).

a conceptual truth, which, as such, is applicable to every conceivable intellect.[20] Moreover, by referring to the consciousness of the cognizer ("in its own consciousness"), he is underscoring the point that a cognitive judgment is a self-conscious or apperceptive act, which a cognizer performs for itself on the basis of a norm-guided evaluation of the reasons underlying the verdict. Otherwise expressed, to make a cognitive judgment is to place oneself in the logical space of reasons and to hold oneself responsible to its norms.[21] Consequently, a cognizer cannot regard itself as determined to judge in a certain way by factors external to the self-imposed norms ("from elsewhere"), since that would require locating the act of judgment in the logical space of causes and therefore as not governed by epistemic norms. Clearly, on this reading, "impulse" [Antriebe] should not be taken literally and narrowly, but broadly as referring to any causal (non-normative) factor that might determine the belief-state of a putative cognizer.

Kant's final step is to spell out the parallelism between reason in its cognitive or theoretical and its practical functions.[22] The point is that just as a cognizer must view itself as a self-determiner with respect to its judgments, so a rational agent must regard itself as determining itself to act on the basis of self-imposed principles and therefore as standing in the logical space of *practical* reasons. And from this Kant concludes that every rational agent must, from a first-person point of view, regard itself as free. As Kant puts it in the concluding lines of the section, "the will of a rational being can be a will of its own only under the idea of freedom, and therefore must, for practical purposes, be attributed to all rational beings."

Kant's claims in this section are hardly immune from criticism, especially his final step; but what is particularly noteworthy is his failure to draw the conclusion that the argument has seemingly put him in position to draw. For if we assume the following four propositions, all of which Kant affirms:

(1) We must necessarily attribute to all rational beings with a will the idea of freedom under which alone it can act.

(2) To act under the idea of freedom is to be free in a practical respect.

(3) To be free in a practical respect is to be subject to whatever laws one would be subject to if the will could be shown to be free on theoretical grounds.

---

[20] As I read Kant, this includes the divine intellect, with its intellectual or creative intuition. Although, strictly speaking, the "taking as" locution cannot apply to such an intellect, since it creates its object whole cloth rather than determining it by bringing it under a concept, for that very reason it could not be conceived as having its object given from elsewhere. Thus, one might say that its activity consists in a making rather than a taking.

[21] The distinction between the "logical spaces" of reasons and causes, the first of which is concerned with questions of justification and the second with questions of explanation, was first drawn by Wilfred Sellars and more recently emphasized in the work of John McDowell. See Sellars (2000) and McDowell (1994). I find it particularly useful in discussing Kant, since it is a close relative of Kant's distinction between the *quid juris* and the *quid facti*.

[22] For a parallel argument see RSV 8: 14; 10.

(4) The reciprocity thesis shows that a free will necessarily stands under the moral law.

We seem to be in position to conclude: (5) Since rational beings such as ourselves have wills, that is, a reason that is practical, we stand under the moral law or, equivalently, the moral law is valid for us.

Instead of drawing this conclusion, however, Kant turns immediately in section three to a new topic, namely, the interest that attaches to the idea of morality, which seems to be at best tangentially related to the subject matter of section two, and in the process he poses the problem of a circle, which he claims can be avoided only by introducing the distinction between two standpoints. Accordingly, we are led to ask: what prevented Kant from drawing the conclusion for which the argument has seemingly prepared the way and to embark instead on what appears to be a digression?

I believe that the solution to this puzzle lies in the first word of the conclusion that Kant does not draw, namely "Since," which to render the argument valid must be replaced by "If." In other words, all that the argument establishes is the conditional: *If* rational beings have wills, that is, a reason that is practical, then they stand under the moral law or, equivalently, the moral law is valid for them. As step two indicates, everything turns on the assumption that the rational beings in question have wills.[23] The argument sketched above assumes this to be the case, but does not argue for it, from which it follows that Kant is not yet in a position to conclude that rational beings stand under the moral law, not to mention the categorical imperative. Accordingly, a major concern of the remainder of this chapter, particularly its final part, is to determine if Kant can be read as providing an argument for this seemingly innocuous thesis.

II

The first four paragraphs of the third section of GMS 3 (448_{25}–50_{17}), constitute the transition from the preparatory consideration of the first two sections to the problematic of the deduction. They may also be read as containing an imaginary conversation between Kant and a virtual interlocutor, who is pressing him regarding his project of grounding morality. This interlocutor is not the familiar skeptical amoralist in search of reasons for obeying the dictates of morality when they clash with self-interest, but the curious and sympathetic meta-ethicist, who is in search of an explanation for the unconditioned normativity of moral commands, the legitimacy of which she does not question. Otherwise expressed, this interlocutor is concerned with the question of how the moral law can be binding or a categorical imperative possible, rather than why

---

[23] The importance of this point has been emphasized by Henrich (1975, esp. 91–100, as well as by Ameriks (1982, 203–4) and Laberge (1982, 746–47).

one should subject oneself to its dictates.[24] Kant has no interest in the latter question because it implicitly reduces morality to a matter of hypothetical imperatives.

The section begins with a statement of what has been accomplished up to this point. Kant claims to have traced the "determinate concept of morality," that is, the principle of autonomy, back to the idea of freedom; but the latter was not proven to be something actual [*Wirkliches*]. Rather, all that has been shown is the necessity of presupposing freedom, if we want to think of a being that is both rational and possesses a will, which is here characterized as a "consciousness of its causality with regard to its actions." Kant also points out, however, that, on the same grounds, we must ascribe the property of determining itself to action under the idea of its freedom to every being with reason and will (GMS 4: 448_{25}–49_6). Thus, Kant once again emphasizes the distinction between the possession of reason as a theoretical capacity and of will as a practical (causal) capacity; though he goes somewhat beyond his previous accounts by calling attention to the fact that volition involves a consciousness of this capacity.

In the second paragraph (GMS 4: 449_{7-23}), Kant begins his formulation of the problematic by noting that there also flowed [*Es floss*] from the idea of freedom the consciousness of a law, namely, the principle of autonomy. By noting that the thought of freedom brings with it the consciousness of this principle Kant puts himself in position to pose the essential question of GMS 3: "Why ought I subject myself to this principle and do so qua rational being and also thereby all other beings endowed with reason and will as well?" (GMS 4: 449_{11-13}). Once again, this question is to be understood as stemming from a concern to understand the grounds of moral obligation, rather than from a need to be convinced that one should heed the dictates of morality. Kant's imaginary interlocutor concedes that this cannot be explained by appealing to some interest that would *impel* [*treibt*] someone to obey the moral law, since this would undermine the categorical nature of moral requirements. But having absorbed Kant's lesson that finite rational agents act on the basis of interests, she also recognizes that the possibility of obeying the moral law requires that one *take* [*nehmen*] an interest in it and wonders how such an interest is possible.

The interlocutor further suggests that the reason this question is so pressing is that, unlike perfectly rational beings, for whom reason is practical without any hindrance, beings like ourselves have a sensuous as well as a rational nature and, as such, are subject to non-moral incentives, which entails that the presumed objective necessity or validity of the moral law is not also subjective. In short, while conceding that *if* one were a perfectly rational being, there would be no puzzlement regarding the grounds for acting as the moral law dictates, she points out that, since we are not such beings, but instead imperfectly rational ones with sensuous incentives that may run counter to these dictates, its applicability to beings like ourselves stands in need of explanation.

---

[24] The basic point has been made by numerous commentators, but I find the clearest expression of it in the recent literature to be by Timmermann (2007a, 129–30).

The third paragraph (GMS 4: 449₂₄–50₂) begins the line of thought that leads to the introduction of the specter of a circle in paragraph five. Reflecting on the previous course of the argument, Kant remarks that it seems that in the idea of freedom we have simply presupposed the moral law, again identified with the principle of autonomy, but could not by itself (independently of the presupposition of freedom) prove its reality [Realität] and objective necessity. Even if this were the case, Kant notes, something "quite considerable" [ganz Beträchtliches] could have been gained, namely, a more precise determination of the principle of morality than would otherwise have been obtained; but nothing substantial would have been accomplished with regard to the demonstration of the validity of this principle and the necessity of subjecting oneself to it.[25] In particular, Kant notes that we would not have provided a satisfactory answer to three essential questions. (1) Why must the universal validity of our maxim as a law be the limiting condition of our actions? (2) On what do we ground the worth that we assign to this way of acting, which is supposed to be so great that there can be no higher interest? (3) How is it that a human being feels his personal worth through it alone, compared to which an agreeable or disagreeable condition is viewed as nothing?

This paragraph raises a number of questions. To begin with, there is the interpretation of "It seems" [Es scheint]. Is Kant simply reporting what he thinks has been shown up to this point or is he implying that more has been established than seems to be the case at first glance? Although the first reading may be more natural, particularly when considered in light of the soon to be introduced worry about circularity, it also appears to dismiss the contribution (preparatory as it may be) of section two. We have seen that Kant there purports to have provided a warrant to presuppose freedom for every being with reason and will and that he also claimed that all the laws that are "inseparably bound up with freedom" hold for a being that can act only the idea of freedom. As noted, this still leaves open the question of whether rational beings have wills and it does not provide any grounding for the moral law that is independent of freedom. Nevertheless, it does indicate that Kant has done more than simply presuppose the moral law by subsuming it under the idea of freedom; for in giving grounds for the necessity of acting under the idea of freedom, he is (in virtue of the reciprocity thesis) giving grounds for recognizing the validity of the moral law as well.

A related problem concerns Kant's statement that what has been accomplished up to this point is merely a more precise determination of the principle of morality. This is puzzling, not because there is any doubt that Kant took himself to have accomplished this with his understanding of the moral law as the principle of autonomy, but because this was already accomplished in GMS 2 and is presupposed in the formulation of the

---

[25] By saying that something "quite considerable" would have been accomplished in a more precise determination of the principle of morality, even if the argument cannot proceed to the next stage of justification, Kant is, in effect, claiming that the argument of GMS 1 and 2 constitutes a self-contained and significant result. This is also the view that Kant later affirmed in the second Critique and that is at least implicitly shared by most sympathetic commentators on GMS, relatively few of whom have anything of substance to say about GMS 3.

reciprocity thesis in the first section of GMS 3. Accordingly, this gives rise to the question of whether Kant is here referring to what has been accomplished in the first two sections of GMS 3 or in the work as a whole up to this point.

Although the context suggests the first alternative, the second makes better sense of the text. As we have seen, Kant set for himself two central tasks in GMS, namely, to search for and establish the supreme principle of morality. The first task was accomplished in GMS 2, not by discovering a new principle, but by providing a precise articulation of the principle implicit in common human reason. We have also seen that the second task was assigned to GMS 3; but rather than focusing on the contributions to this task of its first two sections, which at this point would be premature, Kant is simply calling attention to the fact that the second task has not yet been accomplished. And, as evidence for this, he poses the three above-mentioned questions, which the argument has not yet provided the materials to answer.

The fourth paragraph of the section (GMS 4: 450_{2-17}) returns to the notion of a pure moral interest; this time considered as a possible explanation for the binding power of the moral law.[26] Kant admits that, as a matter of fact, we can take an interest in the quality of one's person, by which he presumably understands the goodness of one's will or the virtuousness of one's character, and that this carries with it no interest in the agreeableness or disagreeableness of one's condition. In other words, we can take an interest in the mere worthiness to be happy, without making the attainment of happiness one's motive for obeying the moral law. But, as Kant points out, this non-empirical or pure interest in the worthiness of being happy cannot be regarded as the source of moral obligation because it already presupposes the importance of moral laws.[27] Accordingly, Kant concludes his preliminary remarks by noting that we still cannot see why we ought to detach ourselves from our empirical interests or, what supposedly amounts to the same thing, "*on what grounds [woher] the moral law is binding.*"

It is at this point and apparently in direct response to the inability of the line of argument that has been formulated in the first two sections of GMS 3 to deal with this binding problem, that Kant interjects a worry about a circle. He writes:

There appears at this point, one must freely admit it, a kind of circle from which there seems to be no escape. In the order of efficient causes we take ourselves to be free, in order to think ourselves as under moral laws in the order of ends, and we think ourselves afterwards as subject to these laws because we have ascribed to ourselves freedom of the will, for freedom and the will's own lawgiving are both autonomy, hence reciprocal concepts, but just for this reason one of them cannot be used to explicate the other or to provide its ground, but at most only for logical purposes in order to bring seemingly different ideas of the same object under a single concept

---

[26] My reading of this paragraph is indebted to that of Timmermann, who characterizes it as an "excursus." See Timmermann (2007a, 131).

[27] This is to be contrasted with Kant's position in the Canon of the first *Critique*, where we have seen he attempted to ground moral obligation in the desire to be worthy of happiness.

(just as different fractions of equal value can be brought to the lowest common denominator). (GMS 4: 450_{18-29})

And, some three pages later, after supposedly resolving the problem by introducing the distinction between the two standpoints and the contrast between the worlds of sense and understanding, Kant concludes:

The suspicion that we raised above has now been removed, namely, that there was a hidden circle contained in our inference from freedom to autonomy and from this to the moral law, that we perhaps presupposed the idea of freedom only for the sake of the moral law, in order afterwards to infer it from freedom, thus we were unable to provide any ground for it [the moral law], but could assume it only by begging a principle that well meaning souls would gladly concede to us, but which we could never establish as a demonstrable proposition. For we now see that, when we think of ourselves as free, we transfer ourselves into the world of understanding [*Verstandeswelt*], and cognize autonomy of the will, together with its consequence, morality; but if we think ourselves as obligated [*verpflichtet*] we consider ourselves as belonging to the world of sense and still at the same time to the world of understanding. (GMS 4: 453_{3-15})

Two questions have fueled and continue to fuel much of the debate regarding these passages. (1) Is there really is a circle or merely the appearance of one? (2) If there is, what is its nature? More recently, these have been joined by a third: Is this circle (whether real or apparent) to be found in Kant's argument in the first two sections of GMS 3 or in a position that he is criticizing? The widely shared puzzlement regarding the first two questions was pointedly expressed by Paton, who wrote:

In plain fact the objection [that there is a circle in Kant's argument] totally misrepresents his argument. He never argued from the categorical imperative to freedom, but at least professed, however mistakenly, to establish the presupposition of freedom by an insight into the nature of self-conscious reason quite independently of moral considerations. Perhaps when he came to the objection he was beginning to see dimly that the presupposition of freedom of the will did really rest on moral considerations; but it is surely unusual for a man to answer the sound argument which he has failed to put and to overlook the fact that this answer is irrelevant to the unsound argument which alone has been explicitly stated.[28]

What is truly unusual is that a scholar of Paton's stature should so completely misrepresent what Kant actually says in these passages. It is evident that Paton took the circle to which Kant referred to consist in roughly the following course of reasoning: (1) we take ourselves as free because we think ourselves as under moral laws; and (2) we think ourselves under moral laws because we have taken ourselves as free.[29] Such a line of argument is suggested by the reciprocity thesis, which no doubt explains why Paton and many others appear almost reflexively to

[28] Paton (1958, 225).
[29] This formulation is taken from Quarfood, who does not attribute it specifically to Paton, but treats it as a common misinterpretation of Kant's claim, which it certainly is. See Quarfood (2006, 288).

attribute it to Kant, as if this must have been what he had in mind.[30] An examination of the text, however, indicates that this is not what Kant says.

Consider the first of the two passages cited above. Kant there expresses the problem in terms of a contrast between an order of efficient causes and an order of ends. This reflects Kant's view that the idea of freedom is that of a kind of efficient cause (one the causality of which is not brought about by an antecedent cause) and this both calls to mind the contrast drawn in GMS 2 between the realms of ends and of nature and anticipates the distinction that Kant is about to draw between the worlds of sense and of understanding. The essential point, however, is that nowhere in GMS does Kant suggest that freedom is inferred from the premise that one stands under moral laws. The worry is rather that we supposedly assume our freedom in the first order in order to think ourselves as under moral laws in the second; but then we proceed to regard ourselves as subject to moral laws because we have assumed that we are free. Thus, the only inference to which Kant refers is from the presupposition of freedom to standing under moral laws and the problem is that there is no independent grounding for this presupposition, not that this grounding is provided by the presumption that rational beings stand under moral laws.

Moreover, a consideration of the second circle passage yields essentially the same result. There the worry, which had supposedly been removed in the interim, was that a "hidden circle" is contained in the inference from freedom to autonomy, that is, from negative to positive freedom, and from this to the moral law. Again, there is no mention of an inference from the moral law to freedom, and the inference to which Kant refers proceeds in the opposite direction. To be sure, a major part of the worry is that freedom was only presupposed for the sake of the moral law, which meant that the latter was left without any real foundation; but presupposing freedom so that one could then infer the moral law from it is quite distinct from inferring freedom from the moral law. And it is only the latter that would generate a vicious circle.

The upshot of the matter, then, is that, even though the procedure that Kant describes is logically dubious, it is not a case of circular reasoning, at least on the standard understanding of such reasoning as an argument in which the conclusion is already contained in a premise. Moreover, as has been noted in the recent literature, there is a passage in *Kant's Lectures on Logic* (§92) that bears directly on this point.[31] In distinguishing between a *petitio principii* and a *circulus in probando*, as two closely related types of logical fallacy, Kant writes:

By a *petitio principii* is understood the acceptance of a proposition as ground of proof as an immediately certain proposition, although it still requires a proof. And one commits a *circle in*

---

[30] For a list and discussion of the views of many of those who have interpreted the circle in this way, see Schönecker (1999, 349–56). Since he has provided what is by far the most thorough account of the circle problem and the literature regarding it, my account is indebted to his at several points.

[31] See Schönecker (1999, esp. 333–39) and Quarfood (2006, 289–92).

proof if one lays at the basis of its *own* proof the very proposition that one wanted to prove. (JL 9: 135; 629).[32]

Given these definitions, it seems evident that the fallacy to which Kant is alluding is a *petitio* rather than a *circulus in probando* (a circular argument). In fact, Kant himself suggests as much when in the second passage he remarks that presupposing the idea of freedom for the sake of establishing the moral law, might be considered as begging a principle [*Erbittung eines Princips*]. Accordingly, the question becomes: what principle (or proposition) has been accepted as immediately certain without proof? Clearly, it cannot be the reciprocity thesis, since Kant argued for it in section one. And, equally clearly, it cannot be the moral law, since that is presented as the conclusion of the supposedly fallacious argument.

This apparently leaves us with the proposition that rational beings like ourselves, or perhaps all rational beings, possess a free will, from which the conclusion that rational beings stand under the moral law follows straightforwardly by means of the reciprocity thesis. And, in support of this, it could be argued that, in Kant's account this proposition is, indeed, accepted without proof because: (1) Kant readily admits that it is impossible to prove freedom of the will thorough the theoretical use of reason; and (2) Kant's alternative to a theoretical proof, namely, the appeal to the necessity of presupposing or acting under the idea of freedom, really amounts to the assertion of an immediate certainty in the sense that it claims that from the practical point of view one cannot coherently doubt one's freedom (one cannot act under the idea of being unfree).

Although I believe that the above account of Kant's reasoning is roughly correct, I also believe that it does not provide a complete diagnosis of the line of thought underlying the circle or, better, the *petitio*, at least not if the latter is to be located in the argument that Kant actually provides in the first two sections of GMS 3. This is because Kant does not there draw the inference that involves the fallacy in question. This inference (from the presupposition of freedom to the moral law) is to be found rather in the natural extension of Kant's argument, which was spelled out at the end of the first part of this chapter. Moreover, this answers the third of the above-mentioned questions, namely, whether the circle or *petitio* is to be found in Kant's actual argument or one that he is criticizing, and, in so doing, it helps to explain why so many interpreters have such difficulty in finding it. They are looking in the wrong place.[33]

---

[32] See also R3314: 16: 774; LB 24: 233–34; LH 24: 414; LD-W 24: 510.

[33] The interpreter who introduced the third question into the discussion was Brandt (1988, 169–91). He argues that the circle is not to be found in Kant's own argument, but in "the metaphysics of morals (in the narrow sense)," by which Brandt understands the analytic procedure of the Wolffian view, which he sees as underlying Kant's claims that (1) a free will is an autonomous will, that is, one subject to the categorical imperative and vice versa (what I have referred to as the reciprocity thesis) and (2) a rational being is free in its own self-representation and can and must be taken by us as free in its own self-representation. The circle arises for Brandt when Kant endeavors to proceed from these analytic premises to the synthetic *a priori*

Finally, if this is correct, we are in a position to specify more precisely the source of the *petitio*. For if we locate it in the extended argument rather than in what Kant actually argues for in the second section of GMS 3, then the root of the difficulty does not lie simply in the presupposition of freedom, but in the assumption under which this presupposition is made, namely that freedom is to be attributed to rational beings with wills. That rational beings like ourselves have not only reason but wills, that is, *practical* reason is, I submit, the proposition that "well meaning souls would gladly concede . . . but which we could never establish as a demonstrable proposition."[34] And it is the same proposition that is also begged in the presupposition of freedom. Accordingly, our next task is to consider whether the distinction between the two standpoints and the correlative contrast between the worlds of sense and understanding, which Kant introduces as the only recourse [*Auskunft*] available (GMS 4: 450₃), may be taken as addressing this problem, thereby justifying the presupposition of freedom and with it the proposition that every rational being with a "consciousness of its causality with regard to its actions" stands under the moral law. As has already been noted, this would not be enough to show that this law (in its imperatival form) is binding on such beings, but it would show that that they must recognize its validity, which is a necessary step in the attempt to establish its bindingness.[35]

III

The final section of this chapter covers the last eight paragraphs of section three of GMS 3 (GMS 4: 450₁₈–53₁₅). It is concerned with Kant's distinction between the two standpoints, its justification, and the uses to which he puts it. In an attempt to make it easier to follow Kant's complex argument, the discussion is divided the into four parts: (A) an analysis of the nature of the distinction between the two standpoints and Kant's reasons for drawing it; (B) an excursus containing a sketch of my interpretation of transcendental idealism; (C) a comparison of this idealism, so construed, with what Kant appears to say about it in the text under consideration; (D) an analysis of the

conclusion regarding the necessitation of the will by the categorical imperative. For my analysis and critique of Brandt's interpretation, see Allison (1990, 219–21).

[34] Kant may well have had Crusius in mind here. As a voluntarist and chief opponent of the Wolffians in eighteenth-century German philosophy, Crusius regarded the will as the chief power of the mind and maintained that it has an executive function that presupposes, but cannot be performed by the intellect. Accordingly, he denied that God could create a being with understanding but no will. See Crusius (1964, 866–67 and 885–86). This seems to be directly contrary to Kant's view that there is at least conceptual space for rational beings without wills and his apparent need to justify the claim that rational beings who are conscious of their reason as having causality really have wills. Obviously, the latter is not a worry that could arise for a voluntarist. Indeed, it could not arise for a Wolffian either, since they deny that there is a faculty of volition distinct from the cognitive faculty.

[35] At GMS 4: 449₂₉–₃₀ Kant appears to distinguish between the validity of the moral law and the necessity of subjecting oneself to it, which is what, on the reading offered here, one would expect him to do. Admittedly, however, no such isolated text can be considered decisive for interpreting the overall structure of his argument, since Kant seems to slide rather too easily from the question of validity to bindingness.

course of Kant's argument from the introduction of the concept of a world of understanding to a deduction of both the presupposition of freedom and the moral law.

(A) The two standpoints

This distinction, which Kant presents as the only hope for avoiding the circle (or *petitio*) to which the preceding analysis has supposedly led, is between two ways in which we can represent oneself and one's actions to oneself: (1) as a cause "efficient *a priori*," which we do when we consider ourselves as acting under the idea of freedom, and (2) when we represent our actions "as effects that we see before our eyes" (GMS 4: 450_{30-34}). The idea is that each of these modes of representation involves the assumption of a different standpoint. And by relegating each of the ways of considering one's actions to a different standpoint, Kant endeavored to dispel the thought that there is any contradiction between them.

Inasmuch as this amounts to a restatement in somewhat different terms of the resolution to the third antinomy in the first *Critique*, one might wonder what bearing it has on "the suspicion ... that there was a hidden circle contained in our inference from freedom to autonomy and from this to the moral law." The answer, which Kant does not make explicit, is that any such worry stems ultimately from a more fundamental worry concerning the impossibility of ascribing freedom to *any* human action because of its incompatibility with the presumption that the same action is explicable in accordance with laws of nature. The claim that we act only under the idea of freedom loses much of its force, if it can be shown that any action under this idea contradicts the laws of nature. Otherwise expressed, Kant's real concern at this juncture is to justify the presupposition of freedom and from this point of view the worry that this might require a prior acceptance of the validity of the moral law is something of a red herring, which Kant apparently used as a rhetorical device for the introduction of the two standpoints.

It also seems reasonable to assume that Kant recognized the need to show, without dragging in the elaborate architecture of the *Critique*, that this distinction between the two standpoints is not merely an *ad hoc* device, dreamt up in order to resolve the problem at hand, but is necessary, quite independently of its usefulness in accounting for the presupposition of freedom, because it is grounded in the very nature of our cognitive faculties. Moreover, the strategy that Kant adopted to attain this end requires showing that this distinction is recognized, at least implicitly, by the ordinary human understanding.

Kant's discussion begins with a lengthy paragraph (GMS 4: $450_{35}-51_{36}$) in which, after some remarks on sense perception, which are intended to reflect the views of the ordinary, pre-philosophical understanding, he introduces the distinction between appearances and things in themselves, proceeds from this to a distinction between a world of sense or sensible world [*Sinnenwelt*] composed of the former and a world of understanding [*Verstandeswelt*] composed of the latter, and applies this distinction to the self. I shall briefly discuss each step in turn.

(1) Kant begins with the observation, which he claims requires no subtle thinking, but can be recognized by "the commonest understanding" [*der gemeinste Verstand*], if perhaps only by an obscure feeling, that representations that come to us passively, that is, through the senses, enable us to cognize objects only as they affect us, not as they are in themselves. In other words, the claim is that the very fact that a cognizer is passive in the representation of an object, in the sense that the representation results from the subject being affected by the object, is taken by such an understanding to entail that it cannot cognize the object as it is in itself.[36]

One could challenge this observation, viewed as a claim about the commonsense view of experience, on the grounds that the latter is best regarded as naïve realism.[37] Of greater relevance, however, is its lack of accord with Kant's own "critical" view. The problem is not that Kant thought that sense perception acquaints us with things as they are in themselves, since he obviously did not. It is rather that he denied this on the basis of a premise that is here omitted and that is not shared by the "commonest understanding," namely, that the subject is equipped with certain *a priori* forms of sensibility (space and time) in terms of which what affects the mind is given in empirical intuition.

(2) The second step is the assertion of the necessity of assuming "behind the appearances something else that is not an appearance, namely the things in themselves" (GMS 4: 451₁₃₋₁₄). Although the text is not completely clear, the emphasis on passivity strongly suggests that Kant is here offering what might be termed an instance of the causal version of the inference from appearances to things in themselves, which is one of the two versions of this inference that he provides.[38] On this reading, appearances are viewed as "mere representations," that is, subjective objects comparable to Berkeley's ideas; whereas things in themselves are mind-independent and unknowable entities, which must be posited in order to account for the existence of these representations, a task which they fulfill by "affecting" the mind, thereby producing sensations. The problems with this view are obvious and have frequently been noted; particularly the point that attributing existence and causal powers to objects

---

[36] Ameriks refers to this as Kant's "passivity argument" and suggests that it serves merely "to introduce a supposedly helpful *association* between the passive and merely phenomenal on the one hand and the active and noumenal on the other hand" (2003, 181). Although I agree with Ameriks' evaluation of this argument as "crude" and his claim that it does not serve an essential role in Kant's deduction of freedom and morality, I differ from him in seeing it as part of a deliberate (and ultimately unsuccessful) strategy to present his views in a manner accessible to the ordinary understanding.

[37] For example, this is how Hume apparently viewed the matter in his treatment of "scepticism with regard to the senses" in the *Treatise*. See Hume (2000, 125–44). But apart from Hume, Kant's observation would also be challenged by many other philosophers. In fact, the view that Kant here attributes to the common understanding is basically that of Locke, a point which Kant apparently acknowledges. See Pro 4: 289; 84.

[38] The other is the semantic version, according to which the necessity of appealing to the concept of a thing in itself follows from an analysis of the concept of an appearance. See, for example, KrV A251–52 and B306. Perhaps the clearest statement of the causal version is Pro 4: 314–15; 107. For my discussion of this issue, which includes an analysis of the concept of affection, see Allison (2004, 50–73).

that are presumed to be unknowable is both inconsistent with "critical" principles and incoherent.[39]

(3) The third step consists in what might be termed the globalization of this distinction between these two kinds of entities: knowable appearances and unknowable things in themselves. Indicating that he views this globalization as the direct consequence of the distinction between appearances and things in themselves, Kant remarks that,

This must yield a distinction, however crude, of a world of sense from the world of understanding, the first of which can be very different according to the difference in the sensibility of the many types of observers of the world, while the second, which its foundation, always remains the same. (GMS 4: 451_{18-21})

In addition to the fact that this yields a contrast between two worlds rather than between two standpoints on a single world, the interesting aspect of this formulation is the claim that the sensible world varies according to the differences in the sensibility of the percipients, while the world of understanding is invariant. This contention contains an important ambiguity, which I shall discuss below.

(4) Rather than explaining how this contrast between the two worlds, one relative to the point of view of the observer and the other not, is to be understood, Kant turns immediately in the fourth and final step to the application of the distinction between appearances and things in themselves to the I or self. The basic point is that just as we cannot know external objects as they are in themselves, so we cannot cognize ourselves as we are in ourselves, that is, independently of how we become acquainted with ourselves in inner experience. According to Kant, this is because inner experience, like outer, is receptive, that is, the product of affection. In this simplified account, Kant does not bother to explain that affection is to be understood as self-affection, which, together with its complement, the doctrine of inner sense, is one of the more difficult notions in the *Critique*.[40] Instead, assuming an isomorphism with the preceding account of outer sense, Kant concludes that, even though the self can cognize itself only as it appears to itself,

---

[39] The classical critique along these lines, which has been reiterated countless times, is by F. H. Jacobi, who famously claimed that "without the presupposition [of the thing in itself] I cannot enter the [critical] system, and with that presupposition I cannot remain in it" (1968, 304).

[40] Although Kant refers to inner sense in the first edition of the *Critique*, he only discusses its unique features and its connection with self-affection in the second edition and therefore subsequently to the publication of GMS. In addition to the Refutation of Idealism, two main places in which this conception is discussed are a note added to the Transcendental Aesthetic (KrV B66–68) and the Transcendental Deduction (KrV B153–56). Other important discussions of the topic are found in various *Reflexionen* bearing on the Refutation of Idealism. See, for example, R5653 18: 306–7; R5655 18: 313–16; R6319 18: 633; and R6354 18: 633. I discuss Kant's conceptions of inner sense and self-affection, together with the thesis that we can know ourselves only as we appear to ourselves and its relation to the Refutation of Idealism in Allison (2004, 275–303).

[B]eyond this constitution of his own subject, which is composed of mere appearances, he necessarily supposes something else lying at its foundation, namely his I, as it may be constituted in itself, and thus with respect to mere perception and the receptivity of sensations, he must regard himself as belonging to the *world of sense*, but with respect to what there may be of pure activity in him (which reaches consciousness not through affection of the senses but immediately) he must count himself as belonging to the *intellectual world* [*intellectuellen Welt*], of which he still knows nothing further. (GMS 4: 451₂₉₋₃₆)

The contrast between passivity and activity here assumes a central role; for we learn that it is with respect to a consciousness of its activity (which at this point remains undefined) that a subject is constrained to regard itself as a denizen of an intellectual world, presumably on the grounds that one cannot become consciousness of this activity through sense perception.[41] Since this is a central feature of Kant's account, which he discusses in subsequent paragraphs in this section, we shall examine it in some detail. But before we are in a position to proceed, we must consider Kant's idealism, both as it is expressed in the paragraph under consideration and how it is to be viewed in light of a more comprehensive reading of the Kantian texts.

(B) The nature of transcendental idealism

The longstanding dispute regarding Kant's transcendental idealism turns on the question of whether the distinction between appearances and things in themselves is between two ontologically distinct set of objects, which is usually referred to as the "two world" or "two object" view, or between two ways in which a single set of objects can be considered, as they appear and as they are in themselves, independently of the subjective conditions under which they appear, which is usually termed the "two" or "double aspect" view. As already noted, the former view involves notorious difficulties and those who propose it as a reading of Kant's position are generally highly critical of transcendental idealism.[42] Although Kant's idealism on the latter interpretation seems free from these difficulties, it comes with its own set of problems. Foremost among these is that it threatens to degenerate into a form of skepticism in which objects only *appear* to have spatiotemporal properties and whatever else is predicated of them as objects of possible experience, whereas *in reality* they do not.

In order to avoid both sets of difficulties and to preserve the robust sense of empirical realism to which Kant was clearly committed, I have argued for a modified version of the second approach. In addition to insisting on the thesis that Kant's transcendental

---

[41] We shall see that this activity for Kant is both theoretical (cognition) and practical (deliberation and choice). One of the more interesting and largely neglected texts bearing on the former is a fragment entitled "Answer to the Question: Is it an Experience that we think?" See 18: R5661 318–19. I discuss it in Allison (1983, 275–78).

[42] Perhaps the most influential formulation of such a critique in the recent literature is Strawson (1967, esp. 33–48 and 235–73). A recent critic who adopts a two-world reading of transcendental idealism and defends it as a sophisticated form of phenomenalism is Van Cleve (1999, 143–50). His account includes a critique of my interpretation to which I respond in Allison (2004, 42–45).

distinction is between two ways in which the objects can be considered in a philo-sophical reflection on the conditions of their cognizability, the essential feature of this approach is that it takes seriously Kant's contrast between transcendental idealism and transcendental realism as two all-inclusive and mutually exclusive meta-philosophical standpoints. In other words, every position, apart from transcendental idealism, counts as a form of transcendental realism, which for Kant means that it (erroneously) considers "mere appearances" as if they were things in themselves.[43] As already noted, this parallels Kant's view in practical philosophy, where all moral theories that are not based on the principle of autonomy, that is, all theories besides Kant's, are considered as forms of heteronomy.

Basically, this amounts to an attempt to interpret transcendental idealism in terms of what it denies, which again parallels Kant's meta-ethical procedure, where we under-stand autonomy by contrasting it with heteronomy. What makes this approach fruitful is that transcendental realism encompasses a wide variety of metaphysical and episte-mological views, just as heteronomy encompasses a wide variety of moral theories, such that its common thread cannot be equated with a particular metaphysical or epistemological position, but must instead be regarded as a shared meta-philosophical standpoint. I have suggested elsewhere that this standpoint can be described as a commitment to a theocentric model of cognition, that is, the assumption (often merely tacit) that human knowledge is to be measured and evaluated in terms of its conformity (or lack thereof) to the norm of a putatively perfect divine knowledge. And I have further suggested that this commitment is shared by all non-critical philosophies. Moreover, since, *ex hypothesi*, the objects of divine cognition are things as they are in themselves, it follows that all forms of transcendental realism regard appearances, that is, the spatiotemporal objects of human experience, as if they were things in themselves, that is, as if they possessed their spatiotemporal properties and relations independently of their cognitive relation to the human mind.[44]

It follows from this that transcendental idealism must likewise be regarded as a second-order meta-philosophical position rather than as a first-order metaphysical theory, competing, for example, with the metaphysics of Leibniz or Berkeley. Specifi-cally, it is characterized by a commitment to an anthropocentric model of cognition, which is epitomized in the famous metaphor of a Copernican revolution. Its central point is that we must look to the human mind rather than the divine for our epistemic norms, just as we must look to the human will for our moral ones.[45] Since these norms are conditions under which objects can be cognized by the human mind, I have termed

---

[43] See KrV A369, A490–91/B518–19.

[44] For my fullest recent accounts of the relationship between transcendental idealism and transcendental realism, see Allison (2004, 20–49, 384–95; 2006b and 2006c, and 2007).

[45] See Allison (2004, 35–37).

them "epistemic conditions." They include space and time (the forms of sensibility), which are conditions under which objects can be given, and the categories or pure concepts of the understanding, which are the conditions under which objects can be thought. And since both conditions, working collaboratively, are necessary to cognize an object, while the pure categories (apart from their schemata) are sufficient for the thought of an object as such, it follows that uncognizability does not entail unthinkability or, as Kant succinctly put it, "To **think** an object and to **cognize** an object are . . . not the same" (KrV B146). We shall see that this is crucial for understanding Kant's account of freedom and, more generally, of a pure practical use of reason.

(C) Transcendental idealism and the two standpoints

Our immediate problem, however, is that whatever virtues this may have as a reading of Kant's overall position, it does not seem to provide an accurate account of what he says in the text just considered. For what Kant appears to have affirmed here is an unvarnished statement of the two-object or two-world view. Thus, he speaks of appearances and things in themselves as distinct objects, with the latter underlying the former and even serving as a source of the latter by affecting the mind. Moreover, not only does Kant distinguish between the two types of object, he also regards the tokens of each as constituting two distinct worlds. It therefore appears that if one were to attempt to construct an interpretation of Kant's transcendental idealism on the basis of this text, one would end up with a two-object or two-world reading.

Nevertheless, if one approaches the text in light of what Kant says elsewhere on the topic, particularly in the first *Critique*, and with an awareness of the basic contours of the ongoing interpretive debate, things seem considerably less clear. To begin with, in addition to speaking of objects that affect us, thereby producing appearances, Kant also remarks that what they [these affecting objects] may be in themselves "remains unknown to us" (GMS 4: 451_{3-5}). And later, in a passage that functions to introduce the contrast between the world of sense and the world of understanding, he remarks with respect to things in themselves that, while we can know how they affect us, we can never know "what they are in themselves" (GMS 4: 451_{16-17}).

Taken literally, Kant seems to be saying in these passages that we cannot know things in themselves *as they are in themselves*. If not incoherent or confusingly redundant, this is, to say the least, an odd locution, which pulls us in two directions. If "things in themselves" is taken to refer to a discrete set of entities underlying appearances, it makes no sense, since Kant's view is that we cannot know such things *at all*, not merely as they are in themselves. It is perfectly intelligible, however, if it is taken as referring to the things that appear to us, qua considered *as they are in themselves*, that is, as they are independently of the conditions under which they appear. In short, although the two-world language seems to predominate, in reality both ways of construing the contrast between appearances and things in themselves can be found to exist side by side in the text, which perhaps helps to explain why the interpretive question appears to remain open after over two centuries of Kant interpretation.

Moreover, Kant's account of the appearance/thing in itself distinction in GMS suffers from an ambiguity between an empirical and a transcendental version of this distinction to which he calls attention in the first *Critique* and which reflects the ambiguity of the distinction between the invariability of the world of understanding and the variability of the world of sense referred to earlier. Thus, in an important passage in the Transcendental Aesthetic Kant writes:

> We ordinarily distinguish quite well between that which is essentially attached to the intuition of appearances, and is valid for every human sense in general, and that which pertains to them only contingently because it is not valid for the relation of sensibility in general but only for a particular situation or organization of this or that sense. And thus one calls the first cognition one that represents the object in itself, but the second only its appearance. This distinction, however, is only empirical. If one stands by it (as commonly happens) and does not regard that empirical intuition as in turn mere appearance (as ought to happen), so that there is nothing to be encountered in it that pertains to anything in itself, then our transcendental distinction is lost, and we believe ourselves to cognize things in themselves, though we have nothing to do with anything except appearances anywhere (in the world of sense), even into the deepest research into its objects. (KrV A45/B62)[46]

As the passage indicates, Kant acknowledges the appropriateness of using the distinction between appearance and thing in itself at the empirical level to distinguish between what seems to be the case to a particular observer under certain condition, and is therefore variable, and what is judged objectively to be the case, and is therefore invariable with respect to the condition of the cognizer. His point, however, is that this is not to be confused with the transcendental distinction. According to the latter, *everything having to do with sensibility*, not merely the content provided by sensation, which varies from observer to observer and, indeed, for the same observer under different conditions, but also that which is supposedly invariant for all human observers, that is, the objective spatiotemporal properties of objects, is attributed to appearance; while the thing in itself, transcendentally considered, is denuded of all its spatiotemporal properties. Clearly, what is doing all the work here is Kant's theory of sensibility, according to which whatever is sensibly given has both an empirical and variable content stemming from sensation and *a priori* forms (in the case of human sensibility space and time). And it is with respect to these forms that we must

---

[46] In the remainder of the passage Kant illustrates the point by noting that (at the empirical level) we would term a rainbow in a sun shower a "mere appearance" and the rain drops the "thing in itself" [*die Sache an sich selbst*] and he notes that such language is perfectly appropriate, as long as the latter expression is taken in a "merely physical sense" (which here is equivalent to empirical). But, he continues, if we consider this empirical object simply qua an empirical object and ask whether the rain drops represent an object in itself, then the question becomes transcendental and the answer is negative (KrV A45–46/B62–63. Other important texts in which Kant makes the same point include Pro. 4: 289–90; 84–85 and Fort. 20: 269; 361.

understand the transcendental sense of the invariability. Simply put, there is one space and time in which all objects of human experience (phenomena) are located.[47]

The crucial difference between what Kant says about the distinction between appearances and things in themselves in our text from GMS and what he says in the first *Critique* is that, whereas in the latter Kant warns against confusing the empirical and the transcendental versions of the distinction, in the former he seems to invite this very confusion by trying to show that even the common understanding has at least a crude grasp of the transcendental distinction. Given the importance for Kant of connecting his account of the two standpoints with the ordinary understanding, this new approach is understandable. Unfortunately, however, it leads to a complete distortion of the "critical" view. Moreover, Kant himself virtually admits as much, when, after remarking that a thinking person must draw this inference, he reiterates his earlier claim that this inference (to a domain of things in themselves underlying what is given in experience) is also to be found in the commonest understanding, on the grounds that the latter is inclined to expect behind the object of the senses something that is invisible and self-active. But then he laments that this understanding proceeds to spoil things "by soon making this invisible object into something sensuous, i.e., by wanting to make it into an object of intuition, and thereby does not become any wiser" (GMS 4: 442$_{4-6}$). To say that this understanding "does not become any wiser" is to admit that it does not possess the concept of something non-sensible, which is the precise opposite of what Kant was trying to show.[48]

(D) Completing the argument of section three

After this lengthy digression, we are in a position to return to a consideration of Kant's argument. As we have seen, the line of thought which led to the introduction of the transcendental distinction was initiated by a worry regarding circularity in the argument for the presupposition of freedom. Kant claimed that the only way out of this difficulty was to distinguish between two standpoints under which the self and its

---

[47] It is also the case, however, that for Kant variability also enters the picture at the transcendental level, since space and time are invariable forms only of *human* sensibility and Kant leaves at least conceptual space for other (non-human) species of rational beings, presumably with other, similarly invariable, forms of sensibility. See, for example, KrV A26/B42.

[48] The awkward situation in which Kant finds himself as the result of his effort to connect the transcendental distinction between appearances and things in themselves, which is grounded in the sensible/non-sensible (or phenomenal/noumenal) contrast, with a distinction that is familiar to the ordinary understanding calls to mind his dispute with Garve regarding the role of popularity in philosophical discourse, which was discussed in Chapter 2. Although he displayed some ambivalence on the matter in his various treatments of the topic, we saw that Kant rejected Garve's view that every philosophical doctrine should be capable of being made popular in the sense of being comprehensible to the educated but not philosophically trained public. In particular, he exempted from the popularity requirement whatever pertains to the "systematic critique of the faculty of reason itself, along with all that can be established only by means of it; for this has to do with the distinction of the sensible in our cognition from that which is supersensible but yet belongs to reason" (MS 6: 206; 366). Inasmuch as the problem Kant encountered in the present context arose precisely from his failed attempt to render the contrast between the sensible and the supersensible (or non-sensible) popular, he might be faulted for failing to abide by his own principle.

activities can be regarded. One involves taking these as part of the sensible world. With respect to this standpoint, the appeal to transcendental idealism yields the result that, qua considered part of the sensible world, the self, like all other objects is cognized only as it appears (to itself), not as it is in itself.

In accordance with this strategy, Kant's next step is to introduce the second standpoint, that of a subject or agent, and to show that, considered from this standpoint, the subject warrants membership in an intelligible world. This occurs in the following passage:

Now a human being actually finds in himself a capacity, which distinguishes him from all other things, even from himself, insofar as he is affected by objects, and that is *reason*. This, as pure self-activity [*Selbstthätigkeit*], is elevated even above the *understanding* in that, though the latter is also self-activity and does not, like sense, contain merely representations that arise when one is affected by things (and thus passive), it nevertheless can produce no other concepts from its activity than those which serve merely *to bring sensuous representations under rules* and thereby to unite them in one consciousness; without which use of sensibility it would think nothing at all; whereas reason under the name of ideas shows a spontaneity so pure, that it thereby goes far beyond anything that sensibility can ever provide it, and proves its foremost occupation by distinguishing the sensible world and the world of understanding from one another, thereby delineating the limits of the understanding itself. (GMS 4: 452$_{7-22}$)

The question raised for us by this passage concerns its relationship to Kant's earlier discussion in section two, where he first argued that reason must regard itself as free in its cognitive capacities. Although Kant did not there distinguish between the spontaneity (or self-activity) of reason and that of the understanding, the basic point of the two accounts seems to be essentially the same, namely, that in the consciousness of our epistemic spontaneity we are directly aware of a capacity that we cannot conceive as sensibly conditioned.[49] Thus, the problem is that if this passage does not add anything of material significance to the argument of the earlier one, it is difficult to see how it could help to alleviate the deficiencies in that argument which supposedly led to the worry over circularity. In short, one wonders how something that was previously viewed as part of the problem can now be considered part of the solution.

The most obvious difference between the two passages is that the one presently under consideration features the contrast between the spontaneity of the understanding and of reason. This is an important distinction for Kant's practical as well as his theoretical philosophy, since it is the capacity of reason to think the unconditioned that makes it (not the understanding) the source of the moral law. Nevertheless, this cannot be the salient difference between the two passages; for Kant could easily have included the contrast between the two levels of epistemic spontaneity in the earlier discussion without materially changing things.

---

[49] Kant expresses a similar view in the first *Critique*, where he speaks of the self-consciousness attained through apperception as contrasted with inner sense. See KrV A547/B575.

If the relevant difference between the two accounts does not lie in the nature of the epistemic spontaneity to which they appeal, it must lie in the use that is made of this appeal. We have seen that in the earlier account this appeal led directly to a parallel claim regarding the spontaneity of reason in its practical capacity and this, in turn, raised the question of the grounds for assuming that it has a practical capacity, that is, that rational beings like ourselves have wills or a reason that is practical. But rather than arguing directly from the possession of theoretical reason with its high level of spontaneity to the possession of practical spontaneity or will, Kant now argues from the spontaneity of theoretical reason to membership in the world of understanding or the intelligible world. Thus, immediately after his account of reason, Kant remarks:

On account of this a rational being must view itself, *as intelligence* [*als Intelligenz*], (thus not from the side of its lower powers), as belonging not to the world of sense but to the world of understanding; hence it has two standpoints from which it can consider itself, and recognize laws for the use of its powers, and consequently for all its actions: *first*, insofar as it belongs to the world of sense, under laws of nature (heteronomy), *second*, as belonging to the intelligible world [*intelligiblen Welt*], under laws, which, independent of nature, are not empirical, but are grounded merely in reason. (GMS 4: 452$_{23-30}$)

As this and the preceding passages make clear, Kant took a being's possession of theoretical reason to justify its conception of itself as a member of the intelligible world in virtue of the kind of self-activity that the use of reason involves, namely, one that, unlike that of the understanding, is completely free from any sensuous contribution.[50] If the preceding analysis is correct, the next and decisive step should be to connect this membership with possession of a will and the freedom and practical capacity of reason that goes with it. Moreover, this is essentially what Kant does at the beginning of the next paragraph, where he writes:

As a rational being, hence as a being belonging to the intelligible world, a human being can never think of the causality of his own will otherwise than under the idea of freedom; for independence from the determining causes of the world of sense (such as reason must always ascribe to itself) is freedom. (GMS 4: 452$_{31-35}$)

I have said that this is *essentially* what Kant does because this formulation is somewhat misleading. Strictly speaking, it is not, as the text suggests, that a rational being is conscious of the causality of its will and what needs to be shown is that the latter can be thought only under the idea of freedom. Since will, as here understood, just is practical reason, that is, reason regarded as a causal power, and since it is analytic for Kant that the causality of reason can be thought only under the idea of freedom, there is no such

---

[50] I suspect that it may have been because of his recognition of the confusion that would be caused by arguing from the possession of reason to membership in the world of understanding after drawing this sharp distinction between understanding and reason that Kant replaces the *Verstandeswelt* with the *intelligiblen Welt*.

need.[51] The issue is rather whether this consciousness is genuine or illusory, which is equivalent to the question of whether rational beings have wills, that is, are genuine actors or mere conduits in a causal process of which they are spectators rather than active participants.[52]

I have also suggested that a worry about this possibility is what prevented Kant from concluding early on that we are free agents and therefore by the reciprocity thesis, stand under the moral law. But before proceeding further, more needs to be said about why this was a genuine worry for Kant and how the adoption of the second standpoint helps to resolve it.

With regard to the first point, the basic problem has been noted by both Wilfred Sellars and Dieter Henrich. According to Sellars, whose remarks are directed at Kant's agnosticism about agency in the Dialectic of the first *Critique* rather than GMS 3 but are equally applicable to the latter, "Kant is leaving open the possibility that the being which thinks might be something 'which is not capable of imputation'. It might, in other words, be an *automaton spirituale* or *cogitans*, a thinking mechanism." On Sellars' reading, Kant's point is that we are certain that we are conscious of ourselves as something more than such a thinking mechanism, but he is concerned with the possibility that this "more" might be illusory, a "figment of the brain."[53]

Henrich, whose focus is on the argument of GMS 3, developed a similar analysis in somewhat different terms. According to Henrich, the root of the problem lies in the contrast between two conceptions of freedom at work in Kant's argument. One, which following Kant's use of the expression he calls "logical freedom" (R5442 18: 183), and the other is transcendental freedom. By the former is to be understood the freedom of judgment or theoretical thought referred to earlier in the chapter and by the latter the freedom of the will with which Kant is concerned in GMS. Henrich's claim is that at one stage in his intellectual development Kant had thought that the inference from logical to transcendental freedom was sound, but that the recognition of

---

[51] In the first *Critique*, Kant refers both to causality through (or of freedom), which is contrasted with the causality of nature, and the causality of reason. The former expression occurs most often in the thesis and antithesis of third antinomy and the latter in Kant's lengthy account of the resolution of the antinomy, as well as in the brief discussion of freedom in the Canon. Simply put, the point is that the causality of reason is necessarily conceived as the causality of freedom, since it involves in its very concept, an absolute spontaneity. The converse does not hold, however, because the idea of a causality of freedom is introduced in the cosmological context of the third antinomy, where it is conceived as a cause that is itself uncaused and therefore constitutes an absolute beginning (see KrV A444–45/B472–73). It is when applied to the will that such causality is conceived as the causality of reason and the question, noted but not answered in the first *Critique*, is whether reason has such causality. This is precisely the question that Kant is addressing in GMS 3.

[52] Since it explicitly concerns the power of reason, Kant's worry differs from the objection, given its classical formulation by Hume, that our first-person experience of freedom (the "liberty of indifference" in Hume's terminology) is illusory. See Hume (1999, 158n and 2000, 262).

[53] Sellars (1974, 80–81). The first *Critique* passages in which this agnosticism is expressed and at which Sellars' remarks are directed include: "Now that this reason has causality, or that we can at least represent something of the sort in it, is clear from the **imperatives** that we propose as rules to our powers of execution in everything practical" (KrV A547/B575); "Now let us stop at this point and assume it is at least possible that reason actually has causality in regard to appearances" (KrV A548–49/B576–77).

the possibility of a "transcendental fatalism" led him to reject this inference, which, in turn, created the problem with which Kant wrestled in GMS 3.[54]

Although Sellars' and Henrich's accounts are broadly similar, I believe that Sellars' is somewhat closer to the worry that actually concerned Kant. As we have seen, this worry is that our consciousness of agency might be illusory, that though we have reason, this reason is not practical, which is nicely captured by Sellars' suggestion that we might be nothing but thinking mechanisms. Moreover, Kant has an account of what this would involve, that is, of what the alternative to reason as a moving force would be, namely, instinct, which he took to be the prime mover in non-rational animate nature. We have already seen evidence of this in Kant's teleological excursus in GMS 1, where he suggests that if nature's end for the human race were happiness, instinct would have been a better choice than reason. Moreover, strong confirmation of this is to be found in a passage near the end of the work in which, after reiterating his view that freedom is a mere idea, Kant notes that,

It holds only as a necessary presupposition of reason in a being that believes itself to be conscious of a will, i.e., of a faculty different from a mere faculty of desire (namely a faculty of determining itself to action as an intelligence, therefore according to laws of reason, independently of natural instinct). (GMS 4: 459$_{9-14}$)

In addition to reinforcing the view that Kant regarded instinct as a viable alternative to reason as the moving force in purposeful action, something which we have already seen in Chapter 3, this passage is noteworthy because it calls attention to the distinction between the will and the faculty of desire, which is implicit in the entire account. For Kant, the faculty of desire [*Begehrungsvermögen*] is, together with cognition and the feeling of pleasure and displeasure, one of the three fundamental powers of the mind. Kant defines it as "a being's *faculty to be by means of its representations the cause of the reality of the objects of these representations*" (KpV 5: 9n; 144).[55] In beings for which reason has causal power this faculty is termed "will." Conversely, in the *Anthropology* Kant writes that, "the inner *necessitation* of the faculty of desire to take possession of [its] object before one even knows it [*ehe man ihn noch kennt*] is instinct" (A 7: 265; 367).

It was also noted in Chapter 3 that the interplay between instinct and reason as motivating forces in human nature is a central theme in Kant's historical essays. The basic ideas are that nature has equipped human beings with few instincts compared to other animals, so that they will be forced to rely on reason, and that the transition from animality to a distinctively human condition consists in a break with instinct as the prime mover and a turn to reason, which in its initial manifestation is highly imperfect and is only fully developed in a lengthy historical process in which it is goaded (rather than guided) by nature.

---

[54] See Henrich (1975, 64–70; 1998, 311–16). According to Henrich, for Kant "transcendental fatalism" refers to the Stoic doctrine.

[55] See also Chapter 6, note 24.

This suggests that Kant's worry that reason might be not practical or, equivalently, that our consciousness of ourselves as rational agents might be illusory, is at bottom a worry that the motivating force for humans, as it is for the rest of the animal kingdom, is merely instinct; that we may *think* that we are rational agents and, as such, free, but in reality we are really nothing more than creatures of instinct, differing only from other animals in possessing an inexplicable and practically inefficacious power of theoretical reason. Otherwise expressed, the problem is that, whereas the consciousness of possessing reason as a theoretical capacity is arguably self-certifying, on the familiar Cartesian grounds that any doubt concerning the possession of this capacity already presupposes it, as Sellars' account suggests, this immunity to doubt does not extend to reason as a *practical* capacity.

Assuming that this was Kant's worry, the task is to understand how the appeal to the distinction between a sensible and an intelligible world and the idea of oneself as a denizen of the latter as well as the former is supposed to resolve it. Although Kant can hardly be said to have been clear on this essential question, I take his basic point to be that, considered qua member of the latter, the worry that we might be creatures of instinct, impulse, or any such tropistic property is out of place, since these are only predicable of beings considered qua members of the sensible world. Obviously, this does not suffice to *prove* that our reason is practical or, equivalently, that we have wills. It does, however, provide a warrant for presupposing our agency and therefore our freedom, insofar as we consider ourselves as members of an intelligible world, which, it must be kept in mind, is made necessary by our possession of reason as a theoretical capacity. And, so construed, Kant's argument seems to have something like the following form:

(1) Since it involves an absolute spontaneity, my (self-certifying) consciousness of possessing theoretical reason requires me to conceive myself as a member of an intelligible world.

(2) But in considering myself in this way, I cannot regard my agency or practical reason, which I am also conscious of having, as merely illusory, since, *ex hypothesi*, the factors that could render it illusory are absent when I consider myself in this way.

(3) Therefore, insofar as I consider myself as a member of an intelligible world (as I am constrained to do by my possession of theoretical reason), I am entitled to presuppose that my reason has a practical capacity or, equivalently, that I have free will.

As already noted, since it does not follow from the fact that I must consider myself as free from a certain point of view that I really am free, this line of argument cannot be viewed as demonstrating that I possess free will. But, as has also been noted, this was not Kant's intent. His intent was rather to provide a warrant to presuppose freedom that is sufficient from a practical point of view. Moreover, though not a speculative proof, such a warrant is a genuine deduction in the Kantian sense that it addresses a *quid juris*.[56] And, given the reciprocity thesis, it is also a deduction of the moral law, though not of the categorical imperative, since it does not address the binding problem. The latter requires showing not merely that the moral law is valid for rational agents as expressing a principle of pure reason or even a moral ideal, which, absent competing interests, a rational being would readily obey, but is an unconditional requirement, which such beings are obligated to obey, regardless of their other interests.[57] This is the task of section four of GMS 3, to which Kant gives the heading: "*How is a categorical imperative possible?*" (GMS 4: 453$_{16}$), and it will be considered in the next chapter.[58]

[56] The fullest and most useful account of this issue is by Henrich (1998, 303–41). Henrich distinguishes between deduction and proof and between strong and weak versions of the latter, with these coming in various degrees. However, in spite of agreeing with Henrich on a number of basic points, including the systematic importance to the argument of GMS that rational beings have wills, and the thesis that Kant attempts to provide a deduction of the moral law that is distinct from that of the categorical imperative, I have some basic disagreements as well. The most fundamental of these and the major source of others is his view that Kant does not really mount an argument for either the validity of the moral law or freedom that is logically independent of the moral consciousness and that the thesis that rational beings have wills is based upon the assumption of membership in a moral order. As he puts it at one point, "[E]ven in the *Groundwork* all deduction is in the end referred to the factual self-certainty of the moral being" (op. cit., 331). Here the "even" is to be understood in relation to the second *Critique*, and Henrich's point is that there is an essential continuity between the two works rather than what Ameriks has termed a "great reversal" because, despite appearances, there is no real attempt in the earlier work to derive freedom and the moral law from non-moral premises. Against Henrich, I maintain that the argument discussed in this section of the present chapter is not dependent on any specifically moral premises and, indeed, that Kant's claim to have avoided a circle (quite apart from the question of whether it was successful) must be seen as an attempt to derive his conclusions from non-moral premises, specifically, from the self-certifying consciousness of possessing theoretical reason.

[57] The view that the moral law expresses a moral idea but does not ground any obligation is roughly the position of Philippa Foot, who suggests that moral persons should be regarded as "volunteers" in "the army of duty." See Foot (1981, esp. 170–73).

[58] My present assessment of Kant's deduction of the moral law in GMS 3 is more positive than my earlier one (see Allison, 1990, 227–29). I there claimed that the deduction was a failure on the grounds that it turned on a two-fold slide. The first was from a relatively thin conception of a non-sensible world [*Verstandeswelt*] to a thicker one [*intelligibelen Welt*], which is required to justify the claim that rational beings, who believe that their reason is practical, stand under the moral law. The second was from the assumption that reason is practical to the stronger assumption that *pure* reason is practical, i.e., that it is sufficient of itself to determine the will. Although I am hardly prepared to claim now that Kant's deduction is unproblematic, particularly in light of the view of transcendental idealism (discussed above) in which it seems to be rooted, I believe that my earlier criticism of the argument was too harsh. For I now think that the idea of membership in an intelligible world (understood as a point of view assumed in order to conceive one's reason as practical rather than as a metaphysical thesis about a noumenal self) does provide a warrant to dismiss (from a practical point of view) the worry that we might, at the end of the day, be creatures of instinct and that, given this, the reciprocity thesis suffices to show that we are constrained to regard ourselves as standing under the moral law. But, as has been emphasized throughout, this does not amount to an argument that we are bound by the categorical imperative.

12

The Deduction of the Categorical Imperative and the Outermost Boundary of Practical Philosophy

This chapter is concerned with sections four and five of GMS 3, which are the last two sections of the work, and Kant's brief "*Concluding remark*" (GMS 4: 453_{16}–63_{33}). Section four addresses the question: "*How is a categorical imperative possible?*" which Kant equates with the deduction of such an imperative. Section five and the concluding note address the boundary question, that is, the question of what the practical use of reason is able to achieve and what lies beyond its scope. As such, it constitutes the practical counterpart to the bounds of the theoretical use of reason drawn in the first *Critique* and the *Prolegomena*. The present chapter is divided into two major parts, corresponding to these two topics.

I

Section four consists of three paragraphs. The first contains the actual deduction; the second explains how this deduction accounts for the possibility of categorical imperatives[1] and relates it to the problem of the synthetic *a priori* and the manner in which the latter was treated in the first *Critique*; the third argues that this deduction is confirmed by the practical use of common human reason. Since, in addition to analyzing the three paragraphs of section four, I provide a critical assessment of the deduction, the section is divided into four parts.

(A) The possibility of a categorical imperative

We have seen that Kant initially posed the issue of the possibility of imperatives in GMS 2; first considering it in its general form, then claiming that, while this possibility is easily accounted for in the case of hypothetical imperatives, there are peculiar difficulties regarding a categorical imperative, which led him to postpone considering

---

[1] Kant uses the plural form "imperatives" in this paragraph, even though the original question concerned the possibility of the categorical imperative (singular).

that matter until GMS 3. Since every imperative involves a necessitation [*Nötigung*] of the will, to account for its possibility is to account for this necessitation. In our initial consideration of the topic, we saw that there were two reasons for the relative ease of explaining the possibility of hypothetical imperatives. (1) The practical propositions, which become hypothetical imperatives when expressed in the imperatival mood, are themselves instantiations of the analytic principle (GP): "If A fully wills E and knows that M is indispensably necessary for E and M is in its power, then A will M." (2) The necessitation holds only under the conditions that the addressee of the imperative wants to bring about some state of affairs and is in a position to do so. Given these conditions and GP, nothing further is required to account for the necessitation of the will and therefore for the possibility of the imperatives in which this necessitation is expressed.

What makes the explanation of the possibility of a categorical imperative so difficult is that the conditions that account for this necessitation in the case of hypothetical imperatives are absent. Specifically, what is missing is a presupposed end or object of volition, which grounds the necessitation of the will and which, together with GP, make such imperatives analytic "as far as volition is concerned" (GMS 4: 417_{10-11}). And since the lack of this presupposed condition entails the lack of analyticity of the practical proposition, it follows for Kant that a categorical imperative must be "a synthetic-practical proposition *a priori*" (GMS 4: 420_{14}). Kant then uses this synthetic *a priori* status to justify his reservation of the treatment of the possibility of such an imperative for a critique of pure practical reason, the elements of which he provides in GMS 3.

Although the apparent connection of this to the "critical" project of explaining the possibility of synthetic *a priori* judgment explains why Kant characterized the task of the deduction of the categorical imperative as showing how such an imperative is possible, there are some peculiarities in Kant's procedure that call for comment. To begin with, the self-described goal of the deduction of the categories in the first *Critique* was to show *that* they make experience possible; the question of *how* they do so was treated as a not unimportant but subsidiary matter.[2] In the *Prolegomena*, Kant poses the how question with respect to the possibility of mathematics and pure (*a priori*) natural science; but he there assumes that the latter are actual and, starting with this assumption, he investigates the conditions of their possibility. By contrast, in GMS Kant does not assume that the categorical imperative is actual or real. On the contrary, we have seen that he repeatedly raises the specter that this imperative (and with it morality) might be a merely chimerical idea or phantom of the brain. Thus, one wonders why merely showing how the imperative is possible suffices as its deduction.

---

[2] See KrV A xvi–xvii. This remark applies only the deduction in the first edition, to which Kant assigned both a subjective and an objective side and claimed that only the latter was essential. The deduction in the second edition has an entirely different structure.

In addressing this issue, we must begin with a consideration of the sense of "possible" at work. Clearly, it cannot mean merely logically possible, since that would not be strong enough for the task at hand. Nor can it mean empirically possible, since a categorical imperative is not possible in this sense.[3] And it likewise cannot be equated with what Kant terms "absolute possibility," that is, being possible in all respects, since that is a concept that pertains to the theoretical use of reason.[4] Rather, in order to make sense of Kant's deduction, "possible" must be taken as meaning capable of binding or necessitating. Possibility, so construed, which might be termed "practical possibility," is established by demonstrating that the conditions of the bindingness of the categorical imperative are met by its addressees. If this can be shown, then it will also be shown that moral requirements are legitimate demands of practical reason rather than phantoms of the brain.

Kant's deduction, which is intended to address this question, is compressed into a single paragraph, indeed, into a portion of this paragraph. Following the usual procedure, I shall first quote the text in full (numbering the different sentences for ease of reference) and then comment on each in turn:

(1) The rational being counts itself qua intelligence as belonging to the world of understanding and only as an efficient cause belonging to this world does it call its causality a *will*. (2) On the other side, however, it is also conscious of itself as a piece [*eines Stücks*] of the world of sense, in which its actions are found as mere appearances of that causality, but their possibility cannot be understood from the latter, with which we are not acquainted; rather, those actions as belonging to the world of sense must instead be understood as determined by other appearances, namely desires and inclinations. (3) Qua merely a member of the world of understanding all my actions would therefore conform completely to the principle of autonomy of the pure will; qua merely a piece of the world of sense, they must be taken as entirely in conformity with the natural law of desires and inclinations, hence with the heteronomy of nature. (4) (The first would rest on the supreme principle of morality, the second on that of happiness.) (5) However, because *the world of understanding contains the ground of the world of sense, hence also of its laws*, and is therefore immediately lawgiving with regard to my will (which belongs entirely to the world of understanding), and thus must also be thought of as such, I shall cognize myself qua intelligence, though on the other side as a being belonging to the world of sense, as nevertheless subject to the laws of the first, i.e., to reason, which contains its law in the idea of freedom, and therefore to the autonomy of the will; consequently, [I] must regard the laws of the world of understanding as imperatives for me and actions that conform with this principle as duties. (GMS 4: 453$_{17}$–54$_5$)

Since the first four sentences reiterate the main points of the preparatory argument of section three, the deduction proper is contained in the fifth and final sentence. Because of its importance, complexity, syntactical puzzles, and general difficulty in interpreting, this sentence will require the closest attention. But we must first consider the first four

---

[3] This is the sense of possibility that Kant discusses in the Postulates of Empirical Thinking. See KrV A218–19/B265–67.

[4] See KrV A232/B284–85. Kant connects this sense of possibility with the *ens realissimum* in the chapter on the Ideal.

sentences in order to understand how they are supposed to provide the necessary preparation for the deduction.

(1) The first sentence reminds us that it is in virtue of possessing reason as a cognitive capacity that a rational being takes itself as an intelligence [*als Intelligenz*], that is, as a thinking being conscious of its spontaneity. As such, a thinking being also places itself in the world of understanding. Moreover, it is only insofar as it functions as an efficient cause in this world that such a being designates its causality with the name "will." Presumably, the worry that rational beings might not have wills was eliminated in section three with the avoidance of the circle and the deduction of freedom. At least this must be assumed, if the deduction is to proceed.

(2) The function of the second sentence is to remind us of the second aspect of the two-fold nature of the self-consciousness of a finite rational being. Not only is it conscious of itself as an active being, exercising a spontaneous causal power, but also as a piece of the world of sense. There are two noteworthy features of this sentence: (a) the claim that from this standpoint the rational being's actions are experienced by that very being, as appearances of its causality as intelligence; and (b) that the appearances by which these actions are causally determined are desires and inclinations. Both speak to the previously noted psychological nature of Kant's determinism at the empirical level. The first does so through the characterization of these actions in their phenomenal manifestations *as appearances* rather than *as effects* of this causality. Clearly, the actions must also be experienced as effects; otherwise the agent would not regard them as *its* actions; but characterizing them as appearances suggests something more, namely, that they are the expressions of the agent's intentions.[5] In other words, Kant's focus is exclusively on intentional actions, which are the only natural occurrences that are candidates for the ascription of freedom. This also explains why Kant refers to desires and inclinations as the causal determinates of actions at the phenomenal level. It is not that Kant denied that there are other, non-psychological causes, e.g., neuro-physiological ones, but merely that he does not regard them as relevant to the explanation of the intentional actions of rational beings.[6]

(3) The third sentence combines the results of the first two. As such, it stipulates how the actions of a rational being would be understood, qua considered from each of these standpoints alone, that is, if it were the only standpoint from which such actions could be considered. Since each standpoint brings with its own law, the result would be that

---

[5] In his discussion of the relationship between intelligible and empirical character in the first *Critique*, Kant characterizes the empirical character in various places both as the effect and as the appearance or sensible schema of the intelligible character. For examples of the former, see KrV A546/B574, A551/B579, and A556/B584; for examples of the latter, see A541/B569, A546/B579, A553/B558, and R5611 18: 253. For my analysis of the relationship between empirical and intelligible character in Kant, see Allison (1990, 29–53).

[6] For a clear illustration of Kant's view on the matter, which reflects his judgment concerning the extremely rudimentary state of neuroscience at his time, see A 7: 175–76; 285–86.

all of the actions are seen as conforming entirely to that law. In other words, considered merely qua member of the world of understanding, all of its actions would be located in the logical space of reasons; while, conversely, considered merely qua members of the world of sense, they would be located in the logical space of causes.

(4) Although the fourth sentence is apparently intended merely as a parenthetical addendum to the third, it raises an interesting question to which we shall return below in a different form, namely, what does it mean to say that the actions of a rational being, considered qua part of the world of sense, rest on the principle of happiness? The problem is that this principle, like the principle of morality is a *principle*, that is, a rational norm and, as such, it does not seem to be applicable to a being considered merely qua member of the world of sense. A being, so considered, would pursue its happiness in the sense of seeking fulfillment of its inclinations and desires, which may be all that Kant intended; but this is quite different from acting on the principle of happiness, which involves determining oneself to act on the basis of a practical rule with normative force.

The fifth sentence, which contains the actual deduction, can be broken down into two parts: the first proceeding from "because," the second from "therefore." But since the first part contains three distinct claims and the second two, I shall divide the analysis as follows: $5A_{1-3}$ and $5B_{1-2}$.[7]

($5A_1$) *The world of understanding contains the ground of the world of sense.* The obvious question raised by this claim concerns the meaning of "ground" [*Grund*]. Echoing the causal version of the relationship between things and themselves and appearances, the most natural way to construe the term in the present context is as referring to an intelligible, i.e., noumenal cause. On this reading, Kant is making a metaphysical claim to the effect that the world of understanding (the noumenal world of things in themselves) is the ground of the existence and nature of the world of sense (the phenomenal world).

In addition to yielding the unattractive picture of transcendental idealism discussed in the preceding chapter, this reading generates the further difficulty that it is hard to

---

[7] The most thorough analysis of this sentence has been provided by Schönecker (1999, 364–96; 2006, 308–23). Although my own account is indebted to his, I differ from him in my endeavor to provide a somewhat more charitable reading. According to Schönecker, Kant's whole argument turns on what he calls Kant's "*ontoethischen Grundsatz*" [ontoethical principle], by which he understands a metaphysical-axiological principle to the effect that the bindingness of the categorical imperative for sensuous rational beings is entirely a function of "the superiority of the ontic status of the world of understanding." As he puts it in his English language account: "The human being as a thing in itself and hence the '*eigentliche Selbst*' and its law is of higher ontic value then the human being as an appearance: and this is why the law of the world of understanding the moral law is binding upon the human being (as a categorical imperative) who is a member both of the world of understanding and the world of sense" (2006, 317). While Schönecker insists that Kant must be read as arguing in this way, he also acknowledges that such an argument is unconvincing and contrary to basic "critical principles." For my part, this is sufficient to question such a reading, which can be defended only if all other more charitable alternatives are precluded.

see how this metaphysical picture of the relationship between the two worlds could provide the basis for the desired conclusion. Simply put, even if, for the sake of argument, one were to grant metaphysical primacy to the world of understanding over the world of sense, it does not follow that it also has *normative* primacy, which is what is required for the deduction to succeed.[8] For example, let us assume a theistic position according to which God is the creative ground of the phenomenal world: Kant would be among the first philosophers to insist that this *does not entail* that God is also the source of the normativity of the moral law or of its bindingness in its imperatival form on rational beings who also belong to the world of sense. Accordingly, what is needed is an account of the relationship between the two worlds that justifies the attribution of a nomological or axiological rather than an ontological primacy to the world of understanding over the world of sense.

(5A$_2$) *The world of understanding also contains the ground of the laws of the world of sense*: This step, which Kant presents as an immediate consequence of the preceding, seems intended to address that issue. In other words, it supposedly follows from the fact that the world of understanding is the ground of the world of sense that it is also the ground of its laws or norms. Although the claim seems plausible, its import depends not only, like the preceding, on the meaning of "ground," but also of "laws." Clearly, the laws in which Kant is primarily interested are moral laws; but in order to yield an interesting inference, there must be a generic sense of "law" at work of which moral laws are a species. Unfortunately, Kant is silent on this crucial point.

Within the framework of Kant's philosophy, the most likely candidates for non-moral laws fitting this description are the principles of pure understanding of the first *Critique*. These laws are grounded in the world of understanding in the sense that their source is the human understanding and according to the doctrine of the first *Critique* they pertain to the world of sense because they are the ground of *a priori* laws of nature. Although they are not also the ground of empirical laws of nature, since the latter are underdetermined by these transcendental principles, as conditions of the possibility of experience, these principles provide a set of norms to which any conceivable empirical law must conform.[9]

On this reading, the intelligible world is the ground of the laws of the world of sense in two respects: (1) of the (*a priori*) laws of nature and (2) of moral laws, which in the sensible world take the form of particular categorical imperatives. Further support for this reading is the fact that it corresponds with Kant's conception of a two-fold metaphysic (of nature and freedom), each part of which is presumably grounded in an intelligible world.

---

[8] This objection has been raised by Ameriks (2003, 178).

[9] This reading of Kant's claim that the laws of the world of understanding are the grounds of the laws of the world of sense is suggested by Paton; but he also suggests (and I believe mistakenly) that the thing in itself, considered as the source of sensation or the matter of empirical intuition, is the ground of empirical laws. See Paton (1958, 251).

(5A₃) *The world of understanding is thus immediately lawgiving with regard to my will (which belongs entirely to the world of understanding), and therefore must also be thought as such*: The most confusing part of this sentence is the parenthetical clause, which I have reformulated to give it propositional form. This is evidently intended as a specification of the general principle that the world of understanding is lawgiving to the world of sense; but inasmuch as Kant also characterizes the will to which the world of understanding supposedly gives the law as itself belonging to the world of understanding, Kant ends up saying that the world of understanding gives the law to itself rather than to the world of sense. Fortunately, however, since the problem seems to be more a matter of mangled syntax than philosophical confusion, it can be remedied relatively easily. What Kant intended to say is that, since the will belongs entirely to the world of understanding, it, too, must be considered as giving law to the world of sense.[10]

(5B₁) *Therefore (as may be inferred from 5A₁₋₃) I shall cognize myself qua intelligence, though on the other side as a being belonging to the world of sense, as nevertheless subject to the laws of the first, i.e., to reason, which contains its law in the idea of freedom, and therefore to the autonomy of the will*. This passage contains the crux of the argument, but its interpretation depends on the reading of the parenthetical clause "though on the other side as a being belonging to the world of sense." This can be understood in two ways. On one reading, which is the most natural grammatically, it serves largely as an aside, the function of which is to point ahead to the conclusion, (5B₂), where membership in the world of sense is first explicitly connected with being subject to imperatives. In other words, on this reading, it does not refer to part of what I, qua intelligence, supposedly cognize with respect to myself. On the other reading, which makes better sense of Kant's overall position, what I cognize or am conscious of as intelligence is my membership in the world of understanding and *at the same time* in the world of sense. This makes better sense because it is only qua being conscious of membership in *both* worlds simultaneously that I can be aware of myself as subject to imperatives. Moreover, this corresponds to the situations that Kant describes in his illustrations of FLN, where in each case it is a matter of whether the agent who recognizes the universality requirement, which we can now see stems from its membership in the world of understanding, can at the same time also retain the maxim of action it adopts as member of the world of sense.

(5B₂) *Consequently, [I] must regard the laws of the world of understanding as imperatives for me and actions that conform with this principle as duties*: If one accepts the preceding proposition and Kant's accounts of imperatives and duties, this conclusion follows. And if the argument as a whole is sound, it solves the binding problem by showing how laws that are descriptive for perfectly rational beings are prescriptive for imperfectly rational ones like ourselves with both a sensuous and a rational nature.

---

[10] Similar analyses are provided by Paton (1958, 251) and Schönecker (1999, 371–75; 2006, 312–13).

(B) Kant's explanation of the deduction

The second paragraph of section four consists of a single sentence, which attempts to show how the argument of the preceding paragraph explained the possibility of categorical imperatives and to connect this explanation with the quintessential "critical" problem of the possibility of synthetic propositions *a priori*.[11] To facilitate its analysis, I shall once again cite the text in full, enumerating and discussing its constituent elements.

(1) And so categorical imperatives are possible, because the idea of freedom makes me a member of an intelligible [*intelligibelen*] world,[12] whereby if I were only that, all my actions *would* invariably conform to the autonomy of the will, (2) but since I intuit myself at the same time as a member of the sensible world, they [my actions] *ought* to conform to it; (3) which *categorical* ought represents a synthetic proposition *a priori*, since to my will affected by sensuous desires there is added the idea of the very same [*ebendesselben*] will, but belonging to the world of understanding, pure and practical by itself, which contains the supreme condition of the former according to reason; (4) which is roughly the way in which concepts of the understanding, which by themselves signify nothing but lawful form as such, are added to the intuitions of the sensible world, and thereby make possible synthetic propositions *a priori*, on which all cognition of a nature rests. (GMS 4: 454_{6-19})

(1) Although syntactically the first clause suggests that the fact that the idea of freedom makes me a member of an intelligible world is a *sufficient* condition of categorical imperatives, it is clear from the passage as a whole, as well as from what we have already learned, that it is only a *necessary* condition. Thus, Kant proceeds to add that if one were considered merely as such a member, all one's actions would automatically conform to the principle of autonomy, in which case there would be no imperative. Also worthy

---

[11] Because of the latter, it has been claimed by Timmermann that it is here, rather than in the preceding paragraph, that we find the actual deduction of the categorical imperative or, more precisely, of the synthetic *a priori* practical proposition in which it is expressed. See Timmermann (2007a, 141–42). I do not, however, find Timmermann's argument, which is directed specifically against Schönecker, persuasive. First, the synthetic *a priori* proposition to which he refers, namely, "an absolutely good will is that whose maxim can always contain itself, considered as a universal law" (GMS 4: 447_{10-12}) is not mentioned in the paragraph. Second, although it is synthetic *a priori*, this proposition is not in imperatival form. Accordingly, justifying or "deducing" it cannot be equated with providing a deduction of the categorical imperative. Finally, as an additional argument for locating the deduction in the second rather than the first paragraph, Timmermann refers to Kant's remark at the beginning of the third paragraph that "the practical use of common human reason confirms this deduction" (GMS 4: 454_{20-21}). But this move seems lame; for Kant's reference at this point to a confirmation of the deduction is perfectly compatible with the view that he was referring back to the first paragraph.

[12] Although Kant had used the expression "*intelligiblen Welt*" previously (GMS 4: 452_{31}), this is its first appearance in section four, which up to this point had referred to the "world of understanding" [*Verstandes-welt*]. Kant's use of these expressions suggests that he viewed them as equivalent and this is reflected in the fact that some translations render both as "intelligible world." In my earlier treatment of the topic, I had suggested that "*Verstandeswelt*" referred to the noumenal in a merely negative sense (not-sensible), whereas "*intelligiblen Welt*" referred to the noumenal in the positive sense. I no longer think that this contrast is justified by Kant's use of the terms. For my earlier view, see Allison (1990, 227–28).

of note here is Kant's claim that it is the *idea* of freedom (not its reality) that makes one a member of an intelligible world. Presumably, Kant understands by this not merely the intellectual capacity to *think* this idea, but the capacity to determine oneself to *act* on the basis of it, which is what it means to have a will.

(2) Kant here introduces the *ought* in a manner that is highly confusing. Taken literally, what Kant says is that it is because one intuits oneself as a member of the world of sense that one's actions ought to conform to the principle of autonomy, which is the law of the intelligible world. This is a *non sequitur*, for an ought-claim cannot be derived from the mode of cognitive access that one has to oneself. Nevertheless, since it seems reasonably clear that Kant's way of putting the matter is due to his clumsy attempt to link the categorical ought with the synthetic *a priori* rather than to some deep confusion, this can be set aside. What is important is not the epistemological grounds for locating oneself in the sensible as opposed to the intelligible world, but the previously made point that it is only qua member of *both* worlds that one is subject to categorical imperatives.

(3) This is brought out in the next step, where, in attempting to account for the synthetic *a priori* status of the categorical ought, Kant also fills in a lacuna in the deduction contained in the previous paragraph. This lacuna concerns the identification of the part of the world of sense to which the will, qua member of the world of understanding, gives the law. Given the principle of autonomy, the obvious answer is that the will gives the law to itself, that is, to the "very same will," but we saw that this was rendered problematic by Kant's puzzling claim that the will belongs *entirely* to the world of understanding.

If the latter were the case, the notion of the will giving the law to itself would be vacuous, if not incoherent; since this presupposes a distinction between the will considered qua legislator or giver of the law, in which respect it belongs entirely to the world of understanding, and considered qua addressee and executor of the law, in which respect it belongs to both.[13] Moreover, we have seen that this is precisely the distinction that Kant later expressed by means of the contrast between *Wille* and *Willkür* as two functions or aspects of a single faculty of volition (*Wille* in the broad sense). Accordingly, when viewed retrospectively, it is again easy to see that it is Kant's lack of having at hand the terminology in which his point can best be expressed that forced him to rely on awkward circumlocutions.

(4) Kant here compares the tasks of accounting for the possibility of synthetic propositions *a priori* and the categorical imperative. But since he describes the similarity as rough or approximate [*ungefähr*], it is difficult to determine how much weight to

---

[13] It must be considered as belonging to *both* worlds, rather than, as Kant's formulation suggests, merely to the world of sense, because the will qua addressee and executor of the law, which is part of the sensible world, must be considered as free. I shall return to this issue in the assessment of Kant's argument.

attach to it or how far it should be pushed.[14] In any event, the comparison breaks down in at least one significant way; for in the theoretical realm concepts and intuitions for Kant are radically distinct, and it is this distinctness that ultimately guarantees the syntheticity of judgments in which concepts are applied or "added" to sensible intuitions. By contrast, in the case of the categorical imperative, it is, as we have seen, a matter of the relation of the will, which has both an intellectual and a sensible side, to itself. And while this is clearly not an analytical relation of a predicate to the concept of the subject, the practical proposition in which the will or, more precisely, the law of the will qua belonging to the world of understanding, that is, the "pure will," is "added to" the sensuously affected will qua member of the world of sense is also not obviously synthetic.[15]

(C) The confirmation of the deduction

The stipulated function of the third and final paragraph of section four (GMS 4: 454_{20}–55_9) is to provide confirmation of the deduction of the categorical imperative by appealing to the practical use of common human reason. In reality, however, what Kant provides is not so much a confirmation of the argument of the deduction, which as concerned with the difficult philosophical question of the conditions of the possibility of such an imperative would hardly fall within the purview of common human reason, as it is of the latter's acceptance of the axiology on which the deduction is based.

In an attempt to strengthen his case, Kant chose as his exemplar not an ordinary person but the most malicious scoundrel [der ärgste Bösewicht], with the proviso that this scoundrel is accustomed to the use of reason. The claim is that if such a person were to encounter instances of genuine moral goodness, he would not only recognize them as such but wish that he were similarly disposed [so gesinnt seyn möchte]. And since this scoundrel realizes that what stands in the way of this are his impulses and inclinations, he also wishes that he were free from them (GMS 4: 454_{21-29}).[16]

Applying the preceding account of the will to this scenario, Kant suggests that by means of this wish, the scoundrel transfers himself (in thought) to an order of things that is radically different from the one defined in terms of his inclinations and impulses.

---

[14] The deeply misleading nature of this analogy is pointed out by Henrich, who sees it as an expression of Kant's intent to model his deduction on that of the categories in the first Critique. See Henrich (1975, 98).

[15] Once again, the point is that Kant assumed that the analytic–synthetic distinction is exhaustive. Consequently, in order to establish that a judgment is synthetic, it is sufficed to show that it is not analytic. For a discussion of this with respect to judgments of taste, see p. 167 note 45.

[16] The German text states that because of these inclinations and impulses the scoundrel can "nicht wohl in sich zu Stande bringen" (GMS 4: 454_{27-28}). Most English translations take Kant to be claiming that the inclinations and impulses actually make it impossible for the scoundrel to become the kind of person he

In justification for this he points out that the scoundrel's newly wished for end would not satisfy any of the latter, but would produce only a greater inner worth of his person. Kant further suggests that with this transfer to the new order of things, through which the scoundrel assumes the standpoint of a member of the world of understanding, comes a will that is free of sensuous impulses. In providing this idealized portrait of the morally awakened scoundrel, however, Kant neglects to point out that all that the latter has acquired is the *wish* for such a will, which is quite different, not only for its attainment, which according to Kant is impossible for a finite agent, but also from a determination to strive for one.[17] In short, as far as character is concerned, he is still the same scoundrel, a point which Kant, apparently for rhetorical reasons, largely glosses over.[18]

Instead, Kant focuses on the positive side of the putative experience of the scoundrel. This contains three aspects, each of which is in some way problematic:

(1) That it is the idea of freedom, understood negatively as independence from determination from sensuous impulses, which necessitates the change of standpoint (GMS 4: 455$_{3-5}$). Although Kant has argued that the positive concept of freedom can be derived from the negative, we have seen that this concerns a conceptual relationship. In the present case, however, the issue is not between concepts but modes of consciousness, and it is far from obvious that this same relationship applies in this domain. Nevertheless, this is precisely what Kant seems to be maintaining, when he suggests that the scoundrel's consciousness of his negative freedom leads him to recognize the supremacy of the moral law. In this respect, Kant's account in the second *Critique*, according to which it is the consciousness of standing under the moral law that leads to the consciousness of independence from determination by one's sensuous desires or needs, seems more to the point.

(2) That as a result of this change of standpoint, the scoundrel is conscious of a good will (the will of his idealized self), which he acknowledges constitutes the law for the evil will that he actually has (GMS 4: 455$_{4-8}$). What is problematic here is the quasi-Manichean view of the self that this and, indeed, the whole paragraph, suggests, a view that is at total variance with Kant's position. I shall return to this matter below.

---

would like to be; but this is obviously incompatible with Kant's view of freedom. Thus, following Timmermann, I take Kant's point to be that these factors make it difficult but not impossible for the scoundrel to attain this end. See Timmermann (2007a, 143, n51).

[17] This passage is to be compared with Kant's accounts of moral conversion or regeneration, which requires a fundamental dispositional change (RGV 6: 46–48; 91–92 and 66–74; 108–14) and of the imperfect duty to strive after an unattainable moral perfection (MS 6: 446–47; 566–67).

[18] In fairness to Kant, he does not completely ignore the point, since he suggests that the scoundrel continues to transgress the law, even while recognizing its authority; but he makes this point only in passing. See GMS 4: 455$_{6-7}$.

(3) That the moral ought [*Sollen*] is what Kant's scoundrel would necessarily will [*Wollen*] qua member of the intelligible world and he regards it as an ought only insofar as he also considers himself as a member of the world of sense (GMS 4: 455₇₋₉). Although this accurately reflects Kant's account of the conceptual relationship between the moral law and the categorical imperative, from a psychological point of view it gets things completely backwards. From that point of view, to which Kant is presumably appealing in order to confirm his deduction, it is clearly the consciousness of the ought [*das Sollen*] that comes first and the idea that if one were unencumbered with a sensuous nature there would be only *ein Wollen* is at most an afterthought, which a philosophically minded scoundrel might entertain.

Overall, Kant's confirmation of his deduction of the categorical imperative is disappointing. First, as a bit of psychology it seems highly implausible. Indeed, it seems much more likely that the malicious scoundrel would scoff at the manifestations of goodness that Kant describes rather than being transformed by them, even if only in thought. Moreover, judging by what Kant says elsewhere in his more cynical moments, it is not difficult to imagine that he would agree with that assessment.[19] Second, as already noted, much of what Kant says in this paragraph appears to conflict with central tenets of his moral psychology. This is largely manifested in the quasi-Manichean view of the self alluded to above, which gives the deeply misleading impression that what prevents the scoundrel from identifying with his good will qua member of the intelligible world is simply that he is tied by his sensuous nature to his evil will qua member of the world of sense. Although the passage does not state this, it certainly leaves that impression, which is totally at variance with Kant's conception of freedom, not only in his later writings, such as *Religion*, where he attempts to deal with the foundation of evil in freedom rather than one's sensuous nature, but already in GMS.

(D) Critical assessment of the deduction

Turning from Kant's confirmation of his deduction of the categorical imperative to the deduction itself, I think it fair to say that it has not been particularly well received. Moreover, there are good reasons for this, not the least of these being the fact that Kant himself apparently repudiated it three years later in the second *Critique*. In an effort to structure my assessment of this deduction, I have organized it around three issues: (1) the problem of idealism; (2) the problem of the status of the addressee of the categorical imperative; and (3) the problem of accounting for a pure moral interest.

(1) *The problem of idealism*: Despite the efforts of many Kantians to avoid dealing with the matter, which might well be characterized as the third rail of contemporary

---

[19] This more cynical view can be found already in GMS. Consider, for example, Kant's sarcastic critique of those who attempt to derive or confirm moral principles by appealing to the experience of human behavior (GMS 4: 407₁₇–8₁₁).

Kantianism, I think it evident that because of its inseparability from the problem of freedom, the deduction of the categorical imperative presupposes transcendental idealism. Accordingly, the question is not *whether* this deduction requires an appeal to this idealism but *how* the latter is to be understood.

We have seen that this idealism initially appears in the deduction as a dualistic metaphysical theory, in which one set of objects or "world" (the world of understanding), is assumed to be ontologically distinct from and to ground another (the world of sense), even though the former is unknowable, while the latter, though known, as a realm of "mere appearance," is something less than fully real. Closely related to this, we also saw that there was a difficulty in understanding how the *metaphysical* superiority of the world of understanding, which is expressed in its status as *ground*, is translated into a *normative* or *axiological* superiority to the sensible world, as the argument evidently requires.

Although many writers on Kant, who accept this picture of transcendental idealism, will find nothing amiss here, at least as a reading of Kant, they will also likely dismiss this conception as incoherent; and I concur with that assessment. I have also suggested, however, that Kant's appeal to this metaphysical picture at the beginning of section four can be viewed more charitably as the result of his misguided effort to present his transcendental idealism in a manner that is accessible to the "commonest understanding." That Kant made such an effort is clear; but we also saw that Kant himself at least implicitly acknowledged the futility of this project, when he noted that such an understanding is incapable of attaining a proper grasp of the transcendental distinction, since it sensualizes the supposedly noumenal world, thereby inadvertently creating a second (but unknowable) phenomenal world underlying the first. If the world of understanding is conceived in this manner, then the whole point of Kant's distinction is lost, including its relevance to understanding the possibility of a categorical imperative.

Fortunately, however, the whole of Kant's argument does not depend upon this interpretation of transcendental idealism. On the contrary, we have seen that when Kant first interjects this idealism into the picture in section three (albeit without characterizing it as such) it is in the guise of a distinction between two standpoints, which is intended to resolve the worry over a circle or *petitio*. Indeed, it was only in order to illustrate this distinction between the two standpoints in a way that would be accessible to the common understanding that Kant introduced a metaphysical distinction between appearances and things in themselves, which corresponds to what for Kant is the empirical rather than the transcendental version of his distinction.[20]

---

[20] I am not suggesting that this is the only place where Kant presents the distinction between appearances and things in themselves as holding between two entities, one of which is conceived as the cause or ground of the other. Obviously, there are many such places; otherwise interpreters would not have attributed such a view to Kant. For my full treatment of the matter see Allison (2004, chapter 3).

Moreover, a difference of standpoints is not a metaphysical difference between things, but a difference between how the same entity or state of affairs, in this case the self, can consider itself. To consider oneself as a member of the world of understanding is to consider oneself as subject to certain norms, the most important of which is the moral law; whereas considering oneself as a member or, as Kant also puts it, a "piece" of the world of sense, is a more ambiguous matter, depending on whether one is considering oneself in a theoretical or in a practical manner.

It is also the case that by interpreting Kant's distinction as between two standpoints taken on one and the same thing, rather than as between two types of entity, the puzzle concerning how a metaphysical supremacy could translate into a normative or axiological one disappears. First, since there is only a single entity, there is no metaphysical supremacy, at least not of the sort envisaged by the criticism.[21] Second, there is no special difficulty in seeing how one standpoint on something could bring with it greater normative significance than another, without this implying any corresponding metaphysical or ontic supremacy. Consider, for example, a copy of *Hamlet*. Regarded as containing a great work of literature, this object certainly has a greater value (aesthetically, economically, and perhaps in other ways as well) than would the same object regarded as a collection of pieces of paper bound together and containing printed marks. Moreover, continuing with the analogy, one could also say that the text of the play (the world of understanding) is the "ground" in the sense of being the final cause or *raison d'être* of the physical book (the world of sense) and even of its "laws," understood as the arrangement of the printed marks on the various pages.

One of the major sources of obscurity in Kant's account is its failure to explain the connection between the two ways in which his distinction between the world of understanding and the world of sense are characterized in GMS 3. And since it is the metaphysical version, as expressed in terms of the ground–grounded relation, that is operative in the deduction of the categorical imperative, the impression is left that it is this that is fundamental and that the two-standpoint contrast must somehow be understood in terms of it. Nevertheless, a quite different picture emerges if we focus on Kant's remark, to which we shall return in the second part of this chapter, that, "The concept of a world of understanding is . . . only a *standpoint* that reason sees itself necessitated to take outside appearances, *in order to think of itself as practical*" (GMS 4: 458_{18-20}).

---

[21] This is not to deny that a distinction between standpoints could not itself be metaphysical in nature. This would be the case, if, as is sometimes done, one equates the standpoint associated with the world of understanding, which involves a consideration of things as they are in themselves, and that associated with the world of sense, which involves a consideration of the same things as they appear, as a contrast between how things *really are* and how they *seem to be* under the subjective conditions of human cognition. But in addition to the notorious difficulties which such an interpretation of transcendental idealism involves (for example, it commits one to the view that we only *seem* to be causally determined by antecedent causes, whereas in reality we are not), this could not explain the *normative* superiority of the world of understanding to the sensible world.

(2) *The problem of the status of the addressee of the categorical imperative*: The problem is that the contrast between the world of understanding and the world of sense, even when interpreted in terms of standpoints, does not seem adequate to account for the necessitation of the will expressed in the categorical imperative. Considered qua legislator of the law, the subject unambiguously belongs to the world of understanding; but contrary to what Kant's distinction between standpoints suggests, the same subject, considered qua addressee or recipient of this imperative, cannot unambiguously be located in the world of sense. The reason for this asymmetry is that the addressee must be regarded as capable of responding to the requirements of this imperative, which means that it must not only, as intelligence, have the intellectual capacity to recognize these requirements, but also the volitional or practical capacity to meet them, even when they conflict with the inclinations and impulses that it has qua part of the world of sense. In short, the addressee must be conceived (and conceive itself) as having both intelligence and will, which on Kant's account cannot be done, if it is considered merely as part of the latter world.

This asymmetry reflects the fact that the distinction between the two standpoints is initially introduced on the basis of theoretical considerations, but is then applied to the practical. From the theoretical point of view, there is a simple dichotomy and no asymmetry, at least not of the kind that emerges when the distinction is applied to the practical use of reason. To consider the addressee of the categorical imperative as a member of the world of sense (understood in the theoretical sense) is to consider it as it appears to itself, or as a phenomenon. Here the only difference from other phenomena is that it is cognized through inner rather than outer sense. And from this point of view, the subject's impulses and inclinations are experienced as causal determinants of its behavior. That is why from this point of view there is no freedom. Correlatively, from the theoretical point of view a consideration of the subject as a member of the world of understanding, which is equivalent to the thought (though not the cognition) of it as it is in itself, has no positive content. Its concept is that of "the noumenon in the negative sense" (KrV B307).

By contrast, the practical application of the two standpoint distinction, which is based on the introduction of the idea of freedom, involves two major changes. First, the concept of a world of understanding receives positive content by means of the moral law. Second, in virtue of the introduction of the idea of freedom, the relationship between the subject (now considered as the addressee of the law) and its inclinations and impulses is radically transformed. Rather than being the causal determinants of its behavior, the latter are now seen as sources of reasons to act, which are grounded in the sensuous nature of subject and which ought to be (but not always are) subordinated to reasons stemming from the subject's *reiner Wille*, that is, from the law.

I believe that it was Kant's failure to distinguish carefully between these two very different ways in which the contrast between the two points of view can be taken that led to the quasi-Manichean view of the self alluded to in the preceding section. More specifically, this view is the direct result of carrying over to the practical understanding of the relationship between the world of understanding and the world of sense the conception of the latter that is operative in the theoretical version of the relationship, which means that membership in the world of sense is understood in straightforwardly causal terms. I also think that similar considerations explain the previously noted slide in Kant's account of heteronomy (from heteronomy$_1$ to heteronomy$_2$). As we have seen, in GMS 2, Kant introduces the heteronomy of the will as a meta-ethical principle, opposed to autonomy (heteronomy$_1$), where, as a *principle* of the will, it was seen as applicable only to rational agents, defined as beings that act in accordance with their conception of laws or on principles. By contrast, in GMS 3 it mainly refers to behavior that belongs to the world of sense in the sense that it falls under natural laws rather than under principles of any sort (heteronomy$_2$).^{22}

Although Kant himself was largely responsible for this confusion, partial mitigation is provided by the limited focus of GMS. As has been noted repeatedly, Kant limited himself to the twin task of searching for and establishing the supreme principle of morality. By keeping to this program, Kant was forced to limit his explicit treatment of freedom to the vital, yet narrow issue of its function as a condition of the moral law. But inasmuch as the search for the supreme principle of morality was conducted largely by means of an investigation of the nature of rational agency, we have seen that a much richer and more complex conception of freedom is implicit in his account from the beginning. And while it is true that Kant did not integrate these conceptions in something approaching an overall theory of freedom, he can be excused on the grounds that such an account would not fall within the scope of GMS.

(3) *The problem of accounting for a moral interest*: Strictly speaking, the problem of moral interest is that of accounting for a pure, non-empirical interest, which a moral theory based on the principle of autonomy and the concept of a categorical imperative requires. But since we shall see that Kant explicitly denies the possibility of explaining such an interest, even while insisting on the necessity of assuming that one exists, our problem is to understand how Kant could have thought that a deduction of the categorical imperative is possible, given the impossibility of explaining the former. In order to appreciate the problem, we need only keep in mind that the goal of such a deduction for Kant is to explain how a categorical imperative is possible, which, as we have seen, comes down to the problem of accounting for a bindingness or constraint that is not based on any presupposed interest. But since in order for an agent to regard itself as bound by a principle it must take an interest in what the principle requires and

---

^{22} For the latter view of heteronomy see GMS 4: 452_{28} and 458_{33-35}. The former view is also found, however at 460_{25-26}. See also Paton (1958, 214–15) for the distinction between two kinds of heteronomy.

since the categorical imperative requires that its addressee take a pure interest in its dictates, we seem to be led ineluctably to the following line of reasoning:

(1) The deduction of the categorical imperative requires showing how such an imperative is possible (by stipulation).
(2) The categorical imperative requires that its addressee take a pure moral interest (from an analysis of the concept of such an imperative).
(3) It is impossible to account for the possibility of such an interest (by Kant's own admission).
(4) Therefore, a deduction of the categorical imperative is impossible.

Since Kant clearly accepted all three of the premises and yet rejected the conclusion in GMS, it appears that he must either have failed to notice the problem, which is highly unlikely, or that he did not consider that these premises jointly entailed the conclusion. In particular, he must not have regarded the third premise as incompatible with the possibility of a deduction of the categorical imperative along the lines he attempted. Yet it is also difficult to see how Kant *could not have* thought them to be incompatible, given the fact that explaining the possibility of such an interest appears to be an essential part of explaining the possibility of a categorical imperative. Moreover, Kant gave a strong indication that he was aware of this point, when, in a passage alluded to in the previous chapter, he asks rhetorically:

But why, then, ought I subject myself to this principle [the categorical imperative] . . . ? I am willing to concede that no interest *impels* me to do this, for that would not yield a categorical imperative; but I must still necessarily take an interest in it, and see how this comes about [*einsehen, wie das zugeht*]. (GMS 4: 449₁₃₋₁₆)

Assuming that the phrase "see how this comes about" refers to the moral interest, it also seems reasonable to assume that the place where this is supposed to be accomplished is the deduction in section four. As we have seen, however, Kant does not deal there with the question of interest. In fact, he only returns to it in section five, where, rather than referring to it as something that has been established in the deduction, he eliminates it entirely from the agenda of practical philosophy on the grounds that it lies outside its scope.

Following Kant's account, we shall revisit this issue in the second part of this chapter. For the present, I wish merely to note that I take Kant's procedure as indicating an ambivalence on his part regarding prospects for a deduction of the categorical imperative already at the time of the composition of GMS. On the one hand, in the deduction in section four, Kant gives the impression that he took himself to have provided a fully adequate answer to the question that the deduction was intended to answer: how is a categorical imperative possible? On the other hand, in section five, he seems to acknowledge the point I have raised; but nonetheless maintains that he has provided a sufficiently comprehensive account of the condition of the possibility of a categorical imperative to warrant calling it a deduction.

II

This portion of the chapter is concerned with section five of GMS 3 (455_{10}–63_2), and Kant's "*Concluding remark*" (GMS 4: 463_{4-30}). Although Kant's heading for this section is "*On the outermost boundary of all practical philosophy*," only the last of its three parts actually deals with the boundary question, which is a counterpart to the discussion of the determination of the bounds of pure reason delineated in the *Prolegomena*.[23] The first two parts deal respectively with the role of speculative vis-à-vis practical philosophy, which concerns largely the resolution of the apparent conflict between freedom and natural causality, and the legitimate domain of practical philosophy. Accordingly, including comments on the "*Concluding remark*," the discussion will be broken down into four parts.

(A) Theoretical prepares the way for practical reason (GMS 4: 455_{10}–57_2)

Not surprisingly, the theoretical question that is of direct concern to practical reason is freedom of the will, since this serves as the fundamental presupposition of its entire enterprise. Indeed, without the presupposition of freedom there could no such thing as the practical use of reason and therefore no practical philosophy as Kant construed it. Although theoretical reason in its speculative use cannot provide practical reason with a demonstration of freedom, Kant maintains that it can do the next best thing, namely, show that any attempt to demonstrate the impossibility of freedom necessarily fails.[24] Moreover, echoing the claim that he had already made in the second section of GMS 3, Kant insists that this is sufficient for practical purposes.

According to Kant, speculative reason accomplishes this task by showing that the view that there is a contradiction between freedom and necessity according to laws of nature is based on a deception [*Täuschung*]. So described, Kant's position might be regarded as a form of compatibilism, roughly similar to the compatibilisms of the Leibnizians, Hume, and many present-day philosophers, for whom there is no contradiction in saying of one and the same human action that it is both free and causally determined. But while Kant's position is undoubtedly compatibilist in this sense, it differs from the more familiar forms of compatibilism with respect to the conception of freedom that he held to be compatible with natural necessity. Whereas compatibilists of the traditional stripe usually understand by freedom simply voluntary action, we have seen that Kant understood it as transcendental freedom. Accordingly, I find

---

[23] See Pro 4: 350–65; 140–53.

[24] According to Kant, "A theoretical cognition is **speculative** if it pertains to an object or concepts of an object to which one cannot attain in any experience" (KrV A634/B662). This is contrasted with its natural use, which pertains to objects that can be given in a possible experience. In the text currently under consideration, Kant refers on several occasions to the speculative (rather than the theoretical) use of reason and contrasts it with its practical use. Accordingly, in order to follow Kant's argument, we need to introduce a further distinction, which he does not here draw, between a dogmatic and a critical use of speculative reason. Obviously, Kant's positive references to the task of speculative reason are to be understood in the latter sense.

appropriate Wood's paradoxical characterization of Kant's project as an attempt to show "the compatibility of compatibilism and incompatibilism."[25]

Kant's analysis is closely modeled on his treatment of the Third Antinomy in the first *Critique*. He emphasizes that freedom and nature or, more precisely, causality in accordance with laws of nature, are non-empirical concepts, both of which are necessary for their respective domains: the former for morals; the latter for cognition. But since Kant notes that "freedom is only an *idea* of reason, the objective reality of which is doubtful, while nature is *a concept of the understanding*, which proves, and must necessarily prove its reality by examples from experience" (GMS 4: 455_{24-29}), he grants to the latter the superior epistemic credentials. In fact, Kant acknowledges that if the idea of freedom were shown to contradict either itself or nature, "it would have to be given up altogether in favor of natural necessity" (GMS 4: 456_{9-11}).[26]

Kant does not find this drastic expedient necessary, however, since he regards the view that there is such a contradiction as based on a deception. This deception is what Kant refers to in the *Critique* as transcendental realism, understood as the affirmation of the "**absolute reality** of appearance" that is, the view that appearances are things in themselves.[27] In other words, it is only if one adopts the spurious standpoint of transcendental realism that there is even the appearance of a contradiction between the claims that a subject, considered qua appearance, is causally determined according to laws of nature and considered as it is in itself, apart from the conditions of sensibility through which it is cognized, is subject to the causality of freedom. Although Kant does not here use the expression "transcendental realism," the thought, if not the terminology, of the *Critique*, is clearly at work. As Kant puts it,

[I]t is impossible to avoid this contradiction if the subject, who regards itself as free, thought of itself *in the same sense*, or *in just the same relation* when it takes itself to be subject to the law of nature with respect to the very same action. (GMS 4: 456_{12-16})

Kant infers from this that in order to avoid the apparent contradiction involved in considering a subject as both free and determined in accordance with laws of nature with regard to the very same action, it is necessary to take this subject and its action in two distinct senses and relations. One of these senses is as it appears and the other is as it is in itself. As we have seen, the former involves considering the subject in relation to

---

[25] Wood (1984, 74).

[26] It is not clear what Kant meant by the possibility that the concept of freedom is *self*-contradictory, since the contradiction to which he refers and which is at issue in the Third Antinomy is with the lawfulness of nature. Indeed, if the concept of freedom were self-contradictory then the thesis of the Third Antinomy would be as well, which is a view that Kant could hardly endorse, since it eliminates even the appearance of an antinomial conflict.

[27] See KrV A536–37/B564–65. Also, at KrV A543/B571 Kant writes: "If we would give in to the deception of transcendental realism, then neither nature nor freedom would be left." It is crucial to distinguish between this deception [*Täuschung*] and transcendental illusion [*Schein*]. The former is avoidable by appealing to transcendental idealism, but the latter is not. Kant's view, however, is that transcendental idealism makes it possible to avoid being deceived by this illusion. For the definitive account of Kant's conception of transcendental illusion, see Grier (2001).

the sensible conditions under which it is cognized (or cognizes itself) in experience and the latter involves considering the same subject apart from this epistemic relation, as an object of pure thought. As we have also seen, this is equivalent to considering the subject from two distinct standpoints. The unspoken, but underlying assumption is that only transcendental idealism allows for the possibility of these distinct modes of considering.[28]

Kant, however, not only claims that it is possible to avoid this contradiction in the manner described above, he also regards it as a duty incumbent on speculative philosophy to do so, in order to clear the way for practical philosophy (GMS 4: 456$_{27-29}$). Since according to Kant only transcendental idealism is capable of performing this task, this seems to imply that every speculative philosopher, that is, every metaphysician, has a duty to become a transcendental idealist! But Kant's point can be expressed less tendentiously by simply stating that dealing with this problem is not a matter of discretion for the philosopher, since to neglect it would leave what he terms "a *bonum vacans*, which the fatalist could justifiably [*mit Grunde*] take possession of and banish all morals from it as occupying it without title" (GMS 4: 456$_{31-33}$). In other words, unless speculative philosophy resolves this problem, which does not fall within the bailiwick of practical philosophy, the latter would be defenseless. But it must also be kept in mind that the task that Kant assigns to speculative philosophy is a limited one, as is befitting his critical stance. It is not to show that freedom is actual or even really possible but merely that freedom and natural necessity in one and the same action do not contradict each other.[29]

(B) The legitimate domain of practical philosophy (GMs 4: 457$_4$–58$_5$)

Assuming that speculative philosophy has prepared the way, practical philosophy begins for Kant with "the legitimate claim to freedom of the will of even common human reason," a claim which is supposedly grounded in "the consciousness and the granted [*zugestandene*] presupposition of the independence of reason from merely subjective determining causes," all of which fall under the general label of sensibility (GMS 4: 457$_{3-9}$). Although Kant does not specify exactly who grants this independence to reason, presumably it must be common human reason itself, whose claim to freedom of the will was threatened by a worry regarding its compatibility with natural causality. In other words, common human reason for Kant, at least in the practical domain, is not intrinsically problematic, and only becomes such when confronted with a challenge from speculation, from which a critique of pure reason has safeguarded it.[30]

---

[28] The reason why only transcendental idealism allows for this two-fold way of considering the subject is that only it recognizes the existence of *a priori* forms of sensibility, which provide the basis on which the distinction is drawn.

[29] See KrV A557/B585.

[30] See, for example, GMS 4: 391$_{20-24}$. In the second *Critique*, Kant considers a second and more traditional challenge to freedom from the side of speculation, namely, its compatibility with divine causality

Following the line of thought introduced in section four, Kant further claims that common human reason, apparently without any prompting from philosophy, arrives at the view that human beings not only can but must consider themselves from two standpoints: as intelligent beings with wills, which, considered as such, inhabit the world of understanding, and as phenomena in the world of sense. Kant's argument for this claim is basically phenomenological in nature, inasmuch as it appeals to the two-fold consciousness that human beings have of themselves: as rational agents subject to norms and therefore as independent of determining causes in the world of sense, and as sensibly affected beings, which considered as such are parts of the latter. In spite of the robustly metaphysical nature of much of Kant's language, I once again think that his basic point is nicely captured by the Sellarsian distinction between the logical spaces of reasons and of causes. To consider oneself in the former manner is just to place oneself and one's actions in the space of reasons and in the latter manner in the space of causes.

Precisely because of its apparent conflict with Kant's metaphysical language, how-ever, such a seemingly anodyne reading cries out for further justification. And my claim is not that Kant *must be* read in this way, but that he *may be* and that doing so makes better sense of the text. There are two reasons for this, both of which have already been noted. First, it avoids the notorious difficulties associated with the two-world reading of transcendental idealism. Second, even if these difficulties be ignored or somehow finessed, a reading of the deduction that turns on the ontological superiority of the intelligible world (as ground) to the sensible world (as grounded) fails to address adequately the question of the *normative* superiority of the laws of the former to those of the latter, which is presumably the task of the deduction of the categorical imperative to establish. Granted, this does not justify the normative reading that I have suggested as an account of what Kant actually thought; but it does suggest that something like this reading, which focuses on the distinction between two standpoints rather than two worlds, provides the best means for salvaging anything of the argu-ments of sections three and four in GMS 3.

Apart from the previously discussed account of the world of understanding as the ground of the world of sense and its laws, which provides the fundamental premise on which Kant's deduction of the categorical imperative in section four is based, the main impetus for the metaphysical reading of Kant's contrast between the sensible and intelligible worlds is provided by his references to the "proper self" [*eigentliche Selbst*] in section five.[31] Accordingly, the issue on which the conflict between the metaphysi-cal and the normative reading of Kant's argument turns may be defined in terms of how one construes this expression. If it is taken to refer to a real or noumenal self (the self as it is in itself), then, in spite of the difficulties to which it leads, fidelity to the text

---

(KpV 5: 100–2; 220–22). But Kant deals with this challenge in a similar way and the problem is not noted in GMS.

[31] This metaphysical reading is strongly endorsed by Ameriks (2003, 178) and, of course, by Schönecker in light of his attribution to Kant of the "*ontoethischen Grundsatz.*"

requires us to interpret Kant's deduction of the categorical imperative as resting primarily on the ontological primacy of this to the merely phenomenal self. But if, as I hope to show, the expression is capable of a different, non-metaphysical interpretation, which accords with the contrast between two standpoints as previously analyzed, then the way is open for a somewhat different, more positive evaluation of Kant's position.

To begin with, Kant refers three times to the proper self in section five and in each case it is equated with the will: in the first case implicitly and in the other two explicitly. In the first of these, after referring to the intelligible world of which an agent knows nothing other than that in it not simply reason, but pure reason, independently of sensibility, gives the law, Kant remarks that "since he is there his proper self only as intelligence (whereas as human being [*Mensch*] he is only an appearance of himself) . . . those laws concern him immediately and categorically" (GMS 4: 457_{33-36}). In the second reference, which immediately follows upon this, Kant explicitly equates the proper self with the will (as intelligence) and adds that, though we do not attribute to the latter inclinations and desires, which pertain to the self qua member of the sensible world, we do attribute to it any indulgence that might be paid to these insofar as they oppose the requirements of reason (GMS 4: 458_{2-5}). In other words, the proper self is the subject of imputation. In the third, after again equating the proper self with the will as intelligence, Kant adds that, "*what belongs to mere appearance is necessarily subordinated by reason to the nature of the thing in itself*" (GMS 4: 461_{3-5}).

In all three passages, the proper self is connected with the intelligible world. In the first, the metaphysical reading, according to which the proper self is identified with the real or noumenal self, is strongly suggested by the contrast with the human being, characterized as "only an appearance of himself." In the second, this metaphysical language is absent; but by indicating that the proper self is responsible for the motivational weight given to inclinations, if not for the inclinations themselves, Kant seems to be alluding to the incorporation thesis, which in his later terminology is connected with the freedom (absolute spontaneity) of *Willkür*. Finally, in the third, Kant appears to relate the conception of the proper self directly to the ontological subordination of appearances to things in themselves, which is affirmed in the deduction.

Although these passages are compatible with the metaphysical reading as characterized above, they do not require it. To the contrary, further consideration lends support to a normative reading, which as previously suggested is connected to the two-standpoint distinction and, as such, does not turn on the ontological superiority of the intelligible to the sensible world. Essential to this reading is the identification in all three passages of the proper self with the will in one of its aspects.

In the first, it seems to be identified with the pure will, which serves as the source of a law (the moral law) that is valid independently of any sensuous conditions. This will is clearly noumenal in the sense of being merely intelligible, but it is a capacity rather than an entity (as a self presumably is for Kant). Moreover, if this is the case, it is difficult to see how the human being could be regarded as the *appearance of* this proper self. In fact,

Kant does not actually make the latter claim. Rather, he merely states parenthetically that "the human being is only an appearance of *itself*" [my emphasis], which, apart from the question of its intelligibility, seems to be a gratuitous addition to the central point regarding the intelligible nature of a pure will.

The key to unraveling the third passage lies in Kant's claim that the necessary subordination of what belongs to mere appearance to the nature of the thing in itself is said to be performed "*by reason*." Kant does not say whether he is referring to speculative or practical reason; but the context (Kant is concerned with the bounds of *practical* reason) strongly suggests the latter. And if this is true, it seems evident that the subordination required by reason must be understood in terms of norms or values rather than grades of being. In other words, what Kant is saying is that the norm derived from the sensuous side of our nature ("what belongs to mere appearance"), namely, happiness, must be subordinated to the one derived from our proper self, or pure will, namely, the moral law, which is presumably what a deduction of the categorical imperative must show.

I have reserved discussion of the second passage for last, since it poses a separate problem. Simply put, it is that, whereas the first and third passages refer to what Kant will later term *Wille*, in the sense of legislative will, the second appears to refer to what he will term *Willkür* (executive will or choice). Since Kant had not yet arrived at the *Wille–Willkür* distinction in 1785, he obviously could not appeal to it at this point. Instead, he refers simply to *Wille*, which he presumably understood as involving both the legislative and executive functions and which was latter identified with *Wille* in the broad sense. Setting that aside, however, once again the main point is that *Willkür*, like *Wille*, is a *capacity* not an *entity* and, as such, cannot be identified with the real or noumenal self; though it might be regarded a capacity of such a self.

In view of these considerations, I believe that "the proper self" is best understood in normative rather than metaphysical terms and in light of Kant's conception of the autonomy of the will. As we have seen, to attribute autonomy to the will is to claim that it is a law to itself, which leads to the question of the source within the will of its legislative authority. It is this source, which may be described as the source of normativity, that is to be identified with the proper self in the sense that it is what one obeys when one obeys oneself. And since, according to Kant, this source is the pure will as defined above, it is this that constitutes the proper self. Correlatively, the human being, who is the addressee of this law, may be described as an appearance of itself in the sense that it is sensibly affected and in this respect part of the phenomenal world; though, as we have also seen, qua addressee, it is not *merely* a part of the latter.

Even if this is granted, however, it may still be objected that this reading fails to do full justice to Kant's metaphysical language, not only in his discussion of the proper self, but also in his deduction of the categorical imperative. I have three points to make in response to this objection. First, it must be kept in mind that this language was first introduced by Kant in order to show that the distinction between the two standpoints, which provided the means through which he endeavored to avoid the circle or *petitio*, was already grasped by common human reason. In other words, it is the distinction between the two standpoints that "wears the trousers" in Kant's account and the metaphysical interpretation of this distinction in terms of two worlds or ontologically distinct sets of entities is intended to illustrate this distinction in a way that accords with the common understanding. Second, we have seen that Kant himself virtually admits that this attempt fails, since the common understanding is unable to grasp the concept of a non-sensible ground. Finally, it is essential to keep in mind Kant's previously cited claim that, "The concept of a world of understanding is . . . only a *standpoint* that reason sees itself necessitated to take outside appearances, *in order to think of itself as practical*" (GMS 4: 458_{18-20}), which is difficult to reconcile with the view that the world of understanding (or, equivalently, the intelligible world) is to be understood metaphysically as referring to a distinct realm of being.

Nevertheless, the fact remains that this characterization of the world of understanding as only a standpoint stands together in the text with the overtly metaphysical language that has already been noted. And to this commentator at least, this suggests that there is a certain tension in GMS 3 between metaphysical and normative strands of argumentation. But while this tension may not have been successfully resolved by Kant, I think that it is in principle resolvable, if we keep in mind that GMS 3 is intended as a transition to a critique of pure *practical* reason. Here the point is simply that, apart from the postulates, which are not here at issue, practical reason is neither concerned with theoretical claims nor dependent for its normativity on a metaphysical superstructure. Moreover, I take this to accord with the task of section five, which is to determine the boundary of practical reason.

(C) Determining the outermost boundary of practical reason

It is not until the final eight paragraphs of section five (GMS 4: 458_6–63_2) that Kant turns to the boundary question, for which everything said up to now can be regarded as preparation. The decisive contrast on the basis of which Kant draws the boundary is between *thinking* oneself [*hineindenken*] into a world of understanding and endeavoring to intuit or feel oneself in it [*hineinschauen, hineinempfinden*] (GMS 4: 458_{6-8}). The former is deemed permissible, since it is only a negative thought (the world of understanding is non-sensible); whereas the latter is impermissible because it aims at a positive cognition that transcends the capacity of human reason (whether speculative or practical).[32] But as we have already seen and as Kant reminds us, in spite of being merely negative with respect to the world of sense, the thought of a world of understanding is not vacuous from a practical point of view. In fact, it yields not only the negative conception of freedom (not being causally determined by anything

---

[32] This reflects Kant's distinction between the noumenon in the negative and positive senses: the thought of something as not an object of sensible intuition as opposed to the thought of something as the object of a non-sensible (intellectual) intuition. See KrV B 307–8.

in the world of sense), but also the positive conception of it as a causality of reason, which is identified with the will.

Kant characterizes the law of this will as "so to act that the principle of one's actions accords with the essential nature of a rational cause, i.e., with the condition of the universal validity of the maxim, as a law" (GMS 4: 488_{13-16}). This constitutes a fresh formulation of the moral law and what is fresh about it is its reference to "the essential nature of a rational cause."[33] Presumably, the essential nature of a rational cause is just to be rational; and as Kant's gloss on this indicates, this means not merely acting only on maxims that are universally endorsable, but doing so *simply because of* their universal endorsability. In other words, for a will for which this principle serves as its law, universal endorsability would not be merely a necessary condition in the sense of constituting a litmus test or filter, but also the single motivationally sufficient reason for its volitions.[34] Clearly, a will governed by this law would not be the human will, since for the latter happiness is a necessary natural end and as such is the source of legitimate reasons to act, provided that they do not conflict with the demands of morality.[35] It is rather a pure or perfectly rational will.[36]

For present purposes, however, the crucial point is neither the details of this law nor its relation to the various formulations of the categorical imperative, but the fact that in order to conceive of such a law and of the pure will for which it is a law, it is necessary to "think oneself into" a world of understanding. And what makes this crucial is that this pure will and its law are normative for the human will. Accordingly, if morality as Kant understands it is to be possible, this world of understanding must lie within the bounds of practical reason. Moreover, it is in an attempt to explain why the concept of a world of understanding lies within these bounds that Kant makes the claim to which reference has already been made on more than one occasion, namely, that "The concept of a world of understanding is ... only a *standpoint* that reason sees itself necessitated to take outside appearances, *in order to think of itself as practical*." I have already suggested that Kant's characterization of the concept of this world as "only a *standpoint*" may be seen as an effort to block a metaphysical reading; while the claim that "reason sees itself necessitated to take [such a standpoint] ... *in order to think of itself as practical*" points to the normative function of this standpoint.

---

[33] This is a statement of the moral law rather than the categorical imperative because it is a descriptive law that describes the *modus operandi* of a pure will.

[34] As such, this principle is stronger than FUL and, indeed, any of the formulations of the supreme principle of morality in an imperatival form. We have seen that these are construed as tests of the permissibility of maxims, whereas this principle serves as a positive requirement.

[35] As we have seen, this is the point of the inclusion of "at the same time" [*zugleich*] or "also" [*auch*] in Kant's various formulations of the categorical imperative. It should be noted that there is no such expression in the formulation of the law currently under consideration.

[36] This could include, but need not be limited to a holy will, since purity or complete rationality requires only that the will be determined solely by *a priori* principles, not that it have no connection with a sensuous nature.

Kant is equally, if not more insistent that this is as far as practical reason can legitimately go. And, as an example of an unjustifiable outreach, he cites the attempt to provide an object of the will, that is, a motivational cause [Bewegursache] from the world of understanding. Such an endeavor, Kant notes, would transcend the bounds of practical reason because it presupposes the cognizability of something to which human reason has no cognitive access (GMS 4: 458_{16-18}).[37] Moreover, most of the remainder of section five is devoted to the specification of further ways in which practical reason could overstep its bounds. The list, which presumably is not intended to be exhaustive, contains three items: trying to explain how pure reason can be practical; how freedom is possible; and how it is possible for human or, more generally, rational beings with a sensuous nature, to take an interest in moral laws, which is equivalent to explaining the possibility of a pure moral interest. Although Kant notes that these issues are intimately related, since they all turn ultimately on freedom, I shall briefly consider the first two together, since Kant explicitly equates them, and then discuss the third in somewhat more detail, since it is directly relevant to the deduction of the categorical imperative. The discussion of section five will conclude with a look at what I take to be Kant's reconsideration of his deduction of the categorical imperative in light of these restrictions on the scope of practical reason.

(1) *The inexplicability of the practicality of pure reason and of freedom*: Since the idea that pure reason is practical contains two components: that it is the source of the law (*principium diiudicationis*) and that it can of itself, without appealing to any sensuous interest, move the will (*principium executionis*), the question of its possibility likewise has two components. But it is clear from the context that Kant is here interested only in the second, since it is only this component that can be equated with explaining the possibility of freedom. Moreover, the reason why these tasks are equivalent is that they both require explaining the possibility of a kind of causality (a causality of reason) that defies the conditions of causal explanation. Kant writes:

For we can explain nothing but what we can trace back to laws, the object of which can be given in a possible experience. But freedom is a mere idea, the objective reality of which can in no way be exhibited according to laws of nature, and therefore also not in any possible experience. (GMS 4: 459_{3-7})

---

[37] If we examine Kant's account of practical reason in the Canon of the first *Critique* in light of his position here, we find that he was guilty of precisely this error; for Kant there argued for the necessity of God and a future life as conditions of a moral incentive. Although Kant reaffirmed the necessity of these postulates in the second *Critique* and his later writings, it was not for the purpose of providing a moral incentive. Rather, Kant's revised view of these postulates turns on the theses that we have a duty to promote the highest good and that it is only by assuming the existence of God and a future life (as objects of a practical faith) that we can conceive of this obligation as capable of fulfillment. Presumably, Kant thought that this kept these postulates within the bounds of practical reason.

Kant concludes from this that freedom has the status of a necessary presupposition of reason, something of which we have been aware since section three of GMS 3. But Kant goes a bit beyond this by suggesting that, when explanation ceases, that is, when we go beyond appealing to laws of nature, there remains room for defense. Unfortunately, the proffered defense is weak. Once again, it is directed against those who deny that freedom is possible on the grounds that it contradicts laws of nature; and it consists in the reiteration of the distinction between appearances and things in themselves, together with the claim that these critics ignore this distinction. The problem is not that this defense relies on transcendental idealism, since that is unavoidable. It is rather that Kant once again appeals to this distinction in a crude and misleading form, suggesting that it is reasonable to "admit that behind the appearances there must lie things in themselves (though hidden) at their foundation, and one cannot demand of the laws of their operation that they be the same as those under which their appearances stand" (GMS 4: 459_{27-31}). In so doing, Kant once again presents his transcendental distinction as one that is, or at least ought to be, readily acknowledged by common human reason, thereby ignoring the "critical" view that transcendental realism, which is what these critics are effectively charged with affirming, is the common view and that it can only be countered by a full transcendental critique.

(1) *The inexplicability of moral interest*: Kant here makes a two-fold claim. On the one hand he maintains that the "subjective impossibility" of explaining an interest in morality is the same as explaining the possibility of freedom of the will (GMS 4: $459_{32}-60_1$).[38] On the other hand, he insists that the fact that we take an interest in morals laws is undeniable; and he suggests that the foundation of this interest lies in moral feeling.[39]

Although one might think that the latter claim itself amounts to a kind of explanation of moral interest, Kant's further discussion indicates that he takes the expression "moral feeling" to refer to an inscrutable capacity, which is itself deeply problematic, rather than to an empirically accessible property of human nature that could provide a genuine *explanans*.[40] According to Kant, what makes moral feeling inscrutable is that it

---

[38] In a note appended to this text, Kant defines an interest as "that by which reason becomes practical, i.e., becomes a cause determining the will" (GMS 4: 459_{34-35}). See also GMS 4: $413n_{26}-14_{37}$. I discuss Kant's conception of interest, including these definitions, in some detail in Chapter 3, with particular emphasis on their connection with maxims.

[39] Kant's claim that human beings really do take an interest in moral laws (GMS 4: 460_{1-2}) might be taken in either a strong or a weak sense. Taken in former sense, the claim would be that we know as a matter of fact that, at least on some occasions, human beings act solely from an interest in morality, i.e., from duty; taken in the latter sense the claim is that we know as a matter of fact that moral considerations are experienced as providing a (subjective) reason to act, even though we may seldom, if ever, act solely for these reasons or from that interest. But it is clear from our previous consideration of Kant's moral psychology that his claim must be understood in the latter sense.

[40] Kant's conception of moral sense here differs from that of the moral sense theorists such as Hutcheson in two respects. First, he denies that such a sense provides the standard of moral judgment. This is the point that

presupposes "a capacity of reason to *induce* [*einzuflössen*] *a feeling of pleasure* or of delight in the fulfillment of duty" (GMS 4: 460$_{9-11}$). In other words, moral feeling, like freedom of the will, is inexplicable because it must be attributed to a causality of reason, which, as such, violates the conditions of possible explanation, which are also those of a possible experience. And since a moral interest would have to be based on moral feeling, so construed, it is likewise inexplicable.

This characterization of moral feeling as "*a feeling of pleasure* or of delight in the fulfillment of duty" is peculiar for a number of reasons. First, it conflicts with what Kant says elsewhere, including in GMS. As we saw in examining the argument of GMS 1, Kant there characterizes the feeling for the moral law as respect. Although like the feeling described here, respect is viewed as produced by reason and therefore as qualitatively distinct from other feelings, which are attributable solely to our sensuous nature, Kant there describes it as having both a positive and a negative side, with the former being analogous (though not identical) to inclination and the latter being analogous (though not identical) to fear (GMS 4: 401$_{17-22}$). But while it might be argued that inclination is not too far from pleasure, it must be kept in mind that this is only one aspect of this complete feeling and that Kant insists that this aspect is merely analogous to inclination. Moreover, in the more substantive and presumably definitive discussion of respect in the second *Critique*, Kant again emphasizes its two sides, this time identifying the negative side with pain resulting from humiliation, and the positive with self-approbation [*Selbstbilligung*], which he distinguishes sharply from pleasure.[41] Finally, moral feeling, understood as respect, is connected by Kant primarily with the recognition of the *demands* of the moral law (which is what enables it to function as an incentive) rather than with their *fulfillment*. To be sure, Kant does refer elsewhere to a feeling of self-contentment [*Selbstzufriedenheit*] that is connected with the fulfillment of duty, but he denies that this could serve as the moral incentive and he distinguishes it from happiness, which is essentially connected with pleasure.[42]

It must also be noted, however, that Kant's conclusion to his account of the aetiology of moral interest is not completely negative since he remarks that at least one thing is certain, namely, that the validity of the law for us does not derive from the fact that it interests us (since that would be heteronomy), but, rather, that it interests us because it is valid for us. Kant further claims, in a previously cited passage, that this validity stems from the fact that the law "arose from our will as intelligence, therefore from our proper self"; to which he adds by way of an explanatory clause that "*what belongs to mere appearance is necessarily subordinated by reason to the nature of the thing in*

Kant here emphasizes and it reflects his fundamental tenet that that moral principles must be grounded in reason. Second, he rejects the view that a moral sense is a property of human nature that can be understood in naturalistic terms or, as in the case of Hutcheson, on the basis of a providential naturalism.

[41] On the last point see especially KpV 5: 77; 202 and 80; 204.

[42] See KpV 5: 117–19; 234–35.

itself." But having already discussed this claim, I shall turn to Kant's final reflections on his deduction of the categorical imperative.

(D) Revisiting the deduction (GMS 4: 461₇–63₂)

After concluding his account of the inexplicability of moral interest, Kant returns to the original question of the deduction: how is a categorical imperative possible? But, as previously noted, his final answer appears to involve a considerable weakening of his initial claims. As a result of his analysis of the boundary of practical reason, Kant acknowledges that the question is not completely answerable, mainly because of the inexplicability of a moral interest, which we have seen to be essential to the possibility of a categorical imperative. Accordingly, he now maintains that the question of the possibility of a categorical imperative can be answered

to the extent that one can state the only presupposition on which alone it is possible, namely the idea of freedom, and that one can likewise see the necessity of this presupposition, which is sufficient for the *practical use* of reason, i.e., for the conviction of the *validity of this imperative*, and hence of the moral law as well; but how this presupposition is itself possible can never be understood by any human reason. (GMS 4: 461₈₋₁₄)

Two aspects of this admission regarding the limitations on the possibility of a deduction are particularly worthy of note. First, the deduction, so construed, is capable of yielding only a necessary condition of the possibility of a categorical imperative, but not conditions sufficient to account for its possibility, which was the explicit task of the deduction as Kant initially defined it. Second, what Kant here claims to have shown, namely, the necessity of presupposing the idea of freedom from a practical point of view, was accomplished already in section three. Accordingly, if we accept these remarks as Kant's second thoughts on the matter, we seem led to the conclusion that, even though he was quite explicit in insisting that it was in section four that the deduction is carried out and that it consists in showing how a categorical imperative is possible, whatever real work is done in GMS 3 is done in the first three sections, which Kant himself describes as merely preliminary, and that it consists essentially in the justification (from a practical point of view) of the presupposition of freedom, from which the validity of the moral law for all rational agents as such, follows by means of the reciprocity thesis.

In light of this, one might argue, as some have done, that the bindingness of the categorical imperative for rational beings with a sensuous nature is a relatively trivial consequence of the validity of the moral law for rational agents as such.[43] The argument would be that if a principle is necessarily followed by a perfectly rational agent, then it *ought* to be obeyed by imperfectly rational ones. But despite its *prima facie* plausibility, such a claim is deeply problematic and, I believe, would not have been

---

[43] This is maintained by Paton (1958, 247). In my initial treatment of this topic I agreed with Paton; consequently, my present account amounts to a rejection of my earlier view. See Allison (1990, 226–27).

endorsed by Kant, at least not in this form. The basic problem, which has already been noted, is the necessity of distinguishing between the validity and the bindingness of a moral principle. As we have seen, one could consistently acknowledge the validity of the moral law for perfectly rational agents, while denying that this law poses an obligation on oneself. Thus, one might recognize it as a valid moral ideal and perhaps like Kant's malicious scoundrel even wish that one were the kind of being capable of following it; all the while continuing with business as usual on the grounds that one is not such a being.

This is because for Kant we are not simply imperfectly rational in the Platonic (and Wolffian) sense that we lack a clear and distinct (or adequate) idea of the good (or perfection), but because our "imperfect rationality" consists also (and primarily) in the fact that our sensuous nature is an independent source of ends, which are encapsulated in that great natural end: happiness. And because of this, the question naturally arises: why should the laws describing the behavior of a perfectly rational agent be the grounds of obligations for us, when they conflict with *true needs* that derive from our nature as sensuous beings?[44] In spite of the rationalism of his moral theory (and general philosophical orientation), Kant was sufficiently aware of the limits of rationalism to recognize the seriousness of this problem, which is why the concept of obligation lies at the heart of his moral theory and, as we saw in Chapter 2, is the fulcrum of his critique of the Wolffian universal practical philosophy.

Moreover, if we approach the matter in this light, we can understand both why Kant saw the necessity of a deduction of the categorical imperative that went beyond that of the moral law from the presupposition of freedom in section three and why this deduction took the form that it did. The latter is the case because Kant evidently thought that the best (perhaps the only) way to establish the normative supremacy at which he aimed was to ground it in an ontological supremacy. But we have seen that this effort failed for two main reasons. The first is the general point, which was illustrated by the example of God's will, that normative supremacy is not entailed by the ontological variety, a thesis with which Kant, as a committed anti-voluntarist, would have to concur. The second, which is specific to Kant's account, is that its sharp contrast between the sensible and the intelligible, appearance and thing in itself, is too blunt an instrument to provide an understanding of how the rational agent, qua addressee of the categorical imperative, can, as it must, be considered as a member of both worlds simultaneously.[45]

---

[44] True needs must be emphasized here because the conflict between true and apparent or essential and subordinate needs can be resolved on purely prudential grounds, without any need to appeal to moral considerations. I have also chosen the expression "grounds of obligation" rather than simply "obligations" in order to bypass issues regarding the distinction between perfect and imperfect duties.

[45] The point is noted by Henrich (1975, 97).

(E) Kant's concluding remark (GMS 4: 463₄₋₃₃)

(E) Kant's concluding remark (GMS 4: 463_{4-33})

The central topic of Kant's brief concluding remark is a comparison of the speculative and the practical uses of reason, which gestures toward the idea of the unity of reason that was referred to in the Preface as necessary for a complete critique of pure practical reason. In contrasting these two uses of pure reason, Kant notes that both lead to the conception of absolute necessity: the former to that of some supreme cause of the world, the latter to *laws of action* of a practical being as such. Kant further notes that this striving for a consciousness of the necessity of its cognition is an essential principle of all use of reason, just as its inability to grasp this sought for necessity of either what exists, happens, or ought to happen unless a condition is available as its ground is its endemic fate. In short, reason in both its speculative and practical use is condemned to a Sisyphean quest for the unconditioned.

The rhetoric of this remark calls to mind the famous opening lines of the Preface to the first edition of the first *Critique*, where Kant remarks that,

Human reason has the peculiar fate in one species of its cognitions that it is burdened with questions which it cannot dismiss, since they are given to it as problems by the nature of reason itself, but which it also cannot answer, since they transcend every capacity of human reason. (KrV Avii)

But whereas in the first *Critique* Kant limited this "peculiar fate" to "one species of its cognitions," namely, the speculative variety, he here explicitly extends it to the practical use of reason as well.

Moreover, Kant uses this common feature of reason as justification for the limited nature of the results that he has been able to achieve in GMS 3. Thus, he claims that it is not a criticism that can be raised against his deduction of the supreme principle of morality, but against human reason as such, that it cannot make comprehensible an unconditional practical law. As before, the argument turns on the principle that to make something comprehensible or, equivalently, to explain it, is to derive it from a condition; but in the case of the categorical imperative this is impossible, because, *ex hypothesi*, it is unconditioned.[46] And from this Kant concludes, evidently endeavoring to make a virtue of a necessity, that while "we do not indeed comprehend the practical unconditioned necessity of the moral imperative, we nevertheless do comprehend its *incomprehensibly*," to which Kant adds that this is "all that can reasonably be required of a philosophy that in its principles strives up to the boundary of human reason" (GMS 4: 463₂₉₋₃₃).

If one is to understand the development of Kant's moral philosophy during the "critical" period, it is essential to realize that this position is unique to GMS; for in neither the first nor the second *Critiques* does Kant associate such a Sisyphean quest

---

[46] It should be clear that the same applies, *mutatis mutandis*, to a pure moral interest, which is unconditioned because of its independence from any incentive stemming from our sensuous nature.

with *practical* reason. In the first *Critique* or, more precisely, the first edition of that work, Kant did not envision such a worry because, as previously noted, he had not yet arrived at the principle of the autonomy of the will, which involves the conception of pure reason as practical, independently of both any sensuous incentives to motivate obedience to the law or of any theoretical (if not speculative) use of reason to ground its validity.[47] As we have seen, in the Canon of that work Kant endorsed the quasi-eudaemonistic view that, while, on the one hand, the moral incentive is "pure" in the sense that it is defined as the desire to be *worthy* of happiness rather than simply to be happy, on the other hand, Kant also thought that this desire could not be practically efficacious without at least the hope that those who are truly worthy of happiness will be rewarded proportionally to their worthiness of it. And, as we have also seen, this hope is supposedly grounded in the postulation of God and immortality, both transcendental ideas, which, as such, are products of the speculative (not the practical) use of reason.

By contrast, in the second *Critique* Kant rejects the idea that pure practical reason could, like speculative reason, overstep its proper bounds. Instead, the worry is that it does not have any pure, i.e., non-empirical use, which would undermine the possibility of a categorical imperative. Accordingly, Kant there defines the task as showing "*that there is pure practical reason*" and that this involves a critical evaluation of "reason's entire *practical faculty*" (KpV 5: 3; 139), which is why he calls it simply a critique of practical reason rather than of pure practical reason. Showing that there is pure practical reason or, more simply, *that* pure reason is practical, is quite distinct from showing *how* a categorical imperative is possible, which would involve showing how pure reason can be practical, a task which Kant admits in GMS 3 cannot be accomplished by human reason. Moreover, this reconceptualization of the grounding task explains why, rather than attempting to provide a deduction of the categorical imperative, Kant appeals to the fact of reason. To try to show that pure reason is practical is to regard its practicality, as expressed in the categorical imperative, as a peculiar kind of fact or, as Kant also more carefully put it, a "fact as it were" [*gleichsam als ein Faktum*] (KpV 5: 47; 177).

I cannot here discuss this new and likewise deeply controversial strategy on Kant's part, since it would take us well beyond the scope of a commentary on GMS.[48] Instead, I would like to close this work with the observation that, in spite of being generally recognized as one of the classical, if not *the* classical work in modern moral philosophy, if looked at from the perspective of the development of Kant's moral theory from the first *Critique* on, GMS is in many ways a transitional as well as a foundational work.

---

[47] The qualification "in the first edition" is important here because, even though the major first *Critique* discussion of practical reason, namely, that which is contained in the Canon, is also contained unchanged in the second edition, which postdates the publication of GMS, this is because, apart from some minor changes, Kant chose not to rewrite the portion of the *Critique* subsequent to the Paralogisms. What a 1787 version of the Canon, had Kant decided to write one, would look like is, indeed, an interesting question.

[48] I do analyze it, however, in Allison (1990, 230–49).

It is foundational because of its introduction of the revolutionary principle of the autonomy of the will, which Kant juxtaposes to the principle underlying all previous moral theories and which, as I have tried to argue, must itself be seen as the result of Kant's attempt to derive the concept of morality implicit in common human reason from the highly abstract concept of a rational agent as such. It is transitional not only because Kant's later sharp distinction between a doctrine of right [*Rechtslehre*] and a doctrine of virtue [*Tugendlehre*] in the *Metaphysics of Morals* seems to involve an abandonment of the core idea of GMS that there must be a single principle of morality, and because Kant's expression of his views suffers at key points from a lack of the *Wille–Willkür* distinction (as well as other refinements to be found in his later writings), but also (and primarily) because its account of the grounding of the categorical imperative occupies a position that is mid-way between those of the first two *Critiques*. But while an awareness of its transitional elements is crucial for students of Kant's moral theory and can lead to a more nuanced and sympathetic reading of GMS, it is its foundational element that accounts for it ongoing importance. Although moral philosophers may reject Kant's approach to the foundations of morals, they cannot ignore it. And this, in my view, is the true mark of a philosophical classic.

Bibliography

Adickes, Erich. *Kant und die Als-Ob-Philosophie*, Stuttgart: Fr. Frommanns Verlag (1927).

Allison, Henry E. *The Kant–Eberhard Controversy*, Baltimore and London: Johns Hopkins University Press (1973).

—— *Kant's Transcendental Idealism: An Interpretation and Defense*, New Haven: Yale University Press (1983).

—— "The Concept of Freedom in Kant's 'Semi-Critical' Ethics," *Archiv für Geschichte der Philosophie* 68 (1986a), 96–115.

—— "Morality and Freedom: Kant's Reciprocity Thesis," *Philosophical Review* 95 (1986b), 393–425.

—— *Kant's Theory of Freedom*, Cambridge: Cambridge University Press (1990).

—— *Idealism and Freedom: Essays on Kant's Theoretical and Practical Philosophy*, Cambridge: Cambridge University Press (1996).

—— "We Can Act Only Under the Idea of Freedom," *The Proceedings and Addresses of the American Philosophical Association* 71 (1997), 39–50.

—— "Ethics, Evil, and Anthropology in Kant: Remarks on Allen Wood's *Kant's Ethical Thought*," *Ethics* 111 (2001a), 594–613.

—— *Kant's Theory of Taste: A Reading of the Critique of Aesthetic Judgment*, Cambridge: Cambridge University Press (2001b).

—— "On the Very Idea of a Propensity to Evil," *Journal of Value Inquiry* 36 (2002), 337–48.

—— *Kant's Transcendental Idealism: An Interpretation and Defense*, revised and enlarged edition, New Haven: Yale University Press (2004).

—— "Kant and the Two Dogmas of Rationalism," in *A Companion to Rationalism*, ed. Alan Nelson, Oxford: Blackwell Publishing (2005), 343–59.

—— "Kant on Freedom of the Will," in *The Cambridge Companion to Kant and Modern Philosophy*, ed. Paul Guyer, Cambridge: Cambridge University Press (2006a), 381–415.

—— "Kant's Transcendental Idealism," in *A Companion to Kant*, ed. Graham Bird, Oxford: Blackwell Publishing (2006b), 111–24.

—— "Transcendental Realism, Empirical Realism and Transcendental Idealism," *Kantian Review* 11 (2006c), 1–28.

—— "Debating Allison on Transcendental Idealism" (response to Allen Wood and Paul Guyer), *Kantian Review* 12 (2007), 24–39.

—— *Custom and Reason in Hume: A Kantian Reading of the First Book of the Treatise*, Oxford: Clarendon Press (2008).

Ameriks, Karl. *Kant's Theory of Mind: An Analysis of the Paralogisms of Pure Reason*, Oxford: Clarendon Press (1982).

—— "Kant on the Good Will," in *Grundlegung zur Metaphysik der Sitten, Ein kooperativer Kommentar*, ed. Otfried Höffe, Frankfurt am Main: Vittorio Klostermann (1989), 45–65.

—— *Interpreting Kant's Critiques*, Oxford: Clarendon Press (2003).

Aune, Bruce. *Kant's Theory of Morals*, Princeton: Princeton University Press (1979).

Baker, Judith. "Counting Categorical Imperatives," *Kant-Studien* 79 (1988), 389–406.

Baron, Marcia. "The Alleged Moral Repugnance of Acting from Duty," *Journal of Philosophy* 81 (1984), 197–220.

—— "Freedom, Frailty, and Impurity," *Inquiry* 36 (1993), 431–41.

—— *Kantian Ethics Almost without Apology*, Ithaca, NY: Cornell University Press (1995).

—— "Acting from Duty (GMS, 397–401)," in *Groundwork of the Metaphysics of Morals*, ed. Christoph Horn and Dieter Schönecker, Berlin and New York: Walter de Gruyter (2006), 72–92.

Baumgarten, Alexander Gottlieb. *Metaphysica*, in *Kant's gesammelte Schriften*, herausgegeben von der Preussischen Akademie der Wissenschaften, Berlin and Leipzig: Walter de Gruyter & Co. (1926), vol. 17, 5–206.

—— *Initia philosophiae practicae prima acroamatice* (1760), reprinted in *Kant's gesammelte Schriften*, herausgegeben von der Preussischen Akademie der Wissenschaften, Berlin and Leipzig: Walter de Gruyter & Co. (1934), vol. 19, 7–91.

Beck, Lewis W. *A Commentary on Kant's Critique of Practical Reason*, Chicago: University of Chicago Press (1960).

—— *Studies in the Philosophy of Kant*, Indianapolis, New York, and Kansas City: Bobbs-Merrill Company Inc. (1965).

—— *Early German Philosophy, Kant and His Predecessors*, Cambridge, MA: The Belknap Press of Harvard University Press (1969a).

—— *Kant's Foundations of the Metaphysics of Morals, Text and Critical Essays*, trans. Lewis White Beck and ed. Robert Paul Wolff, Indianapolis: Bobbs-Merrill Company Inc. (1969b).

—— *The Actor and the Spectator*, New Haven: Yale University Press (1975).

Beiser, Frederick C. *The Fate of Reason German Philosophy from Kant to Fichte*, Cambridge, MA: Harvard University Press (1987).

Bennett, Jonathan. *Kant's Analytic*, Cambridge: Cambridge University Press (1966).

Bittner, Rüdiger. "Maximen," in *Akten der 4 Internationalen Kant Kongress, Mainz 1974*, ed. G. Funke and J. Kopper, Berlin: Walter de Gruyter, 485–98.

—— *Moralisches Gebot oder Autonomie*, Freiburg/Munich: Verlag Karl Alber (1983).

—— "Das Unternehmen einer Grundlegung zur Metaphysik der Sitten," in *Grundlegung zur Metaphysik der Sitten, Ein kooperativer Kommentar*, ed. Otfried Höffe, Frankfurt am Main: Vittorio Klostermann (1989), 13–30.

Brandt, Reinhard. "Der Zirkel im dritten Abschnitt von Kant's *Grundlegung zur Metaphysik der Sitten*," in *Kant Analysen-Probleme-Kritik*, ed. Hariolf Oberer and Gerhard Seel, Würtburg: Königshausen & Neumann (1988), 169–91.

Brewer, Talbot. "Maxims and Virtues," *Philosophical Review* 111 (2002), 539–72.

Carnois, Bernard. *The Coherence of Kant's Doctrine of Freedom*, trans. David Booth, Chicago and London: University of Chicago Press (1987).

Cicero, Marcus Tullius, *De officiis*, with English translation by Walter Miller, Loeb Classical Library, London: William Heinemann, New York: The Macmillan Co. (1893).

Cramer, Konrad. "Hypothetische Imperative?" in *Rehabilitierung der praktischen Philosophie*, vol. 1 ed. Manfred Reidel, Freiburg: Rombach (1972), 159–212.

Crusius, Christian August. "Anweisung vernünftig zu leben." *Die Philosophischen Hauptwerke*, vol. 2 Hildesheim: Georg Olms Verlagsbuchhandlung (1969).

Darwall, Stephen. *The British Moralists and the Internal 'Ought': 1640–1740*, Cambridge: Cambridge University Press (1995).

Dean, Richard. *The Value of Humanity in Kant's Moral Theory*, Oxford: Clarendon Press (2006).

Dennett, Daniel C. "Mechanism and Responsibility," in *Essays on Freedom of Action*, ed. Ted Honderich, London: Routledge & Kegan Paul (1973), 159–84.

—— *Elbow Room: The Varieties of Free Will worth Wanting*, Cambridge, MA and London: MIT Press (1984).

—— *The Intentional Stance*, Cambridge, MA and London: MIT Press (1989).

DesJardins, Gregory. "Terms of *De Officiis* in Hume and Kant," *Journal of the History of Ideas* 28 (1967), 237–42.

Dietrichson, Paul. "Kant's Criteria of Universalizability," in *Kant: Foundations of the Metaphysics of Morals, Text and Critical Essays*, ed. Robert Paul Wolff, Indianapolis: Bobbs-Merrill Company Inc. (1969), 163–207.

Duncan, A. R. C. *Practical Reason and Morality: A Study of Immanuel Kant's Foundations for the Metaphysics of Morals*, London, Edinburgh, Paris, Melbourne, Toronto, and New York: Thomas Nelson and Sons Ltd. (1957).

Düsing, Klaus. *Die Teleologie in Kant's Weltbegriff*, Bonn: H. Bouvier. Co. Verlag (1968).

Eisenberg, Paul. "From the Forbidden to the Supererogatory: The Basic Ethical Categories in Kant's Tugendlehre," *American Philosophical Quarterly* 3 (1966), 255–69.

Engstrom, Stephen. *The Form of Practical Knowledge: A Study of the Categorical Imperative*, Cambridge, MA and London: Harvard University Press (2009).

Fleischacker, Samuel. "Kant and Adam Smith," *Kant-Studien* 82 (1991), 249–69.

Foot, Philippa. "Morality as a System of Hypothetical Imperatives," in *Virtues and Vices*, Berkeley and Los Angeles: University of California Press (1981), 157–73.

Freudiger, Jürg. *Kants Begründung der praktischen Philosophie*, Bern, Stuttgart, Wien: Verlag Paul Haupt (1993).

Fricke, Cristel. Maximen, *Recht und Freiheit in der Philosophie Kants, Akten des X. Internationalen Kant-Kongresses*, ed. Valerio Rohden, Ricardo R. Terra, Guido A. de Almeida, and Margit Ruffing, Berlin: Walter de Gruyter (2008), vol. 3, 125–35.

Garve, Christian. *Abhandlung über die menschlichen Pflichten in drei Büchern aus dem Latinischen des Marcus Tullius Cicero*, Übersetzt von Christian Garve, Breslau: Wilhelm Gottlieb Korn, 4th edition (1792a).

—— *Philosophische Anmerkungen und Abhandlungen zu Cicero's Büchern von den Pflichten, Anmerkungen zu dem Ersten Buche*, Breslau: Wilhelm Gottlieb Korn (1792b).

—— *Uebersicht der vornehmsten Principien der Sittenlehre, von dem Zeitalter des Aristoteles an bis auf unsre Zeiten*, Breslau: Wilhelm Gottlieb Korn (1798).

—— *Versuche über verschiedene Gegenstände aus der Moral, Literatur und dem gesellschaftlichen Leben* (in Henrich, 1967, 134–38).

—— "The Garve Review," in *Kant's Early Critics: The Empiricist Critique of the Theoretical Philosophy*, ed. and trans. Brigitte Sassen, Cambridge: Cambridge University Press (2000), 59–77.

Gibert, Carlos Melches. *Der Einfluss von Christian Garves Übersetzung Ciceros "De officiis" auf Kants "Grundlegung zur Metaphysik der Sitten,"* Regensberg: S. Roderer Verlag, (1994).

Green, T. H. *Prolegomena to Ethics*, ed. David O. Brink, Oxford: Clarendon Press (2003).

Gregor, Mary J. *Laws of Freedom: A Study of Kant's Method of Applying the Categorical Imperative in the Metaphysik der Sitten*, Oxford: Basil Blackwell (1963).

Grier, Michelle. *Kant's Doctrine of Transcendental Illusion*, Cambridge: Cambridge University Press (2001).

Guéroult, Martial. "Canon de la raison pure et critique de la raison pratique," *Revue de Philosophie* 8 (1954), 331–57.

Guyer, Paul. "The Possibility of the Categorical Imperative," in *Kant's Groundwork of the Metaphysics of Morals, Critical Essays*, ed. Paul Guyer, New York and Oxford: Roman & Littlefield (1998), 215–46.

Hamann, Johann Georg. *Briefwechsel*, volume 5, ed. Walther Ziesemer and Arthur Henkel, Frankfurt (Main): Insel Verlag (1965).

Harbison, Warren G. "The Good Will," *Kant-Studien* 71 (1980) 47–59.

Hegel, G. W. F. *Phenomenology of Spirit*, trans. A. V. Miller, Oxford: Oxford University Press (1977).

Henrich, Dieter. *Kant, Gentz. Rehberg, Über Theorie und Praxis*, edited with introduction, Frankfurt am Main: Suhrkamp Verlag (1967).

—— "The Proof-Structure of Kant's Transcendental Deduction," *Review of Metaphysics* 22 (1969), 640–59.

—— "Die Deduktion des Sittengesetzes. *Über die Grunde der Dunkelheit des letzten Abschnittes von Kants 'Grundlegung zur Metaphysik der Sitten'*," in *Denken im Schatten des Nihilismus*, ed. Alexander Schwan, Darmstadt: Wissenschaftliche Buchgesellschaft, (1975), 55–112.

—— "The Deduction of the Moral Law: The Reasons for the Obscurity of the Final Section of Kant's *Groundwork of the Metaphysics of Morals*," trans. Paul Guyer, in *Kant's Groundwork of the Metaphysics of Morals, Critical Essays*, edited Paul Guyer, New York and Oxford: Roman & Littlefield (1998), 303–41.

Henson, Richard. "What Kant Might Have Said: Moral Worth and the Overdetermination of Dutiful Action," *Philosophical Review* 88 (1979), 39–54.

Herman, Barbara. "On the Value of Acting from the Motive of Duty," *Philosophical Review* 90 (1981), 359–82.

—— *The Practice of Moral Judgment*, Cambridge, MA: Harvard University Press (1993).

Hill, Thomas, E. Jr. *Dignity and Practical Reason in Kant's Moral Theory*, Ithaca and London: Cornell University Press (1992).

—— "Kant's Argument for the Rationality of Moral Conduct," in *Kant's Groundwork of the Metaphysics of Morals, Critical Essays*, ed. Paul Guyer, New York and Oxford: Roman & Littlefield (1998), 249–72.

—— (co-ed. with Arnulf Zweig). *Kant, Groundwork for the Metaphysics of Morals*, Oxford and New York: Oxford University Press (2002).

Höffe, Otfried. "Kants kategorischer Imperativ als Kriterium des Sittlichen," in *Ethik und Politik*, ed. Otfried Höffe, Frankfurt: Surkamp (1979), 84–119.

Horn, Christoph. "Kant on Ends and Human Agency: The Teleological Argument (GMS, 394–396)," in *Groundwork of the Metaphysics of Morals*, ed. Christoph Horn and Dieter Schönecker, Berlin and New York: Walter de Gruyter (2006), 45–71.

Hume, David. *An Enquiry concerning the Principles of Morals*, ed. Tom L. Beauchamp, Oxford Philosophical Texts, Oxford: Oxford University Press (1998).

—— *An Enquiry concerning Human Understanding*, ed. Tom L Beauchamp, Oxford Philosophical Texts, Oxford: Oxford University Press (1999).

Hume, David. *A Treatise of Human Nature*, ed. David Fate and Mary J. Norton, Oxford Philosophical Texts, Oxford: Oxford University Press (2000).

Irwin, Terence. "Morality and Personality in Kant and Green," in *Self and Nature in Kant's Philosophy*, ed. Allen W. Wood, Ithaca and London: Cornell University Press (1984), 31–56.

Jacobi, F. H. *David Hume über den Glauben, oder Idealismus und Realismus, in Über den transzendentalen Idealismus, Werke*, ed. F. Roth and F. Köppen, Darmstadt: Wissenschaftliche Buchgesellschaft (1968), vol. 2, 291–310.

Kemp, J. "Kant's Examples of the Categorical Imperative," in *Kant: Foundations of the Metaphysics of Morals, Text and Critical Essays*, ed. Robert Paul Wolff, Indianapolis: Bobbs-Merrill Company Inc. (1969), 230–44.

Kerstein, Samuel J. *Kant's Search for the Supreme Principle of Morality*, Cambridge: Cambridge University Press (2002).

—— "Deriving the Formula of Humanity," in *Groundwork for the Metaphysics of Morals*, ed. Christoph Horn and Dieter Schönecker, Berlin and New York: Walter de Gruyter (2006), 200–21.

Kobusch, Theo. *Die Entdeckung der Person. Metaphysik der Freiheit und modernes Menschenbild*, Freiburg, Basel, Wien: Herder Verlag (1993).

Köhl, Harald "The Derivation of the Moral Law (GMS, 402, 420f)," in *Groundwork for the Metaphysics of Morals*, ed. Christoph Horn and Dieter Schönecker, Berlin and New York: Walter de Gruyter (2006), 93–117.

Korsgaard, Christine. *Creating the Kingdom of Ends*, Cambridge: Cambridge University Press (1996).

Kuehn, Manfred. *Kant: A Biography*, Cambridge: Cambridge University Press (2001a).

—— "Kant and Cicero," in *Kant und die Berliner Aufklärung, Akten des IX. Internationalen Kant-Kongresses*, vol. 3, ed. Volker Gerhardt, Rolf-Peter Horstmann, and Ralph Schumacher, Berlin and New York: Walter de Gruyter (2001b), 270–78.

Laberge, Pierre. "Du passage de la philosophie morale populaire à la métaphysique des mours," *Kant-Studien* 71 (1980), 418–44.

—— "L'Espèce de cercle dont, à ce qu'il semble, il n'y pas moyens de sortir," *Dialogue* 21 (1982), 745–53.

—— "La Volonte, la representation des lois et la fin," in *Grundlegung zur Metaphysik der Sitten. Ein kooperativer Kommentar*, ed. Otrfried Höffe, Frankfurt am Main: Vittorio Klostermann (1989), 83–96.

Leibniz, G. W. "Monadology," in *Philosophical Essays*, trans. and ed. Roger Ariew and Daniel Garber, Indianapolis & Cambridge: Hackett Publishing Company (1989), 213–25.

Lewis, C. I. *An Analysis of Knowledge and Valuation*, La Salle: Open Court Publishing Co. (1947).

Liddell, Brendan. *Kant on the Foundation of Morality: A Modern Version of the 'Grundlegung'*, translated with commentary, Bloomington and London: Indiana University Press (1970).

Ludwig, Bernd. "Kant's Hypothetical Imperatives," in *Groundwork for the Metaphysics of Morals*, ed. Christoph Horn and Dieter Schönecker, Berlin and New York: Walter de Gruyter (2006), 139–57.

—— "Kant, Garve, and the Motives of Moral Action," *Journal of Moral Philosophy*, 4 (2007), 183–93.

Marshall, John. "The Syntheticity of the Categorical Imperative," in *Proceedings of the Sixth International Kant Congress*, ed. G. Funke and T. Seebohm, Washington: Center for Advanced Research in Phenomenology University Press of America (1989) Vol. II/2, 185–200.

McCarthy, Michael H. "Analytic Method and Analytic Propositions in Kant's Groundwork," *Dialogue* 15 (1976), 565–82.

—— Kant's Application of the Analytic/Synthetic Distinction to Imperatives," *Dialogue* 18 (1979), 373–91.

McDowell, John. *Mind and World*, Cambridge, MA: Harvard University Press (1994).

Meerbote, Ralf, "Kant on Freedom and the Rational and Morally Good Will," commentary on Terry Irwin's, "Morality and Personality in Kant and Green," in *Self and Nature in Kant's Philosophy*, ed. Allen W. Wood, Ithaca and London: Cornell University Press (1984), 57–72.

Meier, Georg, Friedrich. *Allgemeine practische Weltweisheit*, Halle: Carl Hermann Hemmerde (1764) (reprinted by Georg Olms Verlag AG, Hildesheim, 2006).

Millgram, Elijah. "Does the Categorical Imperative Give Rise to a Contradiction in the Will?" *Philosophical Review* 112 (2003), 525–60.

Miltz, Bernhard. "Zur Analytizität und Synthetizität der *Grundlegung*," *Kant-Studien* 89 (1998), 188–204.

Muller, Paul. *Chr. Garves Moralphilosophie und seine Stellungnahme zu Kants Ethik*, Borna-Leipzig: Buchdruckerei Robert Noske (1905).

Nell (O'Neill), Onora. *Acting on Principle: An Essay on Kantian Ethics*, New York and London: Columbia University Press (1975).

—— (O'Neill). *Constructions of Reason: Explorations of Kant's Practical Philosophy*, Cambridge: Cambridge University Press (1989).

Nietzsche, Friedrich. *Beyond Good and Evil*, trans. Marianne Cowan, Chicago: Henry Regnery Company (1955).

Nowell-Smith, P. H. *Ethics*, London: Penguin Books (1954).

Paton, H. J. *Groundwork of the Metaphysics of Morals*, annotated translation and analysis, New York: Harper & Row (1956).

—— *The Categorical Imperative: A Study in Kant's Moral Philosophy*, London: Hutchinson & Co, 3rd edition (1958).

Patzig, Günther. "Die Logischen Formen Praktischer Sätze," *Kant-Studien* 56 (1966), 237–51.

Petrus, Klaus. "Kant und Garve, 'Beschrieene Dunkelheit' und 'Seichtigkeit'," *Kant-Studien*, 85 (1994), 280–302.

Piper Adrian M. "Kant on the Objectivity of the Moral Law," in *Reclaiming the History of Ethics: Essays for John Rawls*, ed. Andrews Reath, Barbara Herman, and Christine Korsgaard, Cambridge: Cambridge University Press (1997), 240–69.

Pippin, Robert. *Kant's Theory of Form*, New Haven: Yale University Press (1982).

Pogge, Thomas. "The Categorical Imperative," in *Kant's Groundwork of the Metaphysics of Morals, Critical Essays*, ed. Paul Guyer, New York and Oxford: Roman & Littlefield Publishers (1998), 189–213.

Pohlmann, R. "Autonomie," in *Historisches Wörterbuch der Philosophie*, vol. 1, ed. Joachim Ritter, Wissenschaftliche Buchgesellschaft: Darmstadt (1971), 701–19.

Prauss, Gerold. *Kant und das Problem der Dinge an sich*, Berlin: Walter de Gruyter (1971).

—— *Kant über Freiheit als Autonomie*, Frankfurt: Vittorio Klostermann (1983).

Quarfood, Marcel. "The Circle and the Two Standpoints," in *Groundwork of the Metaphysics of Morals*, ed. Christoph Horn and Dieter Schönecker, Berlin and New York: Walter de Gruyter (2006), 285–300.

Rawls, John. *A Theory of Justice*, Cambridge, MA: The Belknap Press of Harvard University Press (1971).

—— *Lectures on the History of Moral Philosophy*, ed. Barbara Herman, Cambridge, MA: Harvard University Press (2000).

Reath, Andrews. *Agency & Autonomy in Kant's Moral Theory: Selected Essays*, Oxford: Clarendon Press (2006).

Reich, Klaus. "Kant and Greek Ethics (I)" (trans. W. H. Walsh), *Mind* 48 (1939a), 446–63.

—— "Kant and Greek Ethics (II)" (trans. W. H. Walsh), *Mind* 48 (1939b), 337–54.

Reinhold, Karl Leonhard. "Erörterung des Begriffs von der Freiheit des Willens," in *Materialien zu Kants Kritik der praktischen Vernunft*, Herausgegeben von Rüdiger Bittner und Konrad Cramer, Frankfurt am Main: Suhrkamp Verlag (1975a), 252–74.

—— "Einige Bemerkungen über die in der Einleitung zu den 'Metaphysischen Anfangsgrüunden der Rechtslehre' von I. Kant aufgestellten Begriffe von der Freiheit des Willens," in *Materialien zu Kants Kritik der praktischen Vernunft*, Herausgegeben von Rüdiger Bittner und Konrad Cramer, Frankfurt am Main: Suhrkamp Verlag (1975b), 310–24.

Rickless, Samuel C. "From the Good Will to the Formula of the Universal Law," *Philosophy and Phenomenological Research* 68 (2004), 554–77.

Ross, Sir David. *Kant's Ethical Theory*, Oxford: Clarendon Press (1954).

Rousseau, Jean Jacques. *Discourse on the Origin and Foundations of Inequality Among Men*, in *The First and Second Discourses*, ed. Roger D. Masters, trans. Roger D. and Judith R. Masters, New York: St. Martin's Press (1964).

—— *On the Social Contract with Geneva Manuscript and Political Economy*, ed. Roger D. Masters, trans. Judith R. Masters, New York: St. Martin's Press (1978).

Sartre, Jean-Paul. *The Transcendence of the Ego: An Existentialist Theory of Consciousness*, trans. Forrest Williams and Robert Kirkpatrick, New York: The Noonday Press (1957).

Sassen, Brigitte (ed. and trans.). *Kant's Early Critics: The Empiricist Critique of the Theoretical Philosophy*, Cambridge: Cambridge University Press (2000).

Scarano, Nico "Necessity and Apriority in Kant's Moral Philosophy: An Interpretation of the *Groundwork*'s Preface," in *Groundwork for the Metaphysics of Morals*, ed. Christoph Horn and Dieter Schönecker, Berlin and New York: Walter de Gruyter (2006), 3–22.

Schaper, Eva. "The Kantian Thing-In-Itself as a Philosophical Fiction," *Philosophical Quarterly* 16 (1966), 233–43.

—— *Studies in Kant's Aesthetics*, Edinburgh: Edinburgh University Press (1979).

Schlipp, Paul Arthur. *Kant's Pre-Critical Ethics*, 2nd edition, Evanston, IL: Northwestern University Press (1960).

Schmucker, Josef. *Die Ursprünge der Ethik Kants*, Meisenheim am Glan: Verlag Anton Hain KG (1961).

Schneewind, J. B. Introduction to *Lectures on ethics*, ed. Schneewind and Peter Heath, trans. Peter Heath, *The Cambridge Edition of the Works of Immanuel Kant*, Cambridge: Cambridge University Press (1997).

—— *The Invention of Autonomy: A History of Modern Moral Philosophy*, Cambridge: Cambridge University Press (1998).

Schönecker, Dieter. "Zur Analytizität der *Grundlegung*," *Kant-Studien* 87 (1996), 348–54.

—— *Kant: Grundlegung III Die Deduktion des kategorischen Imperativs*. Freiburg/München: Verlag Karl Alber (1999).

—— "What is the 'First Proposition' Regarding Duty in Kant's *Grundlegung?*" in *Kant und die Berliner Aufklärung, Akten des IX. Internationalen Kant-Kongresses*, vol. 3, ed. Volker Gerhardt, Rolf-Peter Horstmann, and Ralph Schumacher, Berlin and New York: Walter de Gruyter (2001), 89–95.

——and Wood, Allen W. *Kants "Grundlegung zur Metaphysik der Sitten," Ein einführender Kommentar*, 2nd edition, Paderborn, München, Wien, Zürich: Ferdinand Schöningh. (2004).

—— "How is a Categorical Imperative Possible?" in *Groundwork for the Metaphysics of Morals*, ed. Christoph Horn and Dieter Schönecker, Berlin and New York: Walter de Gruyter (2006), 301–23.

Schultz (Schulze, Schultze), Johann, "Zur Rezension von Eberhard's Magazin (II. Band)," *Kants gesammelte Schriften*, vol. 20 (1942),400–23. English translation: *The Kant-Eberhard Controversy*, Appendix B, 171–77.

Seel, Gerhard. "*Sind Hypothetische Imperative analytische praktische Sätze?,*" in *Grundlegung zur Metaphysik der Sitten. Ein kooperativer Kommentar*, ed. Otfried Höffe, Frankfurt am Main: Vittorio Klostermann (1989), 148–71.

Sellars, Wilfred. *Essays in Philosophy and its History*, Dordrecht/Boston: D. Reidel (1974).

—— "Empiricism and the Philosophy of Mind," reprinted in *Knowledge, Mind, and the Given*, ed. William deVries and Timm Triplett, Indianapolis: Hackett Publishing Company Inc. (2000).

Sensen, Oliver. "Kant's Conception of Human Dignity," *Kant-Studien* 100 (2009), 309–31.

—— "Dignity and the Formula of Humanity," in *Kant's "Groundwork of the Metaphysics of Morals": A Critical Guide*, ed. Jens Timmermann, Cambridge: Cambridge University Press (2010), 102–18.

Sidgwick, Henry. "The Kantian Conception of Free Will," in *Groundwork for the Metaphysics of Morals*, ed. Lara Denis, Peterborough, Ontario: Broadview Press Ltd. (2005), 181–87.

Siep, Ludwig. "*Wozu Metaphysik der Sitten? Bemerkungen zur Vorrede der Grundlegung,*" *Grundlegung zur Metaphysik der Sitten. Ein kooperativer Kommentar*, ed. Otfried Höffe, Frankfurt am Main: Vittorio Klostermann (1989), 31–44.

Silber, John. R. "The Ethical Significance of Kant's Religion," in *Immanuel Kant's Religion within the Limits of Reason Alone*, trans. Theodore M. Greene and Hoyt H. Hudson, New York and London: Harper Torchbooks (1960), lxxix–cxxxvii.

Smith, Adam. *The Theory of Moral Sentiments*, ed. D. D. Raphael and A. L. Macfie, Indianapolis: Liberty Fund Inc. (1982).

Strawson, P. F. *The Bounds of Sense: An Essay on Kant's Critique of Pure Reason*, London: Methuen (1967).

Timmermann, Jens. *Kant's Groundwork of the Metaphysics of Morals: A Commentary*, Cambridge: Cambridge University Press (2007a).

—— "Simplicity and Authority: Reflections on Theory and Practice in Kant's Moral Philosophy," *Journal of Moral Philosophy* 4 (2007b), 167–82.

Timmons, Mark. "Contradictions and the Categorical Imperative," *Archiv für Geschichte der Philosophie*, 66 (1984), 294–312.

Timmons, Mark. "The Categorical Imperative and Universalizability," in *Groundwork for the Metaphysics of Morals*, ed. Christoph Horn and Dieter Schönecker, Berlin and New York: Walter de Gruyter (2006), 158–99.

Vaihinger, Hans. *The Philosophy of 'As If'*, trans. C. K. Ogden, London: Kegan Paul, Trench, Trubner & Co. Ltd., 2nd edition (1935).

Van Cleve, Jay. *Problems from Kant*, Oxford: Oxford University Press (1999).

Ward, Keith, *The Development of Kant's View of Ethics*, Oxford: Oxford University Press (1972).

Willaschek, Marcus. "Practical Reason," in *Groundwork for the Metaphysics of Morals*, ed. Christoph Horn and Dieter Schönecker, Berlin and New York: Walter de Gruyter (2006), 121–38.

Wolff, Christian. *Preliminary Discourse on Philosophy in General*, trans. Richard J. Blackwell, Indianapolis: Bobbs-Merrill Company Inc. (1963).

—— *Vernünfftige Gedancken von der Menschen Thun und Lassen, zu Beförderung ihrer Glückseligkeit*, edited with an introduction by Hans Werner Arndt, Hildesheim and New York: Georg Olms Verlag (1976).

—— *Philosophia Practica Universalis, Methodo Scientifica Pertractata*, ed. Winfred Lenders, Hildesheim and New York: Georg Olms Verlag (1979).

—— *Vernünftige Gedancken von Gott, der Welt und der Seele des Menschen, Auch allen Dingen überhaupt, Den Liebhabern der Wahrheit mitgetheilet* (1751), reprinted Ann Arbor: UMI (2005).

Wolff, Robert Paul. *The Autonomy of Reason: A Commentary on Kant's Groundwork of the Metaphysics of Morals*, New York: Harper Torchbooks (1973).

Wood, Allen W. "Kant's Compatibilism," in *Self and Nature in Kant's Philosophy*, ed. Allen W. Wood, Ithaca and London: Cornell University Press (1984), 73–101.

—— *Hegel's Ethical Thought*, Cambridge and New York: Cambridge University Press (1990).

—— "Unsociable Sociability: The Anthropological Basis of Kantian Ethics," *Philosophical Topics* 19 (1991), 325–51.

—— *Kant's Ethical Thought*, Cambridge: Cambridge University Press (1999).

—— "Humanity as an End in Itself," in *Kant's Groundwork of the Metaphysics of Morals, Critical Essays*, ed. Paul Guyer, New York and Oxford: Rowman and Littlefield Publishers (1998), 165–88.

—— (trans. and ed.). *Groundwork for the Metaphysics of Morals*, New Haven and London: Yale University Press (2002).

—— "The Good without Limitation," in *Groundwork for the Metaphysics of Morals*, ed. Christoph Horn and Dieter Schönecker, Berlin and New York: Walter de Gruyter (2006a), 25–44.

—— "The Supreme Principle of Morality," in *The Cambridge Companion to Kant and Modern Philosophy*, ed. Paul Guyer, Cambridge: Cambridge University Press (2006b), 342–80.

—— *Kantian Ethics*, Cambridge: Cambridge University Press (2008).

—— "Kant's Fourth Proposition: The Unsocial Sociability of Human Nature," in *Kant's Idea for a Universal History with a Cosmopolitan Aim: A Critical Guide*, ed. Amélie Oksenberg Rorty and James Schmidt, Cambridge: Cambridge University Press (2009), 112–28.

Zweig, Arnaulf (trans. and ed.). *Correspondence, The Cambridge Edition of the Works of Immanuel Kant*, Cambridge: Cambridge University Press (1999).

Index